DEVELOPMENTAL PSYCHOLOGY

DEVELOPMENTAL PSYCHOLOGY

CHILDHOOD AND ADOLESCENCE

W. Andrew Collins

UNIVERSITY OF MINNESOTA

Stanley A. Kuczaj II

SOUTHERN METHODIST UNIVERSITY

MACMILLAN PUBLISHING COMPANY
NEW YORK

COLLIER MACMILLAN CANADA
TORONTO

Editor: Christine Cardone
Developmental Editor: Madalyn Stone
Production Supervisor: Charlotte Hyland
Production Manager: Pamela Kennedy Oborski
Text and Cover Designer: Robert Freese
Cover Photograph: Roger Malloch/Magnum Photos
Photo Researcher: Elsa Peterson
Anatomical Illustrator: Laura Pardi-Duprey
Illustrations: Graphic Typesetting Service

This book was set in Palatino and Goudy type by Ruttle, Shaw & Wetherill, Inc.,
and was printed and bound by Von Hoffmann Press, Inc.
The cover was printed by Von Hoffmann Press, Inc.

Macmillan Publishing Company
866 Third Avenue, New York, New York 10022

Collier Macmillan Canada
1200 Eglinton Avenue East, Suite 200
Don Mills, Ontario M3C 3N1

LIBRARY OF CONGRESS CATALOGING-IN-PUBLICATION DATA

Collins, W. Andrew, 1944–
  Developmental psychology : childhood and adolescence / W. Andrew
Collins, Stanley A. Kuczaj II.
      p.   cm.
  Includes bibliographical references and index.
  ISBN 0–02–377010–4
  1. Child psychology.   2. Adolescent psychology.   3. Child
development.   I. Kuczaj, Stan A.   II. Title.
BF721.C5828   1991
155.4—dc20   90–45609
                     CIP

Printing: 1 2 3 4 5 6 7   Year: 1 2 3 4 5 6 7

Acknowledgments: Photo credits appear on pages 7–688, which constitute a continuation of the
copyright page.

To Carolyn, Caroline, and Drew Collins

To Abe and Ben Kuczaj

Preface

The study of human development is one of the liveliest, most productive areas of psychology. Human capacities for change—both positive and negative—by turns intrigue, dismay, and inspire both the average person and the earnest student of human behavior. In the past two decades, developmental psychologists have achieved an understanding of these capacities that was once thought to be impossible to reach.

Today the field of developmental psychology is in one of the most extensive periods of growth in its history. Not only are greater numbers of people entering the field than in the previous ten years, but also new professional societies and scholarly journals are springing up to encourage and strengthen efforts to tackle a wider range of problems and approaches than in the past.

We have written this book to give a picture of developmental psychology as it is today: an expanding, multifaceted enterprise devoted to understanding both basic principles of psychological development and the circumstances that create new opportunities and demands for children and adolescents in the 1990s. To make this picture as faithful as possible, we have given special attention to five characteristics of developmental psychology as a field of study:

Orientation

- *Topical and chronological approaches.* The study of development includes both an interest in particular topics or domains of human functioning (e.g., perception, cognition, and emotions) and an interest in distinctive developmental features at different times in the life cycle. Working developmental psychologists typically do not think of the field in either a fully topical or a consistently chronological perspective. Currently, for example, topical interests overlap and coexist with chronological interests in two periods especially: infancy and adolescence.

Therefore we have combined a topical perspective with an emphasis on these two age periods in our text. The early sections of the book emphasize the questions and answers that have resulted from the work of researchers who study the early years of life. The final two chapters focus on what we have learned from research by addressing questions of special interest during adolescence. In both cases, however, we have tried to show how what we have learned about infants and adolescents indicates that these periods of life are quite distinctive; however, they also expand our understanding of basic developmental principles that we have seen at work in other developmental periods. These chapters serve as "bookends" for a series of topical chapters (e.g., perceptual development, language development, cognitive development, and social and personality development). This organization captures, we hope, the real-life synergism between an interest in developmental periods and in domains and contexts of growth in developmental psychology.

- *Continuous emergence of new knowledge.* Developmental psychology frequently experiences a rapid emergence of new knowledge as a result of "explosions" of activity in certain areas of research. Recently, for example, emotional development has captured the attention of a number of researchers; as a result we now have valuable new insights about this fundamental aspect of human psychology. Because of the vitality of this area, we have taken the somewhat unusual step of devoting an entire chapter to emotional development. Similarly, research on the second decade of life has grown enormously since 1980, and we have recognized this expanded productivity in two comprehensive chapters. Finally, throughout the book we have called attention to current emphases in research and newly emerging knowledge about the principles and processes of development. Every chapter includes special Research Focus boxes, many of which report examples of new directions in the field.

- *Process emphasis.* In picturing the study of children and adolescents as a dynamic, growing enterprise, we are also attempting to convey a sense that *why* is as important as *what* to a developmental psychologist. To be sure, it is important to know *what* aspects of behavior, and *what* changes in these aspects, are especially important to human experience; but developmental psychologists also want to know *why* these behaviors are significant and *why* changes occur as they do. We have sought to focus on individual growth and change in a way that combines a recurring emphasis on the processes that contribute to the flow of development from one period of life to the next, with constant reminders that our knowledge of the process of development is still open and is itself constantly changing.

- *Theoretical eclecticism.* The aforementioned openness means that developmental psychology today, more than in the past, is guided by a variety of theoretical formulations that provide useful perspectives on the complex processes of growth and development. This eclecticism marks a change from earlier periods in the history of the field. In the mid-twentieth century, behaviorism dominated research on development; cognitive-developmental perspectives enjoyed a similarly extensive influence in the decades of the 1960s and 1970s. Such theoretical orthodoxies have given way to more diverse, integrative ways of thinking about behavior and development. We have attempted to capture this pluralistic state of affairs—another sign of the current vitality and expansion of the field.

• *Attention to the environments of childhood.* We have attempted to make clear the relevance of basic processes to the everyday worlds of children and adolescents in this diverse society. A growing understanding of the important role of contexts of development led us to devote chapters to developmental processes in environments in which children grow and develop (families, peer groups, school, and the societal institution of the mass media). In addition, we have included not only numerous references to research that has grown out of the overlap between research and application, but also discussions by experts on such issues as the treatment of babies born with severe problems, teenage pregnancy and parenthood, and the policy issues associated with the growing number of "latchkey" children in U.S. society.

Organization

This book is about how children and adolescents develop the behaviors and competencies necessary to live and work as adults. It has two purposes. First, it is meant to give you a general *description* of human development from birth to young adulthood—the changing behavior patterns, thoughts, perceptual and language capabilities, emotions, and relations with other persons that characterize the course of growth as it is currently understood. Second, the book is intended to help you understand some possible *explanations* for these changes in individuals as they mature. In other words, the book provides an introduction to developmental psychology, the study of the changes in thought and behavior that typically occur during the human life cycle.

Part One. The Study of Development: Biological Foundations and Infant Development. Part One consists of four chapters that lay the groundwork for addressing this complex topic. Chapter 1 addresses the question: How do psychologists answer questions about children, adolescents, and their development? You will see that behavioral scientists have been studying the unique characteristics of childhood and adolescence for a relatively short time. Today, a variety of methods are used to describe and explain developmental changes and their implications.

Chapters 2 and 3 provide overviews of information about two very early stages of human development: the nature of the fetus and the newborn infant, and the significance of these very early stages of human life for subsequent growth and psychological development. In these chapters you will see that developmental psychologists have been particularly interested in very early development for two basic reasons. One is that research on the prenatal and newborn periods enables scientists to examine the biological foundations of individual development, including genetic factors and innate abilities common to all healthy infants. The second is to trace the impact of certain environmental influences that, even before birth, can affect the growth of the fetus and the capabilities of infants and children. Chapter 4 gives close attention to a particular type of early experience involving interactions with other people. Throughout this section, you will be reminded that psychologists wish to understand the early phases of human life to better understand the links between them and development in later periods of life.

Part Two. The Development of Perception, Cognition, and Language. Part Two consists of four chapters in which the development of perceptual, language, and cognitive abilities is examined in detail.

Chapter 5 addresses a basic question in psychology: How do humans perceive the world around them? After reviewing the nature of perception generally, the chapter examines how perceptual abilities change as a result of experiencing the objects and events that constitute the everyday world. In Chapter 6, the focus is on the development of language. A key question is how infants and toddlers make use of the speech sounds of their parents and others to acquire the ability to form words and sentences on their own.

Chapters 7 and 8 take up the topic of intellectual abilities. A key question is how children make use of the information acquired through perceptual processes to gain new knowledge and reach increasingly more mature understanding of the world around them. In addressing this question, the chapters consider how intellectual abilities and the changes in them can be described and assessed and how psychologists and others can best identify the essential experiences that support optimal intellectual growth.

Part Three. Foundations of Personality and Social Development. Part Three is the first of two parts devoted to the developmental significance of children's experiences with other persons. To set the stage, Chapter 9 provides an overview of the major theoretical perspectives of why social relations are important in development. Following the path laid down in Part One, Chapter 9 addresses the key question of how children develop the different patterns of social behavior and responsiveness to other persons to which the term *personality* refers.

Following this overview are two chapters that discuss aspects of individual development that are fundamental to all aspects of personality and personality development. Chapter 10 examines perceptions and understanding of the persons and relationships that comprise the social world. Chapter 11 focuses on children's emotional expressions, their responsiveness to emotion-arousing experiences, and their awareness of emotions in their own behavior and the behavior of others.

Part Four. Social Contexts and Relationships and the Development of the Individual. Human beings develop in a world in which other persons are perhaps the most significant features. Interactions with parents, teachers, other children, and a variety of incidental acquaintances dominate childhood experiences beginning in early life. The impact of these interactions on the patterns of individual characteristics that mark each child as a distinct individual is the primary focus in the study of personality and social development. Part Four considers both the most common and salient sources of influence in the lives of most children and several aspects of development in which these influences seem especially important to the behavior patterns of individual children.

Chapters 12 and 13 address four important sources of influence in personality and social development: family, schools, mass media, and peers. The chapters make it clear that these sources are closely intertwined. Although all may influence development in unique and important ways, each of the four also helps to determine how much and what kind of impact the other three will have on a developing child.

The interwoven effects of family, school, mass media, and peer influences are especially apparent in the aspects of individual development considered in Chapters 14 and 15. These forces all help to shape children's concepts of themselves as male or female, their knowledge of gender roles, and their expectancies regarding the adoption of these roles. Family, friends, and social institutions also influence the development of children's abilities for self-regulation, including not only the capacity for positive, socially desirable behaviors but also the stimulus and inhibition of antisocial behaviors.

Part Five. Beyond Childhood: Development During Adolescence. Because adolescence has so often received special attention, Part Five is devoted to examining information about how this stage appears to differ from earlier periods of development. Chapter 16 begins with an overview of the physical changes of adolescence. For adolescents themselves, these changes often require considerable psychological adjustments that affect behavior, thought, and emotions. Chapter 17 examines the common belief that social relationships change and that behavioral and emotional problems multiply during adolescence. Throughout these chapters, the linking of adolescent development to the processes outlined in previous chapters illustrates the continuous operation of developmental principles as children grow toward maturity.

Boxed Discussions. Two types of boxed discussions are in the text. Research Focus boxes appear in every chapter. In these we show how the principles and methods of developmental psychology can be applied to some of the pressing real-life questions about children. The longer, *Controversy* discussions appear in every part. These are discussions written by experts concerning controversial issues such as the treatment of babies born with severe problems; the biased nature of ability tests; whether the developmental processes of girls differ from those of boys; the policy issues associated with the growing number of "latchkey" children in U.S. society; and teenage pregnancy and parenthood.

Significant Features

Part Introductions and Chapter Outlines. Each of the five parts of our text begins with an overview of the focus of that part and a description of its significance to the specific area of development being addressed. It also provides an overview of the individual chapters within the parts. Every chapter begins with a chapter outline of the major sections to be covered and a chapter introduction. These features preview the material and place it in a developmental context for the students.

Tables, Illustrations, and Photos. The tables and illustrations have been carefully crafted to summarize, elucidate, and reinforce the concepts being discussed in the text. While the photos have been painstakingly selected to be representative of all elements of the population and to illustrate important points in the text, we also hope they will add a measure of relevancy and student interest. We have included four 4-page color inserts that capture the nature of prenatal development, infancy, childhood, and adolescence. Special mention must be made here of the stunning 4-color photographs by Lennart Nilsson that appear in the insert devoted to prenatal development. These photos, taken in 1990, are an example of cutting-edge technology revealing the wonders of conception. We are pleased we were able to obtain them for this edition of our text.

Methodological Appendices. Appendices appear at the end of selected chapters. Their purpose is to explain basic statistical and methodological points, sometimes with the aid of illustrations, and to help students understand the details of common research procedures.

Chapter Summaries. At the close of each chapter, the Summary reviews the main points from the chapter, highlighting their relevance to the four main unifying themes of the text: (1) the origins of focal aspects of development; (2) the course of development of changes from infancy to adolescence; (3) the relationships between different aspects of individual functioning; and (4) the nature of especially significant environmental influences.

Suggested Readings. A short list of suggestions for further readings on main topics discussed within the chapter, plus materials on related topics, follows each chapter.

Glossary. An end-of-book glossary briefly defines the special, central terms of the discipline. These terms appear in bold-faced type the first time they are mentioned in the text.

Ancillary Materials

The text is accompanied by the following ancillary materials that have been carefully developed with authors' collaboration.

Study Guide. The Study Guide to accompany this text was written by James Ramsey Speer of Stephen F. Austin State University. Using the PQ4R Method of Study, this Study Guide was designed to help increase student learning of the text material and improve their performance.

Each chapter of the Study Guide contains an introduction, chapter outline, learning objectives, study questions, review questions (terms and multiple choice), and application questions. Integrative questions help students focus on material in the text as well as on lecture notes from the instructor.

Instructor's Manual. This instructor's resource has been prepared by Suzanne K. Getz of the College of William and Mary. It includes chapter learning objectives, chapter summaries, lecture focus sections (that amplify the text discussions of key topics), a suggested reading list, and an annotated bibliography for outside materials and class activities.

Testbank and Computerized Testbank. Melvyn B. King and Debra E. Clark, of the State Univesity of New York at Cortland, have proposed a testbank of 2,000 multiple-choice questions. Each test item is referenced by page and to the chapter content, and is identified by type of question (factual, applied/conceptual). The testbank is available in book form and computerized versions for the IBM or MacIntosh computers.

Acknowledgments

We have been fortunate to have a number of colleagues and coworkers help in pulling together these rather complex views of developmental psychology today. Chief among these is John C. Masters, whose contributions to the earlier drafts of the manuscript were of inestimable value. We are grateful to him for his scholarship and professional support. Two other colleagues, Daniel Keating and Natalie Torrey, contributed draft materials in the very early stages of the project, and we are grateful to them as well. Like most other textbook authors, we owe a special debt to the reviewers of successive versions of the manuscript. In our case, the following provided helpful commentaries: Alan Keniston, University of Wisconsin-Eau Claire; Thomas S. Parish, Kansas State University; Kathryn N. Black, Purdue University; Kathleen Preston, Humboldt State University; William Gnagey, Illinois State University; Frank C. Keil, Cornell University; Reed Larson, University of Illinois at Urbana; Pamela Blewitt, Villanova University; Matthew J. Sharps, California State University-Fresno; Claire Golumb, University of Massachusetts; Susan W. Goodwyn, University of California-Davis; and Bruce B. Henderson, Western Carolina University. We also wish to thank Macmillan staff members Madalyn Stone, Charlotte Hyland, and Christine Cardone for their supportive approach to the project. In addition, we want to express our enormous gratitude to our many co-workers and students who provided valuable assistance in various stages of manuscript preparation. In Minneapolis, we thank Lonnie Behrendt, Caroline Collins, Elizabeth Greene, Catherine O'Geay, and Nelson Soken. In Dallas, our thanks go to Virginia Kirkpatrick and Ann Wassel.

Finally, we thank our families—particularly Carolyn Collins and Abe and Ben Kuczaj—for their support and forbearance.

W. Andrew Collins
Stanley A. Kuczaj II

Brief Contents

Contents

PART TWO

The Development of Perception, Cognition, and Language 130

CHAPTER FIVE

Perceptual Development 132

CHAPTER SIX

Language Development 166

CHAPTER SEVEN

The Nature and Measurement of Intelligence   204

CHAPTER FOURTEEN

Gender and the Development of Gender Roles 470

CHAPTER FIFTEEN

Self-Regulation: The Development and Control of Prosocial and Antisocial Behavior 500

DEVELOPMENTAL PSYCHOLOGY

Part One consists of four chapters that lay the groundwork for addressing the dual goals of this book: describing development from birth through adolescence, and examining possible processes of change during these years. Chapter 1 poses the question: How do psychologists answer questions about children, adolescents, and their development? You will see that behavioral scientists have been studying the unique characteristics of childhood and adolescence for a relatively short time. Today, a variety of methods are used to explain developmental changes and their implications.

Chapters 2 and 3 provide overviews of information about two very early stages of human development: the nature of the fetus and the newborn infant, and the significance of these very early stages of human life for subsequent growth and psychological development. In these chapters you

PART ONE

The Study of Development: Biological Foundations and Infant Development

will see that developmental psychologists have been particularly interested in very early development for two basic reasons. One is that research on the prenatal and newborn periods enables scientists to examine the biological foundations of individual development, including genetic factors and innate abilities common to all healthy infants. The second is to trace the impact of certain environmental influences that, even before birth, can affect the growth of the fetus and the capabilities of infants and children. Chapter 4 gives close attention to a particular type of early experience, one involving interactions with other people. Throughout this section, you will be reminded that psychologists wish to understand the early phases of human life to better understand the links between them and development in later periods of life.

3

Studying Child Development

Introduction

Picture a human infant, one you know personally or an "ideal" baby that appears on television or in newspaper advertisements. Your mental infant may be either female or male, a member of any racial or ethnic group. To the student of child development, the differences between the child you picture and the children others may imagine are striking and challenging. Children are individuals, and their individuality is usually apparent from an early age. The questions of how differences in thought and behavior originate and the degree to which they are influenced by heredity versus experience are at the heart of psychology as a field of study.

For developmental psychologists an equally compelling question is, what are the common features of the process through which these infants grow into childhood, adolescence, and adulthood? To answer this question, researchers work toward careful *descriptions* of how thought and behavior change and *explanations* for those changes.

This book is designed to introduce you to the study of psychological development from infancy through adolescence. In this chapter we begin our survey by addressing three broad questions: First, we ask what we mean by the term *development*. Second, we turn to recurring issues that have marked the study of development. Third, with these two questions setting the stage, we turn to the question of how we can attain valid and useful descriptions and explanations about development.

What Do We Mean by Development?

A crystal created by dipping a string into a supersaturated solution may grow larger and larger, but we would not say it had "developed." Although the term *development* implies growth and change, it is not limited to the accumulation of characteristics that humans acquire as they mature. Instead, the term *development* is commonly reserved to refer to human growth that includes distinctive new thought and behavior patterns.

Let us examine two examples of apparent developmental change in children:

- Consider a two-year-old child who has been using correctly the past tenses of irregular verbs. One day she was heard saying, "I ran there." Later she begins to say *runned* instead of *ran* ("I runned there"). This apparent step backward signifies a realization that merely adding "-ed" to a verb often turns it into the past tense. It is an overregularization that gives clear evidence that a common rule of grammar has been acquired, although at the cost of a temporary incompetence. Further developmental steps, which appear to take place without direct teaching for most children, will enable the child to apply the "add -ed" rule properly and to recognize the existence of irregular verb forms as well.

- Think of a preschooler and a fifth grader faced with the following task: An adult shows them three beakers: two identical beakers that are short and fat and one that is tall and thin. The two fat beakers contain the same amounts of water; the thin one is empty. Both children tell the adult that the two fat beakers contain the same amount of water. The adult then pours the water from one fat beaker into the tall, thin, empty beaker and asks whether the amount of water is still the same. The preschooler says the tall, thin beaker has more than the short, fat beaker, but the fifth grader says both contain the same amount. Because the column of water is higher in the thin beaker than in the fat one, it looks as if the amount is greater, and this apparently convinces the preschooler that the amount of water is different. The older child seems to go beyond appearances, perhaps realizing that even though the height of the column in the thin beaker is greater, the equally important dimension of the width of the beaker is less.

These two examples illustrate the idea that development involves an observable change in behavior that seems to signify that the person has a more complex capability to carry out everyday tasks, solve problems, and interact with other persons.

The Concept of Process in Development

Developmental psychology is the science of the changes in thought and behavior that typically occur during the human life cycle. It addresses questions about why people of different ages behave the way they do and how change occurs. These are questions about the *processes* that alter thought and behavior. The concept of process is ordinarily used to refer to mechanisms that cause developmental change. In other words, the focus is on explaining *how* and *why* changes in capabilities and behaviors occur, rather than on simply describing the changes. Think about language acquisition. We can readily chart the growth of a young child's vocabulary, as parents often do with lists posted on refrigerator doors. This *describes* a child's growing lingusitic competence, but it does not tell much about the underlying process by which children learn new words or their meanings. Research on *how* parents, teachers, and peers talk to young children and the ways in which this helps children learn words and their meanings, however, tells us something about *why* change occurs. The social context of language acquisition and some of the other processes influencing early language learning.

Developmental researchers formulate theories about the course and processes of change in the many aspects of human functioning: language, perception, cognition, emotion, and social interactions and relationships. Out of these theories hypotheses are drawn to direct research. On the basis of findings, theories are refined and, often, further research is undertaken in the hope of identifying principles of human growth and change.

A Historical Perspective on the Study of Childhood Development

Interest in understanding the nature of development has been determined historically by current social practices and views concerning human nature.

Concepts of Childhood in History.   Childhood and adolescence have not always been viewed as distinct periods of life, separate from adulthood. During the middle ages, children under the age of seven were considered infants; after age seven, they were treated as adults (Aries, 1962). This is quite different from today's world in which most people perceive at least four categories of individuals: infants, children, adolescents, and adults. Some draw even more distinctions, dividing the life span into infancy, early childhood, middle childhood, early adolescence, middle adolescence, late adolescence or youth, young adulthood, middle age, and old age. Even within the field of developmental psychology today, there are reminders that our implicit partitioning of developmental eras is less differentiated than is needed for the careful study of developmental change. For example, we often neglect the differences between children in early elementary school and middle school. Similarly, we often fail to notice the difference between early- and middle-adolescent groups, although recent evidence points to the years from age 10 to age 14 or 15 as a distinctive and developmentally significant period (Carnegie Council on Adolescence, 1989; Collins, 1984).

Historically, the failure to conceive of childhood as distinct from adulthood, with its inherent lack of sensitivity to developmental progression, was accompanied by very different treatment of children than we are accustomed to in the twentieth century. Noisy or bothersome children were sometimes quieted by alcohol or narcotics. If they were unwanted, the children might simply be abandoned, left to die on the streets. Even if fortunate enough to be taken in by a foundling home, the children's survival was uncertain. By one report (Kessen, 1965), less than one-half of one percent (fewer than 50 out of more than 10,000) of the children in one Irish foundling home survived the experience. At about age seven, when they became "adults," children became full-fledged members of the adult work force at the same age that children in today's industrialized societies enter elementary school. In Georgian England, children as young as seven or eight were treated as adults in criminal cases and received harsh sentences such as long-term deportation to prison colonies in Australia and to some areas of the pre-Revolutionary American colonies (Burns & Goodnow, 1985).

Gradual changes in social and economic conditions and in views of human nature affected concepts of children and childhood, as well, and these in turn affected interest in children's welfare. During the 17th and 18th centuries, economic progress and technological change contributed to the development of a middle class and created a demand for workers who had some degree of skill and education. Consequently, special provisions had to be

According to current views of human development, each child in this family represents a distinctly different period of the life span.

made to send children to school or to tutor them at home. Furthermore, improved living conditions and medical care in the rising middle class led to reduced mortality rates among infants and very young children, and greater economic security reduced the need for children to contribute to the work force. Factors such as these increased the attention given to children within the family at ages beyond infancy and produced a growing recognition of childhood as an important period of development between infancy and adulthood.

This historical perspective helps us to see that concerns about the nature and course of development—and even the existence of distinct periods of human development itself—have always been embedded in the social, political, and philosophical milieu of human societies. Even today, the importance of infancy and early childhood to research on human development is tied partly to a series of economic and political questions about the status of women in our society and their participation in the work force. As increasing numbers of women contribute to family incomes, the question of whether these early periods of child development will be impaired by out-of-home care and education has become more important. As a result, instead of viewing the preschool years as one period, a finer breakdown into infancy, toddlerhood, and early childhood has begun in order to understand the implication of varied experiences and arrangements for care during these years. Similarly, the increase in drug use and out-of-wedlock pregnancy and childbearing in the very early years of adolescence appears to be generating concerns about the unique characteristics of development at the ages of 12, 13, and 14.

Scientific Interest in Child and Adolescent Development. As early life was seen as a distinct point in human development, theoretical and empirical efforts

9

arose to increase understanding of the pre-adult years. One of the first examples of this was the emergence of a number of baby biographies prepared by educators, philosophers, biologists, and other parents who recorded their observations of their children's early development. These biographies were subject to the criticism that the observer's beliefs or theoretical perspective had affected the record. For example, consider Charles Darwin's (1877) diary describing the early development of his son. Darwin felt that *ontogeny* (the development of the individual) and *phylogeny* (the development of the species through evolution) were similar, and that the study of one could enhance the understanding of the other. In fact, Darwin (1877) wrote that through carefully observing infants, one could see the different periods of human evolution recapitulated by the successive phases of the infant's development. Despite their sometimes biased accounts of development, baby biographies lent credibility to the study of children and fostered the belief that learning about child development was an important scientific goal.

The establishment of developmental psychology as a field of study is usually credited to G. Stanley Hall (1846–1924). Hall was an important and influential figure in American psychology. A founder of the American Psychological Association and president of Clark University, he was the first person to welcome the Viennese psychiatrist Sigmund Freud to the United States, even before Freud's theory of psychoanalysis was widely accepted. His own interest in developmental psychology was heavily focused on one aspect, how children view and understand the world around them. Hall examined the developmental changes in children's views of many subjects, from religion to sex. His research illustrated how information could be used systematically to describe the behavior and thought of children at different ages, and he also made a number of inferences to explain what caused development. Although his theoretical and empirical contributions have not

G. Stanley Hall (seated, center), shown here with participants in a 1909 psychology conference at Clark University, is credited with establishing developmental psychology as a field of study.

made a lasting contribution to the field, Hall greatly advanced the science of child and adolescent development by lending his considerable prestige to this area of study in its early years.

It is worth noting that major theories that have guided child development as a science through the years have been associated with particular aspects or *domains* of development. Sigmund Freud, for example, stressed the importance of early experience primarily in terms of the child's social and emotional development. The German ethologist and Nobel laureate Konrad Lorenz focused on early experience from the perspective of early perceptual development and the role of instinct in behavior. Swiss psychologist Jean Piaget developed a stage-based theory of cognitive development, emphasizing the active role of children in their own intellectual development. Throughout the text, we will examine these historical contributions more fully in the context of the domains of development to which they have been particularly central. We will also see how the fundamental notions of development represented in early views have been transformed and refined in subsequent work in developmental psychology.

Dominant Questions in the Study of Development

Let us now turn to the heart of knowledge about child development. Regardless of the theoretical stance we take or the methods we use in studying development—regardless even of whether we are studying language, perception, cognition, or social behavior and relationships—certain core questions repeatedly emerge. These questions are basic to the picture of development that researchers are beginning to piece together. We introduce these questions in this section and will use them as a framework for the topics we address in each of the subsequent chapters.

What Are the Origins of Behavior?

The infant that you were asked to imagine at the beginning of this chapter appears in many ways to lack social and intellectual capabilities. As we will see in Chapters 2 through 4, the recent discovery of extensive and significant abilities in very young infants has dramatically changed popular ideas about what infants can do. At the same time, these findings have emphasized the importance of considering the origins of abilities and behaviors and of attempting to understand how those abilities and behaviors change from their initial to their mature forms.

The obvious fact that infants know very little, in the sense that older children and adults have acquired a good deal more specific information about the world around them and how to get along in it, was considered for centuries to indicate that infants were devoid of capabilities. The origins of behavior were widely assumed to exist in the experiences that infants en-

11

countered after birth. The most famous statement of this view came from the philosopher John Locke (1632–1704) who wrote in the late 17th century. Locke considered the mind of an infant to be a *tabula rasa* or a blank slate on which experience imposes both content and structure. Although recognizing that some inherent characteristics existed, Locke was confident that the primary influence on development was children's experience with the world and others in it. Locke's view was consistent with many popular ideas about children and development—then and now—and was influential in helping to justify the importance of formal education in the development of social and intellectual competence.

Persistent though it has been, the *tabula rasa* view of the origins of behavior has had powerful competition from the view that development is at least partly impelled by factors internal to the child. Among the early proponents of this view, called *nativists*, were the 17th-century philosophers René Descartes and Immanuel Kant. According to Descartes and Kant, human beings are born with an innate set of ideas and abilities, which govern their interpretation of information about the world. For Descartes and Kant, experience with the world is relatively unimportant in determining how infants perceive the natural world. Instead, these nativists argued that all human beings possess innate concepts of space, time, and matter, and these innate concepts determine how we interpret the information provided by experience. There are contemporary parallels to these ideas in hypotheses that assume that infants have innate perceptual skills (see Chapter 5) and innate knowledge of language (see Chapter 6).

A somewhat different view was proposed by the French philosopher Jean Jacques Rousseau (1712–78). Writing only shortly after Locke, Rousseau argued that development might unfold in a natural sequence if the infant were provided with the opportunity for experience without an adult imposing any particular design. He objected to the view that children were incomplete adults who needed only to be supplied with the detailed knowledge that adults could instill. Seeing the child's behavior as the product of a continuous interaction between the child's inborn impulses and the demands of the environment, Rousseau emphasized the importance of allowing children to engage the world in terms of their own understanding and purposes (Borstelmann, 1983). He cautioned against a strict socialization for the purpose of teaching self-denial and delayed gratification and opposed formal and focused education that was for the purpose of training children for particular positions in society.

The debate over nature versus nurture has continued far past the pronouncements of Locke and Rousseau. In one form the issue has focused on the relative emphasis given to native impulses as determinants of behavior and development or to learning and experience. Even Rousseau did not question that experience was influential in development, but favored letting the internal readiness of children direct their experiences. Nor did Locke, who acknowledged "native propensities," think experience was the only source of children's competencies. Although this balanced approach has not always characterized discussions of this issue, most responsible experts today recognize that both inherent characteristics and experience contribute to development. Consequently, in the survey of development in this textbook, we will ask, what are the apparent origins of this aspect of children's capabilities and behavior? This topic is particularly central to Chapter 2 on genetic and prenatal influences on development.

Different aspects of behavior follow different developmental timetables. For example, as we will see in Chapter 4, many basic perceptual skills are present at birth or in the first few months of life and change little after that time. Grammatical competence is achieved largely by the end of the third year, although vocabulary and conceptual aspects of language undergo considerable development in later years. Children show remarkable capacities for social responsiveness in early life, but, as they mature, interpersonal relationships develop different forms and functions. Thus, describing changes in thought and behavior is central to the study of development.

What Are the Nature and the Course of Behavior Change?

Differentiation and Integration. Developmental psychologists have also been particularly interested in describing the form of developmental changes. One influential hypothesis has been that development is, simultaneously, a process of *differentiation* and *integration*. This characterization comes from the study of embryology. A developing fetus begins as one cell, then divides into two, which divide into four. In addition, different capacities for functioning outside the mother's womb emerge at different points during the gestation period. This is a result of the progressive differentiation of cells. By saying that behaviors become *differentiated* in the course of development, we are implying that individuals' repertoire of skills and abilities become more complex and specialized as they develop. Continuing the embryological metaphor, the different types of tissue that result from cell differentiation gradually become coordinated into organs and, eventually, into an incipient human organism. By extension, this process of *integration* implies that, psychologically, many specific skills and abilities become coordinated into effective patterns of thought and action. An influential theory of development, the *organismic–developmental theory* of Heinz Werner (1948), has sought to explain how thought and action both increase in complexity and become more organized and coherent as children develop. Werner's view implies that children follow the principles of differentiation and integration in psychological development, as well as in biological functions.

Continuity Versus Discontinuity. A recurring controversy about the course of development is whether development should be considered *continuous* or *discontinuous*. If development is continuous, then early development should predict later development because later development is built directly on early development. If children suffer neglect or abuse at an early age, for example, their later development would inevitably be damaged. If development is *discontinuous*, however, the effects of early trauma might be diminished, perhaps even overcome, by later positive, enriching experiences. The issue of continuity versus discontinuity in development has arisen in connection with every aspect of growth and change. For example, if children are not exposed to language at early ages, is it possible for normal language learning

13

to occur at a later age? If children are deprived of intellectual stimulation in infancy, but enter an enriched and supportive environment later on, will the later environment affect intelligence test scores and school performance? If children lack the opportunity of playing with other children at young ages, can they develop appropriate interpersonal skills when the opportunity becomes available? In some cases, such as in the current discussion of the effects of out-of-home child care for infants and preschoolers, the question of continuity versus discontinuity is central to public debates about the welfare of children.

For developmentalists, one manifestation of the continuity versus discontinuity controversy is a continuing debate over whether development can be described in terms of a series of *stages*. The idea of a stage implies that development is divided into a series of relatively discrete periods in which one particular capability or behavior pattern predominates. For example, in Jean Piaget's theory of intellectual development, young children are considered to function primarily in terms of concrete objects and observable events, whereas at later stages abstract thought and reasoning are more characteristic. Similarly, in Sigmund Freud's famous theory of psychosexual development, infants are viewed as being in the oral stage first, where they are particularly sensitive to close interactions with caregivers, whereas in later stages they are increasingly sensitive to interactions with others besides the main caregiver. In both the Piagetian and Freudian examples, experiences in the earlier stage are considered essential as a foundation for the achievement of the later stage. Although there is apparent discontinuity in that the dominant characteristics of a child's functioning differ in the different stages, there is continuity in the sense that later functioning is built on earlier functioning. This idea that stages fall in a particular order, and individuals must pass through one (successfully or not) before proceeding to the next, is referred to by the term *epigenesis*. In each chapter that follows, we will have an opportunity to address the questions: To what extent does change in this area follow a continuous pattern versus a discontinuous, *epigenetic,* or stage-like, pattern? What form does the pattern take?

These first two questions provide a basis for raising our two further questions: Given that development results from an interplay of native endowment and environmental influences, what environmental conditions are especially significant for developing a particular behavior? Also, in what ways are different aspects of development interrelated with one another in a maturing person?

What Environmental Conditions Affect a Given Aspect of Behavior or Capability and Its Course of Change?

We noted earlier that most experts now view development as an interplay of inherent characteristics and experiences with the outer world; they would agree that the relative contribution of each varies from one phase of development to another. Although it is generally impossible to specify how much of a behavioral pattern or capability is attributable to heredity, virtually all behaviors show some degree of environmental influence. Indeed, developmental psychologists have devoted a great deal of attention to correlations between environmental conditions and the occurrence of specific behaviors

Developmental psychologists frequently examine how stimulating versus impoverished environments effect cognitive, behavioral, and emotional development.

and to research explaining these links. For example, the effects of stimulating versus impoverished environments in infancy, the impact of parental discipline and teaching methods, and the effectiveness of interventions to improve children's social behavior and school learning are all well known research topics in the study of development. A question to raise in connection with the topics to be discussed in later chapters, then, is what conditions or social influences have been found to be particularly important in how behaviors and capabilities show themselves at different ages?

Although we discuss the development of perceptual abilities, language skills, or social behaviors as though they are distinct and independent aspects of human behavior, we are after all attempting to understand a human infant, child, or adolescent. Consequently, when we talk about changes in behavior in one area, we need to consider the implications for other aspects of functioning. For example, the ability to walk alters the nature of the physical settings children encounter, including the potential for harm to themselves and the kinds of interactions they have with others. The shift from childhood to adolescence entails a variety of changes as well: in physical appearance, social contacts, opportunities for previously unavailable recreational and work experiences, and so forth. As we will see in Chapters 16 and 17, adolescence is a time when both internal changes and external experiences contribute to multiple developmental changes.

What Are the Significant Links Between Behavior Change in One Area and Other Areas of Functioning?

One behavior affects another behavior in ways that are not always clear. For example, although it is commonly assumed that cognitive skills are essential components of successful social interactions, it is also apparent that social interactions foster cognitive development. As we will see in Chapters 4 and 11, emotional states are affected by cognitive maturity, but emotions can also either facilitate or interfere with cognitive functioning. When in later chapters we raise the question of interrelatedness, we will focus on the diverse links that can occur among multiple aspects of development.

15

The complexities of human development, which are already apparent in the early years of life, grow even more so as the number of potential influences and the accumulation of past experiences grow. Questions about origins (e.g., heredity or environmental influences), change, environmental impact, and interrelatedness of behaviors and capabilites can be addressed fruitfully at every time of life. These questions are at the heart of research on child and adolescent development and a better understanding of human nature.

How Do We Study Development?

To get useful information about the core questions in developmental psychology, we need good descriptions of the typical behaviors and abilities of children at different ages and an understanding of how change occurs. Developmentalists rely on the tenets of science to obtain reliable and valid information. As background for the overview of research findings that will come in later chapters, we now turn to a brief overview of common principles and methods of research used by developmental psychologists.

Formulating Hypotheses

Hypothesis testing is the backbone of any science. Sometimes hypotheses emerge from the careful observation of behavior. Sound description is essential in any science that studies the behavior of organisms in natural environments. At other times, hypotheses are derived from theories of human behavior and development.

In either case, hypotheses are tested in an effort to provide knowledge and to advance theory. For example, finding that an increased level of viewing violent television programs leads to greater levels of aggression in children provides important information about television influences on social behavior. At the same time, the finding contributes to the evaluation of theory, in this case to theory regarding how children learn from observing the behavior of others, such as fictional characters on television.

A constant tension in devising hypotheses about behavior and development is that one must be able to both prove and disprove hypotheses. Hypotheses that allow the researcher to predict several different outcomes without specifying factors that produce one outcome rather than another are not open to being disproved. "Common sense" knowledge is in many ways a set of naive hypotheses about the world that is attractive partly because it is not falsifiable and, thus, can readily "explain" a great deal—at least, in hindsight. Consider the following two adages: "Absence makes the heart grow fonder" and "Out of sight, out of mind." Both may be true in some instances, but neither alone can explain a great deal about separation and a person's reactions to it, because both statements fail to tell us under which conditions the theories would most likely hold true. For example, we have no clue about the conditions under which "absence makes the heart grow

Observing children in classrooms is one way of gaining insight into the environmental influences that contribute to development.

fonder" and how they differ from the conditions that lead to a person's being "out of sight, out of mind."

Testing Hypotheses

Testable hypotheses raise specific questions about behavior and its development. Developmental psychologists usually go about answering these questions through one or more of several commonly recognized research methods. In this section, we briefly survey these methods, to prepare you to understand the descriptions of research and findings that will be presented in later chapters. In particular, we want to introduce some of the terms that developmental psychologists use to communicate their methods and findings to others.

As groundwork, let us consider the general goal of research: to identify a specific set of conditions under which a particular aspect of behavior may occur.

The aspect of behavior is referred to as a *variable*. Variables are usually examined for one of two purposes. One purpose is to determine the relations among variables (for example, between inconsistent discipline by parents and coercive behavior by the child). The second purpose is to discover conditions under which behavioral variations occur, as between one group of children and another (for example, those who have been trained to control aggression and those who have not), between children of one age and another, or between children having different characteristics (for example, boys vs. girls).

Let us apply this distinction to an example. Suppose your hypothesis concerned the relation between parental authority and how children respond to it. Parental authority can vary on a dimension that ranges from strict (such as, sharp limits on behavior and angry reactions to misbehavior) to lenient (such as, few limits and tolerance for many instances of misbehavior). Children's behavior is also variable, for example, it might be rated as obedient or rebellious. If one variable (such as, parental authority) is believed to be an important condition affecting the other variable (such as, child behavior), the former is referred to as an *independent* variable and the second is considered to be the *dependent* variable.

Strictly speaking, many psychological variables are not observable. One cannot see a motive, for example, or intelligence or a child's understanding of a grammatical rule. What can be observed are overt behaviors that reflect the psychological variable in question. In our earlier example of the child who begins to say "runned" instead of "ran," we can *infer* that a grammatical

17

rule has been acquired. Because we must deduce psychological processes from observable behavior, we rely on research strategies to strengthen *inferences* about psychological development.

A basic issue in research is how to assess the relation between variables. The following three methods are the most commonly used for this purpose: (1) correlational studies, (2) mean-difference studies, and (3) experiments.

Correlational Studies. Studies of associations between variables that do not assume that one variable causes changes in the other are called *correlational studies*. For example, a study may examine the association between warmth and acceptance toward the child and the child's moral development. Parental behavior might be given high scores if it is very warm and accepting and low scores if it is less so, and children's scores on a measure of conscience development would also vary from high to low. The measures of these two variables would then be used to compute a statistic called a *correlation coefficient*. A coefficient at or approaching +1.0 indicates that, across all the parent-child pairs you studied, high levels on one variable are associated with high scores on the other variables and low levels on the two variables are similarly associated. In the parent-child example, the more warm and accepting the parent, the higher level of conscience shown by the child, and the less warm and accepting the parent, the weaker the conscience shown by the child. A correlation coefficient of −1.0 means that high levels on one variable are associated with low levels on the other (for example, the less warm and accepting the parent, the higher the conscience level of the child, or the more warm the parent, the less the conscience level of the child). A value of 0 would indicate that there is no association between the parental warmth and acceptance and the child conscience variables.

The degree of correlation between two variables is typically evaluated on the basis of the *statistical significance* of the correlation coefficient. A significant association is one that would be expected again if the study were repeated. In terms of learning about the association between parental warmth and child behavior, we might use the correlation as an indicator of whether we should attempt to understand the process by which the two might be linked. If the association is statistically significant, there is an empirical reason to take the next step in research.

Mean-Difference Studies. Another approach to assessing the relation between variables is to examine differences between groups of individuals. The groups are separated on the basis of known differences on one variable and then assessed to determine whether they also differ on other variables. Continuing the example of parental warmth and children's development of a conscience, an investigator might assess the warmth and acceptance of a large number of parents and then divide their children into two groups, those whose parents are above average in warmth and acceptance and those whose parents are below average. Then, after assessing the children's level of development of a conscience, the researcher could test the hypothesis that children whose parents are warm and accepting will tend to have a higher average level of conscience development than those whose parents are colder and less accepting. In this example, it is easy to see the similarity between correlational and mean-difference methods. Instead of computing a correlation coefficient between two variables, we compute the mean, or average, score on the second variable for children in two or more groups, which have been formed on the basis of the variation in the first variable, that of parents' level of warmth and acceptance. The mean scores of the two groups are then compared statistically. The appendix to this chapter illustrates how data on the relation between parental warmth and conscience development might be studied using either a correlational or a mean-difference method and explains the process of testing the significance of correlation coefficents and mean differences.

In neither correlational nor mean-difference studies does a statistically significant result indicate that one variable causes another. In the case of a signficant correlation between parental leniency and child obedience, for example, it might be that parental strictness induces the children's obedience or rebelliousness, or it could be that obedient children influence their parents to be more lenient because strictness is not needed. Correlation alone gives us no information about the direction of the effect. Similarly, significantly higher conscience measures for the children of warm, accepting parents could indicate that "good," trustworthy children elicited greater warmth and acceptance from their parents.

Experimental Studies. The term *experiment* is reserved for studies in which one variable is manipulated or controlled by the investigator (for example, teachers are instructed to be strict or lenient in the classroom) and its effect on another variable is measured (for example, observers rate children's subsequent behavior as obedient, rebellious, attentive, and so on). The manipulated variable is the *independent variable,* and the one left free to change is the *dependent variable.*

The control over one or more variables in research provides a sounder basis for inferring causality. The basic premise for inferring causality is that the cause precedes the effect. Experimenters controlling when a particular behavior occurs, for example, are initiating a cause-effect sequence they have hypothesized. If the expected dependent variable does not reliably follow the introduction of the independent variable, however, their hypothesis is disconfirmed.

Suppose we wish to study differences in mathematical problem-solving ability at different ages. Mathematical performance is the dependent variable. In order to study a variable, it must be operationalized, that is, it must be given a dimension that can be measured. In this instance, mathematical problem-solving ability might be measured by school mathematics grades or by a standardized test of mathematical ability.

In addition to the dependent measure, the hypothesis specifies age as another variable of interest. Furthermore, because differences between boys and girls in mathematical ability have frequently been hypothesized and reported, it also makes sense to consider gender. Thus, both age and gender are independent variables; they are under the control of the experimenter who chooses the children to participate in the study. Ideally, equal numbers

19

of boys and girls at each age would be randomly drawn to be experimental subjects.

Suppose that we wish to test a somewhat more specific hypothesis: that boys and girls are different in mathematical problem-solving ability because girls are pressured to achieve in school earlier than boys, although boys eventually experience such pressure as well. This hypothesis would lead to the prediction that girls' achievement would be greater than boys' during elementary school, but would not differ in high school. If this prediction were confirmed, it would not not rule out other explanations, however. Teachers may expect girls to do better when they are young and may, therefore, give them more help toward earning higher grades, or they might expect girls to need more help than boys. Teachers might also expect boys to be less attentive and less interested in school and, in turn, give them less help.

Experimental manipulation in the laboratory usually allows for greater control over extraneous variables that might mask or interfere with observing the cause-effect sequence. Because experimenters cannot measure or manipulate everything that is likely to influence behavior, however, a common feature of experimental designs is a *control group.* In developmental studies, the control group is typically composed of children who are selected for participation according to the same criteria as the children in the experimental group. In other words, researchers assume that control group children are subject to the same extraneous factors as the experimental group children, but control subjects are not manipulated by the independent variable, as the experimental group is. If the scores on the dependent variable are different for the experimental group than for the control group, we have a stronger basis for inferring that the manipulation caused the difference.

A potential drawback of greater control in laboratory experiments is that the laboratory—although intended to parallel real-life circumstances—may be so different from children's typical experiences that the relation observed in the laboratory is not a good indication of how children would behave in real life. Two variations of the laboratory experiment enable researchers to observe the effects of manipulations under more natural conditions. In one, the *natural experiment*, the experimental manipulation occurs within the natural environment. Instead of changing the environment artificially, the researcher selects children according to their different experiences. For example, in the past, researchers interested in the effects of television on children have sometimes been able to compare communities in which television signals could not be received with those into which television was just being introduced (see, for example, Williams, 1986). The lives of the people in these communities were otherwise very similar, despite the geographical conditions that made television viewing possible in one community and not in the other. Before the introduction of television, the children in the two villages were very similar behaviorally and intellectually. The post-introduction differences in the children in the two communities could, thus, be attributed to the introduction of television.

In the other type of relatively natural experiment, the *field experiment*, the experimenter controls the independent variable or variables, but does so in circumstances where children are ordinarily found. For example, some experimenters (for example, Friedrich & Stein, 1973) have studied the effects of television by introducing special "diets" or television shows into children's everyday activities over a period of months. By observing children in nursery school play, these researchers documented behavioral differences that paralleled differences in what the children were watching on television. Although they were not able to control the children's viewing habits at home during this period, the experimenters did use parents' reports of children's typical viewing in analyzing their results. Thus, although less controlled than a laboratory study of exposure to television, this study provided some evidence that different types of television programming can affect children's play behavior.

A sensible, but rarely pursued, strategy is to test hypotheses using a combination of methods. For example, correlational methods and natural experiments can be used to gather initial evidence that a relation between variables generally fits the pattern predicted by the hypothesis, even under complex natural circumstances, and carefully designed laboratory analogues can then be used to test the causal link between some of the relevant variables and others.

The three types of studies for testing hypotheses provide different kinds of information about the relations among variables.

Testing Hypotheses About Development: Cross-Sectional Versus Longitudinal Designs

For many developmental hypotheses, however, an additional choice must be made: how best to get information about the capabilities and behavior of children of different ages. Think back to our example of Piaget's famous beaker study. Piaget tested children ranging in age from preschoolers to the late-elementary school years and then compared their responses to a series of questions about the effect of pouring water from one beaker to another, differently shaped beaker. As we have seen, the preschool children's answers were more affected by the shape of the beaker than the older children's were, and Piaget inferred that the older children had developed capacities for inferring on the basis of factors other than the appearance of the water in the beakers. This design was *cross-sectional*, because it sampled from a cross-section of children of several different ages. An alternative—although an expensive and time-consuming one—would have been a *longitudinal* study, in which Piaget retested the same children year after year between preschool and late adolescence.

The main advantage of a longitudinal design is that the findings clearly indicate stability and changes in the same child across the age periods of interest. Let us say that we tracked a sample of children from preschool to middle adolescence and found that, overall, there was a steady, gradual decrease in dependence on adults across these years. We might have obtained the same downward trend from one age group to another from a cross-sectional comparison of three or more age groups (say, ages 3–4, 7–8, 11–12, and 15–16). There are, however, several pieces of information we can obtain from the longitudinal data that are not available in a cross-sectional comparison. For example, we can assess the extent to which dependency is a stable characteristic of individuals by looking at the extent to which the same

21

Observational Research

A common avenue for studying behavior is simply to observe and record it. This is frequently done under natural conditions, differing from laboratory studies where children's behavior is controlled.

One paradigm for observational research is that of *structured observation*. In this design, children may be placed in a structured situation; their behavior is constrained very little. For example, children might be brought to a small play room with some blocks and given the opportunity to build a tower. From behind a one-way glass, the experimenter would record instances of cooperative and helpful behavior, as well as the frequency of noncooperation, competition, or perhaps even hindering or interfering. Giving the children a specific task increases the likelihood that certain classes of behavior will occur, without imposing specific requirements on how those behaviors are displayed. Of course, it might be possible to see instances of the same types of behavior by simply watching children in a playroom together, but there would undoubtedly be fewer of them. Consequently, it would take much

longer to see enough samples of the behavior to study it reliably. When the experimenter sets up a situation, however, the situation may not be representative of the natural environment in which behavior and development occur.

Despite limitations such as fewer occurences of a specific behavior, *naturalistic observation* is an important avenue to study behavior, particularly when it is important to know that the behavior in question does occur in the "real world." As noted above, the range of behaviors would be greater and would include many that were not pertinent to the issue under study. Of course, these extraneous behaviors need not be recorded by observers.

One key to quality in observational research is careful preparation of the categories of behavior to be observed. Another is careful training of observers, who must have a common understanding of what each category includes and excludes. Observational research is the best avenue to learning directly from children, but it requires hard and consistent effort by the experimenter to be sure that learning is reliable and valid. ❦

Observing children's behavior in controlled laboratory settings allows developmental psychologists to infer the effect of specific conditions on behavior (see above box).

individuals ranked high, medium, or low in dependency from one age to another. If we find similar levels of dependency, *relative to other children of the same age,* we can conclude that, even though the level of dependency may be generally lower at age 11–12 than at age 3–4, children who were relatively high or low in dependency in the preschool years also tended to be *relatively* high or low as they approached adolescence. In later chapters, there will be many instances in which longitudinal data have provided information that could never have been obtained from cross-sectional studies alone.

Longitudinal designs also avoid a problem known as *cohort effects.* A cohort is a group of individuals who were born at about the same time. In times of rapid social change, such as the years since 1960 in the United States, children born only a few years apart can be exposed to different demands and constraints. For example, children born in 1948 and those born in 1953 experienced different levels of political activism and social consciousness during their childhood years. Consequently, a cross-sectional study of these two age groups in 1970 (at ages 22 and 17) would not be a valid method for investigating the relation between age and political and social attitudes. The children's attitudes and behaviors as measured in 1970 were likely to be quite different, not just because one group was five years older than the other, but because of the differences in their experiences at earlier ages. Because longitudinal designs follow the same cohort from one age period to another, measuring longitudinally the political and social attitudes of both the 1948 and 1953 cohorts would provide better information about the age-attitude relation.

For virtually all aspects of development reviewed in later chapters, we will find a mixture of longitudinal, cross-sectional, field, laboratory, observational, and other types of research methodologies. Periodically, you may want to refresh your understanding of the advantages and limitations of those procedures.

Ethical Considerations in Developmental Research

Although developmental research must always strive to be objective, it must first take into account the well-being of the individuals who participate. In research with children, this is a particularly sensitive issue because the participants may not be capable of granting their own consent to participate in research. Thus others, such as parents or guardians who are charged with the responsiblity for children, must be involved in deciding whether a child can participate in research.

Concerns about research ethics grew out of the universally denounced use of prisoners as unwilling subjects of alleged "research" in German prisons during World War II. Following the Nuremberg trials, regulations for protection of human subjects began to be developed. In the United States, professional societies such as the Society for Research in Child Development and the American Psychological Association have developed codes of ethics for research and clinical practice. The federal government has initiated requirements that institutions receiving federal funds for research must establish an institutional review board to examine research projects by individual scientists and confirm that subjects are not placed at undue risk of harm. Regulations have been developed to guide such judgments for adult subjects as well for children, as well as other groups more vulnerable or less able to understand and consent in a fully informed way to participate in research. These regulations are periodically updated. Many institutions voluntarily use institutional review boards to ensure the ethical character of research under their sponsorship.

In addition to a basic judgment that a research project does not put an individual at undue risk for harm or violate rights of privacy and confidentiality, the central issue of ethical research concerns the prerogative of the person to consent or decline to participate in a given study. For children or other potential research subjects who are under another's legal guardianship, this may quickly become a complex issue. There are some common basic protections, however. First, a minor child may not participate in a study without the *informed consent* of a parent or guardian. This means that the investigator must provide a fully understandable description of the research and the experiences to be encountered by a participating individual. Generally, the person giving consent must sign that description to show that it has been read and understood. One task of institutional review boards is to review consent forms for fullness of disclosure and clarity.

Even if a parent or guardian consents on behalf of a child, the child must also consent to participate (without undue pressure to do so) and must be clearly given the option of discontinuing at any time. For children, consent is usually obtained verbally, but for older ones (for example, a child over 12 years of age), a signature indicating consent is sometimes also obtained.

These are just some example of procedures to ensure that the scientific pursuit of knowledge about development is conducted ethically. In an ethical experiment, children and adults are treated with respect and dignity and kept free from undue risk of harm if they freely consent to participate in research. 🐦

Summary

Developmental psychology consists of the description of changes in human thought and behavior and a search for explanations about how those changes occur. The term *development* ordinarily refers to growth that includes new or different thought and behavior patterns in some aspect of a child's functioning. Although questions about the nature of and changes in children's thought and behaviors have been addressed by philosophers for centuries, the empirical study of development is a relatively recent product of social changes emphasizing childhood and adolescence as distinctive periods in the life span. The establishment of developmental psychology as a field is usually attributed to G. Stanley Hall.

In searching for explanations of changes in thought and behavior in infancy, childhood, and adolescence, developmental psychologists have sought repeatedly to answer four core questions. The question of the origins of behavior is perhaps the most pervasive of these. Early attempts to address this question gave rise to the nature–nurture controversy, a clash between *nativists'* belief that development is caused by factors internal to the child and *environmentalists'* argument that experience imposes structure and content that determine behavior and changes in behavior. Responsible scholars now recognize that complex interactions between inheritance and experience both determine the nature and course of development.

The second question requires both descriptions of how competencies change over time and what causes these changes to occur. Whether development is continuous or discontinuous is one part of this question. The third question concerns the most important environmental conditions or determinants of change. The fourth concerns how aspects of development are interrelated, emphasizing that neither physical, intellectual, nor social growth occurs independently of the others.

These questions have been addressed by developmental psychologists following the tenets of the scientific method. Researchers formulate hypotheses based on theories of child thought, behavior, and development or on empirical observation. They then test those hypotheses in one of three general ways. In *correlational studies*, measures are taken of two or more variables, and *correlations* are computed to determine whether and how the variables co-vary with one another. *Group-difference studies* involve comparing two or more groups that differ in pertinent ways and determining whether these groups are reliably different from one another on a measure of some particular variable. *Experiments* usually involve creating a laboratory analogue of conditions, observing the behavior of children under those conditions, and again computing differences between the groups. These different approaches may involve cross-sectional designs, in which measurements are taken at only one time, or longitudinal designs in which measurements are taken repeatedly over a period of time, usually months or years.

Using these methods, developmentalists are gradually finding answers to questions of origins, the nature and course of development, the source and nature of environmental influences on development, and the interrelations of different aspects of developmental changes.

Suggested Readings

Achenbach, T. (1978). *Research in developmental psychology: Concepts, strategies, methods.* New York: Free Press.

Aries, P. (1962). *Centuries of childhood.* New York: Knopf.

Kessel, F. S., & Siegel, A. W. (Eds.) (1983). *The child and other cultural inventions.* New York: Praeger.

Mussen, P. H. (Ed.), & Kessen, W. (Vol. Ed.) (1983). *Handbook of child psychology* (4th ed.), Vol. 1: *History, theory, & methods.* New York: Wiley.

Appendix

CORRELATION VS. MEAN-DIFFERENCES: METHODS AND STATISTICS

There are many different ways that research may be conducted to answer questions about children's behavior and development. These different ways of proceeding often require that we use different statistical methods to determine whether the results are likely to have occurred by chance.

An example comes from the correlational and mean-difference methods described in Chapter 1. Remember that the example used in describing the differences between these methods involved measuring parents' warmth and acceptance toward the child and the child's strength of conscience. Some hypothetical scores on these two measures appear in Figure 1-1a. These data can be examined in two ways.

In correlational studies, a correlation coefficient was computed between parents' scores and children's scores. The correlation coefficient is a numerical summation of the information shown in Figure 1-1b. As you can see, the numbers on the graph almost form a straight line, indicating that in most cases, the greater a parent's score on warmth and acceptance, the greater the child's conscience score. This almost perfect relation between the two results in a very high correlation coefficient: $+0.98$.

In a mean-difference approach, the children are divided into two groups: those above average on conscience development, and those below average, as shown in Figure 1-1c. Then, taking these two groups separately, an average score for parents on warmth/acceptance was computed for each group. In this case, the mean score for the above-average group is 62; for the below-average group, it is 29. A t-test on the difference between these two mean scores indicates a t of 4.45.

Both the correlation coefficient and the t statistic in this example are highly significant. Remember that statistical significance refers to the degree to which findings exceed a result that might occur by chance. The statistic that is used to report statistical significance is p, or the probability that a result could have occurred by chance. In the case of the correlation coefficient and t in our example, $p < .01$. This indicates that the correlation is so high and the mean difference so large that there is no more than 1 chance in 100 that the result is a fluke. If we repeated the studies 100 times, we would expect to find a nonsignificant result no more than once, if that.

These data are not from an actual study, but were made up to illustrate the statistical principles of correlation, group differences, and significance. If they were real data, it would be reasonable to conclude that children's level of conscience is strongly related to the degree to which their parents are warm and accepting toward them. Remember that we would *not* be justified in inferring that parental attitudes *caused* high levels of conscience—or even that children with good consciences elicit warm, accepting behavior from their parents. We would need other methods, incorporating the conceptual control that we only obtain from experiments, to draw a causal inference.

Child	Children's Conscience Score	Parental Warmth/Acceptance Score
Maria	45	70
Drew	20	40
Kirby	10	25
Matt	30	50
Eva	5	15
Marta	40	60
Jerri	25	45
Jason	35	55
Jim	15	20
Lara	50	75

(a)   Mean (Average):   27.5   45.5

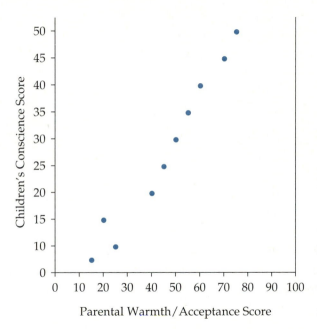

(b)   Parental Warmth/Acceptance Score

FIGURE 1-1
Correlational versus mean-differences approaches to the same data. (a) The data: Children's conscience (0–50, high score = high conscience); parental warmth/acceptance (0–100, high score = high warmth). (b) The distribution, depicted as a cross-tabulation or scatter plot (r = .98). Conclusion: High conscience in children tends to be very strongly associated with high warmth and acceptance by parents. (c) The mean difference approach (t = 4.45, $p < .01$). Conclusion: Children with high conscience levels tend to have parents who are more warm and accepting than do children with low conscience levels.

Children Above the Mean on Conscience		Parental Warmth/Acceptance Score
Maria	45	70
Matt	30	50
Marta	40	60
Jason	35	55
Lara	50	75

Mean Parental Warmth/Acceptance scores for these children: 62

Children Below the Mean on Conscience		Parental Warmth/Acceptance Score
Drew	20	40
Kirby	10	25
Eva	5	15
Jerri	25	45
Jim	15	20

(c)   Mean Parental Warmth/Acceptance scores for these children: 29

27

CHAPTER TWO

Biological Bases of Development and Prenatal Influences

Introduction

The question of the origins of behavior requires that developmental psychologists delve into biology. In fact, not one, but several areas of biology are necessary for understanding how, even before birth, some aspects of individual potential and the forthcoming course of development are determined. To understand how development is affected by the characteristics children inherit from their parents, we must draw from *genetics*. To gain insight into how behavior is affected by the nervous system, including the brain, and its development, we must turn to *neurobiology*. To describe the development of the organism itself from conception to birth—the nature and course of development in its initial stages—we turn to *embryology*. Developmental psychologists are interested in these processes because of what they can tell us about the raw material of development.

From the very moment of conception, however, psychologists also have reason to think about the role of experience. It is now known that a number of environmental factors can damage genetic material and can interfere with the normal development of the embryo, including the brain and nervous system. In short, the nature–nurture controversy that we discussed in Chapter 1 is as completely relevant to development before birth, as it is to development after birth.

The Nature–Nurture Controversy

The tendency to view the development of human capabilities and behaviors as resulting *either* from heredity (nature) *or* the environment (nurture) has gradually given way to the assumption that the *interaction* between heredity and the environment is the most significant factor in these developments. As we shall see in the remainder of this text, most contemporary theories of human development, regardless of whether they are concerned with cognition, perception, or personality, emphasize the interaction of innate predispositions with experience. We now know that development does not take place in a vacuum, and so consideration of the role of experience is essential for any viable theory of human development. However, we also know that human beings are not born as *tabula rasa*, but instead are equipped with certain capabilities and predispositions that are either present at birth or mature shortly after birth. Thus, the goal of developmental psychology is to determine the extent to which innate capabilities interact with different experiences to yield both general patterns of development and the wide range of individual differences within this general pattern that makes each member of our species unique.

General Versus Specific Heredity

A member of a species possesses both a general inheritance and a specific inheritance. The general inheritance consists of the hereditary material necessary to make the organism a member of its species: It is what the organism has in common with all members of its species. General inheritance is the reason that dogs differ from cats, apes from human beings, and moths from butterflies. Although the members of a species share a common general inheritance, each member (except in the case of identical siblings) is also genetically different from all other members. These differences are due in part to differences in hereditary material and in part to differences in experience. The differences in hereditary material among members of the same species reflect *specific inheritance*, the unique combination of hereditary material provided by parents to each of their children. Except for identical siblings, parents provide different combinations of hereditary material to each of their offspring, which is why nonidentical siblings are different from one another. Nonetheless, the hereditary material provided by one set of parents to each of their offspring does overlap. Thus, although parents do provide a unique combination of hereditary material to each of their children, their children share some hereditary information simply because they have the same parents. In addition, they share other hereditary material because they are members of the same species.

Evolution as an Example of the Interaction of Heredity–Environment

General inheritance and specific inheritance are important notions in evolutionary theory, which attempts to account for the similarities of parents and offspring as well as for the enormous differences between the ancestors of a species and its present-day members. The basic assumption of evolutionary theory is that the continued existence of a species depends on the species' ability to adapt to its environment. In evolutionary theory, the emphasis on species–environment interaction for species survival rests on the premise that organisms that are better adapted to their environment are more likely to survive to the age of reproduction and, therefore, are more likely to produce offspring. In general, the more offspring that a species produces, the more likely it is that the species will survive. The exception to this rule occurs when a species is too successful at producing offspring (as human beings seem to be). In such cases, the increasing numbers of the species place too severe a strain on the environmental resources; the resulting change in the environment threatens the continued existence of the species.

31

General inheritance and specific inheritance are both important determinants of a species' continued existence. If a species is well adapted to its environment, then it is important for the species to maintain its existing characteristics in order to remain well adapted. In such cases, general inheritance is probably more important than specific inheritance in determining the likelihood of a species' continued survival. Despite this emphasis on general inheritance for well-adapted species, the significance of specific inheritance remains. Environments do change, and a changing environment can threaten a once well-adapted species with extinction. As an environment changes, characteristics that were once valuable in assuring a species' survival may become nonadaptive, while characteristics that were once nonadaptive may become adaptive. Therefore, in order to survive changes in the environment, species must provide for both stability across generations (general inheritance) and the possibility of change (specific inheritance). Evolution depends on two seemingly contradictory processes: one that maintains stability from generation to generation and one that assures a small but steady trickle of variability in the population. For such change to be observed within one or two human generations, changes must occur in a species with a brief life span and the changes must be observed in a clearly changing environment. One well-known example that fits both criteria is that of a moth native to England. The particular species was relatively light in color and well adapted to resting on trees and foliage. As industrialization occurred and smoke stacks poured black smoke and debris on trees and houses, the light colored moths became easier targets for their predators. Moths slightly darker than their unfortunate light colored brethren were more likely to survive in those environments than were the lighter moths. Over time, more and more dark moths appeared in the population, until the dark moth became the most frequent example of this species of moth.

The Basic Units of Heredity

The Cell. Cells are the basic building blocks of all living things. Cells come in all shapes and sizes. Some cells are shaped like rods, others like spirals, others like snowflakes, and still others like blobs of jelly. A cell can be as small as one 250-thousandth of an inch in diameter, as in the case of a pleuropneumonia microbe, or as large as a tennis ball, as in the case of the yolk of an ostrich egg. A cell can exist in isolation, as in the case of single-celled organisms such as the amoeba or paramesium. Or cells can exist as members of a community, with each cell having a specialized function. An example of such a community is the human being, a complex living organism comprised of millions of specialized interdependent cells.

All of the activities within a cell are controlled by the nucleus. In addition to its function as the control center of the cell, the nucleus contains all of the hereditary information necessary for the cell to reproduce itself. This information is carried in chromosomes, which contain the genes. Genes consist of deoxyribonucleic acid, or DNA. Genes store all of the heritable information that is transmitted from generation to generation. Hence, in the remainder of our discussion, we will refer to the information provided by heredity as genetic information.

Cellular Reproduction: A Closer Look at Chromosomes

The genetic information contained in chromosomes is duplicated whenever a cell reproduces itself. The significance of this phenomenon is underscored when we realize how many genes must be reproduced when a cell reproduces itself. A normal human cell contains 46 chromosomes, and each chromosome is responsible for the duplication of thousands of genes. A human cell has been estimated to contain more than 200,000 genes (Winchester, 1972). However, the precise number of genes carried by an individual chromosome is unknown. Table 2-1 shows the number of chromosomes found in the cells of various living organisms. Although the number of chromosomes varies from species to species, it is not the case that organisms with more chromosomes necessarily have more genes. A crayfish cell, for example, has 200 chromosomes, but fewer genes than a mouse cell, which has 40 chromosomes. Crayfish chromosomes are shorter than mouse chromosomes, with each of the crayfish chromosomes containing fewer genes than those of the mouse.

The 46 chromosomes contained in the normal cell of a human being are arranged into 23 pairs. The chromosomes in 22 of these pairs are autosomes. They are "homologous," that is, the members of a pair are similar to one another, but different from all other pairs. In addition to the 22 pairs of autosomes, there is a 23rd pair. This pair is made up of the sex chromosomes. In the human female, each cell contains two similar sex chromosomes, both designated X. In the male, each sex cell contains two dissimilar chromosomes, one X (as in the female) and one Y. This full complement of 46 chromosomes

TABLE 2-1

The diploid number of chromosomes found in the cells of a variety of creatures.

Organism	Diploid Chromosome Number	Organism	Diploid Chromosome Number
Ascaris univalens (parasitic worm)	2	Ambystoma (tiger salamander)	28
Drosophila melanogaster (fruit fly)	8	Honeybee	32
Garden pea	14	Domestic swine (hog)	38
Onion	16	Mouse	40
Corn	20	Man	46
Opossum	22	Monkey (Cebus)	54
Bullfrog	26	Crayfish	200

SOURCE: adapted from Winchester, 1972, p. 44.

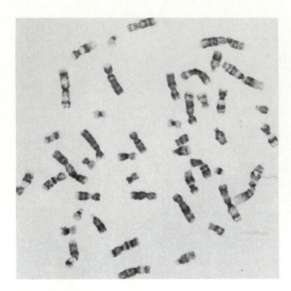 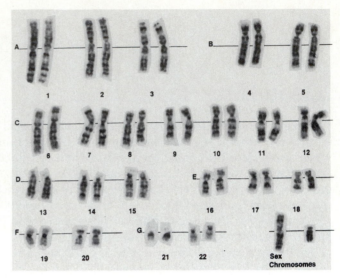

FIGURE 2-1

The picture on the left shows the chromosomes found in the cell of a normal human male. The picture on the right shows the chromosomes arranged by pairs according to length. Given that these chromosomes are from a male, the 23rd pair consists of an X and a Y. If the chromosomes were from a female, the 23rd pair would consist of two Xs.

Source: from Winchester, 1972, p. 60.

(22 pairs of autosomes plus 1 pair of sex chromosomes) is known as the diploid number of chromosomes. The 46 chromosomes found in the cells of a normal human male are pictured in Figure 2-1.

Mitosis

The process of mitosis occurs whenever a cell with the diploid number of chromosomes reproduces itself. In the initial phase of mitosis, the nucleus halts normal cell activity. The nucleus begins to dissolve and the chromosomes contained within it begin to duplicate themselves. For each original chromosome, two identical chromatids are formed, connected by a small structure called the kinetochore. For the normal human cell, this results in 46 pairs of chromatids. Following the formation of the chromatid pairs, all of the pairs line up along the equator of the cell. The kinetochore holding the chromatids together then splits, and each chromatid migrates toward opposite sides of the cell. A new cell membrane is then formed along the equator of the cell. As a result, there are now two cells, with each cell an exact duplicate of the single parent cell from which it derived. Mitosis is shown schematically in Figure 2-2.

Germ Cells and Sex Chromosomes

In contrast to the normal body cell, the mature ovum and the mature sperm (which are called germ cells) have only the haploid number of chromosomes. In other words, each human germ cell has 23 chromosomes, 22 nonpaired

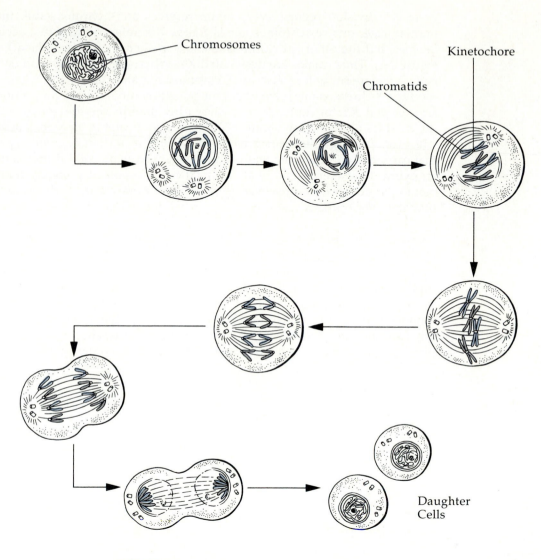

FIGURE 2-2

Schematic representation of the stages of mitosis.

Source: adapted from Winchester, 1972, p. 45.

autosomes and 1 sex chromosome (either an X or a Y). If an ovum is fertilized by a sperm following intercourse, it is then called a zygote and will again have the diploid number, having received 23 chromosomes from the ovum supplied by the mother and 23 chromosomes from the sperm supplied by the father. The sex chromosomes, as suggested by the name, help to determine the sex of the child. In the normal female, each sex chromosome is large and looks like an X. Thus, the sex of a female is designated XX. When

35

germ cell division occurs, every ovum receives an X chromosome. In the normal male, one sex chromosome is a large X similar to those that occur in females, but the other sex chromosome is a smaller one shaped like a Y (see Figure 2-2). Thus, males are designated XY. When germ cell division occurs, half of the sperm will receive an X chromosome and half of the sperm will receive a Y chromosome. Given that the genetic combination is XX for normal females and XY for normal males, the father determines the genetic sex of the child (as illustrated in Figure 2-3). Sperms that contain an X chromosome will produce a genetic female when implanted in an ovum, while sperms that carry a Y chromosome will produce a genetic male child if they fertilize an ovum. However, as we shall see in the discussion of prenatal development, the absence or presence of certain hormones during the course of prenatal development also influences sexual development.

Meiosis

Germ cell division is accomplished by the process of meiosis. Sperm and ovum production are not identical processes. Spermatogenesis, or sperm production, occurs in the male's testes. Human testes are made up of small tubules, which contain cells called spermatogonia. Each spermatogonia contains 46 chromosomes. In the initial stage of spermatogenesis, the spermatogonia change into primary spermatocytes. The primary spermatocytes begin to duplicate themselves, but unlike mitosis, the chromosomes of the primary spermatocyte in meiosis pair with their homologous mates, with the

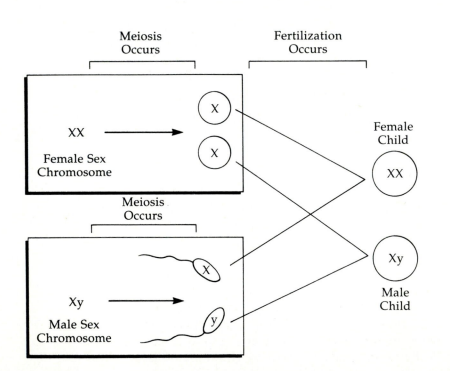

FIGURE 2-3

Chromosome exchange in sex determination.

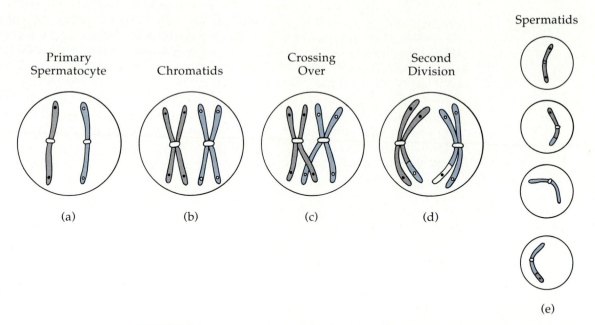

Spermatids

Primary
Spermatocyte   Chromatids

Crossing
Over

Second
Division

(a)   (b)   (c)   (d)

(e)

FIGURE 2-4

A schematic representation of the process of crossing over. (*a*) Two homologous
chromosomes before meiosis. (*b*) Each chromosome is duplicated, forming two
chromatids in the process. (*c*) One chromatid from each chromosome exchanges
part of itself with a homologous chromatid from the other chromosome. This is
crossing over. (*d*) The two chromosomes pull apart from one another. (*e*) Four spermatids, or one ootid and three polar bodies. (Note that two of the four resulting
germ cells contain crossover chromosomes and two do not).

Source: adapted from Winchester, 1972, p. 262.

result being a group of four chromatids linked to one another (as opposed
to two in mitosis). During this period, a phenomenon called crossing over
may occur. Crossing over involves the exchange of chromosome segments
by homologous pairs (see Figure 2-4). Crossing over results in additional
combinations of genes occurring in individual chromosomes, which in turn
contribute to increased variability among members of a species. Cell division
follows this initial stage of meiosis, resulting in two cells, called secondary
spermatocytes. Each of these cells contains 23 chromosomes, but each of
these chromosomes consists of two chromatids rather than one. The second
division of meiosis immediately follows the first division. No duplication of
chromosomes is involved in the second division. Instead, the two chromatids
are divided, with each of the resulting spermatids containing 23 single chromosomes. Each spermatid grows into a mature sperm without any further
cell divisions. The DNA of the mature sperm is concentrated in its head,
which is also coated with enzymes that help the sperm to break through the
barriers presented by the ovum.

37

Ova are produced in the ovary via a process called oogenesis. Initially, a primary oocyte is formed. During the initial phase of oogenesis, the chromosomes duplicate themselves just as they do in spermatogenesis. However, the chromosomes cluster to one side of the cell rather than in the middle. As a result, the cell does not divide into two equal cells, but into one large cell (called the secondary oocyte), which contains the chromosomes and one small cell (called a polar body). The secondary oocyte also divides into two unequal cells, producing another polar body and the ootid egg. The polar bodies are byproducts of oogenesis and serve no further function in the reproduction process. Only the ootid egg develops into a mature ovum that may be fertilized by a sperm. The processes of spermatogenesis and oogenesis are shown in Figure 2-5.

Chromosome Aberrations

The process of meiosis is not always free from error. Approximately 1 in every 200 live human births involves either an abnormal number of chromosomes (usually 45 or 47 instead of 46) or a change in the structure of a chromosome. One aberration of particular interest to psychologists is *nondisjunction*. This aberration occurs when either the homologous chromosomes do not separate in the first division or the chromatids do not separate in the second division. As a result, one of the germ cells contains only 22 chromosomes and the other germ cell contains 24 chromosomes. If such a germ

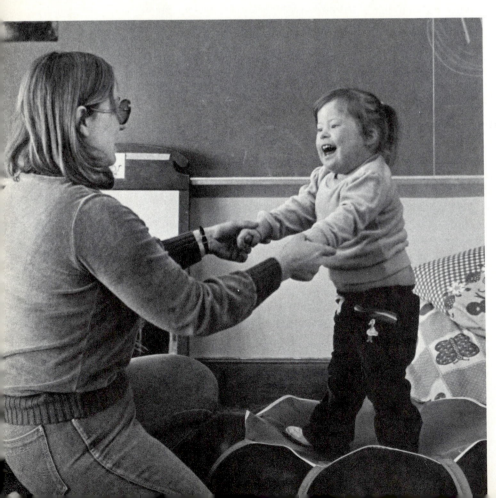

A youth with Down's syndrome engaging in playful exercise at a special school.

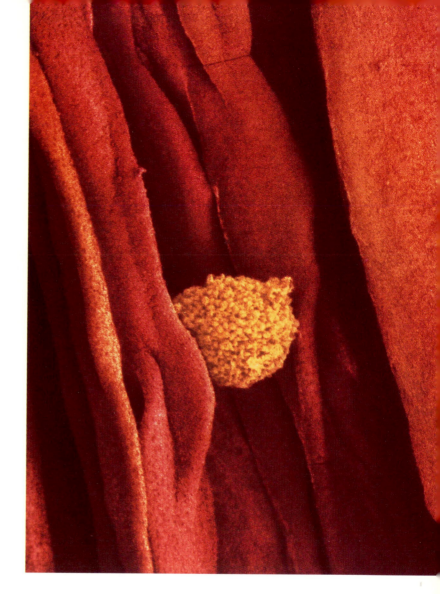

COLOR PLATE 1
An unfertilized ovum in the folds of the
fallopian tube (magnified 100 times).

Prenatal Development

Much of what has been discovered about prenatal development during
the past 20 years rests on the pioneering photographic techniques developed by Lennart Nilsson. As you admire the amazing photographs that
comprise this section, remember that some of the photographs are of
microscopic organisms (the ovum, sperm, and blastocyst), and that the
depicted events represent normal prenatal development. Contrasting
the blastocyst, the 4½-week-old embryo and the 5-month-old fetus will
illustrate the magnitude of the changes that rapidly occur during the
period from conception to birth.

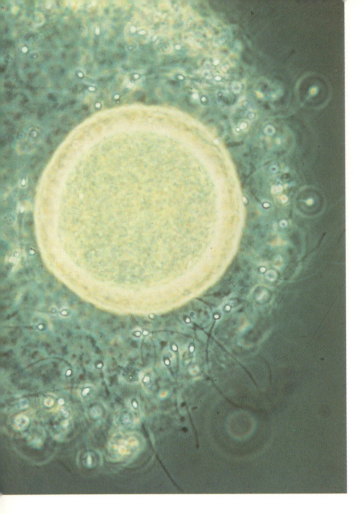

COLOR PLATE 2
Sperm surrounding the ovum. Notice the difference in size between the ovum and the sperm.

COLOR PLATE 3
Sperm approaching the outer membrane of the ovum.

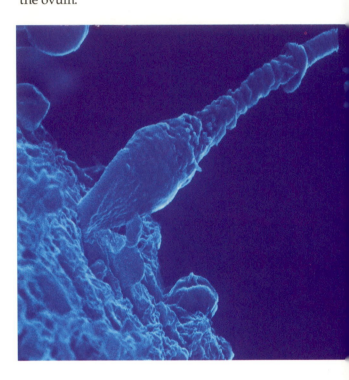

COLOR PLATE 4
A sperm has begun its penetration of the outer surface of the ovum.

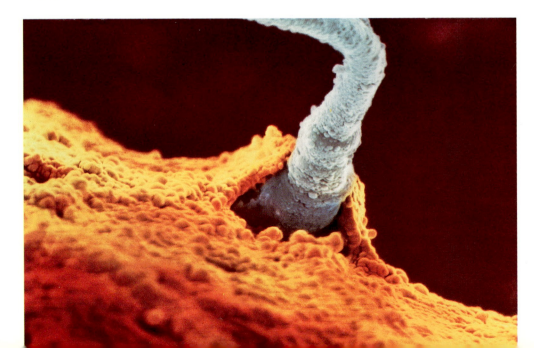

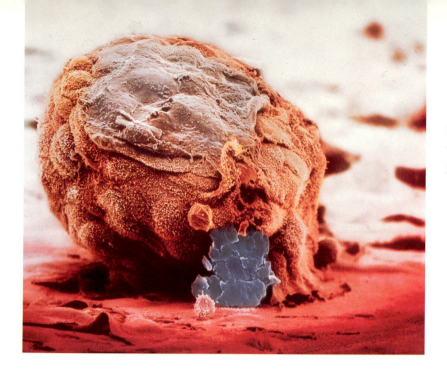

COLOR PLATE 5
The blastocyst facilitates its landing on the uterine wall with leg-like structures composed of sugar molecules.

COLOR PLATE 6
At 4½ weeks, a rudimentary heart has already been formed, as well as an early eye. The tail will disappear, leaving behind shrunken vertibrae.

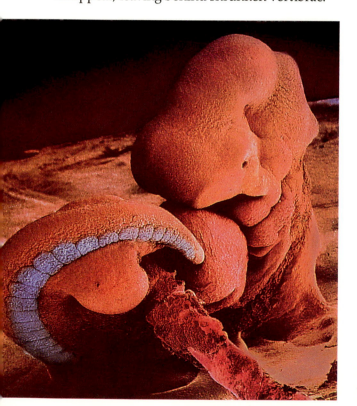

COLOR PLATE 7
A 5-week-old embryo with head bent down toward chest. The arms and legs are rounded buds.

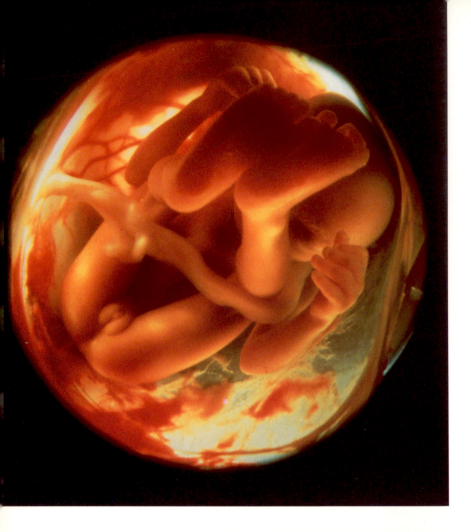

COLOR PLATE 8
Photograph of a 5-month-old
female fetus. This little girl is
approximately 10 inches long.

COLOR PLATE 9
A fetus at 5½ months
after conception. This
fetus is about 12 inches
long.

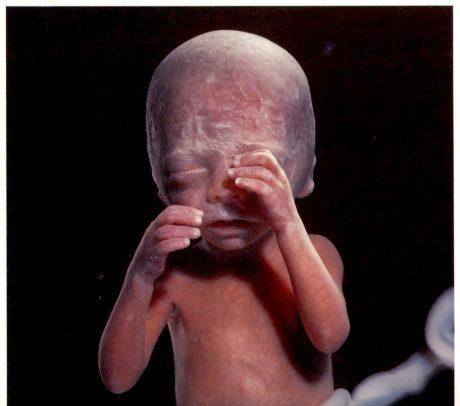

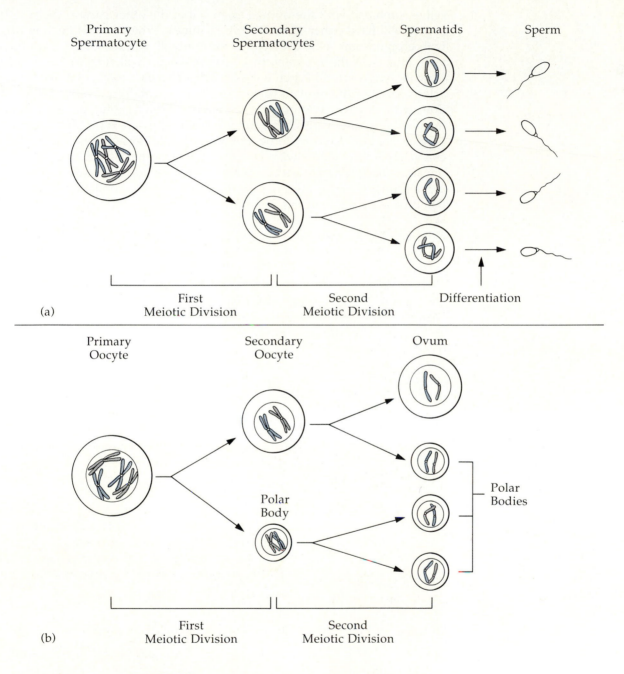

FIGURE 2-5

Schematic representation of the processes involved in (*a*) spermatogenesis and (*b*) oogenesis. Note the similarities and the differences in the formation of sperm and ova.

Source: adapted from Winchester, 1972, p. 64.

39

cell is combined with the normal germ cell of the other parent, the resulting zygote will have either 45 or 47 chromosomes. When nondisjunction occurs with chromosome #21, the zygote with only 45 chromosomes will not survive. However, the zygote with 47 chromosomes will survive but will have Down's syndrome. Children with Down's syndrome have a number of characteristics that differentiate them from normal children (Volpe, 1984). Children with Down's syndrome are mentally retarded, although the degree of mental retardation varies from child to child. They are typically cheerful and gregarious, but also tend to be stubborn. In addition to these psychological characteristics, children with Down's syndrome have a number of unique physical characteristics. Facial characteristics include a prominent forehead, a projecting lower lip, a large protruding tongue, and slanting eyes. As a result of poor muscle tone, children with Down's syndrome acquire motor skills, such as sitting, crawling, and walking, much later than do normal children. For example, normal children begin to walk around the age of 12 months. Children with Down's syndrome may not learn to walk until two or three years of age. As shown in Table 2-2, maternal age is closely related to the incidence of Down's syndrome. The older the mother is at the time of conception, the greater the risk that the child will have Down's syndrome. However, the age of the father is not related to the incidence of Down's syndrome. This differing affect of parental age seems to reflect biological differences in regard to the formation of ova and sperm. Whereas men create new sperm throughout the course of their lives, women are born with all of the primary oocytes fully formed. Apparently, the longer these cells are held in the body prior to the process of oogenesis, the more likely that chromosome aberrations such as nondisjunction will occur during oogenesis.

Nondisjunction can also occur among the sex chromosomes. Klinefelter's syndrome is characterized by one too many X chromosomes. Individuals afflicted with Klinefelter's syndrome have 47 chromosomes, with two X sex chromosomes and one Y sex chromosome, a condition that occurs in approximately 1 out of 900 children. The result is an individual with male characteristics. However, the sex organs are only one-half the normal size and are always sterile. In addition, individuals with Klinefelter's syndrome are prone to mental retardation and other psychiatric problems.

The aforementioned aberrations are characterized by the presence of an extra chromosome. Deletion of normal chromosome material may also result

TABLE 2-2

Relation of maternal age to incidence of Down's Syndrome

Mother's Age at Birth of Child	Incidence of Down's Syndrome
Under 30	1:1500
30–34	1:1000
35–39	1:300
40–44	1:100
45 and over	1:40

SOURCE: Karp (1976), p. 76.

in abnormal developments. For example, Turner's syndrome is characterized by the absence of a chromosome. Rather than having an XX or an XY combination, these individuals have only a single X chromosome. Victims of Turner's syndrome have female characteristics, but will not develop mature, functional sexual organs. However, injections of estrogen (a female hormone) may result in a more normal outward female physical appearance.

At this point, you may be unduly alarmed by the potential problems that can occur in meiosis or conception. Although it is important to recognize that reproduction is not free of error, it is equally important to remember that there are no problems in the majority of cases. And, as we shall see in the next section, the normal processes of conception and prenatal development are remarkable.

Conception

Despite legal and theological controversies concerning the precise moment at which life begins, there is no doubt about the moment at which development begins. Development begins when a single sperm cell pierces the wall of the ovum, resulting in the conception of an individual.

Typically, a woman produces one ovum per month from one of her two ovaries. This usually occurs approximately midway between two menstrual periods. The ovum travels from the ovary down the fallopian tube toward the uterus (see Color Plate 1). If it is not fertilized by a sperm, the ovum gradually disintegrates and is expelled as part of the next menstruation. However, when intercourse occurs, millions of sperm are deposited in the vagina. In the attempt to travel through the cervix and the uterus, several thousand sperm survive to reach the fallopian tubes (see Color Plates 2 and 3). If an ovum is about to be released by an ovary or is already present in the fallopian tubes, a sperm may manage to penetrate the wall of the ovum, the result being the conception of a human being (see Color Plates 4 and 5). Although the common notion is that conception occurs because millions of sperm attack the ovum, recent research suggests that the ovum plays a significant role in the conception process (Schatten & Schatten, 1983). Following the initial contact with the sperm, the ovum extends tiny hairlike structures (called microvilla) that embrace the sperm and may even assist the sperm's attempt to penetrate the ovum. Simultaneously, the ovum engages in activity to fend off the other sperm that surround it. This protective activity takes two forms. First, an electric block is formed, which changes the ovum's outer membrane from negative to positive, repelling the interested sperm. This electric block lasts about thirty seconds, and is immediately followed by the formation of a hard outer coating that forces away all sperm except the one held by the microvilla. Once conception has occurred, the ovum continues to travel down the fallopian tube and implants itself in the wall of the uterus.

41

The Stages of Prenatal Development

As noted earlier, a new human being begins to develop as soon as a sperm and an ovum unite. The fertilized ovum is called a zygote. Development from conception to birth is called *prenatal development*. During this time, which averages 38 weeks, the microscopic zygote evolves into a functioning newborn baby. Development during the prenatal period is the most dramatic and rapid of any developmental period, a claim that is easy to justify given the changes that occur in the organism between conception and birth. Prenatal development is divided into three periods: the germinal period, the embryonic period, and the fetal period.

The Germinal Period. The germinal period begins at the moment of conception and continues until the fertilized ovum (now called a zygote) is implanted in the wall of the uterus. Following conception, the zygote travels through the fallopian tube and into the uterus. The journey through the fallopian tube to the uterus takes approximately three days. The zygote then floats freely in the uterus from four to six days before it is implanted in the uterine wall. Although the germinal period only lasts from eight to ten days, considerable development occurs.

As the zygote travels down the fallopian tube, it begins the process of cell duplication and differentiation that will eventually result in a newborn baby composed of millions of cells (see Figure 2-6). This process begins about 24 hours after conception and continues at such a rapid rate that the developing organism will consist of thousands of cells by the time it is implanted in the uterine wall. Initially, the multiplying cells are identical to one another, and the process of cell duplication occurs without the zygote taking nourishment from its surrounding environment. As a result, each cell duplication results in more but smaller identical cells. Approximately five days after conception, the cells within the zygote begin to take nourishment from the uterine environment. Once this happens, the developing organism is called a blastocyst. More significant than this name change from zygote to blastocyst is the cellular changes that occur. As the blastocyst receives nourishment from the uterine environment, the cells that comprise the blastocyst begin to differentiate. One set of cells forms the *inner cell mass* and provides the cellular basis for the developing organism itself. The other set of cells forms a protective layer around the inner cell mass. This protective layer of cells is called the *trophoblast* and also plays an important role in the implantation process. Once the blastocyst is sufficiently developed, the cells in the trophoblast attach themselves to the spongy wall of the uterus. Once implantation is complete, the germinal period of prenatal development is complete.

The Embryonic Period. This period of prenatal development begins when the blastocyst becomes anchored to the uterine wall and connections are established between the blastocyst and the mother. It lasts until approximately eight weeks after conception. During this developmental period, the developing organism is called an embryo (see Color Plates 6 and 7).

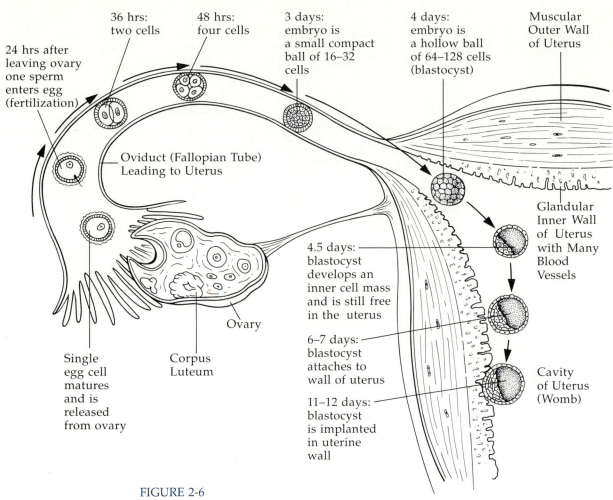

FIGURE 2-6

Representation of a zygote's journey down a fallopian tube to the uterus.

Once implantation has occurred, the small organism is continually sheltered and nourished by the mother. The original trophoblast is transformed into the *amnion* and the *placenta*. The amnion contains the amniotic fluid that surrounds the embryo. The amniotic fluid functions as both a support and a cushion for the embryo. The placenta is a protective but permeable barrier that surrounds the amnion. The placenta allows nutrients to reach the embryo and also allows the embryo's waste products to pass into the mother's bloodstream. The embryo is linked to the placenta via the *umbilical cord* (see Figure 2-7).

At the beginning of the embryonic period, the embryo is about one-fifth of an inch long (approximately 10 thousand times larger than the original fertilized egg). Following implantation, the cells in the inner cell mass begin

43

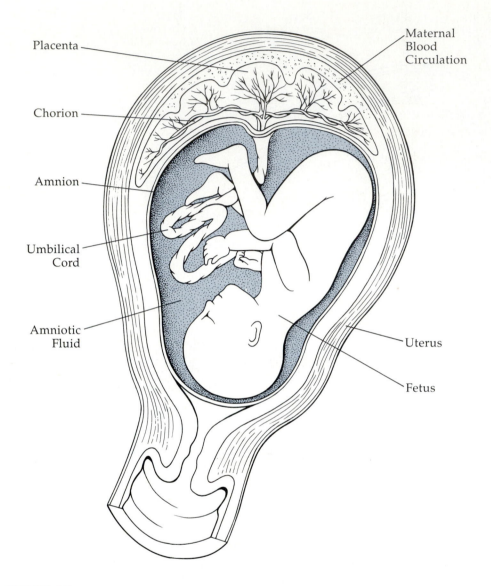

Placenta

Maternal
Blood
Circulation

Chorion

Amnion

Umbilical
Cord

Amniotic
Fluid

Uterus

Fetus

FIGURE 2-7

Representation of an embryo (fetus) in amniotic fluid, amnion, placenta, and umbilical cord.

to differentiate into three basic layers from which the various tissues and organs will be formed. One of the first layers to emerge is the *ectoderm*, which will eventually yield cells to produce the skin, eyes, ears, nose, mouth, and central nervous system. Another is the *endoderm*, which will result in such body organs as the liver, pancreas, thyroid gland, and lining of the intestinal tract. The remaining layer is the *mesoderm*, which will produce the circulatory,

44

muscular, and skeletal systems, and emerges shortly after the other two layers (Moore, 1982). By the end of the embryonic period, the embryo is between 1 and 1½ inches long and resembles a miniature human being. In addition, all of the major organs have become differentiated from one another.

The Fetal Period. This is the longest of the three prenatal developmental periods, lasting from eight weeks after conception until birth. During this period, the developing organism is called a fetus. During the fetal period, the fetus is transformed from the miniature, 1-inch long organism at eight weeks to a fully functioning newborn baby at birth. At 16 weeks after conception, the fetus is between 6 and 7 inches long and weighs about 4 ounces. Although the fetus now looks remarkably like a miniature baby, the internal organs are not sufficiently developed to maintain life outside of the womb. At 24 weeks following conception, the fetus can open and close its eyes and seems to have a favorite sleeping position (see Color Plates 8 and 9). During the last four weeks of pregnancy, the fetus gains an average of ½ pound per week, resulting in an average full-term newborn who weighs in at approximately 7 pounds and is about 20 inches long.

Sexual Differentiation During Prenatal Development

The process of sexual differentiation begins at the moment of conception. Recall that the ovum always contains one X chromosome, whereas the sperm may contain an X or a Y chromosome. If the sperm contains an X chromosome, the resulting XX combination yields a genetic female. If the sperm contains a Y chromosome, the resulting XY combination produces a genetic male.

During the first weeks after conception, the blastocyst develops a *primordial gonadal streak.* If the organism has XX chromosomes, the streak develops into ovaries. If the organism has XY chromosomes, the streak develops into testes. The transformation of the primordial gonadal streak into ovaries or testes represents the first step of gender differentiation (Moore, 1982).

The next stage of gender differentiation depends on hormonal secretion. The testes formed in the preceding stage begin to secrete the hormone testosterone six to eight weeks following conception. The presence of testosterone results in the formation of the testicles and penis during the next stage of sexual differentiation. The absence of testosterone results in the development of the vulva and clitoris (Halpern, 1986). Figure 2-8 illustrates the stages of sexual differentiation.

Each stage of genital development is independent of the others. Although early development is not reversible by external factors, such factors can

45

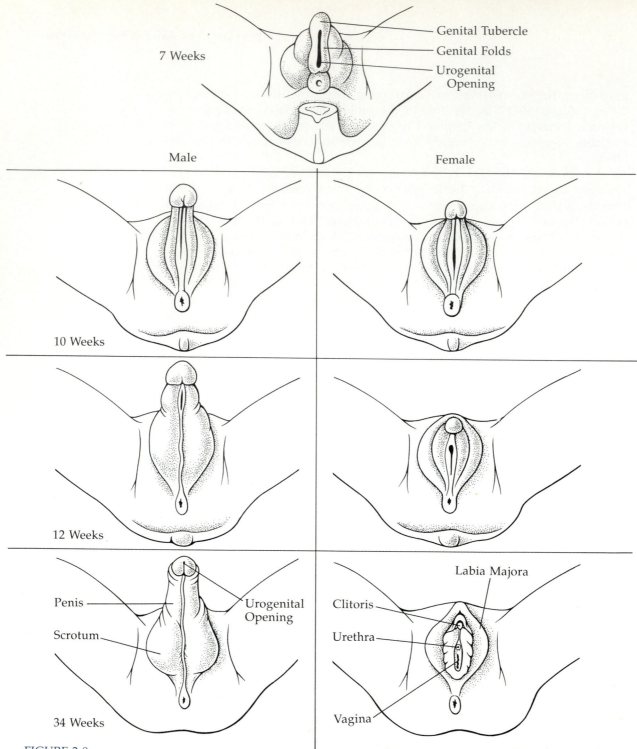

FIGURE 2-8

Human male and female sex organs develop from a common embryonic beginning.
The undifferentiated sex organs consist of a genital tubercle, a urogenital opening,
and a pair of genital folds. For males, the genital tubercle enlarges to produce a
penis and enclose the urogenital opening. The genital folds form the scrotum,
which will contain the testes. For females, the genital tubercle forms the clitoris,
and the urogenital opening will form the openings of the urethra and the vagina.
The genital folds form the outer lips, the labia majora.

Source: adapted from Winchester, 1972, p. 161.

prevent subsequent "normal" developments from occurring. For example, during the early 1950s, women at risk for miscarriages were given hormonal treatments to reduce the chances of a miscarriage. Some of the hormones were converted by the women's bodies into testosterone. If the testosterone was present after the third month of pregnancy, genetic females (those who had XX chromosomes) had normal ovaries (which had developed before the mothers were given the hormonal treatments), but had male external genitalia.

The Development of the Brain

The past 25 years have resulted in a wealth of evidence demonstrating the connection between the structure and function of the brain and various kinds of behaviors. Although we are still quite far away from a comprehensive descriptive model of the relation of brain development to behavioral development, we have learned much about the development of the brain in recent years (Aoki & Siekevitz, 1988; Greenough, Black, & Wallace, 1987; Nowakowski, 1987).

Four cellular processes are involved in the physical development of the brain. These are cell proliferation, cell migration, cell differentiation, and cell death. Each of these processes plays a different role in the development of the brain.

Cell Proliferation. Cell proliferation results in the production of nerve cells. Recall that shortly after conception, the developing embryo forms various differentiated layers of tissue that will eventually give rise to the various organs and tissues that constitute a functioning human being. The outer layer of tissue for the human embryo is the ectoderm. Part of the layer of tissue right below the ectoderm is the chordamesoderm. By the middle of the third week following conception, the chordamesoderm has caused a change in the part of the ectoderm that lies just above it, causing this area of the ectoderm to become primitive neural tissue.

The neural tissue is initially shaped like a flat disc, but soon rolls itself into a long tube, which is closed off at both ends. Once the neural tube is formed, a single layer of cells on the inner surface of the tube begins to produce nerve cells (see Figure 2-9). This process continues throughout prenatal development, and is virtually complete at birth. Although nerve cells will be added to the human cerebellum in the months following birth, cell proliferation is most evident in the prenatal period. Hence, the increase in the size of the brain during prenatal development is primarily a function of an increase in the number of nerve cells (see Figure 2-10). Following birth, the growing size of the brain is caused primarily by an increase in the size of individual nerve cells, rather than the addition of more cells.

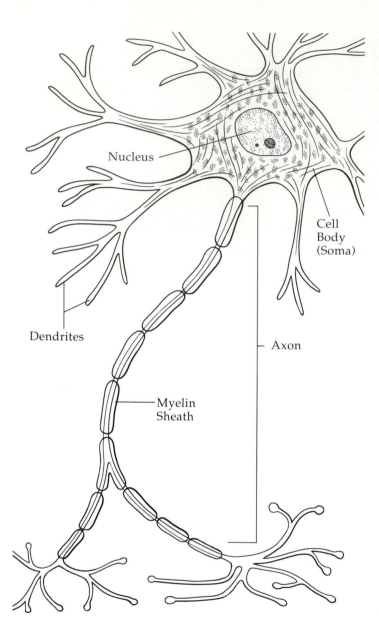

Nucleus

Cell
Body
(Soma)

Dendrites

Axon

Myelin
Sheath

FIGURE 2-9
Schematic representation of a nerve cell.

Cell Migration. Although cell proliferation results in billions of nerve cells being formed, the nerve cells do not remain in place once they are created. As the nerve cells divide and duplicate themselves, they also begin to migrate from place to place within the neural tube, gradually building the brain from the inside out. This process is called *cell migration.* Nerve cells do not migrate randomly, but instead seem to be guided to various locations by other nerve

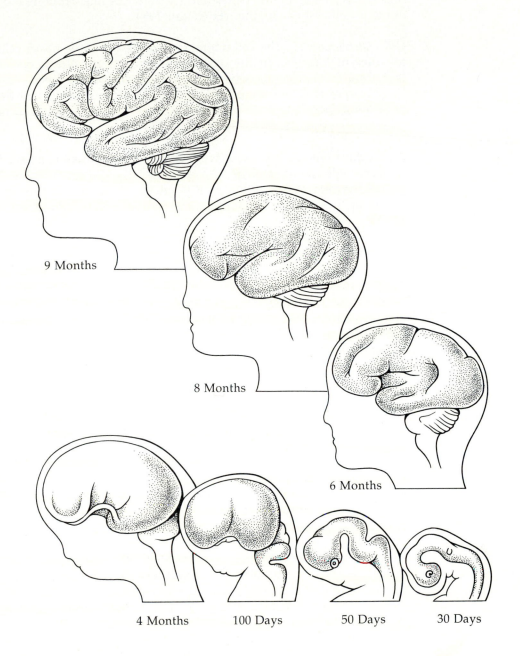

9 Months

8 Months

6 Months

4 Months   100 Days   50 Days   30 Days

FIGURE 2-10

Illustration of the growth of the brain (in size and shape) during prenatal development.

49

cells (Rakic, 1985) and by biochemical substances that promote the adhesion of nerve cells to one another (Edelman, 1984).

Cell Differentiation. The cell migration process involves nerve cells moving to different locations in the developing brain. Once the nerve cells reach their final destination, they begin to change into specific types of nerve cells. This process is called *cell differentiation*. The type of nerve cell that results depends in part on where in the brain the cell is located and in part to the other nerve cells that surround it.

Cell Death. One perplexing aspect of brain development concerns the death of nerve cells, called *cell death*. As many as 50% of all nerve cells die during prenatal development. Although it is unclear why so many nerve cells die, it is clear that there is considerable competition among nerve cells for survival.

One aspect of brain development that seems to be related to cell death concerns the links among nerve cells. Once nerve cells have reached their destination, they begin to congregate with one another. As nerve cells congregate, they also begin to develop dendrites and axons, which allow them to begin communicating with one another. Nerve cells that manage to congregate and link up with one another are more likely to survive than those that do not.

Although most nerve cells are formed and in their proper location at birth, development of the brain continues after birth. The mature adult human brain weighs approximately four times as much as the brain of the newborn infant. One factor that is involved in postnatal brain development is *myelinization,* the formation of the *myelin sheath* around the axon of nerve cells. The myelin sheath is an insulating cover that increases the effectiveness of nerve cell communication. Myelinization begins about 24 weeks after conception, but is largely incomplete at birth. Most myelinization occurs in the first year of life and follows a predictable pattern. The nerve cells along the spinal cord are myelinated first and are followed by nerve cells in the hindbrain. Myelinization next spreads to nerve cells in the midbrain and finally proceeds to the nerve cells that comprise the forebrain.

Another aspect of brain development following birth concerns connections among the brain cells. At birth, there are relatively few connections among the nerve cells. The number of connections increases throughout the early years of life, the result being an overabundance of nerve cell connections in children's brains (Huttenlocher, 1979). In fact, children's brains may contain as many as 50% *more* connections than those of adults (see Figure 2-11). Children seem to develop most of their neural connections by two years of age. Their subsequent experience determines which connections survive and which do not. Connections that are used are likely to survive, whereas those that are not used are unlikely to survive (Greenough, Black, & Wallace, 1987). Just as the development of the nerve cells during prenatal development is characterized by competition among the cells to survive, the development of nerve cell connections following birth is characterized by competition for

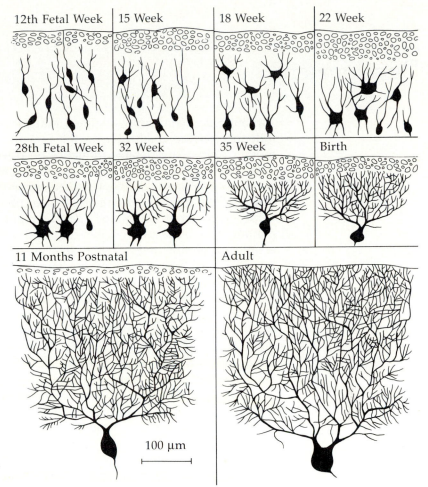

FIGURE 2-11

Illustration of nerve cell connections in the brain and how such connections change with development.

survival among the connections that are formed. At present, it is unclear what consequences this pruning process has, although it seems likely that it may influence cognitive capacities and perhaps even behavior (Goldman-Rakic, 1987).

Recent research has also suggested that there are significant developmental changes in the amount of energy used by the brain, as indicated by changes in the metabolic activity of the brain. During the first year of life, the metabolic rate of the infant's brain is between 60 to 70% that of the adult. By two years of age, the metabolic rate of the child's brain is equal to that of an adult. However, sometime between the ages of three and four years the metabolic rate of the child's brain increases to approximately twice that of an adult. It is not until the age of 10 that the metabolic activity of the brain begins to decrease, eventually falling to the adult rate at 13 or 14 years. Again, it is not yet clear what the developmental differences in metabolic activity mean in regard to cognition and behavior.

51

Environmental Influences on Prenatal Development

Although it is commonly assumed that the environment begins to exert its influence on the child at birth, the prenatal environment provided by the mother exerts considerable influence on development. In fact, during prenatal development the mother *is* the environment. For example, the mother is the only source of nutrition for the developing organism. Thus, maternal diet is an important environmental factor for prenatal development (Winick, 1974). It has been suggested that a pregnant woman should consume a minimum of 2,700 calories per day, and that her diet should include the essential vitamins and minerals (Hayes, 1987). Maternal diets deficient in calcium, phosphorus, iodine, or vitamins B, C, and D are associated with high frequencies of abnormal fetuses. In fact, approximately 50% of infants born to malnourished mothers have congenital abnormalities (Metcoff, 1974). The size of fetal organs is also affected by maternal malnutrition. The brain and the heart are least likely to be affected, while the liver and thymus are most likely to be affected (Sinclair, Saigal, & Yeung, 1974). Given that the fetus gains an average of one-half pound per week during the last two months of pregnancy, maternal malnutrition during this period is most likely to affect the fetus' growth and subsequent weight at birth (Rush, Stein, Cristakis, & Susser, 1974).

The placental barrier that separates the child from the mother is permeable to a variety of molecular substances. This is necessary for the placenta to allow nutrients from the mother to reach the developing organism. As a result, any substance ingested or produced by the mother during pregnancy may affect the development of the organism. Environmental agents that may harm the developing organism are known as *teratogens*. Known teratogens include AIDS, alcohol, cigarette smoking, herpes simplex, radiation, rubella, and thalidomide.

Acquired Immune Deficiency Syndrome (AIDS). The AIDS virus may be transmitted from an infected mother to the developing organism in one of two ways. The virus may pass through the placental barrier. Or the fetus may be infected by coming into direct contact with the mother's blood during delivery (Weber, Redfield, and Lemon, 1986).

Alcohol. Excessive drinking by the mother during pregnancy may result in *fetal alcohol syndrome.* Newborns with this syndrome have small heads, small eyes, underdeveloped brains, and congenital heart disease. Children with fetal alcohol syndrome are more likely to be irritable infants and to suffer from retarded physical and cognitive development throughout their lifespan (Hanson, Streissguth, & Smith, 1981; Volpe, 1984).

Radiation. Women who are exposed to large doses of radiation during pregnancy are more likely to experience spontaneous abortion (Moore, 1982). If the amount of radiation is insufficient to kill the developing organism, it may nonetheless damage its development. For example, mental retardation occurred in 64% of the infants born to women who were pregnant and within 1,500 meters of the atomic explosions at Hiroshima and Nagasaki toward the end of World War II.

Rubella. Rubella, or German measles, has little effect on women who contract it during pregnancy. However, the consequences for the developing organism may be quite serious. Mothers who contract rubella during pregnancy run a greater risk of producing infants with cataracts, heart defects, deafness, and mental retardation (Stevenson, 1977). The seriousness of this teratogen was revealed in a Rubella epidemic in 1964–65 that resulted in more than 30,000 stillbirths and 20,000 newborns with congenital defects (LaVigne, 1982).

Thalidomide. For a six-year period beginning in 1956, thalidomide was prescribed to pregnant women in Europe in order to alleviate the morning sickness associated with the early stages of pregnancy. Thalidomide had no negative consequences for the mothers, but resulted in various types of deformities among their newborn infants. Some infants had malformed arms and legs, while others had hearing defects, underdeveloped intestinal tracts, or heart defects.

The above list of teratogens is by no means complete. Nonetheless, it should provide you with a good idea of how critical the mother's habits and experiences are for the developing organism. In prenatal development, the infant often becomes what the mother ingests and experiences.

Sensitive Periods

The developing organism seems to be particularly susceptible to specific forms of experience during certain developmental periods. These are called *sensitive periods*. Such periods are another example of the interaction of heredity and environment that is responsible for development. The ages associated with sensitive periods are set by genetic influences. The nature of the experience that organisms undergo during sensitive periods is determined by the environment. For example, Konrad Lorenz (1957) found that shortly after hatching, young ducklings will follow the first and closest large moving object that they encounter. This phenomenon is called imprinting. It occurs only if the ducklings encounter a moving object within the first 24 hours of life. Ducklings who are prevented from seeing a moving object (usually the

The incidence of fetal alcohol syndrome is related to the average number of drinks the mother has during pregnancy (Abel, 1984). Approximately one out of three pregnancies in mothers who consumed five or more drinks per day during pregnancy resulted in newborns with fetal alcohol syndrome. However, it is possible that any alcoholic intake during pregnancy may harm the developing organism (Bolton, 1983). Until the effects of moderate consumption are determined, total abstinence from alcohol would seem to be the safest policy.

Cigarette Smoking. Women who smoke cigarettes during pregnancy run the risk of damaging the health of their child as well as their own health (Bolton, 1983; Butler, 1974). The incidence of premature births and stillbirths is higher among mothers who smoked during pregnancy than among mothers who did not smoke. Mothers who smoke during pregnancy are also likely to produce lower birth weight infants than are mothers who do not smoke. Finally, smoking during pregnancy may increase the incidence of congenital heart disease among newborns.

Herpes Simplex. This form of herpes, also know as genital herpes, may be transmitted to the developing organism in one of two ways. The herpes virus may pass through the placental barrier and so infect the developing organism while it is still in the womb. Or the fetus may encounter herpes lesions on the mother's genitals during birth. To avoid this latter possibility, the fetus of an infected mother is often delivered via Cesarean delivery. Those unfortunate infants who are infected by the mother's herpes simplex virus may experience blindness and/or brain damage.

Types of Mental Retardation

Mental retardation afflicts between five and seven million people in the United States and may result from a number of conditions. These include chromosome abnormalities, inherited metabolic disturbances, infections during prenatal development, injury to the brain, and severely deprived environments.

Individuals classified as mentally retarded fall into one of four categories: (1) *mild retardation:* individuals with mild retardation comprise approximately 90% of the mentally retarded population. They develop much more slowly than normal children, but are sufficiently intelligent by the end of adolescence to lead independent lives. Such individuals often marry and have children. (2) *moderate retardation:* Individuals with moderate retardation are capable of taking care of themselves, but usually live in special homes. They rarely marry or become parents. (3) *severe retardation:* Individuals with severe retardation can be trained to perform simple tasks, but require considerable supervision throughout their lives. (4) *profound retardation:* Individuals with profound retardation are usually institutionalized, since they are unable to care for themselves. They may not be able to speak, although they understand simple instructions. ❦

mother duck, although Lorenz himself was imprinted upon) during this period fail to imprint on moving objects that they subsequently encounter. Thus, imprinting occurs only if a moving object is encountered during a particular developmental period. Possible examples of sensitive periods for human development include the times when visual perception and language are developed (see Chapters 4 and 5). The lack of various sorts of visual stimulation during the early days of life seems to lead to later deficits in visual functioning, suggesting that the visual system needs to be sufficiently stimulated early in life in order for normal development to occur (Aslin, 1981). Children's acquisition of their first language is most readily accomplished during the first five years of life, after which the language learning capability diminishes quite rapidly (as evidenced by the difficulty that most adults experience when attempting to learn another language).

Although the notion of sensitive periods is usually associated with optimal development, it is also possible to identify sensitive periods in which the developing child is most at risk when exposed to teratogens. Rubella (German measles) in mothers, for example, has been found to be more damaging to the developing child when it occurs early in pregnancy (Stevenson, 1977). Mothers who contract rubella during the first month of pregnancy have a 50% chance of producing an abnormal child. The likelihood of rubella producing an abnormal infant drops to 22% if the mother contracts it during the second month of pregnancy, and falls to 7% for mothers who contract rubella in the third month of pregnancy. Moreover, particular abnormalities are associated with the period of pregnancy in which the mother contracts rubella. Maternal rubella at four weeks of pregnancy will most likely result in cataracts and heart defects, whereas maternal rubella at seven weeks of pregnancy will most likely result in mental retardation (Dekaban, O'Rourke, & Corman, 1958).

There are also sensitive periods for the negative consequences of smoking and thalidomide on prenatal development. The effects of smoking on the newborn child's birth weight are greatest if the mother smokes during the last five months of pregnancy (Butler, 1974). Recall that the fetus gains most of its weight during the last months of pregnancy. Mothers who smoke during this period are likely to produce low birth weight infants. The effects of thalidomide also depend on the age of the embryo at the time the mother ingests the drug (Lenz, 1962). The sensitive period for thalidomide is the third and fourth week of prenatal life. Mothers who took thalidomide during the beginning of the third week of pregnancy produced infants with deformed ears. Use of the drug toward the end of the third week or during the beginning of the fourth week of prenatal development resulted in deformed arms, underdeveloped intestinal tracts, and heart defects. Deformed legs occurred when mothers had used the drug toward the end of their fourth week of pregnancy.

The effects of alcohol and radiation on the developing fetus also depend on the developmental period during which the developing organism is exposed to these teratogens. Alcohol seems to do the most damage if the

55

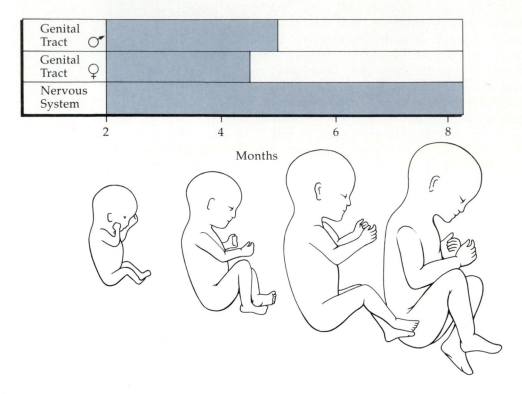

FIGURE 2-12

A schematic representation of sensitive periods (following conception) in the human embryo for the development of certain characteristics.

Source: from Tuchmann-Duplessis, 1969, p. 246.

mother imbibes during the first few months of pregnancy (Vorhees & Mollnow, 1987). Exposure to alcohol during this period affects the migration of the brain's nerve cells. For unknown reasons, alcohol results in the nerve cells passing their target locations, causing them to end up in inappropriate locations. Exposure to alcohol during this developmental period may also result in smaller-sized brains that have fewer convolutions than their normal-sized counterparts. Similarly, radiation is most likely to result in mental retardation if radiation is experienced between the 8th and 16th weeks of pregnancy. Radiation during this developmental period appears to interfere with nerve cell migration. It stops neurons short of their intended targets. Results such as these demonstrate that teratogens will produce the most damage to the child developing in the womb if they are taken by the mother at a time when certain types of prenatal development are occurring. Figures 2-12 and 2-13 illustrate the sensitive periods for certain developments that occur between conception and birth.

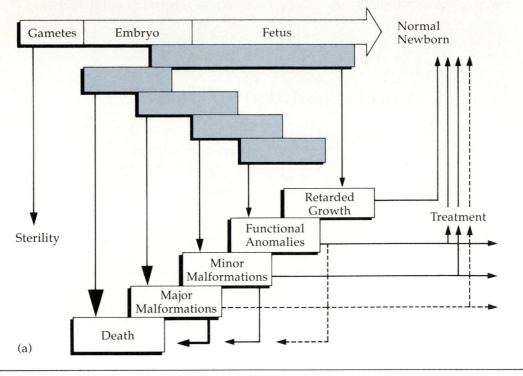

Sterility

Retarded Growth

Functional Anomalies

Minor Malformations

Major Malformations

Death

Treatment

(a)

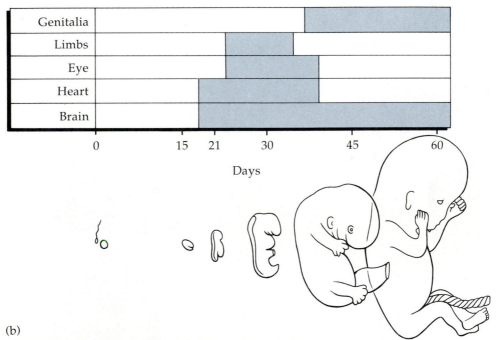

	Genitalia							
	Limbs							
	Eye							
	Heart							
	Brain							

0   15 21   30   45   60

Days

(b)

FIGURE 2-13

(*a*) Schematic representation of the action of teratogenic agents at various stages of reproduction. (*b*) Sensitive periods (following conception) in the human fetus for the development of the main structures.

Source: from Tuchmann-Duplessis, 1969, p. 248.

Diagnosis and Treatment of Prenatal Disorders

During the course of prenatal development, the embryo and later the fetus are enclosed within a protective cover called the amniotic sac, which contains amniotic fluid, a clear, waterlike substance. The fetus continually recycles this fluid by swallowing and resecreting it; one result of this is that the amniotic fluid contains discarded fetal cells. Amniocentesis is a process by which amniotic fluid is withdrawn for biochemical and chromosomal analyses in order to discover the status of the fetus. This process is illustrated in Figure 2-14. Amniocentesis is usually recommended for pregnant women over 35 and for those with a family history of genetic abnormalities.

Physicians have also used a technique known as ultrasound diagnosis to take "photographs" of the developing organism in the prenatal environment. This technique involves the use of sounds to create an image, much the same way that early sonar was used to help navigators detect underwater reefs or submarines. Sounds pass through liquids, but "bounce" off solid matter, such as stone, metal, human tissue, or bone. By analyzing the sounds that

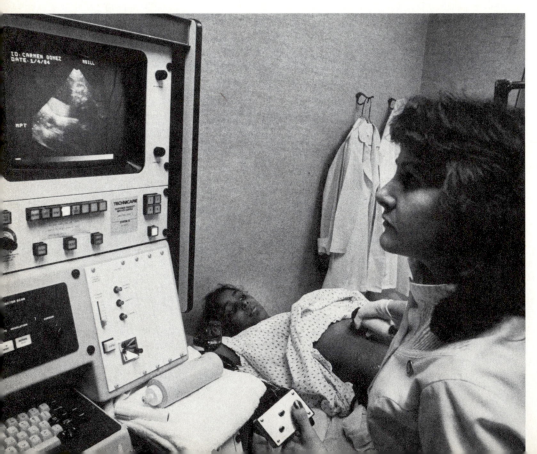

A mother looking at the ultrasonic image of her developing child produced by an ultrasound machine during a prenatal examination.

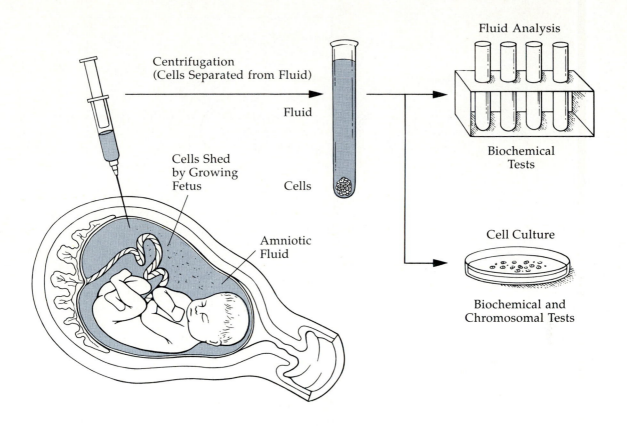

FIGURE 2-14

A schematic representation of amniocentesis.

Source: from Volpe, 1984.

bounce back in an ultrasonic examination, physicians have been able to "see" whether the zygote has attached itself to the uterus, whether the embryo and fetus are developing normally, and if there is one, two, three, or more developing children. Ultrasonic examinations appear to be totally harmless to the developing child and have helped to further our understanding of prenatal development as well as being a useful diagnostic tool.

Advances in the diagnosis of prenatal conditions made possible by techniques such as amniocentesis and ultrasound have also led to the creation of a variety of techniques that are used *in utero* to correct the condition. Two of these techniques are shown in Figure 2-15. Advances in prenatal diagnosis have also led to ethical dilemmas for parents. If the analyses reveal severe developmental defects, the parents must decide whether to continue the pregnancy or to abort it. Regardless of one's ethical convictions, such decisions are not easy.

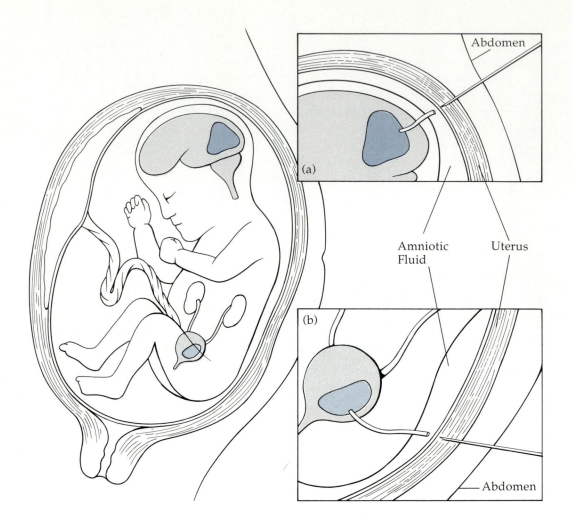

FIGURE 2-15
Schematic representation of two prenatal treatments. (*a*) Hydrocephalus is a
buildup of fluid in the fetal brain. A drainage tube is inserted to relieve pressure.
(*b*) Hydronephrosis is a blockage in the urinary tract. A drainage tube is inserted to
relieve pressure.

Behavior Genetics   *The Relationship Between Genotype and Phenotype.*   So far, in this chapter, we
have considered the manner in which genes contribute to the development
of an individual. We have also emphasized the fact that the environment
interacts with the genetic givens to produce an individual. *Genotype* refers to
the genetic makeup of an individual. *Phenotype* refers to the outward appearance of an individual. It is important to remember that genotypes and

60

phenotypes are *not* equivalent terms. As we shall see, a given genotype might result in many phenotypes, depending on the environment. Or different genotypes raised in similar environments might appear to be identical phenotypes. In either case, it is difficult to determine the genotype from the phenotype, or vice versa.

One striking example of the difference between genotype and phenotype was described by Imperato-McGinley (1981). She studied a group of individuals from three intermarrying rural villages in the Dominican Republic who appeared to be female at birth and who were raised as females by their community. However, at puberty, these individuals who had been *phenotypically* female began to change into males. These changes included the descent of the testes, the deepening of the voice, and the development of a muscular, masculine physique. Subsequent analyses of these individuals revealed that they were genotypically male (they had one X and one Y chromosome). However, they also possessed a defective gene that resulted in their inability to convert the male hormone testosterone into another male hormone, dihydrotestosterone. Although these individuals had normal levels of testosterone, they lacked dihydrotestosterone altogether. The lack of dihydrotestosterone results in a phenotypic female at birth, but the presence of testosterone during puberty results in the emergence of masculine characteristics and a phenotypic male. Although this is an extreme example, it serves to illustrate the point that it is sometimes difficult to infer the genotype of an individual from its phenotype.

The study of the interaction between genotypes and environments to produce phenotypes is called *behavioral genetics.* Given the many possible interactions between genotypes and environments, it should be clear that the study of behavioral genetics in its present form is limited because of the generality of its findings. Nonetheless, behavioral genetics has shed considerable light on nature–nurture interactions. In the following section, we shall review certain assumptions and methodologies associated with this area of research.

One technique that is commonly used in behavioral genetics studies involves the use of twins. Twins differ from all single-borns in that they shared a common prenatal environment. However, identical twins also share an identical genetic background. Identical twins occur when one ovum divides into two after it has been fertilized by a sperm. For this reason, identical twins are called monozygotic twins. Each of the cells produced by the division of the single fertilized ovum is genetically the same as the cell from which it was duplicated. As a result, each of the two cells develops into an individual who is genetically identical to the individual who results from the development of the other cell. Thus, identical twins (triplets, and so on) are the only individuals who are genetically identical to one another. Fraternal twins result when the woman produces two ova, each of which is fertilized by a separate sperm. Fraternal twins are dizygotic, produced by two fertilized ova. Given that each fraternal twin evolves from a different ovum and a different sperm, fraternal twins share no more genetic material than any siblings who were conceived at separate times by the same parents. It has been estimated that

61

Twins are often used in developmental studies. The pair on the left are identical twins, and the pair on the right are fraternal.

the odds of two dizygotic twins being genetically identical are 1 in 251 trillion (Winchester, 1972). Given the genetic differences between monozygotic twins and dizygotic twins, comparisons of the two types of twins are useful in the study of behavioral genetics. One type of comparison involves concordances and disconcordances between twins for particular traits. Twins are *concordant* for a trait if each twin possesses the trait. Twins are *discordant* if one twin has the trait of concern and the other twin does not. Comparing the concordance rates of monozygotic and dizygotic twins allows us to better determine the relative influence of genetics on the characteristics of concern. If monozygotic twins exhibit a higher concordance rate than do dizygotic twins, then the characteristic being studied is thought to be more influenced by heredity than by the environment. If monozygotic twins and fraternal twins exhibit similar concordance rates, then the importance of heredity is minimized for the emergence of that phenotype.

Concordance rates for monozygotic twins and dizygotic twins for a variety of characteristics are summarized in Table 2-3. Monozygotic twins exhibit higher concordance rates than do dizygotic twins on a range of characteristics, ranging from the site of cancer to a criminal record, suggesting that genetic information influences the emergence of these characteristics. Similarly, the results in Table 2-4 show the correlations that have been found among twins' personality test scores. Monozygotic twins share higher correlations than do dizygotic twins for personality characteristics such as in-

TABLE 2-3

Concordance rates for monozygotic and dizygotic twins with respect to certain characteristics

Trait	Monozygotic Twins	Dizygotic Twins
Cancer	61	44
Clubfoot	32	3
Congenital dislocation of the hip	42	3
Criminal record	68	28
Diabetes mellitus	84	37
Down's syndrome (mongolism)	89	6
Epilepsy	72	15
Handedness (right or left)	79	77
Harelip	33	5
Manic-depressive psychosis	77	19
Measles	95	87
Mental retardation	97	37
Rickets	88	22
Schizophrenia	86	15
Site of cancer (in cases where both twins have cancer)	95	58
Tuberculosis	65	25

SOURCE: Adapted from Winchester, 1972, p. 532.

TABLE 2-4

Correlations of monozygotic and dizygotic twins for personality test scores

Personality Measure	Monozygotic	Dizygotic
Introversion–extroversion	.52	.25
Social closeness		
Social potency		
Impulsivity	.48	.29
Neuroticism	.52	.22
Social anxiety		
Physical anxiety		
Total anxiety		
Defensiveness (lie)		

SOURCE: Adapted from Scarr and Kidd, 1983, p. 417.

troversion–extroversion, impulsivity, and neuroticism, suggesting that heredity plays a role in the emergence of some personality characteristics.

Although findings such as the above suggest that heredity influences the emergence of a variety of characteristics, it is important to note that heredity is not the sole determinant of these phenotypes. The concordance rates are not 100% for any of the characteristics, suggesting that the environment is also a factor in the emergence of the characteristics under discussion.

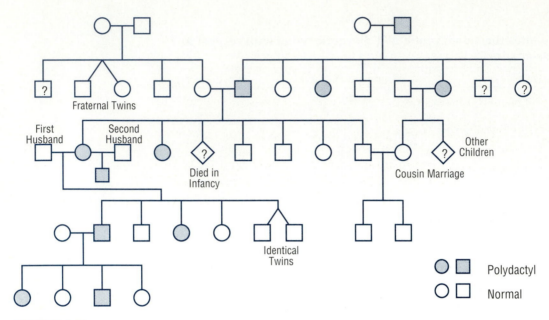

FIGURE 2-16

Pedigree analysis showing family ancestry for polydactyly. Squares represent males. Circles represent females.

Source: from Winchester, 1972, p. 17.

FIGURE 2-17

Pedigree analysis showing family ancestry for color blindness. Note that color blindness skips generations and only occurs in males.

Source: from Winchester, 1972, p. 18.

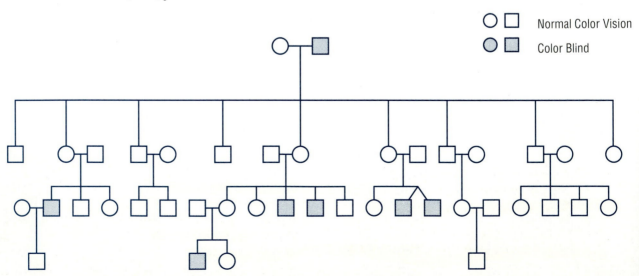

Another type of research used in the study of behavioral genetics involves family pedigree analysis. By examining the frequency with which characteristics are passed from generation to generation within a family, it becomes possible to determine the genetic transmission of such characteristics. For example, polydactyly is a condition in which a child is born with six fingers on each hand and six toes on each foot. Pedigree analysis of this trait has shown that polydactyly only occurs when one parent has the trait (see Figure 2-16). Moreover, when at least one parent has polydactyly, it will be transmitted to approximately one-half of the children. Boys and girls are equally likely to exhibit this trait, demonstrating that it is not linked to the sex chromosomes. In contrast, color blindness is sex-linked. Only males can inherit color blindness and only if their grandfathers had it (see Figure 2-17).

The Twin Method

The use of twins as subjects in research in developmental psychology reflects a concern with unraveling the intracacies of the nature–nurture debate. If an investigator compares two randomly selected children on a measure (for example, rate of physical growth), differences between the children could be due to either environmental factors (such as, the children could have had different environments), to hereditary factors (for example, the children could have different genotypes), or to some combination of environmental and genetic factors. However, if the investigator had compared identical twins, then any observed differences would be due to environmental factors since identical twins have identical genotypes. Here, then, is a very simple illustration of how research with twins can help to pinpoint environmental influences on development.

Researchers who have used twins to answer developmental questions have actually gone far beyond simple comparisons of identical twins. One example of a sophisticated research design employing twins is the following:

- Group 1–identical twins reared together
- Group 2–fraternal twins reared together
- Group 3–identical twins reared apart
- Group 4–fraternal twins reared apart

This design allows a number of important comparisons. Since identical twins share identical genotypes and fraternal twins are no more genetically similar than any pair of siblings, comparing these two types of twins allows the researcher to better determine the importance of heredity. If heredity is important, then identical twins should be more similar than are fraternal twins. In studies of twins, similarity is often measured in terms of concordance. If both members of a twin pair share a characteristic (such as those listed in Table 2-2), then the twins are concordant for that characteristic. A concordance rate refers to the percentage of twins who are concordant for a characteristic. Thus, if heredity is the important determining factor for a characteristic, then identical twins should have a higher concordance rate than fraternal twins, regardless of whether the twins are reared together (and so share the same environment) or reared apart. If the environment is the more important factor, then twins reared together should be more similar than those reared apart (regardless of whether the twins are identical or fraternal).

Despite the obvious advantages of using twins in developmental research, this research technique has its pitfalls. Identical and fraternal twins are not as easy to find as are non-twin children, especially if a researcher wants to find twins who have been reared apart. Thus, twin research usually involves smaller numbers of subjects than comparable studies with non-twin children. ❧

Summary

In this chapter, we have introduced and considered the implications of the nature–nurture controversy. Advocates of the nature position argue that heredity is the most important determinant of development. Advocates of the nurture position argue that the environment influences development much more than does heredity.

Every living thing contains a unique set of genetic information (with the exception of identical siblings). All members of a species possess both a general inheritance and a specific inheritance. The general inheritance is the genetic material that all members of a species have in common. The specific inheritance is the genetic material that is unique to an individual. The term genotype refers to the genetic make-up of an individual. The term phenotype refers to the outward characteristics of the individual. It is difficult to determine an individual's genotype from his or her phenotype. The study of the relation of genotype and phenotype is known as behavioral genetics.

Cells are the basic building blocks of all living things. The cell nucleus contains the chromosomes, along which are located the genes. Genes carry all of the heritable information that is transmitted from generation to generation. The normal human cell contains 46 chromosomes, arranged into 23 pairs. This is the diploid number of chromosomes. Cells duplicate themselves through the process of mitosis. The result of mitosis is two duplicates of the original parent cell. The exception to this involves the sperm and the ovum. They contain only 23 chromosomes, the haploid number of chromosomes. Sperms and ova are formed through the process of meiosis. During meiosis, crossing over may occur which results in increased genetic variability among members of the species.

The period from conception to birth is called the prenatal period. Development during this period is divided into three stages: the germinal period, the embryonic period, and the fetal period. Sexual development during the prenatal period begins at conception. If the fertilized ovum has received two X sex chromosomes, the child is a genetic female. If the fertilized ovum has received one X sex chromosome and one Y sex chromosome, the child will be a genetic male. Hormones released later during the prenatal period influence the development of sexual characteristics.

The brain begins to develop in the germinal stage of the prenatal period. At birth, virtually all of the nerve cells of the human brain are formed, as are some of the connections among the cells. After birth, the nerve cells will grow in size and the connections among brain cells will increase in number as children grow older. As a result, young children's brains contain more nerve cell connections than do adult brains. Experience appears to play an important role in determining both which nerve cells and which connections survive.

The environment provided by the mother to the developing child in the womb is very important. Deficits in maternal diet, maternal smoking, use of drugs, and alcohol consumption during pregnancy have all been shown to result in atypical prenatal development. The effects of teratogens (substances that are harmful to the developing organism) such as thalidomide depend on the age of the developing embryo or fetus when exposed. Thus, the effects of teratogens depend on whether the developing organism is in a sensitive period (a developmental period of high susceptibility to particular environmental influences).

From our consideration of the issues and developmental phenomena in this chapter, it should be clear that development proceeds as a result of the interaction of genetic predispositions and environmental experiences. As you shall see in the remaining chapters, certain aspects of development seem to be more influenced by the environment than by heredity, while other aspects of development are more influenced by heredity than the environment. However, in all cases, genetic predispositions interact with experience to produce development.

Suggested Readings

Apgar, V., & Beck, J. (1974). *Is my baby all right?* New York: Pocket Books.

England, M. (1983). *Color atlas of life before birth: Normal fetal development.* Chicago: Yearbook Medical Publishers.

Farber, S. (1981). *Identical twins reared apart: A reanalysis.* New York: Basic Books.

Lewotin, R. (1982). *Human diversity.* New York: Scientific American Books.

Nilsson, L., Ingleman-Sundberg, A., & Wirsen, C. (1981). *A child is born: The drama of life before birth.* New York: Dell.

Plomin, R. (1986). *Developmental genetics and psychology.* Hillsdale, NJ: Erlbaum.

Stechler, G., & Halton, A. (1982). Prenatal influences on human development. In B. Wolman (Ed.), *Handbook of developmental psychology.* Englewood Cliffs, N.J.: Prentice Hall.

CHAPTER THREE

The Newborn Infant and the Effects of Early Experience

Introduction

The time from conception to birth is about 260 days, allowing for some variation from one mother to another. The course of development during that time is both dramatic and critically important for the later health and growth of the child. As we saw in Chapter 2, much of prenatal development is determined by the nature of our species and by the genetic material passed on to the fetus from its parents. In addition, scientists now know that prenatal experiences, such as the quality of nutrition that the mother gets and whether or not she uses alcohol and tobacco, strongly affect the development of the brain and other organ systems. In other words, experience plays a role in development even before a child is born.

In this chapter we describe the newborn child and the effects of experiences during birth and in the first few weeks of life. Among the questions we will address are the following: Are there capacities that can be detected at birth that foretell whether an infant is likely to develop normally? Once these early signs have been detected, can we change the course of development? To what extent can experiences that occur very early in development affect what a person is like in childhood, adolescence, and adulthood?

We can answer these questions far more completely today than we could only a decade ago. In recent years psychologists and others who study infant behavior have learned a great deal about how to assess the competencies of newborns. Furthermore, they have studied the development of children whose birth or early experiences were somehow different from those of typical children. The resulting advances in knowledge enable us to specify what typical newborns can do and to identify and better understand children whose capacities are different in some way from the capacities of healthy newborns.

We begin with a brief overview of the birth process and then turn to a discussion of the newly born child. We will then consider some problems in development for children whose birth experiences have deviated somehow from normal. Finally, we will discuss the development of children who, in the days and weeks just after birth, experience environmental deprivations.

Birth

Birth begins when the mother's uterus contracts repeatedly, in an effort to push the infant from its sealed world inside. The contractions occur at widely spaced intervals at first and serve primarily to dilate (widen) the cervix, the opening from the birth canal into the uterus. This opening must be enlarged to 10 or 12 centimeters so that the baby's head and body can pass through it. Contractions gradually become stronger and more frequent, moving the infant out of the uterus and into the vagina, or birth canal. In most cases, the baby's head appears first, although in about 10% of births feet or buttocks appear first. This position is known as a breech birth and can present serious difficulties for the baby and the mother, as we will discuss below in the section on infants at risk.

When the baby is fully delivered, the physician or midwife ties off the umbilical cord several inches from the baby's body and cuts it. Uterine contractions continue until the placenta (commonly known as the afterbirth), the remainder of the umbilical cord, and the fetal membranes come out of the mother's body, as well. Figure 3-1 summarizes the phases of the birth process. The length of time required for this process varies widely from one birth to another. Some births take 22 or more hours from the beginning of contractions, whereas others—particularly if the mother has given birth previously—take as little as 4 to $4\frac{1}{2}$ hours.

Attitudes toward childbirth and methods of delivery have changed considerably during the past century. In the first half of the period, the most pronounced change was using surgical procedures to help with birth. In earlier times, babies were often born at home, often without the attention of a physician. Once physicians began to attend births, births rapidly came to be considered surgical procedures, and birth was marked by the routine of other types of surgeries. Mothers were anesthetized, and fathers were relegated to waiting rooms until delivery was completed and their spouses were "waking up" from the anesthesia.

In the past two decades, however, the trend toward using surgery has been modified in several ways. In general, the extent of medication used in childbirth has been reduced, so that mothers are conscious and involved in the birth process. Fathers—and sometimes other family members or friends—typically are present in hospital delivery rooms or other childbirth facilities. As one physician put it, we have stopped thinking of birth as a medical procedure and begun to view it again as an integral part of family life.

One reason for this change in childbirth practices is that advances in medical technology make it easier to monitor both mother and infant for any signs of difficulty or distress. Thus, it has not been considered essential that only medical personnel be present in cases where emergency procedures are needed. As an example, devices can be used to tell if the infant is suffering from a shortage of oxygen or if there are irregularities in heartbeat; and technology and well-established medical procedures are available to resolve these problems. In fact, although more than 98% of births still take place in hospitals, the medical staff members in attendance are not always physicans; sometimes trained midwives carry out the procedures of routine delivery, with a physician on call in case of emergencies. A small number of parents prefer to have their babies born at home, but most experts advise parents to take advantage of the medical resources now available at progressive hospitals. Although relatively few births require doctors to intervene with drugs, surgery, or other means, it is sometimes necessary to protect the health and even the lives of mother and baby.

71

First Stage

Before Labor Begins

Transition: just before the baby's head enters the birth canal

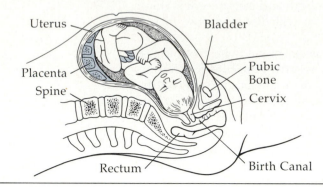
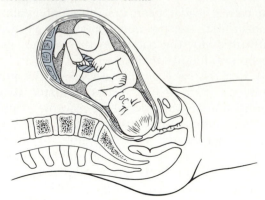

Second Stage

The Baby's Head Before Crowning   The Head Crowning   The Head Emerging

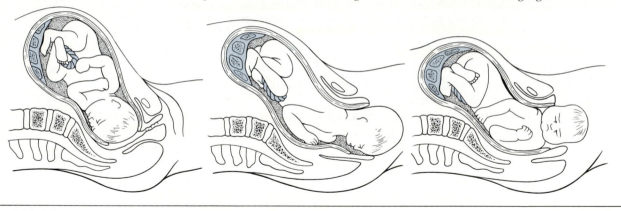

Third Stage

The Third Stage of Labor: the placenta coming loose and about to be born

The Pelvis After Delivery

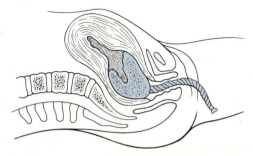
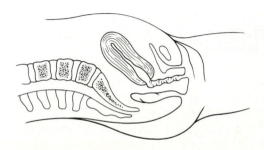

FIGURE 3-1
The three phases of childbirth.

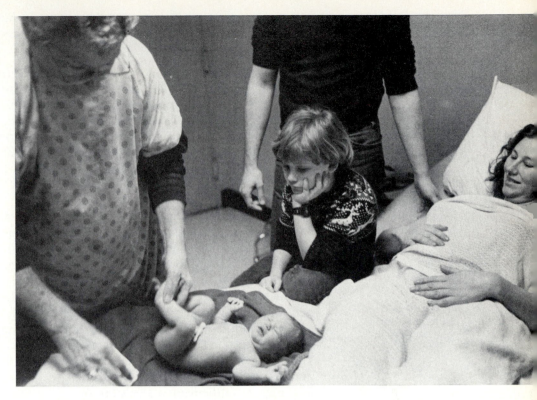

In the past two decades, birth has become a family affair for many parents and children, with fathers and even siblings attending the arrival of a new family member.

Most hospitals now also make special efforts to soothe and comfort infants immediately after birth, typically by handing them to their mothers to be held close or even to be breast fed. Some even follow the gentle birthing suggestions of the French obstetrician Leboyer (1975) by immersing the newborn baby in a warm bath to simulate the conditions of the womb.

What happens during birth can affect a newborn's responses immediately after birth and even months and years later. In later sections, we will consider the characteristics of babies for whom the birth process has been unusual.

The Newborn

A half-century ago, one well-educated father justified his lack of interest in his newborn son by saying, "He has nothing to say to me, nor I to him." Newborns appear to be passive, helpless creatures. If they are capable of any but the most elementary reactions, the casual observer does not see it, because the limitations on infants' movements and expressions deny us access to what they see, hear, and remember. Consequently, until very recently most adults have assumed that the newborn period was a necessary, but largely uninteresting prologue to a later time when the capacity to experience and react to the surrounding world would finally emerge.

Today, however, it is clear that newborns are equipped with a remarkable array of capabilities and potentials. In the past 25 years, researchers have devoted considerable study to the period between birth and 28 days of age,

73

which is called the neonatal period. (We use the terms neonate and newborn interchangeably to refer to infants under 1 month of age.) In this section, we will first examine the capacities of normal newborns. Next we will give an overview of the methods that psychologists and pediatricians use to discover what newborns can do. Then, in subsequent sections of the chapter, we will consider the circumstances in which newborn behavior deviates significantly from normal patterns and the long-term effects of this deviation.

The Behavior of Newborns

Let us turn first to a question that is both of great interest to parents and has guided scientists in their search for knowledge about newborn infants: What do the behavior patterns of newborns reveal about their capacities for responding to the varying demands and challenges of their environments? This question raises two more specific issues. One is the kinds of stimulation to which infants are capable of responding. The other is how these responses help to prepare infants for the experiences that they will encounter.

When parents first have an opportunity to interact with a new baby, they are rarely attuned to the details and implications of what the baby does. They will probably notice if the baby seems to be looking back at them with interest (which some parents will be eager to interpret as recognition!). A few may move their fingers or a brightly colored object from one side to the other in front of babies' faces to see if they follow with their eyes. Many will talk and coo as though the babies understand their words, and they may smile with bared teeth and move their heads up-and-down or side-to-side as though to engage the infants in conversation.

Depending on how alert or sleepy the baby is, the average newborn will have noticed many of these overtures. Babies have extensive abilities for sensing the world around them. They see faces and objects—although their visual acuity is not as good as it will be a few months later, and distant objects appear somewhat blurry. Parents who want to be recognized would do well to put their faces fairly close to the baby at first. Babies spend a good deal of time "scanning" their environments, picking up the outlines of faces and objects before noticing the details. They are also quite good at following moving objects, especially slowly moving ones. Babies can hear sounds and can discriminate human speech sounds from one another, so that parents' conversation-like talking is actually an important early source of stimulation of an innate ability. Babies seem to be predisposed to react to human faces, voices, and movements—characteristics that are primary to participating in the exchanges of social life. The father who refused to interact with his son, as though the child was an unresponsive lump, could have scarcely been more wrong, as the accompanying Research Focus 3-1 indicates.

In addition to these basic sensory abilities and capabilities for response to others and to the environment, psychologists now know that the behavior of infants follows patterns of organization that give us important clues about the human organism and its potentials. These are especially apparent in research findings about four aspects of newborn behavior: (1) cyclical states of alertness, (2) sleep patterns and functions, (3) crying, and (4) responsiveness to contingencies.

RESEARCH FOCUS 3-1

How Newborns Cope with Stress

Newborns are ordinarily thought of as exceptionally fragile. Certainly, their need for care and nurturance is great, but infants are born with a remarkable capacity to tolerate stress and to resume normal functioning very quickly afterward.

This capacity is evident in recent studies of circumcision. The majority of male infants in the United States undergo this procedure sometime between the second and fourth day of life. The surgical removal of the foreskin of the baby's penis is ordinarily done without anesthesia, and babies show intense distress while the surgery is being done. Tests of hormone levels in their blood before and immediately after circumcision typically show sizable increases in the amount of cortisol, a hormone that is associated with high levels of stress (Gunnar, Malone, Vance, & Fisch, 1985). Remarkably, however, within a few minutes of the procedure, most infants are capable of calm, normal interactions when their mothers feed them (Marshall, Porter, Rogers, Moore, Anderson, & Boxerman, 1982). How do infants manage this amazing recovery?

In a recent study, psychologist Megan Gunnar and her collaborators (Gunnar et al., 1985) observed newborns for periods lasting from 30 minutes before circumcision to as long as 4 hours following the surgery. She was interested both in the levels of cortisol that appeared in the babies' blood samples and also in the behavioral states that they were showing at different intervals following circumcision. Consequently, she examined 20 of the infants only 30 minutes after their surgeries. In another group, 20 babies were tested 90 minutes after their circumcisions. Two additional groups of 20 each were tested 120

minutes (2 hours) and 240 minutes (4 hours), respectively, after their operations. Finally, they observed a group of babies whose parents had elected not to have them circumcised.

Circumcision is clearly a highly stressful event for these infants. Their serum cortisol levels are elevated substantially during the surgery and for several hours thereafter. The Gunnar team also noted that babies appear to have remarkable abilities for overcoming the physiological stresses associated with this painful procedure. Their study showed that the babies' cortisol levels returned to the precircumcision level within 2–4 hours after the surgery. (They report that their other studies have indicated that the average time for reaching normal cortisol levels is $2\frac{1}{2}$ hours.) In other words, within a fairly short time after having surgery without anesthesia, these newborn boys no longer showed hormonal evidence that their bodies had experienced stress.

One factor in the recovery from circumcision may have been sleep. Circumcised infants typically remained awake 30 minutes after their operations, but the babies tested at 90, 120, and 240 minutes were very likely to be in quiet sleep, or non-REM sleep. Compared to babies who had not been circumcised, the circumcised groups showed noticeably higher levels of quiet sleep in the 4 hours following their surgeries. Gunnar speculates that quiet sleep helped the infants dampen the natural tendencies of their bodies to produce cortisol in reaction to stress, thus explaining why the amount of cortisol dropped so quickly from the high levels created by the circumcision itself. 🍎

States of alertness. Psychologists use the term *organization* to refer to the ways in which the seemingly random, meaningless behaviors of an organism seem to be related to important elements of that organism's functioning or environment. In the case of newborns, psychologists have found important clues to behavioral organization in the study of the infant's states, or different levels of alertness or consciousness. For example, at any given time, 2-week-old Tara may be asleep with eyes closed and face and limbs relaxed, or her sleep may be somewhat more irregular and restless, with some writhing and stirring, facial grimaces, and eyelid movements. Jacob, also 2-weeks-old, is sometimes alert, following movement with his eyes, but inactive and with a relaxed face; at other times, when awake, he is more active, making diffuse movements with his arms and legs, and attentive to objects and people around him. Thus, infants are not simply either asleep or awake. They normally vary in how active they are and how much they are attending to things around them, whether they are asleep or awake. These and other variations in states have been described by Peter Wolff (1966), as shown in Table 3-1.

Wolff and others (Lamb & Campos, 1982) have speculated that the alert inactivity state has special significance for growth and development because it is the time when infants are likely to be most attentive and positively responsive to stimulation from both persons and things around them. At the same time, it is clear that all states and changes in states provide a window on how and why infants respond differently to different experiences. This point is illustrated by research findings on the two most extreme states described in Table 3-1: sleeping and crying. We will discuss these two in more detail.

Sleep. The popular impression that newborns sleep most of the time is well founded. During the first 15 days of life, infants typically sleep about 16 hours a day. The characteristics of their sleep tell us that, during much of

TABLE 3-1
Classification of Infant States

Regular sleep: The eyes are closed and the infant is completely still; respirations are slow and regular; the face is relaxed—no grimace—and the eyelids are still.

Irregular sleep: The eyes are closed; the infant engages in variable gentle limb movements, writhing and stirring; grimaces and other facial expressions are frequent; respirations are irregular and faster than in regular sleep; there are interspersed and recurrent rapid eye movements.

Drowsiness: The infant is relatively inactive; the eyes open and close intermittently; respirations are regular, though faster than in regular sleep; when eyes are open, they have a dull or glazed quality.

Alert inactivity: The eyes are open and have a bright and shining quality; the infant can pursue moving objects and make conjugate eye movements in the horizontal and vertical plane; the infant is relatively inactive; the face is relaxed and the infant does not grimace.

Waking activity: The infant frequently engages in diffuse motor activity involving his whole body; the eyes are open, but not alert, and the respirations are grossly irregular.

Crying: The infant has crying vocalizations associated with vigorous diffuse motor activity.

SOURCE: Adapted from Wolff, 1966.

that time, they are not simply resting passively. Paradoxically, studying infants' sleep has given us new information about the need for stimulation in the early weeks of life.

The contrast between infants' sleep and the sleep of older children and adults helps to make this point. Throughout life, part of a person's sleeping time consists of REM (rapid-eye-movement) states, in which there are not only rapid eye movements, but also changes in heart rate and blood pressure. These states are often called dream sleep, because adults dream during REM states. Beginning about age 2 and continuing into adulthood, REM sleep comprises about 18–25% of total sleeping time (Roffwarg, Muzio, & Dement, 1966). In adults, REM sleep ordinarily follows non-REM sleep.

By comparison, in newborns, 50% of sleep time is spent in REM states (Roffwarg et al., 1966). You can see in Table 3-1 that the irregular sleep state is characterized by noticeable movement of the closed eyelid, an indication of rapid eye movements. Not only is there proprotionally more REM sleep, but REM and non-REM patterns are distinctive in newborns. Instead of falling into REM sleep after a period of non-REM sleep, babies under the age of 6 months usually go directly into REM sleep from one of the waking states (Kligman, Smyrl, & Emde, 1975; Korner, 1972).

What do these different patterns tell us about the significance of REM sleep in infancy? The most plausible theory is that, for newborns, REM sleep serves as autostimulation. The mental activity associated with rapid eye movements may stimulate the brain, thus contributing to the development of the central nervous system (Roffwarg et al., 1966). Once piece of evidence that supports this is that infants who received a lot of stimulation spent less time in REM sleep than comparison infants who did not receive much stimulation (Boismier, 1977; Emde, Harmon, Metcalf, Koenig, & Wagonfeld, 1971). As infants mature, they may have more opportunities for stimulation and rely less on REM sleep to provide an optimal amount of stimulation. Consequently, their sleep patterns resemble adult patterns more. For newborns, sleep time may also be an essential time for mental development.

Crying. It is obvious from Table 3-1 that sleep states are different from one another. Differences in infant crying are less apparent, but recent research shows that babies give quite different cries at different times. Furthermore, it is now clear that those different cries serve as important signals to caregivers about the state and the needs of their infants (Lester, 1983). In other words, crying states are an early and largely effective means of communication.

Infants spend 6–7% of their waking time crying, on the average, although the amount varies from day to day and from one baby to another (Korner, Hutchinson, Koperski, Kraemer, & Schneider, 1981). Through careful observation of many normal infants, researcher Rudolph Schaffer (1971) identified three distinctive patterns of cries:

1. A basic pattern, in which crying starts at low intensity and without a distinctive rhythm, but gradually becomes both louder and more rhythmical. It usually consists of these phases: cry, rest, take in

RESEARCH FOCUS 3-2

Assessing the Newborn and Instructing the Parent

Psychologists and pediatricians have devised a number of procedures to determine whether newborns have normal neurological and sensory capacities. One of the most famous, the Brazelton Neonatal Behavioral Assessment Scale (BNBAS), has been used widely not only to assess babies' status, but also to help parents learn what their babies are like and how they might enhance the infants' development (Brazelton, 1979).

The Brazelton is one of the most extensive neonatal assessment techniques in existence. It includes tests of the reflexes, the organization of behavior, the extent to which babies modulate their states, such as, crying and alertness, and responses to others in interaction. The information from the test indicates the capacity to make smooth transitions from one state to another, to be attentive to differences in social stimuli, and to coordinate motor responses. In short, the Brazelton gives a good indication of infants' neurophysiological capacities and their potential for adaptation to the world around them (Kopp, 1983).

Parents may not always be able to appreciate the richness of information that a skilled tester can get from a Brazelton examination. But several recent studies show that parents can nevertheless learn a great deal from watching their babies being tested with the Brazelton. For example, psychologist Tiffany Field (1983) compared two groups of mothers of high-risk infants. One group watched the Brazelton tests being given to their babies, and the second group did not. Afterwards, Field observed that the mothers who had seen the Brazelton demonstration were more responsive to face-to-face interactions with their babies than the mothers in the other group. When Field retested the babies 1 month later, she found that the group whose mothers had seen the Brazelton scored higher on the 1-month followup than the babies in the no-demonstration group. Apparently, being able to watch a skilled tester work with their babies helps to convince the parents of high-risk babies that their children can respond normally and, perhaps, gives them some clues about being sensitive to their children's reactions. As a result, even though their babies may be less responsive and more irritable than other babies, the mothers were able to adjust their own behavior to take fuller advantage of the capacities their infants did show.

The Brazelton has also been used with parents or normal babies with positive results. Even when babies are not at any special risk, seeing the Brazelton seems to help parents become more quickly acquainted with their children and their babies' unique abilities for responding to others (Myers, 1982). ❧

---

breath, rest, and so on. The basic cry is associated with hunger, but can also be related to other conditions.

2. A "mad" or angry cry, which follows the same sequence of phases as the basic pattern, but each of the components lasts a longer time.
3. A pain cry, which begins very suddenly and loudly. Its phases are as follows: a long cry, followed by a long silence (during which the infant holds his breath), followed by a series of short gasping intakes of breath.

Researchers have found that mothers can recognize these different types of cries. For example, mothers who heard a tape recording of a pain cry from another room showed distress and concern; but when the tape was altered to change the length of the phases, the mothers were more relaxed and less bothered by what they heard (Wolff, 1969). Experience helps adults decipher the meaning of infant cries. For example, mothers recognize the difference between pain cries and "mad" cries when the crying infant is their own, but not when it is someone else's child. Fathers are generally less able than mothers to tell the two types of cries apart, even when the infant is their own (Wiesenfeld, Malatesta, DeLoach, 1981). Adults, such as nurses and childcare workers, who have extensive contact with infants are more accurate at recognizing different crying patterns than those with less infant contact (Lester, 1983). In short, although crying may seem to be much the same from one time to another, there are important nuances to infant cries that give them special communicative significance in the infant's own world.

Responsiveness to contingencies.   The fact that crying and caregivers' responses seem to be so well attuned to each other points to another capability that is present very early in infancy: the ability to detect relations between actions and their consequences. These relations are referred to as *contingencies*, and infants' sensitivity to them is illustrated by an experiment conducted by John S. Watson and Craig Ramey (1972). Using a special remote-controlled mobile, these researchers compared the behavior of three groups of infants. One group was given pressure-sensitive pillows, so that when the babies moved their heads, the mobiles hanging above their cribs turned slightly. In other words, the movement of the mobile was contingent on the action of the baby's head.

Over a period of 14 days, these infants gradually increased the number of times they moved their heads. Furthermore, these infants' mothers reported that their babies showed a great deal of pleasure and excitement when the mobile responded to their head movements. A second group of infants also had a mobile that could move, but the movements were not contingent on the babies' head movements; instead, the mobile was regulated by a timing device that caused it to turn periodically by itself. In a third group, the infants' mobiles were stationary. Neither of these second groups showed a general rise in amount of head turning. Several weeks later, Watson and Ramey put their special mobiles in the infants' cribs again, but this time they set up the experiment so that all of the babies could have control over the turning of the mobile. However, the babies who had not originally been able to regulate their mobiles did not learn to do so under this new arrangement. Even when they had the opportunity to make the mobile move, they seemed unable to recognize the new contingency or to act on the basis of it (Watson, 1979).

Studies like Watson and Ramey's illustrate the importance, early in life, of opportunities to achieve a sense that one's actions can make a difference. The effects babies create may be very simple, for example, the appearance of the caregiver when the baby is in distress or a parent's facial expressions and conversation-like talking when the baby makes expressive movements or noises. Without experiences that teach them that their actions can produce effects, however, infants may not learn that they can exercise some control over their environments.

Assessing the Health and Sensory Capacities of Newborns

Ask expectant parents what is their greatest concern about the impending birth, and they are likely to say it is the health of their baby. Most would probably agree that they mean not only that the infant not have some critical health problem, but also that they mean the infant has normal abilities to hear, see, feel, and, generally, to respond to the world around him or her as other humans do. Fortunately, what scientists have learned about the capacities of newborn infants has provided a basis for useful techniques for assessing the health and the sensory capacities of newborns. We will first discuss two categories of infant capacities that underlie many assessment methods: (1) their repertoire of inborn reflexes, or involuntary responses to stimulation, and (2) their tendency to habituate to a touch, sight, or sound that has been experienced repeatedly. Next we will describe two widely used assessment procedures that have been built on the growing body of knowledge about newborn capabilities and behavior patterns.

Reflexes. Reflexes cause normal infants to behave in certain highly predictable ways. Most of these highly automatic behaviors are essential for survival and growth. For example, when their cheeks are stroked, infants turn their heads in the direction of the stroking and open their mouths. This rooting reflex helps to orient babies to the breast or bottle and thus aids in feeding, as does the sucking reflex when an object is placed in the mouth. Other examples of these survival reflexes are breathing, blinking, and swallowing. Most of these are permanent human responses, although the rooting reflex gradually weakens over the first 6 months of life.

Knowing about the normal newborn's repertoire of reflexes has enabled psychologists and medical practitioners to identify several important signs of whether a newborn in functioning normally. The characteristic of reflexes that makes this possible is their automatic quality. When you stimulate a baby in a way that stimulates a reflex action, you can count on getting the same response time after time from a normally functioning infant. If you do not get the reflex response, there is reason to suspect that the baby's neurological system is impaired in some way. For example, stroking the sole of a baby's foot from heel to toe ordinarily causes the toes to fan upward (the Babinski reflex), but this does not happen in babies who have defects of the lower spine. A sudden loud sound or jarring or a sudden lowering of the baby's body causes the arms to be thrown out and then quickly brought toward each other (the Moro reflex), but babies with a serious disturbance of the central nervous system do not react in this way or do so in a consistently weak manner. Neither the Babinski nor the Moro reflex is present in adults; both disappear during the first year of life. But they and several others like them are important indicators of neurological functioning in infants, as Table 3-2 indicates. Thus, testing reflexes has become an important part of neonatal examinations.

Habituation. Another inherent capability of infants that has been important to assessing newborns is that of *habituation*. Infants habituate, or become less responsive to a stimulus after they have been exposed to it over a period of

TABLE 3-2
Major Newborn Reflexes

Name	Stimulation	Response	Developmental course	Significance
Blink	Light flash	Closing of both eyelids	Permanent	Protection of eyes from strong stimuli
Biceps reflex	Tap on the tendon of the biceps muscle near elbow	Short contraction of the biceps muscle	In the first few days it is brisker than in later days	Absent in depressed infants or those with congenital muscular disease
Knee jerk or patellar tendon reflex	Tap on the tendon below the kneecap	Quick extension or kick of the knee	More pronounced in the first two days than later	Absent or difficult to obtain in depressed infants or infants with muscular disease; exaggerated in hyperexcitable infants
Babinski	Gentle stroking of the side of the infant's foot from toes toward heel	Dorsal flexion of the big toe; extension of the other toes	Usually disappears near the end of the first year (8–11 months)	Absent in defects of the lower spine
Withdrawal reflex	Pinprick is applied to the sole of the infant's foot	Leg flexion	Constantly present during the first 10 days, present but less intense later	Absent with sciatic nerve damage
Plantar or toe grasp	Pressure is applied with finger against the balls of the infant's feet	Plantar flexion of all toes	Disappears between 8 and 12 months	Absent in defects of the lower spinal cord
Palmar or automatic hand grasp	Press rod or finger against the infant's palm	Infant grasps the object	Increases during the first month and then gradually declines; disappears at 3 to 4 months	Response is weak or absent in depressed babies; sucking movements facilitate grasping
Moro reflex	(1) Sudden loud sound or jarring (for example, bang on the examination table); or (2) head drop—head is dropped a few inches; or (3) baby drop—baby is suspended horizontally and the examiner lowers his hands rapidly about 6 inches and stops abruptly	Arms are thrown out in extension, and then brought toward each other in a convulsive manner; hands are fanned out at first and then clinched tightly; spine and lower extremities extend	Disappears in 6 to 7 months	Absent or constantly weak moro indicates serious disturbances of the central nervous system

SOURCE: Adapted from Prechtl & Beintema, 1965; Knobloch & Pasamanick, 1974.

time. Responsiveness in very young infants can be assessed using several different physiological and behavioral measures (Lipsitt, 1978). For example, when infants encounter a novel stimulus, their heart rates typically accelerate; when the stimulus becomes familiar, heart rate acceleration is lower at each new presentation. Another indicator of responsiveness to a stimulus is the rate at which an infant sucks on a pacifier. Infants increase their rate of sucking when a new stimulus (for example, a new tone or a different human voice) appears. After they have seen or heard the same stimulus for a time, the responsiveness declines. The introduction of a new stimulus, however, increases the sucking rate again (Aslin, Pisoni, & Jusczyk, 1983).

The principle of habituation permits us to use simple behaviors of which all neonates are capable to infer the presence of other abilities that cannot be observed directly. Suppose you want to know whether an infant can hear. You can begin by sounding a tone of a certain pitch. The baby's rate of sucking is likely to increase in response to this new stimulus, as it will in response to other new sensory experiences. If you continue sounding the tone, the sucking rate will gradually return to normal. The baby has habituated to this particular stimulus. Now sound a different pitch. Most newborns show an increase in sucking rate again. Why? Because they recognize that this is a different sound than the one to which they had grown accustomed. By allowing the infant to habituate to one pitch, you determine whether the baby can discriminate one pitch from another (Aslin, Pisoni, & Jusczyk, 1983; Steinschneider, Lipton, & Richmond, 1966). By using this idea with other aspects of sound, such as loudness and duration, it is possible to determine not only whether babies can hear, but what aspects of sound they are especially sensitive to. Other procedures for assessing infants' sensory capacities based on the principle of habituation will be discussed in Chapter 5.

Neonatal Assessment Devices: Some Examples. Parents can usually obtain immediate information about the general health of their baby from the medical staff members who attend the birth. A standard procedure in most delivery rooms is a simple assessment devised by pediatrician Virginia Apgar (1953). Dr. Apgar recommended checking the infant's heart rate, breathing, muscle tone, color (an indication of blood circulation), and reflexes at 1 minute and again at 5 minutes after birth. Table 3-3 shows how infants are rated on these characteristics. As you can see, possible scores range from 0 to 10. Infants who score 4 or lower on the 5-minute Apgar test need immediate medical attention, without which they might not survive. Those with scores between 7 and 10 are considered not to be in any immediate danger.

The Apgar test gives an immediate indication of whether additional medical intervention is needed and, if so, how quickly. However, it provides only part of the information needed to assess a baby's overall health and capacities. In recent years, it has become possible to get information about the functioning of newborn infants' nervous systems and behavior patterns. For example, Prechtl (1977) has devised a scale for testing the soundness of the nervous system. The original scale, which contains many neurological and

TABLE 3-3
The Apgar Test

Characteristic	Score		
	0	*1*	*2*
Heart rate	Absent	Slow (less than 100 beats per minute)	Over 100 beats per minute
Respiratory effort	Absent	Slow or irregular	Good, baby is crying
Muscle tone	Flaccid, limp	Weak, some flexion	Strong, active motion
Color	Blue or pale	Body pink, extremities blue	Completely pink
Reflex irritability	No response	Frown, grimace, or weak cry	Vigorous cry

SOURCE: Adapted from Apgar (1953).

reflex items, is very lengthy, and a more recent version has been created that can be completed in a 10-minute screening examination to check babies for weakness, problems on one side of the body, and nervous excitability (Kopp, 1983).

Another example of assessment of general functioning is the Brazelton Neonatal Behavioral Assessment Scale, devised by pediatrician T. Berry Brazelton (1979). The Brazelton is widely used to measure newborns' neurological functioning. The Brazelton Neonatal Behavioral Assessment Scale is administered when an infant is 3 days old and again a few days later to check on the accuracy of the assessment. Examiners check 20 reflexes and also note the baby's responses to 26 situations, such as cuddling, orientation to face and voice, and the sound of a rattle. Extremely low scores may indicate brain damage or some other neurological impairment. Higher scores indicate that infants do not appear to suffer from neurological deficits and, indeed, are responding in normal ways to various kinds of social stimulation. Like the Prechtl, the Brazelton relies heavily on knowledge of infant reflexes and the "bias" of infants to attend to the human voice and other characteristics of persons. Such assessment procedures give physicians and others a good idea of how an infant compares to other babies in the newborn period and provides important clues about which babies should be monitored with particular care.

Infants at Risk: Newborns Who Face Possible Developmental Problems

In describing birth and the newborn infant's remarkable capacities, we have drawn a picture that applies to most babies, but not to all. As we saw in Chapter 2, a number of conditions that occur before birth can create potential difficulties for infants' health and later growth and development. Infants who encounter teratogens (substances that may damage the developing fetus) prenatally are said to be at risk for, or particularly likely to show, physical, cognitive, and social–emotional difficulties in later development. In this section, we will present information on infants who are at risk because of conditions surrounding their birth or because of the nature and quality of environmental experiences during the first month of life. These infants may face health problems at birth and immediately afterwards, and they may show impairments of functioning both in infancy and in later periods of development.

At the same time, it is important to note that risk to newborns today is much lower than it was 30 years ago in one sense: Infants are more likely to survive in spite of difficulties at birth. Statistics indicate that, between 1965 and 1980, the number of newborns who died because of the most common birth complications (asphyxia or lack of oxygen, and birth injuries) decreased by 80–90%, and the number of deaths from premature births declined by almost 70% (Kopp, 1983). One reason for this is the remarkable advances made in medical knowledge and treatment of infants who experience these conditions. A subspecialty of pediatrics, called neonatology, is now devoted specifically to the intensive care of high-risk newborns. As we discussed in Chapters 1 and 2, these advances have been accompanied by a complex array of issues regarding survival of the infant versus the prospects for long-term health and normal functioning for some preterm and birth-traumatized infants. These issues are examined in greater detail in the discussion of ethical issues in treating severely impaired newborns.

Despite these improvements in the survival rates of infants at risk, infant mortality in the United States is still higher than the rate in many other industrialized countries. For example, in 1973 the mortality rate for U.S. Caucasian infants was 14.8 per 1,000 births, which was higher than the 9.6 per 1,000 births reported for Sweden (Chase, 1977). These figures imply that medical factors alone are not sufficient to counteract the problem of infant mortality. Changes in social, cultural, and economic conditions will also be needed (Emanuel, 1977; Kopp, 1983). Particularly needed are better prenatal care and more extensive programs such as "well baby" clinics for low-income and at-risk mothers and infants.

Another way in which risks to newborns have declined in recent decades is in the likelihood that there will be long-term effects of early problems. In the early 1960s, almost half of preterm infants showed neurological and cognitive problems at later ages (Drillien, 1964). Twenty-five years later, preterm infants have a better than 70% chance of developing normally, depending on their birthweight and whether or not they have health problems other than their early birth.

To examine some of these points further, let us turn to a discussion of the three most common categories of risk factors in the newborn period: factors related to timing of birth (particularly to birth before babies have reached full gestational age); factors related to complications of birth, such as asphyxia and medication during the birth process; and factors related to deprivation during the newborn period itself. In each case, we will consider both the risks, or potential problems, for infants who experience these conditions and also the possibilities that these risks can be overcome by appropriate interventions and care.

"Timely" births refer to babies who are born between the 37th and 43rd weeks following conception (Guttmacher, 1973). Before the 37th week, births are considered preterm and babies are thought of as premature; after the 43rd week, births are postterm and the infants are considered postmature. These untimely circumstances of birth may have serious implications for later development. Postterm births are slightly more at risk for oxygen deficiency (anoxia), a likelihood that is thought to be due to less efficient food and oxygen distribution by the "aging" placenta to the fetus (Brown & Dixon, 1978). Preterm births are more common than post-term births, constituting 8–9% of births in the United States. Preterm births also carry more potentially problematic consequences than postterm births.

Timing of Birth

Risk from Preterm Birth. The problem of being born before the full gestation period is that infants are unlikely to have the full extent of capacities that enable normal, full-term babies to survive and to show the adaptive patterns of behavior that we described in the previous section. The risks to preterm newborns are not equally severe in all cases, however. The most serious problems occur when infants weight less than 1,500 grams at birth and when they have health problems in addition to early birth. For example, it is common for preterm babies to have breathing problems because their lungs are not properly coated with a substance called surfactin. This substance ordinarily appears during the final month of a full-term pregnancy. A deficiency of surfactin can cause hyaline membrane disease, which makes it difficult or impossible for the infant to breathe. Infants who weigh between 1,500 and 2,500 grams and those who do not have problems like hyaline membrane disease are less likely to have problems as newborns or in later development (Kopp, 1983).

Environmental Factors in Preterm Risk. In addition to differences in their physical maturity, preterm infants have quite different experiences than do full-term babies, and the effects of birth timing are sometimes difficult to separate from the impact of these different environmental influences. As we saw in Chapter 2, prenatal factors like maternal health and malnutrition and use of alcohol, tobacco, and other substances can affect the timing of birth, as well as subsequent development (Kopp, 1983). Mothers of preterm infants are often from less advantaged economic circumstances than mothers in the full-term group; teenage mothers are more likely to deliver prematurely than older mothers (Garn, Shaw, & McCabe, 1977). These prenatal and socioeconomic factors are also frequently the causes of low birth weight in full-term babies. These small-for-date infants suffer many of the same risks for developmental problems that preterm babies do (Kopp & Parmelee, 1979). In short, the environmental correlates of low birth weight mean that the effects of preterm birth per se are often hard to identify.

RESEARCH FOCUS 3-3

SIDS: A Tragic Risk in Some Infants

Every year in the United States, about 8,000 infants die suddenly, without obvious warning signs that their bodies may not be functioning normally. The common name for such tragedies is crib death, because they occur while the infant is asleep. The technical label is Sudden Infant Death Syndrome, or SIDS.

A common belief in such cases is that there is no cause of death. The babies have not suffocated or strangled after regurgitation. When they are discovered, there are no signs of pain or struggle. However, it is illogical to say that these are "deaths without causes" (Lipsitt, 1978). The problem is that no single condition has been identified that explains why such unexpected deaths occur. There may be a number of different causes. Consequently, physicians use the term *syndrome* until more is known about the most frequent or likely causes.

Experts now know a great deal about the circumstances that increase an infant's risk for this condition. SIDS is most likely to occur between 2 and 4 months of life. Victims are most likely to be males. The deaths are most likely to occur in the winter months, often after the infant has had some common respiratory infection. This latter finding has raised the possibility that a virus may be a cause of SIDS, but as yet no particular virus has been identified as a factor in these infant deaths. In comparisons between the neonatal records for SIDS victims and the records of infants who survive their first year, several differences have emerged: (1) more of the victims were low birth weight, weighing less than 2,500 grams at birth; (2) more had Apgar scores lower than 7; (3) more needed resuscitation in the first 5 minutes after birth; and (4) more had required intensive care and longer hospitalizations after birth. These babies generally had not been viewed as highly unusual cases or as being particularly at risk, and, indeed, the majority of babies who show these characteristics do not fall victim to SIDS. Nevertheless, there are more signs of an early fragility in groups of SIDS victims than in groups of babies who survive (Lipsitt, 1978; Steinschneider, 1975).

A particularly important clue concerns the sleep patterns of SIDS victims. These infants often have irregular breathing patterns, including periods of apnea (spontaneous interruptions in breathing) that are very frequent and last for unusually long periods (Steinschneider, 1975). Some experts now believe that SIDS may occur because these infants have not organized their sleep patterns to overcome such interruptions. It may be especially difficult for babies who have some congestion that blocks or narrows their breathing passages to do so. Psychologist Lewis Lipsitt (1978) has suggested that the period between 2 and 4 months of age may be an especially dangerous time for these infants. The basic reflexes with which the baby is born are in transition at these ages, and more of the infant's behaviors must be controlled voluntarily, rather than by reflex. But some infants may make this transition more smoothly than others, and SIDS victims may be among those who have not yet gained the necessary degree of voluntary control. Consequently, when their breathing passages are blocked, these infants do not act to overcome the obstruction. The reasons for this kind of delay in development for some babies have not yet been identified.

All the information to date suggests that the tragedy of SIDS cannot easily be avoided, but parents often blame themselves for not being as attentive as they should have been. Perhaps as we learn more about the causes of these early tragic deaths, psychologists and physicians can discover more specific signs of risk and more effective ways to prevent SIDS. ❧

Preterm and small-for-date babies are likely to be treated differently than full-term infants from the moment of birth. The first days or weeks of their lives are spent in heated isolettes to help maintain their body temperatures and to protect them from infection. There is little of the physical contact or cuddling that babies usually have, because the "preemies," as preterm infants are popularly called, are fed, cleaned, and changed through portholes in the isolettes. Sometimes, the babies remain in the hospital for several weeks or months, and this separation from the mother and other family members can have lasting effects on the quality of the interpersonal interactions (Kopp, 1983; Leifer, Leiderman, Barnett, & Williams, 1972).

Because of their history and, perhaps, their current levels of responsiveness, preterm infants' interactions with others are likely to be quite different than the interactions of full-term infants. Preterm infants may elicit less attention or more negative attention from others because they often look more fragile than full-term babies and also because they may be more irritable and less responsive to the overtures of others. Several research groups (Bakeman & Brown, 1980; Crnic, Ragozin, Greenberg, Robinson, & Basham, 1983; Field, 1982; Greenberg & Crnic, 1988; Lester, Hoffman, & Brazelton, 1985) have recently compared the interactions of mothers with their preterm infants to those of mothers whose babies were full term. They found that the mothers of preterm infants spend as much or more time interacting with their babies as do the full-term mothers, but the preterm mothers' behaviors seem less keyed to the infants' responses. This active, but somewhat inattentive and insensitive behavior by the mothers appears to be an attempt to stimulate infants whom they expect to be less responsive than normal. However, it has been found that when mothers were instructed to be less intrusive, their babies' activity and responsiveness increased. Preterm babies may need milder, not more strenuous, stimulation than other babies because of the relative immaturity of their nervous systems (Field, 1982).

Preterm birth may mean that infants are more likely to encounter developmental problems, but recent medical advances have made it possible to deal with many of the physiological complications.

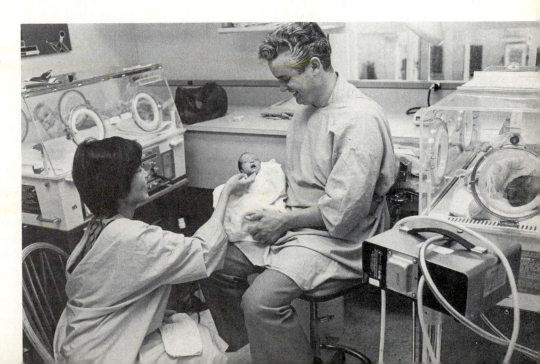

The effects of environment on preterm infants remind us that we must not only think of the risk to the infant because of birth timing, but also the extent to which risk may be exacerbated or alleviated by the caregiving environment.

Complications During the Birth Process

A second set of conditions that create developmental risks are complications during the birth process. Most births proceed normally and without threat of damage or difficulty for the infant. In some cases, however, traumatic events occur.

Asphyxia. The most common problems involve asphyxia, a loss of consciousness as a result of a shortage of oxygen (anoxia) accompanied by a buildup of carbon dioxide. If the brain is deprived of oxygen for only a few minutes, brain damage can occur. Asphyxia is one of the dangers that accompany the circumstances of breech birth that we described in the beginning of the chapter. Infants in the breech position can remain too long in the birth canal and, consequently, get too little oxygen. Sometimes the umbilical cord, through which infants get oxygen and dispel carbon dioxide may become pinched or tangled during birth, causing anoxia.

Anoxia or asphyxia is the leading cause of death in the prenatal and neonatal periods (Adamsons, 1975; Volpe, 1977). Infants who have survived anoxia or asphyxia may show effects that range from mild to severe, although not all show long-term effects. Relatively mild effects are irritability in newborns and lower than average performance on motor skills and some cognitive areas during the first 3 years of life (Kopp, 1983; Rose, Feldman, McCarton, & Wolfson, 1988; Sameroff & Chandler, 1975). Follow-up studies show that these early mild effects gradually lessen until early school age, when they are scarcely apparent (Corah, Anthony, Painter, Stern & Thurston, 1965).

More serious long-term effects include cerebral palsy, which causes difficulties in controlling muscles of the head or the limbs (Apgar & Beck, 1974; Kopp, 1983). Anoxia and asphyxia are also the cause of some cases of mental retardation. The ways in which anoxia and asphyxia may affect later development are not always clear, because deprivation of oxygen is frequently combined with other conditions and birth complications, such as low birth weight, or with prenatal risk factors.

Maternal Medication. Medications in childbirth, such as pain-killing drugs, sedatives, or stimulants to induce or speed up uterine contractions, are used much less extensively today than in the past. A major reason for this is the strong evidence that such medications may affect the infant adversely and that these negative effects may persist for long periods after birth. Newborns whose mothers have had sizable dosages of medication during childbirth appear more sluggish and irritable, smile less, and are less responsive in feeding and cuddling than other newborns. Furthermore, in 1-year follow-ups, these same infants were less advanced in physical and mental development than the comparison babies (Brackbill, 1979).

The reasons for the powerful effect of drugs on the newborn are not clear. One may be that the size of the dosages required to have an effect on the

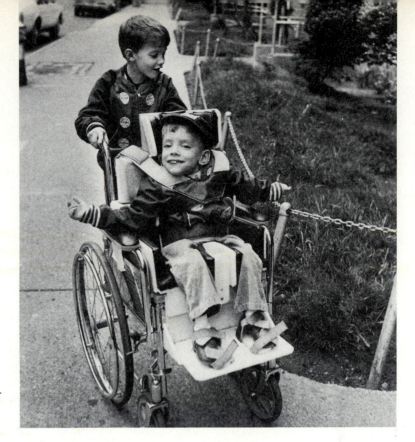

Long-term effects of preterm birth include cerebral palsy and some forms of mental retardation.

mother are simply too powerful for the tiny infant. Reaching the baby through the umbilical cord before delivery, the drugs may actually damage or overpower the child's nervous system. Another possibility is that the heavy dosage requires a longer period to dissipate in a small system. Finally, it is possible that the sluggishness that results from the drugs causes the infant to take in less and benefit less from stimulation than other children, thus slowing the normal pace of cognitive growth.

Preterm birth, asphyxia, and obstetric medication increase the risk of abnormal or delayed development due to circumstances associated with birth. We turn now to a set of conditions occurring after birth that may be significant to development.

The uncomplicated birth of a healthy infant is, generally speaking, a powerful indicator that development will proceed normally. Unless there is some traumatic event—an accident or a serious illness—or a chronic condition that interferes with the usual experiences of growth, it is reasonable to expect that the child will develop within the range that is typical of the majority of children in a society.

Some infants do experience conditions that deprive them of essential care and stimulation, and the implications for development are potentially serious. For example, children must have a diet with an adequate amount of nourishment. Malnutrition slows or even suppresses physical growth. If the malnutrition is brief or not extremely severe, children seem to grow even faster in order to catch up with the growth trajectory they would have followed under optimal conditions. Children who suffer prolonged malnutrition between birth and age 5 can show lasting effects, however. In adult-

Deprivation of Care and Stimulation

89

hood, these individuals are likely to be shorter than more adequately nourished peers. Furthermore, long periods of nutritional deficiency can have lasting effects on brain growth and, thus, on cognitive development (Pollitt, Garza, & Leibel, 1984; Tanner, 1978). Famine conditions in Third World countries in recent years have raised concerns about the effects of hunger on entire populations, but the effects on infants and young children have been of special concern, for good reason.

Another example of deprivation is less common today than it once was. Infants who have little chance to see the world around them, to touch and manipulate objects, to hear language, and—most importantly—to be cuddled or stimulated by face-to-face interactions with others, typically lag behind other infants in both cognitive and social competencies (Casler, 1967; Kagan & Klein, 1973). Sensory deprivation was often characteristic of institutional environments for children, such as orphanages (Goldfarb, 1955). Infants in such institutions were often left alone for long periods, in relatively bland, austere environments with few opportunities for either sensory or social stimulation. After observing the development of children reared in these settings, several psychologists and psychiatrists raised the possibility that social and sensory deprivation had serious negative effects on development.

The Work of Bowlby and Spitz.   The devastating effects of World War II in Europe and Great Britain included, for many families, disruptions in time together and the orphaning of children. After the war, the World Health Organization commissioned a report by the British psychologist John Bowlby, which documented the development disorders that followed early deprivation, particularly deprivation resulting from separation from the mother (see Bowlby, 1969; 1973). His observations were consistent with those made at about the same time by the psychologist Rene Spitz. Spitz (1946) compared infants in a foundling home, which provided very little social contact or stimulation, to those in a more family-like nursery setting. He found that the foundling infants were less healthy physically, showed socially inappropriate reactions to strangers, and showed other delayed cognitive and social de-

Institutional child-care facilities like orphanages, now virtually nonexistent in the United States, frequently failed to provide the intellectual stimulation and nurturant care that fostered optimal growth for the children who lived in them.

velopment. Subsequent studies of children and adolescents who were deprived as infants have shown persistent developmental problems, including emotional maladjustment, restlessness, hyperactivity, aggression, low achievement, and problems of concentration (Goldfarb, 1946, 1955; Provence & Lipton, 1976; see review by Rutter, 1979).

Because child welfare policies in the United States now favor alternative methods of care, such as foster home placement, children today rarely live in institutional arrangements. Deprived environments may occur naturally, however, and may even be a part of the normal childrearing practices of a society or culture. For example, Jerome Kagan and Robert Klein (1973) studied infants in a remote farming area of Guatemala. The infant care practices in this area provided very limited sensory stimulation:

> During most of the first year, the infant is tightly clothed and restricted to the inside of a windowless hut. . . . The infant has no conventional toys with which to play and adults are minimally interactive with him. . . . Play and vocalization directed at the baby by others occurred less than 10 percent of the time, in contrast to 25 to 40 percent of the time in American homes (Kagan, 1976, pp. 106–107).

During the first year these infants were far behind infants from the United States of the same ages in cognitive development and social skills.

Even in the United States, where relatively enriched, responsive environments for infants are thought to be the norm, there is considerable variation in the degree to which babies experience early stimulation. For example, let us take the case of Terri and Mark Bauer, a middle-class, well-educated couple who recently became first-time parents. The Bauers were surprised to find that they had very different views of appropriate care for a newborn. Terri believed in a great deal of holding, cuddling, and talking to her daughter, Courtney, whereas Mark felt the baby should not be greatly stimulated. He, supported by his mother, argued that the baby should be left in her crib or left to lie on a pillow in another room unless it was necessary to feed or change her.

Researchers have recently found that homes vary greatly in how much stimulation is provided to infants; and these differences—all of which are considered to be in the normal range in our society—seem to be correlated with differences between children. For example, in one study, psychologist Leon Yarrow and his colleagues (Yarrow, Rubinstein, & Pedersen, 1975) observed the reactions of mothers when their 5-month-olds vocalized (made a gurgling sound or any of the other range of prelanguage sounds that babies make) or gave a distress sound. Some of the mothers responded with attention and stimulation, while others ignored the infant or only reacted minimally. The infants whose mothers gave them attention and stimulation were more developmentally advanced than the infants of mothers who did not. In addition, the infants who had access to a variety of play materials and household objects that they could hold and play with were more advanced in reaching, grasping, exploratory behavior, and preference for novel stimuli than infants who had fewer of these opportunities. Other studies have found that older (12–14-month-old) infants were more cognitively advanced if their home environments provided many opportunities for exploring varied objects, spaces, and places (Wachs, 1976; Wachs & Gruen, 1982). Although none of the children in these studies actually experienced deprivation, those who experienced less stimulation and opportunities for exploration developed at different rates than those whose sensory experiences were richer.

The term risk is meant to convey that children who have experienced environmental deprivations in infancy, similar to those who have experienced preterm birth or traumatic birth events, face greater than average possibility of developmental problems in later life. How great is the risk? To what extent can early difficulties be overcome?

Can the Effects of Early Deficiencies Be Reversed?

Today, most infants who encounter the risk conditions described above develop normally (Kopp, 1983; Sameroff & Abbe, 1978; Sameroff & Chandler, 1975). Supportive environments, including improved medical care and broader awareness of the need for early stimulation and nurturant, attentive care, contribute to overcoming the effects of very early problems. When developmental problems do occur, socioeconomic disadvantages and family factors, such as drug use and abusiveness, are generally more important causes than are early experiences.

Psychologists Arnold Sameroff and Michael Chandler (1975) have suggested that we should think in terms of a continuum of caretaking outcomes. They point out that a developmental risk factor must also be viewed in terms of the potential for recovery, conditional on the environmental supports and opportunities available to the child. In our discussion of preterm birth, we pointed out that the amount of developmental risk is a result both of the extremity of birth conditions and the extent to which parents and others are able to provide optimum growth conditions. Allowing for differences in birth weight and health, a preterm baby born to a poor teenage mother who lacks both economic advantages and an adequate social support system may do poorly physically and may not develop cognitively and socially in later years as other children do (Drillien, 1969; Kopp & Parmelee, 1979). In contrast, a baby of similar weight and initial health status born to a middle-class family in which proper nutrition, medical care, and nurturance are available is likely to overcome the difficulties of early birth (Beckwith & Parmelee, 1986; Cohen & Parmelee, 1983; Sameroff, 1981). A recent 5-year longitudinal study showed that the intelligence test scores of 100 5-year-olds who had been born preterm were not related to birth or newborn experiences, but to home–environment variables such as the mother's education level (Cohen & Parmelee, 1983). A consistently attentive, appropriately stimulating environment is critically important in the long-term outcomes for children born preterm (Beckwith &

Parmelee, 1986; Cohen & Parmelee, 1983; Sameroff, 1981). The idea of a continuum of caretaking outcomes applies to all developmental risk factors, not to preterm births alone.

The concept of a continuum of caretaking outcomes has been underscored by the findings of a recently completed longitudinal study of children born on the Hawaiian island of Kauai (Werner, Berman, & French, 1971; Werner & Smith, 1977, 1982). All 670 children born on the island in 1955 were included in the study. Of special interest were the 47% of these children who had some kind of risk as newborns. Thirty-one percent of the sample had mild problems around the time of birth, 13% had moderate complications, and another 3% had severe difficulties in the newborn period. The question was, to what extent would these complications in the newborn period predispose the children to intellectual and behavioral problems in later years?

Psychologist Emmy Werner and her colleagues retested the children at ages 2, 10, and 18. At age 2, only 12–16% of the 670 children showed deficiencies in social, intellectual, and health status. The children who continued to have problems were those who had experienced more severe stresses as newborns. However, the quality of the children's environment determined how pronounced the effects of early problems were at age 2. Of the infants who had experienced severe problems as newborns, those who lived in low socioeconomic families with mothers of low intelligence were more deficient in cognitive skills than were those with stable, high-socioeconomic environments and mothers of high intelligence.

When they were measured at age 10 and age 18, the children of Kauai showed few long-lasting effects of early risk. A relatively large number of the 18-year-olds who showed mental health problems, retardation, and teenage pregnancies had experienced moderate or severe complications as newborns, but the overall incidence of these difficulties was small. In general, IQ scores were not correlated with complications in the newborn period, but were associated with parents' IQs and their socioeconomic status. Lowerclass children's IQ scores were markedly lower than middle- and upper-class children's scores. In the words of the researchers, "Children who were raised in more affluent homes, with an intact family and a well-educated mother, showed few, if any, negative effects from reproductive stress, unless there was severe central nervous system impairment" (Werner & Smith, 1982, p. 31). Apparently, during childhood, the impact of early problems has increasingly been overcome by the impact of other variables that affect development, such as economic advantages, the qualities of family environments, mental health problems, and—undoubtedly—genetic factors. All in all, the researchers noted that the number of children who had problems related to poor environment was 10 times greater than the number whose problems could be related to newborn risk factors.

The role of environmental factors was especially striking in comparisons between subgroups of the 18-year-olds: one group of individuals who had been considered high risk in infancy, but who had not developed problems (resilient children), and another group who had less positive outcomes. The researchers concluded that the resilient group had been protected by several

Protective Factors in Development: The Children of Kauai

93

factors that were common to their environments and that were not characteristic of the problem group. The resilient teens had been rated in infancy as having "easy," adaptable temperaments; their families were relatively small; their parents' attitudes were positive and supportive; their families had relatively little conflict; overall, they had fewer stressful experiences; and counseling and remedial assistance were available to them.

The histories of the children of Kauai make it clear that, in most cases, protective factors in children's lives far outweigh early conditions in determining the long-term developmental pattern for children at risk.

Effects of Change in the Environment

Equally dramatic evidence of the role of environmental factors comes from studies of changes in children's environments that provide the opportunity for recovery from initially damaging experiences. One example is the findings of a comparison involving the Guatemalan infants studied by Kagan and Klein (1973). As we noted in the last section, these children experienced a restricted environment that resulted in comparatively poor cognitive and social skills during the first year of life. Once they learned to walk, however, these infants' environments changed greatly. As Kagan describes it:

> By 13 to 16 months when the baby becomes mobile and is allowed to leave the hut, he encounters the greater variety inherent in the outside world . . . domestic animals, other children, trees, rain, clouds. . . . The 8–10 year old is assigned tasks and responsibilities, such as helping the father in the field, caring for infants, cooking, cleaning, and carrying water (Kagan, 1976, p. 107).

Kagan and Klein tested a group of 10-year-old Guatemalan children and found that they performed on a par with children from the U.S. on memory and perceptual tests. Assuming that these children had, as infants, experienced the same deprivations as the group of infants studied by Kagan and Klein, the effects of early environments had apparently been overcome by middle childhood. A longitudinal study following Guatemalan village children from infancy to age 10 would be needed to confirm this conclusion, however.

Similar compensatory effects were also seen in a study of providing an enriched environment for institutionalized children. Psychologist Harold Skeels (1966) studied a group of children who had spent much of their infancy and childhood in an orphanage that was a deprived environment, both socially and perceptually. In the late 1930s, overcrowding in this institution caused half of the children to be sent to another institution, a center for mentally retarded children. This new center, because of its more enlightened caregiving practices and better physical facilities, offered a more stimulating environment than the orphanage had, including more varied opportunities for exploration and for social contact and attention from adults. At the time of the transfer, this latter group of children had an average tested IQ of 64.3, compared to an average of 86.7 for the children who remained in the orphanage. Within two years, however, Skeels found that the group from the enriched environment had gained 28.5 IQ points on the average, whereas the orphanage group had actually declined by an average of 26.2 IQ points. Most of those in the enriched environment group were subsequently adopted, and later tests showed that their IQ scores improved still further. Of the children who remained in institutions in both groups, there were further drops in IQ scores.

By following up these children 21 years later, Skeels documented that the children who had been moved to the enriched environment many years before were all self-supporting; furthermore, none showed any signs of intellectual deficits. They were not noticeably different from the rest of the U.S. population, as described in the 1960 census. Their children had normal IQs and were making normal school progress. By contrast, the adults who had remained in the orphanage in childhood, had much lower levels of education, lower level occupations, and lower incomes than their more fortunate peers. The comparison between these individuals strikingly demonstrates the effectiveness of enriched environments in overcoming the risks imposed by early deprivation.

Environmental changes need not be as extensive as those observed in Kagan and Klein's Guatemalan village or in the institutional arrangements described by Skeels in order to overcome the effects of early problems. For example, interventions with parents to help make interactions with preterm infants more like those of normal infants can have a positive effect on development (Rauh, Achenbach, Nurcombe, Howell, & Teti, 1988; Sameroff & Abbe, 1978). Psychologists Sanford Zeskind and Richard Iacino (1984) found that encouraging mothers to visit their preterm infants in the neonatal intensive care unit had beneficial effects on the infant's physical condition and on the mothers' adjustment to their babies' circumstances. A different intervention (Barrera, Rosenbaum, & Cunningham, 1986) involved a year-long program to train parents in observational skills and emotional support techniques and to inform them about community resources. Special attention was given to the importance of sensitivity to the infants' signals and responses during interaction. The program was effective in changing the home environment of the parents who participated, compared to a control group of parents who did not receive the training. There were also effects of the intervention on the infants' cognitive development to the age of 18 months.

How "Plastic" Is Human Development?

Findings such as these have led many psychologists to argue that human beings are extraordinarily resilient, plastic organisms who can tolerate serious difficulties and still function in normal ways (e.g., Kagan, 1984; Lerner, 1984). Although it is unlikely that a child can develop normally in the face of overwhelmingly negative circumstances, many children and adults do overcome remarkable problems to lead normal lives. As we learn more about protective and corrective factors in children's lives, we become more able to identify ways in which children at risk might be helped to develop the essential capacities to achieve skills and to live independently and competently as adults.

At the same time, it is important to note that there is considerable evidence that early experiences can continue to affect children throughout their lives. The effects may not only pertain to intelligence, sensory capacities, or competence to carry out tasks and responsibilities. A long-term effect of particular importance concerns the role of the quality of early social relationships on personality characteristics and differences among children and adults in their social and emotional lives. In the next chapter, we will consider these aspects of early experience.

Summary

Understanding of newborns' behavior and capabilities has greatly increased during the past 25 years. As a result, psychologists and medical practitioners today know much more about optimal care for newborns and the risks associated with difficulties during birth or with deprivation in the neonatal period (the first month following birth).

The birth process is less often treated as a medical problem than it was two decades ago, so mothers are given fewer obstetric medications and fathers are typically present and often active in giving support during childbirth. Most births still take place in hospitals, however, and medical knowledge and technology now make it more possible to intervene in complicated deliveries to protect the health of the mother and child.

In the neonatal period (birth to 28 days of age), remarkable capacities are already apparent in infants. The *origins* of these capacities lie in the genetic makeup of the human organism, although these capacities may be modified by the conditions of prenatal development. Normal newborns have capabilities for experiencing the world through their senses. Procedures have been devised to test vision and hearing, using the psychological principle of habituation (the decline in responding after extended or repeated exposure to the same stimulus). In addition, infant behavior is organized in characteristic ways. Normal infants move in and out of behavioral states that vary in levels of alertness or consciousness. Examples are crying, sleeping quietly, sleeping somewhat restlessly or irregularly, and alert inactivity. Very young infants' sleep patterns appear to be organized differently from adult sleep patterns, perhaps indicating that sleep serves different purposes in infant development than in adult psychological life. Crying apparently serves important communicative functions for caregivers, with distinctively different types of cries indicating different infant need states. Infants are also able to detect contingencies between actions and their consequences, which provides an important foundation for developing a sense of control over the environment and effectiveness in social interactions.

A number of tests can now be performed to judge the health and responsiveness of newborns, as compared to norms for babies in the first few days of life. The Apgar test is widely used to assess the general health of newborns immediately after delivery and to judge the need for immediate medical attention in cases where infants have respiratory or other problems. The Prechtl Scale and the Brazelton Neonatal Behavioral Assessment Scale make it possible to assess an even wider range of neurological capacities and behavioral responses in the newborn. A primary feature of these procedures is checking the infant's reflexes (involuntary responses to stimulation), which, if not present, may indicate neurological deficits.

Several categories of problems associated with birth and the experiences of newborns may create a risk for difficulties in the later *course* of development. Preterm birth is a major cause of health problems after birth and may also be a warning of intellectual and social difficulties at later ages. However, in recent decades the number of deaths from preterm birth have declined dramatically; and the probability of long-term difficulties has been reduced as well. Complications during the birth process may lead to asphyxia or anoxia (deprivation of oxygen), which can cause motor dysfunction and retardation. Administering medications to the mother during delivery may affect the child as well, causing developmental delays for long periods after birth, but current medical practices involve less use of medication in childbirth than previously. Finally, deprivation of proper nutrition and sensory stimulation may affect the rate at which infants develop cognitive skills and social responsiveness.

Researchers have found that *environmental influences,* in the form of attentive care and stimulating environments, can do much to reduce the risks to infants who have experienced birth problems or environmental deprivations. The most likely long-term effects of problems during birth and in the newborn period occur when the infant's nervous system itself sustains serious damage or when the quality of caregiving and environmental supports do not foster normal development. In other cases, there appears to be considerable plasticity in human development, meaning that the human organism can tolerate serious difficulties and still function in normal ways later in development. The evidence of the *interrelations* of early physical and social experiences with a variety of aspects of behavior in later life is an important focus of research for developmental psychologists.

Suggested Readings

Apgar, V., & Beck, J. (1974). *Is my baby all right?* New York: Pocket Books.

Falkner, F., & Macy, C. (1980). *Pregnancy and birth.* New York: Harper & Row.

Kopp, C. B. (1983). Risk factors in development. In P. H. Mussen (Ed.) & M. M. Haith & J. J. Campos (Vol. Eds.), *Handbook of child psychology (4th ed.), Vol. 2: Infancy and developmental psychobiology* (pp. 1081–1188). New York: Wiley.

Kopp, C. B., & Kaler, S. R. (1989). Risk in infancy: Origins and implications. *American Psychologist, 44,* 224–230.

Tanner, J. M. (1978). *Fetus into man: Physical growth from conception to maturity.* Cambridge, MA: Harvard University Press.

Severely Impaired Newborns: A Synopsis of Ethical Issues

John D. Arras, Ph.D.

Biomedical technology is a two-edged sword. It can help physicians save the lives of infants who surely would have died 10 or 20 years ago from severe prematurity, chromosomal anomalies, neural tube defects, and other life-threatening conditions, but in some cases the life it saves is of such low quality that parents, caregivers, and society have come to doubt the wisdom of applying technology without regard for its long-term consequences. Such doubts pose agonizing questions: Who should live? Who should be allowed to die? Who should decide? A recently completed survey by the Hastings Center's Project on Imperiled Newborns highlighted the following issues (Hastings Center Project, 1987).

1. *Standards for Decision Making.* If some catastrophically impaired newborns shall be allowed to die, what ethical standards should guide decision-makers? Although all sides seem to agree that *dying* children need not be subjected to further "heroic" measures, consensus ends there. The proponents of a "sanctity of life" ethic contend that infants who are not dying must receive all "medically indicated" treatment, no matter what the child's anticipated quality of life (Ramsey, 1978). This position is contested by those who insist on the importance and inevitability of qualify of life judgments. These critics make a crucial distinction between "comparative" judgments of quality of life, which compare (usually unfavorably) the impaired child to some standard of normalcy, and "non-comparative" judgments that focus on the child's own experience of life. They then argue that in some extreme cases marked by intractable and severe disability and pain and suffering, continued life would be worse *for the child* than an early death (Arras, 1984). For the most catastrophically impaired children—for example, those with Trisomy 13, severe birth asphyxia, or those in a persistent vegetative state—even this "best interest of the child" standard is inadequate, since such children do not appear to have the requisite mental capacities to sustain "interests" other than the avoidance of pain. In such cases, a strict "comparative" standard, for example, the absence of any capacity for human relationships, has been suggested as the appropriate measure (McCormick, 1974; Arras, 1984).

2. *The Problem of Uncertainty.* No matter what substantive ethical standard we use, our deliberations will be plagued by pervasive medical and social uncertainty. We know that some conditions, such as very low birthweight accompanied by intraventricular bleeding, are very serious, but we usually cannot predict accurately the exact extent of any particular child's disability in the future, or how well the child's family will cope with his or her disabilities. The following three strategies have evolved to cope with this uncertainty: (Rhoden, 1986) (1) The "wait until near certainty" approach, practiced widely in the

United States, contends that we should treat every potentially viable infant until it is certain that the baby will either die or clearly meet one's substantive standard for non-treatment. (2) According to the "statistical" approach, a child should not be treated if he or she fits a particular statistical profile—for example, in Sweden infants below 750 grams are rarely placed on ventilators. The first approach will save all who can possibly be saved, but at the cost of saving some for a horrible quality of life, whereas the second approach avoids the latter problem, but at the cost of allowing some to die who could have lived good lives. (3) A third, more "individualized" approach makes tradeoffs in both directions; it would begin treatment for every infant, but allow decision makers to terminate treatment before it is absolutely certain that the child will either die or meet the substantive criteria for non-treatment.

3. *Who Will Decide?* Traditionally, parents have been charged with medical decision making for their own children. This tradition reflects our beliefs that parents usually have the best interests of their children at heart and that the state should intrude as little as possible into the privacy of family matters. Recently, however, various federal "Baby Doe" initiatives—for example, the 1984 Amendments to the Child Abuse Prevention and Treatment Act—have attempted to seriously curtail parental discretion (Rhoden, 1985).

By contrast, a presidential commission has recommended that parents should be allowed to decide either when further treatment is contrary to the child's best interests or when it merely promises very uncertain benefits (President's Commission, 1983). Thus, parents should retain discretion to decide cases that fall into the gray area of medical uncertainty. This discretion should end, however, when it is determined by caregivers, hospital ethics committees, state child protection agencies, or courts that the parents' decision clearly threatens the best interests of the child.

4. *Social Issues.* Although public attention has recently been focused nearly exclusively on the ethical dilemmas in the neonatal nursery, equally important social issues require discussion. First, there is the problem of accessibility to prenatal care for poor women. It is now generally recognized that many of the problems encountered in the neonatal nursery can be directly traced to the consequences of poverty (for example, to poor nutrition and lack of prenatal medical care). When the federal government cuts back on programs targeted at poor mothers, we can be sure that the result will be increased rates of severe prematurity, chronic lung disease, and intracranial bleeding in their children. Guaranteeing access to prenatal care is thus an ethical issue of the greatest magnitude (Lantos, 1987).

Second, society confronts equally troubling ethical issues after the new neonatal technology has worked its magic. What will become of the "graduates" of these nurseries and their families? In many cases, imperiled children will have been saved to lead severely debilitated lives, propped up on pillows and tethered to expensive and time-consuming machines. The care of such children poses extreme challenges—financial, psychological, and social—to their parents and other siblings. What are the limits, if any, of parental obligations to such children? And what are the responsibilities of the state to help parents cope with such unprecedented burdens (Hastings Center Project, 1987)?

John Arras teaches Biomedical Ethics at Albert Einstein College of Medicine—Montefiore Medical Center and at Barnard College in New York City. He is editor of Ethical Issues In Modern Medicine.

CHAPTER FOUR

Attachment and Early Social Relationships

Introduction

One of the hallmarks of early development is the formation of attachments between infants and those who care for them. The research described in Chapter 3 on the role of quality care in overcoming early developmental risk shows the importance of social relationships in the first years of life. In addition, early relationships provide the basis for responding to others that is necessary to function as a member of the human community. Indeed, the fundamental question developmental psychologists ask about social and personality development is how responsiveness to others develops and how it contributes to the healthy growth of the individual child.

Studies of early social development have been among the most numerous and important in the field of developmental psychology in the past 20 years. In this chapter we review the information that has come to us from those studies. Several questions provide a framework for our discussion: How are attachments formed? How can we observe the attachment of an infant to other persons? What is the importance of early attachments for later development?

Theories of Attachment

Attachment is generally defined as strong affectional ties with one's most intimate companions—in the case of infants, their most frequent caregivers. The nature of the relationship between child and caregiver has been of great interest to theorists in every major tradition of thought about psychological development. In this section, we provide brief summaries of the three most influential theoretical perspectives on human attachment.

Psychoanalytic Theories

In psychoanalytic theory, the quality of the early interaction between infants and their mothers was considered particularly important for both early psychological development and as the foundation for later social relationships and personality development. Sigmund Freud believed that the most significant early interactions were those that involved *oral gratification*. He considered activities such as sucking, mouthing, and biting to be infants' way of reducing strong, inborn biological drives. Because caregivers are so often associated with these oral pleasures when they feed the baby, they become especially important persons to the infant. This special relationship with the caregiver subsequently plays an essential role in the child's development. One critically important result of attachment is *identification*, which causes children to model themselves after the parent in order to adapt to the surrounding world (Waters, Hay, & Richters, 1986).

Freud himself viewed the mother–infant bond as "the prototype of all later love relationships." If caregivers fail to provide food when the infant is hungry or are otherwise derelict in their caregiving, psychological problems can result both during infancy and in subsequent periods of development. Other theorists with particular interests in the determinants of psychopathology have speculated extensively about problems in the early attachment relationship. Rene Spitz (1946) attributed emotional difficulties in childhood and adulthood to emotional deprivation and lack of warmth. Levy (1943), in contrast, felt that adjustment problems are often related to extremely intense relationships, such as maternal overprotectiveness. Margaret Mahler (Mahler, Pine, & Bergman, 1975) has argued that failure to separate from the mother, while maintaining attachment to her, results in personality difficulties in later life. These views, like the ideas of Freud himself, were drawn largely from clinical observation and not from programs of controlled research.

Social learning theory is concerned with the socializing impact of experience with parents or other caretakers, their rewarding and punishing behaviors, and the examples for affection and independence set by those who interact with an infant. In this view, responsiveness to the caregiver is not considered to be innate, but is *learned* because the caregiver is always present when the baby's basic needs are being met. As in psychoanalytic theory, this learning

Social Learning Theory

Receiving physical nourishment has been viewed by many theorists as a key element in the formation of attachments between children and their caregivers.

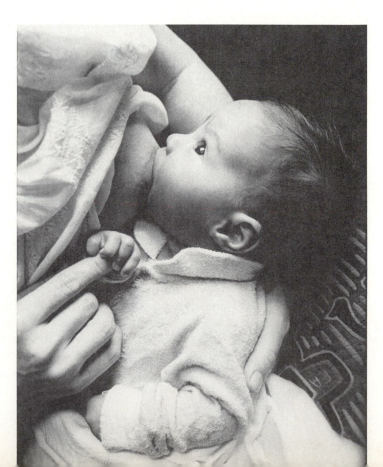

takes place because of the caregiver's association with the satisfaction of bodily needs, such as hunger and thirst. Once learned, the responsiveness to caregivers then generalizes to others, so that a child is more likely to respond to other persons. Gradually, the child learns to discriminate among individuals and responds most readily to those with whom there have been previous rewarding experiences. In short, the caregiver–child bond is seen as an important source for social responsiveness in general.

Research findings (Brokaw & McLemore, 1983; Buss, 1983; Gewirtz & Baer, 1957; Stevenson, 1965) indicate that social contact with others is rewarding to both children and adults for many different reasons. Caregivers' responses may be valuable because they demonstrate to infants that the infants' own actions can produce an effect. As we saw in Chapter 3, Watson and Ramey (1972) demonstrated that infants become emotionally responsive even to nonhuman objects, like an attractive mobile, if the movement of the mobile is made dependent on the infant's actions. These early experiences of cause and effect may help to create a sense of efficacy and control on the part of infants. Because caregivers are in the best position to respond to actions by infants, their sensitivity to the babies' cues may be one reason why babies learn rapidly behaviors that attract caregivers' attention and enable infants to be in contact with them.

Ethology

Empirical interest in attachment has been spurred by the ideas of British psychiatrist, John Bowlby, who proposed an ethologically based theory of human infant attachment (Bowlby, 1969, 1973, 1980). *Ethology* is the study of the characteristic behaviors of species, including their adaptation to the demands and opportunities presented by their typical environments. In Bowlby's theory, the attachment relationship is viewed as an evolved mechanism that helps humans adapt to the social world. The tendency to form attachments became well established in human behavior during the hunting and gathering period in human history. Human infants are more immature at birth than the young of some species and, thus, more in need of care from others; in a society in which it was necessary to move quickly and widely to find food, it was particularly important for children and caregivers (typically mothers) to remain close so that the mother could attend to the infant's needs. It was also necessary to have signal systems (calling, crying) that could effect reunion if a separation did occur. The accompanying Research Focus 4-1 describes an aspect of a mother's attachment to her baby that has received widespread attention.

In short, attachment behaviors serve an essential goal for survival, namely achieving, maintaining, or reestablishing contact between a child and caregiver. The extremely young infant's attachment behaviors are thought to be governed by mechanisms that rigidify into *fixed action patterns* (for example, relatively automatic crying when frightened or separated from the mother). As the child matures, attachment becomes more flexible, so that the older, more mobile infant can adapt to a variety of contexts. This flexibility is possible because of a *goal-correction mechanism* that operates much like a thermostat, activating attachment behavior patterns when necessary to re-

Maternal Bonding

Attachment is a two-way street: parents must form a bond with their babies, as well as infants with their parents. There are strong social norms for parents to be nurturant toward their young; and the feeding and other caregiving that begin very early in most babies' lives confirm parents' acceptance of these norms.

In recent years, however, it has been widely suggested that the parental bond is facilitated in humans, as it is in some lower species, by immediate contact between mother and baby after birth. Pediatricians Marshall Klaus and John Kennell (1976) have argued that skin-to-skin contact immediately after birth promotes the bonding of mother to infant and have raised the possibility that medical procedures associated with birth in Western countries interfere with this natural process.

Researchers have attempted to test Klaus and Kennell's hypothesis, and many of their findings support the idea that early and extensive contact promotes affectionate involvement of mothers with babies. This is especially likely when the child is a first born, when the infant is premature, or when the mother is especially young or from an economically disadvantaged group. Such mothers are more likely than others in their situation to breast feed and to do so more frequently, to touch their babies affectionately and hold them closely, to be sensitive to signals from their babies, and to engage them in face-to-face interaction (Maccoby & Martin, 1983).

The difficulty of studying differences between experiences in the first few minutes after birth have made it impossible to tell whether the effects of skin-to-skin contact are the result of the timing of the experience (that is, very soon after birth), the amount of exposure encouraged or allowed between mother and child in the first few days of life, or the kind of contact (for example, nude skin touching). Neither do we know

The opportunity to be close to a newborn baby is satisfying to parents and may help to promote affectionate involvement with their infants, but it is unlikely that early contact is essential to a healthy relationship or to optimal development of the child.

whether the experience of early contact affects the mother–child relationship in later life. Thus far, mother–infant pairs have only been followed through the first 18 months, at most (Goldberg, 1983). These same limitations apply to studies of the effects of birth attendance and early contact by fathers (Palkovitz, 1985).

For parents under stress at the beginning of their relationship with infants, early contact appears to help the relationship to begin well. It is clearly *not* the case, however, that a lack of early contact will mean that mothers or fathers will fail to be affectionately bonded to their babies. ❧

duce anxiety caused by a separation from the caregiver or the presence of a stranger. In addition, more complex correction mechanisms may adjust the form of the behavior to suit the particular circumstances. For example, a child may cry louder if the mother is farther away or if a stranger is particularly frightening.

In Bowlby's conceptualization, both the caregiver and the infant behave in ways that show their attachment, but most attention has been concentrated on the behavior of the infant. Especially significant in Bowlby's theory is the idea that infants affect caregivers, as well as benefiting from the caregiver's ministrations. Two classes of infant attachment behavior have been of particular concern. First, there are *signalling behaviors,* which may alert a caregiver to an infant's location or need for help, or simply maintain contact across a distance. Common signalling behaviors include smiling, crying, or calling. Second, there are *executive behaviors,* whose function is to achieve contact or overcome separation. These include touching, clinging, or following. Thus, the infant is active in forming and maintaining relationships with caregivers.

With these views of the nature and importance of attachment in mind, we now turn to a review of information on attachment in the first few years of life.

Behavioral Signs of Attachment

Observing attachment, like observing other qualities of young infants, is difficult because both the nature and existence of an attachment relationship must be inferred from indirect signs. For example, when an infant cries at the departure of her mother, the crying is generally accepted as an index of attachment behavior because it is considered evidence of disruption in an emotional bond between the baby and her mother. Touching and clinging are considered to be signs of that emotional bond, as are behaviors for maintaining contact across a distance, such as looking and calling to a parent or caregiver. Independent and exploratory behaviors are used to study how children achieve and regulate separation from a caregiver. In this section, we will consider how behavioral signs like this are used to characterize the attachment between infants and their caregivers.

The Emergence of Attachments in the First Year

The meaning of attachment becomes clearer when we see how individual infants begin to show signs of emotional bonds with others. In a classic longitudinal study, Schaffer and Emerson (1964) interviewed mothers of 60 Scottish infants about the infants' reactions to separation. The interviews began when the infants were only 5 to 23 weeks of age and were repeated monthly until the babies were 18-months-old. Three types of attachment behavior were examined: *indiscriminate attachments,* in which infants tended to protest (cry) over separation regardless of the specific identity of the person leaving; *specific attachments,* in which babies actively sought contact with a

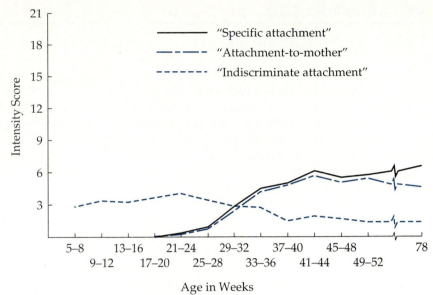

FIGURE 4-1

Developmental course of attachments.

Source: from Schaffer & Emerson, 1964.

particular person or persons and protested when separated from those persons; and *attachment to mother* as a particular instance of specific attachment.

Figure 4-1 shows the changes in patterns of attachment during the 1½-year study. In the first 6 weeks of life, Schaffer's and Emerson's infants reacted to many different persons and rarely protested at being approached or being left by any of them; in other words, there was little evidence of attachment in these early weeks. Thereafter, up to 6 or 7 months of age, the babies showed indiscriminate attachments, preferring human company and protesting when people left, but not reacting to familiar persons more than to strangers. However, at about 7 months on the average, infants began to protest when separated from a specific individual—in this study, usually the mother—and when they encountered unfamiliar persons. Schaffer and Emerson (1964) intepreted this as the emergence of specific attachments. Within a few weeks, the range of attachments broadened to include a number of different figures. Most mothers reported that their babies showed some degree of protest over separation from persons other than themselves or other individuals to whom they appeared to be attached (such as, father, grandparents). In other words, the infants formed multiple attachments, in some cases as many as five.

It seems likely that the emergence of specific attachments partly reflects infants' growing abilities to recognize others and to know the differences between familiar and unfamiliar persons. For example, calling or crying for a person who is out of sight means that the baby is aware that persons continue to exist, even when they are not immediately visible. This awareness is similar to the concept of *object permanence*, which is one of the hallmark cognitive achievements of the first year of life. Although infants show evidence of object permanence earlier than the emergence of specific attach-

107

RESEARCH FOCUS 4-2

Fathers as Attachment Figures

Being a father was once popularly viewed as a distant, uninvolved role—a biological necessity, but a social accident, according to one famous definition. As social roles of men and women have been widely reconsidered in the United States, however, "fathering" has become a widely discussed topic in settings ranging from popular magazines and television talk shows to PTA meetings and informal support groups.

Researchers have also devoted considerable attention to the unique aspects of the father's role. Do fathers serve the same functions for infants as mothers? That is, are they interchangeable as caregivers? What are the implications for the infant's development if a father, rather than a mother, is the primary caregiver?

Several conclusions can now be drawn from these studies:

- Fathers show interest in their babies from birth, and they show their interest in much the same way and to about the same degree that mothers do: by holding, touching, vocalizing, and kissing them (Parke, 1981).
- Infants can and do become attached to their fathers in much the same way as they form attachments to their mothers. Whether the attachment is classified secure or anxious is reflected in the child's reactions to the father as caregiver, just as it is for the mother. In one study, infants were observed to see whether they would prefer the mother over the father as a source of comfort in the presence of an unfamiliar person. The babies were just as likely to seek contact with their fathers as with their mothers (Lamb, 1977).
- At the same time, fathers and mothers interact somewhat differently with their infants. When with their babies, fathers are more likely to engage in physical play and stimulation and to introduce unusual or unpredictable games; whereas mothers are more likely to spend their time holding and soothing their infants, caring for their needs, and playing more traditional games (Lamb, 1981). This difference holds true even in "nontraditional" households where the father is the primary caregiver.

Clearly, the question—once a hotly contested one in United States society—of whether fathers can be adequate caregivers that provide a healthy basis for development for their children can be answered "yes."

A more important question, however, may be how the children's relationships with both parents jointly contribute to their growth. A partial answer to this question was provided in a study of 43 infants and their parents by Mary Main and Donna Weston (1981). Each child's attachment to father and to mother was assessed in the Strange Situation when the child was 12 months old. Of the 43 infants, 12 were securely attached to both parents and 11 were anxiously attached to both; 11 were securely attached to mother but not to father, and 10 were securely attached to father but not to mother. Main and Weston then exposed each infant to a friendly, but unfamiliar, person dressed in a clown suit, who spent several minutes trying to get the child to play. Infants who were securely attached to both parents were the most responsive to the clown, and those who were anxiously attached to both were the least responsive. However, babies who were securely attached to one parent—no matter whether it was the mother or the father—were notably more responsive than those who were anxiously attached to both. The opportunity to have two relationships with caregivers, either or both of which can lend security to a child's experience, is one indication of the significance of the father's role in development. 🐾

ments, the concept may well be linked to babies' developing an attachment to their main caregivers. Similarly, the ability to distinguish between familiar and unfamiliar persons may be one reason for fearfulness toward strangers, which commonly emerges near the middle of the first year. Such fearfulness is more likely when infants are left alone with an unfamiliar person. Babies may recognize such a situation as an unfamiliar one and, therefore, be frightened by it, even though at an earlier age they might have shown no awareness of being cared for by an unfamiliar, rather than a familiar, person (Campos et al., 1983; Rheingold & Eckerman, 1973).

Schaffer's and Emerson's findings are an *average* picture of the emergence of specific attachments in the infant's life. From one baby to another, there was considerable variation in the time at which specific attachments emerged. For example, one infant showed evidence of a specific attachment at only 22 weeks of age, while two infants did not show these similar attachments until after 1 year. There was also some variation in the sequence of reactions that are thought to indicate attachments. Protest over the approach of a stranger typically began about 1 month after the onset of specific attachments, but one infant in four in Schaffer's and Emerson's study showed apparent fear of strangers even before there had been evidence of specific attachments. We will examine some possible reasons for these differences in a later section. Despite some variation in timing of attachments, Schaffer and Emerson's description seems to capture the pattern shown by most infants.

Attachment may be signified by a number of different specific behaviors, like clinging, touching, and crying at separation. These behaviors probably grow even more diverse as we grow older, so that strong affectional ties to another person, like a spouse or close friend, may be indicated in subtle and very private ways that are quite unlike the behaviors of infants and toddlers toward their caregivers.

A number of experts believe that these varied behaviors share a common characteristic: namely, they make possible the formation of relationships that give us a feeling of *security*. Psychologist Mary D. S. Ainsworth (Ainsworth & Wittig, 1969; Ainsworth, Blehar, Waters, & Wall, 1978) has argued that attachment behaviors vary in the degree to which they reflect this feeling of security. Ainsworth's ideas build upon the ethological theory advanced by John Bowlby. In infancy, security means that the baby feels confident of the caregiver's availability and responsiveness. This confidence is essential to healthy psychological growth, because it allows securely attached infants to move away from their caregivers to explore the world around, with the assurance that they can return to the caregiver as a safe haven if threatened. Insecurely attached infants are those who feel uncertain that their caregivers will respond quickly and appropriately to their needs for nurturance, whether physical or emotional. Their lack of confidence will inhibit exploration and impede the development of independence and competence that is essential to psychological health and to the growth of motor, intellectual, and other skills (Waters, Hay, & Richters, 1986). In short, early attachment serves a fundamentally important function in individual development by establishing

Security: A Fundamental Element in Attachment

109

a sense of security that permits the infant to experience the environment without fear of being isolated or separated from caring, nurturant persons.

Erik Erikson (1963) expressed a similar idea. He referred to the confidence in the caregiver as infants' *sense of trust* that their needs would be met; if caregivers behaved in such a way that this sense of trust was not established in infancy, Erikson felt that the children's subsequent development of a healthy sense of self would be impaired. (Erikson's ideas will be discussed in more detail in Chapter 9.)

The Strange Situation. The concept of security underlies one of the most widely used systems to classify attachment in infants. This technique, called the Strange Situation procedure, was developed by Ainsworth and her colleagues (Ainsworth & Wittig, 1969). The Strange Situation consists of a series of eight 3-minute episodes in which the infant is brought into an unfamiliar room. Subsequently, the baby is shown a set of toys, encounters an unfamiliar adult, and experiences two brief separations from the parent. Table 4-1 outlines the sequence of events in this procedure.

TABLE 4-1
Summary of Episodes of the Strange Situation

Number of episode	Persons Present	Duration	Brief Description of Action
1	Mother, baby, and observer	30 sec.	Observer introduces mother and baby to experimental room, then leaves.
2	Mother and baby	3 min.	Mother is nonparticipant while baby explores; if necessary, play is stimulated after 2 min.
3	Stranger, mother, and baby	3 min.	Stranger enters. Min. 1: stranger silent. Min. 2: stranger converses with mother. Min. 3: stranger approaches baby. After 3 min. mother leaves unobtrusively.
4	Stranger and baby	3 min.* or less	First separation episode. Stranger's behavior is geared to that of baby.
5	Mother and baby	3 min.† or more	First reunion episode. Mother greets and comforts baby, then tries to settle him again in play. Mother then leaves, saying bye-bye.
6	Baby alone	3 min.* or less	Second separation episode.
7	Stranger and baby	3 min.* or less	Continuation of second separation. Stranger enters and gears her behavior to that of baby.
8	Mother and baby	3 min.	Second reunion episode. Mother enters, greets baby, then picks him up. Meanwhile stranger leaves unobtrusively.

* Episode is curtailed if the baby is unduly distressed.
† Episode is prolonged if more time is required for the baby to become reinvolved in play.
SOURCE: Campos et al., 1983.

This series of events allows researchers to observe how the baby behaves with the parent in settings that vary in their familiarity, opportunities for exploration, and potential for distress. For example, let us observe Lisa and Margot, two 18-month-old girls who participated in the procedure on the same day at different times. When Margot and her mother entered the room, Margot soon moved away from her mother to play with the toys and otherwise explore the new environment. Lisa, by contrast, stayed near her mother and seemed nervous and overly clinging. The most significant part of the procedure for the researchers, however, occurred when the mothers and their daughters were reunited after the brief periods when the mothers go out of the room. Margot had been playing with the toys, and when her mother returned, she called out to her, getting a smile and a wave in return; Margot then quickly went back to her play. Lisa had played while her mother was away as well, but she had been aimless and less involved in her play than Margot. When her mother returned, Lisa ignored her; even when her mother went over to her, Lisa turned away and said, "No."

These two girls illustrate some of the different reactions that the Strange Situation elicits. Experts believe that infants who are securely attached feel free to explore the room and to become involved with the toys. For some, separation is not particularly distressing, and reunions are positive, causing a relatively smooth return to exploration and play. For others, separation may cause distress, but upon reunion the infant approaches the parent and can be quickly comforted. In contrast, infants who feel less secure with their caregivers typically show very different reactions to separation and reunion. They may become angry, may find it difficult to reestablish and maintain contact when their caregivers return, and/or may not settle down when the caregiver tries to comfort them. These latter infants are considered to have *anxious attachments*. Experts sometimes distinguish between insecurely attached infants who, like Lisa, actively avoid their parent on reunion (*anxious avoidant* attachments) and those who both seek, yet resist, physical contact and are difficult to comfort (*anxious resistant* attachments) (Waters, Hay, & Richters, 1986).

This three-part classification—secure, anxious avoidant, and anxious resistant—may not capture all of the relevant differences among attachments for all children everywhere. For example, some researchers have found that there are many variations within the secure attachment classification, as well as between secure and insecure groups (Lamb, Thompson, Gardner, Charnov, & Estes, 1985). As we will see in the next section, there may be culturally influenced differences in the way parent–infant pairs deal with separation and reunion, and these may complicate the classification of attachments. Nevertheless, the concept of security has proven to be a powerful basis for describing individual differences among the attachments shown by infants around the world (Campos et al., 1983; Waters, Hay, & Richters, 1986; Sroufe, 1987).

One indication that the Strange Situation gives us information about some fundamental qualities of attachment is that infants are typically classified in the same way at both 12 months and 18 months (Connell, 1977; Main &

111

Weston, 1981; Waters, 1978). Changes can occur, of course. Sometimes family stress will cause a child who was classified as securely attached at 12 months to behave anxiously in the Strange Situation 6 months later (e.g., Vaughn, Egeland, Sroufe, & Waters, 1980). Similarly, insecure attachment might occur at an early time, with signs of a secure relationship appearing later (Rutter, 1979).

Attachment and Exploration: An Example of Developmental Change. The Strange Situation helps to show why theorists have considered attachment to be such an important aspect of human development: A sense of security formed in early relationships helps children achieve a balance between contact with their caregivers and exploration of the world around them. The ways in which this balance changes as the child matures is suggested by a longitudinal study conducted by psychologists Eleanor Maccoby and Shirley Feldman (1972).

Maccoby and Feldman followed a group of 48 children for a period of 1 year, testing them in the Strange Situation procedure at ages 2, $2\frac{1}{2}$, and 3. In this study, the parent who participated in the procedure with the child was always the mother. Figure 4-2 shows the differences in behavior at different ages when the mother was present and when she was absent. You can see that, when the mother was present, play with toys was quite high and crying was quite low at all three points in time. When the mother was absent, however, the response depended upon the age at which the child was tested. At ages 2 and $2\frac{1}{2}$, play with toys was noticeably lower than when the mother was present, and crying was much more typical, especially at age 2. By age 3, there was very little change in the children's reactions when the mother left the room.

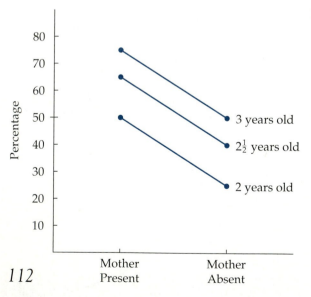

FIGURE 4-2

Percentage of five-second time intervals in manipulative play at different ages when mother is present or absent.

Source: from Macoby & Feldman, 1972.

An especially interesting finding of this study is that, across the year from age 2 to age 3, the children greatly increased in their abilities to recover from separation. At age 2, more than half of the children resumed play immediately or within 30 seconds after being reunited with their mothers. By age 3, 90% of the children resumed play almost immediately.

Maccoby and Feldman's study indicates that the particular signs of attachment may be different for a 3-year-old than for a toddler. Rather than looking for differences between individuals in each age group, these researchers emphasized the ways in which 3-year-olds, on the average, respond differently to separation than 2-year-olds do. Developmental differences, as well as individual differences, determine the ways in which attachment affects a child's behavior (Sroufe & Waters, 1977; Waters & Sroufe, 1983).

Individual Differences and Development Outcomes

Attachment is a basic human response that serves fundamental needs for all children, but attachments can and do differ from one child to another. Much research attention has been focused on the origins of secure and insecure attachments. In this section, we will discuss the consequences of attachment for development. Among the questions we will consider are the following: Can some children be shown to be more intensely attached than others? Do such differences between children remain true from one age to another, so that one 2-year-old who is more securely attached than another will show a more secure attachment at age 4. Also, does a particular type of attachment at one age lead to developmental consequences that become apparent at a later time?

Attachment occurs between two individuals. Consequently, both individuals potentially contribute to the characteristics of the attachment that is formed.

Sources of Individual Differences in Attachment

Caregiver Effects. Attachment is a characteristic of the *relationship* between a child and a particular caregiver, not a trait of either one or the other of them. The behaviors that mark the attachment between 1-year-old Randy and his father may be different from those that are typical of the attachment between Randy and his mother (Bridges, Connell, & Belsky, 1988). Nevertheless, variations in attachment often result from characteristics of the caregiver such as emotional state, or circumstances that influence caregiving, such as whether the mother is employed.

SENSITIVE RESPONDING. When interacting with their babies, mothers of securely attached infants are more sensitive, accepting, and emotionally expressive than mothers of insecurely attached infants (Ainsworth, Blehar,

Waters, & Wall, 1978; Sroufe & Waters, 1977; Sroufe, 1987). In secure attachments, mothers hold their babies more tenderly (Ainsworth et al, 1978) and are more responsive to the infants' signals (such as, crying), and they adjust their interactions to the infants' own pace and current needs (Ainsworth et al., 1978; Clarke-Stewart, 1973; Weber, Levitt, & Clark, 1986). For example, they begin feeding when hunger arises and also end it readily when infants indicate they are full. Mothers of securely attached infants have also been found to participate actively in their children's play, providing support and assuring successful outcomes (Pastor, 1981). Similar differences have been reported between fathers of securely attached infants and those of anxiously attached babies (e.g., Chibucos & Kail, 1981; Lamb, 1981). Attentiveness and clear responses to the child's actions and other cues are an important ingredient of parents' influences upon children at all ages (Maccoby & Martin, 1983). In contrast, infants who have been ignored, rejected, neglected, or abused can be almost uniformly characterized in the Strange Situation as being insecurely attached (Campos et al., 1983; Egeland & Sroufe, 1981; Lyons-Ruth, Connell, Zoll, & Stahl, 1987).

Several conditions may affect the degree to which parents can respond sensitively. Two especially important ones are the caregiver's own emotional health and the availability of social support to help cope with stress.

The *parental emotional state* is likely to affect whether parents can be as attentive to a child's needs as is desirable or, if aware of needs, whether they can make an adequate response. This problem has recently been the focus of a research program at the National Institute of Mental Health (Radke-Yarrow, Cummings, Kuczynski, & Chapman, 1985). The purpose of the study was to compare attachment in 2- and 3-year-old children of depressed mothers to attachment in children of nondepressed mothers. The researchers reasoned that depressed mothers would be less emotionally available and less capable of sensitive responding than the nondepressed mothers, thus putting their children at risk for insecure attachment. In all, 99 children and their mothers participated. A battery of psychiatric and psychological tests were used to diagnose the mothers' emotional functioning. Eventually, 56 of the mothers were categorized as having major depressive symptoms, 12 as having minor depression, and 31 as having no history of emotional disturbance. The mothers and children participated in the Strange Situation procedure to assess the security of attachment.

The findings showed that insecure attachment is more likely in mother-child pairs in which the mother has major depressive disturbance. Of this group, 55% of the children were rated as insecurely attached, compared to 29% of children of nondepressed mothers. Children of mothers with minor depression were insecurely attached at about the same rate (25%) as children of nondepressed mothers. The risk of insecure attachment associated with the mother's depression became even greater when the mother was without a husband. In some of the families studied, both mother and father were depressed, but attachments in this group were more likely to be more secure than in the group of depressed, single mothers.

How might the depressed mothers' actions have affected the processes of attachment? These mothers showed more negative and less positive emotion toward their children than did other mothers in the study and, thus, did not offer the warmth and nurturance that seems to make secure attachment more likely. Another possibility is that depressed mothers may be highly unreliable in their responses to the child. Among the depressed group in this study were some manic–depressive mothers, whose extreme mood swings may be tantamount to an unstable, chaotic environment for their children. The latter form of depression has a strong genetic component, and it may be that the biological underpinnings of the emotional disorder affected both mother and child in these pairs as well. Clearly, emotional difficulties of mothers can interfere with a secure relationship.

A second factor is the amount of *social support* available to the mother. Mothers who have persons to help with their babies or just someone to talk to about the normal stresses of taking care of an infant, seem to be better able to respond sensitively. Susan Crockenberg (1981; Crockenberg & McCluskey, 1986) has studied the effect of social support on the ability of mothers to respond sensitively to somewhat difficult childcare problems arising from a fussy, irritable infant. She found that sensitive responding was more highly correlated with having good social support than with the amount of irritability shown by the baby. As a result, the babies of mothers with good social support were more likely to be securely attached than were babies whose mothers had poor social support.

Why does social support make such a difference? It may be that the persons who offer social support also help directly in providing sensitive care for the infants of these mothers. Another possibility is that social support helps relieve the mothers' stress and makes it possible for them to be attentive and caring toward their babies. In any case, mothers who lack social support appear to be at risk for unresponsiveness to their infants, with potential harm to the security of the babies' attachment.

MATERNAL EMPLOYMENT AND MULTIPLE CAREGIVERS. The social trend in the United States toward larger numbers of two-career families raises questions about the implications for children, particularly infants. Many theoretical views emphasize the importance of consistent caregiver–infant relationships; consequently, the need for substitute care while parents work has led to concerns that it might be difficult for infants to form adequate attachments.

To date, the research evidence shows that maternal employment does not inevitably have negative effects on infant attachment. Rather, the effects of employment depend on the mothers' attitude toward her out-of-home work. When mothers are highly career oriented, infants show less separation protest than when mothers are ambivalent about their work commitments. Several studies have indicated that the infants of employed mothers who value both their out-of-home work and parenthood tend to be securely attached (Benn, 1986; Owen, Chase-Lansdale, & Lamb, in press; Thompson, Lamb, & Estes, 1982).

115

Maintaining proximity to caregivers is one indication that children have formed an attachment.

Because babies of working parents must be cared for by others, however, one question of widespread concern is whether having multiple caregivers affects the security of attachment. Research findings indicate that out-of-home care does not inevitably create problems in attachment (e.g., Belsky, 1984; Snow, 1983). Rather, day-care children often show attachment both to their mothers and to day-care personnel who consistently care for them (Campos et al., 1983; Farran & Ramey, 1977; Kagan, Kearsley, & Zelazo, 1978). Effects on social, emotional, and intellectual development do vary according to the *quality* of day care, however (Howes, 1988). Research on different types of child-care settings indicates that, in centers and family day-care homes in which group size is modest, staff–child ratios are low, and staff training is high, caregiving tends to be more stimulating, responsive and positively affectionate; it also tends to be less restrictive (Belsky, 1984). These characteristics are also consistent with the kind of sensitive care that seems to promote secure attachments. However, the effects of different types of day-care settings on the quality of attachment are not yet known. Research Focus 4-3, which discusses quality criteria in choosing day care, outlines some of the implications of comparative research on day care.

It is clear that the attachment relations between the infants or young children and those who care for them are an important social foundation for subsequent development. As children grow older and become more socially

116

active and interactive, they form relationships with others and these relationships, too, become an important aspect of social development. We will deal more thoroughly with the family as a context for development in Chapter 12.

Characteristics of the Infant. Parents and researchers alike have long found it useful to think in terms of differences in babies' emotional expressiveness. Such differences are often referred to as *temperament*. This term is defined as individual differences in the expression of emotion and responsiveness to stimulation that influence both the internal and interpersonal life of persons. For example, some babies are considered "cuddly" (Schaffer & Emerson, 1964) and others are "irritable" (Wolff, 1969). Since attachment involves both infant and caregiver, the effects of infant characteristics may affect the nature of the relationship that can develop between them (Campos et al., 1983).

Most research findings, however, give equivocal answers to questions about the relationship between infant temperament and attachment (Campos et al., 1983). Some insecurely attached infants have been found to be "difficult" from birth. However, these studies have been criticized as not measuring temperament in a way that is sufficiently different from the Strange Situation paradigm itself; consequently, temperament and the Strange Situation classification may be based on the same characteristics of the child, rather than showing the effects of one on the other. Furthermore, Sroufe (1985) has pointed out that attachment should be related not to infant difficulty alone, but to the combination of the child's responsiveness and the unique ways in which caregivers respond to the child. In short, attachment cannot be adequately explained by measures that focus on the child alone, but require some information about the interaction between the child and the caregiver.

A somewhat different problem arises from using the term temperament inappropriately to refer to characteristics of high-risk infants. For example, two risk factors that we discussed in Chapter 3, low birth weight and low Apgar scores, are among the factors that predict later insecure attachment as assessed in the Strange Situation (Connell, 1976; Waters, Vaughn, & Egeland, 1980). However, the difficulties faced by these babies and their parents arise from physiological sources, rather than from inherent personality orientations. For example, measures of physiological maturity and responsiveness in the newborn period have been found to be related to patterns of secure versus anxious attachment at the age of 1 year (Waters, Vaughn, & Egeland, 1980). High-risk infants are likely to be relatively immature or impaired physiologically to some degree, and this may affect their ability to be full partners in the kinds of interactions that form the basis of secure attachments. As we saw in Chapter 3, parents of high-risk newborns may also have difficulty matching their behavior to the particular needs of their infants, and this problem in "meshing" may affect the quality of attachment. These problems do not arise from inborn personality or emotional dispositions, however, but from the baby's maturity and general health. The role of the infant in attachment is a topic that needs considerable additional research.

RESEARCH FOCUS 4-3

"Quality" Day Care: The New Quest

More than 40% of women with children under the age of 3 are now employed outside of the home in full-time or part-time jobs. Most must entrust the care of their children to a day care provider other than a member of their own family in a setting other than the child's own home. As a result, one of the problems now facing expectant or new parents is, "What is the best care that I can arrange for my child?"

Research on the effects of day care on early development indicate that the question of the *quality* of the care is a more important one than when the mother goes back to work or how much time the child spends in day care. But how can parents assess the quality of the day-care possibilities they are considering? One expert, Dr. Charles Snow (1983), has outlined several criteria of quality care, based on research comparing the effects of different types of day care:

- *Caregiver qualifications.* Staff members with training in the development and care of young children deliver better care and are more likely to stimulate positive development. Characteristics such as commitment and concern for children and their families and skills for interacting with parents are also important.
- *Caregiver continuity.* Having the same caregivers over long periods of time is important, especially for children from broken families. Centers with high staff turnover may present problems in this regard.
- Physical environment. Sufficient space is important, because studies show that aggression increases as space decreases and crowding increases. The arrangement of

appropriate equipment and materials is important because it helps facilitate interaction with other children and a desirable amount of safe physical activity.
- *Group size.* The smaller the number of children, the more likely the child is to receive quality care. In centers, the ratio of children to staff members is important, with 4 to 1 being the maximum and 3 to 1 being preferred. The center's total enrollment is also important. Those with 30–60 children seem to provide higher quality care than those larger than 60, even when staff ratio and physical environment are good.
- *Daily program.* A planned curriculum, or program of activities, is important both to the child's intellectual development and to the opportunity to develop cooperation and other social skills. Research findings indicate that children in *highly structured* programs tend to show less independence, initiative, and imagination, but do better on intelligence and achievement tests, whereas children in *open,* or less structured, programs tend to be more independent and persistent and do better on tests of creativity, problem solving, and inventiveness. Most programs fall somewhere between these two extremes and offer the best of both worlds, with gains in creativity and self-esteem as well as in intellectual achievement.
- *Parents' involvement.* Research findings indicate that the more parents are involved in the program, the more children benefit. In fact, parent involvement can help bridge the child's two worlds of home and day care. ❧

Quality day-care programs have a low ratio of children to caregivers.

Effects of Culture. Cultures vary in terms of their expectations of children's behavior, and these expectations may affect the extent to which children are seen as securely or insecurely attached. For example, in West Germany, where a great deal of attachment research has been carried out, the general level of resistance to parents observed in the Strange Situation is higher than that found in U.S. studies (Grossmann & Grossmann, 1982). The proportion of babies who are avoidant toward parents in Japanese studies (Miyake, 1983; Takahashi, 1986) and Israeli studies (Sagi, Lamb, Lewkowicz, Shoham, Dvir, & Estes, 1985) is also higher than in Western studies.

Several aspects of cultural differences in attachment behavior may explain these contrasts. In some societies, independence may be more highly valued. Therefore, the parents' behavior in the Strange Situation may actually be perceived as discouraging proximity seeking. The usual criteria for security of attachment would not apply in that society as it does in the United States. In other countries, the Strange Situation may depart more markedly from typical experience than it does in the United States. The greater stress experienced by children in those countries could produce behavior that appears less secure than a more culturally appropriate test would. Cross-cultural research on attachment, as in other areas of developmental psychology, requires careful attention to the cultural context in which attachment is assessed (Campos et al., 1983).

119

Effects of Attachment on Later Development

Early attachments appear to be a foundation for many types of competencies. Greater experience with both the social and physical world, achieved via freer exploration in infancy and early childhood, seems to be a natural avenue for the development of competence. An increasing number of longitudinal studies indicate that early attachment history seems to be linked to children's capacities in many different areas of normal experience. In this section, we review the information that is now available on these links. We also consider how the links might be formed across the course of development.

Attachment and the Development of Social Competence

The most general finding is that children who were securely attached as infants have been found to demonstrate enhanced social competence at a later stage of development when compared to children who were anxiously attached. Three aspects of competence have been especially linked to early attachment: flexibility and resilience in social interactions and problem solving; competence in interactions with others; and incidence of problem behaviors and psychopathology.

Flexibility and Resilience. Researchers now believe that secure attachment serves as a *prototype* of cognitive and interpersonal functioning that is carried forward into later life. The sense of safety that children gain from a trusted caregiver should make it easier to form patterns of exploring the environment widely and confidently and also to "lose themselves" in a task or problem that needs solving. This function of attachment security implies that individual children's styles of problem solving and exploration of new environments are likely to persist beyond the early childhood years. For example, children who, as preschoolers, tend to become highly involved in problem solving and who show persistence in and enjoyment of these tasks will very likely show the same characteristics in problem solving when they are older. The particular problems will change and the ways in which they manifest their interest, persistence, and enjoyment might be superficially different, but the underlying qualities of behavior are likely to remain the same from one age to another (Block & Block, 1980; Waters & Sroufe, 1983). The appendix to this chapter addresses some of the problems in identifying measures that show these underlying qualities and explains how the associations across time between measures are assessed.

A study by psychologists Richard Arend, Frederick Gove, and Alan Sroufe (1979) offers some details on how attachment can affect later flexibility and resiliency. These researchers studied a group of nursery school children (ages 4–5) whose attachment classification on the Strange Situation had been determined when they were 18-months-old. The purpose of the study was to see whether attachment classification at 18 months predicted differences in behavior in the nursery school classroom. Each child was rated by the nursery school teachers, who did not know the attachment classification from earlier years.

The results showed that children who had been classified as securely attached at 18 months of age were more resilient in solving problems, overcoming obstacles, and tolerating frustration than were children who had been insecurely attached at an earlier age. Children who had been securely attached were also rated higher in curiosity in the nursery school. Similar results have been reported by other researchers. For example, secure attachment in the first year of life has been found to be related to more complex exploration of the environment at age 2 (Main, 1973) and to both higher self-control and lower dependence on teachers in preschool (Egeland, 1983; Sroufe, Fox, & Pancake, 1983). These findings apply to children from disadvantaged and high-risk families, as well as to the children of middle-class parents (Waters, Hay, & Richters, 1986).

Interactions with Others. In addition to being more flexible and more likely to invest themselves in tasks and problem solving, individuals with a history of secure attachment appear to be more successful in forming appropriate relationships with adults other than their parents and with other children, as well. The accompanying Research Focus 4-4 describes some classic research on the benefits of early social contact for competence in relationships with others.

The behavior of babies in the Strange Situation indicates why early relationships may affect later interactions with entirely different persons. Some infants—those who are securely attached—are characteristically positive and responsive to their caregivers, maintaining appropriate closeness or distance and needing only moderate amounts of reassurance and comfort. Others appear to be more anxious about how others will respond to them and thus either seem too demanding and sensitive or too distant and unresponsive. If these characteristics are manifested in interactions with others, as many experts think they are, the child with a history of secure attachment is likely to fare better than the child whose early attachments had an anxious quality (Waters, Hay, & Richters, 1986; Waters & Sroufe, 1983).

Interactions with Adults. This pattern of attachment can be seen in follow-up studies of children's responsiveness toward adults. In the first year of life, babies who are securely attached show more readiness to respond positively to new adults than anxiously attached infants (Main & Weston, 1981). The secure youngsters showed more interest in the adults and showed more appropriate and empathic responses to the adult's attempts to be playful and to get emotional reactions from the infant. Differences in early attachment

121

RESEARCH FOCUS 4-4

The Benefits of Early Social Contact

Pleasure in social relations, like pleasurable emotions in other situations, can often be inferred from smiles and other positive facial appearances and also can be inferred from whether or not contact with the other person is sought repeatedly, whether it appears to facilitate the child's social adjustment, and so forth. This more extensive view of the role of pleasurable emotions in development can be seen in the classic studies of the social relations of Rhesus monkeys by Harry Harlow and Stephen Suomi (Harlow, 1959; Suomi, 1978). Harlow initially demonstrated the importance of pleasurable contact with others in a famous experiment in which four infant Rhesus monkeys were isolated from their mothers and, instead, placed in cages that were equipped with two surrogate "mothers." The surrogates were shaped like monkeys, but were made of wire. One was equipped with milk so that the infant could get food. The other did not provide food, but was covered with soft terrycloth. To Harlow's—indeed, most psychologists'—surprise, the infant monkeys preferred to spend time near the cloth surrogate and fled to "her" for comfort when they were frightened, even though food was available only from the less comfortable surrogate. Harlow's research indicated that pleasurable emotions were associated with the tactile stimulation of the terrycloth surrogate, which probably resembled the comfort from contact with a human body. The findings struck a blow against learning theorists' view that social attachments resulted from conditioning of a positive response to caregivers through their association with the satisfaction of hunger.

In Harlow's later studies of these isolates reared by surrogates, even the presence of a comfortable surrogate did not prevent major problems in the young monkeys' later adjustments, however. The isolate monkeys were ineffective in their interactions with other monkeys when they were returned to the peer group. Instead of

In Harry Harlow's classic experiment, infant Rhesus monkeys, when threatened, sought refuge with a cloth-covered surrogate mother rather than a wire surrogate that provided food.

interacting, they sat alone, groomed themselves rather than each other, often held themselves autistically and rocked back and forth. They were inept in sexual relations; and if they did bear children, the females were neglectful and abusive parents. In other words, the monkeys who were isolated from their mothers and other monkeys during the first year of life, did not recover from the social deprivation they suffered. Early social contact is functional for normal social adjustments; and the pleasurable emotions implied by the isolate monkeys' preference for the cloth surrogate probably play an important role in facilitating social contact. This hypothesis has been supported further in later research by Stephen Suomi (1978). Young monkeys have been reared in a variety of circumstances: total isolation; rearing with mother only; rearing with peers only; rearing in a normal community; and so forth. The findings indicate that it is social contact generally, not just contact with the mother, that facilitates social adjustments. In fact, monkeys who were reared only with peers, adjusted to adult society better following isolation than those who were reared with mother alone.

Obviously, the possibility that contact with others is inherently pleasurable does not rule out the possibility that pleasurable feelings in many social relationships are the result of learning. Preference for particular companions may result from previous pleasant, rewarding experiences with them—or even with others who are like them in some important respects. Harlow's findings simply indicate that the effects of pleasurable emotions, however derived, may extend to a variety of social outcomes for the individual. 🐛

---

have also been found to be correlated with children's interactions with strangers at the age of 3 years (Lutkenhaus, Grossmann, & Grossmann, 1985). Children who had been tested in the Strange Situation at 12 months of age were observed in their homes at age 3. Those who had been classified as securely attached at 1 year entered interactions with an unfamiliar visitor more quickly and smoothly than those who had been initially classified as anxiously attached. Furthermore, when playing a competitive game with the visitor, the securely attached children reacted to failure with increased effort, while those with an early history of insecure attachment reacted to failure with decreased effort and with open sadness. In short, differences in early attachment classification seem to be correlated with children's later abilities both to interact effectively with adults other than their parents and to maintain resiliency in the face of competitive disadvantage.

Early attachment history may also be related to children's potential for being influenced by adults. In a series of studies, it has been shown that children with a history of secure attachment in the first year of life later show greater attentiveness to adults, a greater disposition to obey, and greater self-regulation of behavior even when they think no one is watching (Stayton, Hogan, & Ainsworth, 1971; Londerville & Main, 1981; Matas, Arend, & Sroufe, 1978). The security of attachment has been shown to be related to children's relationships with their preschool teachers at age $3\frac{1}{2}$ through $4\frac{1}{2}$, with anxiously attached children experiencing more interventions from teachers, who had low expectations that these children would obey and follow their directives (Motti, 1986).

These interpersonal effects of attachment history hold for children from economically disadvanaged families as well as those from middle-class households. For example, infants from disadvantaged families who were rated as securely attached at 12 months were more sociable and compliant both with their own mothers at the age of 2 and with their preschool teachers at age $4\frac{1}{2}$ (Erickson & Crichton, 1981; Erickson, Farber, & Egeland, 1982; Pastor, 1981).

123

Interactions with Peers. Attachment history is also correlated with children's interactions with other children. As we will see in Chapter 13, peer relationships offer important advantages in socialization, including the opportunity to learn to interact with others as equals, the regulation of assertiveness and aggression, and the capacity for cooperation. Children with an early history of secure attachment to caregivers appear to be more likely to interact with peers positively and competently (Hartup, 1983; Jacobson & Wille, 1986; Pastor, 1981).

This link has been documented by Alan Sroufe (1983) in a longitudinal study of 40 children from economically disadvantaged backgrounds. Many of these children were born to unmarried mothers living in poor economic circumstances. The children's history included a good deal of instability. Their mothers moved frequently, many had a series of different male partners, and most had unusually high levels of life stress. At the age of 12 months, only about 33% of the sample were classified in the Strange Situation as being securely attached. When the children were $3\frac{1}{2}$ years old, Sroufe and his colleagues observed them in a special nursery school class composed entirely of participants in the longitudinal study. The nursery school teachers did not know the children's attachment histories, nor were the observers aware which children had been classified as securely or anxiously attached. Nevertheless, children who had been classified differently at 12 months showed contrasting patterns of behavior in the nursery-school classroom. Teachers reported securely attached children as having a higher number of friends than anxiously attached children, and the other children in the classroom rated their classmates with secure attachment history as more popular. Teachers also rated securely attached children higher in social competence and skills, self-esteem, empathy, and positive emotional expressions and lower on negative emotional expression than anxiously attached children—all characteristics that could contribute to differences in peer relationships. Indeed, the classroom observers noted that securely attached children more commonly initiated, responded to, and sustained interactions with others in a positive way and were less whiny, aggressive, and negative in their responses to others.

Emotional Adjustment and Behavior Problems. The correlation beween secure attachment and positive relationships with others carries the converse implication that a history of anxious attachment is related to less successful relationships with others. Research findings also indicate that anxious attachment is correlated with a variety of emotional and behavioral problems in early childhood and in the school years (Waters, Hay, & Richters, 1986). For example, in a disadvantaged sample of 267 children, including the 40 children studied by Sroufe, children with anxious attachment at ages 12 and 18 months were more likely to develop behavior problems in preschool than securely attached children were. When children with different attachment histories were compared, children who had been classified as anxiously attached at both 12 and 18 months had the most school behavior problems and those who had been rated as securely attached at both times had the fewest, with mixed classifications showing wide variability (Erickson, Sroufe, & Egeland, 1985).

Furthermore, the particular types of problems shown by children at later ages have been found to be linked to the nature of the early relationships with caregivers. In the group of 40 children studied by Sroufe, the particular types of behavior problems shown depended on whether the anxious attachment involved resistant or avoidant behavior. Children whose early attachments had been classified as anxious–resistant were rated by their preschool teachers as either impulsive and tense or helpless and fearful; whereas children with anxious–avoidant early attachments showed hostility and isolation from peers (Sroufe, 1983).

The characteristics of children's interactions with peers are often linked to the qualities of relationships between caregivers and children.

Not all infants who are insecure will have later problems, of course. Psychologist Michael Lewis and his coworkers (Lewis, Feirling, McGuffog, & Jaskir, 1984) studied a sample of middle-class children and found that 40% of the boys who were insecurely attached at 1 year of age showed problems at age 6, whereas 60% did not. By looking closer at the problem and nonproblem subgroups within this originally insecurely attached group, these researchers shed some light on the conditions under which early problems may be carried forward into later childhood. The 40% of boys with problems at age 6 were different from the other subgroup in that they also experienced a number of negative environmental factors: Their births were unplanned, they and their families had experienced a number of stressful events, they tended to be second-, rather than first-born children, and they reportedly had few friends. Does this simply mean that the difference between the problem and nonproblem boys resulted from environmental difficulties that had nothing to do with their early attachment history? When Lewis and his colleagues compared the insecurely attached group who had experienced the difficulties to children who had originally been securely attached and had experienced these same environmental problems, they found that the children with an early history of secure attachments showed significantly fewer problems at age 6 than those who had been insecurely attached. It may be, therefore, that secure attachment in the early years serves as a protective factor (see Chapter 3) against the negative effects of later or continuing environmental difficulties.

The consistency of findings indicating that early attachment history is related to later functioning is impressive. It is important to note, however, that the evidence that early relationships and later development are correlated with each other does not prove a cause–effect relation between the two. It simply documents that children with certain kinds of early histories also seem more likely than we would ordinarily expect to solve problems and tackle tasks in certain ways and to show characteristic orientations toward others. An important question is how we might explain the consistency of this pattern across studies and across middle-class and disadvantaged samples.

Why Do the Effects of Early Relationships Persist?

Several possibilities exist to explain the striking correlations between early relationships and later development. The most obvious is that the security of attachment shapes the child's personality so extensively that later experiences reflect early learning without themselves having an impact on behavior. However, as we saw in Chapter 3, the effects of experiences in infancy are rarely irrevocable. Early insecure attachments may also be overcome to some degree by later interventions that foster security and the development of skills; and—unfortunately—early secure attachments may be undermined by later stress, abuse, or neglect (Rutter, 1979). It seems more likely that, for most children, relationships with caregivers continue to exert an influence later in childrens' development. Perhaps the nature of the parent–child relationship is similar from one age to another, with the result being that the

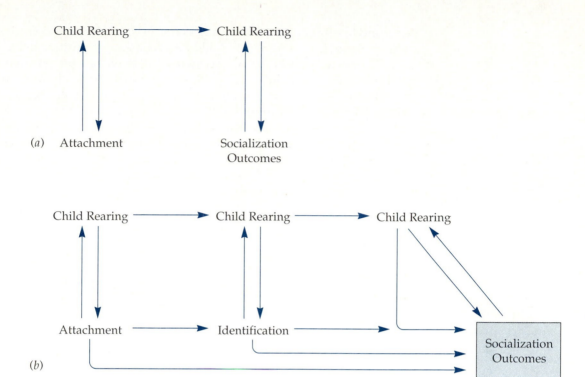

FIGURE 4-3

Alternative models of the relation between early attachment and outcomes of parental socialization in later childhood.

Source: from Waters, Hay, & Richters, 1986.

child shows the effect of a continuing relationship, rather than the relationship in infancy per se. This possibility is diagrammed in Figure 4-3a.

A different view, diagrammed in Figure 4-3b, has recently been suggested by psychologists Everett Waters, Dale Hay, and John Richters (1986). They have proposed that the continuing interactions between parent and child may be influenced by the quality of the relationship formed during infancy. As Figure 4-3b shows, Waters, Hay, & Richters think that two important aspects of caregiver–child interactions are established in infancy. One of these is the caregiver's *expectations* regarding the child's subsequent behavior and responsiveness, which may affect the caregiver's methods in rearing the child and also the degree of confidence caregivers feel about their abilities for influencing the child in general. Second, the early relationship affects the child's *identification* with her caregivers, which affects the degree to which the child tends to behave consistently with parental behaviors and wishes. Identification refers to the degree to which the behaviors of caregivers are adopted by children. In secure attachments, the child is more likely to be attentive to caregivers, to prefer them, to reproduce their characteristic ac-

127

tions, and to respond to the caregiver's control. Caregivers who feel confident about their ability to influence a child and who expect positive behaviors are likely to provide the kinds of experiences that will foster positive growth appropriate for the child's age. In insecure attachments, children are likely to avoid or resist caregiver influence and caregivers may feel powerless, resentful, and detached from the child. Thus, even after infancy, the influence of the caregiver on the child may depend heavily upon the expectations and the degree of identification that began to be formed in the early months of their relationship.

The topic of the role of social relationships in development will be discussed again in Chapters 9 through 15 and in Chapter 17. In those chapters, you will see again how the quality of relationships shapes the nature and course of individual growth throughout the childhood and adolescent years.

Summary

The formation of attachments between infants and their caregivers is a hallmark of development in the first year of life. Extensive research has been devoted to questions of how attachments are formed, why attachments differ from child to child, and how early relationships may influence later development. Developmental theories vary in their views on the *origins* of attachments, but all emphasize the importance of early relationships to later behavior and psychological health.

The attachment of children to caregivers is indicated by a variety of behaviors. In infancy, the most widely known of these behaviors is protest at being separated from others. The typical *course* of development of attachment is that protests are initially *indiscriminate*, with infants crying when they are left by a variety of other persons. The *specific* attachments, signaled by protests when they are separated from a particular caregiver, especially in the presence of unfamiliar persons, become common at about the age of 7 months. Many infants begin to protest at earlier or later ages, however. Although infants also protest separation from other persons, it is most common to see protest at separation from the main caregiver first and then at separation from a group of familiar, consistent caregivers.

The Strange Situation, a method for examining the quality of attachment, has emphasized not only separation protest, but also the behavior of children when they are reunited with caregivers. This approach permits the classification of attachment as secure or insecure. Secure attachment seems to serve the function of allowing infants to leave their caretakers and explore their environments without fear of permanent separation from the caregivers. Insecurely attached infants and toddlers show less willingness to explore and are more avoidant or ambivalent toward their caregivers when the two are reunited following a separation.

Variations in the security of attachment appear to be related to *environmental conditions,* such as parental behavior, including extreme conditions like abuse, neglect, or rejection, arrangements for care (for example, regular day care outside the home), and social class and cultural norms for caregiving relationships and child behavior. Certain individual characteristics of the infant are also important factors. For example, risk factors associated with low-birth weight infants have been associated with problems in establishing secure attachments.

Findings from long-term studies indicate significant *interrelations* between the early caregiver–child relationships and a wide variety of personality characteristics, emotional patterns, and interpersonal behaviors. If there has been secure attachment in early life, children are more likely to show competence in the preschool years by problem solving in a flexible way, showing responsiveness toward adults and peers, seeking and accepting help when needed, and adjusting well to school and other situations. Although it is not clear why the effects of early relationships persist in later development, some experts believe that early relationships form the basis for caregivers' expectations about children and for children's identification with caregivers, both of which in turn affect later socialization.

Suggested Readings

Campos, J. J., Barrett, K. C., Lamb, M. E., Goldsmith, H. H., & Stenberg, C. (1983). Socioemotional development. In P. H. Mussen (Ed.) & M. M. Haith & J. J. Campos (Vol. Eds.), *Handbook of child psychology (4th ed.), Vol. 2: Infancy and developmental psychobiology* (pp. 783–916). New York: Wiley.

Hartup, W. W. (1989). Social relationships and their developmental significance. *American Psychologist, 44,* 120–126.

Hinde, R. A., & Stevenson-Hinde, J. (Eds.) (1988). *Relationships within families: Mutual influences.* Oxford, England: Oxford University Press.

Tronick, E. Z. (1989). Emotions and emotional communication in infants. *American Psychologist, 44,* 112–119.

Waters, E., Hay, D. F., & Richters, J. E. (1986). Infant-parent attachment and the origins of prosocial and antisocial behavior. In D. Olweus, J. Block, & M. Radke-Yarrow (Eds.), *Development of antisocial and prosocial behavior: Research, theories, and issues* (pp. 97–126). New York: Academic Press.

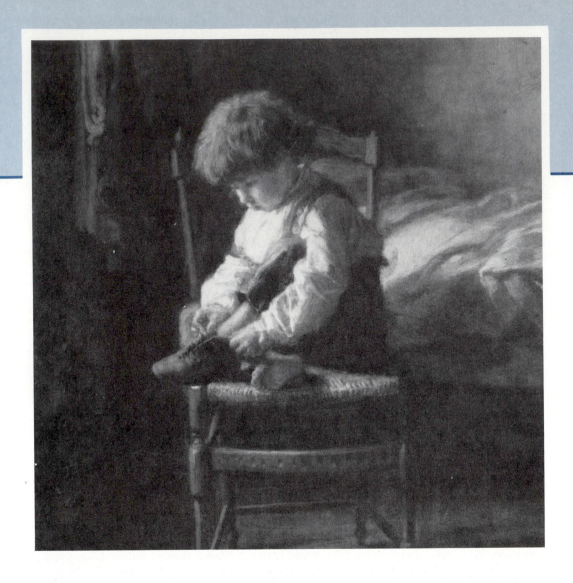

Healthy human infants have surprising capacities for responding to the environment, as Part One has indicated. Nevertheless, the story of development from infancy to adolescence is marked by a growth of knowledge and skills that extends far beyond the remarkable potential now attributed to infants. Part II consists of four chapters in which the development of perceptual, language, and cognitive abilities is examined in more detail.

Chapter 5 addresses a basic question in psychology: How do humans perceive the world around them? After reviewing the nature of perception generally, the chapter examines how perceptual abilities change as a result of experiencing the objects and events that comprise the everyday world. In Chapter 6, the focus is on the development of language. A key question

PART TWO

The Development of Perception, Cognition, and Language

is how infants and toddlers make use of the speech sounds of their parents and others to acquire the ability to form words and sentences on their own.

Chapters 7 and 8 take up the topic of intellectual abilities. A key question concerns how children make use of the information acquired through perceptual processes to gain new knowledge and reach increasingly more mature understanding of the world around them. In addressing this question, the chapters consider how intellectual abilities and the changes in them can be described and assessed and how psychologists and others can best identify the essential experiences that support optimal intellectual growth.

Perceptual Development

Introduction

During the course of a typical day, we are exposed to a wide range of information about the external world and our relation to it. For example, consider the seemingly simple act of driving an automobile on a freeway, an activity that many adults in the United States perform on a daily basis, oftentimes without much conscious thought. Drivers who are planning to enter a freeway must be aware of the location of their own automobile, the speed they are traveling, and the maximum amount of acceleration the automobile will provide if needed. In addition, people must be aware of the locations of automobiles already on the freeway, gauge their speeds, and determine when it is safe to attempt entrance. Integrating information about their automobile's location and speed with information about the location and speeds of other automobiles is also necessary for maneuvering while on the freeway and for exiting the freeway. The ability to perceive and integrate information such as this involves a number of abilities. In this chapter we will consider the nature and development of those abilities most directly involved in our *perception* of the world. Other abilities, such as those involved in analyzing and comparing information and making decisions, will be considered in Chapters 7 and 8.

The way children make sense of the world has fascinated scholars for centuries. Some scholars have argued that children are born with the capacity to perceive the world accurately. Others believe that experience is necessary for children to acquire perceptual abilities. At this point, you probably recognize these views as opposite sides of the nature–nurture controversy. Nativists believe that perceptual skills are part of our biological heritage and require little if any experience to blossom. Nurturists believe that perceptual skills arise from experience. In this chapter, we will examine the origins and developmental course of a variety of perceptual skills. In so doing, we will consider the roles of heredity and experience in the development of these perceptual skills. As you read this chapter, keep in mind that perceptual skills are involved in all of development—cognitive, emotional, language, personality, and social development. If humans could not perceive such things as objects, words, the feelings of others, or changes in the weather, human life would be considerably different.

The Nature of Perception

When asked to consider how we perceive the world, many people begin by stating the obvious. We *see* the world with our eyes. We *hear* the world with our ears. We *feel* the world with our skin. We *smell* the world with our nose. We *taste* the world with our tongue. The relation between our perceptions

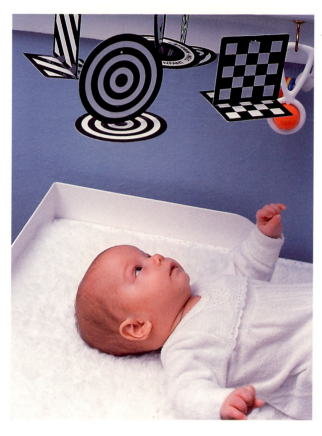

Primary Motor and Perceptual Development

From birth, infants are prepared to undertake, in some measure, the tasks that mark every period of life: acquiring the knowledge and skills needed to master the everyday world of people, objects, and places; and exploring their own characteristics that can be used, to adapt themselves to the constraints, demands, and opportunities of the world. Although their skills are rudimentary by adult standards, infants are capable of remarkable comprehension of the world around them. Their repertoire of innate reflexes enables them to respond to sound, visual stimulation, touch, and meet their basic needs.

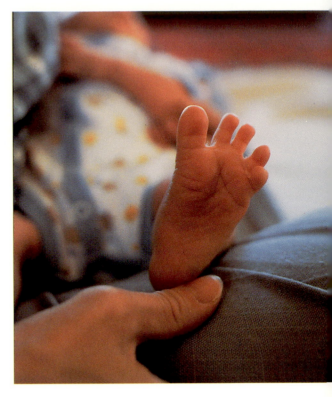

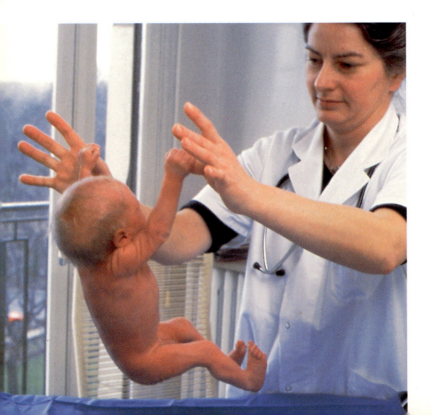

Furthermore, infants discern visual patterns, track moving objects, respond to features of spoken language, and communicate important information about themselves through complex and subtle differences in their cries and by other signals.

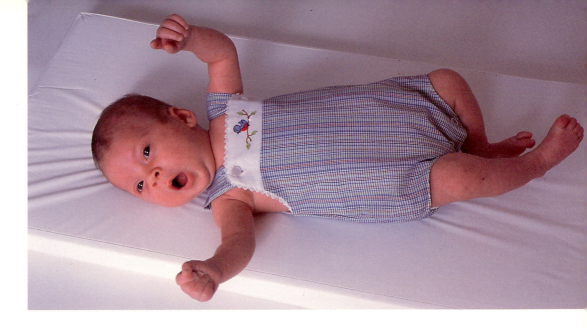

By the end of the first year of life, they expand these already extensive capabilities through locomotion, the beginnings of language, a well-differentiated set of social relationships, and a growing awareness of self and of the people and things around them. Infancy researchers have been stimulated to devise many ingenious methods to discover these innate capabilities, to track their changes and the emergence of new ones.

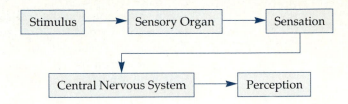

FIGURE 5-1

Relation of stimulus, sensory organ, sensation, and perception.

(seeing, hearing, feeling, smelling, and tasting) and our sensory organs (eyes, ears, skin, nose, and tongue) is obvious to most of us, perhaps even to all normal functioning human beings. Nonetheless, these relations are only part of the picture insofar as perception is concerned. Perception involves a stimulus, a sensory organ that responds to the stimulus, and the interpretation of the sensory organ response by the central nervous system (primarily the brain). In our consideration of perception, then, a *stimulus* is any form of physical energy to which an organism is capable of responding. A *sensation* is a sensory organ's response to some stimulus. A *perception* is the interpretation of the sensation by the brain.

The types of information to which an organism is capable of responding are determined by two factors: the external information available (sound waves, heat, pressure, and so on) and the sensory organs of the organism. Thus, different species have different sensory capabilities. For example, bees are capable of sensing ultraviolet light, whereas human beings are not.

As shown in Figure 5-1, the transformation from a stimulus to a perception depends on both the ability of a sensory organ to produce a sensation coming from the stimulus and the ability of the brain to use the information provided by the sensation to produce a perception. In order to understand perception and its development, we must pay attention to each of the steps involved in perception.

The Development of the Auditory System

The perception of sounds relies on the auditory system. There are many types of sounds in the environment, and our perception of these sounds is influenced by a multitude of factors. These factors include characteristics of the sounds (intensity and duration) and characteristics of the listening task. For example, if people are listening for a sound in order to locate an object (for example, another person), then the listeners will attempt to determine the location of the sound once it is heard. But if people are listening in order to decide if an object is approaching or departing, then they must contrast the intensity of the sounds produced by the object as it moves. If the object is approaching listeners, the sounds will become louder and more distinct as the object nears. If the object is moving away from listeners, the sounds

135

will become softer and less distinct as the object moves further away. Finally, listeners may need to selectively attend to certain sounds and ignore others. For example, if listeners are at a party, they may need to focus on the sounds being produced by one speaker and ignore those produced by other individuals who are speaking at the same time.

Auditory Skills Before Birth

The idea that unborn children respond to sound has existed for some time. Peiper (1924) reported that mothers could feel their fetuses move in response to loud sounds (such as an automobile horn), a finding that was supported by the subsequent work of Sontag and Wallace (1935). Investigations using less gross measures than movement have also supported the notion that fetuses respond to external sounds. Seven months after conception, the heart rate of fetuses increases when a loud sound is presented (Bernard and Sontag, 1947). A recent report suggests that sensitivity to external sounds appears around 26 weeks after conception. Birnholz and Benecerrafa (1983) examined fetal responses to an ultrasound examination, a technique in which

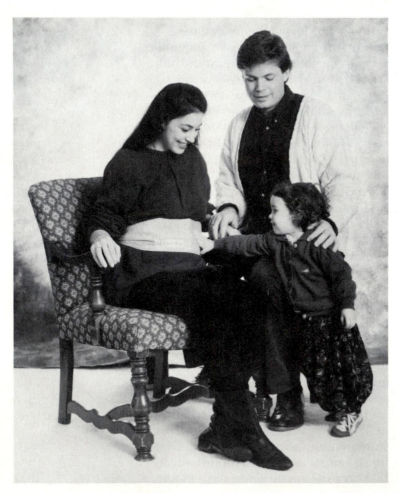

Research suggests that unborn children can hear the voices of their mothers, fathers, and siblings (see Research Focus 5-1).

sound is used to examine fetal growth and characteristics. Fetuses 25 weeks old and younger (from the time of conception) failed to blink when exposed to the ultrasound stimulation, whereas fetuses 26 weeks old and older usually blinked in response to the ultrasound stimulation. These findings suggest that unborn children do have the capacity for auditory perception (at least by 26 weeks after conception). This must be carefully interpreted, however (Aslin, Pisoni, & Jusczyk, 1983). Because sounds must pass through the mother's body to reach the fetus, it is sometimes unclear whether the fetus is reacting to the sound or to the vibrations produced as the sound passes through the mother's body. Nonetheless, the work done on learning in the womb (see Research Focus 5-1) suggests that fetuses can hear human voices in the womb and subsequently discriminate voices they have heard from those they have not.

RESEARCH FOCUS 5-1

Learning in the Womb

When we think of learned preferences, we usually think of experiences that begin at birth. Recently, however, a number of researchers have studied the possibility of learning in a different environment—the womb. For example, De-Casper and Fifer (1980) tested ten 3-day-old infants by allowing them to manipulate a tape recorder by sucking. One sucking pattern resulted in the infants' hearing their mother's tape-recorded voice, while another sucking pattern resulted in their hearing another woman's tape-recorded voice. DeCasper and Fifer found that the newborn infants preferred to listen to their mother's voice, as evidenced by their sucking patterns. This preference occurred regardless of whether the infants were bottle fed or breast fed. Moreover, the infants could discriminate their father's voice from that of another male, but did not prefer to listen to the father's voice. By one month of age, however, they did prefer their father's voice to that of other males. Apparently, the infants had become familiar with their mother's voice in utero and liked to listen to it rather than to a strange female voice. They had become less familiar with the father's voice in their prenatal world, and needed experience in the postnatal world to develop this preference. To fur-

ther test the possibility that fetuses develop auditory preferences in utero, DeCasper and Fifer had pregnant mothers read *The Cat in the Hat* aloud twice a day during the last $6\frac{1}{2}$ weeks of pregnancy. Shortly after birth the neonates were tested to see if they would choose to listen to *The Cat in the Hat* or *The King, the Mice, and the Cheese* (a poem with a very different meter than *The Cat in the Hat*). The infants sucked to hear *The Cat in the Hat*, once again demonstrating that learning in the womb had occurred. Even more striking, 4-day-old infants have been found to prefer to listen to their mother's language rather than to a foreign language (Mehler, Lambertz, Jusczyk, & Amiel-Tison, 1986).

This work is important for two reasons. First, these preferences suggest that hearing is in fact possible during the last few months of prenatal development. Second, young infants' preference for their mothers' voices may also cause mothers to talk more to their infants, since the infants seem to be listening to the mothers. Newborn infants' auditory preferences, then, reveal significant hearing skills, but may also contribute to mother–infant bonding (see Chapter 3) and to language development (see Chapter 6).

Auditory Skills in the Newborn

At birth, infants' ears contain remnants of the amniotic fluid that surrounded them during prenatal development. Despite the presence of this fluid, newborn infants can hear. In fact, newborn infants are sensitive to a wide range of sounds. In some cases, the hearing of newborn infants is better than that of older children and adults. For example, Aslin (1987) has reported that newborn infants can hear very high-pitched sounds, an ability that will be lost as they grow older. However, for most types of sounds, particularly those at low frequencies, the infant's hearing improves with age (Hecox & Degan, 1985; Morrongiello & Clifton, 1984; Sinnott, Pisoni, & Aslin, 1983). This improvement begins shortly after birth, at least partly due to the absorption of the amniotic fluid that was present in the ear at birth, and continues throughout early childhood.

In addition to possessing the ability to hear certain types of sounds at birth, newborn infants also react differently to different types of sounds (Bench, Collyer, Mentz, & Wilson, 1976; Butterfield & Siperstein, 1972; Clarkson & Berg, 1983). For example, newborns react more to complex sounds that involve a variety of frequencies (such as human voices) than to pure tones (Bench et al., 1976). Newborn infants' preferences for complex auditory stimuli may be linked to their ability to discriminate one human voice from another (see Research Focus 5-1).

The Development of the Ability to Discriminate Speech Sounds

Human speech uses sound categories that are called phonemes. A phoneme is a class of sounds that are not physically identical to one another but which speakers of a language treat as equivalent sounds, a phenomenon that is known as *categorial perception*. Human languages differ in terms of the number and types of phonemes they employ. For example, both the [k] sound in "key" and the [k] sound in "ski" are members of the same phoneme in English. This means that English speakers treat the two sounds as if they were equivalent despite the fact that the [k] sound in "key" is aspirated (it concludes with a short puff of breath) and the [k] sound in "ski" is unaspirated (it does not conclude with a short puff of breath). In contrast, the two [k] sounds are members of different phonemes in Chinese; the Chinese people can readily distinguish between the aspirated and unaspirated forms. Thus, speakers of English and speakers of Chinese differ in terms of their ability to discriminate the two sounds. Given that every human child has the capacity to learn any human language (see Chapter 6), developmental psychologists have been fascinated by the question of how children acquire the phonemes of their native language. Recently, scholars have discovered a great deal about categorial perception of phonemes by infants and the roles that nature and nurture play in this phenomenon.

In a pioneering study, Eimas, Siqueland, Jusczyk, and Vigorito (1971) tested 1-month-old infants' ability to discriminate the syllables /ba/ and /pa/. Since a researcher cannot ask 1-month-olds if they perceive the difference between two sounds, Eimas et al. used a nonverbal technique based on boredom. This technique, called the *habituation technique*, involves the presentation of a stimulus until the infant stops paying attention to it (becomes bored) and the subsequent presentation of another stimulus. If the infant pays attention

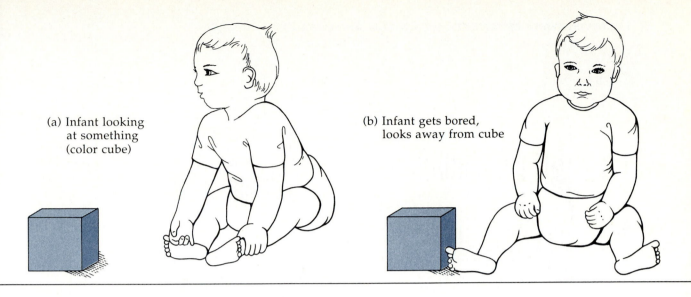

(a) Infant looking
at something
(color cube)

(b) Infant gets bored,
looks away from cube

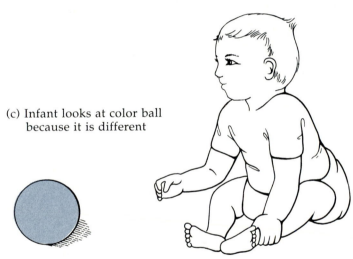

(c) Infant looks at color ball
because it is different

FIGURE 5-2
Illustration of habituation.

to the new stimulus, then one can reasonably assume that the infant can distinguish between the new stimulus and the old stimulus. If the infant remains bored once the new stimulus is presented, then it is unlikely that the infant has noticed the difference between the two stimuli (see Figure 5-2).

Using this paradigm, Eimas et al. found that 1-month-old infants could discriminate the phonemes /ba/ and /pa/. Initially, someone might interpret these results in terms of an ability to perceive absolute differences in sounds. /Ba/ and /pa/ are, after all, sounds that are physically distinct from one another. However, this does not seem to be the case. Remember that the sounds that constitute each phoneme represent a range of possible sounds (see Figure 5-3). For example, there is a set of physically distinct sounds that comprise the syllable class /ba/. Nonetheless, adult speakers of English find

139

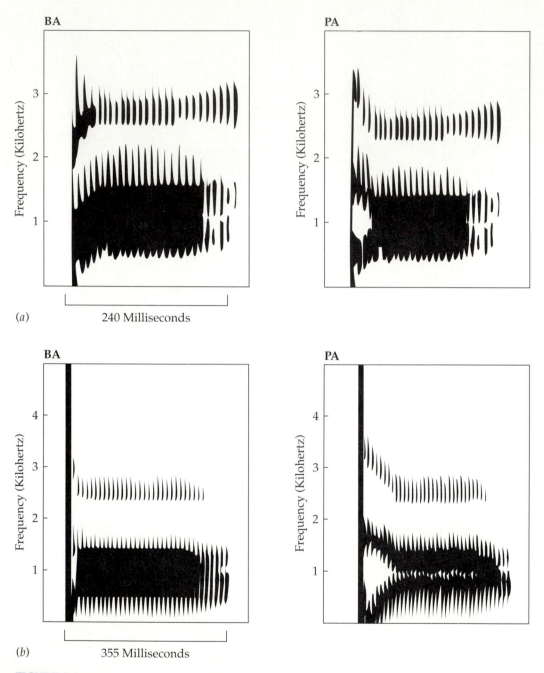

FIGURE 5-3

Illustration of the physical characteristics of two phonemes (|BA| and |PA|). Note that in (*a*), |BA| and |PA| are physically more similar to one another than either is to |BA| or |PA| in (*b*). Despite this, adults and children readily discriminate |BA| from |PA|, and fail to discriminate |BA| from |BA| or |PA| from |PA|. This is categorical perception.

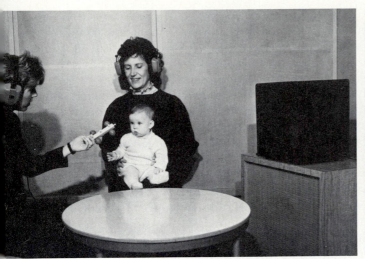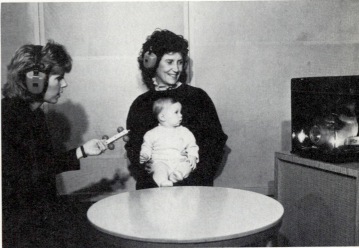

An infant learns to anticipate the illumination of a toy display by attending to the changes from one phoneme to another.

it difficult to discriminate one /ba/ sound from another, even though they have no difficulty distinguishing a /ba/ sound from a /pa/ sound. This is true even if the two /ba/ sounds are more physically distinct than the /ba/ and /pa/ sounds (which is possible given the range of possible /ba/ and /pa/ sounds). Adults can readily distinguish two sounds if the sounds are from different classes (for example, /ba/ versus /pa/), but find it difficult to do so if the two sounds are from the same sound class (for example, /ba/). Interestingly, Eimas et al. found that 1-month-old infants could not discriminate two syllables of /ba/ that were physically as distinct as the difference between a /ba/ sound and a /pa/ sound.

The fact that young infants are able to discriminate phonemes has considerable implications (Eimas, 1985). First, the fact that infants are able to discriminate sounds that represent different phonemes but cannot distinguish different sounds within a phoneme suggests that infants engage in categorical perception. In other words, they are able to perceive differences between categories but not differences within categories. Second, the young age at which infants make these discriminations suggests that such abilities may be innate. This does not mean that young infants can discriminate all phonemes or that infants are born with knowledge of phonemes. Recent evidence suggests that infants' ability to discriminate speech sounds may rest on general auditory processing skills rather than on skills specific to speech (Jusczyk, Pisoni, Fernald, Reed, & Myers, 1983). In other words, infants may be predisposed to categorize sounds in general, a predisposition that influences their perception of speech sounds. This possibility gains support from cross-species research that has demonstrated that nonhuman species such as chinchillas and macaque monkeys are capable of categorical perception of

141

human speech sounds (Kulh & Miller, 1975; Kuhl & Padden, in press). If categorical perception of speech sounds depended on innate knowledge of human phonemes, one would hardly expect species such as chinchillas and macaque monkeys to possess categorical perception.

Regardless of the reasons underlying human infants' capacity for categorical perception of speech sounds, the ability to discriminate phonemes seems to diminish with age. At 6 months of age, for example, infants are able to discriminate a wide range of sounds, including many that are not used in their native language. Since every human child must have the capacity to learn all of the sounds of any human language, the 6-month-old's auditory skills are both impressive and necessary. However, by 12 months of age, infants are quite good at discriminating the sounds of their mother tongue, but are unlikely to discriminate the sounds of other languages (Werker, 1989; see Figure 5-4).

It seems, then, that infants' acquisition of the phonemes of their native language depends on both the innate predisposition for categorical perception of speech sounds and experience with sounds used as phonemes. Children who are exposed to English hear sounds used as English phonemes, and gradually come to distinguish this set of phonemes. Children who hear Chinese are exposed to sounds that function as Chinese phonemes, and so acquire the Chinese set of phonemes. Although it is unclear exactly how experience influences children's acquisition of phonemes, it seems that when

FIGURE 5-4

Infants show a decline in the universal phonetic sensitivity during the second half of their first year, as shown here in the results of experiments performed with babies from English-speaking families and involving non-English syllables from Hindi (*dark bars*) and Nthlakapmx (*light bars*), a language spoken by some native Indians in British Columbia.
Source: from Werker, 1989.

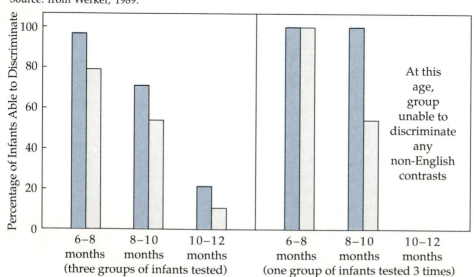

children hear sounds used as phonemes the children then continue to have the ability to discriminate the phonemes, whereas when children lack exposure to phonemic uses of sounds, it makes it difficult to discriminate the phonemes at later ages.

One way in which experience may influence the acquisition of phonemes concerns the types of contexts experience provides. The verbal context in which infants hear sounds seems to influence their ability to discriminate certain sounds from others. Goodsitt, Morse, Ver Hoeve, and Cowan (1984) found that 6½-month-old infants were better able to discriminate sounds when they occurred in a redundant context (for example, ko ba ko) than when they occurred in a nonredundant context (for example, ti ba ko).

The Development of the Haptic System

The *haptic system* is involved in the perception of touch, a form of perception that is both more complex and more important than it might appear at first glance. Touch is involved in a number of reflexes that are present in the very young infant. The brush of a nipple on the cheek causes the infant to turn her head in the direction of the stimulated cheek, a reflex that may have evolved in order to allow even the very young infant to more readily find food. The pain provided by a sharp object elicits a withdrawal reflex that spares the infant further pain and perhaps even actual injury. In addition to the host of reflexes that are elicited by tactile stimulation, the sense of touch eventually allows more complex tactile perceptions. Children (and adults, especially if they are blinded) become increasingly adept at exploring and recognizing objects that they can only manipulate with their hands or which they bump into in a poorly lit room.

Newborn infants have been found to be sensitive to changes in the location of where they are touched, suggesting that shortly after birth their haptic perception is sensitive to where a touch occurs (Kisilevsky & Muir, 1984). Older infants have been found to use haptic information to gain information about the world. For example, Allen (1982) found that 3-month-old infants sucked less on familiar objects than on novel objects, demonstrating that haptic exploration in the form of mouthing allowed infants to discriminate familiar and novel objects. Steri Pêcheax (1986) reported similar results in regard to 5-month-old infants' handling of objects. In this study, objects were placed in the infants' hands without the infants being able to see the objects. The infants habituated to the first objects that they handled and were consequently more likely to handle novel objects than familiar ones. Thus, haptic exploration with their hands seems to provide infants with information that allows them to discriminate objects from one another.

Infants show a preference for haptic exploration using mouthing over that using the hands until approximately 12 months of age. Kopp (1974) presented

8- and 9-month-olds with a solid object and recorded their exploratory behaviors. Although the infants looked at the object (visual exploration) and examined it with their hands, the predominant form of exploration involved mouthing. Despite this preference for mouthing, it is important to remember that infants use a variety of exploratory behaviors in their interaction with objects. By 12 months of age, the preference for mouthing over other exploratory behaviors has diminished (Gibson & Spelke, 1983). Moreover, 12-month-old infants exhibit different manual behaviors in reaction to different properties of objects. For example, they are more likely to squeeze elastic objects and to bang rigid objects (Gibson & Walker, 1982).

The Development of the Taste–Smell Systems

Researchers interested in the sense of smell, which involves the olfactory perceptual system, have demonstrated that even newborn infants can detect noxious odors such as ammonia or vinegar (Engen, Lipsitt, & Kaye, 1963; Sarnat, 1978), and that the sense of smell becomes more acute during the first week of life (Lipsitt, Engen, & Kay, 1963). The newborn's olfactory system even appears to be sensitive to the location of a smell—infants less than 1-week-old will turn their heads away from an offending odor such as ammonia. The early age at which these negative reactions to noxious odors occurs suggests that infants are born with biases against certain types of smells (for example, ammonia). It may also be the case that infants have innate preferences for more pleasant types of odors, but most of what is known about the infant's olfactory system concerns strong noxious odors. The reason for this is straightforward–infants react strongly against offending odors, but may react in much less obvious ways to pleasant odors.

Despite infants' innate reactions against offending smells and the possibility of innate preferences for other types of odors, it is clear that experience will result in other biases and preferences being learned. For example, if you have ever become nauseous after eating a particular food or drinking a particular beverage, it is likely that subsequent experiences with the odors associated with the offending substance became adversive to you. On the other hand, you have probably learned to associate other odors with foods that you find delectable. The earliest example of a learned olfactory preference concerns the mother's body odor. During the first week following birth, infants prefer their mother's body odor to that of other women (MacFarlane, 1975). However, this preference seems to depend on whether the infant is breast fed or bottle fed. Breast fed infants show the preference for their mother's odor, whereas bottle fed infants do not (Cernoch & Porter, 1985). The implication of this finding for differences among bottle fed and breast fed infants in mother–infant bonding is unclear (see Chapter 3).

The sense of taste is highly developed at birth. Newborns can discriminate at least four basic tastes—bitter, salty, sweet, and sour (Crook, 1978; Ganchrow, Steiner, & Daher, 1983; Steiner, 1979). For example, infants given a drop of a bitter solution are likely to stick out their tongues and spit. In contrast, infants given a sweet solution are likely to smile, energetically lick their lips, and suck. In addition, infants less than 3-days-old react differently to various levels of sweetness (Cowart, 1981). Shortly after birth, then, infants are able to discriminate certain types of tastes, and to discriminate different levels of a particular taste. Although the newborn's taste preferences seem to be innate, experience will result in other tastes becoming positive or negative. For both taste and smell, then, the newborn is equipped at birth with basic sensory capabilities, which improve with increasing age. The innate preferences for certain tastes and smells will be supplemented by experience, resulting in certain tastes and odors becoming pleasant and others becoming unpleasant.

The Development of the Visual System

During the past 30 years, researchers have made considerable advances in our understanding of the development of the visual system. These advances have occurred in regard to both our understanding of the development of the anatomy and physiology of the visual system and our understanding of exactly what young infants are able to see.

The eye is the sensory organ involved in visual perception. The similarities and differences between an adult's eye and an infant's eye are shown in Figure 5-5. At birth, the infant's eye is approximately 50% of the size and weight of the adult's eye (Mann, 1964). The pupil is the part of the eye that controls the amount of light entering the eye via the *pupillary reflex*. This reflex is present at birth, but continues to develop during the first week of life (Pratt, Nelson, & Sun, 1930; Beasley, 1922; Sherman, Sherman, & Flory, 1936), although not to any great extent. Other parts of the newborn infant's eye are not sufficiently developed to permit vision similar to that of adults (Gottlieb & Krasnegor, 1985).

The *retina* is the part of the eye that transforms light into signals that are transmitted via nerve impulses along the *optic nerve* to the brain. At birth, neither the retina nor the optic nerve is fully developed. The fovea is the area at the center of the retina where visual information is focused most clearly. The fovea of the newborn infant contains fewer and less mature sensory receptors than does the fovea of an adult, so the infant sees less clearly than does an adult. In addition, the optic nerve is covered by a thin myelin sheath. Recall from our discussion of myelinization in Chapter 2 that the myeline sheath is involved in effective transmission of information in the nervous system. Thus, the newborn infant's optic nerve transmits information from the eye to the brain less effectively than does the optic nerve of an

Anatomy and Physiology

145

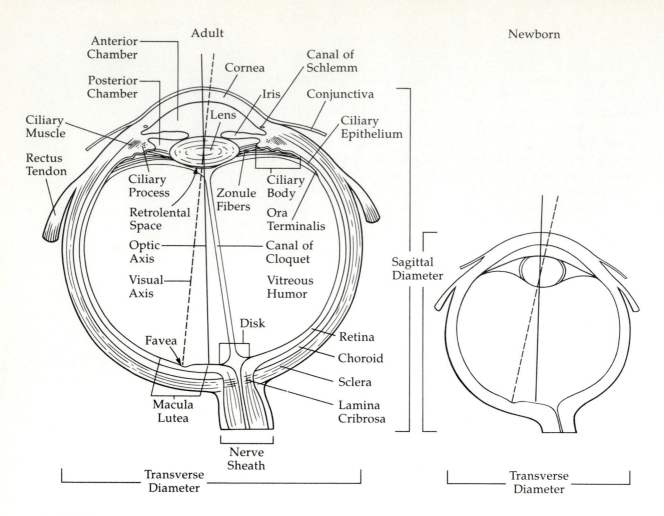

FIGURE 5-5

Differences in the physical characteristics of the infant and adult eye.

adult. The retina and fovea continue to develop until at least the 11th month of life, while the myelin sheath covering the optic nerve achieves adult thickness by the 10th week after birth (Atkinson & Braddick, 1982; Abramov, Gordon, Hendrickson, Hainline, Dobson, & LaBossiere, 1982; Banks & Salapatek, 1983). Finally, the *lens* of the eye is involved in our ability to adjust our focus on objects at various distances from us. The lens of the newborn infant's eye is more spherical than that of an adult's. As a result, the newborn cannot see as clearly as an adult at all distances, perhaps because the immature shape of the lens results in images being focused several millimeters behind the retina rather than on the surface of the retina, where images are focused by the adult lens (Gottlieb & Krasnegor, 1985).

In addition to these differences between the infant and adult eye, the part of the brain involved in visual development also undergoes development after birth (Banks & Salapatek, 1983; Conel, 1939, 1941). This part of the brain, known as the *visual cortex*, has relatively few nerve cell connections at birth. As shown in Figure 5–6, the number of nerve cell connections increases dramatically during the first 6 months following birth.

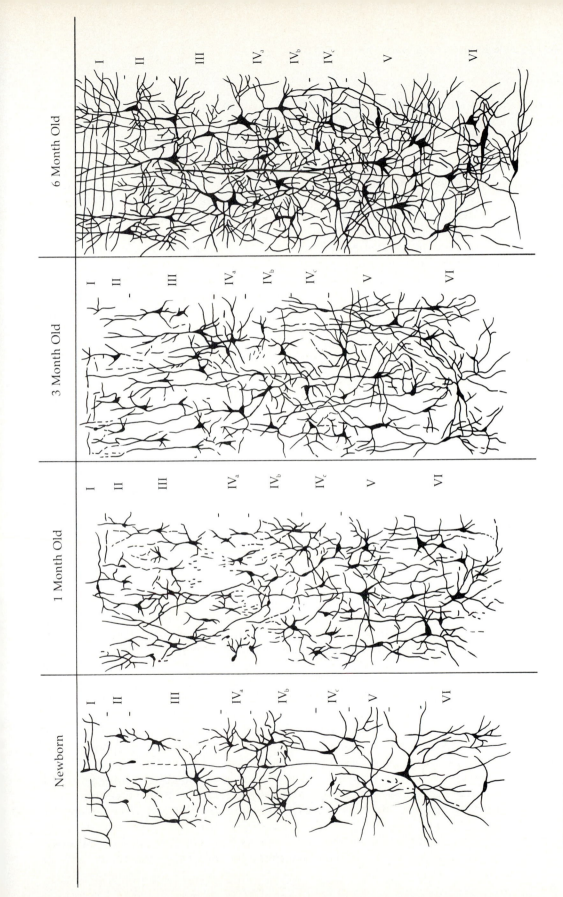

FIGURE 5-6
Illustration of development of nerve-cell connections in the visual cortex.

147

To sum up, the visual system at birth is an immature but intact and functioning system that allows the infant to see. But as we shall see, the newborn infant sees differently from the way in which an adult sees.

Visual Accommodation

When you have looked at photographs, you have probably noticed (and perhaps even been dismayed) that certain objects are clearly in focus while others are fuzzy. By virtue of their design, cameras are only able to focus on one distance at a time—objects that are at this distance are clearly represented in the photograph, but objects both closer and farther away are less clearly focused in the photograph. The human eye is similar to a camera in this regard. The lens of the eye can only focus on one viewing distance at a time. Objects at the focused distance yield clear images, while objects at other distances yield blurred images. Adults find it easy to shift their focus from one distance to another depending on what they wish to see most clearly. This ability is called *visual accommodation*.

In the last 25 years, a number of investigators have attempted to determine the visual accommodation skills of young infants (Banks, 1980; Brookman, 1980; Haynes, White, & Held, 1965). The results indicate that visual accommodation is present at birth, but not fully developed due to the immature shape of the lens. Newborns and 1-month-olds make two types of focusing errors. They overaccommodate for distant objects and underaccommodate for near objects. However, these accommodation errors probably result in fewer blurred images for infants than they would for adults because infants possess a greater *depth of focus* than do adults (Banks & Salapatek, 1983). Depth of focus refers to the distance that an object can be moved and still remain in focus without an accommodation change. So even though young infants seem to make accommodation errors when focusing on objects, the errors may not produce unfocused images. By 3 months of age, these sorts of accommodation errors have vanished; the infant's capacity for visual accommodation is now quite similar to that of adults.

Visual Acuity

Simply put, visual acuity has to do with the ability to detect differences in visual patterns, an ability that is related to visual accommodation. The ability to focus on patterns and thereby see them more clearly is necessary for detecting differences among the patterns. The finer the differences that one is able to detect, the better is one's visual acuity. One measure of visual acuity in infants has utilized infants' preferences for looking at visual patterns. If you present infants with two visual patterns and find that the infants prefer to look at one pattern rather than another, then you would infer that the infants can distinguish the two patterns. We know that newborn infants prefer to look at a patterned visual stimulus rather than at a plain one (Fantz, 1963). However, there is such a thing as too much pattern for newborns. They prefer to look at patterns with 4 squares rather than those with 144 squares (Hershenson, Munsinger, & Kessen, 1965). As their perceptual skills increase, however, infants come to prefer more complex patterns over simpler ones.

Using the fact that infants prefer to look at certain types of patterns, investigators have attempted to determine the limits of visual acuity skills in infants (Allen, 1978; Fantz, 1965; Fantz, Ordy, & Udelf, 1962). For example, Fantz (1965) found that infants preferred to look at striped rather than plain surfaces, and used this fact to chart increases in visual acuity during the first 6 months of life. The basic idea was that infants would look longer at striped patterns than plain patterns only if they could perceive the stripes. Fantz found that infants less than 1-month old could perceive $\frac{1}{8}$-inch wide stripes presented at a distance of 10 inches. By 10 months of age, infants were able to perceive stripes as narrow as $\frac{1}{64}$-inch wide. Although there is some controversy about the actual visual acuity of newborn infants (Fantz, Ordy, & Udelf, 1962; Cornell & McDonnell, 1986), it is clear that the visual acuity is present in newborn infants and increases during the first year of life (Banks & Salapatek, 1983; Banks, Stephens, & Hartmann, 1985; Cohen, DeLoache, & Strauss, 1979).

Our eyes do not remain stationary during visual perception. Our eyes move, both to inspect objects (visual scanning) and to follow the movement of objects (visual tracking). Newborn infants also employ eye movements in their visual exploration of the world (Haith, 1980). Both newborn infants and adults use eye movements called *saccades*. A saccade is a smooth, rapid eye motion that moves a visual image to the center of the field of vision, where it can be seen more clearly. The saccades of newborn infants are slower and less accurate than those of adults, but improve dramatically during the first 6 months of life (Haith 1980).

Visual Scanning and Tracking

In addition to the use of saccades to bring a visual target to the center of the visual field, infants also use eye movements to explore visual stimuli. They do not, however, scan visual stimuli in the same way that adults do. When adults explore a visual object, they scan all of the object (or at least most of it). Young infants tend to scan only part of the object. For example, Salapatek and Kessen (1966) reported that 1-month-old infants concentrate their visual scanning of geometric shapes on areas of high contrast, such as the corners of a triangle or square. Two-month-old infants scan more of the shape, perhaps because they are searching for other areas of high contrast (Banks & Salapatek, 1981), but still fail to scan the entire object. One-month-old infants also limit their scanning to the object's external boundaries, while 2-month-old infants look at both external boundaries and internal features (Bushnell, Gerry, & Burt, 1983; Leady, 1976; Salapatek, 1975). Examples of young infants' scanning behaviors are shown in Figure 5-7.

Older children develop more complex patterns of visual scanning behavior. Specifically, they begin to scan entire forms rather than parts of forms. Zaporozhets (1965) has presented data regarding the manner in which 3- to 6-year-old children scan visual forms. The developmental patterns are summarized by the graphs in Figure 5-8. Although younger children's visual scanning occasionally darts out to the form's boundaries, they generally focus on the circle in the center of the target. Older children spend progressively more time scanning the boundaries. In this experiment children were asked to look at the form for 20 seconds, during which time they were to study it so that they could recognize it at a later time. Perhaps because the older children inspected the actual shape (perimeter) of the form, they were more

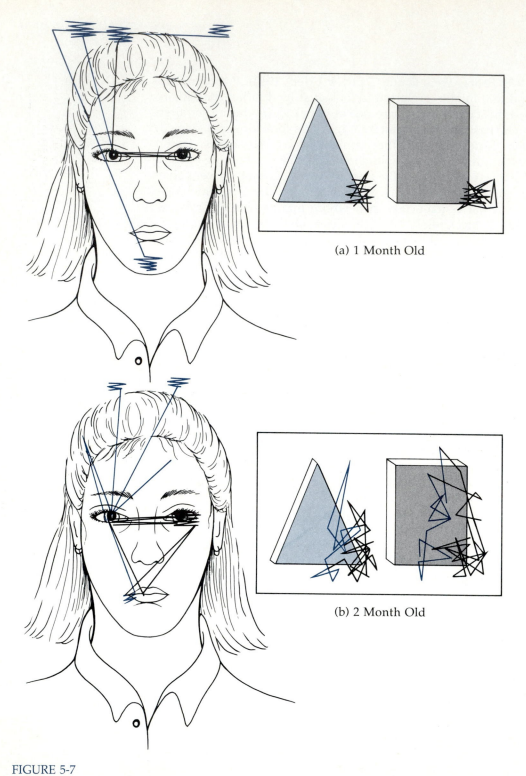

(a) 1 Month Old

(b) 2 Month Old

FIGURE 5-7

Illustration of the visual scanning of 1-month-old and 2-month-old infants for external boundaries and internal features.

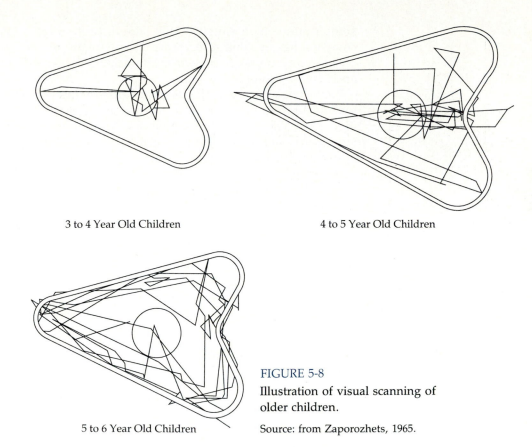

3 to 4 Year Old Children

4 to 5 Year Old Children

5 to 6 Year Old Children

FIGURE 5-8
Illustration of visual scanning of older children.

Source: from Zaporozhets, 1965.

likely to recognize it later. In contrast, the youngest children failed to recognize the figure more than half of the time and oftentimes confused it with a figure that was quite different from the original. This, then, is an example of the relation between visual attention, visual inspection, and memory.

The role of eye movements in the visual tracking of a moving object involves *smooth pursuit eye movements*. These movements are slower than saccades, and allow adults to fixate on and visually follow moving objects. Smooth pursuit eye movements are not present in newborn infants (Aslin, 1981). Newborns do visually track moving objects, but their eye movements are sporadic rather than smooth (Kremenitzer, Vaughn, Kurtzbreg, & Dowling, 1978). Two-month-old infants use smooth pursuit eye movements, but only if the object to be followed is not moving too quickly. Otherwise, they revert to sporadic eye movements. The use of smooth pursuit movements continues to improve until approximately 6 months of age, at which time it is approximately as good as that of an adult.

We have seen that newborn infants are equipped to visually explore their world, and that the mechanisms involved in visual perception mature during the first year of life. The fact that infants prefer to look at complex visual

Perception of Complex Visual Patterns

stimuli rather than simple visual stimuli (unless the visual stimulus is too complex) has enabled researchers to investigate infants' perception of complex visual patterns, in particular infants' abilities to distinguish various types and levels of complexity.

For example, Fantz (1961) demonstrated that newborn infants preferred to look at complex visual targets rather than simple visual targets, as shown in Figure 5-9. The fact that the newborns looked longer at the schematic human face than other visual patterns generated considerable interest, for it suggested that newborn infants could perceive human faces and in fact might even prefer to look at faces rather than other complex visual stimuli. Subsequent research, however, has suggested that young infants react to the number of elements in a visual target rather than to their arrangement in a face-like pattern (Haaf, Smith, & Smitely, 1983; Sherrod, 1979). If newborn infants are presented with schematic faces, such as that used by Fantz, and visual targets in which the facial elements are scrambled, as shown in Figure 5-10, infants younger than 2-months-old are just as likely to look at the

RESEARCH FOCUS 5-2

The Development of Color Perception

Two salient characteristics of visual stimuli are brightness and color. The available evidence suggests that the ability to discriminate and perceive colors is present in young infants. However, it is not clear whether they see colors in the same way adults do. Adults with normal color vision automatically interpret the information available in the visual spectrum in terms of color categories: hues of red, green, blue, yellow, white, black, and so forth. In the early studies of color perception, infants were found to discriminate colors (Peiper, 1927; Trincker & Trincker, 1955), but the colors varied in terms of brightness as well as in terms of hue. Thus, it was unclear whether the infants were able to perceive differences in color or differences in brightness.

Recent work demonstrates that young infants are able to perceive both brightness and color. By holding color constant and varying brightness, Bornstein (1976) found that 3-month-old infants can discriminate brightness differences of 5% (adults can discriminate differences of 1%). Similarly, studies that have held brightness constant and varied color have found that infants can dis-

criminate certain colors. Newborns have been found to discriminate gray from green, yellow, and red (Adams, Maurer, & Davis, 1986). At 1 month of age, infants are able to distinguish blue and gray (Maurer & Adams, 1987). By 3 months of age, infants can discriminate red, blue, green, and yellow from one another, and even seem to prefer reds and blues (Bornstein, 1975; Bornstein, Kessen, & Weiskopf, 1976).

These developments appear to be closely related to the development of the *cones* that are necessary for color vision (Nathans, 1980). Cones are the color receptors in the retina. Although there are functioning cones at birth, Pulos, Teller, and Buck (1980) have suggested that the three main types of cones (those sensitive to red, green, and blue) achieve developmental maturity between 2 and 3 months of age. Although 2-month-olds may have red and green cones, they seem to lack blue cones. Three-month-olds seem to possess all three types of functioning cones. Thus, color perception seems to depend on the development of the necessary physiological receptors more than on experience. ❧

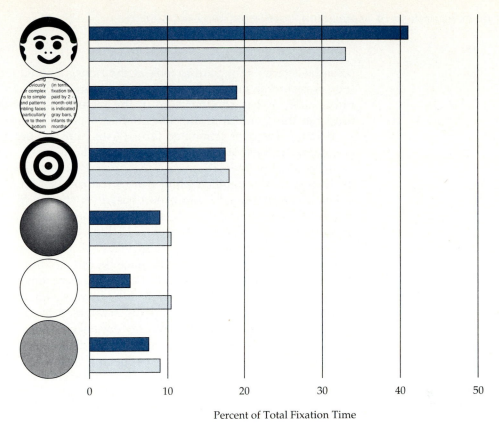

Percent of Total Fixation Time

FIGURE 5-9
Fantz's study of infants' preferences for complex stimuli.

FIGURE 5-10
Illustration of scrambled and non-scrambled
schematic faces, and infants' looking preferences.

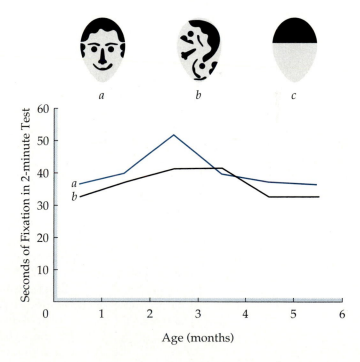

scrambled face as they are to look at the nonscrambled face. Young infants, then, seem to be more influenced by the contrast provided by facial features rather than by the configuration of the features in a human face. It is not until the third month of life that infants exhibit a consistent preference for schematic faces over scrambled faces (Aslin, 1987). Three-month-old infants also prefer to look at photographs of their mother rather than photographs of unfamiliar women (Barrera & Maurer, 1981a) and can also distinguish photographs of unfamiliar human faces (Barrera & Maurer, 1981b).

The aforementioned findings are based on studies in which infants were presented with static displays—schematic representations of faces (scrambled or nonscrambled) or photographs. In life, however, faces are not static. Infants experience faces as moving, visual stimuli, and even seem to especially like to look at the parts of the face that move (the eyes and the mouth). Perhaps static presentation of facial arrays underestimate infants' abilities to perceive faces. In the *first* hour of life, infants will follow a slow-moving schematic face but not a slow-moving scrambled face (Goren, Sarty, & Wu, 1975), suggesting that movement may enhance the newborns' ability to perceive faces. Other work has demonstrated that movement of the internal elements in a visual array increases the sensitivity of infants as young as 1 month of age to changes in the internal elements (Bushnell, 1982). Infant sensitivity to the movement of internal elements is so strong at 3 months of age that they can distinguish videotapes of actual human faces from videotapes of masks of human faces, even when both the faces and the masks have been covered with black makeup and numerous white triangles (Stucki, Kaufmann-Hayoz, & Kaufmann, 1987; see Figure 5-11 for an illustration of the stimuli).

Depth Perception

One of the most studied aspects of perception is the capacity that allows us to experience the world three-dimensionally. This capacity to perceive the dimensions of height, width, and distance is called depth perception and adds much to the richness of our experiences of the world.

The experience of depth depends on extracting information from cues that do not provide any direct three-dimensional sensation. The retina of the eye is a two-dimensional surface that can register only a two-dimensional image. Thus, the perception of depth and distance must be somehow drawn from the information that is available to the central nervous system—from the retinas, the muscles controlling the eye and its parts, and from the visual stimulus itself.

Monocular and Binocular Vision. As discussed in Research Focus 5-3, the ability to perceive depth develops during the first 6 to 8 months of life. What information do infants use in their judgments of depth? *Binocular* vision provides cues for depth because each eye in a human head receives slightly different views of the world. To illustrate this, hold your head still with both eyes open, then close your right eye, open it, and then close your left eye. The image received by the two eyes is quite similar but not identical. In adults, the information provided by different images in the two eyes is

(*a*) Mask

FIGURE 5-11

Photographs of triangle-covered faces and masks used by Stucki et al.

Source: from Stucki, Kaufmann-Hayoz, & Kaufmann, 1987.

(*b*) Face

integrated to produce depth perception. The use of binocular depth cues by infants does not appear until approximately 3 months after birth, and then gradually improves for the next few months (Field, 1977; Fox, Aslin, Shea, & Duais, 1979).

There are also a number of monocular cues available for depth perception, that is, cues that require only one eye rather than two. These cues are often used by artists to depict depth in their paintings, and so are called *pictorial depth cues*. Sensitivity to a number of pictorial depth cues seems to emerge around 7 months of age. For example, *occlusion* occurs when one object is partially hidden behind another, as when a classroom lecturer is partially hidden by a desk. The object that is hidden is farther away than is the object doing the hiding. Granrud and Yonas (1984) reported that 7-month-olds were sensitive to information provided by occlusion, but that 5-month-old infants were not.

155

RESEARCH FOCUS 5-3

The Visual Cliff

The first successful attempt to assess depth perception in human infants used an apparatus called a *visual cliff* (Gibson & Walk, 1960). The visual cliff is a table with a clear glass top divided in two equal halves by an opaque centerpiece. A pattern, usually a checkerboard, is placed under each half of the glass top. The shallow side is that on which the pattern is placed directly under the glass surface, while the deep side is that on which the pattern is placed at some distance (for example, 2 feet) below the glass surface. The essence of the visual cliff is that the shallow side appears to be safe to move onto, whereas the deep side does not—there appears to be a dropoff on the deep side. If an infant is placed on the centerpiece and ventures only to the shallow side, then Gibson and Walk assumed that the infant perceived the apparent differences in depth between the two sides. Using the visual cliff, Gibson and Walk found that 8- to 12-month-old infants consistently chose to venture onto the shallow side of the visual cliff, suggesting that the infants were capable of perceiving depth (see Figure 5-12).

The development of depth perception has been linked to its adaptive nature in the natural environment. Those animals who develop locomotor skills shortly after birth may have depth perception at earlier ages than those who learn to locomote at later ages. Possessing locomotor skills without depth perception could pose real prob-

lems for a species, since many of its infants might walk into danger (off a cliff, into a larger object, and so on). Using the visual cliff apparatus, different species of animals have been found to have very different ages of onset for depth discrimination as indicated by a tendency to prefer the shallow side. Table 5-1 presents some representative findings.

The argument that depth perception is present by the time organisms become capable of independent movement in their environment does not entail that the organisms will always prefer the shallow side of the visual cliff. Using the visual cliff apparatus, Richards and Rader (1981) tested infants who were either early crawlers (began crawling before $6\frac{1}{2}$ months of age) or later crawlers (began crawling after $6\frac{1}{2}$ months of age). All of the infants had been crawling for about 2 months when they were tested, and so the amount of locomotor experience was not a factor. Curiously, the early crawlers did not show a preference for the shallow side, whereas the later crawlers did. Richards and Rader suggested that the early crawlers were not yet able to perceive depth and so relied on tactile stimulation (the feeling of a solid surface) to guide their crawling while the later crawlers had the capacity for depth perception and so relied on visual stimulation. This interpretation has been challenged by Berthenthal, Campos, and Barrett (1984). They reported that regardless of the age at which in-

TABLE 5-1

The ages at which various species have demonstrated depth perception on the visual cliff

Species	Age of Initial Preference for Shallow Side of Visual Cliff
cat	3–4 weeks
chicken	1 day
goat	1 day
rat	3–4 weeks
human infant	6–10 months

FIGURE 5-12

Photograph of infant on the visual cliff.

fants began to crawl, the amount of crawling experience influenced performance on the visual cliff. Infants with 11 days of crawling experience did not show a clear preference for the shallow side, but infants with 41 days of crawling experience did exhibit a preference for the shallow side. At present, then, it is unclear whether maturation of the depth perception system or experience with crawling is the main determinant of successful performance (choosing the shallow side) on the visual cliff.

Although the visual cliff apparatus proved to be a pioneering technique in the study of depth perception, it is clearly limited in its application. Infants must be able to crawl in order for the technique to be effective. They must also have a preference for the shallow side—infants may perceive depth but nonetheless crawl onto the deep side (as in the case of the early crawlers studied by Richards and Rader). Investigators wanting to assess depth perception in younger, noncrawling infants must turn to other measures of depth perception.

One technique involves measures of heart rate as an index of perception. Children and adults respond differently to interesting and frightening events in terms of their heart rates: interesting events tend to produce reduced heart rates (cardiac deceleration), while frightening, alarming, or startling events produce increased heart rates (cardiac acceleration). In one study that used this technique, Campos, Langer & Krowitz (1970) placed infants either 2 or 9 months of age face down on the deep or shallow side of the visual cliff. The heart rate of younger infants indicated that they perceived the greater depth on one side and that it interested them—their heart rates decreased. For older infants, the deep side was perceived clearly, but, since their heart rates increased, it was assigned a different meaning, indicating alarm. Pick (1976) suggested that these results mean that 2-month-old infants are able to perceive the greater depth on one side, but the interpretation of this perception differs for 2-month-olds and 9-month-olds. Presumably, the meaning that older infants come to assign to the perception of vertical depth is the possibility of falling, a possibility that they view with frightened anticipation.

Other monocular cues are *texture gradients* and *linear perspective*. Texture gradients refer to the fact that the texture of near surfaces appears to be more finely grained than does the texture of far surfaces. Linear perspective concerns the fact that if two parallel lines (such as a railroad track) appear to be converging, the closer together the lines appear to be, the farther away that part of the surface is. Seven-month-old infants are sensitive to texture gradients and linear perspective, but younger infants are not (Yonas, Granrud, Atterberry, & Hanson, 1986).

Another monocular cue involves movement, and so is not a pictorial cue. Imagine that you are driving your car on a freeway and notice that a car is rapidly gaining on you. The size of the retinal image of the car is expanding, and you interpret that information to mean that the car is getting closer. Conversely, if the car were getting farther behind you, the size of the retinal image would shrink. Expansion of the retinal image of a moving object means that the object is approaching, while shrinkage of the size of the retinal image means that the object is receding in distance. This cue is used in motion pictures to provide the illusion of objects moving in three-dimensional space, the speed at which the size of the image changes influencing our decisions about how fast the object is approaching or receding. The faster the image changes, the faster the approach (or recession). In research on depth perception, the expansion of the size of the retinal image is known as "looming."

Two early studies of object looming suggested early sensitivity to such information. Bower, Broughton and Moore (1971) investigated the reaction of infants less than 3 weeks of age to the approach of real objects. They reported that the infants engaged in defensive reactions to the approaching objects—their eyes got wider, they moved their heads away from the object, and they moved their hands as if they were attempting to block the object. In a related study, Ball and Tronick (1971) tested the reaction of 4-week-old infants to the expansion of an image on a movie screen. They found that infants reacted defensively to symmetrical optical expansion (which signifies that the expanding object is approaching the looker), but did not react defensively to asymmetrical optical expansion (which signifies that the approaching object will pass the looker without hitting her).

The results of these two studies suggested that young infants could perceive both the approach of an object and the likelihood that the approaching object would hit or miss them. Subsequent research has cast a shadow on these results (Yonas, Cleaves, & Pettersen, 1978; Yonas, Pettersen, & Lockman, 1979). Yonas et al. (1978) presented 1- to 9-month-old infants with three types of optical information: symmetrical expansion, asymmetrical expansion, and a rising contour or a nonexpanding shape (which does not indicate approach). Yonas et al. did not find consistent differences in the infants' reactions to symmetrical expansion and the rising contour until about 4 months of age. This discrepancy illustrates a key difficulty with using natural reactions to stimuli as a research technique with very young infants. The behaviors that indicate defensive reactions are often rather subtle in young infants, leaving too much interpretation to the investigator. Behavior that one investigator counts as defensive might be viewed differently by another investigator. Nonetheless, it seems clear that infants' reactions to looming objects are present by 4 months of age. In fact, by this age infants have learned to respond to the speed of the looming object. Defensive reactions by 4-month-olds do not occur if the object appears to be slowing down, but do occur if the object maintains a constant speed (Yonas, Pettersen, Lockman, & Eisenberg, 1980).

Size Constancy

The research described thus far has been concerned with infants' ability to perceive depth, but tells us little about infants' *size constancy*. When the same object is seen at different distances, it produces differently sized images on the retina. The actual size of the object remains the same, but the size of the retinal image it produces depends on its distance. The closer the object is, the larger the size of the retinal image. Size constancy is the ability to recognize the actual size of an object despite changes in the size of the retinal image. Size constancy depends on depth perception—an observer must be able to relate distance to retinal image size.

However, it is possible to have depth perception but not size constancy. Conceivably, one could perceive distance but not relate it to the size of the retinal image. McKenzie, Tootell, and Day (1980) studied size constancy in infants by habituating them to an object at a fixed distance. They then exposed the infants to the same object at a different distance, so that the object now casts a differently sized retinal image. McKenzie et al. also showed the infants a differently sized object at a distance that would produce the same sized retinal image as had the object to which the infants had habituated. If the infants possess size constancy, they should respond to the object that was actually the same size as the habituated object, even though the two objects cast differently sized retinal images. If the infants did not possess size constancy, they should respond on the basis of retinal image size rather than actual size. McKenzie et al. found that some infants as young as 4-months-old had size constancy, although size constancy was much more likely to be found in 6- to 8-month-old infants.

Shape Constancy

Shape constancy is similar to size constancy in that it involves the ability to recognize that an object has not actually changed despite changes in the retinal image. Shape constancy is the ability to recognize that objects retain their shape despite changes in the shape of the retinal image that occur when the orientation of the object changes. Newborn infants have been found to possess shape constancy (Slater & Morison, 1985), but not size constancy (as discussed above), suggesting that shape constancy is innate whereas size constancy requires experience. If so, shape constancy is likely to play a more important role than size constancy in young infants' categorization of objects. And in fact, young infants seem to be more sensitive to shape information than size information in their recognition and categorization of objects (see Chapter 7).

The Development of Relations Among the Perceptual Systems

Up to this point, we have considered the development of isolated perceptual systems: the auditory system, the haptic system, the taste–smell system(s), and the visual system. Perceptual systems, however, rarely operate in isolation in our perception of the world. The type and magnitude of a sound affects our hypotheses about the nature and size of the object that produced the sound. Certain objects look as if they would feel hard or soft. Some foods look delicious, while others look less appetizing. Although the study of isolated perceptual systems is very useful in terms of increasing our understanding of the development of each perceptual system, an important aspect of perceptual development concerns the development of relations among the perceptual systems. Investigators who have addressed this problem have been concerned with determining whether perceptual relations are innate or require experience to emerge.

Auditory–Visual Relationships

In addition to perceiving sounds and the differences among them, adults are also able to locate sounds in space—whether they come from straight ahead, from the left, from the right, from the rear, and so on. As a result, adults often turn their heads in the direction of a sound source in order to see what produced the sound. Young infants also seem to possess the ability to locate sounds in space. Wertheimer (1961) reported that a 2-minute-old infant looked in the direction of clicking sounds that were produced in the delivery room. Although this finding is based on the behavior of one infant, subsequent research has demonstrated that infants are able to localize sounds during the first week of life (Algeria & Noirot, 1978; Clifton, Morrongiello, Kulig, & Dowd, 1981; Mendelson & Haith, 1976; Muir & Field, 1978).

These results demonstrate that young infants look in the direction of sound, but it is unclear whether the infants actually expect to see something where they look. Young infants may be predisposed to look in the direction of a sound without expecting to see anything or they may expect to see the object that produces the sound. Although we are unable to resolve this issue at present, there is a growing body of evidence that demonstrates specific relations between visual and auditory stimuli in slightly older infants. Horowitz (1974) exposed 1- to 3-month-old infants to a visual stimuli accompanied by a continuous stream of sound. After the infants had habituated to the stimulus, the sound was changed. The infants exhibited renewed interest in the visual stimulus, even though it had not changed. Apparently, the change in the sound led the infants to search for a change in the visual stimulus. If so, 1- to 3-month-old infants may expect changes in sounds to correspond to changes in visual stimuli.

Other evidence for auditory–visual relations in infancy comes from a series of studies involving motion picture films depicting a variety of events (for example, peek-a-boo, pat-a-cake, bouncing puppets). In these studies, two motion picture films of different events were presented side-by-side on a small screen in front of the infant. A sound track that corresponded to *one* of the movies was played along with the two films. Under these conditions, 4-month-old infants have been found to consistently look at the motion picture that corresponded with the sound track (Bahrick, 1983; Bahrick, Walker, & Neisser, 1981; Spelke, 1976, 1979; Walker, 1982). Four-month-old infants, then, seem to be able to relate auditory information to visual information.

Auditory–Haptic Relationships

We have seen that young infants relate visual and auditory information. Do they also relate auditory and haptic information? Wishart, Bower, and Dunkeld (1978) exposed infants to a noise-making toy in the dark and assessed whether the infants reached toward the object even though they could not see it. Infants from 1 to 5 months of age reached toward the object, such behavior peaking at 5 months of age and then declining. Infants 5 months of age and younger seemed to expect to grab (or at least touch) the object that produced the sound. It is unclear why older infants are less likely to reach toward the sound, but it may simply be that they have learned not to grab things that they cannot see. Some things are hot, bite, or sting, and older infants may have developed caution in regard to reaching for mysterious objects, particularly ones in the dark.

Visual–Haptic Relationships

Are infants able to integrate visual and haptic information? In a series of controversial studies, Bower (1971, 1972; Bower, Broughton, & Moore, 1970) exposed young infants to a phantom object. The phantom object was an illusion produced by the apparatus shown in Figure 5-13. The infants could "see" the object even though it was not present. When infants reached for

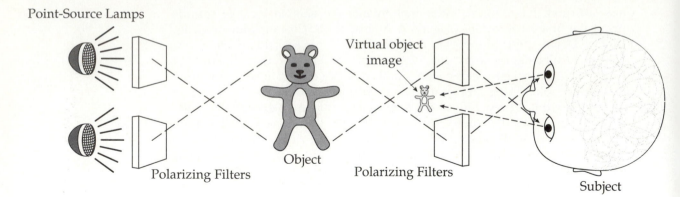

Point-Source Lamps

Virtual object image

Object

Polarizing Filters

Polarizing Filters

Subject

FIGURE 5-13

Illustration of the virtual object experiment. Infants see an illusion (a "phantom object"). They act surprised when they are not able to touch the illusion, but not when they are able to touch the real object.

this object, they acted surprised that they were not able to touch it. However, when they reached for a real object, they were not surprised that they could touch it. Bower found these sorts of responses in children as young as 1 week of age. The finding that infants were surprised when they tried to "grab" the phantom object but not surprised when they tried to grab a real object suggested that the infants expected visual stimuli to have haptic consequences. At this point, you may remember that infants reacted defensively to the visual stimulus of an approaching object, these reactions also supporting the notion that infants react to certain types of visual stimuli as if they have haptic properties. However, as was the case for the looming studies, the phantom object studies are controversial in that subsequent investigations have failed to replicate the infant reaching and surprise reactions reported by Bower and his colleagues for young infants (Dodwell, Muir, & Di Franco, 1976; Ruff & Halton, 1977).

In another study of visual–haptic integration, Meltzhoff and Borton (1979) allowed 1-month-old infants to explore by mouth one of two objects—a smooth object or an object with nubs. The infants were then shown both objects, and looked longer at the one they had mouthed than at the one they had not. These results suggest that 1-month-olds can relate haptic information with visual information, but the results must be interpreted with caution due to a subsequent failure to replicate the results (Baker, Brown, & Gotfried, 1982). However, Gibson and Walker (1984) reported results similar to those of Meltzhoff and Borton. Additional work is clearly needed to clarify the ages at which infants begin to relate types of haptic and visual information.

Summary

Perception depends on a number of components. There must be a physical stimulus (for example, light) in the external world. A sensory organ (for example, an eye) must respond to the physical stimulus in order to produce a sensation. The sensation is interpreted by the central nervous system (primarily the brain) to yield a perception. The study of perceptual development is concerned with the development of the physiological systems (the sensory organs and the central nervous system) and the cognitive abilities necessary to meaningfully interpret information available in the external world.

One hundred years ago, William James (1890) suggested that the world of the newborn infant was a "blooming, buzzing confusion." The notion that newborn infants are poorly equipped to perceive and organize information available in the world held sway for more than 70 years, primarily due to the difficulty of testing perceptual capabilities in young infants. Beginning in the 1960s, however, innovative research by a number of researchers began to unveil the mysterious world of infant perception. Subsequent work has added greatly to our understanding of the development of perception.

The development of the sensory organs and central nervous system begins long before birth (see the discussion of prenatal development in Chapter 2). At birth, the physiological components of the auditory, haptic, taste–smell, and visual systems are functional. Although the physiological components continue to mature throughout the first year of life (particularly for the visual system), the systems are sufficiently developed at birth to yield rudimentary perceptions.

Newborn infants have been shown to possess auditory perception, haptic perception, taste and smell perception, and visual perception. Each of these perceptual systems continues to mature after birth. However, more is known about the development of the auditory and visual systems than the other systems.

Auditory perception may exist prior to birth. At 26 weeks after conception, fetuses react to auditory stimulation. At present, it is unclear whether the fetus actually hears the sound or feels the vibrations produced as the sound passes through the mother's body. However, findings that newborn infants prefer to listen to their mother's voice rather than another woman's voice, prefer to listen to stories previously read aloud by their mothers during pregnancy rather than other stories, and prefer to listen to the language spoken by their mother rather than a foreign language all suggest that fetuses can hear in the womb. These findings also suggest that even though auditory perception is present at birth, experience in the womb may shape the newborn's listening preferences.

An important aspect of auditory perception concerns the discrimination of human speech sounds. Infants as young as 1 month of age have been found to discriminate speech sounds. In fact, infants perceive speech sounds in much the same way as adults, in terms of *classes* of sounds rather than solely in terms of absolute physical differences. The early appearance of this ability, called categorical perception, suggests that the general auditory processing skills that characterize adult speech perception may be innate. Experience with sounds used in human speech is nonetheless important, since 1-year-old infants can more readily discriminate sounds from the language spoken in their society than sounds from languages of other societies.

Although the visual system is functional at birth, both the eye and the visual cortex continue to mature during the first year of life. As might be expected, visual perception also changes as the physiological components associated with it change. For example, the ability to perceive and discriminate colors follows a particular developmental path. Newborn infants can discriminate gray from green, yellow, and red. One-month-old infants can also discriminate gray from blue. Three-month-old infants can discriminate red, blue, green, and yellow from one another. They even seem to prefer reds and blues to other colors. This developmental pattern is related to the development of the cones in the eye that are necessary for color vision.

Visual acuity has to do with the ability to perceive differences in visual patterns. Visual acuity is present in the newborn child, but improves throughout the first 6 months of life. When young infants look at a visual stimulus, they do not scan the entire stimulus. Newborn infants typically look at only one part of the stimulus, usually a part with high contrast. Older infants also look at areas of high contrast, but tend to look at all the areas of high contrast rather than only part of it.

Infants also possess the ability to relate information from two senses. Newborn infants are able to localize sounds in space, as evidenced by their looking in the direction of the heard sound. Young infants also seem to expect a change in an auditory stimulus to correspond with a change in a visual stimulus. Infants may also expect to be able to touch the source of a sound, although the data are less clear on this point. Similarly, infants may expect to be able to touch an object that they see, but the age at which this expectation first appears is controversial.

Perceptual development depends both on the maturation of the sensory organs and the central nervous system, and on experience. The fact that the newborn infant possesses a variety of perceptual skills demonstrates that these skills do not depend on experience. The newborn infant's perceptual skills and preferences (for certain tastes, certain smells, and areas of high contrast in visual scanning) seem to be innately specified. Nonetheless, experience can influence preferences, even if the experience occurs in the womb as seems to be the case for auditory preferences for the mother's voice and language. Experience may also be involved in the development, refinement, and consolidation of other perceptual skills, such as size constancy, visual scanning, and the ability to integrate information from multiple perceptual systems. However, the sensory organs and the central nervous system also mature during the months in which infants perfect their perceptual skills. Thus, it is difficult to determine if experience or maturation of physiological systems results in perceptual development after birth. Most likely, perceptual development results from a combination of experience and maturation.

Finally, this chapter has focused on perceptual development in infancy. The reason for this is straightforward. The basics of perceptual development are completed during infancy. Nonetheless, we urge you to remember that perception is involved in all human endeavors and may be directly implicated in developmental phenomenon as diverse as mother–infant bonding and language development.

Suggested Readings

Bower, T. (1977). *The perceptual world of the child.* Cambridge, MA: Harvard University Press.

Goldstein, E. (1984). *Sensation and perception,* 2nd ed. Belmont, CA: Wadsworth.

Gregory, R. (1966). *Eye and brain.* Hampshire, England. BAS Printers.

Salapatek, P., & Cohen, L. (1987). *Handbook of infant perception, Vol. 1, From sensation to perception.* New York: Academic Press.

Sekular, R., & Blake, R. (1985). *Perception.* New York: Random House.

Language Development

Introduction

Between the time of their birth and their entry into the formal educational system at the age of 5 or 6 years, children accomplish a feat of truly monumental proportions: They acquire the capability to speak and comprehend the language of their speech community. Language is an important part of human life and influences both cognitive and social development. Regardless of cultural differences and differences among the languages to be learned, all normal children acquire their first language with relative ease, leaving most casual observers with the impression that the acquisition of language is a relatively simple task for children. Although it is true that all normal children find language acquisition a natural and spontaneous activity, it is nonetheless a remarkable achievement, one that has amazed and puzzled scholars of language and language acquisition for some time.

In this chapter, we will consider the characteristics of language acquisition and possible explanations for these characteristics. Although the nature–nurture controversy is evident in explanations of many diverse developmental phenomena, the debate between nativists and nurturists is sometimes extreme in explanations of language development. As we will see, all accounts of language acquisition are shaped by assumptions about the nature of human language. For example, if people believe that human language consists of learned associations among words (such as *the* and *boy*), then their account of language development will rest on attempts to explain how children learn such associations. However, if people assume that human language depends on knowledge of abstract classes of words (such as *noun* or *agent*), then their hypotheses about language acquisition will attempt to explain how children learn such abstract classes. Given the importance of assumptions about the nature of language for theories of language acquisition, we will first consider the characteristics of human language.

What Is Human Language?

Human language is primarily a communication system, that is, a means for speakers of a language to communicate facts, opinions, and feelings to other speakers of the language. Communication among its members is not unique to the human species, for species as diverse as bees, lions, and dolphins have been found to possess communication systems. However, to date, none of the communication systems of other species have been found to possess all of the characteristics of human language. Human language appears to be the most complex, diverse, and efficient means of communication known to any species on earth.

Although there is considerable disagreement concerning the precise characteristics of human language, the following definition is one with which most scholars of human language would agree. *Human language is a symbolic, rule-governed system that is both abstract and productive, a system that enables its speakers to produce and comprehend a wide range of utterances.*

Language is a symbolic system in that it involves the use of sounds and combinations of sounds to represent meaning. The sounds and combinations of sounds in a given language are *symbols,* that is, they refer to objects and ideas. The symbols of language are conventional but arbitrary. They are conventional in that the speakers of a language use the same sound or combination of sounds to refer to a given object, class of objects, or idea. For example, speakers of English use the term *dog* to refer to the wide variety of mammals that constitute man's best friend. The symbols are arbitrary in that there is no necessary relation between sounds and their meanings. Consider the word *dog* once again. There is no reason that this sound pattern must refer to the particular class of animals that it does. Speakers of English could just as easily refer to what we call dogs as *morts* or *gatels.* Indeed, it comes as no surprise that different languages use different sound combinations to refer to the same meaning; the English *dog* is *hund* in German, *perro* in Spanish, and *chien* in French.

Language is a rule-governed system, meaning that each human language is constrained by a set of rules that reflects the regularities of the language. For example, in English, words such as *the* and *a* must precede the noun to which they refer: *the boy ate a hot dog* is correct, but *boy the ate hot dog a* is not. The rule system is abstract because it goes beyond the concrete association of individual sounds and words and instead involves the manipulation of abstract classes of words. Thus, rather than saying that *the* must precede *boy,* we may state that articles (the abstract class of words containing words such as *the* and *a*) must precede nouns (the class of words containing words such as *boy*). These abstract classes and the rules that manipulate them deal with the sounds, the words, the combination of words to produce sentences, and the meanings expressed by a language. All of this makes possible perhaps the most important characteristic of human language, its productivity.

Human language is productive in the sense that a finite number of linguistic units (sounds, words, and the abstract classes that contain words) and a finite number of rules are capable of yielding an infinite number of grammatical combinations of words. The idea of an infinite number of utterances is difficult to comprehend, and the reader may be wondering why the capability to produce an infinite number of sentences is such an important aspect of human language. The productivity of language is important not because a given speaker will produce an infinite number of sentences, for this is impossible for mortal speakers. If a speaker of English were to produce a different sentence every second for 100 years, he would have produced 3,215,760,000 different sentences. This is certainly a large number of sentences, but still far from an infinite number. Even though no speaker of any

169

human language will ever produce all of the possible sentences in the language, the capability to do so is important. The productivity inherent in all human languages permits the construction and understanding of *novel* sentences. Speakers of human language are not limited to producing sentences that they have heard before, but may instead produce utterances that they have never heard. They are also capable of understanding sentences that they have never heard before. The ability to produce and comprehend novel combinations of words makes it possible to communicate a wide variety of information. Humans are capable of communicating facts, opinions, and emotions, and may also refer to past, present, and future events. Humans also may communicate fantasy, hypothetical, and possible events. The potential productivity of language and the richness of the human mind combine to make possible the communication of a very broad array of topics. This capability for communicative diversity makes human language the unique communicative system that it is.

The Development of the Phonological System

One of the first tasks facing the young child learning language is that of determining which sounds are important for the language to be acquired. *Phonology* is the aspect of language that is concerned with the perception and production of sounds.

Speech Perception

Deciphering the sounds of the language they hear is a formidable problem, for children are exposed to an undifferentiated series of speech sounds, called a *speech stream*. Children must separate the speech stream into individual sounds and sound combinations in order to learn the phonemes of their language. The following example (from Slobin, 1979) illustrates the complexity of the task facing young children. Consider the following English sentence, written without any word boundaries: "Wheredidyougowithgrandpa." Using your mastery of English and reading, you most likely interpreted this uninterrupted string with ease. Remember that infants are faced with this task at a time when they do not possess any knowledge of language and its sounds. To better understand the difficulty that this causes, consider the following sentence: "dedenlenereyegittinsen."

This is the Turkish equivalent of the English example given above. Unless you are a Turkish speaker, even learning the meaning is of little help in interpreting the string of sounds. The Turkish string is segmented in the following manner: dede-|n-|le|/|ne-|re-|ye|/|git-|t-|in|/|sen.

Despite the inherent difficulty of the task, young children seem to be able to divide up parts of the speech stream at a very early age, before they have had much experience with the speech sounds. The task of segmenting speech may be made easier by the infant's willingness to listen to human speech. Researchers have found that human infants prefer to listen to human speech rather than to other sounds from the environment (Butterfield & Siperstein, 1974; Gibson & Spelke, 1983; Hutt, Hutt, Leonard, Benuth, & Muntjewerff, 1968). Butterfield and Siperstein (1974) found that infants less than 1-week-old preferred to listen to music with accompanying human voices than to music alone. The findings by Hutt et al. support those of Butterfield and Siperstein. In the Hutt et al. study, infants less than 10-days-old showed a preference for sound frequencies that corresponded to those of human speech. The newborn infant's preference for human speech sounds may be due to the fetus hearing the mother's voice (see Chapter 5). Regardless, the infant's sensitivity to human speech undoubtedly facilitates language acquisition and also enhances adult–infant social interaction. For example, the mother's voice is more effective than other sounds at soothing an upset infant (Menyuk, 1971) and is also more likely than other sounds to cause the infant to smile and vocalize (Wolff, 1969).

As discussed in Chapter 5, young infants are also capable of categorical perception, that is, classifying individual sounds as phonemes. Infants have the capability to learn to discriminate the phonemes of any human language, a capacity that diminishes as they learn the phonemic system of their language during the first year of life.

Young infants, then, have impressive speech perception abilities. They can discriminate and seem to prefer speech sounds to nonspeech sounds. They can discriminate some phonemes in the first months of life; the perception of other phonemes depends on the human speech they hear during the first year of life. Experience with human speech also leads infants to discriminate other important aspects of human speech. For example, by the age of 8 months, infants are able to distinguish rising intonation (used to indicate a question) and falling intonation (used to indicate a declarative statement; Kaplan, 1969).

Production of Speech Sounds

Young infants' ability to perceive speech sounds precedes their ability to purposely produce speech sounds. This developmental lag reflects the difficulty of learning to control the complex motor activity of the muscles and organs involved in intentionally producing speech sounds (McCarthy, 1954).

When a human being is not speaking, air flows freely from the lungs, up the windpipe, past the tongue, and out the mouth or nose. When speaking, however, the airflow is impeded in various ways. As shown in Figure 6-1, once air leaves the lungs it travels up the windpipe, where it passes the *larynx*, which contains the *vocal cords*. The expelled air continues to flow through the oral and nasal cavities, which comprise the vocal tract. Vowels and consonants, the two general classes of speech sounds found in all human languages, are formed in different ways. One way that vowels are produced involves the movement of the lips and tongue to change the size and shape of the oral cavity. For example, compare the location of your lips when you produce an [o] sound and an [e] sound. Vowels can also be produced by

171

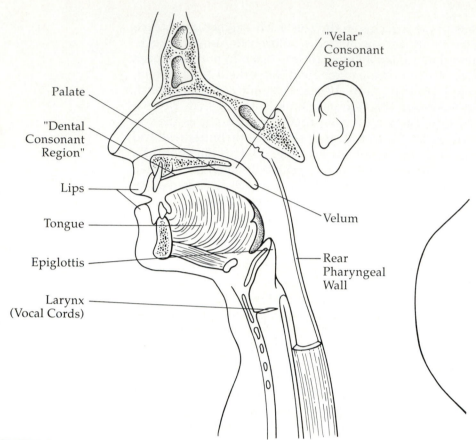

FIGURE 6-1

The physical components involved in speech production.

impeding the air flow through the vocal cords. For example, compare what happens when you produce an [*i*] sound and an [*a*] sound. These sounds are produced by different activities in the vocal cords, not by changes in the location of the tongue and lips.

Consonants are produced by various obstructions in the air flow. The air flow can be completely blocked, which results in *stop* consonants. For example, the consonant [*p*] is produced by putting the two lips together and stopping the airflow. Other consonants, called *fricatives*, are produced by partially blocking the air flow. An example of a fricative consonant is [*s*].

Producing sounds, then, involves considerable control of the vocal cords, mouth, tongue, and lips. Not surprisingly, infants' early vocalizations reflect a lack of control over these aspects of the vocal system. The vocalizations of infants from different cultures seem to develop in much the same way, suggesting that this developmental sequence is strongly influenced by hereditary factors. The course of infant vocalizations seems to follow an invarient sequence of four stages (Kaplan & Kaplan, 1971). However, the transition from stage to stage may be abrupt or gradual, and the age at which each stage first appears varies from child to child (Dale, 1976). The four stages are as follows:

Stage 1: Crying (birth–2 months).   The first month of life yields but one type of infant vocalization—crying. During this period, most infants produce more than one type of cry, suggesting that different cries may mean different things. However, parents are not able to discriminate their infant's cry types if the cries are tape recorded and played to the parents in the absence of an external context (Muller, Hollien, & Murry, 1974). Even if infants are attempting to communicate with their cries, parents are more likely to respond to external context (for example, a wet diaper) than to the type of cry itself.

During the second month of life, different infant cries may communicate different information to parents. Ricks (1972) reported that parents could discriminate the cries of 1- to 2-month-old infants, and that certain cries seemed to convey certain meanings (such as discomfort or hunger). It is unlikely, however, that infants intend to communicate with their cries.

Stage 2: Other Vocalizations and Cooing (1–5 months).   During this period, infants develop a greater variety of cries (which is usually not a source of great joy to parents). Infants also begin to produce a variety of other sounds, combine sounds with one another, and seem to take great joy in repeating sounds (Piaget, 1952, 1962; Wolff, 1969). One sound to emerge in this period, typically by the end of the second month of life, is the *coo*. Cooing, which frequently utilizes the [*u*] sound and typically involves combinations of sounds, is generally interpreted as joyful on the infants' part (perhaps because the infant already enjoys playing with sounds) and so parents reinforce cooing in a different way than crying. The parent–infant interactions following infant cooing are more likely to have a pleasant overtone than are parent–infant interactions following infant crying. In fact, parents often coo back at their child, who may coo back at the parent, and so on. (Parents rarely cry in response to an infant's cry). The reciprocal cooing between infant and parent may help the infant to learn that communication involves taking turns, and this is certainly important in regard to subsequent infant vocalizations. Infants in institutions that provide little infant–adult interaction do not produce many vocalizations and may not even cry (Bowlby, 1951; Spitz, 1965).

Stage 3: Babbling (4–12 months).   As they gain control over their tongue and mouth, infants begin to produce more types of sound combinations. Although some of these combinations sound like words, there is no evidence that infants actually attach meaning to their babbling combinations. Rather than expressing meaning, infants seem to use babbling to experiment with sounds. Jespersen (1922) suggested that infants produce virtually all human speech sounds during the babbling period, but it is now known that this is not true. Nonetheless, babbling is a universal phenomenon that seems to be genetically determined. Infants tend to babble during the same age period

173

An 8-month-old infant communicating to an observer.

and produce a similar range of sounds during early babbling (Atkinson, McWhinney, & Stoel, 1962; Nakazima, 1962). Although some deaf children do not babble (Oller & Eilers, 1988), many deaf children do babble, as do hearing infants of deaf parents (who cannot respond to their infants' sounds, although they certainly do interact with their infants; Lennenberg, Rebelsky & Nichols, 1965; Stoel-Gammon & Otomo, 1986). These results demonstrate that neither hearing human speech nor having others respond to infants' vocalizations are necessary for babbling to occur. Nonetheless, the continuation of babbling beyond the sixth or seventh month of life is rare in deaf infants, suggesting that hearing speech sounds plays a role in later babbling.

Weir (1966) investigated the babbling of infants exposed to various languages. Infants exposed to a tonal language such as Chinese tended to produce monosyllabic utterances exhibiting tonal variation in their later babbling. Infants exposed to a nontonal language such as English tended to produce multisyllabic utterances in their later babbling, but little tonal variation. These results support the notion of *babbling drift,* a hypothesis that infants restrict their later babbling to the sounds that occur in the language they hear. More recent research has questioned the existence of babbling drift, suggesting that later babbling reflects the intonation patterns (for example, English uses intonation to distinguish statements and questions) but not the sounds, of the language the infant hears (Boysson-Bardies, de Sagart, & Durand, 1984; Thevenin, Eilers, Oller, and Lavoie, 1985).

Stage 4: Patterned Speech (12 months on).   The onset of this stage is characterized by a decrease in babbling and the beginning of producing true words.

TABLE 6-1
Children's early words for mother and father in 10 languages

Language	Word for Mother	Word for Father
English	Mama	Dada
German	Mama	Papa
Hebrew	Eema	Aba
Hungarian	Anya	Apa
Navajo	Ama	Ataa
Northern Chinese	Mama	Baba
Russian	Mama	Papa
Spanish	Mama	Papa
Southern Chinese	Umma	Baba
Taiwanese	Amma	Aba

Regardless of the language they hear, the first words produced by infants sound alike. The words begin with consonants, end with vowels, and often involve sound repetition, as in *mama* and *dada*. Many of the early words used to refer to the mother begin with the nasal consonants [m] or [n], as shown in Table 6-1. Jakobson (1968) reported that approximately 55% of the words used to refer to the mother in human languages used the [m] or [n] sounds, but that fewer than 15% of the words used to refer to father used these sounds. This difference might reflect the historical significance of the mother in feeding the infant. While nursing, the infant can produce consonants such as [m] or [n], which may have led to such sounds being incorporated into the words used to refer to the person associated with feeding. Although this is speculative, it illustates the possible ways in which experience may influence the historical evolution of words in a language.

Adult speakers can accurately produce 12–30 sounds per second (approximately 4–10 words, Lieberman, 1984), an ability that takes children years to master. Anyone who has listened to young children speak realizes that they have difficulty pronouncing words. However, some words are easier to pronounce than others. Whenever possible, young children avoid saying words they have difficulty pronouncing (Ingram, 1986; Macken & Ferguson, 1983). Although different children experience different difficulties with the production of sounds, individual children typically have the same problem again and again (Ferguson, 1989). For example, one 3-year-old child consistently

TABLE 6-2
Early milestones of language development

What Child Produces	Beginning Age
Cries	Birth
Cooing	6 weeks
Babbling	6 months
One-word utterances	12 months
Two-word utterances	18 months

175

deleted the [s] sound from the beginnings of words when it was followed by a consonant sound. Thus, *I smell a skunk* was produced as *I mell a kunk*. However, this same child consistently chose the correct form (e.g., *skunk*) in a comprehension task and recognized that his form was the immature form (Kuczaj, 1983). This is illustrated in the following comment that the child made during the comprehension task when asked about the difference between *neeze* (his form) and *sneeze*. "You talk like him. You say *neeze* (sneeze). I can't say *neeze* like you. I say *neeze*. I'll say *neeze* like you when I get big" (Kuczaj, 1983, p. 72).

This finding is consistent with those of other investigators. Young children can perceive phonological distinctions that they cannot produce and so often recognize the difference between their own immature word pronunciations and those of the adults around them (Berko & Brown, 1960; Smith, 1973; Locke, 1979). Moreover, children may be producing phonological distinctions that adults do not recognize. For example, Kornfeld (1971) found that spectrographic analysis (assessing the phonological patterns of speech by machine) revealed that the *gwass* for *glass* and *grass* produced by 2-year-old children were in fact slightly different sounds, even though not distinguishable to the adult ear. The children consistently produced one *gwass* for *grass* and another *gwass* for *glass*; presumably they could also discriminate these differences at the perceptual level.

Developing the capacity to produce sounds and sound combinations reflects a combination of hereditary and enviromental factors. The apparent universality of children's early sounds, babbling, and the sorts of developmental patterns and problems articulating that children exhibit later on suggest that heredity influences these developmental patterns. However, chil-

RESEARCH FOCUS 6-1

Does Learning Humpty Dumpty Help Children Learn to Read?

As discussed in the text, children acquiring their first language must learn to perceive and produce the sounds of the language. Phonological knowledge is important for language use, and may also play a role in learning to read. Bryant, Bradley, Maclean and Crossland (1989) investigated the relationship between exposure to nursery rhymes, phonological knowledge, and reading. Initially Bryant et al. asked 3-year-old children to recite five popular nursery rhymes—Baa-Baa Black Sheep, Hickory Dickory Dock, Humpty Dumpty, Jack and Jill, and Twinkle Twinkle Little Star. The children's phonological knowledge and reading skills were assessed periodically, the last time at the age of 6 years.

Children's phonological knowledge and reading skills at 6 years of age were positively correlated to their knowledge of nursery rhymes at 3 years of age. In other words, the children who were better at reciting nursery rhymes at age 3 were better at reading at age 6. Bryant et al. suggest that nursery rhymes help children to appreciate rhyme and phonemes, and that this increased phonological knowledge makes it easier for children to learn to read. If correct, the implications of the Bryant et al. study are straightforward. Expose your children to nursery rhymes at an early age. Most children enjoy hearing and learning nursery rhymes, and learning nursery rhymes may facilitate later reading.

dren must hear adult sounds to learn which distinctions they must learn to produce in order to master the adult language. Although it has proven difficult to demonstrate the relation of early sounds to later sounds, it seems likely that the entire course of sound production is important in that it enables children to practice and improve their articulatory skills (Vihman, Macken, Miller, Simmons, & Miller, 1985).

The Nature of Semantics and Semantic Development

As children learn the sounds of their first language, they also begin to attach meaning to these sounds. The study of meaning in language is called *semantics*. More specifically, semantics refers to the attachment of meaning to linguistic forms. Although there are many types of meaning, the study of semantic development has primarily focused on the most basic type of meaning, *denotative meaning*. Denotative meaning refers to the use of a linguistic form to refer to something, be it an object, some property of an object, or a hypothetical idea. Thus, the denotative meaning of *dog* has to do with the dogs of the world, the denotative meaning of *furry* has to do with the hairy properties of certain objects in the world, and the denotative meaning of *unicorn* has to do with certain fantasy objects.

The meaningful elements of language are called *morphemes*. There are two classes of morphemes—free and bound morphemes. Free morphemes are words such as *dog, furry,* and *unicorn,* which are called free because they are meaningful even when used in isolation. Bound morphemes are units that alter the meaning of the free morphemes to which they are attached. Thus, the bound morpheme plural *-s* changes *cat* to *cats* and the bound morpheme past tense *-ed* changes *walk* to *walked*. In this section, we will consider the acquisition of free morphemes (or words). The acquisition of bound morphemes will be considered in the next section on syntax.

The acquisition of word meaning depends on the capacity for symbolic representation, the ability to allow a symbol to stand for something else. After all, words are symbols that stand for (represent) meanings. Moreover, the relation between a word and its meaning is an arbitrary, conventional one. The word–meaning relation is arbitrary in that a given word is not necessarily linked to a given meaning. As noted earlier, there is no necessary relation between the English word *dog* and the objects to which it refers. However, the relation is a conventional one. Speakers of English use the word *dog* to convey a certain meaning, and so are able to communicate this meaning among one another. We will concentrate on the development of word meaning only within the context of this arbitrary, conventional relation. Even though some infants may attach meaning to the sounds with which they experiment, such sound–meaning relations are not conventional (although they may be arbitrary) and so are not of interest to us here.

177

The capability to refer to a myriad array of objects, events, and ideas is one of the most significant differences between human language and the communication systems of other species. Every human child, then, is faced with the formidable task of learning thousands of words and their meanings. Children, however, appear to find the task of attaching meaning to words less onerous than might be expected. Children acquire their first word sometime between the 8th and 18th month of life; the average age at which the first word appears is approximately 12 months. By the age of 6 years, children have a vocabulary of 8,000–14,000 words (Templin, 1957). This means that children learn an average of five to eight words a day between their first and sixth birthdays.

The first words that children learn tend to be the names of things that children commonly experience in their everyday environment. Nelson (1973) found that the first 50 words used by children typically include terms for food (*juice, milk,* and *cookie*), body parts (*ear, eye,* and *nose*), clothing (*shoe, hat,* and *sock*), animals (*dog, cat,* and *duck*), household items (*clock* and *light*), toys (*ball* and *clock*), vehicles (*car, boat,* and *truck*), and people (*mama, dada,* and *baby*). More than half (approximately 51%) of the children's early words are *general nominals,* words like *juice* and *dog,* that refer to both specific objects

A mother reading a book to her 1-year-old child. This type of activity helps children to increase their vocabulary.

and classes of objects. The next largest class of words in children's early vocabularies are *specific nominals*, such as *mama*, that refer to particular individuals only.

In spite of these general findings, Nelson (1973) pointed out that there were individual differences in terms of the types of words that children first learn, and that such differences could be represented by a continuum. At one extreme were those children Nelson labeled as *referential*, who first learned words that refer to objects. At the other extreme were *expressive* children, who tended to learn words that refer to personal desires (*want*) or aspects of social interaction (*bye-bye*). Referential children tended to increase their vocabulary at a faster rate than did expressive children (perhaps because there are more objects than personal desires or means of social interaction). Of course, most children fall somewhere between these two extremes.

Interestingly, the mothers of referential children tended to use language that directed their children to objects and object properties in the world. Mothers of expressive children tended to use language to influence the behavior of their children. This suggests that the language that children hear affects their naming practices, particularly in the early phases of semantic development. This possibility is supported by the fact that parents are quite likely to engage in what Brown (1958) called "the original word game," in which parents point to and label objects, and also correct their child's attempts to produce these names. Parents, then, may help children to learn that words are significant and may also help them to learn the correct meaning of at least some terms. Nelson's work suggests that parents may also influence what young children choose to talk about.

The frequency with which children hear a particular word applied to an object may also affect their naming of the object. Schwartz and Terrell (1983) varied the frequency with which 1-year-old children heard novel words used to refer to a variety of objects. They found that the children were more likely to learn the names for the objects that were named more frequently than the objects that were named less frequently, particularly if the children had heard the objects labeled over a long period of time rather than over a short period of time. This suggests that parents could best influence their children's acquisition of words for objects by repeatedly naming objects over a long period of time rather than by repeatedly naming objects during a brief exposure to these objects.

Nonetheless, it must be remembered that children must interpret and organize the information that they hear. Nelson and Bonvillian (1973) exposed 18-month-old children to a group of novel objects that were labeled for the children. Although the children all had identical experiences with the new objects and words, they varied in terms of the words that they learned and the degree to which they used these words to refer to novel objects. This finding shows that children play an active role in their acquisition of words and meanings. Even though the children had identical experiences, their different intepretation of these experiences led them to learn different words and meanings. This experiment reinforces the idea that there is an interaction between experiences and children's interpretation of the experi-

179

ences. Both factors must be considered when attempting to determine the factors that influence semantic development.

To illustrate the interaction of children and experience, we will consider two general developmental patterns that characterize early semantic development: (1) Children learn words for objects more easily than they learn words for actions. (2) Children learn words for certain types of objects before words for other types of objects.

Regardless of the language they are learning, young children's vocabularies contain many more words for objects than words for actions (Gentner, 1982). This is true even if the language the child is learning has verbs occurring in the final position of the sentence and despite the fact that children are known to pay attention to the ends of words and sentences (Kuczaj, 1979; Slobin, 1973). In addition, the early vocabularies of children who are raised in cultures where parents rarely teach children words for objects still contain more words for objects than for actions. It seems that neither the characteristics of individual languages nor parental naming practices can account for children's disposition to learn words for objects. Why, then, do children find it easier to learn object words than action words? Children may find it easier to form object concepts than action concepts because objects exist as distinct entities in the world whereas actions are activities in which objects engage (Huttenlocher & Lui, 1979). The larger amount of object words over action words that exist in children's early vocabularies is more influenced by their cognitive predispositions than their experience (Gentner, 1982).

Children are also more likely to learn object words that are not overly specific or overly general. For example, children are more likely to learn *dog* than they are to learn *spaniel* (too specific) or *mammal* (too general). Terms such as *dog* are called *basic-level* terms (Rosch et al., 1976), and are more common in young children's speech than are terms such as *poodle* or *mammal* (Anglin, 1977). This pattern is influenced in part by how mothers tend to use nouns around their young children. Shipley, Kuhn, and Madden (1983) examined mother–child interactions in which mothers were asked to label pictures for their children. Mothers were more likely to use basic-level terms (e.g., *bear*) than superordinate terms (e.g., *animal*) or subordinate terms (e.g., *grizzly*). Of course, the Shipley et al. data do not demonstrate a direct relation between mother and child naming behaviors, but the similarities between the naming practices of mothers and children suggest such a relationship.

Parents use different sorts of labels depending on the type of word that they want to teach. Parents are more likely to use basic-level terms such as *bear* when labeling a single object, but also use more general terms when labeling more than one object (Callanan, 1989). For example, a parent might point to a group of animals and say "those are mammals." Callanan found that children who heard a term used to label a single object tended to treat the term as a basic-level label, while children who heard a label used to refer to more than one type of object treated the term as a more general label. Thus, parental naming practices are influenced by what the parents are naming and seem to influence the types of words that their children learn.

As parents and children converse about interesting experiences, children are exposed to many aspects of language.

In addition to learning that words are meaningful sounds, children must learn the appropriate limits of the meanings of the words. These limits are called the *extension* of a word. Extension of object words has to do with the objects to which such words may refer. Thus, the extension of the word *dog* is to all of the dogs in existence, but to none of the things that are not dogs. The extension of a word depends on the meaning of the word, which is called the word's *intension*. For example, the intension of *dog* might be "four-legged furry mammal that barks." The relation of intension and extension has led a number of investigators to examine children's extension of words such as *dog* in an attempt to ascertain the meaning (or intension) that children have granted the words.

Initially, children may use a term in an overly narrow sense (Anglin, 1977; Barrett, 1983; Leopold, 1949). For example, *dog* may be used to refer to only a single dog (perhaps the family pet) or *duck* may be used to refer to only a particular toy duck (Barrett, 1986). Such errors are called *underextensions.* However, children also make *overextension* errors in which they use a term to refer to too many objects. For example, *dog* might be used to refer to dogs, cats, bears, and sheep. Word meaning acquisition, then, is more than simply learning a word and attaching some meaning to it. Children must learn exactly the limits of the conventional meaning of a term, so that they can use the term to refer to all the appropriate objects but no inappropriate ones.

Overextensions have been observed more frequently in the speech of young children than have underextensions, perhaps because overextensions are more noticeable than are underextensions. Although it is unclear exactly how frequent underextension errors are in young children's speech, anywhere from one-fifth to one-third of children's first words are overextended (Nelson et al., 1978; Rescorla, 1980). Such errors typically involve children

Children's Extension of their First Words

181

TABLE 6-3
Some overextensions and their bases

Word	First Referent	Subsequent Range of Application	Possible Basis for Overextension
1. Mooi	Moon	Cakes, round marks on windows and in books, round shapes in books, tooling on leather book covers, round postmarks, letter "O"	Shape
2. Bird	Sparrow	Any moving animal	Movement
3. Fly	Fly	Specks of dirt, dust, all small insects, child's own toes, crumbs of bread, a toad	Size
4. Fafer	Sound of train	Steaming coffee pot, anything that hisses, or makes a noise	Sound
5. Bow-wow	Dog	Toy dog, fur piece with animal head, other fur pieces without heads, soft slippers	Texture

SOURCE: Based on Clark, 1975; deVilliers and deVilliers, 1979.

overextending the meaning of a word in terms of certain properties of objects: *movement, shape, size, sound, taste,* or *texture* (Clark, 1975). For example, *ball* may be used to refer to round objects in general, and *candy* to sweet objects in general. Table 6-3 summarizes some of these overextension errors.

What do these errors mean? A child who underextends the meaning of *dog* is using too stringent a criterion for *dog* whereas a child who is overextending *dog* is using too liberal a criterion for *dog*. Clark (1973) and Nelson (1974) originally suggested that children's extensional errors had to do with the meaning (intension) that children had granted the term. If this is so, then one would expect extension errors to be reflected in children's comprehension of the same term. So a child who calls a sheep, *dog,* might also be expected to respond affirmatively when asked if a sheep is a *dog*. However, overextension errors in production are not always reflected in comprehension (Bloom, 1973; Gruendel, 1977; Huttenlocher, 1974; Fremgen & Fay, 1980). Thomson and Chapman (1977) found that when they asked children who called both sheep and dogs, *dog,* to point to a dog, the children typically pointed to a picture of a dog rather than to a picture of a sheep. Results such as these suggest that children's overextension errors in speaking do not necessarily reflect the meaning that children grant the terms.

A slightly different view has been suggested by Kuczaj (1982a). Kuczaj studied the extension of words in production and comprehension by six young children. Each of the studied words was overextended in the children's speech. The comprehension task involved presenting each child with an array of six objects—two appropriate objects, two objects to which the child had overextended the term in production, and two clearly inappropriate objects. For example, a 1-year-old child who had overextended the word

RESEARCH FOCUS 6-2

Overextension Errors in Vervet Monkeys

Overextension errors are not limited to human children. Young vervet monkeys have also been found to produce overextension errors. Adult vervets use different calls to alert their companions to the approach of a predator. A barking sound indicates the approach of a leopard, a "rranp" sound indicates the approach of a martial eagle (an African bird of prey), and a "chatter" sound denots the approach of a snake. The different sounds of warning are important in that the vervets engage in different sorts of evasive action depending on which type of predator is approaching. Young vervet monkeys have been observed to overextend these sounds. For example, they produce the "rranp" sound to indicate any flying object. Adults ignore these infantile "warnings," and the young vervets gradually learn to limit their warning sounds to the appropriate referents (Seyfarth, Cheney, & Marler, 1980; Struhsaker, 1967). 🐛

---

doggie in production was shown two dogs (the two appropriate objects), a bear and a lion (the two overextended objects), and a car and a tree (the two inappropriate objects). Upon being shown the array, the child was asked to give the experimenter a *doggie* and then asked to do so again until the child indicated that there were no more doggies to be given. The results were consistent with previous investigations in that children tended to first choose the correct objects. However, they also tended to next choose the objects to which the term had been overextended in production. These data are shown in Figure 6-2 and demonstrate that overextension may occur in comprehension as well as in production. Similar findings have been reported by Mervis and Canada (1983) and Kuczaj (1986).

It should be clear from this discusion that children must continually refine the meanings that they attach to words until they have determined the appropriate conventional meaning. Kuczaj (1986) has suggested that young children learn object words in the following sequence: (1) The word is underextended (e.g., only some dogs are called *dogs*). (2) The word is overextended and underextended at the same time (not all dogs are called *dog*, but some non-dogs are called *dog*). (3) The word is overextended. (4) The word is used correctly. In Kuczaj's data, the first and third steps might be skipped, but if they did occur, they occurred in the correct sequence.

Fast Mapping.   Although experience is an important factor in children's acquisition of word meaning, children can hazard some guess about a word's meaning from limited experience. Carey (1978) suggested that young children have the capacity to quickly make some reasonable guess about a new word's meaning, a phenomenon that has come to be known as "fast mapping." Basically, fast mapping results when a child interprets the available context to hazard a quick first guess about a novel word's meaning. For example, if a child is first exposed to the word *beige* in the context of the instruction "bring me the beige one, not the blue one," the child might conclude on the

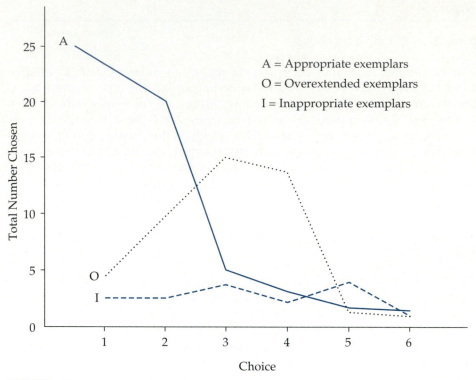

FIGURE 6-2

Total number of different types of objects chosen when children were asked to show the experimenter an instance of an overextended word.

Source: from Kuczaj, 1982a.

basis of this limited information that *beige* is a color term and that it is a color other than blue, assuming that the child knows the meaning of the word *blue* (Carey & Bartlett, 1978).

Although neither the extent to which children engage in fast mapping nor the nature of the circumstances that increase (or decrease) their likelihood to succeed when they do so have been reliably determined, the phenomenon of fast mapping is fairly well documented. Heibeck and Markman (1987) reported that 2-year-old children are capable of making reasonable guesses about a novel word's meaning based on fast mapping (see also Merriman, 1989). However, the extent to which children succeed in their fast mapping attempts depends on their previous knowledge and the type of novel word to which they are exposed. Three- and four-year-old children are more successful when their fast mapping attempts involve a novel animal word rather than a novel color word (Dockrell & Campbell, 1986).

We have seen that what children accomplish in learning word meanings is truly remarkable. They learn thousands of words and meanings. The environment contributes to this process by providing words to be learned and context (albeit oftentimes limited and ambiguous) to assist the child in hazarding a guess about a word's meaning. However, the environment alone cannot account for word meaning acquisition. Children's contributions to word meaning acquisition include general cognitive abilities and predispositions (e.g., Gopnik & Meltzoff, 1987), as well as strategies and predispositions that result in particular developmental patterns (e.g., Gentner, 1982; Kuczaj, 1982b), such as the fact that nouns are more easily acquired than verbs.

The task of word meaning acquisition involves much more than learning to attach meanings to words. Although this is no small task (after all, it takes children considerable time and effort to learn the correct extension of words), children must also learn to relate word meanings to one another. Words are related to one another in terms of a complex set of relationships, and in order to learn the semantic system of their language, children must learn these relationships (Carey, 1985; Kuczaj, 1982b; Luria, 1981; Nelson, 1979). One important type of semantic relation involves lexical opposites. Lexical opposites may be ungradable contrasts, which involve absolute complementary subsets (e.g., *male* versus *female*, *single* versus *married*) or gradable contrasts, which involves comparison along some dimension (e.g., *hot* versus *cold*, *good* versus *bad*). Ungradable contrasts involve either/or decisions. For example, a person is either male or female. Gradable contrasts allow a wider range of comparison. For example, something can be very good or sort of good.

Children may have trouble determining which relation is the relevant one for words that they are trying to relate. For example, a child studied by Kuczaj (1982b) initially treated the terms *hot* and *cold* as if they belonged to an ungradable contrast, and only later learned the relative nature of the terms and their intermediaries *cool* and *warm*. Even after the child had learned that *hot* and *cold* expressed the end points of a gradable dimension, he had

The Acquisition of Semantic Relationships

RESEARCH FOCUS 6-3

Children's Creative Phonological Combinations

Word-meaning aquisition involves learning the relation of particular sounds to particular meanings. We have already seen that young children experience difficulty in learning the proper extension of words such as *dog*. Children also experience difficulty in determining the exact sounds that constitute a word. Vihman (1981) and Hoff-Ginsberg (1983) have argued that children's attempts to understand the phonological regularities of language affect the manner in which they extend the meanings that they have learned. Young children may, for example, produce a *productive work blend*, an error that occurs when children combine the phonological patterns of two words to form a novel *lexical* item. For instance, a child might combine the words *sock* and *shoe* as *sasu*, and use the new term to refer to both socks and shoes. This child would then have to learn that *sasu* is not an English word, and that *sock* and *shoe* refer to socks and shoes, respectively. Word-meaning acquisition is thus a double-pronged problem for young children. They must learn both the correct phonological form of a word and its exact meaning. And they must do this for thousands of words! ❦

The feeding situation provides numerous opportunities for parents and children to communicate.

difficulty learning the appropriate manner with which to express movement up and down the dimension. For some time the child used *cool off* only to refer to changes from one cool state to another cool state and *warm up* only to refer to changes from one warm state to another. For example, when the child was tasting his hot chocolate, he exclaimed "Too hot! I'm gonna let it warm up," meaning he intended to let the hot chocolate change from a hot state to a warm one.

At present, it is unclear which type of contrast (gradable or ungradable) is easier for children to learn. However, the developmental pattern of first learning the words that refer to the ends of a dimension (for example, *hot–cold*) and only later learning the terms that lie between the two extremes (for example, *warm–cool*) seems to be a general developmental pattern in the acquisition of terms that can be ranked along a semantic scale (Kuczaj, 1975, 1982b). This developmental pattern suggests that the extremes of semantic dimensions are more salient to young children than are points between the extremes.

As children grow older, they learn more and more semantic relations. As a result, children are continually refining the nature and structure of their semantic systems. Part of this process involves the refinement of earlier acquired semantic relations. For example, children first learn the general dimensional size pair *big–small,* followed by *tall–short* and *long–short,* then *high–low,* next *thick–thin,* and finally, *wide–narrow* and *deep–shallow* (Clark & Clark, 1977). Thus, just as children must learn to differentiate the meaning of their object words, they must also learn to differentiate their early semantic relations.

186

The Nature of Syntax

Syntax (or grammar) deals with the way words and bound morphemes (such as the *s* on *cats*) are ordered, relative to one another, to produce acceptable and comprehensible sentences. Thanks to the theoretical contributions of linguist Noam Chomsky (1957, 1965), the study of syntactic development dominated the field of language development during the 1960s and the early 1970s.

According to Chomsky, the structure of all human languages is the result of an interrelated set of elements. At one level is *surface structure*, which may be thought of as the spoken sentence. At another level is *deep structure*, which may be thought of as the mental syntactic base for surface structure. Consider for a moment the following two sentences: *The shooting of the hunters was awful*, and *the police couldn't stop drinking*. These sentences are ambiguous; they each have more than one meaning. The first sentence could mean either that the hunters were terrible marksmen or that someone shot the hunters (perhaps a vengeful Bambi). The second sentence means either that the police were alcoholics or that they experienced difficulty in keeping other people from drinking. The important point is that a given surface structure can have more than one meaning. The intended meaning is determined by the deep structure, which specifies that the hunters were either the agents or the objects of the act of shooting, and that the police were either the drinkers or the agents who feebly attempted to maintain the sobriety laws of their district. Deep structure, then, is an important aspect of language structure.

The Development of Syntax

The One-Word Period

Children's acquisition of syntax follows a general pattern. Initially, between the ages of 10 and 18 months, children begin to produce single word utterances. This is commonly referred to as the one-word period. It may not be apparent why this period, which typically lasts several months, may be considered a period of syntactic development. After all, children are producing single words, and syntax would seem to involve the use of at least two words or at least one word and one bound morpheme. Remember, however, that the child in the one-word period is actually producing single word surface structures. The basis for these single word utterances may in fact be deep structures that represent complete sentences. Thus, we must ask whether these one-word utterances are functionally equivalent to words or to sentences. Does the young child who says *milk* mean "milk" or "may I please have another glass of milk?"

187

Over 60 years ago, DeLaguna (1927) suggested that children in the one-word stage actually are intending to produce sentences, and that the task of the listener is to ascertain exactly what the child intends to say (using the available context to assist in the interpretation). According to DeLaguna and to subsequent investigators (see McNeill, 1970, for a more thorough discussion of this topic), single-word utterances function as *holophrases*, single words that function as complete sentences. The notion of holophrases is based on the notion that even though children are limited to *producing* single-word utterances during the one-word period, they are capable of conceiving of and comprehending sentences. Thus, the child who says *milk* while holding her empty glass might be intending to say, "I want more milk," whereas the child who points to spilled milk on the floor while saying *milk* might be intending to say, "I spilled my milk." It is certainly true that most adults interpret children's single-word utterances as if the children mean more than the single word. And it also seems likely that children at this age do intend to communicate more than the single word. However, Brown (1973) and Bloom (1973) both pointed out the dangers of "rich interpretation" (using the available context to interpret the intended meaning of children's utterances). Although the child who says *milk* while holding an empty glass and while pointing to spilled milk is most likely intending to communicate something different in the two situations, it is far from clear that the child conceives of and intends to say sentences. Few of us would be willing to claim that the child who says *milk* while pointing to spilled milk means, "I apologize for spilling the milk, for I know that cleaning up after me is bothersome." Assumptions about what young children mean in the one-word period must be made with great caution (Barrett, 1986). Although young children do seem to intend to communicate more than the meaning of the single word, exactly what they intend to say is most difficult to determine (Greenfield & Smith, 1976). Thus, the implication of the one-word period for syntactic development is unclear.

The Two-Word Period

The next major period of syntactic development is the two-word period. This period, which typically begins between 18 and 24 months of age, is one when children can produce two words at a time. Once children have mastered this period, there is no doubt that they are using syntax, for they are now arranging words relative to one another.

Two-word speech is not produced in a random fashion. Children in the two-word stage consistently use words that convey the most meaning (nouns, verbs, and adjectives) and consistently omit words that convey less information (e.g., articles like *the* and conjunctions such as *and*). They also consistently fail to use prefixes and suffixes. These characteristics of two-word speech led Brown and Bellugi (1964) to label such speech *telegraphic speech*. Given their productive limitations, children talk about the most meaningful aspects of a situation, just as adults do when they are sending a telegram (in a telegram, words cost money, in the two-word period, words cost effort; in both cases, the result is a concentration on the most meaningful elements).

What is the evidence that children know more than they are able to say? Consider the following two-word utterances:

Two-Word Utterance	Semantic Relations
Mommy cook	Agent action
Cook hotdog	Action object
Mommy hotdog	Agent object

These utterances were produced by a 20-month-old child while her mother was preparing lunch. Even though the child was limited to two-word utterances, the child expressed the relations necessary to produce a longer utterance of the form agent–action–object (mommy–cook–hotdog). This example, and even a casual perusal of the meanings that children in the two-word stage typically express, regardless of the language they are learning (see Table 6-4), reveal that children have the conceptual capability to produce longer utterances. However, their productive skills are limited to two words, and so they can only produce part of what they know.

The major accomplishment of children in the two-word stage is learning to express a small set of semantic relations (see Table 6-4). Children's use of these semantic relations is limited (Braine, 1976). For example, children do not consistently use word order to mark semantic relations in the two-word period (Maratsos, 1983; Maratsos & Chalkley, 1980). Children learning English may say *mommy kiss* or *kiss mommy,* regardless of whether mommy is the one doing the kissing or being kissed. When children do use consistent word order, the consistency seems to reflect limited knowledge rather than general rules. For English, the general rule for agent and action would be "agent + action," as in *mommy kiss* when mommy is doing the kissing. Young children's knowledge of this relation is limited to "animate agent + action," so that they are more likely to say "daddy cook" than "ball roll" or "truck hit." Similarly, children's early understanding of the "action + object" relation seems to be limited to "action + inanimate object" (Bloom, Lightbown, & Hood, 1975). Thus, children are more likely to say "give cookie" than "give mommy" or "hit doggie."

Individual differences exist in the two-word speech of young children. For example, one child may decide that location is specified in the second position (*chair here*), while another may decide that location is marked in the first position (*here baby*) (Braine, 1976). Another difference involves the use of pronouns. Some children rarely use pronouns in the two-word stage, while other children use them frequently, as in *I go, me happy* (Bloom, Lightbown, & Hood, 1975). As noted earlier, Nelson (1973) has suggested that this latter difference may reflect how mothers talk to their children. Mothers who use language primarily as a means to teach children about the world have children who use many nouns but few pronouns in the two-word stage (referential children), while mothers who use language to direct their children's behavior have children who use many pronouns (expressive children).

TABLE 6-4
Functions of 2-word sentences in children's speech, with examples from several languages

Function of Utterance	Language					
	English	German	Russian	Finnish	Luo	Samoan
Locate, name	There book That car See doggie	Buch da [book there] Gukuk wau-wau [see doggie]	Tosya tam [Toysa there]	Tuossa Rina [there Rina] Vettä siinä [water there]	En saa [it clock] Ma wendo [this visitor]	Keith lea [Keith there]
Demand, desire	More milk Give candy Want gum	Mehr milch [more milk] Bitte apfel [please apple]	Yeschë moloko [more milk] Day chasy [give watch]	Anna Rina [give Rina]	Miya tam-tam [give me candy] Adway cham [I-want food]	Mai pepe [give doll] Fia moe [want sleep]
Negate	No wet No wash Not hungry All gone milk	Nicht blasen [not blow] Kaffee nein [coffee no]	Vody net [water no] Gus' tyu-tyu [goose gone]	Ei susi [not wolf] Enää pipi [anymore sore]	Beda onge [my-slasher absent]	Le 'ai [not eat] Uma mea [allgone thing]
Describe event or situation	Bambi go Mail come Hit ball Block fall Baby highchair	Puppe kommt [doll comes] Tiktak hängt [clock hangs] Sofa sitzen [sofa sit] Messer schneiden [cut knife]	Mama prua [mama walk] Papa bay-bay [papa sleep] Korka upala [crust fell] Nashla yaichko [found egg] Baba kreslo [grandma armchair]	Seppo putoo [Seppo fall] Talli 'bm-bm' [garage 'car']	Chungu biro [European comes] Odhi skul [he-went school] Omoyo oduma [she-dries maize]	Pa'u pepe [fall doll] Tapale 'oe [hit you] tu'u lalo [put down]

SOURCE: From Slobin, 1979.

Later Grammatical Development

Although it is possible to speak of a one-word period and a two-word period in syntactic development, there is no clear-cut three-word stage. Instead, there is an explosion of grammatical knowledge following the two-word stage, resulting in vastly improved language skills in a relatively short period of time. For example, one of the children studied by Stan Kuczaj was producing two-word utterances such as *kick ball* at 24 months of age and produced the following sentence about 1 year later: *I don't want to go to sleep tonight and dream the dream I dreamed last night.* The difference between this child's competence at 24 months of age and at 36 months of age is substantial, and is characteristic of children in general. How do children accomplish this major developmental change?

Initially, children begin by combining the meanings that they expressed in the two-word stage. The child who could produce *mommy cook, cook hotdog,* and *mommy hotdog* in the two-word stage can now produce *mommy cook hotdog*. In the early phases of grammatical development following the two-word stage, children clearly build upon earlier knowledge.

In order to better consider the development of syntactic skills, consider the following two speech samples (obtained from the same child at two different ages). In the first sample, the child is 24 months of age, in the second, 36 months of age.

ADULT: It is hot.
CHILD: Hot, This hot. This hot this time.
CHILD: Mommy, help me. This hot.
ADULT: Do you want a cinnamon one?
CHILD: Yes.
ADULT: Okay.
CHILD: Cinnamon on them.
ADULT: Cinnamon's already on them.
CHILD: Ow! Hot! This burn my hand.
ADULT: You better be careful.
CHILD: Mommy, put butter on mine.
ADULT: You want butter?
CHILD: Yes. Right there. Right there, mommy. Ow! I burn my hand. I burn my hand.

CHILD: Mom fixed this for me and I don't like it.
ADULT: You don't like bacon?
CHILD: No, Abe's gonna eat rest of it.
ADULT: What?
CHILD: A coupon. Look. For McDonald's.
ADULT: What kind of sandwich would you like?
CHILD: I like a mayonnaise sandwich.
ADULT: Okay.
CHILD: (laughs) That is bad. Mom will come home and not like it.
ADULT: What?
CHILD: This mess. I want a sandwich. Where is my sandwich? I don't want meat. I want not meat. Not peanut butter. Not cheese. Only mayonnaise.
ADULT: Okay.
CHILD: And you put it right here. Okay? Put it right here so I can eat it.
ADULT: Okay. I will after it's made.
CHILD: What kind you gonna make me? I don't want cheese. Only mayonnaise.

191

There are many differences between the speech produced by the child in the two speech samples. Perhaps the most apparent difference is the length of the child's utterances. The utterances in the second sample are considerably longer than those in the first utterance. Moreover, the utterances in the second sample are also more complex than those in the first sample. In the second sample, the child uses a verb ending (the past tense *-ed*), a *be* form (*is*), a modal auxiliary (*will*), and conjunctions (*and* and *so*), none of which were present in the first speech sample.

Even this brief example makes it clear that children learn to use a wide range of linguistic forms and structures after they have passed through the two-word stage. The range of forms that are acquired, the speed with which acquisition occurs, and the explosive nature of the phenomenon make this aspect of language development very difficult to explain.

Speech Errors: Overregularizations

As they learn syntax, children produce a variety of "errors" that demonstrate that they are trying to determine the regularities of their language. These errors may be divided into two types: (1) overregularizations and (2) creative generalizations. English has a number of regular rules governing the use of a variety of morphological and grammatical forms. Overregularizations occur when children apply a regular rule to irregular forms. Creative generalizations occur when children use a linguistic form in a novel context. Children have not heard the forms that they are producing in such cases, so these errors demonstrate that children have succeeded in ascertaining at least some of the regularities of their language.

Plurals. One of the regular rules of English applies to how nouns are made plural. Regular nouns may be made plural by adding the suffix *-s*, as in *cows* and *eyes*. Other nouns have irregular plural forms, such as *feet* and *men*. Soon after children begin to produce correct regular plural forms such as *cows* they also begin to produce overregularized forms such as *foots* and *mouses* (Brown, 1973). They may also produce redundant forms such as *feets* and *mices*. The children's errors demonstrate that they have acquired the notion of a regular plural rule and do not yet understand all of the exceptions to the rule. Significantly, children are unlikely to apply the plural to nouns such as *water* and *air* (McNamara, 1982). Nouns such as these are called mass nouns, and do not have plural forms. Children overregularize the plural form to irregular count nouns (which refer to objects that can be counted) like *foot* and *mouse*, but not to mass nouns, like *water* and *air*, demonstrating knowledge of different types of words even at this young age.

Past Tense. In English, the regular past tense form *-ed* is used to express previous time, as in *walked*, *asked*, and *cooked*. There are also many irregular verb forms used to express past tense, for example, *ate*, *fell*, *went*, *thought*, and *drank*. Children first learn to express the past tense with a small number of irregular forms such as *ate* and *fell*. They then learn the regular past tense form, and soon after begin to overregularize its use, producing forms such as *eated* and *goed*, and occasionally *ated* and *wented* (Brown, 1973; Kuczaj, 1977). Given the large number of irregular past tense forms in English, it is not surprising that children make errors such as *thinked* and *thoughted* well into the school years, for they must learn all of the exceptions to the regular rule. Bybee and Slobin (1982) have suggested that this task may be made easier by children attending to similarities among certain irregular verb forms (e.g., *sing–sang* and *ring–rang* share some obvious similarities), and learning to use these regularities to produce correct irregular verb forms.

Kuczaj and Borys (1988) hypothesized that overregularization errors might depend on phonetic similarity. They exposed 3-, 5-, 7-, and 9-year-old children to novel regular and irregular forms to express large relative size. Half of the children were exposed to 10 regular forms that were phonetically similar (e.g., *fug-ip,gug-ip, kug-ip*), and half of the children were exposed to 10 regular forms that were phonetically dissimilar (e.g., *fod-ip, gir-ip, kip-ip*). In all cases, the addition of the suffix *-ip* indicated that the larger of two objects should be chosen. All children were also exposed to a set of 10 irregular forms, in which *-ip* was not added. As shown in Figure 6-3, children were more likely to overregularize the *-ip* suffix to the irregular forms if they had heard phonetically dissimilar base forms. These results suggest that the generality of the linguistic rules that children learn as they acquire their first language may depend on the nature of the instances that children hear.

FIGURE 6-3

Percentage of overregularization errors produced as a function of age and phonetic similarity of regular forms.

Source: from Kuczaj & Borys, 1988.

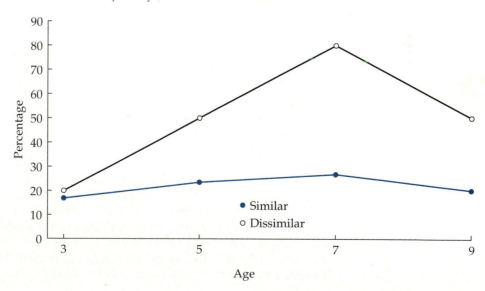

Speech Errors: Creative Generalization of the Progressive

Another type of significant error that has been observed in the speech of young children involves the creative generalization of the progressive -*ing* form. This form is the earliest bound morpheme to be acquired by young children learning English (Brown, 1973). There are no irregular progressive verb forms in English, although there are verbs to which the progressive cannot be attached. For example, *two and two are equalling four* and *I am knowing the answer* are not acceptable English sentences. Children do not err by attaching the progressive to incorrect verb forms. They do not produce forms like *knowing* and *equalling,* and so seem to have learned at an early age which verb forms may take the progressive and which may not (Brown, 1973). However, children do occasionally create new verb forms by treating a noun as if it were a verb, as do adults. They also may use the progressive with these novel verb forms, and so produce sentences like *why is it weathering*? (referring to rain and thunder) and *you're gunning him* (shooting with gun) (Kuczaj, 1978b). These errors, like overregularization errors, demonstrate a type of grammatical knowledge that goes beyond the input. Children do not simply reproduce forms that they have heard. Instead, they create new forms (*goed, shirting*) based on generalities that they have gleaned from the data. As in the case of so many other development processes, the language-learning child is an active rather than a passive creature.

How Can Syntactic Development Be Explained?

We have seen that young children proceed through a number of steps in the course of learning syntax. The speed with which children acquire syntax and the creativity that they exhibit at an early age are important considerations for theorists who attempt to explain children's acquisition of syntax. For example, a theorist might believe that children learn syntax by imitating the speech that they hear. Children learning English do occasionally imitate the speech that they hear (Kuczaj, 1982c), and imitation of adult speech by the Kahuli children of Papua New Guinea is common (Ochs & Schieffelin, 1984). Regardless of the extent to which children imitate adult speech, imitation cannot account for children's creative use of syntax. For example, the child who says *foots* did not learn to produce this form by imitating it. Instead, the child learned a regularity of English—some singular nouns are made plural by adding the suffix -*s*—and applied this regularity to an exception.

Or a theorist might believe that children learn syntax because their parents correct ungrammatical sentences and reinforce grammatical sentences (Skinner, 1957). Braine (1971) reported that he attempted to correct his 2-year-old daughter's use of *other one* as a noun modifier. The following interchange illustrates the interaction between father and daughter.

DAUGHTER: Want other one spoon, daddy.
FATHER: You mean you want *the other spoon.*
DAUGHTER: Yes, I want other one spoon, please, daddy.
FATHER: Can you say "the other spoon"?
DAUGHTER: Other . . . one . . . spoon.
FATHER: Say . . . "other".
DAUGHTER: Other.
FATHER: Spoon.
DAUGHTER: Spoon.
FATHER: Other spoon.
DAUGHTER: Other spoon. Now give me other one spoon.

As this example illustrates, young children are resistant to parental attempts to correct their incorrect syntax. Perhaps because children rarely respond appropriately, parents are unlikely to correct their children's syntax. In fact, parents may give signs of approval to their children's ungrammatical sentences and signs of disapproval to their children's grammatical sentences (Brown & Hanlon, 1970).

CHILD: And Walt Disney comes on Tuesday.
MOTHER: No, he does not.
CHILD: Draw a boot paper.
MOTHER: That's right. Draw a boot on paper.

Parents are about three times as likely to approve of their children's grammatical sentences than their ungrammatical sentences, but are also about five times as likely to disapprove of their children's grammatical sentences than their ungrammatical sentences (Hirsh-Pasek, Treiman, & Schneiderman, 1984). So parents are more likely to both approve and disapprove of ungrammatical sentences. Obviously, parents are responding to something other than grammar. Parents seem to approve of a child's sentence if it is semantically accurate rather than syntactically correct. In other words, parents pay more attention to what their children say than to how they say it. Parents do not teach syntax to their children by correcting their children's errors and reinforcing their correct syntax. In fact, parents who report that they are likely to correct their children's syntax have children who acquire language more slowly than do children whose parents report that they are unlikely to correct their children's syntax (Wells, 1985).

Given the difficulty of explaining syntactic development in terms of the environment (model sentences to be imitated, correction, reinforcement), Chomsky (1972, 1987) suggested that there is an innate Language Acquisition Device (LAD). Chomsky's arguments for the LAD were as follows: (1) Language is a complex system by which deep structures and surface structures are related. (2) The information available to the child is impoverished. It consists of surface structures, which by themselves can provide no infor-

Language Acquisition Device (LAD)

195

RESEARCH FOCUS 6-4

Parental Expansions of Young Children's Speech

Adults frequently expand their children's utterances, adding linguistic forms that were lacking in the child's utterance (Brown, Cazden, & Bellugi, 1969). Adults apparently expand children's utterances in order to check if their interpretation of the child's utterance is correct (Cazden, 1965). The following are some examples of expansions:

CHILD: That Clancy brush.
ADULT: That is Clancy's brush. Do you want to brush him?

YOUNGER CHILD (BEN): Me push Abe. Ben push Abe.
OLDER CHILD (ABE): Ben pushed me in the wagon. You're a big boy.
YOUNGER CHILD: Abe push Ben.
OLDER CHILD: Abe pushed Ben too.
YOUNGER CHILD: Abe boy. Big boy.

These examples demonstrate that expansions of children's utterances (regardless of whether the expansion is given by an adult or older child) build up the child's utterance by adding syntactic and semantic units. Brown and Bellugi (1964) pointed out that expansions should provide the child with a valuable kind of feedback. Because expansions immediately follow the child's utterance and build up this speech, their timing is optimal for the child to contrast them with a preceding utterance. Parents are twice as likely to expand on their children's ungrammatical sentences than on their grammatical sentences, which could alert children to the fact that their ungrammatical sentences need work (Hirsh-Pasek et al., 1984). However, expansions have not proven to be valuable for increasing the rate or changing the course of syntactic development (Cazden, 1965). Sarah, one of the three children in the longitudinal study of language acquisition by Brown and his colleagues, received the *lowest* rate of parental expansions, yet was the *most* advanced in the development of forms like the progressive *-ing* ending and the past tense *-ed* ending, which are among the forms that are omitted in early child speech, but are included and supposedly modeled in adult expansions (Brown, Cazden, & Bellugi, 1969).

Although the significance of expansions for syntactic development has been difficult to demonstrate, Keith Nelson and his colleagues have been able to demonstrate that a slightly different type of response to a child's utterance may facilitate grammatical development. Nelson has termed this type of response a *recast*; the child's utterance is recast by the adult into a sentence with different syntactic form but similar semantic content. Nelson, Carskaddon, and Bonvillian (1973) found that children who were exposed to recast replies by adult experimenters developed syntax more rapidly than did children who were not given an increased amount of recasts.

Nelson et al., (1979) also found that the type of recast influenced development. In these studies, simple recasts were distinguished from complex recasts. Simple recasts are those in which the adult's reply maintains reference to the same basic meaning in the child's preceding speech, with structural change limited to only one of three complex units (subject, verb, object). Complex recasts involve structural change of two or more of the three components. Simple recasts seem to facilitate the child's syntactic development, most likely due to the moderately discrepant nature of the simple recasts, whereas complex recasts impede the rate of syntactic growth. Perhaps complex recasts change too much of the child's original utterance. ❧

mation about deep structures. (3) Children receive little feedback about the grammatical form of their sentences. (4) Despite all this, children acquire syntax relatively quickly.

Some of Chomsky's claims are supported by the data. Children do learn language very quickly, in spite of the fact that they receive little feedback about the grammatical form of what they say (Brown & Hanlon, 1970). However, the input that children receive is not as confusing as Chomsky believed. Chomsky thought that children hear the same sort of language that adults hear. All that one has to do is listen to a lecture, courtroom summation, or ordinary conversation to realize that most adult discourse consists of overly complex speech with many errors. Chomsky reasonably concluded that if children are exposed to such speech, it is unlikely that they will ever learn language without an innate LAD to assist them. However, young children are usually not exposed to the complexities of adult speech. Adults tend to speak to children in short and relatively simple sentences, which are closely tied to ongoing events (Farwell, 1975; Gleason and Weintraub, 1978; Slobin, 1975). Moreover, adult sentences to children are highly repetitive and almost always grammatical. Newport, Gleitman and Gleitman (1975) found only 1 ungrammatical utterance per 1,500 utterances produced by mothers speaking to their young children. They also found that up to 34% of the words and sentences adults say to young children consisted of full or partial repetitions of a previous utterance.

Even though children do hear a simplified version of adult speech, Chomsky (1988) still believes that an innate LAD is necessary. The child may hear short grammatical sentences, but such sentences only provide information about surface structures.

For Chomsky, the LAD is necessary if the child is to relate surface structures and deep structures. The innate knowledge of language that children bring to the task of language acquisition is contained in the LAD. Experience is not necessary for the child to understand language, for he is born with innate knowledge of deep structures and the processes used to change deep structures to surface structures. Experience is necessary for the child to determine the particular surface structures of his language and the relation of the surface structures to the deep structures. According to Chomsky (1981), children need only pay attention to the surface structures they hear to sort out their language. The LAD will automatically construct the child's language for him.

As you might guess, Chomsky's views are controversial. Many theorists dislike the notion of innate knowledge being passed from generation to generation, perhaps because the existence of such information is difficult to test. Even if one believes in the LAD's innate knowledge, it is not clear exactly how much experience with surface structures is necessary for the child to infer specific relations between the heard surface structures and the innate deep structures (Lightfoot, 1989; Snow & Tomasello, 1989). Chomsky's view of language acquisition may be incorrect, but it seems likely that some sort of innate mechanisms are involved in the acquisition of syntax (Slobin, 1986; Maratsos, 1989; Pinker, 1984). Innate mechanisms need not involve

197

innate knowledge, however. To illustrate, consider an example from visual perception (see Chapter 5). We may be born with the ability to perceive colors, but we are not born with the knowledge of what colors are.

Strategies

Children may be innately equipped with a variety of capabilities for language development that they employ in the course of attempting to learn the regularities of their mother tongue. Slobin (1973) suggested a number of strategies that all children may use, regardless of the language that they are learning. One strategy, *avoid exceptions*, may account for the overgeneralizations of forms such as the plural and past tense. Another strategy, *pay attention to the ends of words*, may influence the manner in which children process linguistic information. If children do use this strategy, then they should learn suffixes before prefixes. And in fact, children do learn suffixes at an earlier age than prefixes (Slobin, 1973).

RESEARCH FOCUS 6-5

Evidence for a Critical Period in Syntactic Development

A common assumption in nativist explanations of language acquisition is that there is a critical period for acquiring syntax (Lenneberg, 1967). To test this hypothesis, Johnson and Newport (1989) assessed knowledge of English syntax in native speakers of Korean and Chinese who had immigrated to the United States and learned English as their second language. The subjects had immigrated to the United States when they were between 3- and 39-years-old, and had lived in the United States between 3 and 26 years when their knowledge of English syntax was tested. Johnson and Newport wanted to know if age of arrival in the United States or amount of time spent in the United States was the best predictor of knowledge of English grammar. If the amount of time spent in the United States is the best predictor of knowledge of English syntax, then experience would be implicated as the most important factor in acquiring syntax. If age of arrival was the best predictor of grammatical knowledge, then the existence of a critical period would be supported.

The results support the notion of a critical period. Individuals who had arrived in the United States before the age of 7 years possessed knowledge of English grammar comparable to that possessed by native speakers of English. Individuals who arrived in the United States when they were 8–10-years-old did not know English quite as well as those who had arrived at younger ages, but knew more English grammar than those who had arrived after age 10. For individuals who arrived in the United States between 11 and 15 years ago, the younger they were at the time of arrival, the better their knowledge of English syntax. Those who arrived after age 17 possessed relatively little knowledge of English syntax, regardless of how long they had spent in the United States. Although adults who are learning a second language may surpass children acquiring the same second language during the first year they are learning it (Snow & Hoefnagel-Hohle, 1978), the results obtained by Johnson and Newport suggest that children will eventually learn more of the second language than will adults, even if the children have less previous experience with the second language. The ease with which grammatical knowledge is acquired depends on the age at which one is exposed to the language; the general rule is the younger the better. 🍂

The viability of this strategy was demonstrated in an experimental context by Kuczaj (1979). Preschool children were taught novel suffixes and prefixes. For example, some children heard "the boy drove the ip-car" while others heard "the boy drove the car-ip." Regardless of whether the children had to learn that "ip" referred to "big" or to "red," they were more likely to learn the suffix form than the prefix form. Moreover, chidren were more likely to correctly imitate sentences when "ip" was a suffix than when it was a prefix. Despite the possibility that children may employ strategies in order to ease the burden of language acquisition, it is difficult to determine the extent to which such strategies are innate and the extent to which the environment contributes to their use. And even if children are equipped with a set of language acquisition strategies, they must still determine the regularities that exist in the language they are acquiring. There is controversy over how children do this (Maratsos, 1981; MacWhinney, 1987).

Communication

One of the primary functions of language is communication. Although language serves functions other than communication, (e.g., language is involved in human thought) and although communication is possible without language, human language is the most effective communication system known to exist (even though other species seem to possess complex communicative systems). In this section, we will examine the development of communication skills in children.

One of the important aspects of communication is the intention to communicate. Although people may occasionally communicate something unintentionally (for example, that they are lying or nervous) and may also occasionally fail to communicate exactly what they intend, intention is nonetheless an important component of communication.

When do children acquire the intention to communicate? Although it has been suggested that the cries, vocalizations, facial expressions, and gestures of young infants involve the intent to express a meaning, it is difficult to determine if the communicative intent exists in the child's behavior or in the observor's interpretation of the child's behavior. For example, consider a situation in which children cry, but stop crying when they are given milk. Even though it is clear that giving the child milk resulted in the cessation of the child's crying, it is not clear that the child intended to communicate hunger. The child may have been crying because he was hungry, but with no intent to communicate his state to another.

Although adults from Western societies attribute the intent to communicate to behaviors such as infant crying and vocalizations, this does not hold for all cultures. The vocalizations of Samoan infants are treated as physiologically based reflexes rather than as intentional acts of communication (Ochs, 1980).

In a review of the literature, Shatz (1983) has suggested that it is difficult to determine if intentional communication emerges prior to the onset of language. Although it is possible that language makes intentional communication possible, it is more likely that the onset of language makes the demonstration of intentional communication possible.

In spite of the difficulty of demonstrating intentional communication in preverbal infants, there are many studies that *suggest* communication in infants who have not yet learned to produce any recognizable sounds (Bretherton & Bates, 1979; Chalkley, 1982; Shatz, 1983). In her review of this literature, Chalkley (1982) found that infants had been reported to engage in a variety of preverbal communicative behaviors—ranging from requests for objects, help, or sympathy to the expression of a variety of emotions. Although there are many possible relations between preverbal communication and early verbal communication, the possibilities rest on our interpretation of infant preverbal behavior. We cannot be certain of the communicative intents of preverbal infants, but the range of preverbal communicative behaviors and their apparent relation to early verbal communicative behaviors make it possible (but in no way certain) that preverbal communicative behaviors are the precursors of the communicative functions of language. Of course, the work of Ochs (1980) demonstrates that the parents in all cultures do not necessarily interpret their young infant's behaviors as intentional communication attempts, and so such interpretation on the part of adults is not necessary for the development of intentional verbal communication.

Nonetheless, it is possible that infants from Western cultures benefit from the tendency of adults to act as if the infants are trying to communicate something prior to the emergence of language. One result is the semblance of communicative interaction between parents and infants, often at a very young age. For example, the verbal interactions of mothers and 3-month-old infants have the character of verbal communication. Snow (1977) found certain types of interactions among mothers and young infants that might also help infants learn about the nature of verbal communication. Consider the following exchange cited in Snow (1977):

INFANT: (smiles)
MOTHER: Oh, what a nice little smile! Yes isn't that nice? There. That's a nice little smile.
INFANT: (burps)
MOTHER: What a nice wind as well! Yes, that's better, isn't it? Yes. Yes.
INFANT: (vocalizes)
MOTHER: Yes. There's a nice noise.

This "conversation" is dominated by the mother. As children get older, they become more active participants in terms of both initiating and maintaining conversations (Bloom, Rocissano, & Hood, 1976; Kaye & Charney, 1980; Goelman, 1986; McDonald & Pien, 1982).

In learning to communicate, children naturally learn to communicate a variety of requests. Becker (1982) has suggested that the ability to communicate requests evolves in the following manner: (1) The earliest requests are general desire sounds, names of desired objects, and words like *more* and *want*. (2) The next requests that develop are statements of need, statements of condition (for example, *I'm hungry*), and direct requests that specify the desired act and object (for example, *push dolly*). (3) Location questions (for example, *where's my dolly?*) and claims (for example, *that's mine*) are the next sorts of requests to occur. These types of requests may be viewed as the beginning of the use of indirect requests. Indirect requests imply that some action should be taken rather than explicitly stating the action, for example, stating that *it's hot in here* when one wishes a window to be opened or a fan to be turned on. Preschool children are more likely to use direct requests

Children also learn about language when they interact with their siblings. In this case, a 4-year-old child is encouraging his 1-year-old sister to walk.

when speaking to peers, but to use more indirect requests and polite forms when speaking to older children and adults (Gelman & Shatz, 1977; McTear, 1980). The use of indirect requests increases between the ages of 3 and 5 years (Garvey, 1975), and seems to stabilize between the ages of 5 and 8 years. Thus, children learn to become more subtle in their communication of their wants and needs.

Although children's communicative skills improve with age, they are not always effective communicators. When asked to describe objects, 3-year-old children are likely to produce ambiguous descriptions (Deutsch & Pechmann, 1982). However, 3-year-old children will ask for clarification if they hear an ambiguous message (Revelle, Karabenick, & Wellman, 1981). The fact that 3-year-old children may produce ambiguous messages but ask for clarification when they hear such messages demonstrates that children place too heavy a burden on the listener when the children are speaking. They seem to expect listeners to understand what is said. Children are more likely to blame the listener than the speaker for communicative failures, even when the speaker has produced an inadequate message (Robinson, 1981). Nonetheless, children do pay attention to the needs of listeners, particularly if the listeners are younger children. In what has become a classic study, Shatz and Gelman (1973) found that 4-year-old children change their speech depending on the age of the listener. Four-year-old children produced shorter and less complex utterances when speaking to 2-year-old children than when speaking to either other 4-year-olds or adults. They also speak differently to 2-year-olds, depending on whether they are trying to instruct them or simply playing with them. Subsequent investigations have reported similar findings for 3-year-olds talking to younger children (Sachs & Devin, 1976).

Summary

Language development is actually the intertwined development of a number of systems: the phonological system, the semantic system, the syntactic system, and the communicative system. Each of these systems is an equally important component of language, and so must be accounted for in any viable theory of language development. Children must learn the sounds of their language in order to learn to combine these sounds together to produce meaningful words (phonology). Children must also learn to combine words in sentences in order to communicate more complex meanings (syntax). All of this is necessary in order for children to master the complex communication system that is human language.

Explanations of language development have focused on both hereditary (nature) and environmental (nurture) factors. As we have seen, some explanations have focused on only hereditary influences while others have recognized only environmental influences. Explanations that are exclusively oriented toward either hereditary or environmental factors are too limited, since both hereditary and environmental factors significantly influence language development. Possible hereditary influences on language development include innate knowledge of language, innate strategies that help children to interpret and organize linguistic information, and children's innate need to communicate. Environmental influences may include the manner in which parents attempt to communicate with young, preverbal infants, the kind of speech that children hear, and children's roles in communication interchanges.

Suggested Readings

Ainsfeld, M. (1984). *Language development from birth to three.* Hillsdale, N.J.: Erlbaum.

Atkinson, M. (1982). *Explanations in the study of child language development.* New York: Cambridge University Press.

Bruner, J. (1983). *Child's talk.* New York: W.W. Norton & Co.

Garvey, C. (1984). *Children's talk.* Cambridge, MA: Harvard University Press.

Iwamura, S. (1980). *The verbal games of preschool children.* London: Croom Helm Ltd.

CHAPTER SEVEN

The Nature and Measurement of Intelligence

Introduction

As an adult, you possess an impressive array of mental abilities and a wealth of knowledge that you have accumulated over the years. The mental abilities involved in the organization and interpretation of information are known as *cognition*. Cognitive abilities are involved in all aspects of our interaction with the world because we are constantly interpreting and organizing the information that is available in the environment. You have already been exposed to certain aspects of these abilities. In Chapter 5, we discussed the development of the perceptual skills that are involved in our intepretation of the world. Chapter 6 outlined how children make sense of one important aspect of their environment—their native language. Cognition is involved in all aspects of human behavior and human development; consequently it has generated a considerable number of research investigations and theoretical controversies.

In this chapter and the next, we will consider the nature and development of general cognitive capabilities that are involved in the acquisition and use of knowledge—that is, the mental processes involved in the organization and interpretation of information. In this chapter, we will focus on theoretical attempts to characterize the nature of human intelligence and on attempts to develop standardized tests to measure human intelligence. These goals are related concerns, for how a person attempts to measure intelligence depends on how that person views the nature of intelligence. Many of the disputes in this area of psychology have focused on the nature of human intelligence, the roles of nature and nurture in intellectual development, and the appropriateness of standardized tests of intelligence as measures of intelligence.

What Is Intelligence?

If you ask a group of 50 adults to define intelligence, you are likely to get 50 different answers. The lack of consensus in definitions of intelligence exists among scholars who study intelligence as well as among lay persons. Approximately 70 years ago, the editor of the *Journal of Educational Psychology* asked scholars interested in intelligence to submit their definitions of intelligence. Fourteen scholars did send their definitions to the editor and may have been embarrassed to learn that their definitions did not overlap to any large degree. To the contrary, the 14 definitions were contradictory and may have led to the following cynical definition of intelligence: Intelligence is what intelligence tests measure. This definition is circular as well as cynical and provides no insights into the nature of intelligence or the nature of intelligence tests.

This discouraging picture emphasizes the difficulties involved when scholars attempt to define intelligence, but does not mean that there is no agreement about the nature of intelligence. Adults who are asked to list the characteristics of intelligence are likely to mention three types of abilities (Sternberg, Conway, Ketron, & Bernstein, 1981): (1) practical problem-solving ability, (2) verbal ability, and (3) social competence. The division of intelligence into these three types of abilities is typically made by both lay persons and scholars of intelligence (Sternberg, 1982), which suggests that we possess intuitive ideas about what counts as intellectual abilities. Examples of these three types of abilities are given in Table 7-1.

Adults also have intuitive notions about the intellectual abilities of children, including the idea that what counts as an example of intelligence changes as children mature. Siegler and Richards (1980) asked adults in an introductory psychology course to list five characteristics of intelligent behavior for each of four age groups: (1) 6-month-old infants, (2) 2-year-old children, (3) 10-year-old children, and (4) adults. As shown in Table 7-2, the lists changed depending on the age considered. The intelligence of 6-month-old infants was characterized in terms of perceptual and motor skills, whereas 2-year-old children's intelligence was thought to be more symbolic and focused on obtaining information from the environment. Perceptual and motor skills were not listed as intellectual characteristics of 10-year-old children and adults, whose intelligence was characterized by general reasoning and problem-solving skills.

The characterization of intelligence as sets of abilities such as those shown in Tables 7-1 and 7-2 reflects our intuitions about intelligence and its development. As we shall see, such intuitions have influenced theories of intelligence and attempts to create intelligence tests. We will also see that different theorists have had different intuitions about the significance of various types of intellectual abilities.

TABLE 7-1
Three main types of abilities that adults view as intellectual

Practical Problem-Solving Ability

Accurate intepretation of information, assessment of all aspects of a problem, and logical reasoning

Verbal Ability

Breadth and depth of vocabulary, reading comprehension, ability to speak and write clearly and articulately

Social Competence

Social awareness, ability to make fair judgments, punctuality, and sensitivity to others

SOURCE: From Sternberg, Conway, Ketron, & Bernstein, 1981.

207

TABLE 7-2

Types of intellectual abilities college students attribute to different age groups

Intellectual Characteristic	Age Group			
	6-Month-Olds	2-Year-Olds	10-Year Olds	Adults
Alertness	+			
Vocalizations	+			
Recognition of people and objects	+			
Motor coordination	+	+		
Awareness of environment	+	+		
Curiosity		+		
Language ability		+	+	+
Learning ability		+	+	+
Problem solving			+	+
Reasoning			+	+
Creativity			+	+

SOURCE: From Siegler and Richards, 1980.

Individual Differences in Intelligence

Although there are many models of human intelligence, everyone agrees on one thing: There are individual differences in both intellectual ability and intellectual development. The study of individual differences in intelligence and intellectual development began formally at the beginning of this century and has produced both knowledge and controversy concerning the measurement of cognitive abilities. There is a continual fascination with the topic of individual differences in cognitive abilities, both for theoretical purposes and for the many important practical implications for education. One of the earliest researchers in this field, Sir Francis Galton, had this to say of people who would ignore individual differences: "Their souls seem as dull to the charm of variety as that of the native of one of our flat English counties, whose retrospect of Switzerland was that, if its mountains could be thrown into its lakes, two nuisances would be got rid of at once" (Galton, 1889, p. 2).

It is sometimes tragically difficult to see the "charm" in certain varieties of intellectual differences, as in the case of a profoundly retarded child. Whether we are dismayed or delighted by individual differences, the fact of their existence remains. A group of important and controversial questions also remains: Can we accurately measure a child's level of intellectual development? Is a child's level of intelligence stable or does it change during childhood? What roles do nature and nurture play in this process? What abilities have we not included in our concept of intelligence that ought to be included? What parental variables affect the development of intelligence? Are schools as responsive as they could be to the intellectual needs of the students? Although many of these questions apply to areas other than the study of individual differences in intelligence, the importance of these questions to our everyday lives is reflected in the emotions such controversies generate.

Intelligence Tests

Toward the end of the nineteenth century, the French ministry of education confronted a dilemma. It had made an innovative commitment to the special education of "slow learners" following a series of investigations by pioneers in the study of mental retardation. But a noted psychologist of that time, Alfred Binet, argued that such special provisions would prove fruitless unless better means of selecting children for special classes were found (Binet & Simon, 1905). Prior to Binet's argument, the standard practice had been to have a physician make the final determination of a child's intellectual capacity. However, it was never clear how the decision (or "diagnosis") was to be made. Some physicians looked at the shape of the head, some looked for a certain "gleam in the eye" whose absence indicated deficiency, some asked the child a few basic academic questions, and others used various combinations of such techniques. Binet and his colleagues argued convincingly that these practices were inadequate, resulting in many completely normal children being sent to the special schools and other children for whom the special classes were designed remaining in the regular schools and learning virtually nothing.

The Stanford-Binet Scales

Alfred Binet, the father of standardized intelligence testing (IQ tests).

In what would be recognized as a turning point in the history of psychology, Binet resolved to devise some method by which the necessary decisions could be made both accurately and efficiently. His task was not an easy one, because there was relatively little agreement among educators, researchers, and physicians regarding the nature, causes, or symptoms of mental deficiency. Binet had, however, been studying children's mental abilities for several years and was able to apply that knowledge usefully.

Binet chose a practical route that was simple and elegant, a route that would be followed for decades to come (Sattler, 1988). He decided to look at the relationship between the ability to perform cognitive tasks drawn from everyday life and the age at which children, on the average, could perform them. In other words, Binet decided to establish age *norms* for a variety of intellectual tasks. Some of the first groups of tasks selected for investigation by Binet and his colleague Simon (Binet & Simon, 1908) are shown in Table 7-3.

Binet reasoned that if age norms could be established for a wide variety of tasks, then it would be relatively easy to assess how far ahead of or behind his peers a given child was. Thus, for the first time, it would be possible to talk about relative degrees of mental retardation or precocity. In Binet's terminology, "test norms" refer to some objective standard of comparison relating a given individual's performance to that of a specified comparison group. For example, if someone is testing a 9-year-old middle-class child, the comparison group would be other 9-year-old middle-class children.

Binet never carried out the extensive research that was needed to establish reliable and valid scales (see pp. 216–224 in this chapter for a discussion of these terms) of general cognitive functioning, but the ideas he introduced were elaborated by others, especially in the United States. His use of a broad array of everyday cognitive tasks and his introduction of age norms were

TABLE 7-3

Sample tasks for different age groups from 1908 Binet intelligence test

Three Years
Show eyes, nose, mouth; name objects in a picture; repeat a sentence of six syllables
Five Years
Compare two boxes of different weights; copy a square; repeat a sentence of ten syllables
Seven Years
Indicate omissions in drawings; copy a triangle and a diamond; describe a picture
Nine Years
Give the date (day, month, day of the month, year); name the days of the week; arrange five weights in order
Eleven Years
Criticize sentence containing absurdities; give abstract definitions; place disarranged words in order

TABLE 7-4

Intellectual abilities tested by 1986 revision of the Stanford-Binet intelligence scale

Verbal Abilities	Quantitative Reasoning	Abstract/Visual Reasoning	Short-term Memory
Vocabulary	Mathematics	Pattern analysis	Bad memory
Comprehension	Number series	Copying	Memory for
Absurdities	Equation building	Matrices	sentences
Verbal relations		Paper folding	Memory for
		and cutting	digits
			Memory for
			objects

SOURCE: Adapted from Thorndike, Hagen, & Sattler, 1986.

innovations that would spark a new and controversial field of research: the study of human intelligence and attempts to measure it.

A number of psychological researchers in the United States were immediately interested in the possibilities presented by the Binet Scales. Foremost among these researchers was psychologist Lewis Terman, who had been investigating individual differences since his dissertation at the turn of the century. He lacked a quick and efficient method of estimating individual differences in general intellectual development, and thus the Binet Scales offered him a major breakthrough. While a professor at Stanford University, Terman completed an extensive revision and standardization of the scales, leading to the publication in 1916 of the *Stanford Revision and Extension of the Binet-Simon Scale for Measuring Intelligence* (Terman, 1916) or, as it is more commonly known today, the Stanford-Binet.

Since 1916, the Stanford-Binet has been revised several times, most recently in 1986 (Thorndike, Hagan, & Sattler, 1986). Like earlier versions, the 1986 Stanford-Binet is designed to assess the intelligence of children from 2 to 18 years of age (Table 7-4). Although many other intelligence tests have been constructed since 1916, nearly all of them have been tied in one way or another to the original Stanford-Binet (Jensen, 1980).

The Wechsler Intelligence Scales

David Wechsler constructed three intelligence tests because he believed that the Stanford-Binet intelligence test placed too much emphasis on verbal skills. One of Wechsler's tests is the Wechsler Adult Intelligence Scale (WAIS) and will not be considered here since it emphasizes adult intelligence. The *Wechsler Intelligence Scale for Children* (WISC) was first published in 1949 (Wechsler, 1949) and revised as the WISC-R in 1974 (Wechsler, 1974). The WISC and WISC-R were designed to assess the intelligence of 6- to 16-year-old children. The *Wechsler Preschool and Primary Scale of Intelligence* (WPPSI) was published in 1967 (Wechsler, 1967) and was designed for use with 4- to 6-year-old children. The WISC and WPPSI contain both verbal and nonverbal items, as shown in Table 7-5. The verbal items are similar to those used in the Stanford-

211

TABLE 7-5
Sample items from the Wechsler intelligence scale for children-revised version

Verbal Items

General information: "What is the capitol of Texas?"

Word similarities: "Tell me how *apple* and *orange* are alike."

Arithmetic: "Jane had six donuts. She ate two of her donuts. How many does she have left?"

Vocabulary: "Tell me what an *airplane* is."

Digit memory: "Listen to the following list of numbers and then say them back to me. Six. Three. Five. Nine."

Performance Items

Picture completion: "Look at this picture and tell me what's missing."

Mazes: "Use this pencil to try and find your way out of the maze."

Object assembly: "Here are some pieces of an object. Try to put them together to make the object."

Block designs: "Here are nine cubes. Use these cubes to make the design on the picture I'll show you."

Picture arrangement: "Here are some pictures. Put them in order so that they tell a nice story."

Binet, but the nonverbal items are quite different from those used in the early forms of the Stanford-Binet. The 1986 revision of the Stanford-Binet contains nonverbal items similar to those used in the Wechsler Scales, suggesting that Wechsler was correct when he criticized the earlier forms of the Stanford-Binet for their emphasis on verbal skills.

One of the strengths of the Wechsler Scales is the division of overall intelligence into two components. The *verbal component* assesses intellectual skills similar to those emphasized by the Stanford-Binet and is related to academic success (Hale, 1978; Wikoff, 1979). The *performance component* assesses nonverbal intellectual skills. The performance component provides information about children's nonverbal intellectual skills and also allows educators in the United States to assess the intellectual prowess of children who are not native English speakers or children who have speech and language disorders.

The Peabody Picture Vocabulary Test

The Peabody Picture Vocabulary Test (PPVT) was designed to assess children's knowledge of word meanings (Dunn, 1959, 1965). The PPVT is a popular measure for two reasons. First, it is simple to administer and score. Second, the PPVT does not require a verbal response and so may be used with young children and with children who have speech and language disorders. The child taking the PPVT is shown a page with four pictures on it and asked to point to the picture that corresponds to the word being tested. The PPVT tests children's comprehension of words but does not require children to produce the words. Sample pages from the PPVT are shown in Figure 7-1.

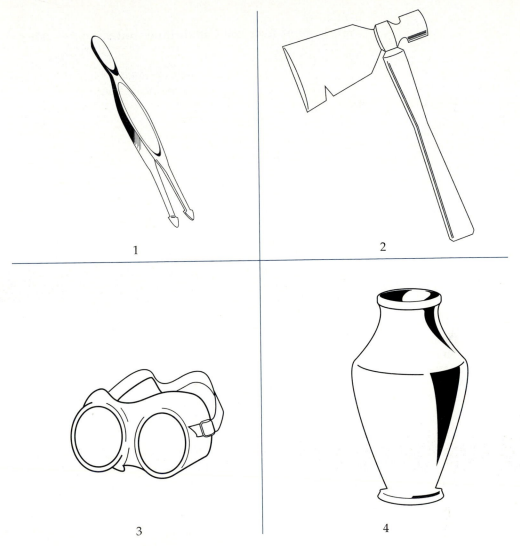

1   2

3   4

FIGURE 7-1

Example of Peabody Picture Vocabulary Test. The child is asked to point to the object that is requested (e.g., tweezers).

Infant Intelligence Tests

The periods of infancy and early childhood seem to be crucial in the development of intelligence. Many kinds of evidence attest to this. The sheer quantity and quality of cognitive development during this period is spectacular (for example, see Chapters 5 and 8) and this period very likely provides the basis for all later cognitive development.

The Cattell Infant Intelligence Scales. The intelligence tests described above are inappropriate for testing children younger than 2 years of age. Tests such as the Stanford-Binet, WPPSI, and PPVT require verbal skills that young

213

TABLE 7-6

Sample items from the Cattell infant intelligence scale

Age (in months)	Task
2	Attends to human voice; visually follows moving person
5	Looks at ringing bell
6	Lifts cup
9	Rings bell
11	Puts cube in cup
12	Marks with crayon

TABLE 7-7

Abilities assessed by Bayley's scale of infant development

Average Age Achieved	Ability
7 weeks	Holds head erect
2 months	Rolls from side to back
$4\frac{1}{2}$ months	Rolls from back to side
7 months	Sits alone
9 months	Plays pat-a-cake
11 months	Stands alone

children, particularly infants, lack. As a result, a number of scholars have attempted to design "infant intelligence tests." One of the earliest infant intelligence tests was the Cattell Infant Intelligence Scales (Cattell, 1950). Examples of the items used by Cattell are shown in Table 7-6.

Bayley Scales of Infant Development. The best known and most widely used infant intelligence test is the Bayley Scales of Infant Development, which contains items for both motor development and mental development (Bayley, 1969). Examples of these items are shown in Table 7-7. In addition, the Bayley Scales rely on an *Infant Behavioral Record,* in which an infant's behavior is rated in terms of dimensions such as fearfulness, purposefulness, and responsiveness.

Determining Scores from Intelligence Tests

Once the basic ideas of how to construct a scale for obtaining a general estimate of an individual's intellectual capacity were understood, the next problem concerned what kind of scores would be most useful and interpretable. The first step was to assign a "mental age" to a child who had been tested. The mental age is the raw-score equivalent of the child's performance. If children answer as many questions correctly as does the average 8-year-old (according to the established norms), then their mental age is 8. Stern, a German researcher, suggested using a quotient which would relate the mental age (MA) of the person being tested to his chronological age (CA). Thus, the notion of the intelligence quotient (IQ) was born (Sattler, 1988). The intelligence quotient was defined as *IQ = (MA/CA) × 100*. Using this formula, if a 6-year-old child performed on the test as the average 9-year-old would, then the IQ would be: (9/6) × 100 = 150. If the same child had scored only as well as the average 4-year-old, then the IQ would be: (4/6) × 100 = 67. The average 6-year-old would have an IQ equal to 100, since (6/6) × 100 = 100. Later the scoring was changed to a *deviation score* rather than the original (MA/CA) × 100 formula. A deviation score records in some standard unit how far above or below the average for a given age a specific child scores. Thus, the average child of any age receives a score of 100, children below average receive scores of less than 100, and children above average receive scores greater than 100. The specific score for children above or below the average is determined by the degree of deviation from the "average" child.

Infant intelligence tests such as the Bayley Scales arrive at a Developmental Quotient rather than an Intelligence Quotient because infant tests measure skills other than intelligence (such as, motor skills). The rationale for determining an infant's DQ is the same as that for determining an individual's IQ. A DQ of 100 means that the infant has achieved an average score for infants his age. A DQ of less than 100 means that the infant's score is less than the average, and a DQ of more than 100 means that the infant's score is greater than the average.

Interpreting Intelligence Test Scores

As we have seen, the average IQ (or DQ) is by definition 100. In the process of standardizing the Stanford-Binet and the WISC, these tests were administered to thousands of school children (Terman, 1916; Thorndike, Hagen, & Sattler, 1986; Wechsler, 1949, 1967, 1974). The distribution of IQ scores that resulted from the standardization process is shown in Figure 7-2. The distribution of scores represented in Figure 7-2 is a *normal curve*, meaning that the

FIGURE 7-2
Normal distribution of IQ scores (for WISC).

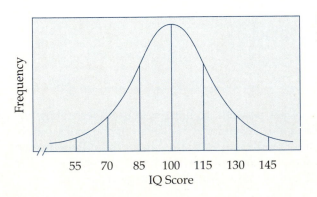

55   70   85   100   115   130   145
IQ Score

TABLE 7-8

The verbal classifications of intelligence test score ranges are shown for the WISC, along with the approximate percentage of children who fall into each category.

IQ	Classification	Percentage Included
130 and above	Very superior	2.2
120–129	Superior	6.7
110–119	Bright normal	16.1
90–109	Average	50.1
80–89	Dull normal	16.1
70–79	Borderline	6.7
69 and below	Mental defective	2.2

SOURCE: From Wechsler, 1949.

scores cluster around the average score in certain ways. The farther away an IQ score is from the average, the less likely it is to occur. The average score of an intelligence test is 100. The standard deviation of scores on the WISC is 15 points. This means that in the case of the normal curve shown in Figure 7-2, 34% of the population has IQ scores between 85 and 100, and another 34% of the population has IQ scores between 100 and 115. IQ scores between 85 and 115 represent the low average to high average range on the WISC, and are the most common scores. Scores lower than 85 or higher than 115 are unusual, while scores lower than 70 or higher than 130 are rare. The standardization of IQ scores into a normal curve has two consequences: (1) IQ scores cluster around the average and become less frequent as they move farther away from the average. (2) An individual's IQ score can be compared with those of other individuals in terms of a *percentile rank.* For example, an IQ score of 115 has a percentile rank of 84, meaning that the individual receiving this score performed better than 84% of the people who took the test.

What does an IQ score mean? An IQ score represents no more and no less than a standard way of expressing a *score on a specific test.* The value and meaning of the IQ score is thus entirely dependent on the characteristics of the test that is used, especially its reliability and validity, topics that we will consider next.

Intelligence Tests: Reliability and Validity

As we have already seen, it is not possible to lump together all intelligence tests as if they are exactly the same. If we look, however, at the most widely used and researched tests, we can see how well they meet the reliability and validity criteria. In the following discussion, we shall consider the reliability and validity of the Bayley, Stanford-Binet, and Wechsler Scales.

The reliability of a test refers to the consistency of the measurement. If we were to measure the length of something, we would want to be certain that the measuring instrument itself were stable: An elastic yardstick would make interpretation of length quite difficult! Similarly, we hope that our estimates of psychological characteristics are not distorted by a highly changeable measure. We cannot normally expect to attain the accuracy of physical measurement, of course, since psychological variables can only be inferred indirectly rather than observed directly. But we can reduce the error in measurement and account for it if proper precautions are taken.

The type of reliabilty that we will be concerned with concerns test-retest stability. If we test a group of children today, wait a week, then return and give the same test to them again, the correlation between the scores from the first testing session to the second should be reasonbly high. (The actual correlations will vary with the size and diversity of the group and the length of time between the two testings. Thus, it is difficult to place a numerical value on "reasonably high." Also, one has different expectations for a new and experimental test as compared to an often-used and well-standardized one. If the correlation is quite low, then there is probably something wrong with the test. At the very least, it is not measuring any stable characteristics of the children in the group, which was the original goal. (If we wished to measure nonstable characteristics, such as moods, we would not have this requirement.) There are many variations of the test-retest method, but the point is simple: If the measure is not fairly stable, then its usefulness is seriously impaired.

The reliability of intelligence tests depends on the amount of time between the first and second testing periods. Tests such as the Bayley, Stanford-Binet, and Wechsler are reliable test instruments *if* the interval between the two testing periods is not very long, and if the tests are administered by competent and experienced examiners. The picture changes, however, when the interval between tests increases.

Scores on infant intelligence tests, such as the Bayley, bear little relationship to scores on the Stanford-Binet or WISC-R obtained in later childhood (Bee, Barnard, Eyres, Gray, Hammond, Spietz, Snyder, & Clark, 1982; Honzik, 1983; McCall, 1983). In retrospect, the reason for the inability of infant intelligence test scores to predict later intelligence test scores seems fairly obvious. Infant intelligence tests measure a different set of abilities than do later intelligence tests. Remember that infant intelligence tests yield a DQ score rather than an IQ score; this distinction means that the two types of tests are measuring different abilities. Thus, a test of the infant's mental and motor skills does not accurately predict the young child's verbal and symbolic skills, let alone the abstract reasoning and symbolic manipulation powers of the adolescent.

Despite the fact that infant intelligence test scores are poor predictors of later intelligence test scores, DQ scores are sometimes useful in predicting developmental delay in later infancy, neurological disorders, and later mental retardation (Escalona, 1968; Honzik, 1983; Siegal, 1981; Werner & Smith, 1982). Nonetheless, this is a far cry from predicting later intelligence. Recent research has been directed toward the specification of individual differences

Reliability of the Bayley, Stanford-Binet, and Wechsler Scales

217

Are Ability Tests Biased?

Rogers Elliott, J. D., Ph.D.

The modern industrial world is complex and becoming ever more so, and it invented widespread schooling as a central institution of socialization to meet the growing need to develop intellectual abilities in its citizens. It was not very long ago in history that most persons could not read or calculate, and such persons in our world would and do appear as having very low abilities. To say that is not to say anything about their innate capacities for intelligence. Intelligence is a *phenotype:* roughly, the currently available "repertoire of acquired skills, knowledge, learning sets, and generalization tendencies considered intellectual" (Humphreys, 1971) are sampled not only by IQ tests, but also by performance in academic subjects, on achievement tests, on SATs, MCATs, LSATs, bar exams, GREs, and other selection tests.

The ability common to all these tests is called general ability, or simply *g,* and it results in an unknown degree from the varying powers of different environments to foster such ability and the varying genetic predispositions of different individuals to respond to any given degree of environmental facilitation of ability. The degree of such genetic predisposition in any individual is unknown—let us call it *Intelligence A* and quickly assign it to the category of attractive but unproductive concepts. The current performances that we call intellectual can be termed collectively *Intelligence B,* and it is the only kind we can ever know. Since the term "intelligence" still carries with it connotations of innateness and fixedness, it is probably better to adopt phrases with less surplus meaning like "developed ability" or simply "general ability."

The dominant culture in all developed modern societies (often thought of as middle class) prizes schools because it prizes the abilities that are developed there and, prior to school, in the home. Though the expression "middle class" in this country is often modified by the adjective "white," in fact all middle classes, black, Chicano, Asian, or otherwise, value and foster general ability and all produce persons of superior intellectual ability. But because the development of abilities is class-tied, and because the disadvantaged children of poverty are, for reasons of historical racism and recent patterns of immigration, disproportionately represented in the lower class and the underclass, there are average racial and ethnic differences in ability that are substantial, not only on IQ tests but on any measure of ability: e.g., black and Hispanic 17-year-olds perform on reading, writing, math, and science tests at about the level of white or Asian 13-year-olds (see the several recent reports of the National Assessment of Educational Progress).

Representatives of disadvantaged minority groups have frequently claimed IQ or other ability tests to be biased, asserting that all groups have the same average degree of innate intelligence, hence all should score the same. It is certainly a reasonable hypothesis that there are no racial and ethnic differences in Intelligence A, but tests can measure, not such innateness, but only the developed ability we see as Intelligence B. And, given the large average racial and ethnic differences that exist in the ability-fostering environments of homes and schools, it would be surprising if there were not also average differences among the major racial and ethnic groups in this country on tests of ability. Differences of equal size exist, for example, among different white groups in this country (Appalachian whites are usually considered the most disadvantaged), or among the various black tribal groups of Nigeria or the several castes of India.

General mental ability is a trait of considerable and growing importance. Class, racial, and ethnic differences are real and have serious social consequences, not only in the allocation of school programs and jobs, but for social harmony and prosperity. If the wealth of a nation inheres in the talent of its citizens, there is still much to be done in America toward building a larger middle class among disadvantaged groups and in improving our schools. The society that has made ability so important a trait, inventing schools to enhance it and tests to measure it, has surely been unfair to certain groups in the past and may continue still to be so.

But if a society that valued height had systemically starved certain of its citizens so that they were shorter on average than the mainstream majority, charging the measures of length with bias would be beside the point, such as, breaking the thermometer because one does not want to know there is a fever. Good measures would in fact be essential to learn whether and to what degree the harm done was being remedied. Mod-

ern tests of ability, although not as reliable as meter sticks and thermometers, are nonetheless very good measures. Assuming reasonable conditions of testing and familiarity with the language of the test, they are valid in content and equally predictive of performance, on average, of the various groups tested. Persons or groups who do relatively well or poorly on tests also do relatively well or poorly on other measures of ability, like grades.

Let us end with a revealing example from a recent lawsuit attacking IQ tests (Larry P. v Riles, 1979). Is the son of a poor black sharecropper with an IQ of 90 more intelligent than the son of a rich white banker with the same IQ? The answer is no, at least not in the short run, and probably not in the long run either, unless critical environments change. If they do change (and *that* is the important work of our society), so will the test scores, but until that happens, similar test scores will predict similar grades and other indices of Intelligence B.

Rogers Elliott is Professor of Psychology at Dartmouth College, where his research and teaching focus on law and psychology and educational psychology. He is the author of the recent Litigating Intelligence, *which concerns lawsuits alleging cultural and racial bias in intelligence tests.*

in infancy that predict later individual differences in intellectual functioning. Fagan and McGrath (1981) have suggested that *visual recognition memory* in infancy may predict later intelligence better than do standard infant intelligence tests. They reported that infants who had greater visual recognition memory had higher IQ test scores when tested at 7 years of age.

Why would such a relationship exist? You may recall from our discussion of perceptual development in Chapter 5 that *habituation* and *preference* for novelty are important aspects of many perception tasks used with infants. Habituation refers to the lack of interest (boredom) that occurs when one is exposed to a stimulus over and over. Preference for novelty refers to the attention that is more likely to be given to unfamiliar stimuli rather than familiar stimuli. In visual recognition memory tasks, the infants are exposed to stimuli until they habituate to them. They are then exposed to both the familiar stimuli and unfamiliar stimuli. Infants who pay more attention to the unfamiliar stimuli are thought to have better visual recognition memory, that is, better memory of the original stimuli. Of course, in order to pay more attention to the unfamiliar stimuli, the infants must also prefer the novel stimuli. Both the speed with which infants habituate to familiar stimuli and the extent to which they exhibit a preference for novel stimuli appear to be positively related to IQ scores obtained in later childhood (Bornstein & Sigman, 1986; Fagan, 1984; Rose & Wallace, 1985). These results suggest that measures of visual recognition memory obtained in infancy are developmentally related to those aspects of intelligence that are measured by standardized intelligence tests such as the Stanford-Binet and WISC.

Even if DQ scores do not predict later IQ scores, it is still possible that an IQ score obtained at one age would predict the IQ score obtained from the same individual at a later age. In fact, IQ scores do seem to become more stable during the preschool years and show increasing stability from the elementary school years onward (Honzik, MacFarland, & Allen, 1948; Sontag, Baker, and Nelson, 1958). In a review of this literature, Bloom (1964) reported the following correlations based on a number of longitudinal studies of intelligence test scores: +.65 for IQ scores at 3 years of age and IQ scores at 17 years of age, +.80 for IQ scores at 5 years of age and IQ scores at 17 years of age, and +.90 for IQ scores at age 8 years and IQ scores at 17 years old (recall that the highest possible correlation is 1.0). You can see that the stability of IQ scores increases as one gets older. By 8 years of age the prediction to age 17 is about as good as is the immediate test-retest reliability.

These correlations were derived from a number of studies involving large groups of children followed for many years. They do not mean that intelligence as measured by tests is "fixed" at age 3 or age 8 for a given person.

IQ test scores are often used to predict an individual's academic potential.

220

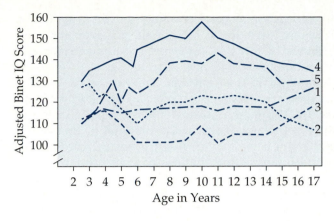

FIGURE 7-3

Five patterns of IQ change found by McCall et al.

Source: from McCall, Applebaum, & Hogarty, 1973.

In each of these studies there were examples of many individuals who exhibited dramatic fluctuations in IQ scores over the years.

Children in longitudinal studies can be grouped by the kinds of changes they show on IQ test scores over the years. For example, McCall, Applebaum, and Hogarty (1973) found the five patterns shown in Figure 7-3.

Although some children did exhibit remarkable stability in their IQ scores as they got older, the more striking finding was that many of the children's IQ scores changed dramatically over time. The average IQ change was 28.5 points, and the IQ scores of approximately one child out of seven showed a change of more than 40 points! In another study, Hindley and Owen (1978) reported changes of over 70 points. These data demonstrate that IQ scores are not the stable indicators of intelligence that we were once led to believe that they were. An IQ score obtained in early childhood is likely to differ from one obtained later for the same individual, sometimes dramatically. Thus, a child labeled as "low average" by an intelligence test score might easily be categorized as "high average" by a later test score. Or a child might go from "bright" to "low average." The basic moral is this: The younger a child is when his first IQ score is obtained, the less likely that this score will be related to a later IQ score. IQ scores do become more stable as we get older, but many important decisions about children's intellectual prowess are made based on tests given at an early age. And such test scores are now acknowledged as being poor predictors of later IQ scores.

Even if we have a highly reliable test, there is no assurance that it is also valid. "In a very general sense, a measuring instrument is valid if it does what it is intended to do." (Nunnally, 1967, p. 75). It is useful to make distinctions among two different uses of the term "validity."

1. Content validity is achieved if the items on a test are a representative sample of the items relevant to the ability being measured. This is difficult if not impossible for global characteristics like "intelligence" but is appropriate for more circumscribed abilities, like "knowledge of algebra I."

2. The type of validity referred to most often in intelligence testing is predictive validity, for which one must demonstrate that scores on a test are

Validity

221

capable of accurately predicting some relevant criterion. The criterion for general intelligence tests has traditionally been academic achievement, most often defined as school grades, A test that could predict this criterion was considered to be better than one that could not.

Are IQ tests valid? The answer to this question depends on the type of validity with which one is concerned. Content validity is concerned with the adequacy of the items used to measure a given characteristic. For example, a test intended to measure your knowledge of the material in this course would have content validity if it sampled the entire range of material that you have read and heard in lectures. A test that has content validity is a fair test of the material or abilities being tested. It has proven to be very difficult to determine the content validity of standardized intelligence tests, since different views of intelligence lead to different types of items being included on intelligence tests. One recurring criticism of intelligence testing is that it has focused on too narrow a range of the intellectual skills that humans possess (Frederiksen, 1986). This may be understandable given the original intention of the tests, which was to predict school performance measured in traditional ways, but it is not adequate if we believe the construct of intelligence to be broader than just standard school learning.

Aspects of Cognition Not Covered by Standard Tests

Cognitive Style.   Cognitive style reflects the fact that individuals approach intellectual tasks in different ways. Cognitive styles are concerned with these differences, and are thought to reflect stable individual differences in how individuals process information (Bjorklund & Curtiss, 1989). Three types of cognitive style have received considerable attention: (1) convergent and divergent thinking, (2) field dependence/field independence, and (3) conceptual tempo.

Convergent and Divergent Thinking.   As long ago as 1950, Guilford pointed out that creativity was a neglected area of psychological research. Since that time, many investigators have tried to define and measure creativity (or creative thinking), especially in terms of the way in which it may differ from the abilities required on standard intelligence tests (Sternberg, 1988; Wallach, 1970). One way in which intelligence tests and creativity tests differ is in terms of the type of thinking involved to do well on the test (Guilford, 1967). *Convergent thought* is appropriate when one must determine the correct answer for a task, as in choosing the correct answers on an IQ test. *Divergent thinking* is appropriate when a task requires flexibility and multiple approaches in order to arrive at a solution. Convergent thought is often associated with intelligence as measured by standardized intelligence tests, while divergent thought is usually associated with creativity (Bjorklund & Curtiss, 1989).

One measure of divergent thinking is ideational fluency. Tasks intended to measure ideational fluency use open-ended questions such as: "Tell me all the different ways you could use a brick" and "Name all the things you can think of that move on wheels" (Torrance, 1955; Wallach & Kogan, 1965). The best measure of divergent thinking in these tasks seems to be the number of responses that children produce (Kogan, 1983). Ideational fluency may be an important aspect of creativity because the generation of many ideas may increase the possibility of coming up with a useful, innovative one. The creative process is not well understood, even by creative individuals, but some combination of divergent thinking and critical thinking seems necessary. The research in this area continues and highlights the importance of recognizing that we do not have all the information about mental ability merely by examining IQ scores. In fact, individuals with high IQ scores are not any more likely to be creative than other individuals (Kogan, 1983; Torrance, 1976), suggesting that the intelligence measured by intelligence tests and creativity are not closely related. In other words, convergent thought and divergent thought do reflect different aspects of intelligence.

Field Dependence/Field Independence.   This cognitive style dimension concerns how individuals process visual information (Witkin, Dyk, Faterson, Goodenough, & Karp, 1962). Field dependent individuals readily perceive the entire visual stimulus as a whole, but are affected by the whole to such an extent that they cannot readily perceive the parts. Field independent individuals are not influenced by the whole to such an extent and so are much more likely to distinguish the parts that make up the whole. This dimension of cognitive style is often measured by an *embedded figures test*, as shown in Figure 7-4. Although field dependence and field independence are not mea-

FIGURE 7-4
Example of Embedded Figures Test.

223

sured by standardized intelligence tests, this dimension of cognitive style is related to performance on such tests. Field independent children tend to perform better on intellectual tasks than do field dependent individuals, a pattern that holds for scientific reasoning and performance on standardized intelligence tests as well as other cognitive tasks (Case, 1974; Kalyan-Masih, 1985; Linn, 1978).

In general, field dependence tends to decrease with age, whereas field independence tends to increase with age (Witkin, Goodenough, & Karp, 1967). However, individual differences on this cognitive style dimension are relatively stable across development. Thus, even though there is a general trend for decreasing field dependence and increasing field independence as children get older, young children who are more field dependent (or independent) than their peers are likely to remain so as they get older.

Conceptual Tempo. This aspect of cognitive style is concerned with the speed and accuracy with which individuals approach intellectual tasks (Kagan, Rosman, Day, Albert, & Philips, 1964). Individuals who approach intellectual tasks in a deliberate and time-consuming fashion and who usually arrive at the correct answer or solution are called *reflective*. At the other extreme are those individuals who make many errors and arrive at these erroneous conclusions quickly. Such individuals are called *impulsive*. Although it is possible to take your time and still be wrong or to arrive at a correct answer quickly, the more general pattern is one in which quick responses are more likely to be incorrect than are more deliberate responses. Thus, research on cognitive tempo has focused on the distinction between reflective and impulsive individuals (Kagan, 1983; Kogan, 1983).

One example of a task in which the reflective–impulsive dimension is relevant is multiple-choice tasks (Bjorklund & Curtiss, 1989). Impulsive individuals are likely to choose the first alternative that seems right, however, this approach leads to many incorrect answers because they fail to consider all of the answers and so often fail to choose the answer that is most correct. Reflective individuals are more likely to consider all of the answers before making their decision; this approach results in more correct choices.

The *Matching Familiar Figures Test* is the most commonly used measure of cognitive tempo (Katgan et al., 1964). Examples of this test are shown in Figure 7-5. Children are shown a target picture and six other pictures and asked to indicate which of the six pictures is identical to the target picture. Both the speed with which children respond and the accuracy of their responses are used to determine if they are reflective, impulsive, or neither.

In general, impulsivity decreases with age (Salkind & Nelson, 1980). Nonetheless, it is still possible that reflective children remain reflective as they get older, and that impulsive children continue to be impulsive as they get older. As it turns out, the stability of cognitive tempo differences seems to depend on developmental period (Gjerde, Block, & Block, 1985; Messer, 1976; Messer & Brodzinsky, 1981). Cognitive tempo is not very stable during the preschool

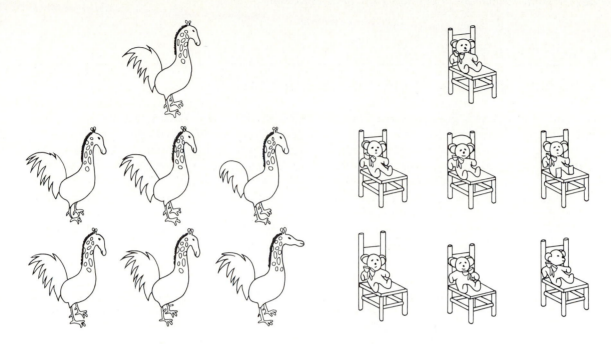

FIGURE 7-5
Example of Matching Familiar Figures Test.

years, but becomes more stable during the early school years. At present, it is unclear whether cognitive tempo becomes more stable as individuals pass through adolescence.

What Do IQ Tests Predict?

We have seen that the test-retest reliability of IQ scores is often questionable, particularly if the first IQ test scores are obtained early in life. We have also seen that the content validity of intelligence tests is suspect, given the narrow range of intellectual abilities assessed by such tests. Having said all this, you may quite reasonably be wondering whether IQ tests have any value. You may recall from our earlier discussion that the original purpose of intelligence tests was to predict school achievement. This type of predictive validity remains the major strength of standardized intelligence tests (Anastasi, 1988; Weinberg, 1989). IQ scores have been found to be related to school grades, scores on standardized achievement tests, and eventual level of education completed (McCall, 1977; Minton & Schneider, 1980; Snow & Yalow, 1982; Tamontana, Hooper, & Selzer, 1988). Not all intelligence test items are equally good at predicting school achievement. Items that are related to verbal skills and acquired knowledge predict school achievement better than do other

225

RESEARCH FOCUS 7-1

Is Impulsivity Always an Inefficient Cognitive Style?

Although impulsiveness is usually considered to be an inefficient approach to solving intellectual problems, a study by Zelniker and Jeffrey (1975) demonstrated that this is not always the case. Their task employed two types of target stimuli and stimuli sets to which the targets were to be compared. Examples of each type of visual stimuli sets are shown in Figure 7-6. One type of stimuli consisted of detailed stimuli, as in the Matching Familiar Figures Test. The other type of stimuli was much less complex. The detailed stimuli require careful comparisons in order to arrive at the correct choice, a task in which reflective children are likely to succeed and impulsive children fail. The less detailed stimuli can be compared in a more holistic fashion. Although impulsive children respond more quickly than

reflective children in both types of tasks, they are just as likely as reflective children to be correct for the less complex stimuli. Thus, impulsiveness may be an efficient information processing approach when the stimuli are suited to holistic processing rather than detailed processing. Smith and Nelson (1988), however, have countered this claim with the suggestion that the apparent holistic processing of impulsive children actually reflects their impressionistic, less effortful cognitive approach. Smith and Nelson found that impulsive children were more likely to make mistakes on matching tasks than were reflective children, even when the matching task favored holistic processing. Additional research is needed to clarify the differences between these two studies. 🍂

FIGURE 7-6

Example of each type of stimuli used by Zelniker and Jeffrey.

Source: from Zelniker & Jeffrey, 1976.

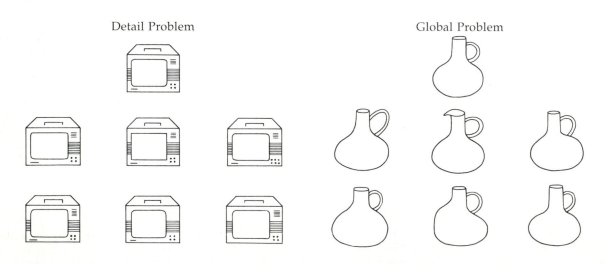

Detail Problem   Global Problem

types of test items (Kaufman, Kamphaus, & Kaufman, 1985; Siegler & Richards, 1982). It is important to be cautious when attributing causality on the basis of correlations, and in this case especially so because the causal connections seem so obvious. "These children did poorly in school *because* they are low on intelligence" is quite different from "Low scores on intelligence tests are associated with poor school performance." For example, another factor, such as, a different language or a handicapping condition, could be working to depress performance in both situations. Moreover, intelligence tests leave a substantial proportion of variance in educational and occupational success unaccounted for. The level of the father's education, for example, is as good a predictor of educational and occupational success as is IQ (McCall, 1977). In fact, a student's previous grades are a better predictor of his future grades than is IQ (Minton & Schneider, 1980). As we have seen, an individual's IQ score is subject to change, but the effort and motivation reflected in a student's past grades seems to be somewhat more stable.

Test Bias

If a test is valid, it is a fair measure of whatever it is supposed to test. In order for a standardized intelligence test to be fair, the sample of children used to standardize the test must be representative of the children who will take the test. Early versions of intelligence tests like the Stanford-Binet used white middle-class children to obtain their age norms and were argued to be biased against nonwhite children from different cultural backgrounds (Williams, 1974; Kamin, 1974). Recent revisions of intelligence tests have used more representative samples of children in the standardization process, but are still argued to be biased against racial and ethnic minorities and children from different cultural backgrounds (Garcia, 1981; Kaplan, 1985; Oakland & Parmelse, 1985; Snyderman & Rothman, 1987). Defenders of intelligence tests argue that the most blatant differences are taken into account in the testing procedure (for example, it is now common practice to test bilingual children in both of their languages) and also that the tests do an equally good, and perhaps even better, job of predicting school achievement for culturally different children as for white, middle-class ones (Sattler, 1988). Other critics of intelligence tests counter that IQ scores reflect motivational and personality variables rather than intelligence or the potential for academic achievement (Zigler & Seitz, 1982). The apparent bias of intelligence tests, combined with the fact that they tap only a limited set of intellectual abilities, makes even the predictive validity of intelligence tests questionable.

Unbiased Intelligence Tests?

One result of this controversy has been the attempt to construct culture-free (unbiased) intelligence tests. One such attempt is Florence Goodenough's (1954) Draw-a-Person test, in which a child is asked to draw a picture of a man or woman. Goodenough reasoned that children's success on such a task depended more on their intelligence than on their cultural background. However, previous experience with drawing might influence the results. Children's drawings of a person for the test are evaluated in terms of the amount of detail and elaboration compared to that found in the tests of other children of the same age. As it turns out, middle-class children tend to score

227

higher on this test than do lower-class children, a difference that may reflect the more frequent opportunities that middle-class children have to draw. In addition, scores on the Draw-a-Person do not predict school performance as well as IQ tests (Scott, 1981). The search for an unbiased intelligence test continues, but seems unlikely to succeed until we agree on exactly what it is that intelligence tests are supposed to measure.

Despite all of the problems with intelligence tests, the scores of such tests have played important roles in a number of theoretical controversies. In the next part of this chapter we will examine some of these controversies.

Psychometric Models of Intelligence

Much of the research conducted in this century on individual differences in intelligence has been based on the *psychometric* approach (Bjorklund, 1989). This approach is based on two assumptions: (1) Intelligence can be described in terms of *mental factors*. (2) It is possible to construct intelligence tests that will reveal individual differences in the mental factors that comprise intelligence (Carroll & Horn, 1981).

Although the psychometric approach to human intelligence assumes that intelligence is best defined in terms of mental factors, there has been considerable disagreement among scholars using the psychometric approach concerning the exact number of factors that comprise intelligence. Attempts to resolve this dispute have relied on a statistical technique known as *factor analysis* (Bjorklund, 1989). Basically, factor analysis involves attempts to determine the relationship of items on an intelligence test. Items that fit together in some pattern are thought to reflect the same factor. For example, an intelligence test might show that the following items are related to one another: reading comprehension items, story completion items, verbal analogy items, and vocabulary items. If so, people who perform well on one of these types of items (such as reading comprehension) should also perform well on the other types of items (such as story completion, verbal analogy, and vocabulary). Similarly, people who score low on one type of item might be expected to also score low on the other types of items. However, reading comprehension, story completion, verbal analogy, and vocabulary might not be related to items involving the rotation of 3-dimensional figures, solving mazes, or placing geometric forms on a board. The latter three types of items might be related to one another, but not be related at all to the first four types of items. If we did find such a pattern, the first set of items might be thought to involve verbal ability, whereas the latter three types of items might be thought to involve spatial ability.

It is rare that sets of test items fit together as well as the aforementioned examples (Bjorklund, 1989). The more typical pattern is one in which items correlate with one another to a certain degree; the significance of such relationships is influenced by the researcher's theoretical and statistical perspective. In addition, the types of items included on a test influence the factors that one might find. For example, if someone creating a test has failed to include items that measure spatial abilities, than people grading the test will not find a spatial factor. Thus, despite the sophisticated statistical techniques available to assist psychometric approaches to human intelligence, there is still considerable controversy concerning the nature of and number of factors that comprise human intelligence. We shall now consider some of the "factor" theories of human intelligence.

A recurring issue in theories of intelligence concerns the number of factors that are necessary to account for human intelligence. Approximately 60 years ago, Spearman (1927) proposed a 2-factor theory of intelligence. According to Spearman, the most important factor was a *general factor*, which he labeled "g" for general intelligence. All aspects of intelligence were thought to depend on this factor, and so Spearman argued that it was the most important factor of human intelligence. For Spearman, individual differences in intelligence reflected differences in this general factor. Despite his emphasis on this general factor, Spearman also recognized that individuals were better at certain intellectual tasks than others. For example, an individual might excel on most items on an intelligence test, but do poorly on items concerning specific types of mathematical abilities. As a result, Spearman also suggested that intelligence had *specific factors*, which he labeled "s." Specific factors have limited generality: Each specific factor is pertinent to only one specific type of intellectual task. According to Spearman, the "s" factors' limited generality made them relatively unimportant for our understanding of intelligence. Consequently, he argued that the "g" factor was the factor that needed to be explained in order to understand human intelligence.

One General Ability or Many Different Abilities?

An alternative model was offered by Thurstone (1938), who argued that intelligence consisted of a set of distinct independent factors, which he labeled *primary mental abilities*. Thurstone believed that there were seven such abilities: memory, numerical reasoning, perceptual speed, spatial ability, verbal comprehension, verbal fluency, and verbal reasoning. Examples of these abilities are given in Table 7-9. Despite the fact that this theory was developed

TABLE 7-9

Average correlations of familial studies of intelligence

	Bouchard and McCue	Plomin and DeFries
Monozygotic twins reared together	.86	.87
Monozygotic twins reared apart	.72	—
Dizygotic twins reared together	.60	.62
Siblings reared together	.47	.34
Siblings reared apart	.24	—
Parent and child living together	.42	.35
Parent and child separated by adoption	.22	.31
Unrelated children reared together	.32*	.25
Adoptive parent and adoptive child	.19	.15

* Average of adoptive/natural (correlation = .29) and adoptive/adoptive (correlation = .34) pairings.
SOURCE: From Bouchard & McCue, 1981; Plomin & DeFries, 1980.

over 50 years ago, a version of Thurstone's Primary Mental Abilities Test (the PMA) is still in use. However, the PMA only represents five of Thurstone's hypothesized factors: verbal reasoning, numerical ability, spatial ability, verbal comprehension, and verbal fluency.

Spearman's and Thurstone's models of intelligence are usually viewed as opposite extremes, with Spearman's model emphasizing a general overriding intellectual ability and Thurstone's emphasizing a set of independent intellectual abilities. The early versions of these theories did reflect such extremes, but Spearman later acknowledged the existence of four group factors (social, numerical, verbal, and visual) and Thurstone later acknowledged a general intellectual factor. Nonetheless, Spearman continued to emphasize the importance of a general factor of intelligence, while Thurstone emphasized the importance of distinct independent factors. The debate generated by these two pioneering theorists continues today (Carroll, 1982).

Guilford's Structure-of-Intellect Model. J. P. Guilford (1967) proposed a model of intelligence in which intellectual abilities were arranged along a set of three dimensions: (1) mental content, (2) mental operations, and (3) mental products. Mental content refers to the type of information that is being employed. Mental operations refer to the type of mental process involved. Mental products refer to the type of of outcomes that should result when certain mental operations are used in conjunction with certain mental contents. In his 1967 theory, Guilford proposed 120 intellectual factors. In a recently revised version of his theory, Guilford (1988) has suggested that 180 intellectual factors exist. These factors result from the interaction of six mental operations, five mental contents, and six mental products, as shown in Figure 7-7. It is far from clear whether so many factors must be used to explain intelligence. In fact, many of the factors proposed by Guilford correlate with one another, suggesting that the factors are not as independent as Guilford assumed (Brody & Brody, 1976; Horn & Knapp, 1974). Nonetheless, the contrast between Spearman, Thurstone, and Guilford illustrates the complexities involved in attempting to determine the nature of human intelligence.

Cattell and Horn's Fluid and Crystallized Abilities. The theory of intelligence proposed by Raymond Cattell and John Horn falls between the extremes of Spearman and Guilford. In this theory, two factors are thought to account for human intelligence (Cattell, 1963, 1971; Horn & Cattell, 1967, 1982). *Fluid intelligence* is one factor; this may be thought of as the thought processes that make incidental learning possible (for example, memory and perception). *Crystallized intelligence,* the other factor in this theory, represents the skills and information that individuals have accumulated during their lives. Cattell and Horn suggest that fluid intelligence is biologically determined. Thus, the skills reflected in fluid intelligence are thought to result more from maturation—the development of the central nervous system—than from experience. Cattell and Horn hypothesized that fluid intelligence would increase dramatically during early childhood as a result of the increasing maturation of

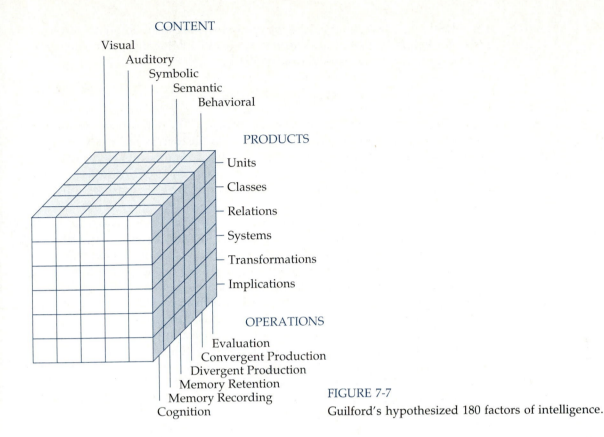

CONTENT
Visual
Auditory
Symbolic
Semantic
Behavioral

PRODUCTS
Units
Classes
Relations
Systems
Transformations
Implications

OPERATIONS
Evaluation
Convergent Production
Divergent Production
Memory Retention
Memory Recording
Cognition

FIGURE 7-7
Guilford's hypothesized 180 factors of intelligence.

the central nervous system. However, the loss of neurons and neural connections that begin in late childhood was predicted to result in cumulative losses in fluid intelligence once adolescence began. In contrast, crystallized intelligence is thought to be influenced by experience rather than maturation. As a result, crystallized intelligence was hypothesized to increase throughout one's life span, although the most dramatic increases should occur early in one's life. Although the available data do support the notion that crystallized intelligence increases with age, there is less support for the notion that fluid intelligence begins to decline in early adolescence (Horn & Cattell, 1967; Horn & Donaldson, 1976; Labouvie-Vief, 1977; Shaie, 1979; Shaie & Hertzog, 1983, 1986).

Jensen's Level I and Level II Intelligence. Arthur Jensen (1969, 1980, 1985) has hypothesized that two different levels of intelligence exist. Level I intelligence involves the ability to form associations. This type of intelligence is involved in remembering telephone numbers, learning the capitals of states, memorizing a song, or learning to say the alphabet. Level II intelligence involves more sophisticated cognitive abilities such as abstract reasoning and problem-solving skills. Level II intelligence is correlated with academic success, whereas Level I intelligence is not. Jensen's view of intelligence has sparked

231

considerable controversy because of his belief that races differ in terms of Level II intelligence (but not in terms of Level I intelligence). We shall consider this issue in greater detail in the next section.

Intelligence in the Context of the Nature–Nurture Controversy

The issue of whether an individual's intelligence is determined by nature (heredity) or nurture (environment) has a long history in the study of intelligence. As we shall see, much of the data used in attempts to resolve this controversy consist of scores obtained from standardized intelligence tests (IQ scores). As we review these data, it is important to remember the limitations of IQ scores as measures of intelligence.

This controversy was rekindled in 1969 by Arthur Jensen, who found that the IQ scores of black Americans and white Americans were significantly different, with black Americans scoring 15 points lower on the average than did white Americans. Based on these data, Jensen suggested that racial groups differed in terms of intellectual capacity. He also suggested that racial differences in intelligence reflected genetic differences between racial groups in terms of their intellectual capabilities. Thus, Jensen was arguing that intelligence is more influenced by nature than by nurture, and that racial groups differ in terms of innate intelligence (views reiterated in Jensen, 1989). Jensen's arguments have been challenged repeatedly (Layzer, 1972; Lewotin, 1976; Kamin, 1974, 1981; Mackenzie, 1984; Scarr & Weinberg, 1983; Snyderman & Rothman, 1987). At present, it seems safest to conclude that racial differences in innate intellectual ability do not exist.

Nonetheless, it is still possible that individual differences in intelligence are influenced by hereditary factors. One approach that has been used to study this possibility is called the *familial method*. This method involves the comparison of the IQ scores of various family members. Two recent reviews of studies using the familial method are summarized in Table 7-9. As you read this table, you will undoubtedly notice that the correlations of IQ scores increase as the genetic similarity of the individuals increase. Thus, monozygotic twins who were raised together show the greatest degree of similarity, followed by monozygotic twins raised apart. As you may recall from Chapter 2, monozygotic twins are genetically identical. Although the pattern of results shown in Table 7-9 suggests that there is a genetic component of intelligence, the extent of the genetic component is far from clear. First, much of the data is based on IQ scores and so must be interpreted in the context of all the controversies surrounding IQ tests. Second, the finding that monozygotic twins reared apart from one another have more similar IQ scores than do other familial pairs (except for monozygotic twins reared together) has usually been cited as strong support for the nature argument. However, many of the cases of monozygotic twins reared apart actually involved cases where the twins were raised by different family members, such as their aunts and grandparents (Kamin, 1974). Thus, the twin's environments were not substantially different even though they had been reared separately. Farber

(1981) compared the IQs of twins reared apart who had had similar environments with twins raised in different environments. She found that the IQ scores were the most similar when the environments were also similar. Finally, the finding that adopted children's IQ scores are more similar to their natural parents' scores than to their adoptive parents' scores is also usually cited as evidence for the nature argument. However, the data also revealed some environmental influences.

Adoption studies have found that two children adopted by the same family end up with similar IQ scores even though the children have no common heredity (Scarr & Weinberg, 1976, 1983). In addition, children born to lower-class parents and subsequently adopted by middle-class parents tend to score about 20 points higher on IQ tests than do comparable lower-class children raised by their natural parents (Scarr & Weinberg, 1975, 1983). Both of these results suggest that the environment plays an important role in intellectual development. However, it is unclear exactly how much of a role the environment plays compared to genetic factors. Perhaps the most important point is that intelligence, at least as measured by standardized tests, can be changed as a function of experience (Angoff, 1988; Horowitz, 1987).

RESEARCH FOCUS 7-2

A Model of Genotype-Environment Interaction

Scarr and McCartney (1983) have offered a model that attempts to explain the interaction of heredity and environment to produce intelligence. They suggest that individuals' genotype (genetic makeup) influences the manner in which they organize their experiences. In this model, both nature and nurture play important roles in intellectual development. However, heredity plays the more important role because it influences both individuals' genotype and how they organize experiences.

Scarr and McCartney suggest that there are three ways in which genotypes influence experience. The first is the *passive* effect, which occurs when children's biological parents provide their rearing environment. Scarr and McCartney propose that passive effects are most influential in the early phases of intellectual development.

The second type of effect is *evocative*. Evocative effects occur when a genetic predisposition influences the manner in which others interact with children. Irritable children elicit different reactions than do well-tempered children. Attentive children also receive different responses than do distractible children. Scarr and McCartney suggest that evocative effects remain constant throughout development.

The last type of effects are *active*, and refer to individuals' actively selecting environments in which they are most comfortable. The basic assumption concerning active effects is that individuals with different genotypes choose different sorts of environments. As a result, they have different sorts of experiences that influence their development. These sorts of effects are thought to increase with age. For example, the parents' role in shaping children's experiences decreases as the children get older, but the children's own role increase as they select their peer groups, favorite leisure activities, and so on.

RESEARCH FOCUS 7-3

Sex Differences in Intelligence

In an effort to better determine the existence of sex differences in intellectual abilities, Maccoby and Jacklin (1974) reviewed the available studies concerned with this issue. On the basis of their review, Maccoby and Jacklin reported the following possible sex differences in intellectual abilities: (1) mathematical ability—males are superior to females, (2) spatial ability—males are superior to females, and (3) verbal ability—females are superior to males.

When considering these sex differences, three things should be kept in mind: (1) The differences are based on averages. There is considerable overlap between the mathematical, spatial, and verbal abilities of males and females. For example, some females are excellent at mathematics, while some males are quite inept at mathematics. (2) The size of the average differences between the sexes is quite small (Plomin & Foch, 1981). (3) The verbal and spatial differences seem to be disappearing (Feingold, 1988). The decrease in sex differences for verbal and spatial abilities suggests that these differences are not biologically determined. If they were, one would not expect the differences to change over time. It may reasonably be assumed, then, that sex differences in verbal and spatial abilities reflected different rearing environments for males and females, and that the decrease in such differences reflects an increasing similarity in the relevant environmental variables for males and females. If this argument is valid, then one must ask why sex differences continue to exist for mathematical ability. This difference could result from different expectations for the mathematical prowess of males and females or from biological differences in mathematical ability between the two sexes (Fox, 1976; Parsons, Adler, & Kaczala, 1982; Raymond & Benbow, 1986). At present, the data concerning this issue are inconclusive. ❧

Atypical Intellectual Development

Mental Retardation and Learning Disabilities

All children do not develop intellectual and cognitive skills at an equal rate. Some children develop more rapidly than the average, and some more slowly. Within a fairly wide range of differences, psychologists tend to set aside these differences and talk about minor variations in normal development. Sometimes, however, the degree of difference is so great that it must be dealt with in special ways: exceptional educational intervention, special training, and the like. Recall that the need to identify extremely slow learners was the spark for the development of the intelligence testing movement. Two kinds of "slow learners" are now recognized as needing special educational help: the mentally retarded and children with special learning disabilities.

The term mentally retarded is applied to children and adults who display a generalized difficulty in dealing with cognitive problems. The typical defining characteristic is a low score on a standardized intelligence test. The group of people who are mentally retarded are really quite heterogeneous.

The range of test scores and the labels applied to different levels of retardation are shown in Table 7-10. The behavioral implications of low intelligence test scores for these groups are very different.

Many "borderline" retarded individuals function quite well in many normal social and vocational settings; their learning problems become apparent only in formal educational settings. Such individuals are unlikely to pursue college degrees, of course, but they can earn a living, raise a family, and participate fully in the life of the community. One of the great human tragedies is that such individuals often suffer because of the "borderline retarded" label; they are denied opportunities for work and training because of the label attached to them. A significant problem for educators is the paradox of trying to provide special learning opportunities, which many of these children need in order to lead the most productive lives possible, without simultaneously branding them with a negative label that can do more harm than the educational intervention can help. The current trend for

TABLE 7-10

Characteristics of the mentally retarded

Category of Retardation	Estimated Incidence in U.S. and Percentage of Retarded Population	Education Possible	Life Adaptation Possible
Mild 50–70 IQ (equivalent to 8–12-year-old)	4,200,000 70%	Sixth grade (maximum) by late teens; special education helpful	Can be self-supporting in nearly normal fashion if environment is stable and supportive; may need help with stress
Moderate 35–50 IQ (equivalent to 6–8-year-old)	1,200,000 20%	Second to fourth grade by late teens; special education necessary	Can be semi-independent in sheltered environment; needs help with even mild stress
Severe 10–35 IQ (equivalent to 3–6-year-old)	400,000 6.7%	Limited speech, toilet habits, and so forth with systematic training	Can help contribute to self-support under total supervision
Profound below 20 IQ (equivalent to 0–3-year-old)	200,000 3.3%	Little or no speech; not toilet trained; relatively unresponsive to training	Requires total care

SOURCE: From Ruch, 1984.

these and many other "different" children is toward *mainstreaming*, which maintains the child in the normal setting, that is, not totally segregated into special schools or classes, while providing special services as unobtrusively as possible.

At the other end of the list in Table 7-10 are the "profoundly" retarded individuals. These individuals, even as adults, need complete care, and may be incapable even of self-maintenance. Much of the training for such individuals concentrates on minimal speech and motor development. Behavior modification techniques have been especially useful with these children.

A further distinction not necessarily related to the labels in Table 7-9 is often made between two categories of retardation based on their etiology. The first category, cultural–familial retardation, represents the lower end of the normal distribution, and the causes are thus the same as the characteristic causes for normal development, i.e., genetic endowment and environmental interaction. Children with cultural–familial retardation are only mildly retarded and are often from economically deprived homes.

The second category includes those cases that can be traced to a specific organic problem. Examples of these types come from two genetic anomalies, Down's syndrome and phenylketonuria (PKU). Down's syndrome results from an extra chromosome; PKU is the result of an enzyme deficiency. In both cases, severe mental retardation may result. It is important to note, however, that although a defect has a genetic origin it does not mean that its emergence is inevitable. A great breakthrough in the treatment of mental retardation was the discovery that PKU is partially treatable; a low-protein diet from birth controls for the enzyme deficiency and makes retardation far less severe. Also, children who have currently nontreatable organic deficiencies such as Down's syndrome appear to go through the same development as other children, although more slowly and with a lower level of eventual development (Cicchetti, 1977).

A different type of atypical development is one which goes by many names: specific learning disabilities, minimal brain dysfunction (MBD), hyperkinetic, special learning and behavior problems (SLBP), and others. As the variety of names suggests, there is little agreement about either the causes or the normal manifestations of this syndrome (Brown & Campione, 1986). The simplest definition is a behavioral description: There are children who, despite average or above average scores on standard intelligence tests, still experience great difficulty in one or more learning situations. The most common problem is difficulty in learning to read, or *dyslexia*.

These problems often show up in the testing situation, where a particular pattern of errors is evident although the overall test performance is adequate or better than adequate. One example of such a pattern is when the score on the performance section of the WISC (for example, block design) is noticeably poorer than on the verbal section. Given the uncertainty surrounding this area, it is not surprising that there are no fully satisfactory diagnostic tools or subsequent treatments. It may well be that these children also do not comprise a homogenous group, and that the different kinds of learning difficulties now lumped together need to be separated and examined indi-

236

RESEARCH FOCUS 7-4

The "Wild Boy of Aveyron"

One major influence on intelligence tests as we know them today was the work of the French psychologist Binet. The French had been interested in the general issue of mental deficiency for more than a century before Binet's first intelligence scale in 1905. The story of a young boy who had been lost in the wilderness for an unknown length of time did much to spark popular, albeit sensational, interest in the subject in early nineteeth-century France.

Jean Marc-Gaspard Itard (1775–1838) wrote in 1801 about his attempts to train and educate an 11-year-old boy who had been found running naked in the forest near Aveyron. The story of the "wild boy of Aveyron" captured the popular imagination and probably contributed to the creation of the atmosphere of support for special education, which assisted later scholars in their efforts to identify and provide for children with special learning needs. The complete background of the "wild boy of Aveyron" was never uncovered, but the popular myth that he was raised by animals is almost certainly untrue.

A remarkably similar story was reported in 1976. A young African boy was reported to have been found living with a troop of chimpanzees and to have a behavioral repertoire similar to the chimps. Several American psychologists flew to Africa to investigate the possibility that the boy had lived out of human contact for some time. The stories were unfounded, however, and the boy's various family and institutional placements could be traced to account for his experiences from birth. His chimp-like behavior was actually just erratic behavior connected to his severe mental retardation.

Despite the continuing appeal of such stories to the public's imagination, no documented cases of nonhuman reared young children exist. 🐦

---

vidually. This possibility is supported by the observation that some children will benefit from treatments, but no single treatment helps all children classified as learning disabled (Ross, 1967). This highlights once again the complexity of the construct "intelligence" and the need to avoid simplistic notions about it.

Children and adolescents who score very high on IQ tests compared to the average for their age are called *gifted children*. Such children were a lifelong interest of Terman, who edited and wrote the 5-volume *Genetic Studies of Genius*, a longitudinal study begun in the 1920s that continues today (Terman & Oden, 1959). The notion of "genius" was dropped after it became clear that the unique achievements of the few whom history calls geniuses were nearly impossible to predict. The term "gifted" was subsequently adopted to indicate children who were especially able intellectually and who might be expected to achieve a great deal. Terman's study debunked two major myths about highly intelligent children that were popular at the time and that have not yet completely disappeared.

The Gifted Child

"Intellectually gifted children are below average in other areas, especially social and physical development." Actually, there is a moderate

237

positive correlation among areas of development, and the stereotype of the child "brain" as a sickly recluse is not based in reality.

2. "Intellectually gifted children are more likely to burn out at an early age." Again, this is not true. Terman's longitudinal studies of high-IQ children revealed that they continued to score above average on intelligence tests through the years, and that they were above average in intellectual pursuits as measured by occupation, awards, publications, and so forth. Since spectacularly negative outcomes of early brilliance tend to get more publicity than routinely good ones, the impression Terman tried to counter still persists (Montour, 1977).

If the normal school experience without alteration is inappropriate for children with learning problems (and it is), then this is also true of highly talented learners. In the childhood years, these students need extra stimulation to avoid boredom and to make efficient use of their ability. Toward early adolescence, when specialized abilities become more salient, educational programs that facilitate specific intellectual strengths are needed (Stanley, Keating, & Fox, 1974; Keating, 1976). These children have often been neglected in educational planning, although recent trends indicate that this situation is changing (Horowitz & O'Brien, 1986).

Summary

Theoretical debates concerning the nature of intelligence and how to best measure it have existed since the beginning of this century. The *psychometric* approach to the study of intelligence and intelligence testing rests on two principles: (1) Intelligence can be described in terms of *mental factors*. (2) It is possible to construct intelligence tests that will reveal individual differences in the mental factors that comprise intelligence.

Psychometric theorists have posited as few as one general mental factor (Spearman, 1927) and as many as 180 specific intellectual factors (Guilford, 1988). It is not yet possible to determine exactly how many factors of human intelligence exist, for the factors that different theorists find depend at least in part on which they are looking for and on the statistical techniques that they employ.

Although many models of human intelligence exist, all theorists agree that there are individual differences in both intellectual ability and intellectual development. One result of the universal recognition of individual differences has been the attempt to develop tests to measure these differences in intelligence. Beginning with Binet's attempts at the beginning of this century and continuing to present attempts to devise culture-free intelligence tests, the use and meaning of intelligence tests have been controversial. Foremost among the problems facing intelligence tests are their lack of stability, the limited array of intellectual abilities that they assess, and the fact that other variables are as good at predicting school achievement as are these tests.

238

Despite the limitations of intelligence test scores as measures of intelligence, these scores have provided the basis for arguments concerning the relative roles of nature and nurture in determining an individual's intellectual prowess. The available data suggest that both nature and nurture are important. However, the amount of intelligence that is determined by nature and the amount of intelligence that is determined by nurture is still unclear.

The study of individual differences in intelligence has revealed that individuals differ in terms of *cognitive style*. *Field dependence/field independence* concerns how individuals process visual information. Field dependent individuals focus on the whole while neglecting the parts. Field independent individuals are better able to perceive the parts as well as the whole. Conceptual tempo refers to the speed and accuracy with which individuals approach problems. *Reflective* individuals are deliberate and usually correct. *Impulsive* individuals reach their conclusion quickly, but are usually wrong. Another dimension of cognitive style distinguishes between *convergent* thought and *divergent* thought. Convergent thought is used when one must determine the correct answer to a problem. Divergent thought is appropriate when problem solving requires flexibility and creativity to arrive at a solution.

Suggested Readings

GARDNER, H. (1983). *Frames of mind: The theory of multiple intelligence.* New York: Basic Books.

GOULD, S. (1981). *The mismeasure of man.* New York: Norton.

HOROWITZ, F., & O'BRIEN, M. (1985). *The gifted and talented: Developmental perspectives.* Washington, D.C.: American Psychological Association.

STERNBERG, R. (1983). *Handbook of intelligence.* New York: Cambridge University Press.

———. (1985). *Beyond IQ.* New York: Cambridge University Press.

WEISBERG, R. (1986). *Creativity: Genius and other myths.* New York: W.H. Freeman and Co.

Cognitive Development

Introduction

The material presented in Chapter 7 focused on the psychometric approach to intelligence, intellectual development, and intelligence testing. One criticism of this kind of measuring has been that it focused on *what* children know and how well they can manipulate this knowledge rather than on *how* children acquire, organize, and use knowledge. The term *cognition* is associated with research to increase our understanding of the mental processes involved in everyday life, such as concept formation, memory, and problem solving. Although studies of intelligence also are concerned with these mental processes, studies of cognition do not rely on intelligence test scores. As we saw in the last chapter, standardized intelligence tests do not sample the entire range of human cognitive abilities (for example, creativity) or predispositions (such as, cognitive style) and may not even be the best measures of the intellectual capabilities they do test (for example, the tests may be biased against individuals with experiences different from those used to standardize the test).

Scholars interested in cognitive development are not interested in comparing the amounts of intelligence that different individuals possess, but, instead, they attempt to determine how mental processes develop from birth onward. Scholars of cognitive development attempt to answer questions such as: How do children make sense of the world? Do the mental abilities of infants differ from those of preschool children? Do the mental abilities of preschool children differ from those of school children? If differences do exist, what are they?

The Cognitive Development Theory of Jean Piaget

The most influential theorist in the area of cognitive development was Jean Piaget, a Swiss scholar who studied children's mental skills for over five decades (the number of pages published by Piaget during this time totaled more than 20,000!). Early in his career, Piaget worked on intelligence tests in Binet's laboratory. Piaget abandoned this work because he noticed that the mistakes children made were often more interesting than their correct responses. Intelligence tests focused on children's correct responses, and Piaget reasoned that analyses of children's incorrect responses to a wide array of cognitive tasks would be necessary to understand cognitive development. This insight led Piaget away from intelligence testing and resulted in many discoveries about how cognition develops.

According to Piaget, each time children (or adults, for that matter) encounter an object, situation, or problem, they attempt to interpret it in terms of what they already know. In other words, they attempt to recognize it by looking back at characteristics of objects, situations, and problems they have encountered before. The process of interpreting the world in terms of existing knowledge is called *assimilation.*

Rarely does an individual encounter a situation in which only assimilation is needed. The more typical situation is one in which children must also engage in *accommodation.* Accommodation involves modifying existing knowledge to incorporate a new experience. For example, young children may interpret their first experience with a shotput in terms of their previous experience with balls. Therefore, they might expect the shotput to be relatively light, to roll, and to bounce (assimilation). However, they will quickly discover that it cannot be bounced and is not light, and so will modify their concept of "ball" (accommodation).

Piaget considered the processes of assimilation and accommodation to be *invariant cognitive functions.* These are processes that are invariant because they are present at birth and are retained throughout life. These functions interact with the knowledge and experience that exist at any one point in life to produce cognitive growth. Piaget suggested that *moderately discrepant events* are the most likely to yield cognitive growth because of the way these events involve assimilation and accommodation. A moderately discrepant event is both familiar and novel. The familiarity provides a basis for assimilation. The novelty provides a need for accommodation. This combination provides optimal cognitive growth. After all, completely familiar objects and events can be handled with assimilation alone, and therefore these result in no cognitive change. Totally novel objects and situations provide no basis for assimilation, and accommodation alone will not result in cognitive growth. Imagine trying to read a book in an unfamiliar language. It would be a unique situation, but there is no basis for assimilation and so little possibility for learning to occur.

Piaget (Piaget & Inhelder, 1969) suggested that cognitive development could best be characterized as a series of stages. The first stage is the *sensorimotor stage,* which typically lasts from birth until two years of age. The second stage is the *preoperational stage,* which usually lasts from two years of age until seven years of age. The next stage is the *concrete operational stage,* which Piaget found to begin around 7 years of age and which lasted until sometime around age 12. The final stage is the *formal operational stage,* which characterizes the thought of everyone who has passed through the concrete operational stage.

There are several points that Piaget emphasized about these stages of cognitive development. First, the rate of development may vary from child to child. Thus, the ages given above are approximations. They describe the development of the "average" child, but normal children may nonetheless pass through the stages more quickly or more slowly than these averages would suggest. Second, the order in which children pass through the stages is invariant. In other words, everyone must pass through the stages in the following order: (1) sensorimotor, (2) preoperational, (3) concrete operational, and (4) formal operational. Third, each stage is qualitatively different from the others. That is, the essential character of thought in each stage is different from the essential character of thought in the other stages. Nonetheless, quantitative changes occur within each stage. For example, Piaget believed that once children enter the preoperational stage they are capable of learning language. As we saw in Chapter 6, children's language skills improve considerably during the preschool years. For Piaget, language acquisition is an example of quantitative development during the preoperational stage. In other words, although the transition from one stage to another represents a qualitative change in children's thought, stages do not emerge fully developed. Development that occurs within a stage is quantitative, whereas the change from one stage to another is qualitative. These ideas are summarized in Table 8-1, and should become clearer as we consider each of the four stages.

The First Stage—Sensorimotor Thought.   Piaget emphasized the role that children's own activity played in cognitive development. Moreover, he argued that this was true for the newborn infant as well as for older children. Piaget's recognition that the human infant is an active organism seeking stimulation rather than a passive, receptive one greatly influenced his theory of cognitive development. This influence is most easily seen in Piaget's account of sensorimotor thought. According to Piaget, the development of sensorimotor thought results from the infant's active search for sensory and motor experiences (Piaget, 1952).

One of the first achievements of the sensorimotor period is the appearance of the *primary circular reaction*, usually around the second month of life. In a primary circular reaction, infants accidentally perform some action that pro-

TABLE 8-1

Description of Piaget's proposed stages of cognitive development

Stage	Ages	Main Characteristic	Major Developmental Task
Sensorimotor	Birth–2 years	Infant's innate schemes provide bases for interacting with the environment	Acquisition of capacity for mental representation
Preoperational	2–7 years	Rigid and inflexible thought	Acquisition and integration of mental operations
Concrete Operational	7–12 years	Capacity for flexible thought, but limited to concrete present stimuli	Acquisition of capacity for abstract and logical thought
Formal Operations	12+ years	Capacity for abstract and logical thought	—

duces an interesting result; infants then attempt to reproduce the action in order to once again experience the result. For example, infants' hands may accidentally touch their own cheeks, which causes the infants to turn their head toward their hands, consequently resulting in the infants sucking on their own fists. In a primary circular reaction, the infants reproduce the actions that led to the interesting result. Thus, the infants will once again bring the hand to their cheeks, turn their heads, and begin to suck on their fists. An accidental behavior thus becomes purposeful because the infants enjoyed what happened as a consequence of the original unintentional behavior. These circular reactions are called primary because the result as well as the action involves the infants' own bodies.

In the next few months, from about the third to the sixth month of life, *secondary circular reactions* appear. Like primary circular reactions, secondary circular reactions first involve a chance action that produces an interesting response, like hitting the side of a crib and making the tiny figures on an attached mobile dance about. Once this result occurs, the infants may repeat their action, producing the same interesting result again and again. In the secondary circular reaction, their action has results in the external world rather than in part of the infants' own bodies.

Toward the end of the first year of life, infants begin to behave as if they intend to achieve a goal. For example, infants who have learned to open and close a box may also learn to push aside a barrier in order to get a hold of the box so that they may open and close it. Shortly after their first birthday, infants also begin to vary their behaviors in order to cause certain effects. Such behaviors, called *tertiary circular reactions* by Piaget, differ from those in the earlier circular reactions in that infants are no longer interested in producing a fixed result. It is the variation in the results that intrigues them. For example, children in highchairs may like the result obtained from dropping their oatmeal on a tray, be intrigued by the difference in the result when they drop some more oatmeal on the floor, and be delighted when both of these results differ from that obtained by throwing some oatmeal on the wall.

According to Piaget, the major developmental task to be accomplished during the sensorimotor stage is the acquisition of the capacity for *mental representation*, an ability that allows one to represent aspects of the world inside one's head. In Piaget's view, infants initially lack the capacity to mentally represent the world, but they will have acquired this ability by the end of the sensorimotor stage. The qualitative difference between the sensorimotor stage and the preoperational stage concerns mental representation. Children in the sensorimotor stage lack mental representation, whereas children in the preoperational stage have it. Given his emphasis on the sensorimotor child's acquisition of mental representation, Piaget looked carefully for evidence of mental representation toward the end of the sensorimotor period. We will consider four types of evidence that Piaget found important.

LANGUAGE. As was discussed in Chapter 6, children begin to use words around 18 months of age. Words are symbols that represent objects, ideas, events, and so on. According to Piaget, the children's symbolic use of words is made possible by their emerging capacity for mental representation. The production and comprehension of words certainly involves mental represen- tation, for word use requires that both the word and its meaning be repre- sented in the mind.

SYMBOLIC PLAY. Children who place a piece of paper on their head and say "hat" are pretending that the piece of paper is a hat. Pretense of this sort is called symbolic play because one object represents another. In our example, the piece of paper represents a hat, and is in a sense a symbol for a hat. Symbolic play, like children's use of words, requires the capacity for mental representation.

IMITATION. Piaget (1962) believed that infants' capacity for imitation changed during the sensorimotor stage. Infants' first imitations occur be- tween the first and fourth month of life, but are strictly limited. Infants can only imitate behaviors that they already possess, such as producing certain sounds. Learning new behaviors through imitation is impossible during this age range. In addition, infants will only imitate behaviors in which they are already engaged. Imitiation during this period is illustrated by the following observation, "I noted a differentiation in the sounds of [my daughter's] laughter. I imitated them. She reacted by reproducing them quite clearly, but only when she had already uttered them immediately before" (Piaget, 1962, p. 10).

Between the ages of four and eight months, infants can imitate an increas- ing number of behaviors, and no longer need to engage in a behavior im- mediately prior to imitiating it. However, infants are still limited to imitating behaviors they already know how to perform. Learning a new behavior by imitating it is still impossible.

The next major change in imitation occurs between 8 and 12 months of age. Infants can now imitate novel behaviors, so that learning through imi- tation is now possible. In addition, infants can now imitate facial expressions. Because infants cannot see their own faces, Piaget argued that the imitation of someone else's facial expression required that infants mentally represent the facial expression to be imitated. The imitation of facial expressions, then, is the first type of imitation to involve mental representation.

The final advance in imitations during the sensorimotor period comes between 18 and 24 months of age. Children are now capable of *deferred imitation*, which Piaget defined as the ability to imitate the past actions of a model. For example, children may observe their mother changing the chan- nels on the television set with a remote control device. The next day children may push the buttons on the remote control even though the mother has not touched it since the previous day. Deferred imitation requires mental representation because a person must be able to remember the model's behaviors to later imitate them.

The most important aspects of imitation for mental representation are infants' imitations of facial expressions and deferred imitation. Recent inves- tigations have suggested that these capacities may emerge earlier than Piaget suggested. Meltzoff and Moore (1977) found that infants younger than one week of age were able to imitate the tongue protrusion and mouth opening

TABLE 8-2

Description of the three types of circular reactions that occur in the sensorimotor stage

Age at which Reaction First Occurs	Type of Circular Reaction	Characteristics
2 months	Primary	Infant accidentally produces a behavior that leads to an interesting result; infant then attempts to reproduce behavior to achieve result again; both the behavior and the result have to do with the infant's own body
4–6 months	Secondary	Same as primary circular reactions, but result now occurs in the environment rather than with the infant's own body
12–18 months	Tertiary	Infant purposely modifies behavior to see what consequences the modifications have on the results

of an adult model. Although it may not surprise the reader to learn that infants will stick out their tongues or open their mouths if they see another person doing so, the Meltzoff and Moore findings were quite surprising to psychologists such as Piaget who believed that such skills were impossible until infants were about 1-year-old. Other researchers have also found imitation of facial gestures and expressions in young infants, sometimes when infants are only hours old (Field, Woodson, Greenberg, & Cohen, 1982; Field et al. 1983; Meltzoff & Moore, 1983; Vinter, 1986). Field et al. (1982) found that newborn infants were able to imitate happy, sad, and surprised facial expressions, findings that support those of Meltzoff and Moore. Vinter (1986) investigated newborn infants' imitation of movement (tongue protrusion and hand opening-closing) and stationary arrays (a stuck-out tongue, open or closed hand), and found that the infants were more likely to imitate the moving models than the stationary models, a finding that may also be interpreted as support for the Meltzoff and Moore findings. Other investigations have failed to find imitation in such young infants (Hayes & Watson, 1981; Koepke, Hamm, Legerstee, & Russell, 1983; Lewis & Sullivan, 1985; McKenzier & Over, 1983; Waite, 1979), suggesting that young infants may not be able to imitate facial expressions.

If newborn infants actually imitate facial expressions, then this ability should remain constant or even improve during the first months of life. In fact, however, imitation of facial expressions declines during this age period. For example, infants' imitation of tongue protrusion peaks around 2 months of age and then declines (Abravanel & Sigafoos, 1984; Fontaine, 1984). This developmental patterns suggests that the imitation of young infants is not purposeful, but instead the function of *innate releasing mechanisms* (Jacobson, 1979; Kaye, 1982). Innate releasing mechanisms, sometimes called fixed-action patterns, refer to behaviors that are automatically elicited by particular types of stimuli (Lorenz, 1973; Tinbergen, 1951). These behaviors, then, are

247

FIGURE 8-1
Photographs of infants imitating facial expressions.

Source: from Field, Woodson, Greenberg, & Cohen, 1982, p. 180.

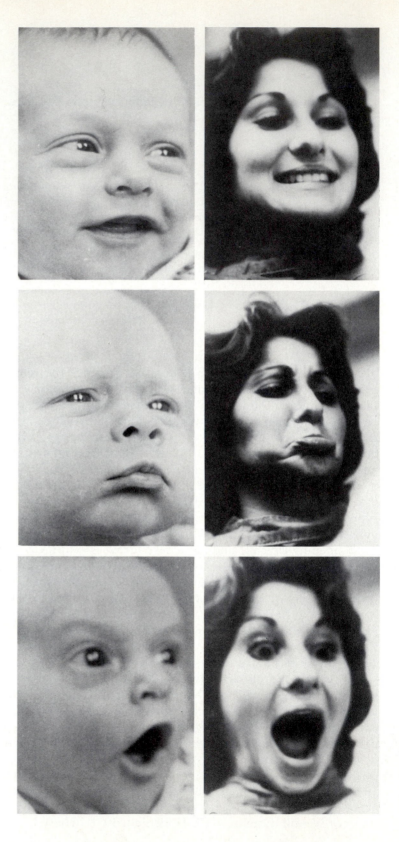

similar to reflexes. If young infants' imitations of facial expressions are reflexive rather than purposeful, then the "imitation" is quite different from the intentional behavior described by Piaget (see Research Focus 8-1).

The debate over the status of young infants' imitations continues, for not all investigators believe that the imitations result from innate releasing mechanisms (Meltzoff & Moore, 1983, 1985). Meltzoff and Moore argue that young infants have been shown to imitate a number of facial expressions, and that it is unlikely that each type of imitation results from a different reflex. The resolution of this debate will be important, for it has implications for the mental capabilities of young infants. Their imitations are either reflexive or intentional. If intentional, they involve mental representation at a much earlier age than Piaget proposed. Regardless of whether the early imitations are reflexive or intentional, young infants' imitations may facilitate early infant–adult interaction because infants' imitations make it seem that they are responding to adults' expressions (Bjorklund, 1987).

Deferred imitation has also been found at younger ages than Piaget reported. Meltzoff (1985, 1988) reported deferred imitation in some 14-month-old infants, and Abravanel and Gingold (1985) found deferred imitation in some 12-month-old infants. These results do not necessarily contradict Piaget's findings because the number of infants who engage in deferred imitation increases as infants get older (see Figure 8-2). Most infants acquire this capacity during the 18- to 24-month-old range, consistent with Piaget's findings.

RESEARCH FOCUS 8-1

What Do Young Infants Imitate?

Jacobson (1979) presented 6-week-old infants with five stimuli to imitate: (1) another person's tongue protrusion, (2) opening and closing hand movements, (3) a pen moving toward the infants' faces, (4) a small white ball moving toward the infants' faces, and (5) a plastic ring attached to a string moving up and down in front of the infants. Jacobson found that the infants were as likely to stick out their tongues in response to the pen and ball as they were to the tongue protrusion. Following this testing session, Jacobson asked the parents of half of the children to stick their tongues out at their children several times a day. As a result, these children were given opportunities each day to practice their imitation of tongue protrusion. The remaining parents were asked not to stick their tongues out at their children. When the children were retested with the same stimuli at 14 weeks of age, the infants who had been provided with practice opportunities imitated tongue protrusions. The infants who were not provided with practice opportunities were less likely to imitate tongue protrusions. These results support the notion of early imitation being caused by innate releasing mechanisms for two reasons. First, the 6-week-old infants did not engage in selective imitation, but also produced tongue protrusions in response to the ball and pen. Second, the positive effects of practice are similar to those obtained for the walking reflex, a behavior that vanishes during early infancy unless it is practiced (Zelazo, Zelazo, & Kolb, 1972).

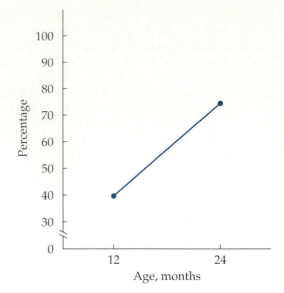

FIGURE 8-2

Developmental progression of deferred imitation in 12- to 24-month-old children.

Source: based on Abravanel & Gingold, 1985.

THE CONCEPT OF OBJECT PERFORMANCE. With the possible exception of discussions in philosophy classes, most of us assume that objects exist independently of ourselves. For example, we believe that objects continue to exist even if they are no longer in our presence. For example, when you leave your classroom, the objects that remain behind continue to exist despite the fact that you can no longer see them. Similarly, if your professor leaves the classroom during the class, you recognize the fact that he or she still exists even though he or she is no longer in your visual field. Despite the seemingly obvious characteristics of these examples, Piaget argued that the concept of object permanence is not present in the young infant. According to Piaget, the concept of object permanence is acquired in a universal invariant sequence that spans the entire sensorimotor period.

Piaget reported that, during the first few months of life, infants act as if they do not remember an object that is out of sight. If an object disappears from sight, the infant acts as if the object no longer exists. Thus, there is no concept of object permanence during the first four months of the sensorimotor period.

During the age range of 4 to 8 months, the infant shows some improvement in object permanence. If an object is partially hidden from infants, they will attempt to retrieve it. However, if the object is completely hidden, infants treat the object as if it no longer exists. This is illustrated by Piaget's observation of his 7-month-old daughter:

> Jacqueline tries to catch a celluloid duck on top of her quilt. She almost catches it, shakes herself, and the duck slides down beside her. It falls very close to her hand but behind a fold in the sheet. Jacqueline's eyes have followed the movement, she has even followed it with her outstretched hand, but as soon as the duck has disappeared—nothing more (Piaget, 1951, pp. 36–37).

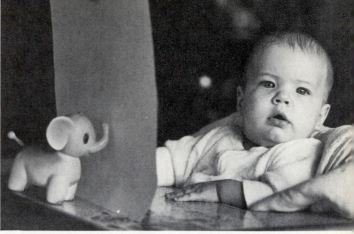

An infant looks at an interesting toy elephant (*left*). Once the toy elephant is hidden from the infant, he loses interest and acts as if the elephant no longer exists (*right*).

Late in this same age range, infants will search for a completely hidden object if they are already moving in the direction of the object. For example, infants who watch their mother hide a toy under a blanket will retrieve it, but only if they are already reaching for the toy when it is hidden.

The age range of 8 to 12 months is often characterized as the most peculiar with regards to the development of object permanence. Although 8- to 12-month-old infants will search for and retrieve objects that are completely hidden, they also are surprisingly limited in their newly acquired ability to find hidden objects. If an object is hidden from infants while they are watching (for example, a towel is placed on the object) the infant will retrieve the object. If this sequence is repeated a few times with the object hidden at the same location each time, infants will consistently retrieve the object from that location. If the object is then hidden at a different location, infants will search for the object at the first location even though they saw it being hidden at the second location. Piaget believed that this curious failure to search where the object *was seen to be hidden* resulted from infants' failure to recognize that the object existed independently of the interesting experience the infant had with it (finding it under the towel at the first location). Bjorklund (1989) provides an observation that illustrates this same process in an infant's everyday experience:

> At approximately ten months [of age], Heidi was seated in her high chair. . . . She was banging her spoon on the tray of the chair when it fell to the floor to her right. She leaned to the right, saw the spoon on the floor, and vocalized to me, and I retrieved it for her. She began playing with the spoon again, and it fell to the right a second time. She again leaned to the right, saw the spoon on the floor, and vocalized until I returned it to her. Again, she played with the spoon, and again it fell to the floor, but this time to her *left*. After hearing the clang of the spoon hitting the floor, Heidi leaned to the *right* to search for the spoon, and she continued her search for several seconds before looking at me with a puzzled expression. Heidi had been watching the spoon at the time it fell. . . . She had both visual and auditory cues to tell her where it must be. But . . . she searched where she had found the vanished object before. She trusted her own past actions with the fallen spoon more than her own perceptions (Bjorklund, 1989, p. 102).

251

This characteristic of 8- to 12-month-old infants' object permanence has been labeled the "A not B" error. As we shall see shortly, this phenomenon is the most controversial aspect of Piaget's proposed sequence of object permanence development.

During the 12- to 18-month-old age range, infants readily shift from the first location to the second location in the aforementioned situation. However, if the object is hidden at location A and then moved from location A to location B without infants' witnessing the change of location, the infants look for the object at place A. This is reasonable behavior, given that the infant last saw the object being hidden at location A. However, once infants fail to find the object, they stop looking for it. Thus, infants are capable of following changes of locations that they witness, but cannot yet cope with changes of location that they cannot see.

The final months of the sensorimotor period (18 to 24 months of age) represent the culmination of the development of the concept of object permanence. Toddlers are able to find the object even if it is secretly moved to another location. According to Piaget, this is made possible by the emergence of the capacity for mental representation that emerges during this stage. The developmental sequence of object permanence posited by Piaget is summarized in Table 8-3.

TABLE 8-3

Summary of Piaget's findings concerning the development of object permanence

(0–4 months)

Out of sight is out of mind; when an object disappears from view, the infant makes no attempt to search for it visually or to retrieve it manually

(4–8 months)

Infants show the first evidence of object permanence; when an object is completely hidden under a cover (e.g., a blanket), infants will not search for it visually or manually; they will search manually for a hidden object only if they were already moving in the direction of the cover at the time the object was hidden; they will search visually for an object if the object is only partially hidden by the cover

(8–12 months)

The infant searches manually for hidden objects; when an object is placed under a cover, the infant will lift the cover and retrieve the object; however, if the object is hidden under several covers successively, with each successive hiding fully visible to the infant, then the infant will search under the first cover rather than the last cover

(12–18 months)

When an object is hidden under several covers, with each successive hiding fully visible to the infant, the infant correctly searches under the last cover; however, if some of the hidings are carried out in such a way that the infant cannot see them (e.g., by moving the object from one cover to another inside an opaque container), then the infant does not search for the object under the last cover

(18–24 months)

Infants solve the invisible hiding problem; they correctly search under the last cover even if some of the steps in the series of hidings were invisible to them

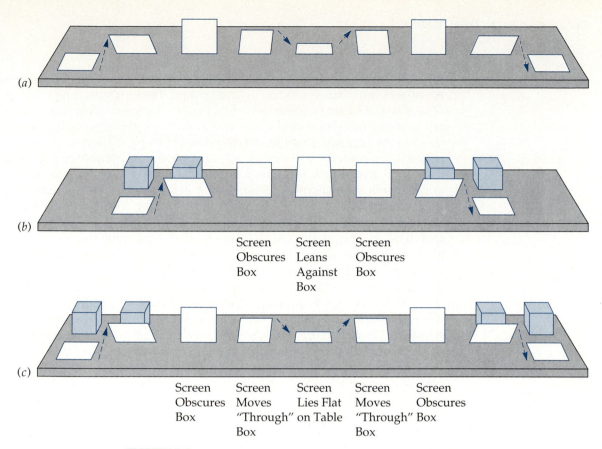

(a)

(b)

Screen	Screen	Screen
Obscures	Leans	Obscures
Box	Against	Box
	Box	

(c)

Screen	Screen	Screen	Screen	Screen
Obscures	Moves	Lies Flat	Moves	Obscures
Box	"Through"	on Table	"Through"	Box
	Box		Box	

FIGURE 8-3

Illustration of object permanence study. (*a*) Habituation Stimulus: Screen rotates back and forth in a 180° arc. (*b*) Possible Event: Screen rotates back and leans against blue box, then returns to original position. (*c*) Impossible Event: Screen rotates back, moves "through" blue box in a 180° arc, and returns to its original position.

Source: based on Baillargen, Spelke, & Wasserman, 1985.

Most investigators concur with Piaget's conclusion that the concept of object permanence is not present at birth but exists almost completely by two years of age (Flavell, 1985). Nonetheless, there is controversy concerning two aspects of the development of object permanence described by Piaget. One controversy concerns the age at which infants first display object permanence. Piaget suggested that this type of knowledge first appeared around eight months of age. Two recent studies suggest that object permanence may be present in 3½-month-old infants (Baillargen, 1987; Baillargen, Spelke, & Wasserman, 1985). In these studies, infants were shown a screen that rotated through a 180-degree arc. After the infants were used to the rotating screen, mirrors were used to make it appear that a box was placed behind the screen. In the *possible* condition, the screen rotated until it bumped into the box and then returned to its original position. In the *impossible* condition, the screen continued its arc by passing through the box until it lay flat on the table and then returned to its original position. These conditions are shown in Figure 8-3. Baillargen and her colleagues found that the infants were more interested

253

in the impossible event than the possible event even though the impossible event was more similar to the original event. These results suggest that the 3½-month-old infants expected the box to stop the screen and were surprised when it did not. Because the box was hidden by the screen during its arc, this in turn suggests that the infants have object permanence.

The other controversial aspect of Piaget's proposed sequence concerns the "A not B" error found in 8- to 12-month-old infants. As you may recall, this error involves the infant searching for a hidden object in a location where they have previously found the object, even though they have seen it hidden in another location. In a recent critique of this literature by Wellman, Cross, and Bartsch (1986), the point is made that searching for hidden objects requires both conceptual knowledge and problem-solving skills. Conceptually, children must know that objects continue to exist even when they are out of sight. However, children must also have problem-solving skills sufficient to the task of finding the object. At present, it is difficult to separate these two aspects of the task, and so it is difficult to explain exactly why and when the "A not B" error occurs (Wellman et al., 1986; Harris, 1986). Recent work, however, does suggest that memory is a factor (Bjork & Cummings, 1984; Diamond, 1985). Diamond (1985) found that the length of the delay between hiding the object and the infant's search for the object was related to the "A not B" error, and that the length of delay necessary to produce such errors changed with age. A delay of only two seconds was sufficient to produce the "A not B" error in 7½-month-old infants, whereas a delay of ten seconds was necessary to produce the "A not B" error in 12-month-old infants. These results demonstrate that infants' memory skills play a role in the "A not B" error, and are shown in Figure 8.4.

FIGURE 8-4

How memory influences the A-not-B error.

Source: from Diamond, 1985.

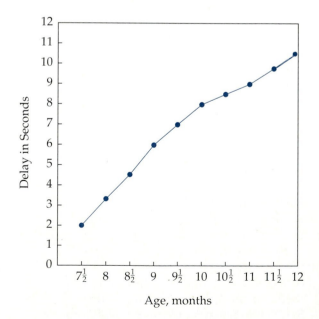

RESEARCH FOCUS 8-2

Representational Thought in Two- and Three-Year-Old Children

In our earlier discussion of infants' skills at imitating, the issue of representational thought was raised. Recall that despite the controversy over the exact age at which infants first imitate the facial expressions of others or engage in deferred imitation, it is generally agreed that infants have the capacity for representational thought. However, as is often the case in cognitive development, the first emergence of a skill in one context does not necessarily mean that the skill will be used in other appropriate contexts. Consider a recent ingenious study by Judy DeLoache (1987). In this study, 2½-year-old and 3-year-old children were shown a room and an exact but much smaller scale model of the room. Initially, children were shown the correspondences between the room and its scale model. Children then saw an object being hidden in the scale model and were told that the object was hidden in the same location in the real room. They were then asked to find the object in the real room. Curiously, only the 3-year-old children were consistently able to find the hidden object. DeLoache suggests that the success of the 3-year-old children reflected their ability to think of the scale model simultaneously in two ways—as an object (the model itself) and as a symbol for something else (the actual room). In contrast, the 2½-year-olds were able to think of the model only as an object; they therefore failed to use the information provided to them regarding the model as information about the actual room. Thus, even though 2½-year-old children clearly have representational skills, their ability to use such skills is limited. If they must view an object as both an

FIGURE 8-5

Photograph of DeLoache's scale model room.
Source: from DeLoache, 1987. Photograph courtesy of Bill Wiegand, University of Illinois.

object and as a symbol, they fail to recognize that the object is also a symbol. On the other hand, three-year-old children are able to view an object in both ways, and so readily succeed on tasks such as that used by DeLoache. 🦋

The Second Stage—The Preoperational Stage. Although Piaget may have underestimated young infants' ability to mentally represent objects and actions, there is no doubt that children are capable of mental representation by the end of the sensorimotor stage. Just as Piaget emphasized that the emergence of the ability for mental representation was the major accomplishment of the sensorimotor stage, he stressed that the major accomplishment of the preoperational stage was the emergence and organization of mental operations. Piaget believed that mental operations originate in overt behaviors, and evolve in the following manner during the preoperational stage. First, children develop the ability to perform a particular overt behavior, such as adding one block to another to create a short tower, Next, the behavior is practiced and generalized to other objects (for example, the child may learn to add more water to a fishbowl). Finally, the general properties of the action (such as, addition) become internalized as a mental operation (addition).

Although mental operations evolve from overt behaviors during the preoperational stage, the mental operations of the preoperational child are not integrated with one another. Instead, the mental operations operate in isolation from one another. As a result, the thought of preoperational children is quite limited. First, it is very *concrete*. Representation, thinking, and reasoning are closely tied to what children can immediately perceive and to the actions in which they engage. As a result, of this concreteness, preoperational thought is also likely to be *inflexible*. That is, the range of possible thoughts about a problem or situation is limited. One evidence of this inflexibility is *centered thought*, a term that refers to young children's tendency to center their attention on a single feature of an object or situation, rather than recognizing all potentially relevant features.

One example of how preoperational children's concrete and inflexible thoughts affect their problem solving is found in Piaget's *conservation of liquid task*. In this task, the children are shown two identical beakers filled with identical amounts of water. After the children have agreed that the two beakers each contain the same amount of water, the water is poured from one beaker into another of a different shape (say a taller and thinner beaker). The children are then asked if the amount of water in the one remaining original beaker and in the tall, thin beaker are the same amount. Preoperational children say no, justifying their incorrect response by focusing on a single aspect of the new beaker. For example, they might say that the tall beaker has more because the water is higher, ignoring the fact that the beaker is narrower than the original. The conservation of liquid task and other Piagetian conservation tasks are illustrated in Figure 8-6.

Preoperational children's centered thought is also reflected in their performance on classification tasks. If you are shown a group of objects (for example, a large red triangle, a large green ball, a small green triangle, and a small red ball) and are asked to put them into two groups, you might decide to use color, shape, or size as the criterion. As long as you employed one criterion consistently, you would produce groups in which every object was similar in some way to every other object in the group.

Piaget and Inhelder (1969) found that if 2- and 3-year-old children are given a group of colored shapes (circles, squares, and rectangles), they use the shapes to make designs or pictures rather than classes of objects. Four- and five-year-olds do produce classes of objects; but they differ in the type of criteria they use for classification. Four-year-old children only use a single dimension (such as, shape) to guide their classification efforts. Five-year-old children use two or more dimensions (for example, size and shape: small squares versus small circles, large squares versus large circles).

In recent years, investigators have been able to demonstrate classification skills in children slightly younger than Piaget reported. Markman, Cox, and

Type of Conservation	Dimension	Change in Physical Appearance	Average Age at Which Invariance Is Grasped
Number	Number of elements in a collection	Rearranging or dislocating elements	6–7
Substance (mass) (continuous quantity)	Amount of a malleable substance (e.g., clay or liquid) 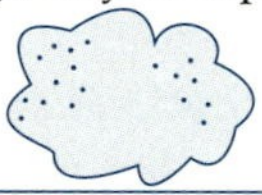	Altering shape 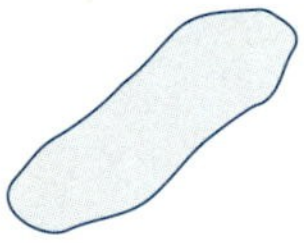	7–8
Length	Length of a line or object	Altering shape or configuration 	7–8
Area	Amount of surface covered by a set of plane figures 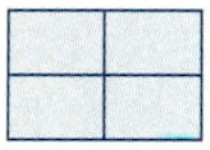	Rearranging the figures 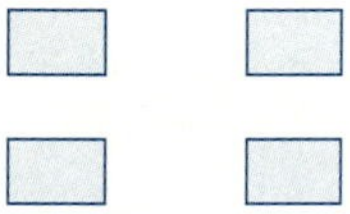	8–9
Weight	Weight of an object 	Altering its shape 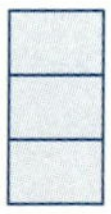	9–10
Volume	Volume of an object (in terms of water displacement) 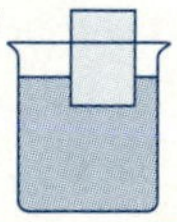	Altering its shape 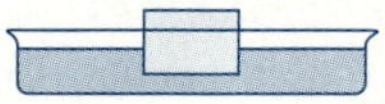	11–14

FIGURE 8-6
Examples of Piaget's conservation tasks, and the average age at which children pass each task.

257

A six-year-old acting on the materials used in Piaget's conservation of liquid task.

Machida (1981) found that 3- and 4-year-old children could classify objects if they were asked to put the objects that were alike into opaque bags rather than into groups on the table in front of them. Markman et al. suggest that 3- and 4-year-old children understand classification, but are distracted by all the objects in front of them when they are asked to create groups that they can see. Thus, they forget to classify the objects and instead begin to play with them.

Although four- to six-year-old children are able to classify objects into groups, they are unable to correctly answer *class inclusion* questions. For example, five-year-old children may have correctly divided a group of flowers into red flowers and white flowers. If there are 10 red flowers and 5 white flowers, the child is also likely to know that there are more red flowers than white flowers. However, if the children are asked whether there are more flowers or more red flowers, they will err by saying there are more red flowers. The children's failure to answer class inclusion questions correctly reflects their concentration on the parts and their inability to simultaneously compare the part (red flowers) and the whole (all of the flowers). According to Piaget, the ability for class inclusion reasoning does not emerge until seven years of age, more than two years after classification skills first emerge. Piaget's results for class inclusion have been supported by similar findings reported by McCabe, Siegel, Spence, and Wilkinson (1982).

The Third Stage—Concrete Operational Stage. By the time children enter the concrete operational stage, Piaget believed that they possessed an integrated set of mental operations. This made possible *decentered thought*, the capacity

258

to consider multiple aspects of a situation or problem. Children at the concrete operational stage succeed on the "class inclusion" problem because they can simultaneously look at the part and the whole. Thus, in the case of the previous example using red and white flowers, they know there are more flowers than red flowers. Similarly, concrete operational children are not fooled by irrelevant changes in the conservation of liquid task. In fact, concrete operational children may act surprised that the investigator has even asked if the amount of liquid is still the same. Children will justify their decision by making an identity argument ("It is still the same water. None has been added or taken away"), a reversibility argument ("You could pour the water back into the original glass. Then you would see that it is still the same amount"), or a comparison argument ("It looks like there's more water in this glass because the water is much higher. But the glass is thinner, so it only *looks* like there's more water").

Although concrete operational children are capable of correctly solving problems such as class inclusion and conservation of liquid, there is one weakness inherent in the thought of this stage. Concrete operational children are unable to think in abstract terms. In order to solve a task such as conservation of liquid, the materials in question must be present. The children will fail the task if they cannot act on the objects themselves, hence the name "concrete" operational stage. It is not until the formal operational stage that abstract thinking is attained.

Another limitation of concrete operational thought is that it is not applied consistently to all tasks. As summarized in Figure 8-6, the conservation tasks employed by Piaget are not solved successfully at the same age, as one might expect if decentered thought is the sole factor that makes success possible. Conservation of number, length, liquid, and mass are correctly solved around seven years of age. Conservation of area and weight are usually understood between 8 and 10 years of age, with conservation of volume being solved only between 10 and 12 years of age.

The Fourth Stage—Formal Operational Thought.   This period is the high point of cognitive development. An adolescent capable of formal operational thought has the same thought processes as a good scientist. Among other facets of thought to appear in this period are the ability to plan ahead, the ability to formulate testable hypotheses, and the ability to consider many possibilities. Consider the following problem. What affects the rate with which a pendulum swings—the length of the string or the amount of weight attached to the end of the string? Suppose that children are given a set of different lengths of string and a set of different weights and asked to solve this problem. Concrete operational children will vary string lengths and weights simultaneously, and so will never determine which variable influences the rate with which a pendulum swings. Formal operational children might vary string length and hold weight constant, and then vary weight and hold string length constant. By doing so, they will discover the correct answer. This is illustrated in Figure 8-7.

259

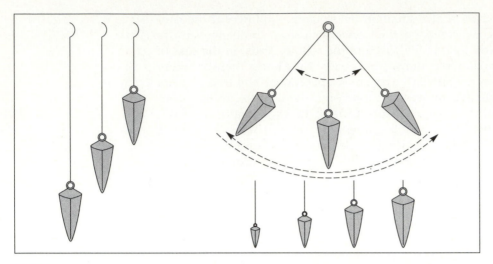

FIGURE 8-7

Example of the pendulum problem used to assess formal operational thought.

Strengths and Weaknesses of Piaget's Theory

In the previous discussion, we have considered the main points of Piaget's theory of cognitive development, highlighting both Piaget's proposed sequence of developmental stages and the major developmental accomplishments of each stage. At the present time, it seems safe to conclude that Piaget's emphasis on mental representation, cognitive functions, moderately discrepant events, and qualitative changes in cognitive development will be remembered as important contributions to developmental psychology. However, as we have seen, there is a growing body of literature that suggests that Piaget may have underestimated children's cognitive capabilities.

Learning

Classical Conditioning

Psychologists interested in learning have attempted to determine how experience influences development. Perhaps the most famous type of learning is that associated with Pavlov (1927). Pavlov discovered that pairing a neutral stimulus with one that triggered a reflex response resulted in the neutral stimulus being able to call forth the reflex response. For example, the sound of a bell ringing is a neutral stimulus. It will not elicit salivation in a hungry dog. However, food is a stimulus that will cause a hungry dog to salivate. In the type of learning that concerns us here, called *classical conditioning*, the food is an unconditioned stimulus and the dog's salivation upon seeing the food is an unconditioned response. If the ringing of the bell is paired with the presentation of the food on a sufficient number of occasions, the ringing of the bell becomes a conditioned stimulus (it becomes associated with the

260

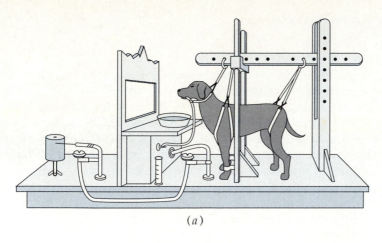

(a)

Before Conditioning

Neutral
stimulus
(bell)

No
salivation

Unconditioned
stimulus
(food)

Unconditioned
response
(salivation)

An unconditioned stimulus produces an unconditioned response.

During Conditioning

Neutral
stimulus
(bell)

Unconditioned
stimulus
(food)

Unconditioned
response
(salivation)

The unconditioned stimulus is presented along with a neutral stimulus.
The unconditioned stimulus continues to produce an unconditioned response.

After Conditioning

Conditioned
stimulus
(bell)

Conditioned
response
(salivation)

The neutral stimulus has become a conditioned stimulus.
It is now capable of producing a conditioned response—the same response
that was previously produced by the unconditioned stimulus.

(b)

FIGURE 8-8

Illustration of the associations involved in classical conditioning.

food). As a result, the ringing of the bell in the absence of the food will cause
the dog to salivate. In classical conditioning, then, the learning organism has
associated two events in the environment such that either event will bring
about the reflex response. These relationships are shown in Figure 8-8.

At present, it is difficult to say if newborn infants can be classically conditioned. The studies that have been done have reported mixed results, but more often than not it has proven difficult to demonstrate classical conditioning in newborns (Olson & Sherman, 1983; Sameroff & Cavanaugh, 1979). Although it becomes easier to demonstrate classical conditioning in infants as they get older, it is also the case that some unconditioned stimulus-conditioned stimulus pairings are easier than others (Blass, Ganchrow, & Steiner, 1984). For example, Brackbill, Fitzgerald, and Lintz (1967) conditioned the pupil dilation of two-month-old infants to either a fixed-time interval or to a tone. In the fixed-time interval condition, a light remained on for 20 seconds, then went off for 4 seconds, then came back on for 20 seconds, then back off for 4 seconds, and so on. The test of conditioning involved leaving the light on and measuring whether the infant's eyes dilated after 20 seconds even though the light had not changed. The infant's eyes did dilate, demonstrating that the infants had associated the conditioned stimulus (the time interval) with the unconditioned stimulus (a change in light intensity), so that the conditioned stimulus by itself could now elicit the response (pupil dilation).

The other condition involved presenting a sound 1.5 seconds prior to a change in the illumination. When presented with the sound but with no change in illumination, the infant's pupils did not dilate, demonstrating that classical conditioning had not occurred. It seems, then, that the likelihood of classical conditioning depends on both the age of the infant and on the nature of the neutral stimulus to be paired with the unconditioned stimulus. Here, then, is another instance of interaction of child and environment.

Operant Conditioning

Another type of learning involves a different sort of association than does classical conditioning. Classical conditioning involves the association of two stimuli—the unconditioned stimulus and the conditioned stimulus. *Operant conditioning*, studied by B.F. Skinner (1938), involves the association of one's own behaviors with some environmental outcome. If the outcome is positive, the likelihood of the behaviors being repeated increases. For example, rewarding a child for saying "please" makes the child more likely to say please. If the outcome is negative, the likelihood of the behaviors being repeated decreases. For example, punishing a child for playing with matches makes the child less likely to play with matches. In both cases, learning has occurred. Although both classical and operant conditioning involve the pairing of events, they differ in one important regard. The events to be associated in classical conditioning both occur in the world, while only one of the events in operant conditioning does so (the consequence). The other event is the child's own behavior. Operant conditioning is possible at an earlier age than is classical conditioning (Appleton, Clifton, & Goldberg, 1975; Watson & Ramey, 1972).

However, for operant conditioning to occur in young infants, the consequence must be immediate. For example, Siqueland and Lipsitt (1966) were able to condition 2- to 4-month-old infants to turn their heads in one direction by rewarding the infants with a mouthful of sugar water immediately after the infants had turned their heads in the correct direction. In this study, the infants heard different sounds as their right cheeks were gently stroked. When the infants heard a tone in this context, they were rewarded with the sugar water if they turned their head to the right. However, if the infants heard a buzz sound, they were not rewarded for turning their head to the right. The infants quickly learned to turn their head after hearing the tone, but not after hearing the buzz. Young infants, then, appear to pay attention to the aspects of the environment that are associated with reward.

RESEARCH FOCUS 8-3

The Saga of Little Albert

Although it is difficult to elicit classical conditioning in children younger than two months of age, it is much easier to do so with older infants. In perhaps the most infamous study of this sort, Watson and Rayner (1920) trained an 11-month-old boy, code-named Little Albert, to fear a harmless laboratory rat. Initially, Little Albert exhibited no fear of the rat. In fact, he reportedly attempted to play with the rodent. However, Watson and Rayner then began a conditioning paradigm in which every time Little Albert saw the rat, a hammer hit an iron bar just behind one of Little Albert's ears. This produced startled responses in Little Albert. He would jump, cry, and attempt to hide his face. Eventually, Little Albert began to make these *same* responses to the rat

alone. Learning in the form of classical conditioning had occurred. The neutral stimulus (the rat) had been associated with the aversive stimulus (the sudden sound). Morever, Little Albert generalized his fear responses to other white furry objects—a rabbit, a dog, a fur coat, and a bearded Santa Claus mask. Although this study is a persuasive example of classical conditioning, it is infamous in that it violates ethical standards for research with human subjects (which were not in force when Watson and Rayner performed the experiment). Procedures that cause harm to the subject are unethical, and it is quite unlikely that a study such as this one would be conducted by contemporary psychologists. 🙢

Once Little Albert became classically conditioned to fear the white rat, he reacted with alarm to other white furry objects, such as a bearded mask.

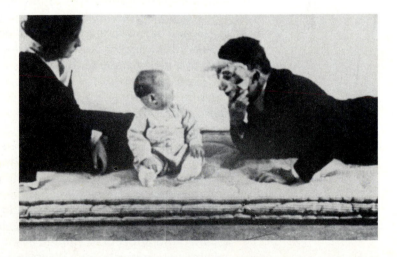

The Development of Problem-Solving Skills

Before one can solve a problem, it is necessary to recognize that a problem exists. DeLoache and Brown (1987) have suggested that even very young children are able to recognize when a problem exists. In fact, young children will often engage in self-initiated learning, creating problems which they then attempt to solve. For example, DeLoache, Sugarman, and Brown (1985) placed a set of nesting cups on a table in front of a child who was told that "these are for you to play with." The children in this study ranged in age from 18- to 42-months-old and were similar to one another in that they began trying to fit the cups together *even though they had not been told to do so.* However, the manner in which children attempted to correct their errors in nesting the cups did change with age. The youngest children used *brute force,* attempting to force the cups into one another. The next stage involved *local correction,* where the child removed one cup from another and then tried another cup until finding one that fit. The final stage involved *construction as a whole.* Children who used this strategy paid attention to all of the relations among the cups, recognizing that the order of largest, next largest, next largest, and so on had to be maintained in order to solve the problem correctly.

What sort of information do children use when asked to solve a problem? Wellman, Fabricius, and Chuan-Wen (1987) investigated 2- and 3-year-old children's ability to consider every available instance in an array. Children were asked to either put a penny into every container in front of them or to take a penny out of every container in front of them. Sometimes the array of containers was in a straight line. Other times the array consisted of randomly arranged containers. The 2-year-old children experienced difficulty in successfully putting a penny in every container, whereas the 3-year-old children were quite successful at doing so. Wellman et al. suggest that the ability to consider every available instance is a fundamental problem-solving skills that first emerges in 3-year-old children.

Sugarman (1987) asked children ranging in age from $1\frac{1}{2}$ to $3\frac{1}{2}$-years-old to find stickers of cats that were hidden under some of the objects in a 16-object array. For example, the 16 objects in one of the arrays consisted of 4 green brushes, 4 yellow brushes, 4 green blocks, and 4 yellow blocks. The stickers of cats were hidden under the green brushes and the yellow blocks. After they had found some of the stickers under the green and yellow blocks, the younger children in this study looked for the stickers only under the remaining green brushes and yellow blocks. This strategy certainly makes sense, since these were the only objects under which the children had found the stickers. However, the $3\frac{1}{2}$-year-old children looked for the stickers underneath all of the objects. Sugarman suggests that the $3\frac{1}{2}$-year-old children were attempting to determine the characteristics of negative instances (those without a sticker) as well as the characteristics of positive instances (those with a sticker). Interestingly, adults who were asked to find the stickers performed similarly to the $3\frac{1}{2}$-year-old children. The ability to consider negative as well as positive instances is an important characteristic of problem solving, and appears to emerge as young as $3\frac{1}{2}$ years of age.

Fabricius, Sophian, and Wellman (1987) asked 3-, 5-, and 7-year-old children to find which of three houses contained "anybody in it," "an empty room," "nobody in it," or "a grown-up and a child in it." Each house had two doors that children could open to look inside. Each door had either one person behind it (an adult or a child) or nobody behind it. Fabricius et al. were interested in whether or not the children realized, after opening one door on a house, that they did not need to open the other door to correctly decide (for example, if they opened a door with an adult behind it when looking for a house with "anybody in it"), and if the children realized that they did need to open the remaining door to make other decisions (for example, if a child opened a door with nobody behind it while looking for an empty house, it is still necessary to open the second door to determine if the house is empty). The authors report that even some 3-year-olds understood whether they had sufficient or insufficient information to make a correct choice, but that this ability increased as children got older. Thus, the ability to make the sort of inferences necessary for correct problem solving is present in 3-year-olds, and becomes strengthened and elaborated as children get older.

Although young children have the capacity to make inferences about sufficient and insufficient information in problem solving, they are not as likely to understand the information that others need to make inferences (Sodian & Wimmer, 1987; Taylor, 1988). Sodian and Wimmer (1987) tested 4- and 6-year-old children's ability to understand the inferences of others in the following manner: Initially, a child and another person were shown a container filled with red balls. Then, while the other person was not watching, the child saw one of the balls moved to a second container. The other person was then told that the object in the second container had been taken from the first container. Despite the fact that the other person had been given sufficient verbal information to correctly decide what was in the second container, most of the 4-year-old children believed that the other person did not know what was in the second container because they had not seen the ball moved. In contrast, most 6-year-old children recognized that the other person did have sufficient information to infer what objects were left in the second container.

Problem-Solving Rules. Siegler (1989a, 1989b) has suggested that an important aspect of cognitive development involves the acquisition of increasingly powerful rules for solving problems. According to Siegler, rules are "if . . . then statements linking particular conditions to actions to be taken if those conditions hold true" (Siegler, 1985, p. 88). Siegler applied this approach to an analysis of a task Inhelder and Piaget (1958) had used to study formal operational thought. This task involved the use of a simple balance scale on which weights could be placed at various distances from the midpoint. Children were asked to decide what would happen once a level that kept the scale from moving was released, correct answers depending on the children's ability to consider both the number of weights on each side of the balance and the distance of the weights from the midpoint. The results obtained by Siegler suggested that children's performance on the balance task reflected their knowledge of certain rules. The task and the rules hypothesized by Siegler are shown in Figure 8-9.

Problem Type	RULE			
	I	II	III	IV
1. Equal weight–equal distance 	100%	100%	100%	100%
2. Unequal weight–equal distance 	100%	100%	100%	100%
3. Unequal distance–equal weight 	0% should say "Balance"	100%	100%	100%
4. Conflict weight (more weight on one side, more distance on the other, configuration arranged so side with more weight goes down) 	100%	100%	33% (chance responding)	100%
5. Conflict distance (similar to conflict weight, but side with greater distance goes down) 	0% should say "Right side down"	0% should say "Right side down"	33% (chance responding)	100%
6. Conflict balance (like the above two problems, except the scale remains balanced) 	0% should say "Right side down"	0% should say "Right side down"	33% (chance responding)	100%

FIGURE 8-9

Siegler's rules for the weight-balance problem.

Concept of Number

Counting Skills. The most significant work on children's developing understanding of the concept of number has been done by Rochel Gelman and her colleagues. This work suggests that children use counting as their principal method for representing the number of objects in a group. According to Gelman, children's counting is governed by five counting principles (Gelman & Gallistel, 1978; Gelman, 1982; Gelman & Meck, 1983).

RESEARCH FOCUS 8-4

Concepts of Appearance and Reality

In a series of ingenious studies, John Flavell and his colleagues have investigated children's ability to distinguish appearance and reality. For example, children were shown a red toy car covered by a green filter that made the car look black. The filter was then removed and children were allowed to inspect the car (which was now clearly a red car). The car was then placed behind the green filter once again, so that it once more appeared to be a black car. Children were then asked: "What color is this car?" "What color does this car look like to your eyes right now?" "What color is this car really and truly?" Thus, children were asked to distinguish the color that the car appeared to be from the color that the car actually was. Three-year-old children were likely to respond "black" regardless of the question, indicating that they focused on appearance. Six-year-old children, on the other hand, responded correctly to the questions, demonstrating that they can distinguish appearance from reality (Flavell, Green, & Flavell, 1986). Similar findings emerged when Chinese children were tested, suggesting that the developmental pattern reflects children's cognitive skills rather than the English phrases "really and truly," "looks like," and so on (Flavell, Zhang, Zou, Dong, & Qi, 1983).

The problem that young children have distinguishing appearance from reality does not seem to reflect an inability to distinguish reality from nonreality. Flavell, Flavell, and Green (1987) gave 3-year-old children both apparent-real tasks and pretend-real tasks. The apparent-real tasks were similar to that described earlier. For example, children were shown a rock that had been painted to look like an egg. They were then asked: "What does this look like to your eyes right now? . . . Let's find out some more about this. It's really and truly a stone that somebody painted. Feel it. It's hard and doesn't break and the paint comes off. . . . What is this really and truly? Is this really and truly an egg or really and truly a stone? Does it look like an egg or does it look like a stone?" In the pretend-real tasks, children were shown an object (e.g., a curved straw) and asked: "What is this really and truly? O.K. Let's pretend that this is a telephone. . . . What is this really and truly? Is it really and truly a straw or really and truly a telephone? What am I pretending this is right now? Am I pretending that this is a straw or am I pretending that this is a telephone?" Children were more likely to correctly respond to the pretend-real questions than to the apparent-real questions, suggesting that the distinction between pretense and reality emerges at an earlier age than does the distinction between appearance and reality. Flavell et al. suggest that the pretense-reality distinction emerges earlier because children have more opportunities to practice and perfect pretending skills than they do appearance/reality skills. In addition, parents often encourage their young children in games of pretend, but it is the rare parent who plays appearance/reality games with his or her child. 🐦

1. *The one-one principle:* According to this principle, each item is counted once and only once, using a different number for each item. Although preschool children do sometimes violate this princple, even 2-year-old children obey the principle if the set of objects to be counted is not too large. Four-year-old children use the one-to-one principle when asked to share things with others (Frydman & Bryant, 1988) and also use number words to refer to the objects they put in one-to-one correspondence (Becker, 1989).

2. *The stable-order principle:* According to this principle, the order in which a person counts should always be the same. For example, 1, 2, 3, 4, and so on. Young children use this principle even though their number sequence may differ from adults. Thus, a 2-year-old child might consistently use the sequence "2, 6" when counting 2 objects. Despite the fact that children may make errors in regard to the number labels that they use, the important point is that they use the labels that they have in a consistent order.

3. *The cardinal principle:* According to this principle, the last number used when one counts an array of objects is the cardinal number value of the array. Thus, if a person counts a set of five objects "1, 2, 3, 4, 5," then 5 is the cardinal number value. Four-year-old children have been found to use the cardinal principle to decide if one-to-one correspondence between 2 sets of objects is possible (Becker, 1989). Four-year-old children do not, however, use the cardinal principle when asked to share objects (Frydman & Bryant, 1988), perhaps because they base cardinality decisions on the last number word in a counting sequence rather than on an understanding of counting principles (Frye, Barisby, Lowe, Maroudas, & Nicholls, 1989).

4. *The abstraction principle:* This principle stipulates that anything may be counted.

5. *The order-irrelevance principle:* According to this principle, the order in which objects are counted does not matter. If a person counts an array of 5 objects, it does not matter in what order the objects are counted. The order in which a person uses numbers is important (the stable-order principle), but the order in which a person chooses which objects to count is unimportant. The outcome will still be the same.

Numerical-Reasoning Skills.   During the preschool period, children acquire numerical-reasoning skills as well as counting skills. They will learn that adding objects to an array increases the numerical value of the array and that subtracting objects reduces the numerical value. They will also learn to tell if one array has the same or different number of objects than another array and to perform simple addition and subtraction (Gelman, 1982; Siegler & Robinson, 1982; Yoshida & Kuriyama, 1986).

The Information Processing Approach to Cognitive Development

Much of cognition is concerned with abilities involved in the interpretation and organization of information that is available in the environment. In general, the information processing approach to cognitive development is concerned with determining the capacity of cognitive systems and the speed

RESEARCH FOCUS 8-5

Counting by Infants?

Although the presence of counting and numerical reasoning skills in 2- to 5-year-old children was surprising to many developmental psychologists prior to Gelman's pioneering work, there is evidence that children understand numbers at an even earlier age. Starkey, Spelke, and Gelman (1980) showed 6- to 9-month-old infants slides of three common household objects. The objects on each slide were different and were shown until the infants became tired of looking at the slides. Once the infants had become habituated to the 3-item slides, they were shown an alternating sequence of 3-item and 2-item slides. The only difference between slides was the number of objects. The infants looked longer at the 2-item slides than at the 3-item slides, demonstrating that they were able to discriminate two items from three items.

In another demonstration of infants' capacity to process numerical information, Starkey, Spelke, and Gelman (1981) showed 6- to 8-month-old infants two slides simultaneously. One slide contained 2 objects. The other slide contained 3 objects. Sometimes while looking at the pair of slides, the infants heard a sequence of 2 drum beats. Other times the infants heard a sequence of 3 drum beats. Starkey et al. report that the infants tended to look longer at the 2-item slides when they heard 2 drum beats and longer at the 3-item slides when they heard 3 drum beats. 🐦

---

and efficiency with which these systems process information (Bjorklund & Frankel, 1989). This common basis has not prevented controversies from appearing in the information processing literature.

All information processing theories assume that the amount of mental space available for digesting information is limited. Robbie Case (1984; 1985) has distinguished between *operating space* and *storage space* in memory. Operating space refers to the amount of space available for dealing with information. Storage space refers to the amount of space available for putting aside information in memory. According to Case, total processing space is the combination of total operating and storage space. Case suggested that total processing space remained constant across development, but that the proportion of space allocated to operating space and storage changed as a function of development. In this view, children become more efficient at processing information as they get older, and so the amount of operating space required to deal with information decreases with age. This in turn frees additional space for storing information. As a result, storage space increases with age.

Case's view is similar to an information processing theory proposed by Sternberg (1985). Sternberg suggested that an individual's behavior on a task depends on the individual's familiarity with the task. If the task is a highly familiar one, then the intellectual processes involved are thought to reflect *automatization*. Automatization refers to the increased efficiency of information processing that occurs as a task is performed over and over. If the task is an unfamiliar one, the intellectual processes involved are active and conscious rather than automatic. For instance, when you were first learning to

One Information Processing System or Several?

read, reading required considerable effort and concentration. As you became a better reader, reading became more and more automatic and so required less effort. You may recall from our discussion of Piaget's theory that he emphasized the interaction of assimilation and accommodation in cognitive development. Although Sternberg's and Piaget's views are somewhat different in terms of their emphases, both views place considerable importance on moderately discrepant events (events that are both somewhat novel and somewhat familiar).

Brainerd and Kingma (1985) have offered an alternative view of the development of the information processing system. They suggest that there are a number of information processing systems involved in memory rather than the single one advocated by Case. Each of these information processing systems has a limited capacity, serves a specific purpose, and is independent of the others. For example, one system might be involved in storing information in memory and another system might be involved in retrieving information from memory. Brainerd and Kingma suggested that the systems also develop independently of one another. At present, it is difficult to determine which view is the correct one. It is hoped that future research will help to resolve this issue (Bjorklund and Frankel, 1989).

Memory Development

Memory is such an everyday part of our lives that we usually take it for granted. Without memory, we would be quite different creatures. We would not recollect the past and or anticipate the future. Instead, we would be tied to our perceptions of the immediate environment. Given the importance of memory in our daily lives, it is not surprising that memory development has been studied extensively. These studies have contributed a great deal to our understanding of memory and to our understanding of children's minds.

Recognition Memory

In its simplest form, recognition memory depends on the ability to determine if a stimulus is a novel one or one that has been experienced before. This skill is very well developed in adults. Two studies will suffice to illustrate this point. In the first, 612 pictures were shown individually to adults who were given a recognition task either immediately following the presentation of the 612 pictures, 2 hours later, 3 days later, 1 week later, or 4 months later (Shepard, 1967). The adults exhibited phenomenal recognition memory skills. In the immediate recognition task, they were able to distinguish all of the novel stimuli from all of the familiar ones. This ability deteriorated slightly after 2 hours, but the adults were accurate for 90% of the pictures after 1 week. The adults' performance after 4 months was at the chance level. These results suggest that the accuracy of recognition memory is best when there is a shorter interval between experience with a stimulus and one's attempt to recognize it.

Nonetheless, accurate recognition of meaningful material persists for long periods of time. Bahrick, Bahrick, and Wittlinger (1975) asked adults to discriminate pictures of their high school classmates from pictures of other high school students 35 years after graduation. Ninety percent accuracy was found. However, the subjects were able to *recall* less than 15% of their classmates' names. In general, accuracy with recall memory is far inferior to that with recognition memory. The reason for this is simple. Recall memory is more demanding than recognition memory because recall requires that the person doing the remembering reconstruct the memory. In contrast, recognition memory requires that the person doing the remembering decide if something has already been experienced.

In order to study recognition memory in infants, researchers must devise a nonverbal recognition memory task since they cannot ask infants if they recognize something. One technique that investigators have devised involves *habituation*. As you may recall, the habituation task involves the presentation of a stimulus until the infant becomes bored with the stimulus.

In a classic study of this mode, Fagan (1973) showed 6-month-old infants checkerboard patterns for 2-minute periods, and then showed both familiar and novel patterns either immediately, 24 hours later or 48 hours later. Regardless of the interval between the original presentation of the stimuli and the recognition task, the infants looked longer at the novel patterns than at the familiar patterns, demonstrating that they remembered the familiar patterns. In a related study, Fagan showed 6-month-old infants black and white photographs of human faces and then exposed the infants to familiar and novel photographs either immediately, 3 hours later, 24 hours later, 48 hours later, 1 week later or 2 weeks later. In every case, infants looked longer at the novel photographs than at the familiar photographs, once again demonstrating that the infants remembered the familiar photographs.

In a slightly different use of the habituation paradigm, Martin (1975) showed 2-month-old, 3½-month-old, and 5-month-old infants a geometric figure for 30 seconds on 6 different occasions on the first day of testing and then repeated the procedure with the same stimulus on the next day. At all ages, infants looked less often at the stimulus on the second day of testing. However, the difference in the amount of looking between the first day and the second day increased with age, suggesting that recognition memory improves between 2 months and 5 months of age.

Given the facility for recognition memory that infants exhibit, it should be of little surprise that older children also have excellent recognition memory skills (Perlmutter, 1984). Brown and Scott (1971) showed 4-year-old children a set of pictures—some pictures were shown once, whereas others were shown twice. Recognition memory was assesed at 1 day and 28 days later. The children were quite accurate in recognizing the pictures after 1 day regardless of whether the picture had been shown once or twice. After 28 days, the children were much better at recognizing the pictures that had been shown twice than those that were shown only once. As one might expect, frequency of exposure seems to improve the accuracy of recognition memory.

271

FIGURE 8-10

Examples of Mandler and Robinson's organized and un-organized scenes.

The meaningfulness of the material to be remembered also affects the accuracy of recognition memory (Hock, Romanski, Galie, & Williams, 1978; Mandler & Robinson, 1978). For example, Mandler and Robinson (1978) presented first-, third-, and fifth-grade children with pictures in which objects were either organized into a meaningful scene or portrayed in unorganized random arrays (see Figure 8-10 for examples of each type of array). All the children were better at remembering the organized scenes than the random arrays. Memory for the organized scenes also improved with age, suggesting that as children get older they get better at using meaningful relationships to assist their memory skills.

Recall Memory

Recall memory is a more complex form of memory than is recognition memory in that there are no external cues to aid memory in recall. Piaget and Inhelder (1973) have suggested that recall is impossible in children younger than 1-year-old because it requires representational skills unavailable to younger infants. However, the difficulty involved in assessing recall memory in nonverbal children makes it difficult to assess this hypothesis.

In one study of recall memory in young children, DeLoache (1986) had 21-month-old children and 27-month-old children watch as a small object was hidden in one of 4 containers. Following this, children were encouraged to play with other toys for 30 seconds and then asked to find the hidden object. When the object had been hidden in one of 4 visually distinct objects (a tin can, a cardboard box, a round woven basket, and an orange plastic flower pot), children of both ages were very likely to successfully retrieve the hidden object. This was true whether the location of the 4 containers had remained the same or had changed during the 30-second interval. In another test, the 4 visually distinct objects were used as cues by attaching each one to the lid of one of 4 identical metal boxes. Once again, both age groups were quite successful at retrieving the hidden object when the locations of the 4 metal boxes had remained stationary. However, when the location of the 4 metal boxes was changed during the 30-second interval, the 21-month-olds were much less likely to successfully retrieve the hidden object. The 21-month-old childrens' performance also decreased when photographs of the visually distinct containers, rather than the objects themselves, were attached to the metal boxes. This was true even when the locations of the metal boxes were not moved. The performances of the 27-month-old children were not affected by movement of the boxes when the actual objects were attached to them as clues or by photographs attached to boxes that were not moved. However, when the boxes with photographs were moved after the object had been hidden in one of them, the performance of the 27-month-olds declined considerably (but still not as much as had the performance of the 21-month-olds).

These results demonstrate that even children as young as 21 months have recall memory, but that their memory skills are fragile. The youngest children studied were successful at retrieving the hidden object only when very few demands were placed on their memory skills. As the demands of the tasks increased, their performance worsened. The 27-month-olds were better able to cope with the increased task demands, but also proved susceptible to such demands. DeLoache suggests that young children have difficulty integrating unrelated information (for example, the object on top of a metal box and its location), so that memory tasks that require integration of such information result in diminished performance.

Ability to recall is easier if the information to be remembered is meaningful. Even adults find it difficult to remember long lists of unrelated material, but can recall considerable detail for meaningful information (for example, the lurid details of a trip abroad, even if it occurred years ago). In one of the early demonstrations of this phenomenon in young children, Brown (1976) showed 3- and 4-year-old children sets of three pictures. Some of the picture sets were shown in a meaningful sequence while others were shown in a scrambled order. Children could recall both types of sequences immediately after their presentation. After a delay, only the meaningful sequences were recalled accurately, suggesting that the children had more difficulty storing the scrambled sequences than the meaningful ones.

The recall memory of children as young as 16 months of age is also influenced by the meaningfulness of the information to be remembered. Bauer and Mandler (1989) presented children with a variety of types of events. Some events contained novel causal relationships, where certain actions had to occur in a particular order. For example, "cleaning the table" consisted of the experimenter spraying the table (with an empty spray bottle), then wiping the table with a towel, and finally throwing the towel away. Other events contained novel arbitrary relationships, where the order of the actions performed by the experimenter did not need to occur in an invariant order. For example, in the "making a picture" event, the experimenter put a sticker on a chalkboard, next leaned the chalkboard against an easel, and finally drew on the chalkboard with a piece of chalk. When 16-month-old children were asked to repeat what the experimenter had done (a form of recall memory), they were better able to recall the temporal sequence for

273

causal events than for arbitrary events. The more meaningful the temporal sequence, the better able the children were to remember it.

In another demonstration of the importance of meaningful material for recall memory, Chi (1978) gave 10-year-olds and adults two memory tasks. In one task, they were asked to recall lists of 10 numbers in a random order. Adults were much better at recalling the lists of numbers than were the children. This is a typical finding. Increased age usually results in improved memory for meaningless material. In the other memory task, the subjects were asked to reproduce stimuli that they had seen in an 8 × 8 array. The children were much better at recalling these arrays than were the adults because the stimuli were chess pieces arranged on a chessboard and the children were skilled chess players, whereas the adults were not. The children were able to use their knowledge of chess to help them remember the arrays, whereas the adults had to attempt to remember what, to them, were random placements of unfamiliar objects in a strange array.

Mnemonic Strategies

Children's memory improves with age. Some of this improvement is due to an increase in memory capacity as children grow older. Older children seem to be able to remember more information than younger children (Brown, 1975; Flavell, 1985). However, the most striking development in the area of memory has to do with the strategies that are used to make memory more effective. Such strategies are called *mnemonic strategies*. Mnemonic strategies are behaviors that we use to help us remember what we want to remember. One such strategy is *verbal rehearsal,* the verbal repetition of the information to be remembered. For example, if you want to remember a phone number until you have dialed, repeating the number until it is dialed increases your chances of remembering it. The rehearsal can be overt (aloud) or covert (saying it to yourself).

In a classic study concerned with children's use of verbal rehearsal to facilitate memory, Flavell, Beach, and Chinsky (1966) asked 5-, 7-, and 10-year-old children to remember a set of pictures. They found that the amount of overt verbal rehearsal increased with age. Only 10% of the 5-year-olds engaged in overt rehearsal, whereas over 80% of the 10-year-olds did so. In a follow-up study, Keeney, Cannizzo, and Flavell (1967) tested 6- and 7-year-old children to determine which children did not engage in spontaneous verbal rehearsal. Keeney et al. then trained these children to rehearse by asking them to whisper the names of the objects they were to remember. Following this training, the children were given a memory task. Seventy-five percent of the children who had been trained to whisper spontaneously engaged in overt verbal rehearsal, which also improved their memory of the material.

Adolescents and adults also work harder at remembering than young children do—they study, rehearse, and practice the things to be remembered. Certainly, naming things is an example of rehearsal, as the study by Flavell, Beach and Chinsky showed. But there are other factors in rehearsal that are more apparent in the behavior of older children than younger ones. For

A third-grader working at memorizing material for class.

example, when children were tested in a study that permitted them to study a group of objects "for as long as they wished" before testing, the older children (in this case, fourth graders) spent more time studying the objects than did kindergarten and second grade children (Flavell, Friedrichs, & Hoyt, 1970). The older children were more likely to name things aloud during their "study time" and to test themselves by first naming the objects and then looking to see if they were right. The difficulty of the material to be remembered also affects the rehearsal of older children more than younger children. Both 9-year-olds and adults have been found to focus their rehearsal on the most difficult items, while 7-year-olds rehearse items in a random fashion (Masur, McIntyre, & Flavell, 1973). We will discuss differences in the information processing skills of children and adolescents in more detail in Chapter 16.

TABLE 8-4

Typical course of development of a memory strategy

	Major Periods in Strategy Development		
	Strategy Not Available	*Production*	*Mature Strategy Use*
Basic ability to use strategy	Absent to poor	Fair to good	Good to excellent
Spontaneous strategy use	Absent	Absent	Present
Attempts to elicit strategy use	Ineffective	Effective	Unnecessary
Effects of strategy use on retrieval	—	Positive	Positive

SOURCE: From Flavell, 1985, p. 222.

Although the successful use of mnemonic strategies increases with age, such strategies have been observed in very young children. DeLoache, Cassidy, and Brown (1985) played a hide-and-seek game with children ranging in age from 18 to 24 months. The children were asked to find toys hidden in various locations in a room (such as, under a pillow or under a chair). After a toy was hidden while the child witnessed the hiding, there was a slight delay before children were allowed to retrieve the object. During the delay, children were observed to engage in a variety of primitive mnemonic strategies: (1) verbalizing about the toy or its hiding place, (2) looking toward the hiding place, (3) pointing toward the hiding place, (4) approaching or hovering around the hiding place, (5) peeking at the hidden toy, and (6) attempting to obtain the object.

In his summary of the work on the development of mnemonic strategies, Flavell (1970) distinguished between *production deficiencies* and *mediational deficiencies*. Children are said to have a production deficiency for a mnemonic strategy if they fail to use the strategy even though the capability to do so is present. Children are said to have a mediational deficiency if their use of the strategy does not improve their memory of the information. The development of mnemonic strategies is summarized in Table 8-4.

Metamemory

Another area of memory in which there has been considerable research during the past 15 years concerns how much a person knows about his or her own memory. Such knowledge is called *metamemory*. Young children seem to have poor metamemory skills. For example, if an adult asks children to predict how many pictures they will be able to remember, young children will consistently *overestimate* their memory performance. They remember far fewer pictures than they predict they will (Flavell, Friedrichs, & Hoyt, 1970; Yussen & Levy, 1976). It is not until children reach the age of 10 years that they become as good predictors of their own memory as are adults.

Markman (1973) demonstrated that children are not poor predictors *per se*. She asked 5-year-olds to predict how many objects they could recall and to predict whether they could jump various distances. The children were quite inaccurate at predicting their memory, but much more accurate at predicting their jumping skills. Thus, children are better at predicting certain of their skills than others.

In an interview study of elementary school age children's knowledge of memory, Kreutzer, Leonard, and Flavell (1975) found that children's metamemory skills improved with age. Older children were more likely than younger children to recognize that meaningfully related information would be easier to remember than unrelated information. The older children also were more likely to understand that it is easier to retell a story in one's own words than in the exact words in which it was originally told. Consider the answer given by a third-grade girl when asked what she would do to remember a telephone number:

> Say the number is 633–8854. Then what I'd do is—say that my number is 633, so I won't have to remember that, really. And then I would think now I've got to remember 88. Now I'm 8 years old, so I can remember, say my age two times. Then I say how old my brother is, and how old he was last year. And that's how I'd usually remember the phone number. (Asked by the experimenter if that was how she usually remembered a phone number) well, usually I write it down (Kreutzer et al., 1975, p. 11).

In a somewhat different approach to metamemory, Foley, Johnson, and Raye (1983) investigated children's ability to remember the origin of their memories. They found that 6-year-old children were as good as 17-year-olds at discriminating memories originating in what they themselves had said earlier from memories originating from what another person had said earlier. However, younger children were not as good at discriminating memories originating from what they themselves had said earlier from memories originating from what they had only thought (but not said) earlier. Evidently, young children find it relatively easy to discriminate memories arising from what they have said from memories arising from what others have said, but find it difficult to discriminate memories arising from earlier thoughts from memories arising from earlier actions (saying something).

Summary

The study of cognitive development is the study of the development of the mental processes involved in the interpretation and organization of information. Scholars of cognitive development attempt to answer questions such as: How do children make sense of the world? Does an infant's view of the world differ from that of a preschool child?

In the history of developmental psychology, Jean Piaget made the greatest contribution to the study of cognitive development. He suggested that throughout our entire life span we interpret the world in terms of two biologically determined functions; *assimilation* and *accommodation*. Assimilation occurs when we interpret the world in terms of existing knowledge. Accommodation occurs when we modify our existing knowledge so that it fits better with new information. Piaget believed that moderately discrepant events were the most likely to produce cognitive development because such events require both assimilation and accommodation.

According to Piaget, cognitive development occurs in a series of stages. The first stage is the *sensorimotor* stage, a period during which the infant acquires the capacity for mental representation. Next comes the *preoperational* stage. Because children lack an integrated set of mental operations during this stage, their thought is inflexible. Children in the next stage, the *concrete operational* stage, possess thought that is logical and flexible. Despite this advance in cognitive skills, children in the concrete operational stage lack the capacity for abstract thought. This ability is not acquired until the final stage of cognitive development, the *formal operational* stage.

Piaget's emphasis on mental representation, cognitive functions, moderately discrepant events, and qualitative changes in cognitive development will be remembered as important contributions to developmental psychology. Nonetheless, there is a growing body of evidence to suggest that Piaget may have underestimated children's cognitive capabilities.

Studies of recognition memory in infancy have demonstrated that young infants have recognition memory. Recall memory is more difficult to demonstrate than is recognition memory. Recall memory is present in children as young as 16 months of age, but is quite fragile. The more difficult the task demands, the less likely that young children's recall memory will be accurate. However, the more meaningful the information to be remembered, the more likely that children (and adults) will remember it.

One of the reasons that children's memory improves as they get older is that they become more proficient at using mnemonic strategies. Such strategies are behaviors that we use to help us to remember what we want to remember. Mnemonic strategies have been observed in children as young as 18 months, but improve with age. John Flavell has suggested that the acquisition of mnemonic strategies is characterized by production deficiencies and mediational deficiencies. Production deficiencies refer to children's failure to use a mnemonic strategy even if they have the capacity to do so. Mediational deficiencies result when children's use of a strategy fails to improve their memory.

Children's awareness of their memory skills and limitations, called metamemory, improves with age. For example, young children frequently overestimate their memory potential. The ability to accurately estimate one's memory improves with age, as do many other metamemory skills.

Children's problem-solving skills also improve with age. Three-year-old children are able to consider every available instance in an array and also look for negative instances are well as positive instances. Children of this age are also able to determine if they have sufficient or insufficient information to make a decision. Still, all of these abilities improve with age.

278

Suggested Readings

BJORKLUND, D. (1989). *Children's thinking*. Pacific Grove, CA: Brooks/Cole.

FLAVELL, J. (1985). *Cognitive development*. Englewood Cliffs, N.J.: Prentice Hall.

KAGAN, J, KEARSLEY, R., and ZELAZO, P. (1978). *Infancy: Its place in human development*. Cambridge, MA: Harvard University Press.

KAIL, R. (1984). *The development of memory in children*. New York: W.H. Freeman and Co.

PIAGET, J. (1962). *Play, dreams, and imitation*. New York: Norton.

SIEGLER, R. (1985). *Children's thinking*. Englewood Cliffs, N.J.: Prentice Hall.

The growth of perceptual, language, and cognitive skills helps to direct and shape every aspect of children's experiences. At the same time, as the chapters in Part Two repeatedly noted, development is also directed and shaped by the opportunities and demands imposed on all children by the environments in which they grow. These environments are comprised largely of interactions among children and other persons, and the impact of these social aspects of children's environments are essential to an understanding of human development.

Part Three is the first of two parts devoted to the developmental significance of children's experiences with other persons. To set the stage, Chapter 9 provides an overview of the major theoretical perspectives on why

Foundations of Personality and Social Development

social relations are important in development. Following the path laid down in Part One, Chapter 9 addresses the key question of how children develop the different patterns of social behavior and responsiveness to other persons to which the term *personality* refers.

Following this overview are two chapters that discuss aspects of individual development that are primary to all aspects of personality and personality development. Chapter 10 examines perceptions and understanding of the persons and relationships that comprise the social world. Chapter 11 focuses on children's emotional expressions, their responsiveness to emotion-arousing experiences, and their awareness of emotions in their own behavior and the behavior of others.

CHAPTER NINE

Personality and Social Development: Theories and Processes

283

Introduction

People have unique histories that make them the children they are and the adults they become. These histories, including physical and hereditary components, are the moving forces behind personality and social development. From the very beginning of life, capabilities are being established for relations with others and for the emergence of enduring and characteristic patterns of behavior that we term "personality."

This chapter begins a series of seven chapters on personality and social development. Because the area covers such a wide array of topics, we are beginning with an overview of ideas and issues that have shaped the work of developmental psychologists. In this chapter you will see that psychologists often have different views of which ideas and issues are most important, depending on their theoretical perspectives on human nature and development. At the same time, all theorists have addressed certain primary questions in attempting to explain personality and social development. A useful first step is to consider the issues that have been common to different perspectives.

Central Issues in Personality and Social Development

Even in infancy, humans are social beings who seek contact with others, are responsive to that contact, and shape the way others behave toward them. Although infants and young children are sometimes classified as egocentric—relating all or most of their experiences and action to their own needs or failing to properly appreciate someone else's point of view—they are certainly sociocentric as well (Hartup, 1989). Chapters 3 and 4 outlined the ways in which this remarkable social potential is manifested in the early months of life. In short, personality and social development is an interdependent process that is a natural consequence of individuals' ongoing interaction with the unique experiences that comprise their social world.

In studying personality and social development, developmental psychologists are attempting to describe and explain how individuals become socialized in their society, developing in the process, the personal patterns of behavior that make them unique, and acquiring the social skills that are necessary for normal social interaction. In general, two questions underlie theory and research in the area:

What is the typical course of development for the characteristic patterns of personality and social interactions? In earlier chapters we have seen models of development that outlined regular and logically coherent progressions, such as the stage–developmental models of Piaget (Chapter 7) and the sequence of social–response patterns obtained from studies of attachment (Chapter 4). Stage models have influenced the study of personality and social development as well, but in general, the course of behavioral development and personality functioning has been derived from extensive observation of children and adolescents of different ages. Describing differences across age periods has been a major goal of research on personality and social development.

What are the processes or mechanisms by which development occurs? Theories of personality and social development address the mechanisms by which behaviors emerge or are acquired in the course of development. Physiological or inheritable factors clearly determine some aspects of personality and social behavior, but *environmental influences,* including people (parents, peers, teachers, bosses, colleagues, friends, and lovers) and institutions (school, community, religious organizations, and the mass media) also help to shape and direct the course of growth. Most research on personality and social development has been devoted to these environmental influences and, increasingly today, to how these external influences affect persons of different ages with different physiological and genetic characteristics (Collins & Gunnar, 1990).

The search for answers to these questions has been directed by several especially influential theories of personality and social development. These theories serve an important function by focusing attention on important categories of behavior and by providing a basis for generating hypotheses about the processes that cause these behaviors to emerge, be maintained, or be transformed in the course of development. Three groups of theories have been especially important: psychodynamic theories, such as classical psychoanalysis as formulated by Sigmund Freud, learning theories, and contemporary cognitive theories, influenced by cognitive–developmental ideas such as those of Piaget and by the study of social cognition in children and adults.

Sigmund Freud's Psychoanalytic Theory

Sigmund Freud (1856–1939), a Viennese physician working around the turn of the century, proposed a theory of personality and social development that has helped define categories of behavior to which developmental psychologists have paid particular attention. Although Freud was primarily interested in understanding the nature of abnormal or disordered behavior, his theory is a developmental theory that applies to both normal and abnormal functioning because it contains a broad description of the origins of children's and adults' behavior patterns, and includes normal as well as abnormal pattern descriptions.

Freud's theory is called a *psychodynamic* view of human behavior because it focuses on internal, psychological processes that are based on a concept of "psychic energy" and how this psychic energy is focused and expended. According to psychoanalytic theory, psychic energy provides the motivation behind all action. *Libido* is the psychoanalytic term for such energy. Libido may be invested in a person, object, or part of the body through a process known as a *cathexis*. A cathexis is a motive to approach, stay near, or in some other way behave positively toward a person or object. Generally, psychoanalytic theory posits that behavior is understandable in terms of the patterns of motivations that result from cathexes formed in the course of early experience. This process is diagrammed in Figure 9-1.

There are two developmental thrusts in psychoanalytic theory: (1) the emergence of basic *structures* of personality, and (2) movement through a series of *psychosexual stages,* or distinct developmental periods during which different experiences have different consequences for a person's eventual personality and interpersonal relations.

FIGURE 9-1

The actual behavior of the individual represents the best, most adaptive compromise the ego can work out.

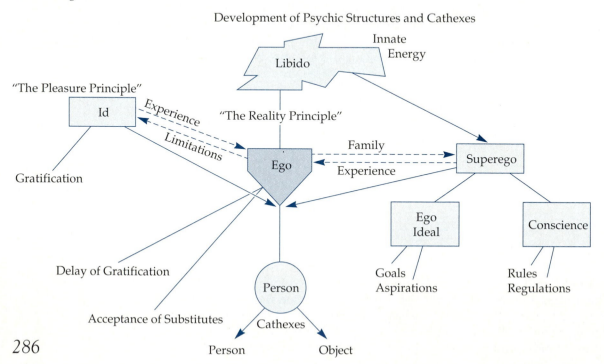

Development of Psychic Structures and Cathexes

One of the best known aspects of psychoanalytic theory is the set of psychic structures that determine behavior: the *id, ego,* and *superego.* The id is innate, the only psychic structure present at birth. It is primarily a repository for the pool of libidinal energy; consequently, behavior governed by the id is chaotic and almost totally undirected. The id's one directional component is the satisfaction of any aroused need. This behavioral pattern is termed the *pleasure principle,* which dictates that the satisfaction of needs is to be achieved immediately in the most direct fashion possible, without regard for the possibility of punishment or other dangers. The needs that demand satisfaction are related to bodily well being: hunger, thirst, elimination, pain avoidance, and sexual interaction. The implication of the id concept is that, whenever any need arises at any period of life, there is a force within the person that clamors for immediate satisfaction of that need.

In the course of development, however, other personality structures emerge that also influence how satisfaction is eventually achieved. The first of these, the *ego,* is developed through experience with reality and the limitations reality poses on the immediate satisfaction of needs. The ego is the executive structure of personality. Its function is that of a central coordinator of behavior that mediates the conflicts that arise when a need clamors for satisfaction, but reality demands either a delay in gratification or the acceptance of a substitute. The ego is thus said to be governed by the *reality principle* (see Figure 9-1). The ego also represents the higher cognitive processes that govern the ability to behave intelligently and in accordance with social rules. Self-control (that is, delaying gratification) or the self-regulation of behavior is an aspect of effective functioning governed by the ego. Unlike the id, the ego is strongly affected by experience. Only if development occurs in a supportive and benevolent social climate will the ego be strong enough to direct behavior effectively.

A third structure of personality, the superego, arises later in development—at about 4 years of age, according to psychoanalytic theory. This structure is a direct reflection of experiences in the family, through which children learn behavior that is appropriate for the society in which they are reared. The superego thus represents the ideals of society in opposition to the id, which presses for individual gratification. The ego, caught in the middle, must attempt to achieve gratification through socially acceptable means.

There are two components of the superego. The *ego ideal* represents the acquired goals and aspirations for appropriate, socially desirable behavior. The *conscience* contains the rules and regulations that define inappropriate or prohibited activity. The two components operate through two processes, in the form of emotions, to provide rewards and punishments that induce the ego to direct behavior in socially acceptable ways. These emotional processes are *pride,* a reward for accomplishment when goals or aspirations are achieved, and *guilt,* a punishment for misbehavior.

In Freud's structural view, then, behavior is shaped both by basic needs and drives and by the social rules acquired by the individual during early experiences with parents, peers, teachers, and others. A person's behavior

The Development of Personality Structures

287

represents the best, most adaptive compromise the ego can work out between the pressures of the id and the constraints and demands of the superego.

Psychosexual Stages of Development

The second developmental aspect of Freud's theory is that all individuals are presumed to go through a biologically determined sequence of stages during growth. The stages are distinguished by a strong cathexis on a particular organ system and, during the stage associated with a particular system, all experiences relevant to that system become particularly important for development. The psychosexual stages are as follow:

The Oral Stage. Beginning at birth and extending through approximately the first 2 years of life, the primary contact between the infant and other persons centers around the act of feeding. Consequently, gratification tends to be associated with the mouth, and the interaction between infants and caregivers during feeding is symbolic of the general dependency of young infants, who could not care for themselves or survive without the benevolence of another. Because of this, experiences during the oral period also influence the development of dependency needs and color all subsequent close relationships.

The Anal Stage. Following the oral period, the major focus of cathexes is the elimination system. This period typically occurs at about the time most societies enforce toilet training, and many of Freud's hypotheses about the psychological significance of this period have to do with the primary motivations for control over elimination pressures: self-control and cleanliness. Toilet training requires that children resist bodily urges that have previously led to immediate release until the proper place and/or time. According to psychoanalytic theory, behavioral traits such as obstinancy or conformity, messiness or meticulousness are likely to arise from experiences during the anal period.

The Phallic Stage. The third psychosexual stage is based on the assumption that the child's genital organs become the focus of cathexes in early childhood. Freud chose the term *phallic,* referring to the penis or phallus, to make the distinction between this early period and the later *genital* period that occurs at puberty. In many ways the phallic period is the most important in psychoanalytic theory because it encompasses the experiences that, in Freud's view, gave rise to the superego and the child's internalization of appropriate sex-typing.

The hallmark of development during the phallic period is the *Oedipus/Electra complex,* or the Oedipal/Electra dilemma. These terms refer to internal conflicts that arise when the shift of libidinal cathexes to the genitals results in sexual motives and desires. According to Freud, young children develop a cathexis, with frankly sexual overtones, for the opposite-sexed parent and also fear of the opposite-sex parent, who is perceived as a rival, albeit a more powerful and threatening one. To resolve this conflict, the child forms a strong identification with the same-sex parent, thereby indirectly obtaining some vicarious satisfaction of the sexual desire for the opposite-sex parent. In addition, there is a *defensive* advantage to becoming as similar as possible to the same-sexed parent. By identifying with an aggressor, one acquires those potencies and characteristics that make such potential aggression fearful; thus, when one is as powerful as another, there is no reason to be fearful.

Freud thought that *internalization* of the same-sex parent by adopting his or her attitudes, values, and orientations resulted in the establishment of the superego—an internalized representation of society's constraints and demands, as embodied in the parent. In addition, he thought that identification with the same-sex parent assured appropriate sexual orientation and sex-role preference, particularly in boys.

The Latency Stage. Once the Oedipal/Electra dilemma is resolved, there is no automatic or immediate progression of libidinal cathexes to a new organ system. Instead a period of relative quiescence in psychosexual development occurs during the years of middle childhood, from about age 5 to the onset of puberty. The term *latency* refers to a temporary diminution of strong libidinal influences on behavior. According to Freud, this respite from pressing inner drives and motives allows a concentration on ego development, during which time children explore their intellectual environment and perfect their adaptive ego skills. Of particular importance are the influences of peers and school experiences and the growth of ego skills such as intellectual coping and mastery and competence in social interactions. Although Freud and other psychoanalytic theorists generally had little interest in this period, it has been the focus of considerable attention in recent years (Collins, 1984).

The Genital Stage. Psychosexual latency is terminated abruptly by the onset of puberty, which revives and intensifies the cathexes on genital organs. The primary characteristics of the genital stage are tumult and chaos, because of the conflict between sudden, strong sexual urges and societal prohibitions against social and sexual contact with members of the opposite sex. Thus, the needs and drives of the genital period often conflict with both reality and the dictates of the superego. In addition, physical changes associated with sexual maturation undermine any sense of continuity individual children may have felt in their own appearance, capabilities, or social roles.

Despite its tumultuous onset, the genital period gradually fades into the relatively controlled sexuality of adulthood. The precise point at which psychosexual development is completed, however, is poorly specified in Freud's theory. In this own writings, Freud behaved as though personality and social development were essentially completed by the end of adolescence.

Freud's views imply that character and personality are the product of the inborn drives and unique experiences that occur in the passage through the psychosexual stages. In addition to the idea that certain traits are likely to be formed during particular stages, two other concepts from Freud's theories are important in understanding how experience achieves its enduring impact. One is *fixation,* which refers to the likelihood that experiences during a particular psychosexual stage affect behavior in regular and characteristic

Behavior Genetics, Personality, and Social Development

All theories of personality and social development include assumptions about the nature of the human organism. In some cases, like Freud's ideas, these theories imply that all individuals are biologically predisposed toward particular patterns of behavior. Recent research findings, however, indicate that some aspects of personality and social behavior may be influenced by genetically determined differences. Although not rooted in a theory of human development like psychodynamic, social–learning, or cognitive–developmental views, these studies imply that our understanding of the nature and course of personality and social behavior depends on a modern version of the nature versus nurture controversy: How children's *experiences* affect, and are affected by, characteristics that are *inherited* from their parents.

Studies of the role of inherited factors in personality and social development are generally referred to as *behavior genetics* (see Chapter 2). The general strategy in these studies is to compare the similarities between persons who are more or less closely related genetically. The most familiar example of this strategy is the *twin study*, which was described in Chapter 2. In this method, identical twins (who are the products of a single zygote, or fertilized ovum) are compared to fraternal twins (who were born from two separate fertilized ova). Identical twins have the same genetic make-up, whereas fraternal twins are no more closely related than any other pair of siblings. In most cases, twin studies compare pairs of siblings who vary in genetic similarity, but share the same family environment. (Often publicized alternatives are studies in which identical twins reared in different families are compared with identical twins reared in the same family.) A second type of behavior-genetic strategy involves comparing birth children with their adopted siblings to assess the impact of similar environments on genetically unrelated children. Other types of behavior-genetic studies are variations on these two common research strategies.

What have we learned about the role of genetic factors in social and personality development? Robert Plomin (1989), a developmental psychologist who is also an expert in behavior genetics, argues that "genetic influences on individual differences in behavioral development are usually significant and often substantial and, paradoxically, also support the important role of environment" (p. 105). Plomin reviewed dozens of studies on such broad dimensions of personality and social behavior patterns as "emotionality," "sociability," and "activity level." He came to the conclusion that as much as 50% of the differences between persons on the aforementioned general characteristics may be attributable to heredity. In other words, if we know what one member of a pair of identical twins possesses on one of these behavioral patterns, our chances of predicting whether the other one possesses that characteristic are about 50%. If the twins are only fraternal, the likelihood of a correct prediction of a characteristic from one twin based on the other is only about 25%. For unrelated individuals, our ability to predict a characteristic from one person to another randomly selected person would be zero.

In underscoring the importance of genetic factors in helping us to understand differences from one person to another, Plomin also pointed out that one-half or more of differences in personality and social development must come from *environmental* influences. For most psychologists, the major task of understanding personality and social development is to determine *which* aspects of the environment are particularly important influences and *how* they exert an impact upon individual behavior and behavior change. In Chapters 11 and 12, we will return to the idea that genetic and environmental influences not only contribute to the constellation of behaviors that make a child unique, but also make it possible for her or him to adapt to society. 🐛

ways in later life. For example, if during the oral period an infant were fed on demand so that hunger hardly arose, the extremely positive gratification of these experiences might result in later emphases on oral behavior and dependency toward others. Similarly, if feedings were often scheduled at intervals great enough to cause hunger, a negative fixation might develop that would also heighten the importance of oral gratification and dependency. In other words, both under- and overgratification can lead to a persistence of behavior patterns that are characteristic of gratifications appropriate to earlier psychosexual periods. The second process that affects the long-term impact of psychosexual stages is *regression*, which is the tendency to return to earlier modes of gratification during periods of stress or frustration in later life. Fixations from the oral period, for example, might incline individuals to smoke or bite their nails, especially before an exam or during a turbulent romantic relationship.

Development never proceeds in a totally smooth, unconflicted fashion, and so it is a part of normal development to produce at least some minor fixations at every stage. These fixations from the several psychosexual stages influence the effects of early experience on later functioning.

Erik Erikson's Theory of Psychosocial Development

The developmental theory of Erik Erikson modified Freud's original theory by emphasizing the importance of early *social* experiences in shaping psychological development. His theory has been termed a *psychosocial* theory of development.

Erikson agreed with Freud that early development could be constructed in terms of stages and that those stages occurred in a specific sequence. However, the primary determining factors for Erikson's epigenetic, or developmental, sequence of stages were not biological, but were based on the social contexts of experience and the types of interaction between children and other important individuals. Erikson was impressed with the regularity with which children in all cultures experience similar types of interactions and relationships with their caretakers at similar points in their development. For example, the immaturity of very young infants means that they must be fed, clothed, and held, thus requiring close intimate interactions. Whereas Freud accounted for the psychological effects of this period in terms of the concentration of the libido on the oral system, Erikson proposed simply that the social experience of caregiving must be primary for very young infants because of their physical dependency upon others. He thus proposed that the experiences during this period were significant determinants of major personality characteristics relating to trust in others, dependency, optimism, and confidence in the good will of those with whom infants interact.

Erikson extended his description of the significance of social experiences in development to encompass the entire life span, proposing eight periods of especially important developmental challenges. The first six stages correspond closely to Freud's five psychosexual stages (Erikson divides Freud's genital stage into two psychosocial stages) and the final two denote what Erikson considered to be important personality developments during adulthood. The importance of each psychosocial stage is expressed in terms of a "developmental task" that the child accomplishes. These tasks are characterized in terms of developmental alternatives, sometimes referred to as crises, that might result from either fortunate or extremely unfortunate social experiences of children during a given stage.

Table 9-1 outlines the significant elements of the social environment for each of the eight psychosocial stages. For example, as noted earlier, the initial task confronting the infant concerns the development of a sense of basic trust in others. The mother is viewed as the significant other person, although the probability that infant care will be rendered by someone other than the

TABLE 9-1

Correspondence Between Freud's Psychoanalytic Theory of Psychosexual Development and Erikson's Psychosocial Theory

| Freud's Psychoanalytic Theory | | | Erikson's Psychosocial Theory | |
Psychosexual (Organ) Stages	Personality Structures	Developmental Task, Sense of:	Radius of Significant Relations	Optimal Outcome
I. Oral	Id Ego	I. Trust vs. mistrust	Maternal person (primary caretaker)	Basic trust and optimism
II. Anal		II. Autonomy vs. shame and doubt	Parental persons	Sense of control over oneself and the environment
III. Phallic	Superego	III. Initiative vs. guilt	Basic family	Goal-directedness and purpose
IV. Latency		IV. Industry vs. inferiority	Neighborhood; school	Competence
V. Genital		V. Identity vs. role confusion	Peer groups; outgroups	Reintegration of past with present and future goals, fidelity
VI.		VI. Intimacy vs. isolation	Partners in friendship, sex, competition, cooperation	Commitment, sharing, closeness, and love
VII.		VII. Generativity vs. self-absorption	Work colleagues; household members	Production and concern with the world and future generations
VIII.		VIII. Integrity vs. despair	Mankind; new generation	Perspective, satisfaction with one's past life, wisdom

mother (either the father or a professional childcare worker, for example) has increased since Erikson proposed his theory in 1950. The crisis of this period is between the development of an enduring sense of basic trust or confidence that others will respond warmly or helpfully, versus a feeling of mistrust and a sense that others are bad or malevolent and that depending on them in any way is threatening.

In the second developmental period, Erikson, like Freud, saw toilet training as a significant social task. Erikson, however, emphasized the potential battleground between infants and parents in which the children's own autonomous control over eliminative functions is limited and shaped to conform with societal rules. Thus, the crisis is one of maintaining some enduring sense of autonomy, capability, and control over one's own destiny, as opposed to a sense of shame and doubt from potentially being exposed to the derision of others and from lacking confidence in the worth of one's efforts or faith in their potential success. Erikson's thinking here underscores the importance of social competence and independence as aspects of behavioral development.

The third crisis faced by the developing child is that of initiative versus guilt. Erikson observed again that physical maturation has important social parallels. Just as the development of voluntary control over the muscles involved in elimination set the stage for toilet training, children's increasing ability to walk and increased capacities to look, listen, and feel provide the opportunity for exploration and intrusion into new places. For amubulatory children, exercising control will either be shaped by positive experiences that arise from successfully initiating exploration of new things or by negative outcomes of accidental misbehavior and violations of privacy. Exploration of their own bodies and mutual explorations in early peer interactions are particularly likely to lead to feelings of guilt because of societal prohibitions. The important social context at this point is the family, although early encounters with peers outside the immediate family (such as in day care) are also important. As was the case in Freud's view of the phallic stage of psychosexual development, the important behavior patterns that are founded in the third psychosocial stage include appropriate sex-role development and aspects of moral development such as ideals for appropriate behavior, self-evaluation, and the capacity for pride or guilt.

Erikson's fourth psychosocial stage corresponds to the psychoanalytic stage of latency. You will recall that psychoanalytic theory analyzed development during this period (the early school years) as free from any focus of libidinal cathexes on a particular organ system. Children are able to concentrate on building skills valued by society that relate to their own cognitive competency. Erikson further emphasizes the task of developing a continuing sense of *industry*, as opposed to one of *inferiority*. Positive evaluations from others for accomplishments in school or for making things that result in a tangible, visible product for everyone to see lead to a continuing sense of industry, an enjoyment of work, and a sense of competency. If the resulting products are poor or the standards for evaluation too high, however, a sense of inferiority

293

may result. Standards of excellence, social comparisons, and competence are important components of individual psychosocial development during the early school years.

In adolescence, which Freud described in terms of a single psychosexual task, Erikson proposed two developmental tasks. One results from the physical changes accompanying sexual maturation. Sensitized by bodily changes, adolescents are tempted to inquire about their social self so that they can discover just who they are and identify the continuities in their social being that integrate them into the world and make each one of them identifiable as a unique person. The important social context at this point is the peer group. Erikson felt that when so much else is changing, young adolescents need to identify those characteristics that remain the same from day to day, the ones that others use to characterize them, that are of worth, and that begin to suggest the future roles they might play in society. If this developmental task is accomplished successfully, it provides the foundation for a continuing sense of identity. The negative alternative in this crisis is identity diffusion, a perceived lack of knowledge about one's self, a sense that a person is of low value to others, or confusion about a person's potential role in society. The quest for identity has often been used as a hallmark of adolescence, and this portion of Erikson's psychosocial theory has played a major role in attempts to characterize and understand common problems and patterns of adolescent behavior. These are discussed in Chapter 17.

In the second psychosocial period of adolescence, the developmental task is one of mastering intimate relationships with others, perhaps primarily with one significant other, which may include sexual interaction. The critical ingredient of intimate relationships is a mutuality of trust. In the absence of intimate relationships, adulthood will be an isolated existence, in the sense that continuing social relationships are likely to be superficial or one-sided and unfulfilling. As in the previous stage, peers rather than adults provide the primary social context for achieving this developmental task.

The final two psychosocial stages concern two additional developmental tasks that characterize middle adulthood and aging. The seventh stage involves the task of achieving a sense of generativity versus self-absorption. The ideal resolution of this stage is a sense that one's life will have consequences for others, primarily the next generation. This is the period of life when individuals focus on their own children and subsequent generations. The eighth stage of development includes a crisis beween ego integrity and despair. In this psychosocial stage Erikson addresses himself to the retrospective analysis individuals do of their entire life, including reflecting on alternatives that they did not choose and the consequences of their lifetime strivings.

Erikson's psychosocial emphasis has extended Freud's ideas to point out the social determinants of individual development. He has also pointed out, as have most other contemporary students of social and personality development, the active role of individuals in their own development through their judgments about the social context and themselves.

Social Learning Theories

The premise of social learning theories is that the complex and continuing behavior patterns that characterize individuals develop as a function of interactions with other persons. Different social learning theorists emphasize different aspects of learning and behavioral development, but there is basic agreement about the primary learning processes, such as reinforcement, punishment, and imitation, upon which social learning theories are built. Social learning theory is, therefore, a theory of processes, *how* development proceeds, and not one of content, *what* behavior patterns and competencies develop. In this section we will first outline the basic principles and processes of social learning as it is understood today. We will also provide a brief overview of two significant extensions of general social learning principles: Dollard and Miller's psychodynamic behavior theory, an early and historically important attempt to re-explain Freud's ideas in terms of the processes of social learning, and cognitive social learning theory, a recent theoretical emphasis on the role of symbolic representation and inferences in learning processes.

Processes of Social Learning

Social learning theories rest on two basic models of how behaviors are acquired and maintained in the course of human development. They are as follows: (1) operant learning and (2) classical conditioning.

Operant Learning. Operant learning refers to the acquisition and maintenance of patterns of behavior that result from experiencing a reinforcing or punishing result. As discussed in Chapter 8, in order for consequences to have an effect on behavior, they must be *contingent,* or reliably related to the behavior. For example, getting approval at the dinner table may be contingent on a child's asking for things politely and chewing with his mouth closed, and this contingency may establish good table manners as instrumental, or as a means, for producing desired social approval.

Classical Conditioning. In social learning, classical conditioning involves acquiring a tendency for a behavior, thought, or emotion to become associated with a particular person or situation. For example, during early caregiving, the distress of hunger, thirst, or being wet is often aroused when the mother or other caretaker is absent, soon to be followed by relief when he or she appears with food, a bottle, or a dry diaper. Similarly, experiencing pain or fear under conditions that were previously neutral may result in a negative emotional response to those conditions. Social learning emphasizes the role of pairings like this in children's endowing other persons and a variety of social situations with positive or negative values. Thus, classical conditioning is important in determining which persons and situations will be positive and attractive to individuals and which will be negative and repellent to them. Several examples may help to clarify this idea. Money is only paper or metal until it is repeatedly associated with the already valued things that it will buy. The grouch on the block is just another person until his or her appearance is repeatedly associated with being yelled at or being sent out of the yard, after which he or she is disliked.

The role of associations between events as a basis for learning does not always occur because children have innate emotional reactions to particular events. Learning also occurs when events simply overlap in time. The results of observed associations, often called *contiguity learning,* means that the appearance of one event or person comes to evoke the other because they have been experienced together so often.

The application of instrumental learning and classical conditioning principles to personality and social development raises two issues. First, what is the *origin* of sensitivity to other persons' behaviors? Second, how do these principles help us to understand the behavioral effects of such common social experiences as social reinforcement (for example, approval from others, rather than material rewards), punishment, and imitation?

Sensitivity to Contingent Responses from Others. In Chapter 4, we saw that early relationships between infants and their caregivers have long-term developmental significance. We turn now to the more specific questions of whether infants respond to the warmth and approval *contingent* on, or in response to, their own actions and what infants' responses mean about the human capacity for social responsiveness.

In a classic study, Rheingold, Gewirtz, and Ross (1956) demonstrated that the contingent physical and social contact provided by caretakers influences the behavior of 3-month-old infants. In this study, when infants were touched under the chin, spoken to, and smiled at each time they vocalized, there was a significant increase in their rate of vocalization. One criticism of this study is that it failed to rule out the alternative possibility that infants were innately responsive to social behavior by caretakers, so that touching and smiling naturally elicited infants' vocalizations. To determine whether the effects of social contact were due to a releasing function or represented an early sensitivity to social contact as reinforcement, Weisberg (1963) contrasted the effects of both contingent and noncontingent social and nonsocial stimulation. For example, when babies' vocalizations (cooing, babbling) were to be reinforced contingently, immediately following the babies' vocalizing, the experimenter popped into the infants' view, spoke to them, smiled, and touched them lightly. When these reinforcers, the sight, sound, and touch of another person, were to be contingent, the experimenter did so only when the babies had *not* just finished vocalizing. Vocalization increased only when the social contact was presented contingently. Social contact that was not dependent on the babies' prior vocalization did not affect vocalizations. This suggests that social contact by itself, with no contingent relationship to infants' behavior, does *not* have a releasing effect.

Research indicating that very young infants are sensitive to contingently presented social events is important because it confirms that even the earliest social interaction between parents or other caretakers and infants may have an effect on infants' behavior through instrumental learning.

Social Reinforcement Processes. There is little disagreement that children are responsive to social reinforcement by others; social attention stands out as perhaps the most frequent and readily documented aspect of interaction to serve a reinforcing function. For example, smiling and calling an infant by name in the studies just described would constitute forms of social attention that are effective in infancy. Other social behaviors typically identified as reinforcers include sharing, smiling, paying attention, granting requests, giving money, toys, and privileges, praising, and thanking—in short, the myriad behaviors that are frequent parts of social interaction and may be dependent on the behavior of a child.

The most important and interesting questions about social reinforcement effects, however, concern *how* social reinforcement affects development. This calls for an *explanation* rather than a *description* of the contributions of social reinforcement. A basic issue is whether social reinforcement leads to *internalization* of behavior patterns so that children will manifest them even when there is no potential for reinforcement. Freud confronted the same issue in his idea of the superego as the personality structure that embodies the children's internalization of socially appropriate behavior and moral standards. Like Freud, social learning theorists have been interested in whether children's reactions to their own behavior might function as reinforcers that cause behavioral control to be internalized. Consider a child's pride over a well-colored picture or the sense of pleasure with having helped another. Once developed, these self-reactions may influence behavior through the process of reinforcement so that behavior that elicits a positive self-evaluation (for example, pride and satisfaction) will become more frequent and behavior eliciting self-criticism will become less frequent. There is clear evidence that children will persist at behavior that takes effort when they react to it with a sense of pride or judge that it is enjoyable, while they abandon that same behavior when they evaluate it negatively or judge it unpleasant (Lepper, 1981). Thus, "social" reinforcement processes in personality development may be either truly social and stimulated by the situation or internalized and operative on a private, personal basis.

Punishment. Punishment involves experiencing an aversive agent, either because something negative happens or because some positive condition is withdrawn. Aversive outcomes can occur either deliberately or unintentionally (as when a child's hand is burned from touching things on the stove). The point is that unpleasant outcomes tend to reduce the likelihood that the behaviors with which they are associated will occur again.

297

The explanation for the effectiveness of early punishment employs the basic learning process of classical conditioning. The reasoning is as follows: When a behavior is punished shortly after it has begun, the unpleasant aspects of the punishment become conditioned to the early thoughts and behaviors in the sequence of that behavior (Aronfreed, 1969; Parke, 1971). The unpleasantness probably is experienced as anxiety by the child, another instance of how reinforcement/punishment processes are frequently linked to emotion and behavior. When children next begin the prohibited behavior, or perhaps even contemplate it, they experience anxiety early in the response sequence and this alerts them to stop. Not only does such an "early warning" system allow inhibition to occur more easily because the behavior is only beginning; it also rewards resistance to temptation by providing relief from the anxiety about performing a previously punished behavior.

Punishment is usually of interest in personality and social development because, for better or worse, adults frequently deliberately use negative consequences to suppress undesirable behavior. Several conditions have been found to increase the effectiveness of punishment in socialization. One is the *nature of the relationship* between children and the people who administer punishment. The warmer and more generally reinforcing the relationship, the more punishment seems to involve not only an aversive consequence for unacceptable behavior, but also an interruption in the nurturance that typically exists between the adult and child (Sears, Maccoby, & Levin, 1957; Parke & Walters, 1967). A second factor is *timing.* Punishment is more effective immediately following a prohibited act than if it is delayed, largely because it is then clearest exactly what behavior elicited the punishment (Walters, Parke, & Cane, 1965). A third factor is the *rationales* or explanations for punishment. In one study (Sears, Maccoby, & Levin, 1957), mothers who reported that they had used both reasoning and physical punishment together said that punishment was a more effective rearing technique than did mothers who used physical punishment without providing specific rationales. Laboratory studies (such as those done by Parke and Murray, 1971) showed that rationales alone are as effective as punishment alone in deterring repetition of unacceptable behavior, but each alone is less powerful than when they are combined.

An important caution should be mentioned concerning the many reasons why punishment is often viewed as a detrimental and ultimately ineffective socialization technique. Foremost among these is the possibility that the emotional reactions that are conditioned in connection with punishment may interfere with a child's learning of adaptive new behaviors in the presence of a person or situation. For example, ridicule of a child's athletic ability by a Little League coach may result in the coach's having less positive influence over the child in the future or the child's being too anxious to benefit from sports involvement or both.

Observational Learning and Imitation. Imitation and observational learning have been defined as processes by which very complex behavior patterns may be acquired as a result of watching others' behaviors, without the necessity for repeated trial and error (Bandura, 1969, 1977; Bandura & Walters, 1963). It is unlikely that the number and variety of behaviors that comprise the social repertoires of most adults could ever be learned without this covert mechanism. Early studies of observational learning and imitation demonstrated the power of observing a model on children's adoption of specific patterns of social behavior. In one of the initial studies, Bandura, Ross, and Ross (1963) demonstrated convincingly that aggressive behavior could be easily acquired by very young children if they simply viewed an adult model who behaved in an aggressive fashion.

These early studies also demonstrated that reinforcing or punishing consequences that follow an observed behavior affect the likelihood of imitation, even when the consequences occur to another person. These vicarious consequences serve as information about the consequences that might occur if the observer adopts the modeled behavior pattern. Consider the likely future behavior of a child who sees another child experiment with smoking and become terribly ill. One of the most interesting aspects of vicarious consequences is that they have different effects on the *learning*, as opposed to the *performance*, of observed behavior. In an early study (Bandura, 1965), children were observed while watching a simulated television program in which an adult exhibited a number of different aggressive behaviors and unique verbalizations ("pow," "right in the nose," "boom," "boom"). In one condition a second adult subsequently appeared on the TV screen and rewarded the model with candy and soft drinks for being a champion. Thus, the model was reinforced. In another condition, the second adult sharply reprimanded the model for being a bully and spanked him with a rolled up magazine, an instance of punishment. There was also a third condition in which there were no consequences for the aggressive behavior. Subsequently, when children were given the opportunity to play alone in a room containing the same toys with which the model had played aggressively, children who saw the model rewarded spontaneously imitated the model's aggressive behavior, but children who had seen the model punished showed little aggression. Thus, *performance* of the observationally learned behaviors was affected by consequences to the model, even though the children experienced no consequences themselves. Later, when the experimenter offered rewards if the children would show him what they had seen the model do, all children demonstrated high levels of *learning* from having watched the model. In short, while the reinforcing or punishing consequences to a model influence the observer's immediate behavior, they do not deter or enhance *learning*, which appears to be a robust, almost "automatic" process by which children acquire many of their social skills and behaviors.

The origin and development of imitation in children remains poorly understood, although some theories have been proposed such as that of Piaget (1932). In a detailed consideration of imitative development, Yando, Seitz, and Zigler (1978) have suggested several types of imitation that children may show and have argued that the point of origin may be different for each type. Early in life, probably about 6 weeks of age, the first imitation may be observed. As we discussed in Chapter 3, at only a few weeks of age infants

299

show a tendency to repeat the facial and manual gestures of adults (Jacobson, 1979; Meltzoff & Moore, 1977). Later in the first year, infants may begin to show spontaneous imitation of familiar acts they have seen parents or other caretakers perform, and still later, they may imitate performances of new and unusual behaviors. Then, between the ages of 12 and 15 months (Valentine, 1930), more complex imitation may occur in which infants appear to be shaping their own imitative behavior from some visual memory of the behavior of another person. At this point, cognitive representation, such as an image, begins to influence imitation, illustrating the way cognitive development and behavioral development are linked.

The frequency of spontaneous and immediate imitation appears to increase during the first few years of life and probably peaks during the preschool years, after which there seems to be a decline (Yando, et al., 1978). Observational *learning,* however, continues to occur throughout the life span. As noted earlier, much observational learning may be "invisible," with imitative performance often being delayed and occurring only when the appropriate circumstances occur, for example, at a later time when observers find themselves in positions similar to those that the model was in earlier.

Two Extensions of Social Learning Theory. Social learning views have been the most influential of all theoretical perspectives in generating research on personality and social development. Although frequently criticized as too impoverished a set of processes to account for the richness of human devel-

Even very young infants may imitate distinctive facial expressions, according to recent research.

opment, principles of reinforcement, punishment, and observational learning have provided important insights into aspects of behavior that are of concern to parents, teachers, and others. Also, despite criticisms that social learning overemphasizes the importance of external influences in directing the course of development, several extensions of the theory clearly incorporate both cognitive and emotional dimensions of individual behavior. We turn now to a brief description of these two extensions.

Psychodynamic Behavior Theory. In their book *Personality and Psychotherapy* (1950), John Dollard, a sociologist and trained psychoanalyst, and Neal Miller, an experimental psychologist, proposed a reinterpretation of Freud's psychoanalytic theory in terms of the psychological learning theory that was prevalent at the time. The theoretical reinterpretation proposed by Dollard and Miller has been termed *psychodynamic behavior theory* because these theorists hypothesized about how the aspects of personality and social development identified as especially important in psychoanalytic theory were *learned* during the course of socialization.

Dollard and Miller's analysis incorporated four primary elements: drives, cue, response, and reinforcement. With respect to drives, Freud's concept of sexual energy or libido is interpreted in terms of *primary drives* such as hunger, thirst, pain avoidance, and sexual arousal. These drives were considered to be innate and to form the basis for all learning and behavioral adaptation, much as psychoanalytic theory viewed libidinal cathexes and the needs or drives of the id as the motivation for all behavior. In development, new drives relating to social interaction are *acquired*. The observation that infants come to care about others and enjoy company was interpreted by Dollard and Miller as an acquired drive for social contact in general. According to psychodynamic behavior theory, acquired drives are established through the process of classical conditioning.

The term *cue* refers to environmental stimuli that serve to guide behavior. The essence of the learning process is not merely producing some random behavior, but tailoring behavior to match the needs and constraints of the moment. To be hungry in the mother's absence may result in taking a cookie from the counter. If the mother is there, however, the correct behavior may be to ask politely if you may have a cookie. In this example, the cookie jar with the mother absent and the mother's presence are both cues that contribute to the behavioral outcome.

Assuming that children have a primary or acquired drive, cues will come to evoke a particular behavior *if* that behavior has previously been successful in reducing the drive—that is, if the cues are reinforced. These last two steps need to be considered together: Behaviors will be performed regularly only if they are reinforced, and, in Dollard and Miller's theory, reinforcement is defined simply as effective behavior that reduces the drive. There may be primary or acquired (secondary) drives, however, by far the majority of all reinforcers are acquired. Infants show no love of money: It will not make them smile or cease crying. For young children, however, money has acquired some reinforcing value, and for adults it is generally a powerful

301

reinforcer. In Dollard and Miller's view, smiles, approval, a playful wink, or simple conversation are not very meaningful to a very young infant, but they grow in value during the course of socialization. An important part of development, then, is the liberation of the infant and child from a narrow sensitivity to only those events and experiences that relate to primary drives. Social sensitivity develops through social experiences with parents, peers, teachers, or even strangers who may contribute to the learned behavior patterns that comprise social and personality development.

Although each individual develops unique needs and patterns of effective behavior, Dollard and Miller also noted some broad commonalities in development. They delineated four common social contexts or related experiences that are likely to be encountered by all children during early development, at least the first three of which correspond quite closely to the initial three psychosexual stages proposed by Freud and the psychosocial equivalents proposed by Erikson.

The first one is *feeding* during infancy. In Dollard's and Miller's theory, the social character of feeding establishes the reinforcing value of social contact by pairing the ministrations of the nurturant caretaker with the pleasure, relaxation, satisfaction and feelings of well being that result from being fed. Differences in individuals could arise as a function of differences in the quality of early feeding or significant related experiences. For example, early weaning and transition to highchair feeding or the extensive use of a propped bottle so that babies feed by themselves would reduce the degree of early close contact and might incline children to be less sensitive to social influences.

The second significant experience involves cleanliness training, primarily *toilet training*. In Dollard and Miller's view, behavioral self-regulation and the capacity for self-evaluation are acquired because of the caregivers' rewards and punishments during toilet training. Through a process of imitation children come to use the praise or rebuke they receive from adults to evaluate their own behavior, thus internalizing standards and shaping their own behavior when it is reinforced by feelings of pride or punished by a reaction of guilt.

The third influential experience in development is the early *sex training* that young children encounter during the later preschool years. Dollard and Miller asserted that early sexual behavior and curiosity are extremely anxiety-provoking for adults, inclining them to punish children severely for early sexual behavior they may exhibit either alone or with one another. The consequence of any early training to inhibit a pleasurable behavior is conflict, which leads to anxiety through the anticipation of punishment when the act is performed or merely contemplated. Thus, sexuality at later ages, when it is expected and valued, may be impaired by conflicts created in early training.

The final core experience influencing social and personality development involves the *socialization of anger* in the child. Dollard and Miller observed that the many frustrations inherent in a child's life are likely to produce aggressive behavior and its emotional counterpart, anger. They also proposed that parents have an intuitive resentment and fear of children's rage or anger

Adults frequently block children's expressions of anger in an effort to socialize alternative patterns of behavior.

and that there is strong cultural support for suppressing anger in children. Parents are thus likely to punish children severely when the children are angry and perhaps behaving aggressively as well. This creates an anger–anxiety conflict: Frustrating situations incline children to aggressive behavior and anger, but anxiety is aroused also, which interferes with an adaptive response to the frustrating circumstance.

Dollard and Miller's psychodynamic behavior theory extended learning principles to an analysis of developmental *processes* that produce characteristic patterns of personality and social behavior. Because the learning theory they utilized in their analysis was the learning theory of the 1940s and 1950s, it does not contain the complexity or cognitive richness of current approaches to social learning. Little recognition was given, for example, to the cognitive, intelligent capabilities or limitations of young children, which might foster or deter their early learning from social experiences. We now turn to contemporary theoretical views that do emphasize the role of cognitive capabilities in learning.

Cognitive Social Learning Theory.   A more recent extension of social learning views emerged in the 1970s in response to the realization that much of learning is under the control of the individual learner. Experiences of reinforcement and punishment, for example, often do not have the effect that might be expected because of their subjective meaning to the recipient. For example, research on threats and on reinforcement has revealed that attempts to control children's behavior by overly powerful positive and negative con-

303

sequences may produce immediate compliance but at the same time incline children against performing the desired behavior in the future (Lepper, 1981).

In a pioneering study, Aronson and Carlsmith (1963) placed children in a situation where they were tempted to play with attractive toys but forbidden to do so. Before leaving children alone with the prohibited toys, the experimenter either told children he would be "annoyed" if they played with the toys while he was gone or said that he would be "very angry" and might tell the child's teacher. In both cases the children obediently avoided playing with the forbidden items while the experimenter was absent. When they had done so in response to only a mild threat (that the experimenter would be "annoyed"), children subsequently no longer found the toys as attractive as they had initially, whereas children who had received a stronger threat still found the toys very attractive. Aronson and Carlsmith proposed that this was due to a cognitive justification process: Realizing that they had not played with the toys during the experimenter's absence, children who heard a severe threat could justify their compliant behavior in terms of the threat alone, which was strong enough to justify their compliance. On the other hand, children who also complied, but in response to a mild threat, had an inadequate justification for their behavior and initiated a cognitive restructuring process to enable a justification: They devalued the toys (found them less attractive) so the mild threat was then sufficient to account for their compliance.

In this case, a threat of social punishment for misbehavior that is only barely sufficient to produce compliance is considered to elicit cognitive changes that might facilitate compliance in the future because the temptation is reduced. For children who expected severe punishment, the toys continued to be attractive so temptation was not reduced, making future self-control more difficult.

Jonathan Freedman (1965) demonstrated these subsequent effects. In his study, one experimenter elicited compliance from children using either mild or severe threats and then, 6 weeks later, a different person took the children to a different setting that contained, among other things, the toys that they had been prohibited to play with earlier. The children were observed while the experimenter was out of the room; children who had earlier complied following a mild threat continued to avoid playing with the toys, whereas those who had received the severe threat did not. These findings suggest that minimally sufficient punishment is more likely to produce the internalization of a prohibition and thus achieve long-lasting effects, while punishment that is overly intense may produce compliance but fails in terms of any longer lasting impact on behavior.

A general conclusion is that social controls that are superfluously powerful may actually have negative effects for long-term socialization. Reinforcement beyond the amount needed to promote a desired behavior may also elicit the desired behavior in the short run, but undermine children's tendencies to act that way in the long run. In an influential study (Lepper, Greene, & Nisbett, 1973), nursery school teachers were asked to introduce various activities into the playroom so that the experimenters could observe how much spontaneous interest children showed in them. Later, children were taken individually to an experimental room in which they were given the opportunity to engage in a target activity in which they had spontaneously shown interest during free play at nursery school. Some were simply asked to do the activity, and others were promised a reward (they would win a "good player award") for doing it. Because the activity was known to be attractive enough to elicit children's interest on its own, the reward was considered superfluous. The findings showed that children who had received the reward for doing the activity at later times showed less interest in it as a free play activity than did children who did not receive a reward. Apparently, having received a reward changed the meaning of the activity from "something I like to do" to "something I do to get a reward." Consequently, although getting a reward is usually expected to make a behavior more likely in the future, in this case the child's own, innate interest in the behavior was actually undermined.

These studies demonstrate that simple processes of social and personality development, like reinforcement and punishment, can become more complex depending on the subjective meaning that children attach to them. They also illustrate the inherent link between cognitive processes, such as what children perceive as their own reason for their acts and the processes of social learning. Children's cognitive capabilities change developmentally, however, as was discussed in Chapter 8. As a result, emerging capabilities for forming ideas, for reasoning, and for making judgments about the self, others, and the values of the larger community have increasingly been seen as significant in children's personality and social development.

Cognitive Developmental Theories

Cognitive developmental theory provides a framework pointing out some of the important components of cognitive development that must be taken into account in measuring how children's experiences affect their behavior differently at different ages. This theory concentrates on the growing cognitive abilities of the child and the ways in which children's developmental level will influence how they interpret the world and their experiences in it.

The cognitive–developmental approach to social and personality development is built upon two assumptions about children's growth. One, which we will discuss first, is that developmental changes in social understanding may underlie changes in social behavior. That is, children may behave more maturely at one age than another because they think more maturely about the causes of others' actions toward them, the alternative responses open to them, and the implications of their own actions. In the words of a pioneer of developmental psychology, James Mark Baldwin (1906): "What we shall think is a function of what we have done. What we do is a function of what we think'' (p. 97). The second, to which we will devote the most attention in this section, is that children's understanding of their social worlds develops in much the same way as their understanding of the world of objects and physical laws.

Links Between Cognitive Development and Social Behavior

The importance of social understanding to social behavior has been the basis for many studies in the field, a number of which have shown that cognition, or understanding, is related to social behavior and personality. This body of research has led to two general views of the relationship between cognitive development and social behavior.

One is a mediational view. This view assumes that the quality of reflective thought a person can bring to bear on a social situation affects the person's response directly. Thus, if Maria can figure out her grandmother's perspective during a telephone conversation, she may be able to communicate more effectively than if she cannot understand her grandmother's need for particular information or her grandmother's particular interests. Similarly, if Kevin is the victim of a mishap and he assumes that it was the result of Bill's intent to harm him, Kevin is more likely to behave aggressively towards Bill. In its simplest form, this view implies that children (and adults) will act on their understanding and, thus, the type of behavior they show will reflect the level of development of their cognitive processes.

A second possibility is that understanding a situation may interact with other influences to determine action in any given circumstances (Rest, 1983). For example, your understanding of the need for laws in a society and the importance of individuals' obeying of them will help you decide whether or not to halt your car at a stop sign in an isolated area. But you will probably act on that understanding differently depending on how hurried or anxious you feel, the presence or absence of consequences (such as a police car parked nearby), your degree of distraction at the moment, and so forth. Children are also subject to cognitive, emotional, and situational factors that may override or color their understanding.

Although most research from a cognitive–developmental perspective has focused on cognitive change, rather than behavioral change, it is clear that the links between understanding and behavior are important elements in personality and social development. We will now turn to an overview of the cognitive changes that may affect personality and social behavior.

The Course of Social–Cognitive Development

Cognitive–developmental theory is most closely associated with the name of Jean Piaget. However, several other thinkers have contributed important ideas to cognitive perspectives on social and personality development, and their work will be discussed both here and in Chapter 10. Among these are Lawrence Kohlberg, Robert Selman, and William Damon, all of whom have proposed influential views of how cognitive development affects social functioning. Several questions have been common to these different views, whether they come from Piaget's theory or not: How can differences in children's social understanding be explained? How does developmental change come about? How do links between social understanding and social behavior occur?

Psychological Structures.   As we saw in the chapter on cognitive development, cognitive–developmental views begin with the idea that the changes in children's thinking as they mature involve changes in mental or psychological structures. The term *structures* within this framework refers to a schematic basis for action and thought that becomes more elaborate and more widely applicable as the child matures. Structures are thought of as including two or more elements, such as perceptions of persons or their thoughts, together with one or more links among these elements in the child's mind. Two examples may help to make the idea clear.

As a first step, let us draw on material from earlier chapters. Recall that Piaget described the child's changing understanding that the amount of liquid in two beakers of different sizes and shapes could be identical. He showed the children three beakers—two identical tall, thin ones (A and B), each containing the same amounts of liquid, and a third short, wide one (C), with no liquid. After seeing the liquid from tall, thin beaker A poured into the short, wide beaker C, five-year-olds thought there was less liquid in the wide beaker than in tall, thin beaker B. These children focused on the height of the column of liquid. In contrast, older children recognized the need to consider the way height and width were linked in determining amount, and they answered that the amount of liquid was the same, despite the physical transformation. In this example, younger and older children's answers seem to involve different numbers of elements—height and width for the older children, but only height for the younger—and, in the case of the older children, the relationship between the two elements. Because Piaget observed similar changes in understanding other physical transformations, he considered this experiment as evidence of different cognitive structures existing in children's minds at different times during their development.

A second example is a social parallel to the conservation of liquids example. Four-year-old Caroline announced at dinner one night that "Jonathan snatched my tablet today at school." Her parents, not having been there and hoping to find out more details about the incident, asked who Jonathan was. Her reply was: "He's the one with Spiderman shirt on." The response was an egocentric one; Caroline could not appreciate that her parents did not know the children in her class and had not observed the incident. She was operating from a recognition of the particulars of the encounter with her schoolmate, but she did not coordinate these with the perspective of her listeners.

Structures that affect social behavior and personality have in common their applicability to concepts of self, concepts of others, and an understanding of

307

the relations between them within a common social world with norms and expectations (Kohlberg, 1969). Thus, the fundamental social–cognitive skill involves role-taking. Social–cognitive development in turn involves increasing understanding of the reciprocity between the self's actions and the actions of others.

Some cognitive–developmental theorists hold that *cognitive structures are abstract patterns that are themselves content-free*, but that can be applied to many different possible contents (e.g., Kohlberg, 1969; Piaget, 1955). For example, in the two previous examples, the tendency of the children to focus on one dimension of an event, regardless of the content of the event, would be viewed as reflecting a common underlying structure. In other words, psychological structures are considered to be applicable to a number of different situations, some of which involve persons and interactions and some of which involve the world of objects. Others view structures as including specific content. For example, knowledge of the general sequence of actions that must be followed in getting food in a restaurant (Schank & Abelson, 1977) or in expressing emotion appropriately (Saarni, 1979) may be thought of as knowledge structures that affect how newly encountered social situations are interpreted (Schank & Abelson, 1977).

The Process of Developmental Change. The transition from relatively simple structures to more complex, mature ones occurs very gradually. Through many experiences, children become aware of additional considerations that need to be incorporated into their typical understanding of social situations. For example, Caroline will become aware of the importance of considering the perspective of others as she is increasingly reminded by listeners that her messages do not communicate her ideas so that her needs are filled. Eventually, role-taking will become an integral part of her implicit structure for social communication.

In Piagetian terminology (see Chapter 8), such experiences involve *assimilation* and *accommodation* to the elements that are pertinent to more mature understanding. The psychological goal is to maintain equilibrium between recognizing the similarity between a new experience and previous experiences (assimilation) and recognizing the ways in which the experience is unfamiliar and requires special adjustments (accommodation). Structural change is sometimes necessary to accommodate to new experiences. Kohlberg (1969) described the experience of encountering new elements to be incorporated into existing structures as cognitive conflict. In interactions with others, children are gradually made aware of what they must consider to make appropriate social responses. Piaget (1965) has particularly stressed the importance of interaction with peers, in which children can be obliged to grapple with the complexities of social interaction without the constraints normally applied by authority figures such as parents and teachers.

Changes across time in cognitive structures are summarized in stage theories of cognitive development, such as Piaget's (see Chapter 8) and in theories of social–cognitive development, such as those discussed in Chapter

Social-Cognitive Development

Stage Theory

Each Stage
Subsumes
the Other

Complexity

FIGURE 9-2
Each successive stage involves more complex behaviors than the previous one, but subsumes the characteristics of those earlier stages as well.

10. In other words, stages are descriptions of successive levels of cognitive functioning, each involving the application of structures that are more complex and that include more of the essential elements of social relations than earlier levels. Stages are hierarchical in nature, meaning that each stage includes awareness of the same elements and relationships that governed thought in the previous stages, as well as new, additional elements and interrelations (Kohlberg, 1969).

Summary

Research in personality and social development is concerned with describing and explaining how children become socialized to their society, developing in the process the personal patterns of behavior that make them unique individuals. Although human beings are socially responsive from the beginning of life, a number of different viewpoints have been advanced that seek to explain the origins of that social responsiveness: how it is affected by the environment and what these effects are for the developing individual. A major question is how social responsiveness contributes to human development.

The classic psychodynamic theories of development, primarily that of Sigmund Freud, provide the historic cornerstone for the study of personality and social development. Freud accounted for many of the conflicts that individuals experience between personal needs and social constraints in terms of three structures of the personality: the id, ego, and superego. In addition, he summarized developmental changes in terms of a series of biologically predetermined psychosexual stages, each of which attains its distinctive characteristics from the particular needs that must be gratified during a given life period. Erik Erikson's "neo-analytic" theory of psycho-*social* stages extended Freud's ideas toward a greater appreciation of social experience as a driving force in development.

Social learning theories generally focus on a group of related processes by which social experiences might affect behavior and development. *Social reinforcement* and *punishment* are processes that help to explain how the consequences of specific behaviors contribute to subsequent actions, and *observational learning* refers to a covert process for encoding and storing information about behaviors that children have seen performed by others, but may not have performed themselves. *Imitation* occurs when observed behaviors are actually repeated by the observer. Together, these processes help to explain how human beings acquire the vast number and variety of behaviors that characterize most adults' social repertoires. Early social learning theorists like John Dollard and Neal Miller showed how learning processes could be used to provide different explanations of the important phenomena identified by Freud.

Recent theorists have proposed cognitive social learning theories that recognize that developing individuals are thinking persons whose cognitive interpretations of the world are "part" of their personalities and at the same time influence how social experiences contribute to their personality development through learning. Theories of cognitive and social–cognitive development, influenced by theorists such as Jean Piaget, also help to explain how changes in understanding of self, others, and social organization may be linked to variations in social behavior.

Several common legacies from these theories are worthy of note. First, all drew the attention of researchers to issues of the *processes* influencing personality and social development. Although theories differ in their precise treatment of these processes, there are significant commonalities that have led to focusing processes, such as the impact of others' actions and the acquisition of self-control. Second, the theories commonly earmark important topics as central to conceptualizing and understanding personality and social development. These include aspects of the environment and the significant others who populate them (such as, family, peers, school) as well as the major categories of behavior and competencies that comprise personality (for example, aggressiveness and self-control). A prime example of commonality is the concept of internalization, a process by which early learning and experience are absorbed to promote enduring developmental consequences. All three types of theories discussed here have fostered and sustained attention to environmental conditions that (1) continue to influence personality and social behavior beyond the time when they are initially acquired (e.g., reinforcements to models who perform the behaviors of interest), or (2) that interfere with the capacity of socialization experiences to cause a significant and lingering impact on development (e.g., inadvertent punishment for the behavior).

Although this chapter focused on theory, we dealt frequently with both the processes deemed central by the various theories and the persons and contexts that influence individual behavior and development. In Chapters 10 and 11, we will continue this dual emphasis by discussing social–cognitive competencies relevant to personality and social behavior and the expression, understanding, and regulation of emotions.

Suggested Readings

Bandura, A. (1977). *Social learning theory*. Englewood Cliffs, NJ: Prentice-Hall.

Erikson, E. (1963). *Childhood and society* (2nd ed.). New York: Norton.

Mischel, W. (1984). Convergences and challenges in the search for consistency. *American Psychologist, 39,* 351–364.

Plomin, R. (1989). Environment and genes: Determinants of behavior. *American Psychologist, 44,* 104–111.

Sulloway, F. J. (1979). *Freud: Biologist of the mind*. New York: Basic Books.

CHAPTER TEN

Perceiving and Reasoning About the Social World

Introduction

Social interactions involve not only behavior toward other people, but also perceptions and inferences about them, their thoughts and feelings, and the events that comprise the social world. Think about how often we describe or refer to things that our listeners do not know about. Think of how we need to understand what has caused some event and, in turn, what may happen because of it. Think about how often we need to evaluate some action or behavior of others or ourselves.

These examples of times when we need to perceive and reason about the social world involve the cognitive skills that we discussed in Chapters 7 and 8. To be sure, it is sometimes more difficult to understand the perceiving and reasoning processes that are involved in social cognition than it is to assess reasoning about impersonal objects and predict relationships among them, as in the studies of cognitive development discussed in earlier chapters. By social cognition, we mean *perceiving* the persons and events that one encounters in everyday life and *reasoning* about the implications of these perceptions for the diverse situations involving others (for example play, getting along with family members, behaving acceptably in school, fulfilling the duties of citizenship). Compared to understanding the nonsocial world of objects and logical relations, social perception and reasoning involve highly variable and unpredictable experiences. When you drop a ball, it always falls. In contrast, in social life, some people respond to a smile by smiling in return, whereas others maintain a neutral expression, look away, or even glare at the person smiling (Hartup, 1988). Social cognition thus involves understanding emotions, beliefs, motivations, and other internal states that vary from one person to another, as well as perceiving observable actions and reactions. To appreciate fully the scope of children's developing cognitive skills and also their changing social behavior patterns, we need to know something about their social–cognitive development.

In this chapter we examine the development of social cognition. We begin by considering how children change in how they understand themselves and other persons. We then turn to their developing understanding of social interactions and relationships. Among the questions we will address is how children change in their understanding of morality and socially conventional behavior. Finally, we will draw on this overview of social–cognitive development to consider how the understanding of self, others, and interpersonal relationships is related to other aspects of personality and social development.

The Problem of Understanding Others: Piaget's View

Jean Piaget studied children's conceptions of others long before other psychologists thought the topic was interesting. He concluded that the growth of children's interpersonal relations and understandings has its *origin* in the development of cognitive skills that are evident in their understanding of the relations between objects or the possibilities inherent in logical thought (Piaget & Inhelder, 1969). For example, during the sensorimotor period, children become more capable of representing people and relationships symbolically, so that they can remember people even when the people are not present. This ability, which is similar to the concept of object permanence discussed in Chapter 7, "results in the formation of . . . lasting sympathies or antipathies toward other people and of a permanent awareness and valorization of oneself" (Piaget & Inhelder, 1969, p. 115).

The problems of social understanding that interested Piaget result mostly from preschool children's tendency to think that their own experiences and perceptions are universal, rather than recognizing that others have independent experiences and perceptions. Piaget's (1955) term for this cognitive tendency is *egocentrism*. Just as a child focuses on the height dimension before acquiring the notion of conservation of liquid (see Chapters 8 and 9), egocentric children center on their own perspective, failing to take account of other possible perspectives. One of the necessary accomplishments in development is separating from our own point of view and coordinating that viewpoint with the perspectives of other persons. Without this ability to coordinate viewpoints, even everyday conversation may be impossible.

The give-and-take of everyday social life provides essential *environmental influences* for developing viewpoints that are coordinated with the viewpoints of others. As we saw in Chapter 9, the cognitive–developmental perspective on social development is based on Piaget's idea that individuals struggle to assimilate new experiences to psychological structures based on past experiences and, simultaneously, seek to accommodate existing schemas to the demand of new social encounters. Thus, interactions with parents, teachers, and other children create pressures on children to take into account such fundamental social elements as the thoughts and feelings of others and the need to adapt their own behavior appropriately. For example, Dunn (1988) has recently argued that early social conflicts with siblings and parents form the basis for social interactions with other people at later ages.

In recent years, a great many studies have helped clarify the meaning and limitations of egocentric thought. This research has given us a more elaborate picture of the many dimensions of perception and reasoning that are involved in perceiving and responding to others and their actions. In some respects, children are far more socially sensitive at early ages than the term egocentrism implies. In the limited respects of Piaget's analysis, however, social–cognitive skills develop very gradually; only in early adolescence do they reach the level of sophistication that is required for many of the complex social tasks required in the adult world. These developments affect children's perceptions and evaluations of other people, their relationships with them, their understanding of basic social concepts and institutions, and the skills they need for social life.

Perceiving and Understanding Persons

The fundamental social–cognitive skill is understanding others and one's self, and the relations between them (Kohlberg, 1969). In this section, we examine the processes that seem to be involved in acquiring and using this skill. The section is in four parts. The first deals with the process of person perception, or noticing those characteristics of persons that make a social impression. The second deals with a particular aspect of person perception: perceptions about one's self and the ways in which these perceptions contribute to children's growing self-understanding. In the third part, we focus on how children of different ages understand those characteristics of persons that are not immediately visible or perceivable, that is, the development of the ability to *infer* what is in the mind of another person. Of special concern are the ways in which inferences about others affect children's abilities for communicating, evaluating the actions of others, and adapting their own behavior to the behavior of others in interpersonal interactions. Finally, the fourth part is concerned with how the ability to understand others affects different types of social relationships: relationships with authority figures, parent–child relationships, and friendships.

In each of the four parts, the underlying question is: What is the *course* of development of children's capacities for perceiving and understanding persons?

Person Perception

Ask 5-year-olds to describe somebody they like a lot, and you will probably hear about the friend's hair color, favorite coat, place of residence, or other observable qualities. By the early tens, the same youngsters are more likely to talk about the friend's more abstract and enduring qualities, such as personality characteristics, skills, and interests. How does this developmental change come about?

Children's descriptions contrast in three major ways that are most pronounced before and after age 8 (Barenboim, 1981; Livesley & Bromley, 1973; Secord & Peevers, 1974; Scarlett, Press, & Crockett, 1971). First, younger children tend to emphasize external characteristics that are readily observable, such as physical appearance, situations, possessions, and activities. Older children may well note these things in their descriptions, but are also likely to mention internal, psychological characteristics—behavior patterns that cannot be directly observed, but must be inferred by the observer. Second, less mature children's descriptions seem more fragmentary than the organized observations of older children and adults. Whereas younger children tend to mention an assortment of characteristics ("is a fast runner," "plays baseball," and "is nice"), an older describer may note that a person displays a coherent pattern of characteristics ("He's a good athlete. He is good at track and baseball—and he's a good sport.") Third, as you can see from these descriptions, young children tend to be vague and global (for example, "nice" or "mean") when they do use summary terms. Older children's characterizations are more differentiated; their descriptions are likely to show that people are "nice" because they are considerate of others, helpful, and pleasant to be with, or that other peers are "mean" because they bully smaller children, upset collaborative play, or show intent to do damage to others. In addition, older children seem less egocentric, in that they seem aware of the subjective nature of their descriptions (for example, they're more careful than younger describers to say, "I think . . ." or "It seems to me like . . ."). Also, older children are less likely to describe other persons only in terms of common activities and experiences. Their view of others seems more objective.

It may not be terribly surprising to know that children talk about others in noticeably different ways, but one must be cautious in inferring the meaning of differences in older and younger children's verbal descriptions. One reason for this is that these descriptions vary both in content, by which we mean *what* children say, and in what terms and structure, by which we mean the way in which content is organized and presented. Age differences may reflect content characteristics. Older children may simply have larger vocabularies and greater verbal fluency than younger children. Young children may recognize the differentiated, dispositional nature of a person they are describing, but their descriptions do not show this recognition in the way that older children's verbal statements do. Consider, for example, this especially striking instance of structural differences in children's social understanding. Younger children tend to characterize someone as "real smart," but teenagers are more likely to exclude implications that don't apply to the person, for example, "He's really smart, but he's not stuck-up or a bookworm" (Leahy, 1976; Livesley & Bromley, 1973, pp. 205–206; Secord & Peevers, 1974, p. 132). These descriptions suggest that children actually perceive persons in a more complex way than younger children do. However, it is possible that vocabulary and other verbal skill differences make contrasts between the thinking of older and younger children seem more pronounced then they actually are. Because of this problem in assessing children's abilities, developmental aspects of person perceptions are often less clear to us than the aspects of cognition that can more readily be studied nonverbally, such as the ordering of physical objects according to size.

Content Versus Structure in Person Descriptions

One way of assessing concepts of others that does not rely heavily on children's verbal description skills is to ask children to make simple predictions about the "future" behavior of hypothetical persons. Using this method, William Rholes and Diane Ruble (1984) asked 5–7-year-old and 9–10-year-old children to predict whether videotaped actors would behave in similar ways in other, related situations. Children in the older group predicted that the videotaped actor would behave consistently in similar situations, especially if they believed his actions were the result of internal, psychological characteristics. Five- to seven-year-olds did not predict similarities in behavior from one situation to another. These findings underscore the developmental differences reported by other researchers (e.g., Gnepp & Chilamkurti, 1988) in children's understanding of persons.

Concepts of Self

The characteristic ways that children describe others are similar to their descriptions of themselves. Secord and Peevers (1974, p. 133) followed their questioning of children about persons they liked or disliked with the query: "Now tell me what you are like." Children's answers to this question were less mature than their answers about others. Kindergarten-age children either could not respond to the question, or they described themselves in terms of their play activities (Secord & Peevers, 1974, p. 133). With increasing age, however, self-descriptions consisted less of concrete details like appearance and activities and more of general and psychological characteristics (Damon & Hart, 1982; Harter, 1983; Markus & Nurius, 1984). The descriptive statements also tended to carry more evaluative connotations. By seventh grade, Secord and Peevers' interviewees were beginning to describe themselves in terms like "lazy," "selfish," "honest," and "shy" (p. 135). Here is a sample self-description:

> I was always so shy with boys—you know, if a boy looked at me, and I saw him looking at me, I thought, it was an insult because I thought he was looking at me—or making fun of me—usually I thought he was making fun of me, you know—look at that funny-looking girl—but after I had some self-confidence—when one did look at me I took it as a compliment (Secord & Peevers, 1974, p. 137).

Although describing oneself objectively appears to be more difficult than being objective about others, the developmental trend is toward self-descriptions in which an objective or third-person viewpoint is increasingly apparent. In addition, self-descriptions gradually become increasingly complex; for example, adolescents, but not children, are likely to attach qualifiers to their statements about themselves ("I like to have a good time, but I don't want to get rowdy") (Leahy, 1976).

Damon's Model of Self-Understanding. Psychologists William Damon and Daniel Hart (1982) have outlined the development of self-understanding from infancy through late adolescence. Their model, diagrammed in Figure 10-1, summarizes what we know from studies of children's self-descriptions.

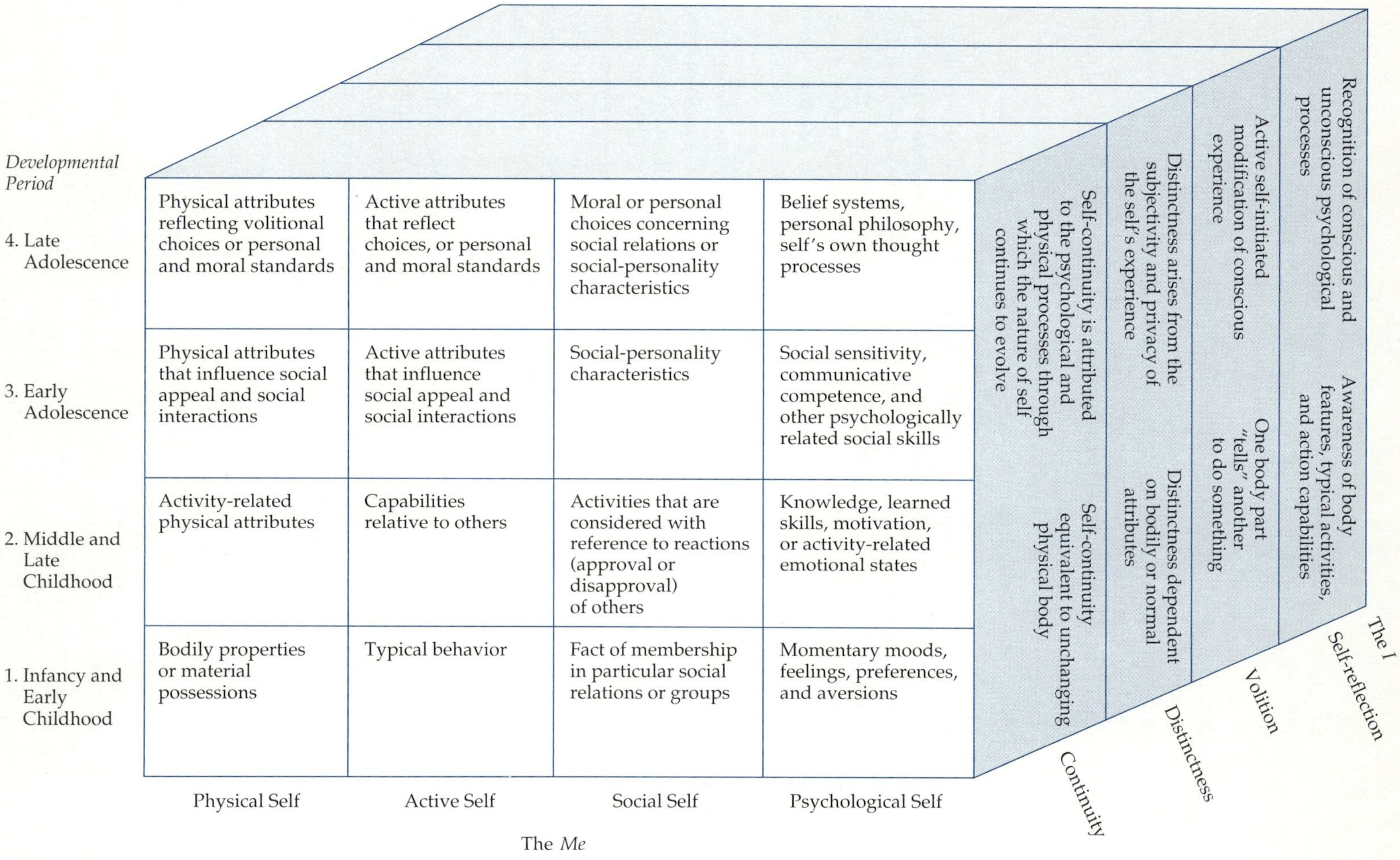

The I

		Self-reflection
Recognition of conscious and unconscious psychological processes	Awareness of body features, typical activities, and action capabilities	
Active self-initiated modification of conscious experience	One body part "tells" another to do something	Volition
Distinctness arises from the subjectivity and privacy of the self's experience	Distinctness dependent on bodily or normal attributes	Distinctness
Self-continuity is attributed to the psychological and physical processes through which the nature of self continues to evolve	Self-continuity equivalent to unchanging physical body	Continuity

The Me

Developmental Period	Physical Self	Active Self	Social Self	Psychological Self
4. Late Adolescence	Physical attributes reflecting volitional choices or personal and moral standards	Active attributes that reflect choices, or personal and moral standards	Moral or personal choices concerning social relations or social-personality characteristics	Belief systems, personal philosophy, self's own thought processes
3. Early Adolescence	Physical attributes that influence social appeal and social interactions	Active attributes that influence social appeal and social interactions	Social-personality characteristics	Social sensitivity, communicative competence, and other psychologically related social skills
2. Middle and Late Childhood	Activity-related physical attributes	Capabilities relative to others	Activities that are considered with reference to reactions (approval or disapproval) of others	Knowledge, learned skills, motivation, or activity-related emotional states
1. Infancy and Early Childhood	Bodily properties or material possessions	Typical behavior	Fact of membership in particular social relations or groups	Momentary moods, feelings, preferences, and aversions

FIGURE 10-1

Four dimensions of self-understanding appear to change with increasing age. Each has effects on subjective and objective views of the self.

Source: from Damon & Hart, 1982.

Changes in understanding of two aspects of the self, first identified by William James (1892–1961), are shown. The first aspect, the self-as-object (the me), reflects how individuals view themselves. Self-understanding is first based on what children know about their physical characteristics. As they develop, children understand themselves in terms of their actions and, later, in terms of their social memberships and relationships. The most advanced understanding of self-as-object involves knowledge of one's own psychological characteristics. As in research on children's understanding of others, the understanding of the self progressively becomes more oriented to the internal qualities of the person.

A second aspect of self-understanding involves the self-as-subject (the I). This refers to children's knowledge of the factors that make them distinctive coherent individuals. Four dimensions of this sense of self appear to change with age. The first concerns continuity of self from one time of life to another. The second has to do with the characteristics that make one distinct from others. The third dimension, volition, refers to the sense that the self can help to control what the person experiences, by directing the self to change internally or overtly. Finally, self-reflection means that a sense of self depends on awareness of personal characteristics, including private thoughts and feelings. Figure 10-1 shows the changes that occur in both self-as-object and self-as-subject over the course of development.

We should note that self-descriptions give information about the cognitive characteristics of children's ideas about themselves. They do not tap into the children's feelings about themselves, which are usually denoted by the terms self-concept and self-esteem. Although individuals' abilities to perceive and label themselves in certain ways partly determines their feelings about themselves (Leahy & Huard, 1976), other considerations, like the quality of social relationships and successful experiences, are also important to how people view them. The development of emotional responses to the self will be discussed in the next chapter.

Inferences About Others: Social Role Taking

Descriptions of others and the self are only two types of information about the development of social thinking and reasoning. Additional information comes from research on children's awareness of how others might think or feel. By asking children to respond to questions about the thought and feelings of others, developmental scholars can assess more objectively the development of their social–cognitive abilities.

Social role taking is the process of making inferences about the internal states of others—their information, ability for understanding, feelings, and personality characteristics. The term role taking includes several different types of inferences about others. *Perceptual role taking* requires a role taker to know what another person sees or otherwise experiences when observing a scene or event from that person's own physical perspective. Piaget and Inhelder's (1956) famous Three-Mountain Experiment shows the remarkable changes that take place between the ages of 4 and 11 years in understanding others' perspectives. Piaget showed his subjects a three-dimensional model of three mountains, allowing them to walk around it to see it from different

According to Piaget, young children may have difficulty estimating where to place a toy pig so that the doll "can't see it."

points of view. He then stationed them at one spot and placed a doll at various other points around the display. The subjects were to select from several pictures the one that showed what the doll could see—that is, the doll's perspective on the three-dimensional model. The youngest children chose their own perspective, even when they were allowed to examine the doll's view and given a second chance to select the correct picture. Somewhat older children showed increasing awareness that the doll's perspective was different from their own, although they had difficulty choosing the correct picture of the doll's view. By age 11, however, the subjects clearly realized that only one perspective—different from their own—would be correct, and they were much more accurate at choosing a picture of it. They rejected their own perspective because they knew the doll's was different and because the task called for information about the doll's perspective.

The term *cognitive role taking* refers to knowing what another person is likely to know, understand, or think about persons, situations, and events. For example, one of the most common tasks of social life is to verbally convey information to another person—in conversation, in providing instruction and assistance, and so forth. In order to accomplish this effectively, people must not only know about the referent (the thing or situation to be described), but must also know something about the other person (what he or she already knows about the referent, reasons for wanting or needing the information, the kind of language the other can best understand, and so on). For example, consider the difference between needing to ask for emergency help on a busy city street where you did not know anyone and asking for the same help if you were with friends or family. Although the problem (the referent) would be the same, the recipients of your communication would be very different. Alone among strangers, you would not know as much or anything at all about what the people around you understood. Think about how that would alter your communication.

Finally, affective role taking refers to the process of recognizing the emotions or feelings of another person; in some respects, it is similar to the common term, empathy. This latter term, however, is often reserved for the observer's actually sharing or experiencing the emotional state of the other person (Feshbach, 1978). We will discuss affective role taking in Chapter 11 in connection with the development of emotional understanding.

The Role Taking Process.   Psychologist John Flavell (1974) has suggested that four separate steps are involved in the role taking process: (1) recognizing the existence of certain characteristics or properties that the other might conceivably possess; (2) recognizing the need to know about the other; (3) inferring the other's characteristics from such information as is available; and (4) applying the inferred knowledge in responding to the other person. Here is Flavell's example of these four steps:

> Supposing S is about to play chess with an unknown opponent (O). He is first of all certain to know the general meaning of such psychological properties as "chess skill," and "knowledge of the game," and also that O could conceivably possess these properties to a greater or lesser extent (Existence). He will also be aware that it would be sensible (Need) of him to try to find out (Inference) just how skillful and knowledgeable O is, so that he can adjust his own game accordingly (Application) (Flavell, 1974, p. 72).

These distinctions help us understand the developmental course of role taking. For example, the fact that a 5-year-old does not infer the doll's view in the Three-Mountain Task accurately does not necessarily mean that the child is unaware of the existence of different views. The difficulty may lie in the complex "computation" of several factors that is required for inference to be put to use, such as the ability to infer the precise information that others do or do not have. Similarly, an 8-year-old's apparent lack of attention to the circumstances of others in a social interaction may indicate problems in applying role taking, but does not necessarily indicate a lack of basic competence to engage in the existence, need, and inference aspects of role taking.

Role taking in social life can vary widely in difficulty. For example, Piaget's Three-Mountain Task involves several objects (mountains) arrayed in 3-dimensional space; as noted above, preschool and even elementary-school children find it difficult to recognize the perceptions of others. However, try showing children both sides of a card with a simple picture on it. Then sit across from the children and turn one side of the card toward them, asking,

"What do I see?" Under this more manageable condition, children as young as 24 months have shown that they can recognize some aspects of another's perceptual perspective (Lempers, Flavell, & Flavell, 1977; Strayer, Bigelow, & Ames, 1973). In short, performance on perceptual role taking at least partly depends on the difficulty of the task.

Role taking also varies in difficulty because some inferences call for more cognitive "computing" than others. For example, Borke (1971) asked young children to say whether story characters would feel happy, sad, or angry in various situations. Three-year-old children were quite accurate in guessing the appropriate affective states. Most likely, they either simply showed they had learned how people typically react in the situations Borke described to them, or they may have been projecting the feelings they themselves would have in such a situation (Feshbach, 1978). The skill is an important one, but it involves less complex reasoning than many role-taking tasks.

In contrast, Chandler and Greenspan (1972) emphasized differences in the complexity of inferences in a reply to Borke's report of her findings. They argued that while this rather simple instance of affective role taking occurs in very young children, more complicated role-taking skills develop much later. To illustrate the differences, Chandler and Greenspan described an accidental happening to children and asked them, in turn, to describe it from the point of view of someone who came on the scene only during the last part of the occurrence. Like Piaget's subjects in the Three-Mountain Task, children did this task reliably only after about age 11. For instance, only about 4% of the 13-year-olds in the study allowed their own information about the event to intrude when they tried to tell the story from the other's viewpoint, while 85% of the 6-year-olds did. This task is simply a more difficult one than Borke required; and estimates of role-taking skills—and the ages at which they appear—vary, depending on the task children are asked to do. Some dimensions of difference among role-taking tasks and their interrelationships can be seen in Research Focus 10-1.

Role Taking and Communication. From a developmental standpoint, young children, whose role-taking skills are less well developed than those of older people, may often behave immaturely because they fail to appreciate the feelings, knowledge, and perspectives of others. Asocial and antisocial behaviors of adolescents and adults are also sometimes attributed to poorly developed role-taking skills.

One type of social behavior for which the effect of developing role-taking skills is well documented is speaking or writing so that another person can understand what you intend to say to them. The importance of recognizing the needs of listeners in oral communication was discussed briefly in Chapter 6. Let us now examine in more detail how social–cognitive skills combine with language skills to make possible social communication. In a classic study, children from second- and eighth-grade classrooms were each required to explain a game to two listeners: one who could see and one who was blindfolded (Flavell et al., 1968). The children themselves had learned the simple game by trial-and-error. No explanation was given to them; an adult

RESEARCH FOCUS 10-1

Differences in Role-Taking Tasks

Inferring the feelings, experiences, or knowledge of another person sometimes requires an elaborate reasoning process and other times demands no more than acknowledging what you would experience under the same circumstances. Since the tasks that psychologists use to assess children's role-taking skills vary in what the child must do to perform well, results often seem contradictory and confusing. Consequently, we have to look closely at the nature of role-taking tasks in order to appreciate children's social–cognitive abilities at different periods in development.

Kathryn Urbeg and Edward Docherty recently analyzed three tasks that have often been used to indicate role-taking ability and two more that they devised themselves. They wanted to examine the different reasoning demands that each placed on children. Here are the tasks they considered:

Task 1, taken from Borke's (1971) research, involved asking children to say whether another child would feel happy, sad, afraid, or angry under certain conditions. The test "stories" included eating a favorite snack, losing a toy, getting lost in the woods at night, being forced to go to bed, and so forth.

Task 2 required a child to identify the feelings of two characters in hypothetical stories. For example, subjects were first shown a picture of two children fighting over a toy truck and then a second picture of a woman handing the truck to one of the children. They are told: "This is a story about you. You and your friend both want to play with that truck. Then the teacher comes over and gives the truck to you. How do you feel? How does your friend feel?"

Task 3, modeled after a procedure reported by Burns and Cavey (1957), also involves a pair of pictures. For example, one picture might show a birthday party scene with cake and presents, and the child would be asked how he or she would feel in that situation. Then a second picture is shown, depicting an identical scene except that it includes a boy with a frown on his face. The child is told: "Here is a boy at his birthday party—how does he feel?"

In Task 4, three pictures are shown, as in a study by Flavell et al. (1968). The first two depict a drastic change in a character's feelings. For example, he or she is at first pleased upon spotting a pretty dog, but then frightened when the dog growls and chases him or her when he or she tries to pet it. Picture 3 shows a new character in the same situation of spotting the dog, and the child is told: "This is you. You are outside and see a pretty dog. You reach down to pet it, but it growls and chases you. How do you feel?" When this question is answered, the child is asked: "You run into the house and shut the door. Then another child comes down the street and sees the dog. How does he feel?"

Task 5 consists of the five stories used by Chandler and Greenspan (1972), after each of which the child must recount the events from his or her own perspective and that of a late-arriving bystander. For example, one story depicts a boy saddened by accidentally dropping his coin down a sewer grating. He is then joined by a friend who can't understand why the boy won't play ball with him. Children first retell the story from their own point of view and then try to reinterpret the same events from the point of view of the friend who came up and wanted to play ball, but didn't know about the lost coin.

These tasks vary along a dimension that shows up in the contrast between Tasks 1–3 and Tasks 4–5. Tasks 1–3 require children to take the role of only one person at a time. Although they must tell about two different viewpoints in Tasks 2 and 3, they may first take one perspective and comment on it, and then do the same with the second perspective. In other words, role taking is sequential. However, in Tasks 4 and 5, simultaneous role taking is required. The child must keep both perspectives in mind to answer correctly, since the information that one character obviously has cannot be allowed to intrude into a description of what the other character knows about the situation.

In addition to this primary difference, other differences between the tasks also make some more difficult than others. For example, Task 1 and the other four tasks contrast in the number of perspectives involved in role taking. Moreover, Tasks 1 and 2 are relatively easy because perspectives can be inferred on the basis of stereotypic knowledge or straightforward projection of one's own feelings. In Task 3, only one of the two inferences (the first) can be answered stereotypically; the other involves information "unique and specific to the individual presented in the story" (p. 199). Similarly, Task 4 involves more stereotypic responses than Task 5.

Urberg and Docherty tested 42 3-, 4-, and 5-year-olds on all five tasks and found that children generally answered correctly on Tasks 1–3 at earlier ages than they could on Task 4. (None of these children could do the complex perspective taking required by Task 5, as Chandler and Greenspan would predict.) In fact, by using role-taking tasks of different degrees of difficulty, Urberg and Docherty were able to identify three levels of role-taking skills among their young preschool subjects:

Level 0—No role taking. Six children (14.3% of the entire sample), with an average age of 3 years, 5 months, passed none of the five tasks, including Borke's very simple affective role-taking exercise. Their performance clearly warrants the label "egocentric."

Level 1—Sequential decentration. The children who passed Tasks 1–3, but not Task 4, demonstrated that they could take the role of one other person at a time. Half of the children, with an average of 4 years, 5 months, performed in this fashion.

Level 2—Simultaneous decentration. The 35.8% of the children (with an average age of 5 years, 4 months) who passed all of the first four tasks demonstrated the ability to reason in terms of two perpectives simultaneously.

Apparently, role taking is not an all-or-none ability, but is more or less possible for children depending on the particular task demands to be met in a given social situation.

To summarize, role-taking skills involve a variety of inference goals, task requirements, and levels of difficulty. Not surprisingly, measures of the skills are typically only moderately related to one another (Kurdek & Rodgon, 1975; Shantz, 1975). That is, a person who is skilled at affective role taking does not necessarily perform well on cognitive role taking and perceptual role-taking, or the converse. ❧

---

simply demonstrated the game for the children, allowing them to alternate with the adult players on "turns" until two entire games had been played. Even the youngest child quickly learned to play. Thus, when the children then explained the game to someone else, they were not imitating the words and phrases used by someone else, but were generating their own explanations. First, a sighted, and then a blindfolded, listener were brought in to "learn" the game from the children. The children's explanations were recorded verbatim and then were examined for the difference between the children's messages to the blindfolded, as compared to the sighted, listener. The older children changed their messages significantly more than the younger ones, who said essentially the same thing to both listeners. The older group provided new information that was essential to learning the game for the blindfolded listeners. Children have also been found to include different information in messages to familiar people, with whom they have shared experiences, than in messages to unfamiliar listeners; but older speakers make more pronounced distinctions between the two than younger ones (Sonnenschein, 1986).

How can these differences be explained? Flavell suggests that, at the very least, the children who did not change their messages for the different listeners should be thought of as *egocentric*, or overly focused on their own viewpoint, and those who did change their explanations as relatively nonegocentric. Figure 10-2 is a diagram of the differences between more and less communicatively skilled children. The diagram fits very well the different kinds of messages given by second and eighth graders in the sighted–blindfolded listener study. Second graders were likely to use pronouns ("that," "this," "it"), together with pointing and gesturing, to describe the game, regardless of whether the listener could see them. Eighth graders' messages for the sighted listener appropriately involved gestures and pronouns in much the same way as the second graders' explanations did. But these older children more typically began their explanations to the blindfolded listener by describing the elements of the game, which they then subsequently referred to specifically: "the red one" rather than "this one."

The role taking involved in this study was quite simple perceptual role taking. Piaget (1955) and others have asked children to explain a mechanical device or retell a complicated fairy tale to other children. In these cases, even relatively mature children seem much less sensitive to the listener's level of information, ability to understand abstract ideas, and so forth. Such communication difficulties stem partly from the complexity of the task and the

FIGURE 10-2

Schemas for (*a*) egocentric and (*b*) nonegocentric communication.

Source: from Flavell, Botkin, Fry, Wright, & Jarvis, 1968.

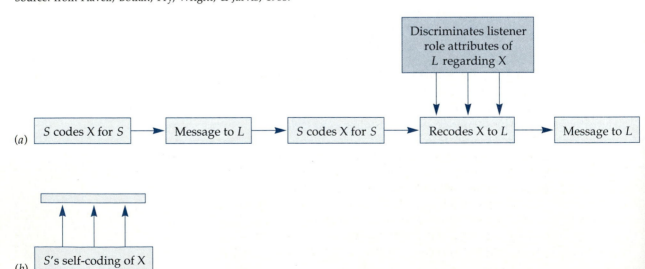

particular types of measures that are being taken. For example, Shatz and Gelman (1973) observed the speech of 4-year-old children to both younger children (2-year-olds) and adults; they found that children's messages to these two different types of listeners were quite different. When talking to younger children, 4-year-olds' language was much simpler, consisting of shorter phrases and more statements designed to get and hold the listener's attention than they used in speech to adults. In other words, even though these young children had performed very poorly on standard tests of ecogentrism, they did adjust their conversation to the different capabilities of their listeners.

In the strict sense of the term, these 4-year-olds were not egocentric. It should be noted, however, that Shatz and Gelman, like many of the other researchers in the field (Garvey & BenDebba, 1974; Garvey & Hogan, 1973; Sonnenschein, 1986), are primarily concerned with evidence of role-taking activity, by which we mean indications in children's messages that they are taking account of their listeners. They are less concerned with the absolute accuracy and adequacy of the message—that is, the extent to which the children's messages enable a listener to respond accurately.

Role Taking Based on Others' Actions.   When children are asked to describe interactions between others, their responses are in many ways similar to their descriptions of persons (Shantz, 1983). For example, when children are asked to recount events from a movie or television show, 6- and 7-year-olds typically describe what people did or said. Older children are more likely to infer thoughts, feelings, and intentions of characters (Collins, 1984; Flapan, 1968). Along with this shift from the overt to the psychological and covert, there is also an increasing effort to explain the interactions; as they mature, children seem to want to make sense of the sequence of occurences they observe. Thus, they are more likely to mention causes of events, relations between happenings, and so forth (Collins, Wellman, Keniston, & Westby, 1978; Collins, 1984; Flapan, 1968). In short, developmental changes in descriptions of events and interactions increasingly involve inferences that "go beyond the information given."

One implication of children's increasing concern with others' intentions is that intentions gradually become a more important part of children's evaluations of persons and their actions. Before about age 6, children tend to assume that all acts are intentional (Barenboim, 1977; Berndt & Berndt, 1975; Rholes & Ruble, 1984; Ruble & Rholes, 1982), but gradually come to realize that some events are accidental. As we will see in a later section of this chapter, the distinction between intentional and accidental acts is one important factor in children's reasoning about morality, values, and justice.

In addition to concern with people's intentions as causes of their actions, children increasingly develop an understanding that events may result from any one of several different causes. For example, an event such as failing a test in school may be caused by internal characteristics of persons, such as their abilities, effort, or attitudes, or it may be caused by factors that are largely outside of the individual, such as the difficulty of the test, the fairness

327

of the teacher, or the child's opportunity to prepare for the test. At this point, we do not have adequate research to determine whether children prefer one particular type of causal explanation, although as we noted above younger children seem to have a bias toward attributing events to personal intent (Ruble & Rholes, 1982).

Research on the development of causal reasoning in social relations does indicate, however, that children do not acquire understanding of some important aspects of causality until middle childhood, roughly, ages 7 to 9 (Karniol & Ross, 1976; Smith, 1975). For example, only in this period do children understand that when there is more than one possible cause for an event, you cannot be sure which possible cause is the actual one. This principle, called the discounting principle, influences most adults' inferences about which of several possible causes can be linked to an event, but preschoolers do not appear to use the principle in making causal inferences. Understanding the cause of others' behavior can be important in determining the responses that we give to them in interaction. For example, we react more negatively to an apparently unfriendly statement if we attribute it to the other person's anger or dislike toward us than if we attribute it to preoccupation or oversight (Dodge & Somberg, 1987).

Role Taking in Relationships

Knowing that other people cannot see the elements of the game you're trying to describe to them affects the way most people behave in straightforward, predictable ways. Recognizing and coordinating the cognitive perspectives of others in everyday life is often much more complex.

Take the case of a person (O) who must recognize not only that he or she infers something about the perspective of Person X, but also that X infers something about O at the same time. In short, O is not only thinking about X, but is thinking about X thinking about O, and so forth. Miller, Shelton, and Flavell (1970) studied children's inferences of this type, which they called recursive thinking; and, not surprisingly, they found pronounced differences among children of the ages 6 to 12 in their ability to think about "people thinking about people thinking about. . . ." All of the children in this age range easily reasoned about two persons simultaneously, and large percentages of them readily conceived of another person thinking about the action of some third person. However, it was not until age 11 or so that children could grasp the notion of persons thinking about others in the kind of endless regress shown in Figure 10-3.

Recursive thought is involved in the sometimes complex task of recognizing the perspectives of other persons in social interactions (Barenboim, 1978). Consider the following dilemma used in research by Robert Selman:

> Tom is trying to decide what present to buy his friend Mike, who will be given a surprise birthday party the next day. Tom meets Mike by chance and learns that Mike is extremely upset that his dog, Pepper, has been lost for two weeks. In fact, Mike is so upset that he tells Tom, "I miss Pepper so much I never want to look at another dog again." Tom goes off, only to pass a store with a sale on puppies; one or two are left and these will soon be gone. The dilemma is whether or not to buy the puppy for Mike's birthday. (Selman, 1976, p. 161).

FIGURE 10-3

Four of the items used by Miller, Shelton, and Flavell (1970) for questioning their subjects show the increasingly elaborate processes that are often required for social perspective-taking. In (a), the simplest case, a boy thinks about two persons in contiguity with one another, but without specifying the thoughts of either. In (b), one of the two persons is also recognized as engaging in thinking, although the content of her thoughts is not inferred. A somewhat more complicated situation exists in (c), where the child thinks about himself thinking about himself. (In other versions of this case, the experimenters showed, for example, the boy thinking about the girl thinking about her father.) This is called *one-loop recursion*. The process pictured in (d) goes one step further: The boy thinks about the girl thinking about her father thinking about her mother—a *two-loop recursion*. Selman argued that these processes enter into recognizing others' perceptives in social interaction.

329

After children had heard this and other similar dilemmas, Selman and his colleagues asked them a series of open-ended questions (for example, "Should Tom buy the puppy for Mike?"). They then categorized the answers in terms of the extent to which children recognized that the two individuals in the stories are aware of each other's perspectives. These researchers have proposed a series of levels of complexity in social perspective taking. The levels are outlined in Table 10-1.

Young children (typically, younger than age 7) usually confuse the attitudes of both persons in the story with their own attitudes—an egocentric response such as those Piaget documened (Level 0). For example, one child said that Mike "is sad, but he'll be happy (when he gets a new puppy)." Asked to explain why, he said, "I like puppies. They make me happy."

Awareness of others' perspectives enters into children's answers with increasing complexity during middle childhood (Selman, 1980). Stage 1 of Selman's sequence involves the recognition that two individuals in a relationship both have different perspectives—that they are subjective. Unlike more mature children, youngsters at the subjective level fail to realize that those perspectives affect one another in interactions. In the case of Tom and Mike, one child recognized Mike's and Tom's different perspectives, but did not appreciate that Mike's perspectives might be affected by Tom's intentions in buying him a new puppy. His answer reflects this: "If (Mike) says he doesn't want a dog, then he doesn't. He'll be angry (if Tom gives him a puppy)."

Gradually, children come to recognize that persons are self-reflective (Stage 2). They recognize that Tom knows that Mike's perspective may be affected by Mike's inferences about Tom's good intentions in buying him a new dog. Children's comments on the dilemmas indicate that the understanding that each of the two characters can base his actions on (1) inferences about the other's perspectives, including (2) the knowledge that the other person is simultaneously making inferences about their perspectives. For example, "Mike says he doesn't want one now. But he'll change his mind later on. If I were in his place, I'd feel like he does, but I'd feel different later on."

Adolescent perspective taking recognizes that both parties can consider their interaction objectively. They are aware both of the simultaneous perspective taking of each other and the possible effects of this mutual activity (Stage 3). For example, "Mike will understand what Tom was trying to do, and even if he doesn't like the dog, he'll appreciate that Tom thought he would when he bought it." This young person's thinking is recursive: She imagines Mike thinking that Tom was thinking about him and his perspective. Such complexity is involved in many instances of social reasoning, and its development is a major achievement in children's social–cognitive growth. We will discuss the achievement further in Chapter 11.

Selman's approach to the development of social perspective taking focuses on one type of social experience: understanding the actions of others. It is not clear whether children's responses to these hypothetical dilemmas involving two other individuals also give us a full picture of what must take place when the children themselves are one of the interactors. In such cases, the children's own perspective might interfere in their efforts to recognize and appreciate the interactive nature of both perspectives. However, Selman believes children's responses to their dilemmas reflect developing concepts of social interactions that should affect children's own behavior, as well as their understanding of others' behavior.

TABLE 10-1
Developmental stages in role taking (Selman)

Stage	Age Range*	Child's Understanding
Stage 0 Egocentric Viewpoint	3–6 yrs.	Child has a sense of differentiation of self and other but fails to distinguish between the social perspectives (thoughts, feelings) of other and self. Child can label other's overt feelings but does not see the cause and effect relation of reasons to social actions.
Stage 1 Social–Informational Role Taking	6–8 yrs.	Child is aware that other has a social perspective based on other's own reasoning, which may or may not be similar to child's. However, child tends to focus on one perspective rather than coordinating viewpoints.
Stage 2 Self-Reflective Role Taking	8–10 yrs.	Child is conscious that each individual is aware of the other's perspective and that this awareness influences self and other's view of each other. Putting self in other's place in a way of judging his intentions, purposes, and actions. Child can form a coordinated chain of perspectives, but cannot yet abstract from this process to the level of simultaneous mutuality.
Stage 3 Mutual Role Taking	10–12 yrs.	Child realizes that both self and other can view each other mutually and simultaneously as subjects. Child can step outside the two-person dyad and view the interaction from a third-person perspective.
Stage 4 Social and Conventional System Role Taking	12–15+ yrs.	Person realizes mutual perspective taking does not always lead to complete understanding. Social conventions are seen as necessary because they are understood by all members of the group (the generalized other) regardless of their position, role, or experience.

* Age ranges for all stages represent only an average approximation based on our studies to date.
SOURCE: Adapted from Damon, 1983.

Concepts of Different Types of Relationships

Children's understanding of the thoughts and behavior of people in relationships depends partly on the type of relationship in question. For the most part, children's understanding of special types of relationships parallels the development of understanding of interpersonal relations, generally. For example, emphasis on one or two persons gradually comes to include an understanding that persons and relationships exist within larger social structures, like communities and nations, which both affect and are affected by the relationships. Also, relationships are largely dominated by self-interest and necessity or rules in the understanding of young children, but are more often seen as bonds that may be entered into on a voluntary basis based on mutual benefit and responsibility as children mature. Young children's views of relationships, like their views of persons, are dominated by concrete, physical characteristics of persons and their actions, whereas older children's views consider more abstract principles such as one person's trust or caring for another.

Detailed knowledge of children's developing thought about specific types of social relationships gives a clearer view of the changes in social concepts that underlie developmental changes in social understanding. Three types of relationships have been given special attention: authority relationships, in which one person has power over another by virtue of age or role; parent–child relationships, and friendships and peer relationships.

Authority. In the first 6 years of life, children are strongly oriented to the demands and approval of authority figures, such as parents, teachers, and other caregivers. Respect for authority remains characteristic of most individuals in adulthood, but the understanding of authority changes during middle childhood and adolescence. In particular, understanding of the rationales for authority and reasons for obedience to authority change during these years.

Psychologist William Damon (1977) demonstrated these developmental changes in concepts of authority in interview studies with children between the ages of 4 and 9. The topics of the interviews were both hypothetical and actual situations in which children were faced with a conflict between authority and their own wishes. Damon found that younger children did not distinguish clearly between what they wanted and what an authority figure demanded of them. At a slightly more complex level of thought, children viewed authority figures as having legitimacy because of superior power to enforce their demands—a "might makes right" viewpoint. Still later, at about ages 6 and 7, children think authority is legitimized by special talents or abilities of the authority figure. At these ages, obedience is rationalized as fair payment for the assistance or service of persons in authority.

Usually beginning about age 9, children's views of authority are based similarly on the special experiences or leadership abilities of authority figures. At the same time, youngsters begin to distinguish between voluntary and cooperative obedience to an authority and arbitrary, constrained obedience. For example, for some children, obedience to a coach of a community softball team contrasts with obedience to a school principal or police officer. Even-

Explaining how to play a game means recognizing the listener's level of knowledge.

tually, ideas of authority involve understanding that authority is invested in some people by the community for the good of many.

Parent–Child Relations. The common authorities for most children are parents. It is not surprising, therefore, that the understanding of parent–child relationships closely parallels the development of authority concepts. Early in development, children view parents simply as adults who supply specific and immediate needs, for example, "Who will make my dinner?" This level and the subsequent levels of thought about parent–child relations are shown in Table 10-1.

Later, children begin to conceive of parents as caretaker–helpers. Instead of dwelling on the physical constraints that parents exercise or the physical needs they meet, children are able to conceive of parents in terms of their characteristics and intentions toward the child. Still later, an understanding of the reciprocal obligations of parent and child toward each other characterizes children's thought. The satisfaction that the child provides to the parent is seen as important, in addition to the ways in which parents meet the needs of children.

In adolescence, understanding reaches a more abstract and complex level in which the bond between parents and children is based on their mutual tolerance and respect. Psychological, rather than merely physical, wants and needs are central to this view. A further complexity of thought during adolescence may involve the recognition that parent–child relationships, like

333

other relationships, change as the individuals involved change. This mature level of understanding may be important in the smooth transition from the parent–child relationships of childhood to the relationships of adult child to aging parents. Parent–adolescent relations are discussed in greater detail in Chapter 17.

In this sequence of ideas about a primary relationship with which almost every child has some direct experience, we see the principles of social–cognitive change that characterize both persons and links between persons within the child's world. Scholars like Selman (1980), Damon (1977), and Kohlberg (1969), view social–cognitive development as highly coordinated from one social topic to another. To date, however, researchers have not always found evidence of coordinated understanding, probably because the topics themselves are so different that tests of social cognition are very dissimilar. At present, researchers are proceeding by examining the development of children's thought in specific areas (Flavell, 1983).

Friendship.   Children without friends are rare (and, as we shall see in later chapters, such children are a matter of concern). Children at every age vary in the number and qualities of their friends, although for a given child these aspects of friendship patterns may be remarkably similar from one age to another (Hartup, 1983, 1984). Notable changes occur across age, however, in the understanding of friendship. The most important of these concern children's beliefs and expectations regarding friends' common activities, acceptance of each other, loyalty, commitment, intimacy, common interests, and similarity in attitudes (Shantz, 1983).

Selman (1980) has charted the sequence of changes in understanding of friendship. As shown in Figure 10-2, the sequence shows many of the cognitive characteristics of the levels of interpersonal understanding and parent–child relations outlined above. At the level of egocentric perceptive taking, friendship is litle more than momentary physical interactions. Young children call their frequent playmates "friends," even when they have little else in common. In the sequence described by Selman, children progressively recognize the reciprocal and mutual nature of friendship. By adolescence, the people that children describe as friends have characteristics in common and share common concerns that go beyond transient activities or superficial resemblances.

In support of Selman's description, researchers have found higher levels of friendship concepts among seventh graders than among second graders (Bichard, Alden, Walker, & McMahon, 1988). Furthermore, between the ages of 7 and 12, children's expectations of their friends increasingly depend on internal, psychological characteristics (Furman & Bierman, 1984). During these years, children increasingly share knowledge of each other and of the similarities and differences between them (Ladd & Emerson, 1984). During the elementary-school years, there are also increases in children's expectation that friends will behave differently toward them than do children who are not their friends (Furman & Bierman, 1984).

Children's reasoning about types of relationships that are central to their everyday lives adds to the findings of studies about the development of social understanding. Later in this chapter, we will review some information about links between social–cognitive growth and changes in specific social behaviors.

RESEARCH FOCUS 10-2

Social Knowledge and Its Effects

The growth of *understanding* about persons and events in social life occurs in parallel to specific *factual knowledge* about feelings and behavior and about the effects of actions on emotions. From preschool to early adolescence, social knowledge not only becomes more extensive, but also gradually includes more subtle details about social actions.

Examples of this growing knowledge come from studies of children's knowledge in two essential areas of social life: how to be effective in *helping* others and how to be successful in regulating one's own impulses in order to *delay gratification*.

Knowledge of requirements for helping. Psychologist Kathleen Barnett and her colleagues (Barnett, Darcie, Holland, & Kobasigawa, 1982) interviewed kindergarten, third-, and sixth-grade children to assess their awareness of the components of providing help to others. They found that kindergarten children recognize the relevance of single elements in the helping process, such as a person's willingness or competence to help and the fact that different actions are needed for helping in different situations. However, only the children in the older two groups recognized the need for combinations of these elements (for example, that an effective helper needs to have the skill to do the task and also be willing to do it). Furthermore, these older children, but not the kindergarteners understood that knowing what the task requires and what the person to be assisted needs are helpful in determining the suitability of different kinds of help. For example, the older children recognized that *indirect* rather than direct intervention is the best way to be helpful to someone else. In short, across ages children showed increasing knowledge that helping involves multiple factors and that the nature of the problem and the needs of the person to be helped should be considered in deciding which of the multiple possible actions to draw upon.

Knowledge of strategies for effective delay of gratification. Harriet Mischel and Walter Mischel (1983) carried out similar interview studies with children ranging in age from preschool age to sixth graders on the topic of what they would do to make it easier for them to tolerate having to wait to get something special. For example, while waiting before you are allowed to eat a sweet snack, you could avoid looking at the treat or put it out of sight, you could think about something else in order to distract yourself, and so forth. They found that preschoolers seemed unaware that they could arrange the situation to make it easier to wait; in fact, these youngest children often endorsed strategies that would have made it harder for them, such as keeping the treat in sight. Sixth graders were aware not only that waiting would be easier if the food were out of sight, but also that they could distract themselves by working on a task or deliberately thinking about something else.

The changes in knowledge about effective behavior that children exhibit at different ages are similar to their changes in concepts of persons and relationships. In addition, experience in social life undoubtedly contributes to children's awareness of what will work in social situations.

Concepts of Morality and Society

Studies of role taking and other social concepts illustrate the development of children's understanding of the knowledge and feelings of others and the effect of those inferences on social responses. Frequently, however, social reasoning goes beyond inferring information to evaluating other people and their actions—whether they are good or bad, right or wrong. These judgments show a striking developmental course in the bases or reasons for the judgments. In this section, we provide an overview of the developmental *course* of concepts of morality and society. Many of the same developmental principles that we have seen in the earlier sections of this chapter apply to these concepts as well.

Moral Judgments

Piaget's View of Moral Development. Piaget noticed, for example, that before the age of 7 or 8 children typically judge others and their actions in terms of the consequences of the actions. Piaget suggested that young children's judgments represent a morality of constraints, meaning that their ideas of good and bad come from the constraints imposed on them by external circumstances. Powerful authority figures are seen as arbiters of what is good or bad. Consequences or damages are external, attention-getting aspects of situations; when they are serious they literally compel a judgment of "badness." By the age of 11 or so, children act as though they view morality as an internal quality of persons, evidenced partly by their intentions. Piaget calls this a morality of cooperation, because he believes children come to recognize this view of morality as a result of the give-and-take of cooperative interaction.

These contrasting judgments appeared in response to story pairs that Piaget presented to children. The two stories in each pair reverse the nature of the causes and consequences being discussed. The best-known story pair concerned two children, one of whom caused 15 china teacups to be broken (severe consequences) while trying to help set the table for dinner (accidental cause). The other child broke only 1 teacup (relatively light consequences), but did so in a fit of anger (intentional cause). Younger children typically say that the boy who broke 15 cups is naughtier than the boy who broke only 1 cup because of the amount of damage done. But, after the age of 7 or 8, children tend to judge the boy in the 1-cup story as naughtier because of his harmful intention.

Kohlberg's Stage Theory of Moral Development. American psychologist Lawrence Kohlberg (1969, 1976) has elaborated on the moral reasoning that Piaget called the morality of cooperation. By analyzing responses to hypothetical moral dilemmas, Kohlberg and his coworkers have developed a typology of the considerations people make when judging the goodness or badness, rightness or wrongness, of other persons and their actions. This typology appears in Table 10-2.

Kohlberg's work focuses on the reasoning involved in making moral judgments. Like Piaget, Kohlberg sees young children as relying largely on concrete, external constraints, enforced by authority figures like parents and teachers. These children, whom Kohlberg characterizes as *pre-moral*, judge "goodness" and "badness" in terms of whether a person or action conforms to the demands of an authority figure and, thus, enables children to avoid punishment. Their reasoning includes little or no consideration of the perspectives of others who may be involved in the situation.

More mature reasoning, however, involves increasingly complicated inferences about the attitudes and values of others and their probable reactions to the action being judged (Kohlberg, 1969; Rest, 1974). Moral reasoning of this type is called *conventional* because it involves sometimes complex considerations about the conventions followed by individuals and groups. A higher level of moral reasoning, the *principled* level, involves consideration of abstract principles or values, such as the interdependence of individuals in a democratic society and the sacredness of human life.

The pre-moral, conventional, and principled levels occur in a predictable order during childhood and adolescence (Walker, 1980; Walker, deVries, & Bichard, 1984). Longitudinal studies of adolescents and adults have charted the development of moral judgments in a sequence of stages that matches Kohlberg's theory (Colby, Kohlberg, Gibbs, & Lieberman, 1983; Rest, Davison, & Robbins, 1978; Rest & Thoma, 1985). These stages have been shown to be closely related to the logical operations described by Piaget (Tomlinson-Keasey & Keasey, 1974; Walker, 1980).

The reason for the predictable order of moral-reasoning stages is that, in Kohlberg's view, children's development involves gradually becoming aware of elements and considerations that have not previously been included in their reasoning. Much as the processes of assimilation and accommodation change children's understanding of the relationship between phenomena, additional considerations are gradually incorporated into their cognitive schemes. These considerations are relevant to relations with others and social responsibilities.

Piaget (1965) has particularly stressed the importance of children's interaction with peers; in these, children can be obliged to grapple with the complexities of moral dilemmas without the structures of authority figures like parents and teachers. Information about a variety of elements in group conflicts can be worked out among equals in the peer group, without fearing violation of absolute standards enforced by more powerful figures. Participation in the peer group and such indices of peer orientation as popularity are often related to more mature moral judgments (Haan, 1985; Keasey, 1971) as well as role-taking skills for effective communication (Rubin, 1972). This correlation may indicate that popular children have the skills necessary for harmonious give-and-take in the peer group—the same skills thought to be essential to higher level moral judgments. At the same time, their greater

337

TABLE 10-2
Developmental stages of moral judgments (Kohlberg)

Stage	Social Perspective	Content of Stage	Individual's Moral Consideration
Preconventional Level			
Stage 1 Punishment and obedience	Egocentric point of view	Literal obedience of rules Avoiding punishment Obedience to authorities, who have superior power. Not doing physical harm to people or property.	A person at this stage doesn't consider the interests of others or recognize that they differ from actor's, and doesn't relate two points of view. Actions are judged in terms of physical consequences rather than in terms of psychological interests of others. Authority's perspective is confused with one's own.
Stage 2 Individual instrumental purpose and exchange	Concrete individualistic perspective	Following rules when it is to someone's immediate interest. Serving one's own or other's interests and needs. Making fair deals to serve both self and other.	A person at this stage separates own interests and points of view from those of authorities and others. He or she is aware everybody has individual interests to pursue and these conflict, so integrates or relates conflicting interests to one another through instrumental exchange of services, need for the other and the other's goodwill, or through fairly giving each person the same amount.
Conventional Level			
Stage 3 Mutual interpersonal expectations, relationships, conformity	Individual in relationship to other individuals; putting self in others' position	Being motivated to follow rules and expectations. Needing to be good (nice) in order to live up to expectations of people close to one. Being concerned about other people and their feelings. Maintaining trust, loyalty, respect, gratitude.	A person at this stage is aware of shared feelings, agreements, and expectations, which take primacy over individual interests. The person relates points of view through the "concrete Golden Rule," putting oneself in the other person's shoes. He or she does not consider generalized "system" perspective.

Stage 4 Social system and con- science maintenance	Societal point of view	Doing one's duty in so- ciety. Upholding the social or- der. Maintaining the welfare of society or the group. Obeying laws, except in extreme cases where they conflict with other fixed social duties and rights.	A person at this stage takes the viewpoint of the system, which defines roles and rules. He or she considers individual re- lations in terms of place in the system.

Transitional Level

Stage 4½ Transitional	Outside society	Choice is personal and subjective, based on emotions. Conscience is relative.	The person at this stage considers himself as an individual making deci- sions without a general- ized commitment or con- tract with society. One can pick and choose ob- ligations, which are de- fined by particular socie- ties, but one has no principles for such choice.

Postconventional and Principled Level

Stage 5 Prior rights and social contrast	Prior-to-society perspective	Asserting basic rights, values, and legal con- tracts of a society, even when they conflict with the concrete rules and laws of the group; but usually obeying them be- cause they are the social contract, which is for the good of all.	The person at this stage is aware of values and rights prior to social at- tachments and contracts. He or she integrates per- spectives by formal mechanisms of agree- ment, contract, objective impartiality, and due pro- cess. He or she considers the moral point of view and the legal point of view, recognizes they conflict, and finds it dif- ficult to integrate them.
Stage 6 Universal ethical principles	Moral point of view	Commitment to univer- sal principles of justice. When laws violate these principles, one acts in ac- cord with the principle.	The person at this stage recognizes that social ar- rangements derive from or are grounded in the moral point of view. He recognizes the nature of morality and represents other persons as ends, not means.

SOURCE: Adapted from Damon, 1983.

popularity may provide more opportunities for such children to develop advanced moral judgments through their interactions with others in the same age group.

Family environments are also highly influential factors in the development of moral judgments (Hoffman, 1970; Holstein, 1976; Leon, 1984) and role-taking skills (Byrne, 1973; Dlugokinski & Firestone, 1974). Parental strategies that induce children to think of the covert feelings of others appear to facilitate moral development (Hoffman, 1970). Engaging in open discussion of family conflicts has a similar advantage (Holstein, 1976). Observing others figuring out dilemmas and, particularly, observing the consequences of their reasoning is another attention-focusing experience (Bandura & MacDonald, 1963; Cowan, Heavenrich, Langer, and Nathan, 1969; Walker, 1983). And, not surprisingly, when children act out the role of a person faced with Kohlberg's moral dilemmas, it affects their judgments, especially if they are at lower stages of development (Arbuthnot, 1975).

Kohlberg's stages have been found to be surprisingly appropriate descriptions of moral development across many different cultures. However, the highest level stages (principled reasoning) are found almost exclusively in complex urban societies and middle-class populations, indicating that Kohlberg's view may be somewhat biased toward these cultural groups (Snarey, 1985).

The system is complicated because Kohlberg has not fully succeeded in separating the general, abstract features of moral judgments from the specifics of the dilemmas his subjects discuss. And in recent years, many of the research and measurement strategies used to study Kohlberg's ideas have been criticized, largely because the results from many studies are inconclusive or conflict with one another (Holstein, 1976; Kurtines & Greif, 1974; Rest, 1983). At the same time, however, the applicability of Kohlberg's developmental scheme has been refined and extended to a variety of problems involving moral judgments (e.g., Gilligan, 1982; Rest, 1983).

An especially serious and pervasive bias has been suggested by Carol Gilligan in her book, *In a Different Voice*. According to Gilligan, Kohlberg's system fails to allow for empathy and caring as justifications for mature moral judgments. Consequently, women are often mistakenly categorized as making judgments at a relatively immature level. For example, because concern about the reactions of others is categorized as Stage 3 reasoning in Kohlberg's system, a woman's emphasis on the negative impact of a theft on the family of a victim might be considered less advanced than a concern about depriving the victim himself of his property. Gilligan has demonstrated that, in terms of logical complexity, judgments based on caring can be as advanced as judgments based on justice (Gilligan & Attanucci, 1988). Most studies show few differences between males and females in moral reasoning, however, except in cases where the two sexes are also different in educational and occupational attainments (Gibbs, Arnold, & Burkhart, 1984; Walker, 1984). Researchers today are sensitive to the dangers of bias from both cultural and sex differences and attempt to avoid them in their studies of moral reasoning.

Role-taking in Moral Judgments.   In Kohlberg's view, moral judgments develop as part of general cognitive growth. Moral reasoning basically involves role taking, a skill necessary for inferring the social perspectives of other persons. At first, role taking skill is required for inferring what another wants or would respond to, an ability that is required for the instrumental–relationist level of reasoning described in Kohlberg's Stage II (see Table 10-2). Role taking gradually becomes more complicated, involving inferences about what would earn approval from members of the immediate social group, from the society, and so forth. In principled reasoning, role taking also takes place, although the role taker may eventually reject the inferences about others' values in favor of moral principles that transcend the inferred needs or wishes of others. Table 10-3 shows the relationship between moral judgment levels and stages of cognitive and role-taking development.

Piaget's work was interpreted by many to mean that young children are cognitively incapable of inferring the internal states of another and, therefore, could not take intentions into account in making moral judgments. However, preschool children are capable of using intentions, but how well they do this depends on how difficult it is to infer the information on which particular moral judgments are based (Austin, Ruble, & Trabasso, 1976; Shantz, 1983). For example, a major difficulty is that, compared to consequences, other persons' intentions or motives are abstract and internal and, thus, are often difficult to know about. Young children may, therefore, base their judgments on consequences because consequences are more concrete, perceptible, and unambiguous than are intentions (Chandler, Greenspan, & Barenboim, 1973). When intentions are made more concrete for children—for example, by using a child's own name in moral judgment stories and asking them to "pretend you" were in the dilemma—young preschool children are more likely to make intention-based judgments than when the stories focused on other persons (Austin, Ruble, & Trabasso, 1976; Keasey, 1977).

Consequences also tend to stand out because so much emphasis is placed on the outcome of actions in children's daily experiences. Research findings now indicate that whether intentions are used in moral reasoning depends on the valence of the consequences. If consequences are negative, intentions tend to be ignored in making judgments, but with positive consequences, intentions affect judgments much more strongly, even for children as young as first graders (Costanzo, Coie, Grumet, & Farnill, 1973). In addition, because consequences are often more concrete and salient than intentions, young children may find them easier to remember than information about intentions (Austin, Ruble, & Trabasso, 1976; Feldman, Klosson, Parsons, Rholes, & Ruble, 1976; Nummedal & Bass, 1976). As children develop, they increasingly integrate both intention and consequence information into their moral judgments (Grueneich, 1982; Leon, 1984; Surber, 1977).

Political Concepts

Developing social–cognitive capabilities are also apparent as children change their concepts of society and societal institutions such as community and law. These topics are very difficult to investigate in studies with children of different ages. Older children know more facts about their own governments

TABLE 10-3

Parallel stages in cognitive, perspective-taking, and moral development

Cognitive Stage*	Perspective-Taking Stage†	Moral Stage‡
Preoperations The "symbolic function" appears but thinking is marked by centration and irreversibility.	*Stage I (subjectivity)* There is an understanding of the subjectivity of persons but no realization that persons can consider each other as subjects.	*Stage I (heteronomy)* The physical consequences of an action and the dictates of authorities define right and wrong.
Concrete operations The objective characteristics of an object are separated from action relating to it; and classification, seriation, and conservation skills develop.	*Stage 2 (self-reflection)* There is a sequential understanding that the other can view the self as a subject just as the self can view the other as a subject.	*Stage 2 (exchange)* Right is defined as serving one's own interests and desires, and cooperative interaction is based on terms of simple exchange.
Beginning formal operations There is development of the coordination of reciprocity with inversion; and propositional logic can be handled.	*Stage 3 (mutual perspectives)* It is realized that the self and the other can view each other as perspective-taking subjects (a generalized perspective).	*Stage 3 (expectations)* Emphasis is on good-person stereotypes and a concern for approval.
Early basic formal operations The hypothetico-deductive approach emerges, involving abilities to develop possible relations among variables and to organize experimental analyses.	*Stage 4 (social and conventional system)* There is a realization that each self can consider the shared point of view of the generalized other (the social system).	*Stage 4 (social system and conscience)* Focus is on the maintenance of the social order by obeying the law and doing one's duty.
Consolidated basic formal operations Operations are now completely exhaustive and systematic.	*Stage 5 (symbolic interaction)* A social system perspective can be understood from a beyond-society point of view.	*Stage 5 (social contract)* Right is defined by mutual standards that have been agreed upon by the whole society.

* Adapted from Colby & Kohlberg (Note 1).
† Adapted from Selman & Byrne (1974) and Selman (1976).
‡ Adapted from Kohlberg (1976).
SOURCE: Adapted from: Walker (1980).

and how they work than do younger children; older children are also likely to be familiar with the meaning of words like government, community, and law. Consequently, when we attempt to study differences between younger and older children's *understanding* of the complex principles and arrangements that underlie political organizations, it is necessary to use methods that avoid confusing factual knowledge and vocabulary differences with differences in the complexity of thought.

Joseph Adelson and his colleagues (Adelson, 1971) partly overcame this problem, however, by interviewing children and adolescents about a hypothetical social organization. These researchers first explained that a group of people had inhabited a distant island; they had no laws, rules, or procedures and were attempting to establish a new community from the start. Children were then asked a series of questions about what would be involved. The results of the interview indicated a general shift in the complexity of reasoning and thinking about such matters between the ages of 13 and 15. Before this age, children's political and social concepts tend to be concrete, absolutistic, and authoritarian. In middle childhood, children are true concrete–operational thinkers, focusing on the particular and the immediate, rather than the inclusive and extensive. For example, preadolescents talk about laws in terms of effects on particular persons (e.g., vaccinations are required to "keep little children from getting sick"). By contrast, adolescents tend to see the effects as societal in scope (i.e., vaccination against disease serves to protect the health of the community). Similarly, preadolescents think of government in terms of the individuals who administer or represent it (for example, the president, mayor, police chief, or simply "they" or "them"). More mature views are more abstract and inclusive; a sense of community emerges, in which social institutions, norms, and principles are the important elements (Adelson & O'Neil, 1966).

This shift parallels the transition from concrete–operational to formal–operational thinking (see Chapters 7 and 16) and the development of moral judgments. The external, authoritarian orientation of the morality-of-constraint child has much in common with the immature political concepts described by Adelson. Perhaps because authority relationships and the consequences of actions are so dominant for them, grade-school children tend to focus on the potential for damage by human beings and to believe, rather ingenuously, that authority is good and just (Adelson, 1971). As Adelson (1971) has written: "The child's orientation to government and law is trusting, uncritical, acquiescent" (p. 1024).

Preadolescents are also affected by their inability to grasp some abstract ideas that are fundamental to the more mature thought of the adolescent political thinker or the morality-of-cooperation moral thinker. Older individuals appear to understand the idea of individual rights, the idea that individuals might have wishes and needs that would go contrary to the demands of the state. For example, older adolescents, but not younger ones, were concerned that a law requiring vaccination might interfere with the rights of persons whose religious principles forbade it. A second cognitive difficulty

343

concerns the notion that laws and institutions can be changed at the behest of the people whom they serve. Preadolescents tend to think such instrumentalities are rigid, fixed, and immutable; they behave as though a law, once it has been made, cannot be changed. Furthermore, they are willing to be rather draconian in enforcing laws, even unsatisfactory ones. Asked about an unpopular law prohibiting cigarette smoking, 9- and 11-year-olds are willing to use martial force to see that citizens did not use tobacco! Fifteen- and eighteen-year-olds saw the possibility and need for legislative action to change the law (Adelson, Green, & O'Neill, 1969).

Political concepts of preadolescents are often contrary to the complex theoretical underpinnings of a political system like democracy. For example, Adelson (1971, p. 1026) notes that preadolescents are more likely to favor one-person rule rather than representative or direct democracy. Consequently, the decline in authoritarian views and the increasing abstractness of political concepts enables adolescents to recognize the relativism that is necessary in a democratic community.

It is important to note that both Kohlberg (1976) and Adelson (1971) point out that the circumstances under which individuals live can affect the extent to which advanced moral reasoning can be applied to real-life judgments. For example, incarcerated delinquents may have the cognitive ability to make complex judgments about right and wrong, but because many institutions are run in an authoritarian manner, most judgments about relations with others inside the institution will necessarily be made at an authoritarian level. Similarly, if the political system under which individuals live does not permit democratic behavior, judgments are likely to be made within the constraints of the system.

Concepts of Social Convention

Evaluations of others often depend on how well their behavior matches social conventions: the practices and rules that are set up, formally and informally, to govern the day-to-day operations of communities and organizations. Unike moral values, which are usually defined in terms of abstract and general principles of justice, fairness, and the value of human life, social conventions can be changed without disrupting society (Rest, 1983). The practice of wearing conservative suits at IBM, uniforms at a school, and white shorts to play tennis are all examples of social conventions. Part of socialization is learning these conventions. In addition, socialization involves the social–cognitive process of understanding what conventions are, how they are arrived at, and how they can be violated or changed. Like moral judgments and political concepts, children's understanding of social conventions changes markedly as they develop (Turiel, 1983).

Psychologist Elliot Turiel and his coworkers have interviewed hundreds of children to determine their concepts of social conventions. They have identified a sequence of seven levels of understanding, shown in Table 10-4. These describe a gradual change from concepts of social conventions as routinized patterns of behavior, without appreciating their connection to the functioning of social relations, toward a sophisticated view of conventions as patterns that groups of people work out as a means of getting along together and achieving certain group goals. The intervening steps in the sequence involve the maturing child's recognition that, even though conventions are created through social agreement and do not represent moral necessities, they may serve useful functions. Turiel points out that questioning the value of conventions, which is a characteristic of thought in early ado-

TABLE 10-4
Major changes in social–conventional concepts

	Approximate Ages
1. *Convention as descriptive social uniformity.* Convention viewed as descriptive of uniformities in behavior. Convention is not conceived as part of structure or function of social interaction. Conventional uniformities are descriptive of what is assumed to exist. Convention maintained to avoid violation of empirical uniformities.	6–7
2. *Negation of convention as descriptive social uniformity.* Empirical uniformity not a sufficient basis for maintaining conventions. Conventional acts regarded as arbitrary. Convention is not conceived as part of structure or function of social interaction.	8–9
3. *Convention as affirmation of rule system; early concrete conception of social system.* Convention seen as arbitrary and changeable. Adherence to convention based on concrete rules and authoritative expectations. Conception of conventional acts not coordinated with conception of rule.	10–11
4. *Negation of convention as part of rule system.* Convention now seen as arbitrary and changeable regardless of rule. Evaluation of rule pertaining to conventional act is coordinated with evaluation of the act. Conventions are "nothing but" social expectations.	12–13
5. *Convention as mediated by social system.* The emergence of systematic concepts of social structure. Convention as normative regulation in system with uniformity, fixed roles, and static hierarchical organization.	14–16
6. *Negation of convention as societal standards.* Convention regarded as codified societal standards. Uniformity in convention is not considered to serve the function of maintaining social system. Conventions are "nothing but" societal standards that exist through habitual use.	17–18
7. *Convention as coordination of social interactions.* Conventions as uniformities that are functional in coordinating social interactions. Shared knowledge, in the form of conventions, among members of social groups facilitate interaction and operation of the system.	18–25

SOURCE: Turiel, 1978.

lescence, may be one factor in the rebellious or challenging behavior of many children during this period of life.

Children's judgments both of hypothetical story characters and of children in their own classrooms and play groups are affected by whether the individuals violate moral rules or social conventions (Tisak & Turiel, 1988). Even preschool-age children give evidence of knowing that some actions are governed by social conventions, while other actions are more subject to individual judgment (Smetana, 1985). In one study (Nucci & Nucci, 1982), children were interviewed about incidents that they themselves had witnessed on their school playgrounds. More than 200 incidents were observed in which social conventions were violated, and children were asked to indicate whether the characters were good or bad and how others should have reacted to the violation of convention. Young children judged the people who violated the conventions more harshly than older elementary-school children, who cited the arbitrariness of many of the conventions involved.

The concepts of community and norms also affect children's notions of deviance and the possibility of personal maladjustment. As in their descriptions of others, younger children generally fail to compare another person's behavior to inferred behavioral norms, the needs and rights of others, and inferences about internal motivating states. Similar tendencies emerge when children are asked to describe others they consider "different," or to explain the behavior of hypothetical characters who are excessively aggressive or suspicious (Whalen, Henker, Dotemoto, & Hinshaw, 1983).

In a study by Coie & Pennington (1976), grade-school children focused on the immediate consequences of others' actions and whether or not they violated established rules. Teenagers were likely to take a more extensive view; they considered actions in terms of the extent to which they fit in with typical behavior by members of the social group. Adolescents also responded in ways that clearly required more complicated role taking than their younger counterparts showed. For example, teenagers tended to talk in terms of psychological disorder or instability—notions that are based on the recognition that the different perspectives of others may not be conventional or typical. Although the behaviors studied by Coie and Pennington—aggression and allegations that other persons are watching you—are perfectly understandable and explainable in some situations, they were not warranted by the situations in the stories. Teenagers implicitly acknowledged that different situations demand different behaviors and attributed the behavior of the story characters to personal idiosyncrasy, rather than to the situation. Grade-school children tended to believe the characters were the real victims of threat or some other common circumstance, even though there was no apparent justification for this belief in the story.

Although age changes in understanding of social convention may reflect increasing verbal sophistication, the observed changes so closely parallel developing cognitive capabilities in other domains that it is reasonable to infer that concepts of convention reflect fundamental transformations in reasoning and thinking skills.

Social Cognition and Social Behavior

Do more mature social concepts imply that a child is likely to behave more maturely as well? The question of interrelations of social–cognitive development and social behavior is a difficult one, largely because factors other than reasoning affect actions at every age. For example, social conditioning and emotional arousal might well override logically derived principles in some instances (Aronfreed, 1976; Rest, 1983). Nevertheless, the notion that the more maturely children reason, the more maturely they will behave, is one reason for the current widespread interest in social–cognitive development.

Let us consider two questions that are pertinent to this issue. First, what are the indications that social–cognitive abilities are related to social behavior? And second, can social behavior be changed by improving social–cognitive skills?

Cognitive Mediation of Social Behavior

Relatively few researchers have studied social reasoning and social behavior in the same studies, but those who have done so report some links between them. For example, children's social reasoning skills during the late childhood and adolescent years are generally associated with the degree to which adults and peers view them as socially competent (Ford, 1982; Pellegrini, 1985). More specifically, helpfulness has been found to be related to role-taking measures in a number of studies (Iannotti, 1985; Underwood & Moore, 1982) and to moral judgments (Eisenberg, Pasternack, Cameron, & Tryon, 1984).

In one study, psychologists William Barrett and Marian Radke Yarrow (1977) observed 5- to 11-year-old children over the course of an 8-week summer camp. The record of children's behaviors included not only instances of helpfulness, but also of aggressiveness and of assertiveness, defined as willingness to become involved in a situation. In addition, the researchers tested children's social–cognitive skills by assessing affective role taking in response to hypothetical stories of children in distress. Social–cognitive skills affected whether children directed their assertive behavior into helpful actions. If children were high in role taking, assertiveness was highly related to helpfulness. In other words, the more assertive children in this group were also more likely to be helpful to other children, compared with low-assertive children. By contrast, children who were low in social–cognitive skills were unpredictable in whether they channeled assertiveness into helpful behavior. These findings suggest that social–cognitive skills affect social behavior, but the particular behaviors affected may depend on motivations and other influences.

Poor social–cognitive skills have been found to be related to problem behaviors in many studies. Disadvantaged preschool children in one study

347

were better adjusted in the classroom according to how skilled they were at generating alternative behavioral responses in hypothetical problem situations (Shure, Spivack, & Jaeger, 1971). Adolescents under treatment for personality–adjustment problems (Platt, Spivack, Altman, Altman, & Peizer, 1974) and for antisocial aggression (Slaby & Guerra, 1988) have been found to perform more poorly than a comparable group of adolescents who have not manifested such problems on a number of social–problem-solving tasks. Elementary-school boys who were treated for learning and peer–relationship problems showed poorer social perspective-taking skills than a comparison group of better adjusted boys (Selman, 1976). Socially rejected preschool children show less flexibility than other children in generating and using alternative social–problem-solving techniques (Rubin & Krasnor, 1985). Being able and willing to manipulate the elements in your environment is associated with well-developed social–cognitive skills.

Poor social–cognitive abilities also appear to characterize children and adolescents who behave antisocially. For example, cheating is more likely for children who make lower stage judgments in the Kohlberg scheme; the higher the stage, the less the likelihood of cheating (Grim, Kohlberg, & White, 1968; Krebs, 1967; Lehrer, 1967). Furthermore, delinquent youths are usually lower than comparable groups of nondelinquent youngsters, both in their moral–judgment stage (Campagna & Harter, 1975) and in their role–taking skills (Chandler, 1973). In short, social–cognitive abilities often correspond to social actions, but the strength of the relationship and the conditions under which it is most important—or irrelevant—vary greatly (Blasi, 1980; Jurkovic, 1980).

Adolescents are likely to view cigarette smoking as a matter of personal choice, whereas younger children may view it as a detrimental act that should be prevented.

Efforts to apply principles of social–cognitive development to improving children's social behavior have involved two steps: first, an attempt to improve the social reasoning of children and adolescents and, second, an assessment of the impact of this intervention on their social behavior. An example of this two-step approach can be seen in studies of efforts to change children's attributions about the causes of poor school performance, followed by assessments of the effects of these changes on their subsequent efforts (see Research Focus 10-3).

A number of interventions have been based on the finding that children change in their awareness that alternatives exist in situations (Rubin & Krasnor, 1985; Spivack et al., 1971). Probably because of the rigidity of immature thinking, children often think in terms of a limited number of outcomes for a given set of circumstances. It is possible that, in their social interactions, individuals who do not develop optimally in the ability to think of alternative solutions may become prematurely frustrated by the failure of a single option in a situation.

Shure and Spivack and their colleagues (Platt et al., 1974; Spivack & Shure, 1974) have investigated individuals' awareness of alternatives and its relationship to their actual social adjustment. Awareness of alternatives is assessed by asking children to respond to a series of hypothetical stories. For example, the child is told that Johnny has been playing with a toy truck for a long time, and now Jim wants to have a chance to play with it. "What can Jim do or say so he can have a chance to play with the truck?" the child is asked. Another series of stories deals with relations with authority figures, for instance, Steve has broken Mother's favorite flower pot and must try to think of something to "do or say so his mother won't be mad at him." Among 4-year-old disadvantaged children, youngsters who showed better ability to generate alternatives for these hypothetical situations also received higher ratings by their teachers of their adjustment in the classroom. Adolescents who were tested by a similar method showed a correlation between the ability to conceptualize alternatives and general personality adjustment.

Spivack and Shure (1974) have developed a preschool curriculum based on the idea that children's social development is enhanced by training them to generate alternative solutions to social dilemmas and to infer causal relationships and the consequences of behaviors in such situations. They report that children who experienced this curriculum for a year scored better on a variety of social adjustment measures in the classroom than did a comparable group whose preschool curriculum did not include this emphasis, although other attempts to use their materials have been less dramatic (Elardo, 1974). A similar attempt to improve the social perspective-taking skills of second and third graders affected the children's interactions in school (Cooney, 1977).

Another type of intervention has involved applying social–cognitive change principles to behavior change with juvenile delinquents. One example is Michael Chandler's (1973) program to improve the role-taking skills of delinquent boys. Chandler reasoned that chronic delinquency might result partly from an egocentric tendency to "misread societal expectations, to misinterpret the actions and intentions of others, and to act in ways that

Changing Behavior Through Improving Social Reasoning Skills

RESEARCH FOCUS 10-3

Retraining Attributions About the Causes of Failure

Explanations about why some actions fail to produce a successful outcome are among the most potent determinants of whether those actions will be repeated. For both adults and children, failure on an intellectual task or an athletic activity appears to be less important than beliefs about the *reasons* for the failure (Dweck, 1986). In general, individuals who believe failure is the result of lack of ability or the difficulty of the task are likely to give up, whereas those who believe their failures are due to lack of effort or just to "bad luck" are more likely to try again. The beliefs may or may not be accurate. Some tasks *are* extremely difficult, and individuals do sometimes lack the abilities necessary for mastering tasks. On the other hand, some individuals habitually expect events to be beyond their control, while others are inclined to make attributions that emphasize the possibility of changing outcomes in the future. In short, attributional biases may develop that cause some individuals to believe that failures are usually the result of factors that they cannot control.

Since 1975, a number of experimental efforts have been devised to test whether attributional biases like these can be overcome by retraining children and adults to attribute failures to causes that can potentially be controlled. For example, retraining might emphasize the possibility that lack of effort, rather than lack of ability, might be responsible for the failure. For example, psychologist Carol Dweck (1975) worked with fifth graders who gave up easily at arithmetic problems when they failed to get the right answer to the first few. She discovered that these children were especially likely to blame their failures on lack of ability. To overcome this bias, Dweck gave the children arithmetic problems to do, and when they got incorrect answers, their teacher was careful to urge them to "try harder" on the next one. After 15 practice sessions like this, the children were much more likely to attribute incorrect answers to lack of effort and were also much more likely to keep working at difficult problems after they had failed to do early ones correctly.

A review of 15 retraining studies (Forsterling, 1985) indicated that interventions like Dweck's have generally been very successful, both in changing attributions and in changing behavior patterns. ❧

---

were judged to be callous and disrespectful of the rights of others" (p. 327). In an attempt to reduce these antisocial tendencies in a group of 11 to 13-year-old delinquent boys, Chandler organized 5-member teams, each of which wrote and acted out brief skits about people their own age doing "real-life things." The groups could choose their own topics, but each skit had to include enough parts for all the boys. The groups replayed the skits five times each, so that each boy could play all the parts. Each time, the skit was videotaped, and the group members reviewed the videotape together to find ways of improving their performances. This role-playing exercise was intended to help the group members see themselves from the perspective of others and to help them appreciate the perspective of others, as well.

At the end of a 10-week period of these group activities, Chandler found that the boys in the role-taking training group improved their social role-taking skills. Compared to other delinquent boys of the same ages who had not undergone role-taking training, the intervention group showed markedly

Playing roles is sometimes used to foster the ability of adolescents to understand the thoughts and feelings of others.

less egocentrism. Following up the boys for 18 months, Chandler found that boys in the role-taking training group were significantly less likely to commit delinquent offenses than were the other boys during this period.

These few, limited efforts to show the socializing effects of social–cognitive interventions underscore the idea that perceiving and reasoning about social matters may be an important dimension of social development. Perceiving and reasoning alone, however, do not always explain why children—or adults—behave the way they do. In the succeeding chapters, other factors in the development of social behavior will be examined.

Summary

Perceiving and reasoning about self and others, and about social relations and events, change markedly in childhood and adolescence. Jean Piaget viewed these changes as having their *origin* in general cognitive changes, so that social reasoning and thinking would follow a developmental course similar to that of cognition about the impersonal world. He described young children's thought as *egocentric* to point out the tendency they have to focus on their own perspective to the neglect of others' viewpoints. Furthermore, Piaget and others, such as Lawrence Kohlberg, believed that one hallmark

351

of children's social–cognitive development was an increasing ability to recognize the relevance of others' perspectives and to coordinate them with their own perspective. Both Piaget and Kohlberg emphasized the role of *environmental influences,* in that ordinary social interaction puts pressure on children to pay attention to an increasingly large number and variety of increasingly subtle social cues in interactions with others.

In general, research findings have supported Piaget's and Kohlberg's view of the *course* of social–cognitive development. Descriptions of other persons and of self become increasingly internal and psychological as children mature, and their understanding of personal motivations for actions grows as well. In addition, the ability and tendency to make inferences about the thoughts, feelings, and experiences of others—called role taking—become more characteristic of social cognition in the later years of childhood and early adolescence. Successful role taking requires children both to infer the other person's perspective, and also to appropriately apply the inference when they respond to the other person. In communicating to another person about an unfamiliar object or event, children must be aware both of what information must be conveyed about the object or event and what additional information the listener needs in order to comprehend the message. In the course of development, children change both in their abilities for inferring the perspectives of others and in using their inferences to facilitate social interaction or to achieve a social goal.

Understanding of social events and relationships also become increasingly abstract and complex as children mature. Young children seem to have a bias toward attributing events to intentions, but gradually come to realize that some events are accidental. Understanding the causes of others' actions affects both children's evaluations of the actions and the responses they make to them. Robert Selman has described the development of children's interpersonal understanding in terms of increasing awareness of the self and other individuals in a relationship—that each is inferring the other's perspectives and that these inferences cause the behavior each shows toward the other. This aspect of the development of social cognition is manifested as children grow up and change their concepts of authorities, parents, and friends.

The growth and change of concepts of society and morality are among the most widely studied topics in social cognition. Lawrence Kohlberg's theory of the reasoning involved in making moral judgments provides a detailed summary of changes in reasoning about good and bad actions in childhood and adolescence. In his view, both logical reasoning abilities and social–cognitive skills like role taking underlie moral development, with higher stages of development requiring more complex logical and social reasoning processes. Social experiences in the family and peer groups are important sources of stimulation to develop mature moral reasoning. Children's understanding of government and law also becomes more complex and more inclusive of the rights of others as children grow, especially for early adolescents. Recent studies indicate that children's concepts of social conventions also change developmentally and may be relevant to understanding many aspects of their social relations.

Social–cognitive skills are *interrelated* with other significant aspects of social and personality development. For example, competence in social reasoning and role taking appears to make it more likely that children and adolescents will be considered socially competent by their peers and by adults. Even more clearly, poor social–cognitive skills are associated with a range of problem behaviors, from being socially withdrawn or rejected to being delinquent. Although other factors clearly enter into these problems for children, social–cognitive skills play a role that is attracting attention from researchers in many areas. Efforts to improve the behavior of children with behavioral difficulties by attempting to change their social–cognitive skills have met with some success, but additional research is needed to show how and under what conditions social–cognitive change results in behavioral change as well.

Suggested Readings

Berkowitz, M. W. (Ed.) (1985). *Peer conflict and psychological growth* (New Directions for Child Development, No. 29). San Francisco: Jossey-Bass.

Damon, W., & Hart, D. (1988). *Self-understanding in childhood and adolescence.* New York: Cambridge University Press.

Higgins, E. T., Ruble, D. N., & Hartup, W. W. (Eds.) (1983). *Social cognition and social development: A sociocultural perspective.* New York: Cambridge University Press.

Overton, W. F. (Ed.) (1983). *The relationship between social and cognitive development.* Hillsdale, NJ: Erlbaum.

Rest, J. (1983). Morality. In P. H. Mussen (Ed.), J. H. Flavell & E. M. Markman (Vol. Eds.), *Handbook of child psychology (4th ed.), Vol. 3: Cognitive development* (pp. 556–629). New York: Wiley.

Shantz, C. U. (1983). Social cognition. In P. H. Mussen (Ed.), J. H. Flavell & E. M. Markman (Vol. Eds.), *Handbook of child psychology (4th ed.), Vol. 3: Cognitive development* (pp. 495–555). New York: Wiley.

Emotional Development

355

Introduction

Development reflects an array of both biological and environmental organizing influences. In the past few chapters, we have seen how nature and nurture combine to affect the emergence of language abilities, intellectual skills, and social concepts and behavior. We have also seen how, in turn, language, cognitive and social abilities play roles in organizing children's further behavior and development.

We now turn to another aspect of the organization of behavior, emotion. In this chapter, we will consider how emotions help to organize both cognitive and social aspects of children's lives and how emotional expression and experiences change in the course of development.

In many respects emotion is an aspect of all behavior. Psychologists have struggled with the study of emotion since psychology's beginnings more than a century ago. One difficulty has been that emotions are so intertwined with other phenomena, such as language, perception, and social behavior that it has not seemed possible to study emotions separately. In addition, emotional responses are difficult to measure. The idea that feelings are hidden from the scrutiny of an observer has hampered researchers who wanted to include emotions in serious studies of psychology and development. In the past decade, however, the study of emotion in infancy and childhood has grown remarkably in several branches of psychology. Researchers have addressed a number of provocative questions that tell us not only about emotions, but also about their role in the development of children (Collins & Gunnar, 1990). We are taking the unusual step of devoting an entire chapter to this topic in order to describe this resurgence of interest in emotions and some of the reasons for it.

The chapter has three parts. In the first, we will review some basic ideas about the nature of emotions, their sources, and their role in development. We will then summarize information about the development of emotional expressiveness and the growth of understanding of emotions in oneself and in others. In the third section, we will return to the question of how emotions organize behavior and contribute to the complex processes of development.

Theories of Emotional Development

The term *emotion* can refer to a child's feelings about a person or event or to the visible signs of those feelings. Emotions can be relatively simple, governed by one dominant feeling like joy or rage, or there can be a mixture of several feelings simultaneously. Emotional experiences can be relatively solitary and nonpersonal, or they can involve any number of other persons and situations. The many variations of emotional life make it difficult to say what emotion is and what changes may occur as children mature.

Four views have been especially important when developmental psychologists have addressed questions of emotional development. All four refer to emotional expressions, or the outward, observable signs of children's feelings. As we have throughout the chapters, we will review these briefly as an overview of ideas about the origins of emotions, the course of their development, the important environmental influences on emotional experience and expression, and the interrelations of emotional and other aspects of development.

In most biological theories, emotions are viewed as unlearned response tendencies that help the individual adapt to environmental pressures (Izard & Malatesta, 1987). For some theorists these unlearned tendencies serve to assure that genes survive into the next generation (e.g., Dawkins, 1976; Wilson, 1975). For example, infants' tendency to smile at human faces very early in life is thought to ensure that other members of the species will provide care until the infant can survive alone. Similarly, signs of fear and distress help to ensure that infants will not fall victim to potentially threatening circumstances by alerting adult members of the group that help is needed (Breger, 1974).

Biosocial Views

In humans' adaptation, this view of the role of emotions helps to explain why humans show varied responses to similar situations. Species below the human level on the phylogenetic scale often show highly stereotyped, rigid action patterns to very specific cues. For example, lower animals may care for their young in quite fixed, stereotyped ways. Humans care for infants in a variety of ways, many of which are equally effective in meeting the child's needs. What is common to these different behaviors is an underlying positive emotional response toward the child (Breger, 1974; Lorenz, 1966; Plutchik, 1980). In the biosocial view, the function of the resulting behavior is the same: to see that the young survive as the next generation and as procreators of a subsequent generation.

Theorists in the tradition of Sigmund Freud emphasize the functions of emotions for the individual child, rather than for the species. Freud's theory of the personality is based on the assumption that all human thought and action are motivated by unconscious instinctual drives, which regularly build up and seek expression through behavior (see Chapter 9). The task of socialization is to channel the expression of these instinctual energies into socially acceptable forms of behavior. In childhood, when many social constraints are still being experienced for the first time, emotional expressions may reflect frustration over the inability to find a socially acceptable channel for instinctual gratification (Rappoport, 1961). The appropriateness of behavior depends partly upon the age of the individual. For example, the forms of gratifying behavior that are acceptable in infancy, such as pleasurable contact with the mother's body while eating, are not appropriate in an older child or adult. At each new age, however, children frequently show age-*in*appropriate modes of gratification.

Psychodynamic Views

Pleasure, which psychodynamic theorists consider to be the primary emotional experience, results from the gratification of instinctual energies. The capacity for pleasure is present at birth. As children develop, however, experience teaches them that some types of gratification also bring pain—in the form of physical hurt or social disapproval, for example. In time, the motivation to discharge instinctual energies in ways that have been associated with painful consequences results in the unpleasant emotion of *anxiety*. In Freud's theory, feelings of anxiety act as signals that a particular type of gratification may also bring pain. Much of Freud's work was concerned with how individuals' responses to anxiety cause them to develop particular modes of gratification. He also gave considerable attention to the emotions of shame and guilt, which are reactions to one's own violations of acceptable standards of behavior. Thus, psychodynamic theorists also view *emotional expression* as an indication that acceptable action alternatives are not available to the individual and that instinctual energies are being discharged through an emotional outburst, such as anger or hostility (Rappoport, 1961).

In recent years, psychodynamic theorists have begun to view emotion as the result of individuals' efforts to integrate experiences. Not only external frustrations, but also tensions associated with attempting to cope simultaneously with internal pressures and external demands, are seen as a source of anxiety, shame, and guilt. Positive emotions are thought to result from successful integration (Breger, 1974; Erikson, 1950, 1968; Loevinger, 1976). We will discuss these views further in a later section of this chapter.

Learning Views

Learning theorists believe that *emotional responses* are acquired, not inherent. In this view, feelings originate in basic physiological responses to an empty stomach, loud noises, or physical pain. A positive emotional state, for example, is the physiological sensation of being satisfied after eating. A negative one is the sudden flood of stimulation from a loud noise. More complex and recognizably social emotions derive from these physiological states through *classical conditioning* (see Chapter 9). For example, the persons who feed a newborn initially have no meaning for the child. Gradually, however, because of frequent pairing with the satisfaction of hunger, a positive emotional reaction to the caregiver occurs. Similarly, in the well known case of Little Albert (discussed in Chapter 5) a child acquired a negative response to white furry objects as a result of pairing the appearance of a white furry object with a loud, unexpected noise. In short, an emotional response that was not a part of the child's previous behavior patterns was learned through a series of frightening experiences.

Emotional responses can also be unlearned or replaced with another response. This process is called *counterconditioning*. A related strategy called *desensitization* also sometimes helps reverse dysfunctional emotional responses by bringing the emotional person into closer and closer contact with the person or object that arouses the undesirable feeling. These strategies are frequently employed in behavior therapy.

Cognitive theories of emotional development focus on the relationship between children's cognitive abilities and their emotional reactions at different ages. In this view emotional responses are heavily dependent on children's abilities to assess the nature and meaning of persons, objects, and situations. The process of perceiving a situation creates a pattern of tension and release that underlies emotional expression (Campos et al., 1983; Schaffer, Greenwood, & Parry, 1972; Singer, 1973; Sroufe, 1979). For example, in the first 6 months of life, when babies encounter unfamiliar persons, they often turn away after a few minutes of staring. If the babies continue to look, after a time they may begin to cry. By contrast, at about 8 or 9 months of age, babies typically show immediate distress when a stranger appears. Why the different reactions? The attention and delayed cry of the younger infant demonstrates that, after trying for a time to recognize the stranger—in Piaget's terms, trying to assimilate the new face to a familiar cognitive scheme—the child is unable to do so. The eventual crying signifies a release of tension built up during the effort to assimilate the face. The older baby's immediate cry indicates that the infant's more mature cognitive functioning made it possible to identify the face as unfamiliar more quickly. In this latter case, the cry is the result of learning about certain categories of persons, rather than a sign of unrelieved tension (Sroufe & Waters, 1976).

In both of these cases, emotional reactions depend on the child's ability to understand the meaning of events—sometimes quite complex ones. Emotion

Fearful reactions to unfamiliar persons are typical of children between the ages of 6 and 12 months.

serves as a register of important cognitive activities in children. Later in this chapter, we will examine further two important aspects of the relationships between cognition and emotion: (1) the ways in which understanding of situations contributes to the emotional experience of children of different ages and (2) the ways in which understanding of emotions experienced by others and by oneself affects the emotional life of children. In summary, emotional expression and its psychological underpinnings are in evidence very early in life. But exactly what will elicit a particular emotion for a particular child probably depends heavily on experience and cognitive growth. In the next section, we begin to examine these aspects by considering the development of emotional expressions in infancy and childhood.

Development of Emotional Expressions

The four contrasting views of emotion remind us that several aspects of emotion in children must be considered if we are to attain a full understanding of this complex topic. One focus must be the forms in which children show emotions. A second perspective is the emotional reactions that appear to be important in development. A third is the developmental course of these significant emotions: how they change from one period of life to another.

The Forms of Emotions

Feelings may be expressed in a variety of ways, but the most recognized way is through temporary changes in facial expression. There are far more studies of the face as an indicator of emotion than of any other channel for emotional expression. One reason for this emphasis on the face is that facial expressions of emotion have been found to be very similar across cultures. Facial expressions of happiness, sadness, disgust, and anger are readily recognizable to members of a number of different cultures (Ekman et al., 1987). The basic emotional expressions also appear very early in life and seem to be readily understandable to adults and children alike. These factors have led scholars to conclude that emotions, as seen in facial expressions, have their *origins* in neural structures. This strong biological component, perhaps established through evolution (Campos et al., 1983; Darwin, 1872/1975; Izard & Malatesta, 1987). Elaborate systems for analyzing facial expressions of emotion have been devised for use in research on emotion in people of all ages and backgrounds.

Avenues of emotional expression other than the face have also been studied. The next most popular avenue of expression is the voice. All of the emotions that have been found to be recognizable in facial expressions have also been found to be communicable vocally, although vocal expressiveness has been studied much less than facial expressions. Autonomic responses such as pupillary dilation, blood pressure, flushing of the face, and galvanic skin response are also used as indicators, although these are more common in studies with adults than with children (Campos et al., 1983).

RESEARCH FOCUS 11-1

On the Face of It

In addition to being a personal experience and a subjective feeling, emotions are social events as well. Happiness, sadness, fear—many, if not all, common emotional states are often communicated to others by facial expressions, body postures, the tone of one's voice, or sometimes simply by direct statement (I'm *so* happy!"). This communication may be accurately interpreted, as when a nursery school teacher correctly recognizes that a child is unhappy about something. It may also be inaccurate, as when a parent, teacher, or friend fails to recognize that a child is sad or angry and says or does something that exacerbates the emotion. Furthermore, individuals may voluntarily control the expression of emotion in order to disguise what they are actually feeling, perhaps even attempting to create the impression that they are experiencing another emotion instead.

Even very young children are capable of recognizing emotions displayed in facial expressions of their peers (Felleman, Barden, Carlson, Rosenberg & Masters, 1983). They are most accurate in recognizing happiness, and somewhat less so in recognizing negative emotions such as sadness or anger. Interestingly, children and adults are equally proficient in identifying emotions in others, and adults, like children, also show a better ability to recognize children's expressions of happiness than their sad or angry expressions. These findings suggest that children's abilities to recognize emotions are well developed by the end of the preschool years and that their spontaneous expressions of their feelings communicate those feelings effectively to others. Box Figure 11-1 illustrates some spontaneous expressions of happiness, sadness, and anger by preschool children.

But what about the intentional communication of emotion to others? We know that children are able to pose emotional expressions, something that they would have to do if display rules are to be effective (Felleman et al., 1983). Interestingly, however, children's posed expressions of emotions are not as recognizable as their spontaneous ones. This suggests that the effective disguising of emotion may be a skill that takes time and practice to develop or perhaps it is so difficult to do well that it is not perfected in early childhood. 🐦

Spontaneous facial expressions of (*a*) happiness, (*b*) sadness, and (*c*) anger by preschool children.

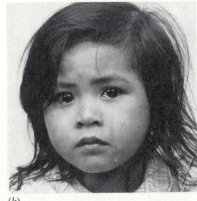
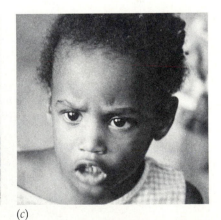

(*a*)   (*b*)   (*c*)

Because of the popularity of facial and vocal signs, we will be referring mostly to these indicators of emotion in this chapter. Underlying our discussion, however, is a widely held assumption, namely, that any single indicator of emotion reflects a state that could be, and may in fact be, manifested in other aspects of expressive behavior at the same time. Some scholars (e.g., Sawin, 1979) have even argued that more than one indicator of emotion should be used to assess children's emotional states, since one indicator alone may mislead us about children's emotional experiences at any given time.

Three Primary Emotions

The functions and forms of emotion become clearer when we examine the development of specific emotions. We now turn to an overview of several emotions that are often considered basic or primary, partly because we observe them and experience them so frequently ourselves. Although previous lists of primary emotions have included as many as 17 entries (James, 1884), we will discuss only fear and wariness, pleasure and joy, anger and rage. We have chosen these three because they have been extensively studied by psychologists and, therefore, serve as examples of research on emotional development.

Wariness and Fear.   Fear refers to "a form of withdrawal or actual or incipient flight from situations for which the individual has no adequate response" (Jersild, 1954, p. 862). This definition obviously refers to human evolutionary history, where fear responses are analogous to physical flight in the face of threatening circumstances. Although physical threats are still very much a part of the environments to which children must adapt, a wide variety of situations may produce the familiar experience of fear in most developed societies. Psychologists have studied fear of unfamiliar persons (e.g., Clarke-Stewart, 1978; Rheingold & Eckerman, 1973; Sroufe, 1979), fear of novel objects or situations (Jersild, 1954; Scarr & Salapatek, 1970), physical fears, such as fear of heights (Bertenthal, Campos, & Barrett, 1983) and fear of objects moving rapidly toward one, a phenomenon called looming (Yonas, 1981). In all three cases, the goal was to understand the principles governing fear reactions and the developmental changes in them.

THE CASE OF STRANGER FEAR. Some experts have argued that infants do not ordinarily show true fear to unfamiliar stimuli until relatively late in the first year of life. Before that time, an attentive, but relatively inactive state called wariness is a more likely response to potentially threatening events (Bronson, 1972; Schaffer, Greenwood, & Parry, 1972; Sroufe, 1979; Sroufe, Waters, & Matas, 1974). By contrast, fear itself is more actively expressed, usually through crying. In the middle months of the first year, this distinction is especially clear, because infants of this age commonly show both reactions. For example, show a 5-month-old a strange looking facial mask that he cannot turn away from, and he will probably spend a few moments staring at the mask without showing any signs of distress. Often, however, after this initial period, he will begin to cry or otherwise show fearfulness.

Commonalities between wariness and fear are significant because they give an indication that different emotional expressions may come from similar processes. However, reactions to novel objects and to unfamiliar persons vary greatly, and they are not always negative (Clarke-Stewart, 1978; Rheingold & Eckerman, 1973). If children can assimilate an unfamiliar person or object to a positive schema, the emotional response would presumably be positive.

One of the most distinctive fear reactions in infancy, the apparent fear of unfamiliar persons, typically emerges in the second half of the first year of life. Even infants who have been unusually sociable and friendly to strangers, smiling and laughing in response to their overtures in the first 6 months, seem to go through a period of less responsiveness and even negative reactions to many adults around the ages of 7 to 10 months. Nine-month-old Nicholas might show a negative reaction to an unfamiliar person, even though at 4 months he had shown a positive reaction to the same person. Biologically oriented theorists attribute this apparent fear to an evolved reaction that signals potentially threatening intrusions from strangers, and a cognitive view emphasizes that stranger fear reflects greater cognitive maturity for discriminating familiar from unfamiliar persons. Regardless of theoretical orientation, stranger fear is viewed as a virtually universal fact of infant emotional life and, thus, as an indicator of biological and cognitive bases of emotional development.

There is now reason to doubt that stranger fear indicates only biological factors or only cognitive ones. Fear responses are common, to be sure, but no study has documented that all children show distress in the presence of strangers between 6 and 9 months, which is considered the prime period for the appearance of stranger fear. On the contrary, many studies have indicated a positive reaction to strangers during this period. Rheingold and Eckerman (1973), for example, report that in a 10-minute play session with a stranger, 8-, 10-, and 12-month-old infants smiled every 16 seconds on the average, and none of them fussed or cried. Other findings indicate that infants react positively to some strangers, but negatively to others (Clarke-Stewart, 1978). For example, reactions to unfamiliar children are generally less likely to be fearful than reactions to unfamiliar adults. Fearful reactions also depend on such factors as infants' prior experience with unfamiliar persons and on whether a familiar, comforting adult is also present when an unfamiliar person appears (Campos et al., 1983).

Some experts argue that discrimination of this sort is consistent with the biosocial view that infants are disposed to behave in a way that assures that their basic needs are met. However, the absence of general stranger fear reactions cannot be taken as evidence of a cognitive deficit; indeed, the ability to discriminate among unfamiliar persons certainly shows that infants have impressive cognitive skills. The emergence of fear reactions to others clearly indicates that the unlearned response of fear can be modified by experience very early in life so that it occurs under some conditions and not others.

FEAR DEVELOPMENT AFTER INFANCY. Specific fears generally become less frequent as children grow older (Rutter & Garmezy, 1983). The fears that do appear follow a fairly common developmental course after infancy. During the preschool years, fears of animals, darkness, and imaginary creatures often occur, but these usually diminish in the elementary school years. Fears about particular situations can arise at any age, of course, and many fears experienced by school children are temporary anxieties about such things as school and out-of-home activities. There are few differences between boys and girls in crying and fearfulness up to school age. Thereafter, specific fears become more common in girls by a ratio of about 2 to 1. Most childhood fears tend to be short lived. If a fear persists, or if the fear is an unusual one for a person of a given age, it may be an indication of psychological problems (Rutter & Garmezy, 1983).

In the preschool and school-age years, fears become increasingly complex, partly because of the growth of language abilities and abstract reasoning skills. The role of language is apparent in the case of a 3-year-old boy who was afraid to go into a lake at his family's vacation spot, although he had previously loved playing there. It turned out that the boy had heard an adult comment on how well the fish were biting in the lake. He told his mother: "Mummy, do you know why I couldn't go in the water one day? I was afraid the fish would bite my feet" (Goodenough, 1934, p. 319). In the later years of childhood and adolescence, fears may more often be associated with relatively remote and abstract possibilities, such as not finding a satisfying career (Jersild, 1954; Zill, 1985).

Children and adolescents in the 1980s express fears that are frequently discussed in the public forums of the day. Nuclear war has become increasingly widely mentioned as a major fear, as has environmental pollution. In addition, fear of physical harm from criminals, fear of failure in school or sports, and fear of social rejection are common (Zill, 1985).

To summarize, fear and related emotional reactions such as wariness are present early in life and are indicators of both maturational and experiential influences on development. Although not the all-important index of biological givens or cognitive maturity it was once thought to be, fear does give us important insights into the bases for early social relations. In later years, fear expressions remind us of the importance of cultural values and expectations, the violation of which is threatening and fear-provoking for people of every age.

Pleasure and Joy. The positive emotions of pleasure and joy are usually inferred from smiling and laughter. Like many of the signs we take to indicate fear, these may often mislead us about the infant or child's emotional state. For example, laughter may betray fear or anxiety, instead of pleasure. In the words of one psychologist, the smile "serves many masters" (Kagan, 1971); therefore, careful consideration must be given to what smiles and laughter mean, even when we clearly intepret them as indicating positive emotional states.

SMILES IN INFANCY. Early smiles, which are usually no more than slight turning up of the corners of the mouth, are called *endogenous* (Spitz, Emde, & Metcalf, 1970) because they are not tied to external stimulation. Recent research also indicates that they are not—as is commonly assumed—the result of gastric activity. Instead, infant smiles result from discharges of excitation in the central nervous system (Emde & Koenig, 1969). Apparently, there are cyclical fluctuations in excitation. Smiling occurs when the level of excitation goes above a certain threshold and then directly drops below it (Sroufe & Waters, 1976). This happens only when the infant is asleep. When awake, the baby engages in motor activity that discharges excitation.

During the first month, *exogenous* smiles begin. These are smiles that are elicited by some external stimulus, such as a smiling, cooing adult.

What do these different responses indicate about development? Smiling and laughter accompany the reduction of tension that occurs for a variety of psychological reasons. Before the third month, smiles often result from visual stimulation—as when an adult vigorously nods his head while talking to the baby. Gradually, infants begin to respond to static visual stimuli, say, a grinning doll or the shapes of a mobile hanging overhead. This is considered evidence that infants are *processing* the stimulus; in Piagetian terms, they are assimilating it to existing schemes, or recognizing it as an instance of something familiar. As we noted above, the effort to assimilate the stimulus induces tension; when the input recognizes the object, the tension is reduced, and this fluctuation in excitation causes the infant to smile (Sroufe & Waters, 1976). The process, which is diagrammed in Figure 11-1, is similar to the pattern of internal events that leads to endogenous smiling, except that in endogenous smiling, tension is induced by the internal cognitive activity associated with assimilation of an experience to existing schemes (Berlyne, 1960; Kagan, 1978).

The cognitive effect described above depends on some degree of novelty in the stimulus. Something that is quite familiar to a child would presumably not generate enough arousal or tension to produce the reduction needed to generate a smile; rather, the familiar object would simply be assimilated straightaway to the infant's existing schemes. In fact, after the third month if an infant repeatedly sees the stimulus that caused him to smile in the first place, he eventually no longer smiles. Apparently familiarity leads to less arousal and, thus, to less smiling. At different times in the course of development, smiling and laughter may result from different types of situations, and the same situations may elicit very different types of emotional responses (Rheingold, 1985; Sroufe, 1979; Sroufe & Waters, 1976).

DEVELOPMENT AFTER INFANCY. The principle that experiences are assimilated to existing schemes, followed by tension reduction that leads to smiling, may be operating when toddlers express glee in a romp with other children and

FIGURE 11-1

Theoretical sequence of events leading to smiles in infancy.

Source: from Sroufe & Waters, 1976.

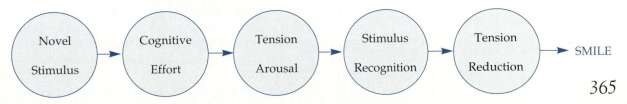

| Novel Stimulus | Cognitive Effort | Tension Arousal | Stimulus Recognition | Tension Reduction | → SMILE |

Preschool children often show pleasure at the novelty involved in clowning around and romping with other children.

when school children and adults laugh at a joke that surprises them by its punch line. In the preschool period, children laugh increasingly more each year, especially in connection with silliness and clowning with other children (Bainum, Lounsbury, & Pollio, 1984). Such clowning often involves both verbal and motor behavior. Some experts believe social episodes like these provide an opportunity to assimilate new and somewhat different interaction patterns to their existing motor schemes (McGrew, 1972). As a result it is not just the relaxation of tension that gives rise to laughter, but the moderate novelty involved in the activity, as well.

Perhaps this is why children who are brighter, according to mental ability tests, and those who are more advanced cognitively have been found to be more likely to laugh at jokes and humorous stories that involved incongruities (Jersild, 1954; McGhee, 1971c). In a series of experiments, Shultz (1972) and McGhee (1971a, 1971b) have demonstrated that incongruities and humorous material requiring other, more complex forms of reasoning are both under-stood better and appreciated more by school children as they grow older. An example is the cartoon of a skier whose skis have left tracks on both sides of a tree. Nine-year-old Caroline laughed uproariously when she saw it, saying: "He can't do that!" Five-year-old Elizabeth did not laugh at all. Seeing the humor in this drawing depends on recognizing the incongruity involved. A preoperational child in Piaget's terms (see Chapter 7) is unlikely to recognize the incongruity that is the basis for the humor in the cartoon. Concrete-operational thinkers are more likely to do so and thus find the cartoon funnier (McGhee, 1971a; Shultz, 1972).

In summary, smiling and laughter are responses that indicate pleasure, including humorous reactions, and reflect arousal and arousal-reduction. The degree of arousal often depends on how situations are construed, which in turn depends partly on the cognitive skills of the child. It is important to remember, however, that pleasurable emotions are fundamentally social; most instances of smiling and laughter occur in the presence of others (Bainum, Lounsbury, & Pollio, 1984). The tendency to smile at others does not change notably from one age to another after infancy. Rather, readiness to give smiles to others seems to be largely a matter of differences among children (Babad, Alexander, & Babad, 1983).

Anger and Rage.   Anger is a focused reaction against something or someone who threatens or blocks a goal. Such reactions do not appear until the second half of the first year of life. As fear has its early roots in wariness, so anger appears to come out of rage reactions, in which the infant becomes agitated, and usually cries over being restrained physically or not fulfilling some motor expectation (Sroufe, 1979; Stenberg & Campos, 1983). For example, restraining a newborn's limbs may cause furious crying. Later, this reaction becomes more obviously tied to the disruption of activities, particularly intentional, goal-directed action. Take a 5-month-old who reaches for a breakable object in his grandmother's living room and finds it efficiently removed before he can get it. The baby might well turn purple faced and scream—an angry reaction, by any standard. Yet the reaction is unfocused; it has no functional purpose either in getting the desired object or retaliating against the person who removed it from his reach. An older child might strike at the adult who prevented him from reaching his goal or say, "I don't like you," or even physically grapple for it. True anger has a focused, intentional quality.

Some of the differences in these behavior patterns reflect older infants' more advanced coordination and skill to do and, later, say aggressive things that are focused at specific others. However, observers of infant behavior see qualitative developmental differences in anger reactions that go beyond better coordination of physical movements. For instance, Sroufe (1979) notes: "The angry reaction is common, though not frequent, in the second half year, because by then the infant persists in its intended acts, will not readily accept substitute objects, and has more specific plans with respect to these objects." The cognitive skills that characterize the development of action and object concepts during the sensorimotor period (see Chapter 5) may parallel anger reactions that are goal-oriented, rather than diffuse rage. Recent research indicates a shift between the ages of 4 and 7 months in directing anger toward persons rather than frustrating events (Campos et al., 1983). In fact, recent findings (Shiller, Izard, & Hembree, 1986) indicate that the predominant reaction to separation from mother at 12 months of age is anger, not fear, as might have been expected.

PHYSIOLOGICAL ASPECTS OF ANGER. What is the nature of anger? At the most fundamental level, anger is a physiological state, the arousal that accompanies not getting a desired object or personal reaction. After events that would be expected to anger a person (such as, being insulted), blood pressure and heart rate are elevated. Presumably, these higher levels are not comfortable and returning them to their normal levels is desirable. Overt anger

367

reactions, like hostility or aggression, whether or not directed toward the person who caused them, accomplish these reductions for the subjects in the research by Hokanson, Willers, and Koropsak (1968).

These same characteristics of physical arousal may also be present in emotional states other than anger, for example, fear. Classic research (Schachter & Singer, 1962) indicates that arousal states are attributed to one emotion or another largely on the basis of social cues or other information that individuals may have about their cause. Thus, a person who is actually aroused because he is experiencing the physiological effects of a drug may show reactions that could be labeled "anxious" or "euphoric," depending on the behavior of an experimental confederate who, the subject believed, had also taken the drug. One would probably label as "anger" as the arousal of persons who have been deliberately insulted, but the arousal may be physiologically undistinguishable from the arousal of a person who was fearful because of a threat.

DEVELOPMENT AFTER INFANCY. Children—and adults—often recognize their feelings as angry because of the situations in which the feelings are elicited. Although the situations that seem anger inducing to them change in subtlety and complexity with age, anger usually comes from challenges to autonomy.

This is especially striking in the most careful research on this problem, done more than 40 years ago by Florence Goodenough (1931b), whose findings are still valid today. Basing her analyses on parents' observation and recording of anger episodes in the home, Goodenough was able to avoid the problem of relying on subjects' or their parents' memories of anger. Her results show that in the first year of life outbursts were most often associated with physical discomforts, often associated with dressing or bathing. At age 2, conflicts with authority—frequently in connection with routine habit training like toilet training—provoke anger, and in the third year, anger arises from these causes and, to a lesser extent, from conflicts with playmates. Social causes of anger predominate over the next few years.

Children's responses to anger do show striking age changes during these same years, however. Here are Goodenough's conclusions from these results:

> With advancing age, behavior during anger becomes more overtly directed toward a given end. At the same time the primitive bodily responses of the infant and young child gradually become replaced by substitute reactions of a somewhat less violent and more symbolic character. As age advances, the proportion of outbursts in which the behavior consists only or chiefly of simple displays of undirected energy decreases, while the frequency of retaliative behavior increases. There are more evidences of persisting generalized reactions toward a single person and more attempts to retaliate by means of indirect attacks designed to hurt the feelings rather than to injure the body of offender. The percentage of observable anger reactions, particularly resentfulness and sulkiness, increases steadily with advancing age (Goodenough, 1931b, p. 245).

Our knowledge about older children, adolescents, and adults is less reliable than Goodenough's reports of younger children because studies of these age

Children often show anger when their activities are disrupted.

groups rely on self-reports. Not surprisingly, grade school and junior high school children report that such personal affronts as being teased, being treated unfairly, or being imposed upon were the most frequent causes of their anger (Hicks & Hayes, 1938). In adolescence, conflicts with parents over independence are often cited (Csikszentmihalyi & Larson, 1984). These indications are similar to the anger-producing circumstances that were observed in preschool children in that they violate "the child's need to protect his pride, his independence, and his self-respect" (Jersild, 1954, p. 885). Only the particulars change as the child grows older.

In summary, the physiological tension or arousal that characterizes anger is produced at different points in development by situations that threaten the person's sense of autonomy. In the earliest years of life, cognitive development plays an important role in producing focused anger reactions, as it does in the emergence of characteristic reactions of fear and pleasure. In fact, the interplay of cognitive and emotional growth is characteristic of development, as is discussed further below.

Fear or wariness, pleasure or joy, and anger or rage are often thought of as "primitive" emotions, because they appear in some form very early in life. There may be other primitive emotions as well (Izard & Malatesta, 1987), although it is difficult for scientists to reach agreement on a definitive "set" of emotions at any age.

The Development of an Emotional Repertoire

There is no doubt, however, that the repertoire of emotions is more extensive in later life than in infancy. How does this repertoire develop? In general, psychologists believe that two processes occur. One process is the differentiation of emotions into more specific subcategories. For example, middle-class adults in the United States typically subdivide anger into "annoyance,"

369

"hostility," "contempt," and "jealousy" (Shaver, Schwartz, Kirson, & O'Connor, 1987). These subcategories imply that a general negative emotion involving agitation and feeling upset can come from very different circumstances and can also have very different results. For example, contempt may result in sneering at or avoiding the offending party, whereas hostility may involve a verbal or physical attack or some other effort to obstruct the activities or wishes of the offender. A second process is learning reactions to new situations that, because of their complexity, might not have originally caused an emotional reaction. For example, in adulthood office assignments are important to many people; the person with the nicer office is assumed to have higher status in the organization. Thus, having a low-prestige office may arouse anger or shame in a 30-year-old person that would not have affected the feelings of an 18-year-old. The prevailing view is that these are not new emotions, but represent more sophisticated eliciting conditions and, perhaps, modes of response than in earlier life (Fischer, Carnochan, & Shaver, 1989).

Some Principles of Emotional Development

Our review of the expression of three emotions—pleasure or joy, fear or wariness, and anger or rage—across the years of infancy and childhood suggests several principles of emotional experience and emotional development. The following four principles, suggested by Joseph Campos and his colleagues (Campos et al., 1983), constitute a summary of research on specific emotions:

1. Certain core emotions are present throughout life. The early appearance of certain emotions supports this idea. Although not every expert agrees on what these "primitive" emotions are, the three discussed above appear on most lists and have been important in helping us to understand human development.

2. Emotions, like actions and thoughts, are subject to socialization. Even universal emotional expressions such as smiling or fearfulness become governed by cultural expectations for how, when, and toward whom emotions are expressed. One implication of this principle is that the potential of a person or situation to arouse emotion may change over time. Even infants may become accustomed to a previously frightening person, who is therefore less likely to cause fear. Also, emotional responses may become linked to previously nonarousing persons and situations through the processes of conditioning and cognitive inference.

3. In the course of development, multiple, complex, and intercoordinated emotions become more evident. This increasingly complex emotional landscape is due to learning new goals, a mixture of experiences that produces both positive and negative feelings about the same persons or situations, and more complex cognitive and social–cognitive skills.

4. Children become better able to control their own emotions and to manage situations to make them more or less arousing. Physical mobility enables a child to move away from a frightening person or situation. By gaining control over a previously frightening event, like a jack-in-the-box, children can transform it into a positive one (Gunnar, 1980).

These principles apply to the emotional experiences and expressions of most normally developing children. However, within this normal range, children vary widely in how readily they react emotionally and in their general tendencies to react positively or negatively. For example, babies differ in how much crying they do and in how likely they are to cry in reaction to simple changes in their environments. Some babies often show pleasure and interest in new people and situations, while others are almost invariably wary or fearful when encountering the unfamiliar (Goldsmith & Campos, 1982; Scarr & Salapatek, 1970; Thomas & Chess, 1977). Recent findings (Izard, Hembree, & Huebner, 1987) indicate that individual infants, followed over a 2-year period, show similar tendencies toward emotional expressiveness from one occasion to another.

To a large extent, such individual differences in emotional expressiveness are determined by biological characteristics of infants. Such characteristics as *responsiveness to stimulation* and *activity level* appear to be based in genetic factors. Identical, or monozygotic, twins are generally more similar on these characteristics than fraternal, or dizygotic twins (Fulker, Eysenck, & Zuckerman, 1980; Plomin & Dunn, 1986). Similarly, tendencies to be inhibited and apprehensive versus outgoing and self-confident are more similar in genetically identical persons than in less related ones (Scarr, 1969). These characteristics undoubtedly affect the degree to which infants and children are likely to express positive or negative emotions to new persons and situations (Gunnar, Mangelsdorf, Larson, & Hertsgaard, 1989; Rothbart & Derryberry, 1981).

Constitutionally based differences in emotional reactivity are one part of what is meant by the frequently used term, *temperament.* This term refers to broad, general patterns of individual differences in the intensity and duration of expressions of arousal and emotionality, as these affect the organization of behavior and social interactions (Campos et al., 1983; Goldsmith, Buss, Plomin, Rothbart, Thomas, Chess, Hinde, & McCall, 1987). Research findings indicate that temperamental differences can be observed very early in a child's life. Some infants have highly irregular sleeping patterns, eat erratically, are easily distressed by new situations, and fuss and cry a great deal; others are calm, generally positive, and adaptable; while others show a mixture of characteristics or do not seem either extremely reactive or calm (Thomas & Chess, 1977).

Such characteristics appear to be manifested in various ways as the child grows (Matheny, 1989). For example, an irritable, fussy baby who is easily distressed by new experiences may have difficulty adjusting to changes in environment and to such life changes as starting school or going away to college (Thomas & Chess, 1977). Although not all experts agree that the idea of temperament is the best way to explain these differences in emotional reactivity, the evidence for some constitutional basis for them is now well established (Campos et al., 1983; Kagan, 1984).

At the same time, it is important to note that differences in emotional reactivity strongly affect the kinds of experiences children have. An infant who fusses or cries a lot requires different kinds and amounts of adult

Individual Differences in Emotional Expressiveness

371

attention than more calm, placid babies do. Furthermore, infants who cry and fuss and lot have less time to survey the environment and to benefit from experiences than do babies who are less upset by stimulation. The ability of parents to adjust to the unique characteristics of their infants seems to be a critical factor. Some parents may find the frequent and intense expression of emotion a sign of their child's awareness, intelligence, and ability to affect the world around her; while others would find the same behavior highly annoying, debilitating, or something to be suppressed for the child's own good (Lerner & Lerner, 1982; Thomas & Chess, 1977). Thus, constitutional differences in emotional reactivity may affect the degree to which others encourage or discourage emotional expressiveness.

In short, emotions appear to have a biological *origin* that strongly elicits particular *environmental influences* beginning early in development. We will examine the role of children's emotional responses in social and cognitive development in a later section. We now turn to another aspect of emotional development that is also integral to development: the ability to recognize and understand the emotions of others and also of oneself.

Recognizing and Understanding Emotions

As children mature, their basic emotions probably change little, but their capacities for recognizing and understanding emotions, including their own feelings, change dramatically. In this section, we turn to the developmental *course* of emotions. First, we consider infants' abilities for recognizing facial expressions of emotion in others and the growth of these abilities during childhood. Next, we consider the development of children's knowledge about emotion—what emotions are, how people feel when they experience particular emotions, how emotions are expressed, and what is socially appropriate in the expression of emotion. You will note that the developmental changes described here are very similar to the developmental changes in perceptions of self and others described in Chapter 10. Scholars view understanding of emotional states as an example of the degree to which learning and cognitive processes are intricately intertwined with emotional experience and expression (Collins & Gunnar, 1990; Harris & Saarni, 1989).

Recognizing Emotional States

When infants seem to know that their mothers are angry or their older sisters or brothers are in pain, they are showing an ability that is essential in social life. In addition, their recognition of others' emotional states tells us that sensitivity to emotion occurs quite early in life. As early as 6 weeks, infants notice differences among facial expressions that usually accompany different emotional states. Although these simple discriminations do not indicate that the infant understands the emotional meaning of the facial expressions (Nelson, 1987), they may represent a first step in the ability to comprehend others' emotional signs.

The recognition that expressions indicate different emotional states appears most clearly at about 4 to 5 months of age. At this time, infants give appropriate emotional responses to angry facial expressions and combinations of angry faces and voices (Buhler, 1930; Charlesworth & Kreutzer, 1973; Klinnert, Campos, Sorce, Emde, & Svejda, 1983). By 9 months, friendly gestures elicit more positive behaviors and emotional expressions than do threatening gestures, even without the sounds that usually accompany gestures in everyday communication (Buhler, 1930). Within the first year of life, then, children react to different configurations of facial characteristics as though they have perceived certain feelings in others (Fox & Davidson, 1988; Termine & Izard, 1988). Vocal expressions elicit similar reactions, although at this point many fewer studies of recognition of vocally expressed emotion have been done.

At about 8 to 9 months, the capability for responding appropriately to others' emotional expressions becomes yet more complex. In addition to recognizing others' emotional states, children can appreciate possible targets of the emotion. For example, infants see their mothers point or gaze at something, and, for the first time, they can identify what they are pointing or gazing at (e.g., Leung & Rheingold, 1981). This advance makes it possible for infants to begin to use others' emotional expressions as a clue to the meaning of an ambiguous event. (We will discuss the developmental implications of this skill in a later section of this chapter.)

The ability to recognize emotions continues to develop throughout childhood and adolescence. Studies of emotion recognition after infancy illustrate this point by comparing the accuracy of children's and adults' recognition of emotional states from the same pictures of children's facial expressions. The pictures themselves are sometimes posed—children are asked to make a "happy," "sad," or "angry" face for the camera—and sometimes show spontaneous facial expressions. Adults are generally more accurate than preschool children in recognizing the depicted emotions (Felleman, Barden, Carlson, Rosenberg, & Masters, 1983; Field, 1982), although both children and adults are quite good at recognizing "sad" faces. When children are asked to *pose* an emotion themselves, their facial expressions are easily recognized by others. This indicates that even preschool children understand a good bit about the facial expressions that go with primary emotional states.

Knowledge About Emotions and Emotional Experience

Knowledge about the significance of expressions of emotion represents only part of the information that is acquired as children mature. Although much of the expression of emotion and even responses to others' emotional expressions appear to be biologically based, many of the "rules" for emotional expression, the value of feeling and expressing emotions, and the management of emotion are the product of learning. Cultures and even subcultures vary considerably in their emotional "rules." Thus, emotions are subject to socialization, just as thoughts and behavior are (Miller & Speery, 1987; Saarni,

373

1987). In this section, we examine some learned aspects of emotion as background for further discussion of children's developing understanding of emotions in others and in themselves.

Labeling Emotional States. Developing emotional knowledge involves learning words that describe emotions and applying them properly to the emotional expressions and correlated states that children know about early on. As with other aspects of language development, most of the acquisition of common emotional labels is completed before children reach school age. *Environmental influences* from parents and others obviously play a large role in this aspect of emotional development, which is one reason for substantial variation from one culture to another in emotional states for which terms exist and in the particular descriptions used for them (Fischer, Carnochan, & Shaver, in press).

Research findings indicate that adults and children classify emotions in similar ways. Consequently, when children use the terms "happy," "sad," "calm," or "relaxed," they tend to mean much the same thing that adults mean when using the same words. Furthermore, the terms are organized in children's minds in much the same way as in adults'. Psychologists James Russell and Doreen Ridgeway (1983) demonstrated this by asking children in grades 3 through 7 to rate themselves on a series of 51 adjectives, such as "mad," "miserable," and "wide awake." Each word was embedded in the sentence "Do you feel——————today?" By identifying the words for which responses were similar, Russell and Ridgeway found clusters of emotion words that closely matched the clusters found using the same procedures with adults. Figure 11-2 shows the resulting clusters. In general, they differ from each other in terms of the degree of pleasure (or displeasure) shown and also in terms of the degree of arousal (or lethargy) shown. Russell and Ridgeway argue that labels for emotion are drawn from a fairly simple two-dimensional structure that children have acquired by the time they are in grade school. One of these dimensions is pleasure–displeasure (for example, "angry" versus "happy"); the other is dimension of degree of arousal (for example, "sleepy" versus "full of energy"). In other cultures, however, children may acquire a quite different array and structure of emotion labels from the information acquired by middle-class children in North America, (Ekman, 1980; Levy, 1973; Lutz, 1982).

Emotion "Rules." Cultures also vary in their implicit expectations for when, how, and toward whom emotions may be expressed and even expectations for which emotions may be shown and which must be masked. For example, in North America children learn that close female relatives are expected to express grief at the death of a loved one, but males are supposed to control their open expression of this emotion. In other cultures, like Tahiti, the expression of grief is taboo, and there is no label for the emotional reaction to loss (Campos et al., 1983; Levy, 1973).

Knowledge of "display" and "feeling" rules develops more gradually

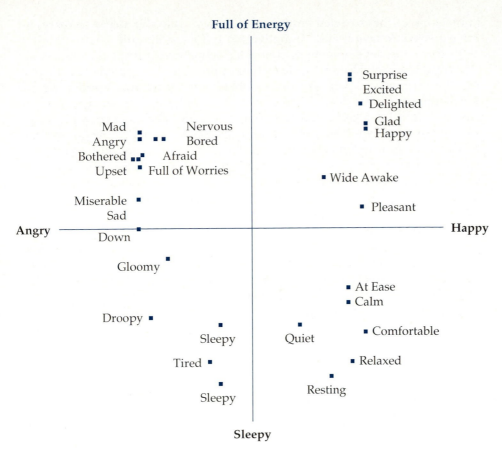

FIGURE 11-2

Common emotion labels as understood by North American children in grades 3 through 7.

Source: from Russell & Ridgeway, 1983.

across the childhood years than does knowledge of emotion labels (Saarni, 1979). In research with children between the ages of 6 and 10 years, psychologist Carolyn Saarni (1979) has found evidence of increased knowledge of rules that apply to photographs of conflict situations. For example, children are increasingly aware that the proper emotional expression is a smile when someone gives you a gift—even if you don't like it. The complexity of the reasons for managing impressions to follow this rule also increased in this sample of elementary school children.

In subsequent research, Saarni (1984) observed children's reactions to the "disappointing gift" situation and also interviewed the children about their own behavior. She found developmental increases in appropriate emotional expressions. In interviews, she found that these differences in management of emotional expressions were related to three aspects of socialization: (1)

375

knowledge of the expected emotional "display" rule, (2) ability to carry out the expected behavior, and (3) motivation to follow the rule.

To study the development of children's actual use of display rules, Saarni (1980) provided children with the actual opportunity to implement a display rule by setting up a situation in which they received a disappointing gift from someone who clearly expected them to like it. The display rule, in words, might have been "look pleased and smile when someone gives you something they expect you to like even though you don't." Approximately half of the 6-year-old children in Saarni's study did indeed "put on a happy face" in this situation, and nearly three-quarters of older children did so. In addition, it was found that girls were more likely to invoke the display rule than were boys. Both of these findings suggest that the implementation of display rules is influenced by socialization and social–cognitive development. That is, (1) children learn to use these rules; (2) they may receive more pressure to use them as they get older or, alternatively, they may simply become more able to identify proper situations and to effectively control their emotion expressions; and (3) there are differential pressures on boys and girls regarding the necessity to use certain display rules. Saarni's findings suggest that girls are more pressured to use the display rule in question. A rule concerning the inhibition of crying or other expressions of disappointment or hurt might be more readily invoked by boys than by girls.

Expectations for appropriate behavior probably become both more complex and more situationally variable as adulthood approaches. In addition, violations of expected display and feeling rules may have more serious consequences for adults than for children. For example, inappropriately emotional behavior by a man or woman in business or professional settings may result in the loss of a job or failure to advance. Childhood socialization in the "rules" of emotional expression may, like other forms of social learning, be a gradual process of building up to more and more complex learning tasks.

Other types of knowledge involving emotion include knowledge of the course of an emotional experience and the link between emotion and memory. For example, age differences have been found in understanding that emotion becomes less intense once the emotion-provoking episode is past, but that emotion-provoking events will be more memorable than events that do not arouse emotions (Taylor & Harris, 1983). The links between knowledge of emotion scripts and children's behavior probably depend on understanding and being able to voluntarily use strategies for appropriately displaying and managing emotions.

Understanding Emotions in Others and Self

Knowledge about emotions, including emotion labels and rules for expression, are necessary parts of the complex task of understanding emotion in social life. In Chapter 10 we discussed the process of inferring the internal states of others and of ourselves. In this section, we examine briefly the process of understanding emotions in others and its development.

Inferences About Others' Emotions. Making inferences about others' emotions has much in common with inferring the perceptual and cognitive experiences of others. That is the reason that we referred to this process as *affective role taking* in Chapter 10. The recognition of facial expressions of emotion that we discussed earlier involves attending only to the emotion cues in the face itself. Role taking involves understanding both emotional expression and other aspects of the situation in which it occurs. Thus, the task is more complex than simple recognition of emotions.

As in the development of role taking generally, young children tend to base their inferences about emotions on attention-getting, salient cues. Consequently, preschool children often find it difficult to comprehend emotions that are inconsistent with the situations in which they occur. For example, when presented with a story in which a child felt sad at her own birthday party, preschool children often erroneously infer that the child feels happiness. Their perception is dominated by the salient information about an ordinarily happy event (the party); they probably assume that the birthday child would feel as they themselves would feel on such an occasion, even when there is other information that contradicts this assumption (Deutsch, 1974). Of course, if the other person's feelings match stereotyped expectations or if the child's facial expression were made very salient, the child's inference would more likely be correct.

How do children develop the ability to infer others' unexpected or complex emotions? Research findings indicate that children notice and remember both emotional expressions and information about situations even at very young ages. However, young children often rely more on one source of information, such as facial expressions, than another in inferring others' emotional states, whereas older children integrate multiple sources of information, even when the information is inconsistent (Gnepp, 1983; Harris, Donnelly, Guz, & Pitt-Watson, 1986). For example, in explaining the sad child at a birthday party, children might focus on explaining the child's facial expression ("She didn't get the present she wanted."). However, older children would be more likely than younger ones to recognize spontaneously the need to explain the discrepancy. The development of affective role taking also involves the increasing understanding that a person can feel more than one emotion at a time. Although young children seem to feel that emotions must be felt one at a time, by age 9 or 10, children more readily understand that a person can feel two quite conflicting emotions (Gnepp, McKee, & Domanic, 1987; Harter, 1982). The birthday party child might, therefore, feel sadness that her father is away on her birthday, but also feel happy that she is having a party.

As in role taking about others' perceptions and cognitions, inferences about others' emotions involve considerations of both internal states and the external demands and constraints of situations (Eisenberg, Fabes, Bustamante, Mathy, Miller, & Lindholm, 1988; Fabes, Eisenberg, McCormick, & Wilson, 1988). A study of children's understanding of their mothers' emotional states (Covell & Abramovitch, 1987) shows an increasing ability between the ages of 5 and 15 to balance their mothers' emotional expressions with information

377

RESEARCH FOCUS 11-2

Personalizing Others' Emotions

Inferring others' emotions is sometimes as simple as reading the expressions on their faces, but sometimes is much more complex. For example, when a person's emotional state is not what we expect for the current situation, we are likely to have difficulty in understanding the reaction. One pertinent piece of information in such cases concerns the previous experiences of the person. If a child shows fear when asked to feed the class gerbil—ordinarily a treat for the chosen child—it helps to know that, when chosen previously, that child was bitten by the gerbil. Adults use such information in attempting to understand others' emotional reactions and, often, raise questions about possible personal factors when information is not readily available.

Even when children have heard or seen information that should help them understand others' surprising emotions, however, young children have a more difficult time than older ones in using the information. Psychologists Jackie Gnepp and Martha Gould (1985) demonstrated this point in a study involving kindergarteners, second, fifth, and eighth graders, and college students. The question of interest was this: If children are first told about an event that causes a person to have a certain emotional reaction, will this information affect their understanding of the same person's emotional reactions in a second situation?

Gnepp and Gould created six stories, each of which contained two events. The first described a child experiencing either a positive or negative event, and the second described a related situation in which the study participants were supposed to appraise the child's emotional state. For example, in one story, the child character was first rewarded for an excellent dive and, second, was given the opportunity to dive again. Another study involved a child's first being spanked for losing things and, then, the same child losing a mitten. The study participants were questioned to be sure they remembered both events and then were asked how the child felt after the second part of the story and the reasons for the emotion. Did the participants use the information from the first story event to understand the child's reaction to the second event?

For the most part, kindergarteners did not. Children of this youngest age were more likely to guess at the characters' feelings and to make up a reason that had nothing to do with the first event. Gnepp and Gould call these situational inferences, because they depend on the immediate situation and not on particular information about the story person. At each successive age, however, children relied more on the information from the first event to predict and explain the character's emotions. These personalized inferences are more mature because of the complex processes of the following: (1) inferring the characters' emotional state in one situation and (2) using this information to understand responses to another situation. College students made personalized inferences about 90% of the time in answering Gnepp and Gould's questions. Second graders did so about 50% of the time on their own and about 80% of the time when the researchers reminded them of the emotional state of the character.

Gnepp and Gould's study demonstrates the cognitive effort involved in understanding the emotional states of others in ways that approach the complexity of emotional experience itself. ❦

about the context. Older children used information about the situation and knowledge of external pressures, rather than relying on their mothers' expressive signs alone, to make inferences about emotions, whereas younger children made inferences from the expressive cues in most cases.

Understanding One's Own Emotions.   Just as concepts of others and self parallel the development of cognitive skills (see Chapter 10), understanding of one's own emotions appears to follow patterns similar to cognitive–developmental sequences. Measures of cognitive ability correlate highly with children's understanding of their own feelings. In one study, more cognitively advanced children were more likely than less advanced children to describe their feelings as an internal experience, rather than describing them in terms of the situation in which they occurred. Similarly, more cognitively advanced children were more likely to spontaneously view their feelings from the perspective of another person, to recognize and understand multiple feelings, and to know that they could change and manage their own feelings (Carroll & Steward, 1984; Nannis & Cowan, 1987). Perhaps these findings partly explain Saarni's (1984) observations that older children both understood the necessary components of appropriate emotional expression and managed their own emotional expressions more appropriately than younger ones.

In the next section, we will examine the functions of emotions and emotional understanding in children's social and cognitive behavior.

Emotion and Behavior

Emotions are commonly believed to disrupt behavior, interfering with one's ability to complete a task, continue an interaction, or conform to expected or required behavior. And emotions do sometimes disrupt behavior. At other times, however, emotional reactions seem to have little effect on the stream of action, usually because the action has become very automatic and is resistant to disruption. Very often, emotions actually help individuals adapt to difficult or complex settings and tasks. For example, emotional responses help to govern attention to relevant parts of a situation or a person's behavior, assuring that the child's responses are attuned to the aspects of the environment that are most crucial at the moment (Easterbook, 1959; Erdelyi, 1974). Memory for persons and situations is also affected by emotional states, a process which may help to establish the value or significance of different events that children remember from their experiences (Bower, 1981; Clark, 1984). In short, from the early days of infancy, emotions help to organize behavior, to give it meaning, and to make it part of the total functioning of the individual.

379

In this section, we examine *interrelations* between emotions and other aspects of behavior and development. These interrelations underscore the organizing effects of emotions and of responses to the emotions of others. In recent years developmental psychologists have discovered organizing effects of emotion in both cognitive development and social behavior.

Emotional Effects on Social Behavior

Emotions may affect how people behave toward each other and also may help to determine the impact of relationships on the behavior of individuals in other aspects of their lives. Warmth and affection from parents increase children's compliance to their requests, perhaps partly because of the positive mood that warm, loving parental behavior fosters in the child (Maccoby & Martin, 1983).

Moods, which are short-term emotional states, help to determine whether and how individuals comply, cooperate, display generosity, and offer help to others in distress (Isen, 1984). In studies of the effects of emotion on children's social behavior, two influences have been especially prominent: social referencing and empathy.

Social Referencing. *Social referencing* is the term applied to the effect of another person's emotional signs on the infant's behavior in an otherwise ambiguous situation. In other words, the responses of others become a reference point in helping children organize their behavior in unfamiliar settings. For example, hearing their mothers' make positive vocalizations made it more likely that infants would approach an unfamiliar toy, while hearing more negative tones inhibited touching and playing with the toy (Hornik & Gunnar, 1988; Svejda & Campos, 1982).

A group of psychologists and psychiatrists (Sorce, Emde, Campos, & Klinnert, 1981) have studied the influence of adults' emotional expressions on 1-year-old infants' reactions to the frightening illusion of the visual cliff. Recall from Chapter 5 that infants are placed on one side of an apparent 4-foot dropoff, made level by a plexiglass plane. The child's mother stands on the other side of the cliff. If infants refuse to cross to the mother, to whom they would ordinarily go willingly, we have evidence that children perceive the dropoff (and, thus, are sensitive to the visual cues that indicate depth). However, Sorce et al. found that the children's responses depend heavily on the emotional signs shown by the mothers. When mothers showed a fearful expression, none of the infants would cross the deep side of the cliff; but when mothers posed a happy face, 15 out of 19 infants in the study crossed the apparent chasm. Further, some mothers were asked to pose angry expressions, while others were asked to feign interest. Under these conditions, 11% and 75% of the infants, respectively, would crawl across the apparent dropoff. Such studies indicate that infants use the emotional responses of caregivers to help give meaning to new or ambiguous circumstances (Campos & Stenberg, 1981).

The emotions and behavior of infants as young as 3 months seem to be affected by emotional cues from significant caretakers (Campos et al., 1983). True social referencing probably emerges when, at about 6 to 8 months of age, infants seem to coordinate the emotional expressions of others with awareness of objects or conditions in the environment. Infants appear to use both mothers and fathers as points of social reference (Dickstein & Parke, 1988). One-year-old children have also been observed to use the expressions of adults other than their parents as references, if the presence of parents make the situation a secure one (Klinnert, Emde, Butterfield, & Campos, 1986). The effect of infants' perceptions of others' emotional expressions on their behavior is a strong indication that, at very early ages, infants have attained some awareness of the significance of particular emotional signs.

Empathy.   The ability to understand the emotions of others also makes possible new opportunities for *empathy,* which is the term used for experiencing the same emotion that another person is experiencing. The capacity for empathy appears to be present very early in life, but in infancy empathy consists of experiencing emotional arousal when others are showing emotion—a kind of emotional resonance (Campos et al., 1983; Hoffman, 1975). As affective role-taking ability increases, empathy may be aroused by inferring what others must be feeling from situational cues or by recognizing the conflicting emotions that a particular situation might arouse for someone. In such cases, a person may feel empathy for someone else, even though the same situation would arouse very different feelings in the empathizer him or herself (Hoffman, 1975). Affective role taking may also make it possible for children gradually to gain knowledge of how their actions might affect others' emotional states. In a study of 5-, 8-, and 12-year-olds' knowledge about what one might do to change the emotional state of another person (for example, from sad to happy), psychologists Charles McCoy and John Masters (1985) found that 5-year-olds tended to mention giving something special to the sad person, regardless of the cause of her sadness, whereas the older children were more likely to fit their approach to the particular causes of the other's emotions.

Empathy has long been considered a critical ingredient in altruistic behavior and in the control of violence and aggression. Although it has been difficult to document these linkages (Eisenberg & Miller, 1987; Parke & Slaby, 1983; Radke-Yarrow & Zahn-Waxler, 1983), positive emotional reactions to others do appear to influence positive social behavior. Elementary school children who reported feeling positive emotions upon hearing an infant's cries were observed to be more helpful in attempting to relieve the baby's distress than children who reported negative emotional reactions (Zahn-Waxler, Friedman, & Cummings, 1983). Programs to train affective role-taking and empathy skills have been effective in reducing aggression and antisocial behavior (Chandler, 1973; Feshbach & Feshbach, 1982), as was discussed in Chapter 10. In these cases, emotional responses appear to facilitate the organization of positive behavior.

381

These developmental patterns are affected, nevertheless, by differences among individuals. The accompanying research focus shows how such differences have been isolated and what they mean for the regulation of emotion.

RESEARCH FOCUS 11-3

Emotional Mastery and Competence

Mastering one's emotions is part of becoming mature, but individuals vary greatly in how that mastery occurs. Many psychologists refer to the various modes of mastering emotions and accomplishing tasks as the distinctive characteristics of individuals. How can these differences in emotional regulation be characterized?

Psychologists Jeanne and Jack Block (1980) have suggested that individuals may be described in terms of two very general dimensions, both of which have to do with the individuals' way of inhibiting and expressing emotion.

One dimension, *ego control*, refers to the way an individual deals with impulses, desires, and wishes. Individuals vary between extremes of undercontrol, or immediate and direct expression of motivations and emotions and an inability to delay gratifications, and overcontrol or the rigid inhibition of feeling and containment of impulses. Moderate control enables a person to express impulses, but in an appropriately modulated, constructive way.

The second dimension, *ego resiliency*, refers to the way in which control is exercised. The resilient person flexibly expresses or inhibits affect, depending on the situation. The "brittle" person is inflexible when the situation changes and new approaches are needed.

Ego control and ego resiliency describe different typical ways of responding. When the extremes of both dimensions are considered, four different patterns of expressing emotion are possible: resilient undercontrollers and overcontrollers, and brittle undercontrollers and overcontrollers. The differences between these groups show how cognitive, emotional, and behavioral factors are organized differently in the personalities of individuals. For example, resilient undercontrollers are energetic, curious, and exploring, while brittle overcontrollers are inhibited, worrying, and intepersonally reserved.

By following a sample of children longitudinally, the Blocks demonstrated that personality organizations—the characteristics of the self—are remarkably stable from age 3 through age 19 (Blocks, personal communication).

In finding this similarity in measures of personality across time, the Blocks have demonstrated an important point about individual development. Children may change in the way that a characteristic is manifested, but the characteristic itself may reflect the same underlying pattern that was present at an earlier age. The Blocks used different tasks and different settings for testing the children at different ages, but similar ways of inhibiting and expressing emotion were apparent, despite the differences. In this respect, the Blocks' approach is similar to the approach used by psychologists who invented mental ability tests, which consist of different types of problems designed to capture certain typical ways of solving problems generally. Although personality is different from mental ability in important ways, the effort to find stable patterns amid the myriad changes in the growing child presents similar challenges. ❧

Emotional states influence learning, memory, and cognitive strategies in many intellectual tasks for children and adults alike (Blaney, 1986; Bower, 1981). When children are in a positive mood they learn happy words better than sad and neutral words (Nasby & Yando, 1982). Similarly, positive moods enhance the speed and accuracy of learning in general compared to neutral or sad moods (Masters, Barden, & Ford, 1979). Even learning from television shows is affected by emotional state: Happy children who viewed a short cartoon subsequently remembered more about the story than did children who were sad while viewing. The sad viewers mostly remembered negative themes from the program (Potts, 1983).

Role taking and other social–cognitive processes may also be affected by the emotions aroused in interactions with others. The complexity of descriptions of liked and disliked persons varies, with liked persons being described more extensively and maturely (Rosenbach, Crockett, & Wapner, 1973). Anger or dislike may short circuit normal processes of social inference so that others' emotional and cognitive states are not correctly inferred (Clark, Milberg, & Erber, 1983; Isen & Shalker, 1982; Shiffenbauer, 1974). Although intense arousal—positive or negative—may interfere with learning, memory, and other cognitive and social–cognitive processes, ordinary fluctuations in emotion may either facilitate or suppress effective cognitive processing depending on the attractiveness of the emotional state and its relationship to the cognitive task.

Effects of Emotion on Cognitive Performance

Even young children express fears about the future, although these concerns are more common among older children and adolescents.

Confident at 11, Confused at 16

Francine Prose

The atmosphere in Carol Gilligan's office at the Harvard Graduate School of Education could hardly be less like my own days as a Harvard graduate student—those seminars mired in torpor from which students were periodically roused by revivifying jolts of pedagogical bad temper. Professor Gilligan's faculty and student colleagues at the Project on the Psychology of Women and the Development of Girls seem relaxed and almost unaccountably buoyant as they gather around the conference table on a rainy Cambridge morning to describe their current work. Indeed the only face in the room that seems less than fully engaged is that of Virginia Woolf, gazing wistfully into the distance from a photograph on the wall.

Perhaps one reason for the group's collective good humor is that Gilligan and her associates see their mission as extending beyond abstract clinical research. As the title of their latest work, "Strengthening Healthy Resistance and Courage in Girls," suggests, they're seeking ways to intervene in the developmental process actively, to help girls weather the crises occasioned by adolescence.

Now the results of a major phase in this project have appeared in a new book. "Making Connections: The Relational Worlds of Adolescent Girls at Emma Willard School" draws on data collected during a five-year study of students at a private girls' school in Troy, N.Y. Gilligan decided to focus on Willard after she was approached by the school's former principal, the late Robert C. Parker. "The school had a question," she says.

" 'How can we make intelligent decisions about girls' education without knowing about their psychological development?' " In the Dodge Study, as it's officially known—funds were provided by the Geraldine Rockefeller Dodge Foundation—extensive interviews and sentence completion tests were used to explore girls' attitudes toward friendship and leadership, sexual morality, politics and violence.

What interviewers kept hearing as they questioned their subjects was that many girls, around the age of 11, go through what Gilligan and her colleagues have come to call a "moment of resistance"—that is, a sharp and particular clarity of vision, an almost perfect confidence in what they know and see, a belief in their integrity and in their highly complex responsibilities toward the world. "Eleven-year-olds are not for sale," says Gilligan.

"I looked at girls at four different age groups, from 7 and 8 years old up to 15 and 16," says Lyn Mikel Brown, just appointed to the Harvard ed school faculty. "And the younger girls had a real sense of outspokenness, of claiming their own sense of authority in the world, being very honest about relationships and the things that hurt them." Responding to the sentence completion tests, the younger girls came up with what Annie Rogers, another member of the faculty, calls "outrageously wonderful statements. One of them was, 'What gets me in trouble is—chewing gum and not tucking my shirt in,' and then, in parentheses, 'but it's usually worth it.' "

But as they get older the girls seem to undergo a kind of crisis in response to adolescence and to the strictures and demands of the culture which, in Gilligan's view, sends a particular message to women: "Keep quiet and notice the absence of women and say nothing." Or as a graduate student, Elizabeth Debold, says: "Girls don't see themselves being what the culture is about. And that has to give them some kind of double vision."

"And by 15 or 16," says Gilligan, "that resistance has gone underground. They start saying, 'I don't know. I don't know. I don't know.' They start not knowing what they had known."

This observation may cause many women to feel an almost eerie shiver of recognition, and inspire them to rethink that period in their lives. It will also be interesting to monitor the responses from psychologists and feminist theorists, for "Making Connections" may well oblige traditional psychology to formulate a more accurate theory of female adolescence (an area that's been virtually ignored until now). Ideally, parents, teachers and therapists who work with girls have begun to find ways to prevent them from "going underground."

Gilligan's discovery of a crisis in female adolescence is thought-provoking and intriguing, but hardly, it would seem, incendiary—until one realizes how small a spark it takes to kindle a conflagration in the academic psychology establishment. Since the 1982 publication of her first book, "In a Different Voice: Psychological Theory and Women's Development," Carol Gilligan's work has generated heated debate in a field in which it is still thought fairly radical to suggest that women's development might be fundamentally different from men's.

One "recurrent problem" Gilligan identified was that previous studies—based largely on male subjects—interpreted the ability to reason from abstract principles as a sign of having reached the highest plane of moral development. But when women were tested (confronted with classical ethics dilemmas—should a poor man whose wife is dying steal the drugs she needs, etc.), many of them apparently failed to reach the "higher" level of putting justice first, and so in the language of the profession were classified as "low stage respondents."

What Gilligan suggested was that the second moral voice (which she termed the "care voice" as opposed to the "justice voice") was not fundamentally inferior and less highly evolved, but simply different—more concerned with human relationships than with abstract principles.

Are there gender distinctions beyond the obvious reproductive functions? However logical it might seem to the casual observer that profound differences in male and female life experience might foster different ways of perceiving the world, this possibility has been vehemently contested in academia; the first volleys of that high-minded shootout continue to echo in the pages of scholarly journals. Yet even those who share Gilligan's beliefs that male/female differences do exist often disagree with her analysis of what those differences are.

By concentrating on girls, the project's new studies avoid the muddle of gender comparisons and the issue of whether boys experience a similar "moment of resistance." Gilligan and her colleagues are simply telling us how girls sound at two proximate but radically dissimilar stages of growing up.

(Continued)

In explaining this difference, project members often refer to one of their interview subjects, a 12-year-old named Tanya who was a classic "resister." On behalf of a homesick younger cousin, Tanya bravely challenged a summer camp rule against campers calling home—she believed and acted upon her conviction that "people are more important than rules." By 15, however, Tanya seemed to have lost some of that uncompromising moral purity, and told an interviewer of having signed "love" to a letter she wrote to someone she did not love. What emerges from talks with Gilligan and her associates is their disbelief and dismay at repeatedly seeing a morally articulate preadolescent transformed into an apologetic, hesitant teen-ager who prefaces every opinion with "this may sound mediocre but. . . ." These teen-agers' syntax "is like a sailboat tacking," says Gilligan. "One sentence goes this way. Another sentence goes that way."

The source of the change, in Gilligan's view, is that, during adolescence, girls come up against "the wall of Western culture," and begin to see that their clearsightedness may be dangerous and seditious; in consequence they learn to hide and protect what they know—not only to censor themselves but "to think in ways that differ from what they really think."

Perhaps Gilligan's most radical challenge to traditional developmental psychology is her emphasis on collectivity—in contrast to "individuation," the establishment of an autonomous self that has until now been seen to mark the highest stage of personality development. The practical benefits of encouraging young people's talent for collaboration are already being felt at schools like Emma Willard, where, in the aftermath of the Dodge Study, teachers and administrators have redoubled their commitment to listen to what girls really have to say. Many Emma Willard students, says Acting Principal Trudy Hanmer, had been "very bright, very articulate, very verbal sixth graders who somehow had changed. They'd got quiet." Consequently the school "de-

mands participation from everyone, until girls who were quiet as freshmen are, by their sophomore or junior year, saying 'I have an opinion that counts.' " Hanmer describes a dramatic rise in the quiz scores of geography students who were organized into map study groups and told that their grades would be the average of all the group members' scores. Relieved of the necessity to compete with their peers, the girls achieved "extraordinarily high grades. Almost everyone got a perfect score."

In the search for more active ways of "strengthening healthy resistance and courage in girls," Gilligan and her colleagues took a group of 11-year-olds from the Atrium School in Watertown, Mass., a suburb of Boston, on a week-long outing last summer during which they wrote, drew and did theater work designed to help the girls function as a group and, as Annie Rogers says, "talk about things they wouldn't ordinarily talk about and bring their voices right out into the public.

"And it worked wonderfully. It did just what we wanted it to do. The kids had to direct and listen to one another, they wrote some beautiful pieces and did some really interesting drawings and formed a community among themselves." These girls will be the subject of follow-up studies for three years, and this year another "Sixth Grade Writing and Outing Club"—its members drawn from Cambridge public schools—will visit the Boston Museum of Fine Arts and Old Sturbridge Village. The girls will also keep journals—in order, says Gilligan, "to amplify their voices for themselves" before these voices can be quieted or silenced.

Carol Gilligan often speaks of her most recent work as "very new" and "very fragile," and again one hears a weariness creep into her voice, as if she is anticipating in advance all the objections that will be raised—debates she fears will resemble those that greeted "In a Different Voice." One can imagine the discussions of whether 11-year-olds are really more or less morally advanced than their older sisters, or what sorts of resistance boys go through when, like the supreme resister, J.D. Salinger's Holden Caulfield, they attempt to hold out against "the phoniness" of adult society. These debates could continue to obscure the real difficulties experienced by women (and men) who, as children, learned to doubt what they know.

Exploring what Freud called "the dark continent" of female psychology, Carole Gilligan describes feeling "like a 19th-century naturalist," and she and her colleagues seem to share a Darwinian sense of mission to excavate the hidden chambers of a common buried past. One can't help noting an extraordinary degree of personal commitment, an appreciation of the connections between their own lives and those of the girls they are studying. "For me," says Gilligan's colleague Elizabeth Debold, "the issues that we're dealing with are issues about my life."

Hearing Carol Gilligan describe the joy and physical freedom of playing tag at the beach with the Sixth Grade Outing Club, one is moved by an almost spooky sense that what she and her colleagues are unearthing is that moment in their own pasts during which they "went underground." "The thing that's so powerful about studying girls," Gilligan says, "is that it takes you back. You remember how you moved in the world, how your body felt when you were 11. You remember how you were with your friends, how your life was—what it was like."

387

Summary

Emotion is an important aspect of the organization of behavior and changes in that organization as the child develops. A recent resurgence of interest in the study of emotions has helped developmental psychologists discover more about the course and effects of emotional development. Theoretical views of emotional development have been offered within the biosocial, psychodynamic, learning, and cognitive–developmental traditions.

Emotional expressiveness develops both in the forms and in the nature of emotions expressed. Facial expressions are the most widely studied form, but emotions can also be communicated vocally quite early in life. Three emotions that appear to be present throughout life illustrate the following: (1) the early appearance of emotional states and, thus, their apparent biological *origins;* (2) the developmental *course* of emotional expression from infancy into later life; and (3) the impact of *environmental influences* in modifying emotional expressions.

For example, the emotions of *wariness* and *fear* are indications of the child's awareness of threat. True fear is thought to appear late in the first year of life and to imply cognitive abilities that enable inferences about potential threat to be made. "Stranger fear," for instance, typically appears in the second half of the first year on occasions when an unfamiliar person appears in the absence of a familiar, nurturant person. Specific fears become less frequent as children mature, although more complex, general fears (such as fear of failure) may increase.

Pleasure or *joy* is usually inferred from smiling and laughter. Infants' very early smiles are believed to result from discharges of excitation in the central nervous system, but social smiles in responses to other persons or to interesting objects may also appear as soon as the first month of life. In childhood, the tendency to smile at other persons depends more on an individual child's emotional expressiveness than on age, although smiling and laughter in response to humor is partly the result of the cognitive capabilities for comprehending the incongruity in the humor.

Anger and *rage* are focused reactions against something or someone who threatens or blocks a goal. In infancy, this reaction is typically rage at being restrained physically; but anger at being prevented from pursuing some goal appears in the second year, possibly as a result of cognitive skills for establishing rudimentary plans and motor capacity to pursue them. Anger, like fear, is partly physiological in nature. As children mature, anger is more likely to be directed toward a person and may take more symbolic, less physical forms.

Although the capacity for these emotions is present at birth, there are marked individual differences in the likelihood of an emotional reaction and in whether emotionality is likely to be positive or negative. To some degree, these differences are biologically based, reflecting genetically influenced differences among children in reactivity to stimulation and in degree of appre-hensiveness. In addition, however, emotional expressiveness is subject to *environmental influences* and change over time, especially in how they are expressed. As children develop, more complex combinations of emotions become apparent, and control of emotions becomes more possible and more likely.

Development also occurs in children's knowledge of emotions amd emo-tional experiences. The ability to recognize others' emotional states increases across the years of childhood, although some recognition ability is present in infancy. Age-related increases also occur in knowledge of cultural norms, or "rules," for the expression of emotion and in knowledge of emotion words or labels. Increasing knowledge and changes in children's abilities for infer-ring the internal states of others result in more complex and more accurate inferences about others' and one's own emotional states.

The *interrelations* of emotional development with other aspects of behavior and development are evident in the extensive organizing role of emotions in social behavior. Emotions determine children's attention to some aspects of a situation or interaction and not others. In addition, the ability to read others' emotional reactions affects children's interpretations of situations and tasks *(social referencing)*. *Empathy* toward others, which involves inferences about others' emotional states and an understanding about their implications, has been linked to both positive and negative social behaviors. Emotions also play an organizing role in cognitive performance and affect what children learn most readily and how effectively cognitive skills can be demonstrated.

Suggested Readings

Campos, J., Barrett, K., Lamb, M., Goldsmith, H., & Stenberg, C. (1983). Socioemotional development. In M. Haith & J. Campos (Eds.), P. Mussen (Series Ed.), *Handbook of child psychology: Vol. 2. Infancy and devel-opmental psychobiology* (pp. 783–915). New York: Wiley.

Cicchetti, D., & Hess, P. (Eds.) (1982). *Emotional devel-opment: New directions for child development.* San Fran-cisco: Jossey-Bass.

Izard, C. E., & Malatesta, C. Z. (1987). Perspectives on emotional development 1: Differential emotions theory of early emotional development. In J. Osof-sky (Ed.), *Handbook of infant development,* 2nd ed. (pp. 494–554). New York: Wiley.

Lewis, M., & Michaelson, L. (1983). *Children's emotions and moods: Developmental theory and measurement.* New York: Plenum.

Tronick, E. Z. (1989). Emotions and emotional com-munication in infants. *American Psychologist, 44,* 112–119.

389

Human beings develop in a world in which other persons are perhaps the most significant features. Interactions with parents, teachers, other children, and a variety of incidental acquaintances dominate childhood experiences beginning in early life. The impact of these interactions on the patterns of individual characteristics that mark each child as a distinct individual is the primary focus in the study of personality and social development. Part Four considers both the most common and salient sources of influence in the lives of most children and several aspects of development in which these influences seem especially important to the behavior patterns of individual children.

Chapters 12 and 13 address four important sources of influence in personality and social development: family, schools, mass media, and peers. The chapters make it clear that these sources are closely intertwined. Al-

PART FOUR

Social Contexts and Relationships and the Development of the Individual

though all may influence development in unique and important ways, each of the four also helps to determine how much and what kind of impact the other three will have on a developing child.

The interwoven effects of family, school, mass media, and peer influences are especially apparent in the aspects of individual development considered in Chapters 14 and 15. These forces all help to shape children's concepts of themselves as male or female, their knowledge of gender roles, and their expectations regarding the adoption of these roles. Family, friends, and social institutions also influence the development of children's abilities for self-regulation, including not only the capacity for positive, socially desirable behaviors but also pressures toward and the inhibition of antisocial behaviors.

CHAPTER TWELVE

Contexts of Social Development: Family, School, and Mass Media

Introduction

Social development occurs in the time and space children share with others. Children require a family that meets early needs, provides attention and affection, models values, and practices discipline. As it becomes more common for both parents to work, the family context may be elaborated by substitute care, such as that provided in day care centers, family day care homes, or with grandparents or other relatives. At age 5 or 6, the school environment becomes yet another important context for development. Both in their own homes and in other settings, the mass media create a pervasive context that portrays people and places that children would not be likely to encounter in their own everyday experience. In terms of our general framework, these contexts constitute a constellation of *environmental influences* that affect the nature and course of children's development.

In this chapter we will consider three primary contexts in which children develop: family, school, and mass media (particularly, television). As in other chapters, we will consider the nature of the influences that occur in these contexts, the ways in which they may change as the child matures, and their links to other aspects of development. To begin, however, we will briefly consider how the different contexts that children experience constitute different *ecologies* for their development.

The Ecology of Development

To envision these contexts in the lives of children, let us consider the Blakes, a typical middle-class family in the southern United States. Both the father, Dan, and mother, Susan, hold jobs outside the home. Two of the three children, a 9-year-old son, Jeffrey, and a 7-year-old daughter, Laura, attend schools to which they must ride a bus. In school Jeffrey participates in a special program for high-achieving students that is not available for children of Laura's age. Both have teachers who emphasize assignments that require cooperation among the children in the class. After school, they both attend an activity program at the school for children whose parents cannot be at home when school is out. A 3-year-old daughter, Stephanie, attends a day care center near the office where Susan works.

The children are all television fans and are allowed to watch television while Susan prepares dinner. When Dan arrives home from work, the family eats dinner together. After dinner, the children watch a favorite television comedy about a middle-class family with three children. Dan reads Stephanie a story before she goes to bed, while Susan insists that Jeffrey do his arithmetic homework. Laura goes to bed about 1 hour after Stephanie, and Jeffrey another hour later. Before bed, Laura and Jeffrey watch Jeffrey's favorite show, an adventure program about an intelligence agent who is skilled at improvising scientific devices to rescue himself from dangerous situations. Dan tucks both older children in, while Susan does the family laundry.

Many U.S. families—although different from the Blakes in number of members, number of parents present, social class, and ethnic and racial background—go through some version of these events each day. We described a middle-class nuclear family as only one illustration of how family, work, school, and media permeate the lives of adults and children alike.

Developmental psychologist Urie Bronfenbrenner (1986) has argued that children develop within a layered array of social contexts. Some of these, like the system of social and economic structures and their historical background, determine the experiences of children in a very global, general way. Other experiences are less global. For example, children who live in poverty experience differing amounts and kinds of stimulation, encounter different physical dangers, have access to different privileges and opportunities, and face different demands for their own behavior than children who live in middle-class homes, like the Blakes. Similarly, adolescents in a capitalist political system experience very different opportunities, demands, and constraints from those in a socialist system. These differences, regardless of whether they are viewed as uniformly positive or negative, do mean that the contexts of children's lives have to be considered in understanding the nature and course of their development.

Bronfenbrenner also notes that contextual differences occur because of children's immediate circumstances. For example, the parents' occupations can affect the expectations that they respond to all day and, thus, the expectations that they have for their children (Kohn, 1974). Similarly, parents' work schedules—whether they are required to travel extensively, and even the distance between work place and home—can produce varying demands and constraints on children from one family to another. For example, the Blake children attend an afterschool care program, whereas some other children in their neighborhood go directly home after school, where they are supervised by their mothers. The characteristics, demands, and opportunities children encounter at school are another example of contexts determined by where a family lives and their comparative economic well-being.

Finally, Bronfenbrenner notes the context of the family itself: the number and roles of individuals present, the characteristics of their interactions, and the goals and values espoused. We now turn to an overview of the family context and its influences in development.

The Family Context

The family can be viewed as a system of interrelated influences. That family may be the common nuclear family of mother, father, and child, or it may be some other form, perhaps a kibbutz or a foster home. In times past, it might have been an orphanage or other group care setting. Regardless of their composition, families provide the primary environmental influences in children's lives during and beyond the first decade of growth and development. Furthermore, as we discussed in Chapter 4, family influences can be observed in other relations outside the family as children mature (Parke, 1988).

In this section we will consider aspects of families that influence the development of children. In doing so we are building on several other chapters where the nature and impact of family relationships on children were given extensive attention. In particular, in Chapter 4, the discussion of social relationships in early life focused heavily on relationships with parents during infancy, and Chapter 17 will address the distinctive characteristics of family relationships during adolescence.

The Emergence of Reciprocity in Family Interactions

A fundamental aspect of development in family relationships is the establishment of reciprocity and mutuality in interactions between caregivers and infants. Reciprocity is a basic characteristic of social relations, as we discussed in Chapter 9. Even in infancy a caregiver's behavior is influenced by the infant's gazing, vocalizing, smiling, crying, reaching, and touching (see Chapters 3 and 4). Crying, for example, can be both a response to discomfort and an effective social act that will result in feeding, a clean and dry diaper, attention and closeness, or some other consequence that relieves the discomfort. Although some might argue that caregivers naturally control interactions with infants, a strong case can be made that infants control a sizable proportion of any given interaction. For example, in a study of mothers and babies during the first year, Pawlby (1977) found that mothers show more imitation of their baby's behavior than their babies do of theirs. Attachment and related behaviors may help to reinforce reciprocity and mutuality between caregivers and infants and, therefore, the establishment of relationships that serve as prototypes for later social life.

As children mature, the particular content of their reciprocal behavior with parents changes, reflecting improvements in the children's social skills and abilities to communicate clearly what they want or to persist until parents comply. In addition, children make better use of information from parents and others in solving problems and reaching goals (Bronson, 1974). Although parents continue to provide resources to children until young adulthood—and sometimes beyond—the extent of dependency on parents for meeting basic needs decreases steadily through the childhood and adolescent years. After early childhood, the reciprocity between parents and children more often consists of duties which each owes to the other (Maccoby, 1984; Selman, 1980). In most Western nations, for example, it is generally assumed that parents owe children continued support and nurturance appropriate to their ages, and children owe parents respect, consideration, responsible self-direction in appropriate activities (such as, schoolwork), and assistance in the maintenance of the household (Goodnow & Collins, 1990). Although parent–child relationships clearly vary in the degree to which either or both parties endorse or fulfill their reciprocal duties, both contribute to the nature of their relationship and to the flow of influence from one to the other.

We now turn to a more detailed consideration of relationships between children and their mothers and fathers. In addition, we will consider the nature of parents' influences on children's behavior and development.

Between birth and age 10, parents are the most important persons in most children's lives. During adolescence and afterward, other persons outside of their families often become increasingly important and influential as well, but most surveys indicate that parents remain among the most significant persons in the lives of their children well into adulthood (Hill, 1988).

Despite a long-standing emphasis on mother–child interactions both in U.S. society and in the study of parent–child relationships, there is now considerable evidence that fathers, when they are regular participants in children's lives, make distinctive and important contributions to development. In this section, we will first discuss mother–child and father–child relationships, noting the similarities and the differences between them at different ages. Then we will turn to the question of the impact of parents on children's behavior and development.

Mother–Child and Father–Child Relationships. The study of the family context was once largely the study of wives and mothers, partly because of social conditions in which men were viewed primarily as breadwinners and women as homemakers. As social patterns have changed toward dual-career families, it has become more common to examine two related questions: How are mother–child and father–child relationships similar to one another? How are they different from one another?

Consider the Blakes, the middle-class family that we described earlier in this chapter. Both parents participated in caregiving and family responsibilities. What might we expect to see in a comparison of parent–child relationships in a family like this?

Mothers and fathers engage in many of the same kinds of activities with their children and have warm, positive relationships with them. As we pointed out in Chapter 4, fathers, as well as mothers, are important attachment figures for their children. Both during and after infancy, in most ways fathers are as significant to their children and as competent in caregiving as mothers (Lamb, 1981, 1986). Fathers are often especially valued as a partner in warm, playful interactions (Russell & Russell, 1987). Even in adolescence, as we will discuss in Chapter 17, father–child relationships are often especially likely to emphasize play and recreation activities, as well as discussion about social and political issues (Montemayor & Brownless, 1987; Youniss & Smollar, 1985).

On the other hand, it is important to note that most surveys show that mothers spend more time with children in all age periods than fathers do. Also, mothers typically are involved with children in a wider range of shared activities than fathers. For example, in infancy, childhood, and adolescence alike, mothers perform more of the caregiving and maintenance routines that require parent and child to be together. Mothers are involved with children in household chores and monitor and help with schoolwork more often than

Parent–Child Relationships and Influences

fathers do. Furthermore, although both mothers and fathers are affectionate toward their children, mothers are more often the parent to whom children turn for comfort and with whom they share personal feelings (Collins & Russell, in press).

In short, as has been frequently reported by sociologists and demographers, the changing participation of women in the work force and men in the family has not completely erased differences between the roles of mothers and fathers in the family. Almost certainly, the continuing differences do not result from women being naturally more competent in caring for children than men. Rather, the differences reflect long-standing social patterns and expectations for men and women and corresponding feelings of personal responsibility for various aspects of family life that may be slow to respond to changing roles outside the home (Lancaster, Altmann, Rossi, & Sherrod, 1987). It is important to note, however, that research in the 1970s and 1980s has clearly documented the important roles that both men and women can play in children's lives (Maccoby & Martin, 1983; Collins & Russell, in press). Several specific effects of fathers and mothers in a fundamental area of development during childhood, sex typing and the development of gender roles, will be discussed extensively in Chapter 14.

Parents as Socializing Influences. Of particular interest was how parents discipline their children. Discipline focuses on techniques of socialization intended to teach children to regulate their own behavior. While much disciplining occurs following infractions of rules and includes punishment (such as, spanking and scolding) of the child, discipline refers to a pattern of activities that may include, but also goes well beyond, punishment. Discipline also includes training in setting limits, calling attention to others who show the desired self-control, or even the direct suggestion of strategies (for example, "On your way home don't walk by the ice cream store. Then you won't be tempted").

Appropriate, effective discipline is a central concern for most parents. In one study, Minton, Kagan, & Levine (1977) observed mothers' reactions to their 2-year-old children's misbehavior, including aggression, tantrums, or damage to household objects. The findings indicated that a concern with discipline predominated in the mother's interactions with her toddler. On the average there was some controlling action on her part about once every 6 or 7 minutes, and almost half of the mother's time with her child was devoted to controlling the child and eliciting obedience. Most frequently, the mother was trying to protect household objects from harm, with relatively few reactions to serious misbehavior by the child such as instances of aggression. Mothers' behavior tended to escalate: Their first responses to misbehavior were mild but increased in intensity if the child failed to obey, and if the child had not obeyed quickly during a preceding interaction, mothers' first disciplinary responses to a new misbehavior were likely to be more forceful.

In later childhood, parents' disciplinary goals are more likely to concern how children behave outside the family and the degree to which they shoulder responsibilities within the family. The general characteristics of effective

398

Fathers' interactions with children often involve play and recreation.

discipline, however, have been found to be similar in infancy, childhood, and adolescence alike. Several studies in the 1980s (Olweus, 1980; Patterson, 1982; Pulkinnen, 1982) pointed to the importance of parental monitoring of the child's whereabouts, activities, and associates when the child is away from home and the importance of showing interest in the child's opinion and daily experiences. Antisocial behavior is viewed as a failure of discipline that results from sporadic, inconsistent attention to children's activities, and the use of power-assertive methods of punishment, unaccompanied by discussion, reasoning, or explanation. We will now discuss the patterns of parents' behavior to give you a further sense of the significance of different parental approaches to discipline.

Patterns of Parents' Behavior.   Being a parent is made up of thousands of specific actions, as well as attitudes and beliefs. It is not always simple to identify which aspects of parents' behavior are especially important in socialization. Many researchers have attempted to describe systematically these different patterns of behavior that parents adopt toward their children. To illustrate this descriptive approach, we will discuss briefly three different systems of categories for linking patterns of parenting to common consequences for the child, particularly personality characteristics and cognitive characteristics.

The first of the three approaches, *the inventory approach*, was proposed by Schaefer (1959) and Becker (1964). This model was derived from parents' own reports of their behavior between themselves and their child. A factor analysis (see the Appendix to Chapter 7) of these reports showed two major

399

Warmth/Acceptingness

		Warm/Accepting	Hostile/Rejecting
Permissiveness/ Restrictiveness	Permissive/ Reasonably Controlling	Socially outgoing Independent Creative Low in hostility	Aggressive Noncompliant Delinquent
	Restrictive/ Overcontrolling	Submissive Nonaggressive Dependent	Quarrelsome Shy Psychological problems

FIGURE 12-1

The Becker and Schaefer models of parenting showing the effects of combinations of warmth or hostility and permissiveness or restrictiveness on children.

dimensions on which a parent's behavior toward the child may vary. The two dimensions appear in Figure 12-1. On one dimension, behavior may range from "extremely permissive" to "extremely restrictive." This dimension indicates the degree to which parents allow their child autonomy and freedom as opposed to setting tight, restrictive limits on what the child may do. The second dimension described the parents' affective stance towards the child, ranging from "warm and accepting" to "hostile and rejecting." Becker (1964) found a correlation between parents' childrearing characteristics and children's behavioral traits. Warm but highly restrictive (overcontrolling) parents had children who were submissive, nonaggressive, and dependent; whereas those who were warm (accepting) but more permissive in their control had children who were socially outgoing, independent, creative, and low in hostility. When hostile, rejecting parents were restrictive, their children tended to be both quarrelsome and shy and to have higher incidences of psychological problems. When such parents were more permissive, children were more frequently aggressive, noncompliant, and delinquent.

A slightly different approach, *the typology approach,* was proposed by Diana Baumrind on the basis of her long-term, repeated observations of parents' behavior with their children (Baumrind, 1971, 1972). Based on her ratings, Baumrind identified three types of parents, each of which was associated with different characteristic behavior by children:

Authoritarian parents are generally restrictive, emphasize rules, expect the child to obey them unquestioningly, and are inclined to punish behavior that deviates from the established code. This type of parent tends to show hostility, as well. Baumrind found that the children of such parents tend to be dependent, with sons also showing hostility and daughters tending to withdraw and to have low self-esteem.

Permissive parents allow children to play a role in establishing standards of conduct, rather than using their superior power to impose rules, and tend to make relatively few demands on their children (for example, in terms of household chores). Children of permissive parents tend to be similar to those of authoritarian parents, with the sons showing hostility and the daughters tending to be socially retiring and to give up in the face of initial failures. It has been proposed that these two rather different types of parenting have similar effects because in both cases the child is insulated from many stresses and given little opportunity to learn to tolerate frustration. In the case of authoritarian parents, this results from overprotection and the constraint-oriented approach to discipline that prevents the child from experiencing a wide variety of social contingencies; with permissive parents, nonpunitive acceptance provides little opportunity to learn limits and tolerance of frustration.*

Authoritative parents set clear limits and standards for behavior, but enforce them with a combination of power and reasoning. Children are encouraged to comform to the limits and standards, but are given the opportunity to play an active role in determining them through their own input to the reasoning process. Baumrind notes that these parents clearly communicate expectations about their children's behavior, but are also realistic in the sense of not being overly or unnecessarily constraining. Both sons and daughters of authoritative parents tend to be appropriately independent and conform to group norms and standards while still maintaining their own individual, generally socially responsible, standards of conduct. Baumrind terms these children instrumentally competent: socially responsible, friendly, yet still independent and assertive. She considers rearing this type of child to be the goal that most parents have for their children, but authoritative parents are the most likely to achieve it.

In a third approach, Maccoby and Martin (1983) have suggested a refinement of the Schaeffer/Becker and Baumrind approaches, based on a broad review of the literature on childrearing practices. They argue that childrearing patterns can be best described in terms of two dimensions: (1) demanding versus undemanding and (2) a multidimensional contrast between accepting, responsive, child-centered methods and rejecting, unresponsive, parent-centered methods. Using terms very much like Baumrind's, Maccoby and Martin (1983) characterize four types of parenting (see Table 12-1). The first two are authoritative–reciprocal and authoritarian–autocratic; these are parallel to Baumrind's authoritative and authoritarian categories. Instead of Baumrind's permissive group, however, Maccoby and Martin propose two new categories: indulgent–permissive, characterized by low demands but acceptance of and responsiveness toward the child; and indifferent–uninvolved, which is

---

* Baumrind also identified a group of *nonconformist parents*, who themselves show rejection of external authority and socially imposed rules, yet they also set limits on their children's behavior and uphold standards of excellence for the child's performance. Baumrind found that this pattern has a more positive effect on sons than on daughters. Whereas the sons tend to be independent and to adopt high standards for themselves, the daughters are dependent and, like those of authoritarian or permissive parents, tend to become socially withdrawn in the face of failure or frustration.

TABLE 12-1

A model of patterns of parenting based on two dimensions: demandingness and responsiveness to the child

	Accepting Responsive Child-centered	Rejecting Unresponsive Parent-centered
Demanding controlling	Authoritative-reciprocal High in bidirectional communication	Authoritarian Power assertive
Undemanding low in control attempts	Indulgent	Neglecting, ignoring indifferent, uninvolved

SOURCE: From Maccoby and Martin, 1983, p. 39.

characterized by parent neglect, indifference, and lack of involvement with children. Maccoby and Martin believe, as did Baumrind, that authoritative parents' behavior is related to optimal child development. Thus, Maccoby and Martin capture both Baumrind's emphasis on variations in parental expectations for behavior and use of different methods to enforce them and also Becker's and Schaeffer's emphasis on the emotional qualities of parent–child interactions and the degree of involvement of parents with children.

Bidirectionality of Influence. In considering the role of the family in socialization, it is important to remember that the child both influences and is influenced by the social context. Among the characteristics of children that affect the behavior of others toward them in interactions are abilities for understanding and making themselves understood, tendencies toward being relatively active and passive (Bell, 1968), responsiveness to influence (Bell & Harper, 1977; Brunk & Henggeler, 1984), and momentary emotional and motivational states (e.g., Carlsmith, Lepper, & Landauer, 1974). Instead of *unidirectional,* or one-way, influence from parents to children, influences in parent–child relationships are *bidirectional,* with each person influencing the other.

A striking example of bidirectional influence and its effects on parental management of children's behavior comes from a recent influential series of studies by Gerald Patterson (1982; Patterson & Reid, 1984). These studies were conducted with distressed families who had one child with notable behavior problems. Patterson and his colleagues observed the interactions in these families, carefully recording the actions of both parents and child. They then demonstrated that problematic, aversive behaviors by the child usually were followed by parental actions that simply encouraged a continuation of the child's problem behavior. Their evidence for this was presented in the form of conditional probabilities, or statistics that indicated the likelihood that certain parental behaviors would be followed by specific types of child actions. This statistical approach is described further in the appendix to this chapter.

402

An example will give you an idea of Patterson's findings. In one case, persistent whining by a child was usually followed by antagonistic behaviors by the mother, which produced more whining; whereas distracting or positive behaviors by the mother caused the whining to stop much more readily. Patterson was able to train mothers and fathers in these families to be more aware of their own responses to children's behaviors and to deliberately substitute reactions that terminated problem behaviors instead of the responses that had contributed to the problem. Patterson's findings illustrate both the effect of child on parent and parent on child.

Children's effects on the behavior of others has led some commentators to argue that children help to determine their own experiences. This is undoubtedly true, although it is a distortion of the research findings—and of logical principles, as well—to imply, for example, that children or adults are responsible for maltreatment by others toward them. The lesson of the research to date is that greater sensitivity to the influence of children on others can often be a useful avenue to improving the kinds of experiences that children encounter.

We now turn to another type of family relationship that has been found to have significant influences on children's development: relationships with siblings.

Sibling Relationships and Influences

For many children the family context includes brothers and sisters who, next to parents, exert among the strongest influences on their development. How can these relationships be described, and what are their influences in development?

Sibling Relationships. The aspect of sibling relationships that has typically received the most attention is that of rivalry and conflict. Recent research indicates, however, that more positive dimensions are also typical of most children's descriptions of their relationships with their sibling. Furman and Buhrmester (1985) conducted a factor analysis of questionnaire responses based on descriptive terms used by siblings in interviews about their relationships. They found that warmth and closeness and comments about the sibling's relative status or power, as well as conflict, were characteristic of relationships. Rivalry, as indicated by statements about parents' being partial to one sibling over the other, seemed to be a relatively minor part of most sibling relationships in this study.

Learning about sibling relationships is often difficult because there are so many different configurations of children in families. Indeed, sibling relationships and their influences vary with both the absolute and the relative ages of children, their birth order, and their gender. For example, older siblings are generally more domineering and aggressive in interactions with their brothers or sisters, and younger siblings are more compliant in these exchanges. At the same time, older siblings initiate more helpful, playful, and other prosocial behaviors than younger siblings do (Dunn, 1983). Generally speaking, relationships of siblings who are relatively close in age show more warmth and closeness than when siblings are further apart. The effects

403

of the age difference seem to diminish during the middle-childhood years, however (Vandell, Minnett, & Santrock, 1987).

Sibling Influences.   Siblings, even when quite young, can influence younger brothers or sisters. Lamb (1978a, 1978b) observed preschool children with younger siblings only a year old and found that for the infants, the older siblings were important objects of attention. They watched their older brothers or sisters, paid attention to the toys they were playing with, and if the opportunity arose for the infants to play with the toys, they tended to imitate the play actions of their older siblings. Frequently the preschoolers talked with their infant brothers or sisters and shared their toys. Lamb also found that preschool girls tended to be more attentive and nurturant to their younger siblings than did boys. In another study, Easterbrooks and Lamb (1979) examined the peer interactions of 1½-year-old infants who did or did not have older siblings. Reflecting their likely success in competing for toys with an older brother or sister, it was found that compared to infants without siblings, infants with older siblings were not as likely to attempt to take toys away from a peer or to get into disputes.

These findings indicate that siblings may serve many functions also served by parents. They may be attachment objects for their younger brothers and sisters and they may serve as behavioral models and teachers. Thus, different constellations of siblings not only affect the relationships that exist among the children in a family, but also make one family environment different from another. Thus, the number, ages, and spacing of siblings contributes to differences in family contexts; and even within the same family, these characteristics and the child's ordinal position in the sequence of children born to the family create different environments for each child.

In this section, we consider three aspects of differences among siblings: ordinal position (for example, whether they are first, last, or middle born), relative age and gender, and differences in parental attention.

First, the *ordinal position* of children among their siblings determines many of children's experiences in the family. Much of the research on the influence of siblings has focused on describing characteristic differences in first-born versus later-born children. Perhaps the most well-known generalization is that first-born children are more likely to be high achievers and leaders, are more likely to go to college, and often have higher IQ scores (Bradley, 1968). They have also been found to be more anxious and to be generally more conservative than later borns (Adams & Phillips, 1972; Breland, 1974). On the other hand, later-born children have been described as more popular with peers, flexible, tolerant, and autonomous or nonconforming.

The finding of achievement differences has been the focus of considerable analysis by psychologists. Zajonc and Markus (1975) have recently proposed a *confluence theory* to account for the effects of ordinal position on children's intellectual development. Since parents are likely to provide intellectual stimulation, larger families—especially those with a number of closely spaced, very young children (requiring much parental care)—dilute some of the

404

stimulation that parents might otherwise give. Furthermore, an older or first-born child surrounded by many younger siblings may not have the stimulating environment that a younger child with one or two older, and more verbal, siblings has. Figure 12-2 illustrates how the model looks when children's intelligence scores are plotted against their birth order in families of various sizes. Although the confluence model has been criticized and does not summarize all the family factors influencing intellectual development, it is a prominent example of how the number and ordinal position of children in the family might be molded into a broader theory of the impact of family interaction on children's development.

Second, *gender and relative age* of siblings affect a child's development. In classic research with two-child families, Koch (1955, 1956) examined four combinations of sibling sex: older brother-younger sister, older sister-younger brother, both brothers, or both sisters. Some of these sibling pairs were only 1 or 2 years apart in age, some were 2 to 4 years apart, and some were 5 or 6 years apart. Koch found that teachers rated children who had a brother as more enthusiastic, ambitious, and competitive than children whose sibling was a sister. Boys who had a brother younger by at least 4 years were more likely than other boys to be perceived as leaders, showing relatively more

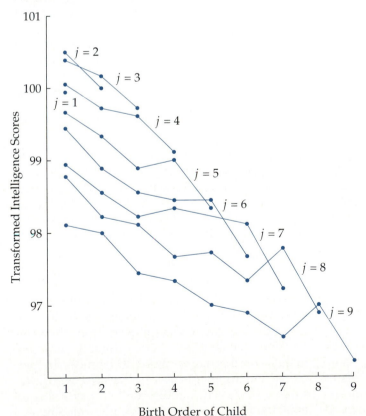

FIGURE 12-2

The relation of intelligence to a child's ordinal position within families of different sizes (j indicates the number of children in the family).

Source: from Zajonc & Markus, 1975.

405

RESEARCH FOCUS 12-1

"Nonshared" Environments in Families

In the longstanding debate over nature versus nurture in determining children's personality and social behaviors, "nurture" has typically been considered to mean children's experiences in the family. Most often, children from the same family have been assumed to share the same environment. Consequently, when studies have shown that adopted children's characteristics are often dissimilar to the characteristics of the biological children of their adoptive parents, the conclusion has been that family environment plays little role in individual development. At the same time, comparisons of identical and fraternal twins (see Chapter 9) indicate that 50% or less of the differences in personality among individuals can be attributed to genetic factors (Plomin, 1989). What then accounts for the differences among persons that are not attributable to genetic factors or common family environments?

Psychologists David Rowe and Robert Plomin (1981), both experts on developmental behavior genetics, have proposed that the unexplained influences come from differences in children's experiences that are not typically assessed in studies of genetic versus environmental influences. After all, children's environments encompass many different features: their neighborhoods, their living accommodations, the childrearing techniques of their parents, typical experiences with their brothers and sisters, characteristics of their peer group, physical and social conditions encountered in school, and so forth. Even siblings living in the same household will have different experiences in many of these aspects of their daily lives. Rowe and Plomin argue that these *nonshared environmental influences* are the environmental forces that are important in producing *differences* among children. Consequently, instead of simply assuming that children have similar environments because they have the same parents and live in the same house, students of development should look more carefully at aspects of their environments that may expose them to different experiences.

Rowe and Plomin suggested that sibling differences could arise from several sources. One is that siblings may have different teachers and almost certainly are exposed to different peer-group influences. Another is that accidental factors, such as injury, illness, or prenatal exposure to harmful substances (see Chapter 3), could be different between children. Even aspects of family life can be different. Being a first- versus later-born child is itself a source of a variety of different experiences for siblings, and whether children are close or far apart in age also affects the similarity of their experiences. Parents may treat children differently, consciously or unconsciously favoring one over the other or finding one easier to manage than the other. All of these environmental factors are relevant to assessing the impact of nurture on children's development, but they are not ordinarily considered in behavior–genetic studies. From this viewpoint, even identical twins who had different teachers, joined different organizations, or pursued different activities would not be presumed to share identical environments.

To illustrate the potential impact of sibling differences, Plomin, together with several colleagues (Daniels, Dunn, Furstenberg, & Plomin, 1985), studied 348 pairs of 11- through 16-year-old siblings throughout the United States. They obtained reports of each adolescent's typical experiences in school and in his or her interactions with parents, siblings, and peers. In addition, they also asked the mothers of these siblings to report on their perceptions of each of their childrens' experiences.

Both the adolescent's own descriptions of their lives and their mothers' perceptions of their experiences indicated that children from the same families encountered very different environments. Furthermore, these differences in perceived environments were correlated with measures of each adolescent's psychological adjustments. More psychologically well-adjusted adolescents also experienced more maternal closeness, more friendliness in interactions with siblings and peers, and more influence in family decisions. Although these findings do not indicate that different environments *caused* different degrees of psychological adjustment, the correlation between the two does indicate that a variety of aspects of experiences should be considered in assessing the role of environments in individual development.

---

responsibility yet being less aggressive; whereas older brothers with sisters had better social skills and were seen as having good rapport with opposite sex peers and with adults. For girls with older siblings, there seemed to be many modeling effects: girls with an older brother were less conforming and often more like tomboys, whereas those with an older sister were more conforming, socially outgoing, and less independent—characteristics that may be interpreted as feminine sex typed. Koch also found the older children whose siblings were not a great deal younger tended to achieve but not to show the higher IQ often attributed to first-born children.

Third, *differences in amount of parental attention* to siblings of different ages may also contribute to environmental differences within the family. Consistent with the ideas of Zajonc and Markus, parents who have more than one child to care for may "dilute" the attention given to each. Younger siblings provide opportunities for older siblings to join in caretaking, while older siblings potentially increase the number of caregivers offering attention to younger ones. *Any* sibling, however, provides the opportunity to compete for resources and attention.

Observational studies have shown that parents do interact differently with various children in the family. Dunn and Kendrick found that a year after the birth of a second child mothers appear to change the way they play with their first-born girls, reducing the amount of time involved significantly (Dunn & Kendrick, 1979, 1980). Baskett (1984) found that in the presence of

Siblings may often provide parent-like assistance to younger, less able children in the family.

their parents and brothers and sisters, oldest children interacted more with parents than with their siblings, whereas youngest siblings divided their interaction between parents and older siblings. She also found that the age and ordinal position of children did not influence the degree to which parents and siblings treated them positively, but older siblings were more likely to receive negative as well as positive responses from parents and siblings.

Clearly, then, both parents and other children in a family are influenced by a child's ordinal position, relative age, and gender. Different children in the same family are likely to be treated quite differently by parents and by their brothers and sisters and apparently, as a result, these children develop characteristically different behavior patterns.

The Family as a System

The family can be viewed as a system of interrelated influences among fathers, mothers, children, siblings, and any members of the extended family who may be present (grandparents, aunts, uncles, and so on). For example, the relationship between husband and wife can influence the relationship of the child with both parents; and the relationship of mother with infant can affect the emotional nature of the husband–wife relationship.

Developmental psychologists have observed these effects on one pair of family members by studying the effect of changes in the composition of families. By comparing the husband–wife relationship before and after the birth of the first child, for instance, it is documented that whether the marital relationship is loving and supportive before the birth affects the degree and the quality of involvement of both parents with the new baby (Belsky, Rovine, & Fish, 1989). A similar technique has been used in studying another transition: the birth of a second child, as it affects the relationship between the mother and first-born child. Feiring, Lewis, & Jaskir (1983) compared the changes in mother–first child relationships beween 12 and 24 months in families into which a second child had been born during the year and families in which a birth did not occur. They found that children with a sibling showed more dependency on the mother and more emotional upset during free play than children without a sibling.

These findings emphasize that both individuals and social relationships are affected by the influences of other persons. Children grow up in a network of persons and relationships that affect each other in sometimes subtle ways. For example, fathers with marital difficulties are more preemptory and intrusive than other fathers when teaching simple tasks to their children, whereas maritally distressed mothers are somewhat more engaged and effective in teaching their children than nondistressed mothers (Brody, Pillegrini, & Sigel, 1987). Although the reasons for the differences are not altogether clear, patterns such as these indicate that understanding relationships within a family is a very important part of understanding the child's social world.

Stresses in Family Relationships

The final quarter of the twentieth century has been a time of dramatic social change for families. Changes in marriage patterns, childbearing, divorce, labor force participation by both parents, and the increasing numbers of families living in economic and social disadvantage are examples of circumstances that affect greater numbers of families than in previous years. There are indications that further changes can be expected by the year 2000 (Cherlin, 1988). From the perspective of social and personality development, these changes raise many questions about the impact of family stresses on children's relationships and development. In this section, we examine two instances of changes in families: the increases in divorce and remarriage, and the increasing incidence of family violence.

Divorce and Remarriage. For the majority of children in the United States, there is not *a* single family context over the course of their childhood and teenage years. Instead, most children experience multiple family contexts. During the 1970s and 1980s particularly, the rate of change and problems in families increased substantially. In the mid-1980s, about 1.1 million children under 18 experienced parents' divorces each year (U.S. Department of Education, 1988).

The effects of divorce are difficult to assess, because divorce often follows a period of great stress in the family and because it can be associated with continued hostility that affects how each parent behaves toward the children. In addition, when a parent leaves, there may be a period of economic difficulties and other pressures. All of these stresses can affect children's emotional well-being and their behavior and adjustment in situations outside of the family, including school. Most studies indicate that the 2-year period following divorce is especially difficult for children. Assuming that the mother has custody of the children, this period is especially difficult for mothers and their sons. Even beyond the 2-year adjustment period, sons show more negative resistant behavior toward their mothers, and mothers show more nagging, angry, and coercive behaviors toward their sons than mothers and sons in nondivorced families (Hetherington, Stanley-Hagan, & Anderson, 1989). If divorce occurs when the children are in the preadolescent years, there are negative effects on mothers' relationships with both sons and daughters (Dornbusch, Ritter, Leiderman, Roberts, & Fraleigh, 1987; Wallerstein, Corbin, & Lewis, 1988).

Remarriage also affects parents' relationships with sons and daughters differently. If mothers and children have passed the 2-year adjustment period and then enter a new marriage, the effect is often positive for sons, perhaps because they appreciate having an adult male in residence. Remarriage appears to be especially difficult for girls, however. Both mothers and stepfathers have generally reported more positive relationships with sons than daughters after remarriage (Clingempeel, Brand, & Sevoli, 1984).

Much is yet to be learned about the effects of divorce and remarriage on children's behavior and development. For example, we do not have good information about the adjustment of children and the effect on parent–child relationships when fathers have custody or when there is joint custody. What is clear, however, is that adjustment to both divorce and remarriage—although rarely easy—occurs more smoothly when both parents and stepparents have mature, responsible attitudes toward each other and toward the children.

409

Family Violence. In the past 25 years concern over the abuse of children has increased substantially. This began with the publication of an article proposing a diagnostic label, "battered child syndrome," that alerted physicians and others to injuries that did not seem reasonably attributable to incidental, unavoidable accidents around the house or on the playground (Kempe, Silverman, Steele, Droegemueller, & Silver, 1962). About 1 million cases of child abuse are reported each year, although many more than that undoubtedly occur (American Humane Association, 1984). The actual frequency of child abuse incidents is difficult to estimate. Increasing reports of child abuse may indicate only that people have become more aware of the problem.

Most research on child abuse has focused on characteristics of the adults who commit abuse, rather than on characteristics of the abused child. Among adults, factors contributing to abuse are immaturity and a lack of understanding of children, plus an undue readiness to use punishment as a form of discipline (deLissovoy, 1973; Steele, 1975). For example, an infant who cries persistently is a trial for any parent, but for parents who do not understand the reasons an infant cries or who attribute the crying to retaliation or malevolence on the child's part may find the crying intolerable. Similarly, adults who have unrealistic notions of what an infant or young child is capable of (for example, in terms of self-control) or who are disappointed when their unrealistically high expectations for the child are unfulfilled are also at risk of becoming abusive (Bugental, Blue, & Cruzcosa, 1989; Terr, 1970).

Abusing parents also tend to have low self-esteem and to be socially isolated from the support of relatives or friends, who can ease some of the burdens associated with child rearing (Steele, 1975). Under stress, abusive mothers have been found to be more defensive, more anxious, more aggressive, and less intelligent than mothers whose care for their children was rated "excellent" (Egeland, Breitenbucher & Rosenberg, 1980).

In November 1987, Lisa Steinberg, aged 6, died from severe beatings inflicted by her adoptive father. Her death was a critical case that made the public more aware of the problem of child abuse.

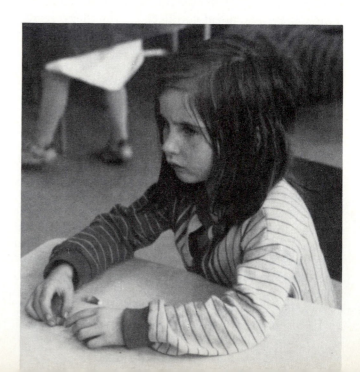

A major concern about child abuse is that abuse may beget abuse. Parents who were themselves abused are more likely than others to abuse their own offspring. However, a substantial number of persons with histories of maltreatment do *not* become abusive toward their own children (Belsky & Pensky, 1988; Kaufman & Zigler, 1987). One important factor in breaking the "cycle of abuse" is social support to the victim of abuse. In childhood that support may come from having one parent who was not maltreating and who ameliorated the negative effects of the other parent's abusiveness. In adulthood, support may come from a spouse or other adults (Egeland, Jacobvitz, & Sroufe, 1989).

In thinking about the implications of abusive parent–child relationships, it is important to remember that clear signs of abuse, like physical injury, may be only one aspect of more generally maladaptive or disordered parent–child relations in abusing families. For example, toddlers from abusing families are much more likely to show disturbances in attachment to their mothers than are children from nonabusing families, and their patterns of attachment are not stable from one assessment to the next (Egeland & Sroufe, 1981). As an example, Bee and her colleagues provided a setting in which parents were to teach their children a simple task (Bee, Disbrow, Johnson-Crowley, & Bernard, 1981). Compared to nonabusing parents and their children, abusing parents were generally less sensitive to their children. These parents did not respond well to cues from the child (for example, questioning looks), they behaved in other ways that were emotionally disruptive, and they failed to support the children's cognitive efforts at the task. Older maltreated children also experience more negative, punitive, and conflictual family environments than do other children (e.g., Patterson & Bank, 1989; Trickett & Kuczynski, 1986).

The principle of bidirectionality in parent–child relationships has raised a question about how children's characteristics and actions may increase the likelihood that they will be abused. In the study by Bee and her colleagues, for example, mothers of abused children proved to be poor teachers, but the abused children gave less clear cues to their mothers and were somewhat more unresponsive in general than nonabused children (Bee et al., 1981). When parents are asked to describe their children, abused children are frequently described as irritable, clinging, restless, hyperaggressive, annoying, and as crying a great deal (Ounsted, Oppenheimer & Lindsay, 1974; Milow & Lourie, 1964; Gil, 1971; deLissovoy, 1973).

It may be the case that abusing parents' perceptions of their children are distorted. Indeed, Frodi and Lamb (1980) found that abusive parents react aversively to smiling, friendly babies, suggesting that abused children may not have behaved differently from nonabused infants at the outset. It is also possible that children who have suffered abuse do behave differently from nonabused children, contributing—at least in some small part—to their continuing to be abused. The behavioral differences themselves may arise from the experience of being abused. For example, the lack of clarity and responsiveness observed in the abused children in Bee's study reflects the uncertainty and confusion that might arise naturally in children who must constantly deal with erratic, extremely reactive parents.

The family context may be even more important to the development of children today than it was a quarter century ago. As the society has grown increasingly urban and complex, the once substantial role of the community has been diminished and relationships with parents, siblings, and a relatively small number of nonfamily adults and peers have become the most common sources of children's relationships and influences. When these relationships are disrupted, children may be at particularly great risk. The study of children in family context, therefore, is especially important in understanding the nature and course of children's social and personality development today.

The School Context

Next to family, school is the most common context of children's lives. It has been estimated that children spend as many as 15,000 hours in school between the time of entrance at around age 6 and graduation from high school (Rutter, Maughan, Mortimore, Ouston, & Smith, 1979). This is almost as much time as they spend at home. Furthermore, the ecology of schools requires children to master a wide variety of knowledge and skills that are not ordinarily demanded by family life. Although teachers serve many of the same functions that parents do, they lack the history and the emotional investment that usually characterize parent–child relationships, and there are fewer common bases on which to build relations with other children than there are in families or even in neighborhoods. As children grow, the school environment becomes increasingly complex. In elementary school the social field that children must master is the classroom, and most interactions are with only one teacher. In the later grades the entire school is the social field, and there are multiple teachers, classrooms, and common spaces (Minuchin & Shapiro, 1983).

Because the purpose of schooling is to convey knowledge that contributes to problem solving and achievement for everyone, the most common questions have to do with the characteristics of school settings that contribute to effective learning by students (e.g., Sizer, 1984). Schools also affect children's social and personality development. In the words of a recent essay on the future of schooling:

> School is a place where children develop or fail to develop a variety of competencies that come to define self and ability, where friendships with peers are nurtured, and where the role of the community member is played out, all during a highly formative period of development. Thus, the building of self-esteem, interpersonal competence, social–problem–solving skills, responsibility, and leadership becomes important both in its own right and as a critical underpinning of success in academic learning (Linney & Seidman, 1989, p. 1095).

In this section, our primary focus is schools as a *social* context for psychological development. We will first examine the characteristics of school contexts that affect children's learning, because academic mastery is an important ingredient of social and personality development. Then we will examine how school characteristics and academic success or failure affect the social and emotional development of children and adolescents.

A primary question in assessing the school context is whether schools effectively promote learning. Some compelling evidence indicates that schools can and often do make a difference in how well their students master academic subjects. For example, comparisons among schools serving very similar populations of students often have very different levels of student achievement, thus implying that some schools are more successful than others in promoting learning (Brookover, Beady, Flood, Schweitzer, & Wisenbaker, 1979; Rutter, Maughan, Mortimore, Ouston, & Smith, 1979). Although earlier surveys (e.g., Coleman, 1966; Jencks, et al., 1972) had contended that variations in school characteristics, such as size and available resources, made little differences in student achievement, later studies of school concentrated on a wider range of possible factors in whether or not students were academically successful. Consequently, it is now possible to point to several aspects of a school's *ecology* that contribute to student achievement. The most important of these are school size, classroom organization of learning activities, teacher behavior, and the school "ethos" or atmosphere related to academic achievement.

School Size. Schools in the United States vary greatly in size. Elementary grade students in rural areas are likely to attend relatively small, compact schools, whereas both elementary and secondary students in urban areas may attend schools with enrollments in the thousands. In general, the larger the school, the lower the average achievement of students (Barker & Gump, 1964; Glass, Cohen, Smith, & Filby, 1982). One reason for this is that large schools tend to have fewer opportunities for involvement in extracurricular activities, student government, and so forth, so that levels of alienation are higher than in smaller schools. Many large schools, however, have been successful in overcoming this problem by creating small learning communities within their schools. These "schools within schools" (Boyer, 1983; Goodlad, 1984) seem to help reduce behavior problems and school dropouts, as well as increasing learning.

Classroom Organization for Learning. Most schools make an effort to organize classroom instruction in a way that will maximize the achievement of individual students. One widely used method has been grouping students according to ability levels ("streaming" or "tracking") as opposed to placing them in more heterogeneous, mixed-ability classrooms. There is little evidence that, overall, children's average academic attainment levels are affected by tracking (Jencks et al., 1972). Furthermore, when attention is turned not to academic attainments, but to children's social attitudes and behavior, there is some evidence that "streaming" has negative effects, with children placed in groups of low ability quickly being labelled "failures" by other children and coming to see themselves in a negative light (Hargreaves, 1967).

413

Working together on classroom projects has been found to promote positive attitudes toward members of different racial groups.

In recent years, a method of classroom organization that emphasizes the importance of small-group cooperation on academic tasks has been found to produce greater learning outcomes for students (Johnson, Maruyama, Johnson, Nelson, & Skon, 1981; Slavin, 1983, 1987). Called *cooperative learning*, this method requires students to work together on classroom assignments and to prepare reports in common. Cooperative learning activities are most successful in increasing learning when both groups and individuals are rewarded for good work. In addition to academic benefits, this method of classroom organization has also been found to improve social relations, particularly across racial lines. It also has been associated with improvements in self-esteem for mainstreamed handicapped students (Slavin, 1983).

Teachers' Behavior. Ask parents about their children's school experiences and the qualities of the teacher will almost certainly be among the first things mentioned. For example, they may mention the teacher's personality or style of interacting with children, how "hard" or "easy" the teacher is, or how innovative or traditional the teaching methods are. Most research findings indicate that teachers' personalities are less important than what they do in the classroom. Although teacher behavior is quite complex, teachers seem to be most successful in helping students to learn when they provide assignments that require active, personal involvement with the material to be learned, communicate high expectancies for students' performance, and consistently give high priority to academic objectives in deciding how classroom time is spent and how the classroom is managed (Brophy, 1986). In general, effective teaching involves moving students through material briskly, but dividing the material into small enough steps that all students can master each step along the way. Each teacher may accomplish these goals differently. The goals themselves, however, are at the heart of successful teaching.

The question of whether teacher expectations about students' ability to master the material sometimes interferes with student learning has attracted a great deal of interest and concern for more than two decades. The concern was born out of the charge that teachers may, unintentionally, interact with and evaluate students differently depending on the teachers' beliefs about whether the student is likely to perform well on academic tasks. For example, Rosenthal and Jacobson (1968) randomly selected certain youngsters in a

414

classroom and informed the teachers that the children had previously shown on tests that they were unusually capable and should make significant gains in intellectual attainments over the next several years. Although these students were no more intelligent or promising than their classmates, the researchers found that the students for whom great expectations had been created in the teachers' eyes actually showed better intellectual gains than would otherwise have been expected. A number of other studies have found that teachers do not necessarily accept test-feedback as indicative of capabilities they do not truly believe a student possesses, trusting their own experience with the student instead (e.g. Pilling & Pringle, 1978).

At the same time, there is evidence that teachers' expectancies do affect their treatment of children in the classroom, and these differences might contribute to eventual differences in academic success. For example, high achievers are often selected for class participation more often, are given more time to respond to teachers' questions, and receive more praise and less criticism than low achievers (Cooper, 1979; Good, 1980). The effect of differences in teachers' treatment of boys and girls in classrooms will be discussed further in Chapter 14, with special emphasis on the implications for male–female differences in academic orientation.

School "Ethos." No matter whether schools are large or small, involve ability "tracking" or not, or have teachers that vary considerably in how they manage their classrooms, an almost overriding factor in whether students learn is the *ethos* of the school. This term refers to the values that characterize the school, particularly in the degree to which there is common agreement among faculty and staff members that the main business of the school is fostering academic achievement. In addition, ethos incorporates the way students are treated and the characteristics of the school as a learning environment.

An example of the role of ethos in promoting student learning comes from a 3-year longitudinal study of 12 secondary schools in inner-city London (Rutter et al., 1979). The investigators assessed characteristics of the students before they entered, tracked the students' performances while they were enrolled in the various schools, and attempted to characterize the schools on dimensions that were relevant to the educational process. Although the schools were in the same area of the city, there were sizable differences from one school to another in students' attendance, delinquency rates, success on Britain's mandatory public examinations, and even the degree to which students tended to stay beyond normal school hours. Different schools clearly produced different levels of students' achievements, even when students' family backgrounds and personal characteristics prior to school entry were statistically controlled.

What were the factors that promoted good or poor student outcomes? Most surprising were the factors *not* related to school effectiveness: the size of the school or the age of buildings and equipment and different kinds of administrative organization did not predict how students performed. What did seem to have an effect were the elements of *ethos* that we described

415

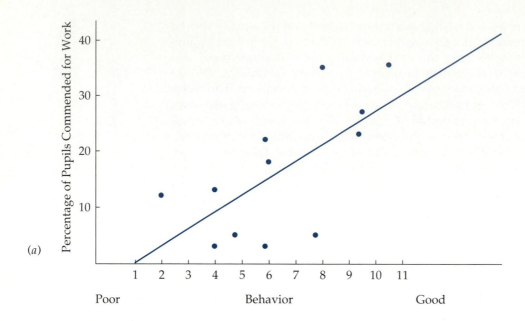

(a)

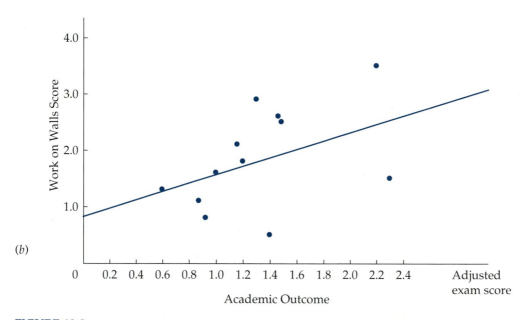

(b)

FIGURE 12-3

The relation between the use of praise for students' good work in different schools and the students' behavior and academic outcomes. The dots in circles represent where each of the 12 schools fell in terms of praise given and the quality of students' behavior or academic outcome.

Source: from Rutter, Maughan, Mortimore, & Ouston, 1979.

earlier. If the school had a strong academic emphasis and if teachers used praise and provided incentives for good work, allowed children to take on responsibilities within the classroom, and spent time interacting with students, average academic achievement in the school was higher than if these qualities were not as apparent. In general, schools tended to rate either "good" or "poor" on both academic and social outcomes. Schools with relatively low delinquency rates, for example also tended to be better in terms of students' successes on the public examinations, and so forth. Figure 12-3, for example, indicates that students behaved better and did better academically in schools where teachers used frequent and public praise for good work or posted good work for others to see. These findings imply that it is the character of the school and the classroom as a social environment for learning that influences educational outcome.

This brief overview highlights an important point about the relation between the effectiveness of schools in cognitive and in social development: School characteristics that contribute to academic effectiveness also tend to have important social benefits as well. The benefits are undoubtedly reciprocal in nature. When students have a feeling of academic mastery and find academic tasks enjoyable and motivating, they are likely to adjust better socially; and when social conditions are perceived positively, students are more likely to respond attentively and enthusiastically to learning assignments. We now turn to some ways in which schools specifically affect social and personality development.

In the United States schools are expected not only to provide basic intellectual skills, but also to help achieve certain social goals, such as preparing students to interact effectively with the diversity of persons who comprise U.S. society. Three major aspects of social and personality development in schools have been given special attention: the effects of schools on individual students' characteristics; the effects of curricula designed to promote moral and effective development; and the effects of schools on interpersonal relations of students.

Social and Emotional Development in Schools

Effects on Individual Development.   Self-concept, including self-esteem, have been two important concerns of parents and educators for several decades (Minuchin & Shapiro, 1983). How children feel about themselves and their abilities has been found to affect their self-confidence and their actual performance on tasks of many different kinds, regardless of actual ability (Dweck, 1986). Academic experiences in school are an important determinant of children's perceived competence (e.g., Harter & Connell, 1982; Rubin, Maruyama, & Kingsbury, 1979). Consequently, children's experiences in schools, where most information about academic competence is encountered, are likely to be one important determinant of self-esteem.

One possible factor in whether children perceive themselves as competent is the degree to which they tend to persist in academic tasks until success occurs. Many children experience failures and, thus, low academic self-esteem because they attribute academic failures to lack of ability or some

RESEARCH FOCUS 12-2

Early Education and Later Success: Economic Perspectives

Questions about the effectiveness of educational programs have touched every level of education in the United States. One striking example has been evaluations of the impact of preschool cognitive enrichment programs, especially their effectiveness for disadvantaged children. These are children who are at risk for poor school performance in later years, for behavior problems and delinquency, and for eventual economic disadvantage in adulthood. In addition to humanitarian concern about the welfare of children with these prospects in life, from a societal viewpoint the costs of remediation, incarceration, and social welfare payments to such individuals are a sizable burden on public funds. Are, then, early interventions to help prepare children for school success a profitable investment in the future well-being and self-sufficiency of disadvantaged children?

Many studies suggest that they are. In one major overview of research findings on the effectiveness of preschool-intervention programs (Lazar & Darlington, 1976), the results of 12 large-scale evaluation studies were compiled. The question was whether disadvantaged children who had attended preschool programs did better in school than similar children who did not have this early opportunity. These studies consistently showed that the preschool program children were less likely to be retained a grade during elementary school; they were also less likely to be placed in special education classes. There is little evidence, however, that there is a consistent advantage for preschool attendees on intelligence tests beyond the early years of schooling. Some experts believe this means that, for children from disadvantaged homes, preschool classes are too little, too late; others believe that the problems lies in too little special attention to such children and their families to reinforce the early benefits of preschool. Nevertheless, the evidence that special education placement and having to repeat grades are lower for children who went to preschool than for those who did not is one sign of the economic value of early education programs.

Other evidence that preschool programs for disadvantaged children pay off economically comes from longitudinal results reported by one group of early educators working at High/Scope Educational Research Foundation in Ypsilanti, Michigan (Weikart, 1983). In their longitudinal projects, disadvantaged children were randomly chosen either to attend structured preschool programs or not to do so. Of those who attended preschool, some had structured curricula that emphasized cognitive development, others had curricula focused on language abilities, and still others had structured programs that emphasized socioemotional growth rather than academic skills. Like the majority of studies on the effectiveness of early programs, the preschool attendees in these projects stayed in school and did better in school than children who did not attend preschool. The type of curriculum to which they were exposed made little difference: attending preschool was the important factor. Beyond these schooling effects, however, the Ypsilanti studies showed long-term effects of early education programs on the personal and social adaptation of disadvantaged children and on their ability to assume financial responsibility for themselves and their families. Preschool attendees generally had lower delinquency rates, resulting in savings for crime victims and in police and court costs. There were fewer welfare payments and other social services to the former attendees, and the attendees earned higher incomes than those who had not attended. In the words of High/Scope's director, Dr. David Weikart:

> The benefits of our preschool education program far outweigh its costs. The benefits included were reduced costs of education, improved future wage earnings, and the value of time while the child was in preschool. The undiscounted benefits of

two years of preschool education (in 1979 dollars) totalled $14,819 per child against the actual two-year program cost of $5,984 per child ($2,992 per year)—a 248% return on the original investment. The internal rate of return . . . (a discount rate which indicates the average earning power of the investment . . .) showed that investment in preschool education was equivalent to an investment receiving 3.7% interest after inflation over several decades (Weikart, 1983, p. 182). ❧

---

other cause that cannot be changed (Dweck, 1986). As we discussed in Chapter 10, interventions have been successful in helping children persist in spite of initial failures. For example, children who tended to give up in the face of difficult math problems were helped by training that encouraged them to view problems as tasks that could be mastered through continued effort. Such persistence may eventually contribute to greater feelings of self-esteem about academic performance.

Because schools are primarily middle-class institutions staffed by middle-class teachers and administrators, children from different social classes and from racial and ethnic minority groups may be particularly likely to not achieve academic successes that would give them the feelings of competence that bolster self-esteem (Rioux, 1968). There is some evidence that teachers assume that middle-class students are more likely to perform well and treat them accordingly (Rist, 1970). Furthermore, parents from lower socioeconomic groups tend to value and encourage conformity and passivity, whereas middle-class parents emphasize self-control and self-direction (Kohn, 1976). Presumably, middle-class teachers' responses to students are shaped by the same values as those of middle-class parents and thus often conflict with the standards to which students from non–middle-class families have been accustomed. The different cultural values and rules of conventional interactions in families of racial and ethnic minority families may produce similar mismatches for students.

The link between school success and self-esteem has led some educators to hope that, by intervening to improve self-esteem generally, children's school performance could be improved. In general, however, efforts to improve self-esteem as a means of improving academic performance have been unsuccessful (Harter, 1983). Apparently, children's sense of themselves as competent in academic endeavors needs to be tied to specific success experiences in learning, not success experiences generally.

Effects of Social Curricula. In addition to the naturally occurring, often unintended effects of school experiences on affective development, formal curricula have sometimes been primarily directed at social development to achieve, indirectly, improved learning and achievement as well. A good example is affective education, whose goals include the clarification of values, a focus on humanism, fostering a sensitivity to group dynamics, or developing sensitivity to the emotions of others (Allender, 1982; Lockwood, 1978). By improving students' capacity for empathic responsiveness, educators hope to reduce aggression and promote prosocial, cooperative interactions,

419

which in turn may reduce the contentious exchanges that disrupt learning in schools.

One program, the Empathy Training Project, includes a set of activities to foster children's emotional responsiveness, their ability to recognize others' emotions, and their capacity to take the perspective of others (Feshbach, 1979). In an initial trial of this program, the curriculum was introduced into an elementary school attended by children from several ethnic backgrounds (white, black, Mexican American). After several weeks, children in the program showed less aggression than children who had not studied the curriculum. The children who showed the largest increases in prosocial behavior and decreases in aggression also had significant gains in cognitive performance.

Findings such as these suggest that some aspects of social skills can be integrated into a formal instructional program with advantages for social and cognitive development alike. Although there have been some large-scale implementations of affect education programs (e.g., Newberg, 1980), evaluations are only preliminary at this point, and it is probably premature to conclude that affect education programs are appropriate as part of the standard curriculum for all children.

Effects on Interpersonal Relations.   For most children, school provides the first opportunity to come into contact with children from a wide variety of social backgrounds. Many of the development benefits of interactions with other children at school will be discussed in Chapter 13. In this section, we will emphasize the specific effect of the school context on relations with children of different racial groups.

The racial composition of most schools in the United States tended to be relatively homogeneous until the 1954 Supreme Court decision outlawing segregation on the argument that separate schools for children of different races were inherently unequal (*Brown* v. *Board of Education of Topeka*, 1954). The Court's decision was among the first to be partly influenced by testimony from behavioral scientists about the consequences of segregated schooling on children and the implications of the decision for school contexts; their developmental effects have continued to be studied extensively (Bell, 1980; Friedman, Meltzer & Miller, 1979; Harris, Jackson & Rydingsword, 1975; Hughes, Gordon & Hillman, 1980; St. John, 1975; Stephan & Feagin, 1980).

Perhaps the most basic expectation about the effects was that desegregated schools would reduce racial stereotyping and promote intergroup relations among children of different races. In 1954, the same year as the Supreme Court decision on desegregation, psychologist Gordon Allport suggested that these goals would be fostered by long-term contact between members of the different groups, institutional rules and sanctions promoting contact and decrying hostility or stereotyped attitudes and behavior, and the establishment of mechanisms to assign equal status to the groups and link them in the pursuit of shared goals. Experience with desegregation has shown that merely assuring that the statistical composition of a student body is racially mixed does not itself accomplish this purpose (Amir, 1976; Carithers, 1970;

Minuchin & Shapiro, 1984; St. John, 1975; Schofield, 1978). Rather, supportive teachers and principals and active changes in teaching practices and content are essential parts of the process. For example, Epstein (1980) found that positive attitudes about members of another race are fostered by such devices as having groups of children of different races work on a school project together or participate on a sports team. There is also some evidence that curricula that promote the concept of equal racial status are effective (Epstein, 1980), although there is some disagreement about the success of multiethnic textbooks, formal discussions about race relations, or courses on minority history (Forehand, Ragosta & Rock, 1976; Slavin & Madden, 1979).

Attention to factors within schools is important because *de facto* segregation can occur intentionally or unintentionally through school organization and procedures. For example, ability tracking systems within a school may *rese*-gregate students if minority children whose past education or family background has ill prepared them for school are generally lumped into a single track (Epstein, 1980; Rist, 1970, 1978, 1979; Rosenbaum, 1978). Consider what happened shortly after integration via the establishment of one magnet junior high school set in a black neighborhood (Rosenbaum and Presser, 1978). Although the school began with a 70% white/30% black balance, children distributed themselves in a racially different fashion within the various specialty courses. The math and science courses in particular were overwhelmingly enrolled with white children. Even though there was no formal tracking system the teachers felt forced to establish an informal one within classes where the minority students were not as well prepared or grounded in the relevant material. Thus, children of one race within the same school may receive a very different educational experience from that enjoyed by other children, and there may be little interaction or contact between children of different racial backgrounds despite the fact that the school appears integrated in terms of its overall racial composition. This may be less likely when ability grouping specifically includes both races (Hallinan & Teixeira, 1987).

One possible effect of desegregation that has been studied with special interest is its impact on children's self-concepts. The general expectation was that minority children would develop a more positive self-concept from being in a desegregated school, on the grounds that attending a racially segregated school promoted feelings of exclusion and reduced worth. Overall, the hypothesis that integration, in and of itself, promotes high or improved self-concepts among minority children has been only weakly supported (St. John, 1975; Minuchin & Shapiro, 1983). There is some indication, however, that the self-esteem of minority students is enhanced if the segregated school has a high proportion of white students (Coleman, Campbell, Hobson, McPartland, Mood, Weinfeld & York, 1966). This effect may be especially likely if children enter integrated schools early in their educational experience (McPartland, 1968).

The goals of the massive changes in U.S. schools brought about by desegregation have been met to some degree, despite a few instances where the contribution of desegregated educational experience has been negative for children. Apparently, although Allport's (1954) proposals sounded simple, they have been more difficult to achieve in practice (Minuchin & Shapiro, 1983).

The Interaction of Family and School Contexts

Children live in families and go to school as well, so their development is inevitably influenced by both contexts interacting. A good illustration of how the family context may mediate the effects from schooling may be seen in research on the effects of congruence between home and school. Children express more satisfaction with school when the authority structure of classrooms is similar to the authority practices they encounter at home (Epstein, 1983). Authoritative parenting, as described in Baumrind's categories, tends to be associated with higher school grades than authoritarian or permissive parent styles (Dornbusch, Ritter, Leiderman, Roberts, & Fraleigh, 1987). Parents' involvement with schools and with children's school-related tasks is also positively correlated with children's school performance (Stevenson & Baker, 1987).

Family perturbations, such as divorce, are also linked to children's school lives. In the first year or two after a divorce, children from one-parent families have been found to be similar to children of two-parent families in their academic aptitude or tested intellectual ability, but they tend to be absent from school more often, study less effectively, and be more disruptive in the classroom (Hetherington, Camara, & Featherman, 1982). At least at first, then, children from single-parent families tend to do less well, achieving lower grades and being perceived by teachers as less effective in the academic setting. In the preschool setting, children from single-parent families resulting from divorce showed not only disturbed social relations with other children, but also were seen by teachers as different in their general social behavior. Girls were seen to be more dependent, and boys were perceived as more aggressive and less able to maintain attention and effort at assigned tasks—and in general as less academically competent (Hetherington, Cox, & Cox, 1979, 1982). On the other hand, children from divorced families may derive emotional support from the school setting (Wallerstein & Kelly, 1980). Especially for older children, the predictability of schedules, expectations for task completion, and the regularity of peer (and adult) contacts may assist their adjustment to the changes in the family context that result from the divorce of parents.

Unfortunately, school personnel are not always sufficiently apprised of the family status for a particular student, something that would allow them to be sensitive to a child's needs or to the family foundation from which he or she approaches the school context and the content of educational materials. Obviously, it is difficult to deal with the range of ways that a child's family context influences his or her performance in and reactions to school, but the interaction still exists. Consider, for example, children from a single-parent family, living with their remarried father, who must come home with instructions for a school assembly where mothers and daughters are expected to

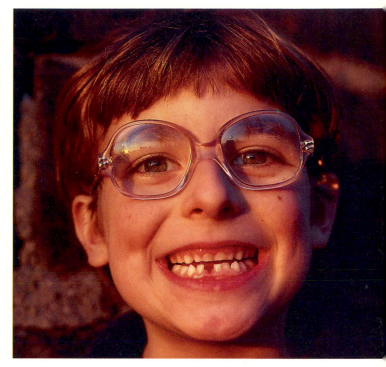

Social and Cognitive Development in Childhood

Childhood, though often spoken of as a single period, encompasses
both preschoolers and preadolescents. The developmental terrain of
childhood is vast. Physical growth and the acquisition of motor and
cognitive skills accounts for many of the changes between the ages of
3 and 12 years, but perhaps as significant is the widening world to
which children are exposed during these years.

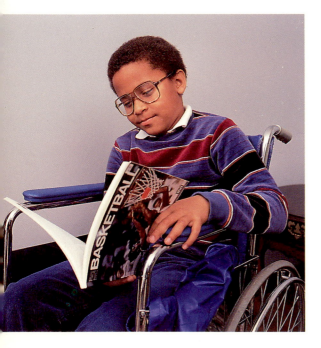

From an environment bounded largely by home or some other care setting, children move on to school and to a greater number and variety of different settings than they have known before.

From a social world dominated by caregiving and adult direction, children move into a world in which they must negotiate their own social arrangements and coordinate their own actions and goals with the actions and goals of others. To make these transitions children must acquire an understanding of others, an appreciation of diverse personal characteristics, and a recognition of responsibilities beyond the gratification of their own needs.

participate together. Consider, on the other hand, how difficult it would be for a large school system to implement procedures that would be sensitive to such individual differences in children's family constellations.

It is important to note also that children who need the support of adults may nevertheless vary in their abilities for drawing effectively on adult help. Some studies have shown that children who could elicit and rely on support from teachers tended also to be more able to draw support from their mothers (Wallerstein & Kelly, 1980). This implies that, although contextual supports should be available, there are still important aspects of children's personal competence that mediate the ability to integrate support from family and school contexts in order to cope with a very difficult family situation.

The degree to which home and school contexts affect one another is often presumed, but rarely examined in detail. Children are products of both. This is sometimes apparent in their use of one context to compensate for difficulties in the other; in other instances, the effect is one of problems in one context being "imported" into the other, as when family problems interfere with school performance. The interface of children's everyday contexts is a force in development that needs much more attention from parents, teachers, and psychologists.

The Mass Media Context

After parents' influences upon children, the aspect of family life that has been the object of the most study is television. Virtually all homes in the United State have at least one television set today, and most have multiple sets. Increasingly throughout the world, even in Third World countries, television is becoming commonplace in daily life (Collins & Korac, 1982; Murray & Kippax, 1979). Although there is some variation in how much people watch television at different times in their lives, television is probably used more consistently at every time in life than any other mass medium. It is not surprising that television has sometimes been considered almost a member of the family.

How does having television as a part of the home environment influence children's development? When parents and educators discuss this question, two general categories of possible influence are usually suggested and researchers have sought information on both: (1) the effects of viewing as an activity and (2) the effects of the content of television programs.

Effects of Television on Children

Activity of Viewing. The first concerns whether the *activity* of viewing television, including the amount of time spent in front of the set, might unduly restrict the amount and kinds of other activities that benefit children's de-

423

Latchkey Children

James Garbarino, Ph.D.

What do you call a 10-year-old child who returns home after school to be alone in his house for a couple of hours? Some would call the child a "latchkey child": That term derives from the fact that such children often carry keys with them to unlock the door latch. Others would say this is "a child in self-care," suggesting that the child is simply assuming responsibility in place of an adult. Others would define that child as being "at risk." Still others would call that child "neglected." Which designation is correct? And what if the child were 6-, 8-, 12-, or 14-years-old?

Surveys suggest that increasing numbers of children are not directly supervised by adults in the hours after (and sometimes before) school. Are these millions of children safe? What are they learning about the meaning of care and responsibility? What messages are they receiving about growing up? What do they do with their time? How do they feel? How will they raise their own children? Why are children living this way? Several researchers have addressed these questions. One of the best attempts to summarize the evidence is contained in a book by Bryan Robinson, Bobbie Rowland, and Mick Coleman entitled *Latchkey Kids: Unlocking Doors for Children and Their Families* (Lexington, MA: Lexington Books, 1986).

The issue of latchkey children will not go away. Once largely confined to blue collar and single-parent families in which the labor force participation of every adult in the household was needed to make ends meet, it has increasingly become a feature of middle-class life as more and more mothers add wage earner to the tasks of homemaker and caregiver.

Some observers argue that we should not be concerned. Their review of the evidence leads them to the conclusion that there is no simple cause and effect relationship between self-care and adverse developmental consequences and thus no real cause for alarm. Others worry about latchkey children for at least two reasons. First, they worry that the younger the children, the greater the children's vulnerability to physical and emotional harm when they are home alone— fires, assaults, accidents, fear, and loneliness. Second, they worry that lack of supervision among older children is related to increased susceptibility to negative peer influence (and thus delinquent and socially undesirable behavior).

What messages are we giving children when we tell them we cannot afford to be home for and with them after school? Are they learning that each member of a family has to shoulder part of the burden of making the family economy work? Are we teaching them that making money rules family decision making? Are they learning that American families cannot afford to subsidize the luxury of full-time childhood anymore, even for affluent kids? Are they learning that growing up and taking care of yourself as soon as possible is what families are all about? This is no easy issue to resolve.

The evidence is not definitive on many of these questions. In some cases, it may never be an open and shut scientific case because personal values play such an important role in the discussion. I am inclined to take the conservative course, by asking: Are there any risks to intensive and prolonged adult supervision? Are kids better off being on their own earlier rather than later? As is clear from the way I put these questions, I think the burden of proof is on those who would substitute self-care for adult supervision. And I think that the burden of proof is greater, the younger the child. Few responsible adults would say that a 4-year-old is capable of self-care. Most adults would agree that a 13-year-old is. Where do we draw the line?

James Garbarino, Ph.D. is President of the Erikson Institute for Advanced Study in Child Development in Chicago, a graduate school and research center specializing in issues of child development. He is author or editor of 10 books, including Children and Families in the Social Environment, The Psychologically Battered Child, *and* The Future as If It Really Mattered.

velopment. Indeed, several studies have indicated that, when television is introduced into a community, children play both outdoors and with friends less frequently (Himmelweit, Oppenheim, & Vince, 1958; Murray & Kippax, 1978). Since play with other children provides important opportunities for the development of intellectual and social skills (Rubin, Fein, & Vandenberg, 1983), excessive television viewing may be displacing significant socialization experiences. The physically passive nature of television viewing has also raised concerns that heavy viewing of television may interfere with the formation of active lifestyles that have been demonstrated to benefit health in adulthood (Shonkoff, 1984).

Time spent viewing may also affect academic performance. Children and adolescents who watch television 4 or more hours a day score lower on academic achievement tests than those who watch for fewer hours (Anderson & Collins, 1988). Heavy viewing has particularly negative effects on children from economically advantaged families, perhaps because television displaces activities available to these children that could stimulate their intellectual growth (Hornik, 1981). Although relatively few studies exist on the effects of viewing *activity,* the evidence to date and the importance of the questions considered indicate that the place of television in children's daily lives deserves further attention.

Content of Programs. The second category of concern about television's influence stems from the *content* of typical television programs. It is now clear that television conveys information effectively and efficiently to both children and to adults (Roberts & Maccoby, 1984). What kinds of information do children acquire from watching television? Are children at special risk for learning things not approved by society?

This question has been raised most frequently with respect to the effects of violence on television. Research studies on the topic, which now number more than 2,500, draw on different samples of children, of different ages, from throughout the world (Pearl, Bouthilet, & Lazar, 1982). The content denoted as violent ranges from slapstick (consider, for example, the Three Stooges) to cartoon representation in which characters readily recover from remarkably violent—if funny—events. Consider some of the antics in Tom & Jerry or Roadrunner cartoons, with the evil intent of Wile E. Coyote and his own violent just desserts.

The studies show that television violence may affect children and adults in a number of ways. For example, one study showed that preschoolers who watched a diet of aggressive programs over a 4-week period not only became more aggressive during nursery school play times, but also were less likely to stay with tasks and obey rules in the classroom and were more intolerant of delays in getting what they wanted (Friedrich & Stein, 1973). These latter effects illustrate how common, implicit aspects of aggression (for example, disobedience or impulsive reactions) that are not themselves violent are also communicated. Repeated viewing of violent programs is associated with antisocial behavior in older children and adolescents, as well (Belson, 1978; Leyens, Camino, Parke, & Berkowitz, 1975). Other research shows that beliefs about real-world crime and violence and about the commonness, effectiveness, and acceptability of violence in solving problems were affected by television portrayals (Hawkins & Pingree, 1982).

To be sure, violent and aggressive content has been a part of children's symbolic worlds for a long time, via channels that predated television but served a similar entertainment purpose. Punch and Judy were hardly a loving couple; consider what happens in Rock-a-Bye Baby, Little Red Ridinghood, Peter and the Wolf, or the Wizard of Oz where even sweet Dorothy commits murder. On this issue, the activity (the quantity of time spent viewing) and the content are almost certainly interrelated. Prior to the advent of television, children probably did not spend the vast amount of time in contact with these sources of entertainment that they do in front of the TV set. This is probably the reason that television researchers, even those interested in content, so frequently cite the impressive statistics regarding the degree to which children today are exposed to television. Although it is impossible to assess the impact of television violence amidst all of the other social pressures for and against aggressive solutions to problems (e.g., Freedman, 1984), the research to date illustrates that television can—and under some conditions does—make antisocial aggression more likely.

Although the number of studies on other effects is smaller, researchers have also examined questions such as: Are children's attitudes and their views of social roles, such as sex roles, affected by the entertainment shows they watch? Does the format of television—the fast pace of most programs, the action, the music and sound effects, and the camera angles—affect children's attention and learning? Do children respond to television commercials differently from adults and, if so, in what ways?

Like the studies of television violence, these studies show that television transmits information and images of social life that children readily remember. The ability of television to attract and hold attention is very great (Rice, Huston, & Wright, 1982). Furthermore, the evidence to date indicates that preschool and young elementary school children are probably most likely to be influenced by what television presents. This is not surprising perhaps, since younger children have the most to learn from any source. However, young children often lack the cognitive skills to understand fully the sometimes complicated story lines involved in typical shows—particularly programs that are produced with older viewers in mind. This difficulty in understanding makes it more likely that young viewers will get the wrong impression from violence and other antisocial acts in entertainment programs and, consequently, may be more likely to emulate television characters (Collins & Korac, 1982).

Commercial Effects.   Television is also an avenue for selling products, in large part because advertising revenues provide much of the financial support for commercial television (an apt phrase!). Although it is the wealth of their parents that they spend or convince their parents to spend, children are considered to be a market and are the target of advertisements for toys as well as foods, primarily cereal and candy (Barcus, 1977; Huston, Watkins, & Kunkel, 1989; Melody, 1973). Research on children's "vulnerability" to advertising suggests that commercials are particularly likely to influence children under the age of 8 (Adler, Lesser, Meringoff, Robertson, Rossiter, & Ward, 1980; Wartella & Hunter, 1983), and older children still do not have the skepticism or sophistication to avoid being influenced by pronouncements, claims, or assertions that are potentially deceptive (Kunkel, 1988; Ross, Campbell, Huston, & Wright, 1981, Ross, Campbell, Wright, Huston, Rice, & Turk, 1984).

Television can be either a positive or a negative influence in development. Children learn about important aspects of the world, how they and others

Television may influence children's development by displacing other significant activities and by providing behavioral models.

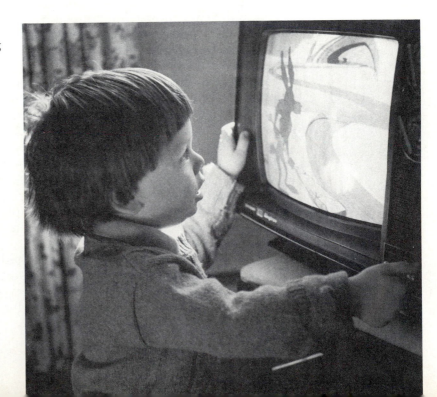

may and do behave, when direct experience alone might not provide such a richness in social and cognitive stimulation, yet misunderstanding or inaccurate (or overly frequent) representations may pervert this impact. As a source of immediate and vivid information about the larger world, it plays a unique role in society today. As an entertainment medium, however, its goals and its functions may not always be beneficial. Studies of its effects on child development may be one way of better understanding its significance.

Summary

Social and personality development takes place in varied interpersonal and institutional contexts that provide opportunities and exert demands and constraints on the course and nature of children's growth. Three significant, interrelated contexts—family, schools, and the mass media—comprise a large proportion of the social experiences that contribute to the development of individual children.

Families are systems of interrelated influences from parents, children, and others (e.g., grandparents, other extended family members, nonresident parents, stepparents). A fundamental characteristic of these influences is *reciprocity* or *bidirectionality,* meaning that children both affect and are affected by their parents and siblings.

Children typically have warm, positive relationships with both mothers and fathers. However, at all ages fathers' interactions with their children are most likely to revolve around playful, recreational activities, whereas interactions with mothers involve a variety of activities including chores, caretaking, and general assistance, as well as playfulness. Parents' influences on children's development are usually described in terms of broad dimensions or patterns of behavior, for example, warm and accepting versus hostile and rejecting, and extremely permissive versus extremely rejecting. A particularly influential system characterizes parents either as authoritarian (restrictive, punitive, demanding, and rule oriented), permissive (low parental expectations for behavior, allowing children to establish standards of conduct, and using discussion and explanation rather than punishment), nonconformist (have standards and rules for children's behavior, but reject external authority and socially imposed rules), and authoritative parents (set clear limits and standards for behavior and enforce them with a combination of power and reasoning). These patterns have been found to be associated with different child personality characteristics. For example, authoritative parents tend to have more achievement oriented, socially responsive children than authoritarian or permissive parents.

Sibling relationships vary with the ages and genders of the siblings as well as with other factors, such as the relative amount and kind of attention parents give to the children. Children, like parents, serve as models and as companions for their siblings. In addition, intellectual development has been found to be related to the constellation of siblings and to a child's ordinal position among the children in a family.

Together, parents and siblings comprise a family system, in which each pair is influenced in some ways by other family members. For example, marital interactions are different in some ways after the birth of the first child than before, and the mother–infant and father–infant relationships are affected by the husband–wife relationship. Similarly, interactions between mothers and first-born children appear to be affected by the birth of a second child, and relationships between divorced custodial mothers and their sons and daughters are affected by remarriage. The potential for transmission of abusive relationships from one generation to the next seems to be reduced by the presence in family systems of persons with whom healthy, supportive, nonabusive relationships exist.

Next to family, school commands more of children's time and activity than any other single social context. Schools have much in common with families in the early years. Children typically interact with a single primary teacher and must master a relatively restricted social environment. In secondary schools, however, the entire school is the social field, providing multiple teachers and others to interact with. The effectiveness of schools in promoting student learning seems to depend largely on the degree to which faculty and staff create an *ethos* that supports academic achievement. School size, classroom organization, and teacher behavior also affect learning and the degree of positive and effective interaction with other students and the development of individual self-esteem and academic motivation.

Schools frequently also attempt deliberately to affect social development and interpersonal relations through special curricula to enhance positive behavior and empathy toward others. The social agenda of desegregating schools has had variable effects in children's relations with peers from different racial groups. Children are generally most socially and academically successful when family and school contexts are mutually supportive and have similar authority systems and values.

The third context, the mass medium of television, is pervasive in U.S. homes and is also often present in schools. Some effects of television result from the time children spend viewing and the loss of other types of experiences because of time spent with television. Other effects result from the content of programs. It is clear that television efficiently conveys information to children about a wide variety of behaviors that the children would not be likely to encounter in their own lives. For example, watching programs in which violent solutions to conflict are heavily emphasized is often followed by more aggressive, destructive actions than watching programs that highlight more positive, constructive behaviors. Although the evidence that particular kinds of social content affects children's behavior is very extensive, it is difficult to determine how important television influences are among the other kinds of social influences that children experience in the home and at school. Television also appears to influence aspects of children's behavior such as consumerism, because of the large amount of advertising that appears on commercial television programs.

Suggested Readings

Dorr, A. (1986). *Television and children: A special medium for a special audience.* Beverly Hills, CA: Sage.

Emery, R. E. (1989). Family violence. *American Psychologist, 44,* 321–328.

Hetherington, E. M., Hagan, M. S., & Anderson, E. R. (1989). Marital transitions: A child's perspective. *American Psychologist, 44,* 303–312.

Hoffman, L. W. (1989). Effects of maternal employment in the two-parent family. *American Psychologist, 44,* 283–292.

Linney, J. A., & Seidman, E. (1989). The future of schooling. *American Psychologist, 44,* 336–340.

Maccoby, E. E., & Martin, J. A. (1983). Socialization in the context of the family. In E. M. Hetherington (Ed.), P. Mussen (Series Ed.), *Handbook of child psychology: Vol. 4. Socialization, personality, and social development* (pp. 1–102). New York: Wiley.

Parke, R. D. (Ed.) (1984). *The family: Review of child development research,* Vol. 7. Chicago: University of Chicago Press.

Wilson, M. N. (1989). Child development in the context of the black extended family. *American Psychologist, 44,* 380–385.

Appendix

CONDITIONAL PROBABILITIES

Conditional probabilities refer to the likelihood that, over many observed instances, a given behavior will be followed by a particular response from another person. An example comes from Gerald Patterson's (1982) studies of families in which one child frequently engages in *coercion.* Patterson uses this term to refer to noxious or aversive behavior that results in another family member's abandoning a circumstance that the coercive child does not like. For example, if a parent refuses to buy a child an ice cream cone during a shopping trip, the child may cry, whine, beg, or become resistant until the parent gives in and buys the ice cream. The giving in essentially ends a period of aversive behavior on both sides.

After carefully observing hundreds of families that had been identified as having problems and also families that had not been considered as having pronounced problems (comparison families), Patterson found that the likelihood of coercion was much greater in problem than comparison families. He determined this by focusing on the events that preceded and followed noxious behaviors by the focal child. After many such observations, several figures can be calculated that help to reveal the patterns of interactions between family members:

- The proportion of times that the child's noxious behavior was *preceded* by some aversive behavior by the other family member.
- The proportion of times that the focal child's noxious behavior was *followed* by giving in on the part of the other family member.

In both cases, you would also want to know how many times each behavior—the noxious action by the child and the provocation and "giving in" by the other family member—occurred *without* the other.

These figures allow you to answer several questions about the degree to which noxious behaviors by the child are *conditional* on behaviors by other family members and *vice versa*. For example: Is noxious behavior by the child more likely following certain "aversive" behaviors by other family members than following other types of behavior? Is noxious behavior more likely to be followed by "giving in" by other family members than by other kinds of responses?

Conditional probabilities then are ways of summarizing information about the degree to which one behavior is regularly related to another in the interactions among persons. These simple statistics enable observers to see the regular patterns that give family relationships their distinctive character.

CHAPTER THIRTEEN

The Peer Context: Peer Influences on Development

Introduction

Unless they are reared in unusually isolated circumstances, children interact with other children from infancy onward, and these social encounters have a significant impact on development. In fact, children's peers are an important part of the social environment in which they mature, influencing socializing in ways that have only recently gained the recognition they deserve (Hartup, 1983).

Before discussing specific areas of concern, however, we must address a problem of definition: specifically, what is a "peer?" The easiest way to identify a peer is to look for an age mate, a child close or identical in chronological age to another. But similarity in age does not always determine which children are peers. Children may be peers in one context and not in another. For example, an athletic child who is also quite successful in schoolwork may have one set of peers on the playground (other athletic children who do not achieve academically) and yet a different set in the classroom (other academically achieving children who are not necessarily athletic). It has been proposed that peer status be established in terms of behavioral complexity (Lewis & Rosenblum, 1975) so that children (or adults, for that matter) who show similar levels of capability or development, should be considered peers even if their chronological ages do not match. While this definition has some minor exceptions, it probably best captures the concept of peer and its intended meaning in discussing development.

Peer Interactions in Infancy

Infants are both socially interested and interactive. Babies less than 6 months of age will pay attention to other infants, especially if the other is crying or engaging in some sort of activity (Buehler, 1930; Durfee & Lee, 1973). Very young infants can only show interest because their mobility is so restricted. Later, when infants crawl and then walk, true interaction between peers develops. When "interaction" does occur in infants less than a year old, it is likely to be simply social action rather than *inter*action: one infant may move toward or make some other social gesture toward another, but the other infant will not act reciprocally. Rather, the other infant is likely to act independently (Durfee & Lee, 1973). However, 1-year-old infants in situations such as day care centers are likely to show a higher proportion of coordinated social interactions than other infants their age.

Although descriptions of peer interactions in infancy are emerging in the research literature, what determines the types of social interaction that are observed is not always well understood. It may be that babies regard other infants more as social *objects* rather than as social beings and respond to them as such. Infants tend to approach and explore inanimate objects largely as a function of the degree to which they provide sensory stimulation: Do they buzz, rattle, feel rough, or push back when squeezed? There is some evidence that sensory characteristics also enhance the likelihood that an infant will be attracted to and interact with a social object. For example, because adults are more active and manipulative toward infants than are other infants, it has been found that babies initially show more interest in adults (Eckerman, Whatley, & Kutz, 1975). Nevertheless, infants themselves are attracted in varying degrees to other infants. In one study of five infants in a day care setting, a clear hierarchy of social attractiveness was found, to the point where one infant was actively sought out and another appeared to be actively avoided (Lee, 1973). When the characteristics of these infants were examined, the "attractive" infant tended to respond reciprocally to social gestures from other babies (for example, when one child would smile or reach, the "attractive" child would do likewise), whereas the avoided or "unpopular" infant was much less reciprocal in social interaction.

Until recently, we have tended to conceive of peer relations beginning during the late preschool years, proceeding in earnest when children enter school where children begin to spend a fair proportion of each day in a peer group, and becoming particularly important in adolescence. Although this may be generally true, it overlooks the fact that even though infrequent, many infants do have contact with other infants or with older children.

Actually, peer contacts for infants may not be rare at all. It has been estimated that over 50% of 6-month-old infants in the United States have some contact with other infants at least once a week, and between 20% and 40% have contact even more frequently (Vandell & Mueller, 1980). Increasing use of group day care for infants (as well as for older preschool children) in our society have served to enlarge the number of peer contacts for infants and young children.

Observations of very young infants indicate that by approximately 2 months of age infants will pay attention to others who are fussing, crying, or active. Although this scarcely qualifies as peer interaction, it is clear that attention to peers is present from an early age. At first, infants are likely to "explore" one another's eyes, mouths, or ears, treating one another more like play objects rather than like other people. By about 6 months, peer interaction becomes more frequent and evolves into a more truly social interchange. Investigators have noted the occurrence of "semi" social acts such as when one infant gives a play object to another who receives it but without looking at or otherwise taking note of the giving infant, as well as those acts that are more clearly social and reciprocal in nature, such as peek-a-boo or imitative acts (Vandell, Wilson, & Buchanan, 1980; Eckerman, Whatley, & Jutz, 1975; Eckerman & Whatley, 1977).

Babies as Social "Objects"

435

Interactions among very young children are rudimentary versions of peer interactions at later ages.

Infant Sharing

Though peer interaction occurs with increasing frequency during infancy, it is still not very frequent. In a group care context such as a day care center, peer contacts between infants may occur about once every 2 minutes (Finkelstein, Dent, Gallagher, & Ramey, 1978) but are not nearly as frequent as contacts between infants and adults (Finkelstein et al., 1978; Vandell et al., 1980). Even in situations most favorable for peer interactions, such as when two infants are placed together in a play pen, contact occurs only about once every 2 minutes (Vandell et al., 1980), or at best once or twice a minute (Eckerman, 1975). Finally, many social actions by one infant toward another are not reciprocated. Reports vary, but they indicate that between 38% and 60% of the social overtures by one infant toward another go unanswered. Although familiarity between two infants (infant "friendship") increases reciprocity in their interactions, it is still infrequent and only during the second year does mutual interaction begin to increase and gain in sophistication, both socially (Mueller & Lucas, 1975) and emotionally (Ross & Goldman, 1976; Mueller & Rich, 1976). At this point the peer interaction of the first year can begin to be called *peer socialization*, interactions that contribute to the social development of each participating child.

An interesting result from recent research has been the documentation of at least one spontaneous prosocial behavior, sharing, in infants as young as 12 months old (Rheingold, Hay, & West, 1976). This is compatible with observations recorded in the early "baby biographies," that infants will part with possessions voluntarily, sometimes actively calling the attention of an adult to an item, holding it up, dropping it in someone's lap, or playing with

436

it while someone else holds it (Preyer, 1988; Shinn, 1909). In fact, this is so common that it has been proposed as a milestone of development.

Though sharing clearly occurs, little is known about what influences its early development. Indeed, studies show that sharing is *not* readily influenced by factors that one might expect. For example, infants share not only with their parents but also with strangers, they share new toys as well as old ones, and they share spontaneously as well as when asked (Rheingold et al., 1976). The one minor factor that did increase infants' pointing to objects (what might be termed perceptual or distal sharing) was the number of items that were around to be pointed to: more sharing tends to occur when there are more things to be shared. More factors probably affect sharing than just the number of items available, but only further research will reveal this. In any event, sharing clearly forms one of the bases for early childhood social interaction with adults, and it may occur in more rudimentary forms between infants (Vandell & Mueller, 1980).

Age Changes in Peer Interactions

There are some common patterns of peer interaction at various ages and, as we have shown, even the earliest peer encounters show the impact of early socialization. Very early interactions in infancy are hardly interactions in the true sense of that word, and it is only later that children's social encounters have much of a "mutual" quality where the two (or more) interacting children treat one another as more than social objects. Nevertheless, it has been demonstrated, for example, that the social overtures to peers made by 1-year-old infants seem to be patterned after the gestures they make toward adults (Eckerman et al., 1975). Children's desire for peer interactions also seems to increase with age, and by the age of two, children will commit more time to peer interaction than to their mothers when the choice is available. Indeed, over the entire course of childhood and into adolescence the peer group in general and peer interaction in particular become increasingly important.

Solitary, Parallel, and Cooperative Play

Increased sociability with age is shown by a variety of different behavior patterns. Within children's play, one of the classic descriptions (Parten, 1932; Parten & Newhall, 1943) characterized initial play as closer to *solitary play* in that the character of the interaction consists essentially of children merely looking at one another while playing rather than playing with each other. This reflects the descriptions presented above of children's initial interactions with one another as social "objects." Parten also observed that children engage in *parallel play*: playing side by side, doing similar or identical things, but not really playing *with* one another. By the time infants are 2 years old, toys become increasingly important in play, and play is for the first time accompanied by displays of affect. Finally, Parten observed that by about 5

437

or 6 years of age, children generally engage in cooperative play, which included reciprocal interactions such as conversation.

Parten's observations have generally proved true over time. The results of a replication study (Barnes, 1971), depicted in Figure 13-1, indicate that these stages are an enduring developmental pattern in play. The replication study also suggested that children today engage in social, cooperative play a bit earlier than they did half a century ago, reflecting, perhaps, more common, early peer experience. One should quickly note, however, that these are simply *common* patterns of play interactions and are not descriptive of every play interaction a child of a given age is likely to have. Nevertheless, they illustrate some of the more global changes that occur in one sphere of children's social activity—play—during the preschool years. It is unfortunate that for so many years these observations have remained descriptive and little, if any, attention has been given to determining the processes that shape children's early social behavior along these lines. That question is likely to be answered soon, however, as interest seems to be shifting from describing peer interaction to clarifying some of the processes that underlie it.

Positive Interactions

Peer interactions are predominantly positive although positive encounters do not come to the attention of adults as often as negative or aggressive ones. While peer aggression appears initially at the end of the first year and clearly increases during childhood, at no time is aggression more prevalent than are positive encounters (Walters, Pearce, & Dahms, 1957). In large part, early

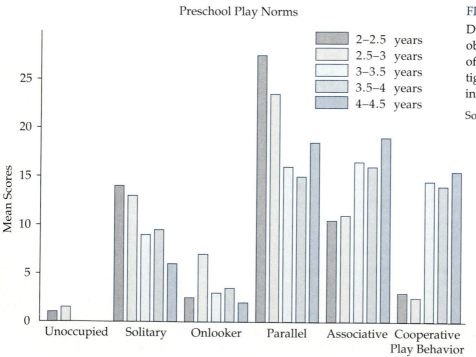

Preschool Play Norms

Legend:
- 2–2.5 years
- 2.5–3 years
- 3–3.5 years
- 3.5–4 years
- 4–4.5 years

Mean Scores (y-axis): 0, 5, 10, 15, 20, 25

Play Behavior (x-axis): Unoccupied, Solitary, Onlooker, Parallel, Associative, Cooperative

FIGURE 13-1

Different types of play observed in a replication of Parten's original investigation of children's peer interactions.

Source: from Barnes, 1971.

Peer interactions provide important opportunities for learning to regulate and cope with aggression.

aggression is intended to achieve a goal (a toy held by another child, for example). Hostile aggression, the punitive expression of anger, is a behavior pattern that begins to occur later in childhood or during preadolescence.

Not only are early peer interactions generally positive but their positive character increases, at least during the preschool years (Charlesworth & Hartup, 1967; Walters et al., 1957). Positive interactions appear as friendships that may be observed as early as 3 years of age. At that age, peer interaction and, thus, friendship occur largely between children of the same sex. Initially, friendships are not frequent or very enduring, but this changes with age. More enduring best friend (Sullivan, 1953) relationships generally occur in later childhood. Interestingly, not all children develop best friend relationships. There is no indication that not having a close friend during early development invariably interferes with later social development, although theorists have argued to the contrary, maintaining that a close friend during the preadolescent years is necessary for sound personality development (Sullivan, 1953). Others (e.g., Gottman & Parkhurst, 1980) have argued that childhood friendships provide enhanced opportunities for children to express emotion, sympathy, support, and so on, and are thus critical in developing the capacity for intimacy in adolescence and adulthood. Nevertheless, there is no large body of research on children's specific friendships, whereas there is more research on their general acceptance (or rejection) by peers. It is, therefore, impossible at this time to do more than speculate about the importance of early friendships for personality and social development.

There is generally consistent evidence, however, that effective peer relations, especially acceptance by one's peers, is important for adequate social development and that peer nonacceptance, particularly rejection, may predict subsequent maladjustment (Suomi & Harlow, 1972; Lougee, Grueneich, &

Effects of Peer Acceptance

Hartup, 1976; Novak & Harlow, 1975; Parker & Asher, 1987). Research has shown, for example, that low peer acceptance is related to, and thus constitutes a risk factor for, dropping out of school early, juvenile delinquency and adult crime, or eventual maladjustment and psychopathology (Parker & Asher, 1987).

The strength of the relationship between peer acceptance and these outcomes varies, and many questions remain unanswered. For example, if a child's status as peer rejected is defined simply in terms of a child not being listed as a friend by classroom peers, that child may be actively rejected and disliked or may simply have a "neutral" status in the eyes of peers, neither liked nor disliked. The apparent negative outcomes from peer rejection for children may apply primarily, or perhaps only, for those children who are actively disliked. Another limitation to this research is a general failure to assess acceptance or friendship beyond the classroom walls. A child may have few or no friends in the classroom but have one or more good friends in another classroom or in the neighborhood and the child, therefore, is not generally unaccepted or without the opportunity for close peer interactions. To illustrate how a general label (for example, that a child is "retarded") may fail to be accurate in all settings, Hobbs (1975) characterized children who perform poorly in the school setting but do fine otherwise (at home, in general community settings) as "six hour retarded children," and it has been suggested that some apparently unaccepted children may not be at risk for later maladjustment because they are only "six hour unpopular children" (Parker & Asher, 1987, p. 365).

Socialization Processes in Peer Interactions

One of the most interesting aspects of peer relations is the way that children's contact with one another influences their socialization. That we all learn from our contact with peers is a given—such contacts influence our development throughout the life span. *How* we are influenced by our peers is a different matter. In addition to more complex elements of peer interaction, such as developing the social skills necessary to make new acquaintances or develop and maintain friendships, two basic processes of social learning have historically received a great deal of attention. These processes are: (1) social reinforcement and punishment between peers and (2) peer modeling, learning by observing the behavior of peers.

Reinforcing and Punishing Behaviors

When children interact they respond spontaneously in ways that can be rewarding or punishing to others. More than two decades ago, long before any definitive research had occurred, B. F. Skinner speculated about some common social behaviors that might have either reinforcing or punishing

The Children of Bulldogs Bank

Through the misfortunes of war and accidents, one may often find experiments of nature that illustrate or elucidate points that could never be studied ethically through experimental manipulation. Toward the end of World War II such an incident occurred. Six German–Jewish children were flown out of Germany to a reception camp in Britain and then forwarded to a country house called Bulldogs Bank, where they were cared for. Anna Freud, a child psychoanalyst and daughter of Sigmund Freud, along with a colleague, Sophie Dann, were placed in charge of these children. The children were all between 3 and 4 years of age.

One reason these children were referred to this special care facility was that they were an inseparable group. They had been together since infancy, living in concentration camps. Their rearing conditions had been extraordinarily poor, and the only continuity in their social environment had been enduring contact with one another. Adult caretakers came and went, providing little care in the process, and so the children had become largely dependent upon themselves. In the process, they developed a pattern of peer interaction that was surely unique, but that illustrates a limiting case (i.e., not generalizable) for the role peers may play in one another's socialization.

Each of the children in this group became a caretaker to all the others, and the group formed a solidarity against the rest of the world. All of their experiences with adults had been transitive and often they had observed atrocities by camp guards against inmates. The apparent result, in addition to a total dependency on one another, was mistrust or antagonism toward adult "outsiders," especially any who dared to infringe on them or attempt to care for them. When they first arrived at Bulldogs Bank, the children were wild, uncontrollable, and extremely destructive. When angry with an adult, they would bite, spit, or hit; but at other times, they would behave as if there were no adults around, not even looking up when one entered the room. The degree to which the children related to one another was as remarkable as their hostility toward adults. In the beginning they were inseparable. One of the children, Ruth, disliked walks and sometimes stayed at the Bank while the other children went out. One time, when the children went without Ruth, they constantly asked about her and after only about 20 minutes they turned back to be with her. The children could not even enjoy special treats if only one child was treated; on one occasion, a boy in the group, Paul, was given a ride in a pony cart, but cried because the other children could not have one too.

Over the course of a year at Bulldogs Bank, the children gradually came to accept adults, their companionship, and their care. What is important about this tragic example is not its happy end but rather its beginning. These children had been deprived of a close and continuing relationship with adult caretakers. In the context of a concentration camp, the adults they had known could do little more than care for their basic physical needs. Nevertheless, the children were neither psychotic nor completely deficient in their abilities to cope with the social and nonsocial world. The only conclusion that can be drawn is that the peer group—in this case, a set of peers who were undergoing the same debilitating experiences—may adequately provide the rudimentary socialization experiences necessary for early personality development and the acquisition of social competence. While no one can argue that peer socialization alone is a poor substitute for the total socialization experience that comprises normal development, the children of Bulldogs Bank underscore the potency of peer experiences in social development and point to their potential for contribution during the earlier years of life. 🍂

effects for individuals of all ages (Skinner, 1953). Although the behaviors Skinner outlined were certainly not exhaustive, they showed extraordinary insight into the ways children and adults influence those with whom they interact. Drawing from Skinner's thinking, Charlesworth and Hartup (1967) proposed the classification of behaviors likely to have reinforcing or punishing effects on children that are listed in Table 13-1.

A primary concern in studying such reinforcing and punishing behaviors in the complex, bustling conditions that characterize a natural social interaction setting is whether behavior can be reliably categorized according to such a system by an observer. If so, a researcher can then study further some of the general characteristics and consequences of reinforcing and punishing interactions among peers. Hartup and his colleagues provided an initial exploration addressing these questions (Charlesworth & Hartup, 1967; Hartup, Glazer, & Charlesworth, 1967) by carefully observing the social behaviors of preschool children and classifying them according to Skinner's categories. On the average, a child would behave in a socially reinforcing manner about 20 times during a half-hour period and in a punitive manner about 5 times. Older preschool children (4 years of age) were more reinforcing in their interactions than were their younger peers, indicating a developmental increase in sociability. In addition, the golden rule seemed to pertain to this action. That is, the more reinforcement children showed to others, the more they received from others. It was clear from these observations that reward and punishment are knit into children's interaction patterns, although the actual consequences of such interactions for other aspects of social behavior and development remain to be demonstrated.

TABLE 13-1

Peer interactions likely to have reinforcing or punishing consequences for peers

Positive Social Reinforcement

1. Positive attention and approval: attending, offering praise and approval, offering instrumental help, smiling and laughing, verbally helping, informing another of a third person's needs, engaging in general conversation.
2. Affection and personal acceptance, physical and verbal.
3. Submission: passively accepting, imitating, sharing, accepting another's idea or help, allowing another child to play, compromising, following an order or request with pleasure and cooperation.
4. Token giving: giving tangible physical objects, such as toys or food, spontaneously.

Punitive Behavior

1. Noncompliance: refusing to submit or cooperate, withholding positive reinforcement, ignoring a peer's overtures.
2. Interference: taking property, disrupting or interfering with ongoing activity.
3. Derogation: ridiculing, disapproving, blaming, tattling.
4. Attack: physically attacking, threatening to attack, making threatening demands.

SOURCE: Charlesworth & Hartup, 1967.

The effectiveness of social reinforcement from peers varies from one context to another. As one might expect, an important factor is the particular peer who is delivering the reinforcement. Hartup (1964) investigated the influence of friendship status on the potency of peer reinforcement by observing 4- and 5-year-old children during a marble dropping game and the frequency with which they inserted marbles in a hold. After a while, a peer who had been trained to tell the subjects what a good job they were doing after each marble was dropped through the hold entered the situation. The peer was not randomly selected, however, and was either another child who was particularly well liked by the subject or one who was disliked.

The interesting finding from this study is that positive comments from a *dis*liked peer had a reinforcing effect, whereas positive feedback from a liked peer had little effect or produced a slight decline in the frequency of marble dropping. The same effect has been reproduced in older children (Titkin & Hartup, 1965) also, but the reasons for the increased effectiveness of reinforcement from disliked peers are difficult to specify. One possibility is that children seldom have contact with disliked peers in everyday interaction and therefore receive less social reinforcement from them. This might enhance the value of and impact on behavior of such reinforcement when it does occur. Another possibility, suggested by Hartup, is that disliked peers are anxiety provoking, at least initially, and reinforcement from them is then more effective or appreciated because it tends to counter the anxiety.

One potential consequence of reinforcing social interactions is developing friendships or personal "popularity." Part of the project by Hartup and his associates included the assessment of friendship nominations, termed sociometric choices, by the children whose social interactions had been observed (Hartup et al., 1967). A child's "sociometric status" is a measurement of acceptance by peers or how often others claim the child as a friend; it is generally assessed by a procedure termed "peer nomination." In this procedure children are asked to name several other children (in the classroom) they like (acceptance) or consider to be their friends, and they may also be asked to name several peers they dislike (rejection). A given child's sociometric status with respect to peer acceptance or friendships can be assigned a numerical value by summing the number or proportion of other children in the classroom who named that child as someone they liked; rejected status can be quantified in terms of the nominations as disliked. It was found that the frequency with which individual children reinforced their peers was related to the frequency those peers selected such children as friends. Similarly, children who interacted frequently with their peers in a punitive fashion were more often disliked by the other children.

Children who are generally well liked and thus "popular" may behave in a generally reinforcing manner toward many different children, including those who do not nominate them as personal friends, and may not act in a reinforcing manner toward some who do choose them as friends. In an observational study (Furman & Masters, 1980) one child was most likely to report that another child was a friend when the two children shared a large

443

number of interactions in which nothing particularly reinforcing or punishing occurred. For example, such things as casual conversations, pointing something out across the room, and so on predicted friendship selection more readily than peer reinforcements or punishments. The relationships that have been observed between children's reinforcing or punitive interactions and their popularity, acceptance/rejection, or friendship status suggest that processes of social reinforcement or punishment contribute to (i.e., determine) sociometric status. The studies we have discussed so far, however, were generally correlational: social reinforcement or punishment was found to be *related* to sociometric status, but there was no direct evidence that it *caused* it. Though perhaps not persuasively, it might be argued that the casual relationship was the reverse, in other words, children reinforced other children because they were disliked.

Thus, if we are interested in determining how social learning processes such as reinforcement, punishment, or modeling actually affect children's peer interactions and sociometric status, this could best be inferred from research in which children's behavior is experimentally manipulated and its consequences for the behavior or attitudes of peers are then recorded. One of the first such studies demonstrated the effects of social punishment (ignoring) and reinforcement (collaboration) on aggressive behavior (Wahler, 1967). In this study, preschool children's social responsiveness toward a peer was manipulated by directing them to attend to or to ignore a particular type of behavior when the peer performed it. For example, Dick was a boisterous and somewhat aggressive child whose shouting, toy throwing, and general aggression in nursery school, usually produced laughter or even collaboration from other children, who merrily joined in. Two peers were taught by an experimenter to carefully ignore Dick's aggressive acts while playing with him and otherwise act normally when he was not being so boisterous. When these peers changed their social reactions, Dick quickly changed his behavior.

The experimenter then told the peers to resume their friendly and collaborative interactions with Dick, even when he was aggressive. The frequency of Dick's aggression rapidly increased. Wahler continued to test the impact of peer reinforcement and reinforcement withdrawal on children's behavior by training different peers to change their behaviors toward other children in the classroom. The doll playing of one little girl was quickly replaced by other activities when her peers ceased to be attentive during doll play.

Similar effects occurred when peer social attention was reduced for cooperative play (for example, two children playing with the same toy, taking turns), indicating that a broad variety—probably the entire range—of children's social behavior is sensitive to the reinforcing behaviors of peers. Observation of another child in the Wahler study indicated that when peer reinforcement increases it produces increases in the likelihood of the behavior that is being reinforced. Jimmy, an unusually isolated child in the nursery school class, spoke very little until some of his peers were carefully instructed to concentrate their attention on Jimmy's speech by responding to him immediately in a positive fashion. In this particular case, peers also concentrated their attention on Jimmy when he behaved cooperatively until he increased both the frequency with which he spoke and the frequency of his cooperative play. The formative impact of peer social reinforcement is clear.

Another major social learning process in which peer interaction may have a socialization impact is modeling (alternatively termed "observational learning" or "imitation"). Even when they are not directly interacting with peers, children turn their attention to other children who are often at a distance, and they enrich their social capabilities from such observations. In fact, the question of *whether* children are socialized by observing their peers has never been raised, probably because the answer is so obvious. Instead, research has focused upon *how* observational learning from peers contributes to development: to clarify the broad range of behavior (social, cognitive, and emotional) that can be affected by observational contact with peers and to clarify some of the characteristics of children or their peers that enhance or detract from the effectiveness of peer modeling.

Modeling

O'Connor (1969) demonstrated that socially withdrawn children may increase their level of social interaction if they are given the opportunity to carefully observe the successful peer interactions of other children. In this study, extremely withdrawn preschool children were shown a 20-minute movie depicting children of the same age who gradually went from being alone, watching some other children play, to joining the other children and engaging in socially rewarding interactions with them (for example, in return, the other children smiled and talked in a warm fashion). To make certain that any changes in social interaction by these children were not due to the pleasant effects of watching a movie, a control group was included in which children watched an enjoyable animal film on dolphins. Only children who saw peers modeling social interaction and acquaintance formation increased their own social involvement in the nursery school setting, and they did so with remarkable enthusiasm, showing 5-fold more social interactions after viewing a mere 20 minutes of successful peer interactions and ultimately engaging in the same level of social interaction as children who had never been socially withdrawn.

It has also been shown that exposure to peer models may affect cognitive operations, such as styles of problem solving. Debus (1970) worked with "impulsive" children who responded too quickly to problems when they were solving them, often blurting out incorrect answers without seeming to think. These children, who were in the third grade, were allowed to observe peers who were more reflective in their problem solving and paused thoughtfully before deciding on a problem solution. Children of both sexes who observed the reflective model significantly slowed their rate of responding after being presented with a problem, indicating that they had spontaneously adopted the reflective style of the model.

Peer modeling may also play a role in shaping emotional reactions and the behaviors these reactions promote. One set of experiments by Bandura and his colleagues clarified some factors that influence the effects of peer models

445

on children's fears. In these experiments, preschool children who were severely frightened of dogs were exposed for very brief periods of time to a single peer model who interacted pleasantly and fearlessly with a dog. In one condition, there were 8 "treatment" sessions in which children watched the model, who interacted briefly (4 minutes) with the dog. In another condition, children were treated to a jovial party atmosphere (balloons, cookies, hats) while watching the model, to determine whether the context within which peers are observed may influence the effectiveness of peer modeling (for example, a pleasant atmosphere might relax the observing child and help reduce fearfulness). In another condition, children saw the dog but without peer modeling interactions, to determine whether mere observation of the feared object in a pleasant context would reduce that fear. Finally, one group of children experienced only the party atmosphere (without a dog in attendance) and served as a comparison condition. To determine the impact of these procedures on children's fear of dogs, they were subsequently given the opportunity to interact with a dog and their behavior was observed. It was found that only when children observed a peer model interacting fearlessly with a dog were they subsequently able to approach and interact with a dog themselves, and the effectiveness of observing the peer models did not depend on the context in which the peer models were observed.

In a subsequent study, Bandura and Menlove (1967) clarified other components of the experience of observing a peer that influenced its effectiveness in influencing emotional responding. In this study, dog phobic children were shown movies of peer models interacting with dogs or movies about animals that were irrelevant but enjoyable (for example, Disneyland, Marineland). In the modeling conditions, some of the children saw a variety of models who interacted with several different dogs that were of different sizes. This experiment included a followup, some 30 days after the modeling experiences. Even after this lengthy period of time, children's increased ability to approach dogs and their reduced fear had persisted.

The effect of observing multiple models was an interesting one. The average tendency to approach a real dog after exposure to peer models was no greater for children who saw multiple models than it was for those who saw only a single fearless peer. As we have seen, there was no difference between the effectiveness of single and multiple models in eliminating fearful avoidance behavior immediately after the treatment period. However, if a researcher examines the types of fearless behaviors children were willing to perform after treatment, an effect from observing multiple models appears. After the 30-day followup, children who had observed multiple models were distinctly more willing to interact with a dog in a way that indicates the fear was completely eliminated. This "terminal" task involved allowing themselves to be confined in a playpen with a dog for a short period of time while the experimenter left the room and they were completely alone. This suggests that observing many different peers performing a certain type of behavior leads to continued observation and possibly even practice of the observed behavior. In the present study, children had the opportunity to practice interacting with dogs during the followup period, and these consequences may have enhanced the impact of the original observation by providing pleasant and perhaps even reinforcing interactions with dogs that further reduced children's fear.

It is safe to say that just about any behavior pattern displayed by a peer model has a potential socializing impact on an observing child. The research cited above was intended to underscore the point that more than just social behaviors may be affected by peer models, and thus cognitive and emotional development may be affected by peers also.

Children's Friendships

Friendship is a special relationship that children have with one another, with a beginning, an end (sometimes), and, most importantly, a period of time when children who are friends feel and behave differently toward one another than they do toward those who are strangers or with whom they are only "acquainted." Our understanding of friendship in childhood and adolescence has moved in two directions, one toward clarifying how children think of friendship and the other toward describing how friends, as contrasted with children who are not friends, interact.

Part of the psychological study of friendship has thus treated it as an aspect of social cognition, an important element of children's understanding of the social world. Even very young children use the term friend, although it is difficult to understand exactly what they mean by it (Hartup, 1983). In terms of the expectations that children have, Bigelow and his colleagues (Bigelow, 1977; Bigelow & LaGaipa, 1975) determined that various elements come to be regarded as typical or important ingredients of friendships and friendly interactions. In the early elementary grades, children say that such things as helping one another, engaging in common activities, or merely being near one another are characteristic of friendship. Somewhat later, acceptance and admiration are mentioned, and toward the end of the elementary years friendships are seen to encompass loyalty and commitment, common interests and genuineness. This progression has been characterized as first involving a concentration on the rewards and costs of friendship, then on social norms such as sharing, and finally on empathy and interactions that include mutual understanding and common interests. Other investigators (Berndt, 1979) have discovered similar trends, with the eventual focus on intimacy and mutual commitment appearing to be particularly prominent among girls.

Friends also behave differently with one another than do unacquainted children, as one might expect. Early research indicated that children tend to spend more time in group play situations with peers whom they consider friends (Challman, 1932; McCandless & Marshall, 1957), although more re-

447

cent work suggests that this may not be as true as had been thought (Chapman, Smith, Foot, & Pritchard, 1979). And, again not very surprisingly, interactions among friends tend to be positive. Children who are friends exchange more reinforcing as well as neutral acts toward one another (Furman & Masters, 1980) and when watching or listening to something funny (e.g., cartoons) there is more laughter among children if they are friends (Foot, Chapman, & Smith, 1977; Smith, Foot, & Chapman, 1977). It has long been known that generosity and sharing are more common among friends, even during the preschool years (Hartup, 1983). When friends work on a joint task, while they may be no more successful than mere acquaintances, they are more interactive and focused on mutuality and equity in shared outcomes, for example, "If we take turns, we'll both make more points" (Newcomb, Brady, & Hartup, 1979).

In some theories of personality development friendship has played a crucial role. Harry Stack Sullivan (1953) proposed that "chums" and "chumships" are of special importance during the middle childhood years, particularly between 8½ and 10 years of age. Sullivan described this relationship as a cornerstone of all close personal relationships, seeing it as the foundation of intimacy when a child develops sensitivity to what matters to another person. The research has supported this general notion, especially in terms of the way concepts such as loyalty or commitment enter into children's views of friendship during the preadolescent years (Bigelow, 1977; Bigelow & La-Gaipa, 1975), although the indications that friends show more helping and other positive social interactions even during the preschool years suggest that the groundwork for mature friendships may be laid earlier.

In fact, there are reports in the literature of devoted and continuing friendships among very young children. Gottman and Parkhurst (1980) followed the interactions of 4-year-old friends, a boy and a girl, over 7 years. The parents of these children were *not* friends and yet, when one family moved out of town, the children carefully planned how they could keep in contact by writing one another or visiting and did so over the next 7 years. These investigators also followed a pair of 4-year-old friends who also suffered a separation due to one family's moving. In the most recent report of this observation (Gottman, 1983), these children also made plans to maintain contact and were still doing so some 3 years after the separation.

While Sullivan, in describing chumship, may simply have been describing what he felt was a common or normative shift in friendships during middle childhood and preadolescence, the reports of Gottman and others suggest that intense and relatively mature friendships may also develop much earlier. Indeed, Vandell and Mueller (1980) report a friendship between two toddler boys, one 8 months old and the other 10 months old, that endured over a several year period and persisted after the children were separated when one family moved. It is not yet clear how much cases like these represent exceptions to the normal time line of friendship development, though it seems safe to conclude that they are not isolated nor particularly rare. Friendships may thus play an important role in development very early in life.

RESEARCH FOCUS 13-2

The Development of Individual Friendships

It is only recently that we have learned much about how children become friends. This is at least in part due to the complexity of any sort of social interaction, especially those that lead to continued interaction or lasting relationships.

In a 1983 monograph, John Gottman studied the early friendship formation process in 3- to 9-year-old children by recording their conversations and then developing an intricate coding system to chart such aspects as children's use of humor, demands on one another, tactics of social "repair" (resolving conflicts that develop), and clarity of referential communication (making it clear *what* one is talking about). Gottman found that children who got along well showed some common factors in their early interactions with one another. They interacted in what might be called a "connected" fashion in which they exchanged information with one another, resolved any conflicts that developed, and established a common ground activity such as finding something to do together or exploring their similarities and differences.

As friendships develop, however, different types of interaction appear to become important. Many of the factors related to the formation of the friendship increase in importance (for example, continuing to communicate clearly or to resolve conflicts), but new ones emerge as well. For example, self-disclosures occur that reveal feelings and not always positive ones. Among Gottman's subjects, two 5-year-old girls were conversing when one began to talk about her mother's boyfriend:

A: Like . . . Jimmy . . .
K: Jimmy who?
A: That big man downstairs.
K: Your brother?
A: He's not my brother. He's a friend of ours.
K: Why does he come over all the time?
A: Because he does. Because my mommy asks him.

K: All the time?
A: She even goes out, he even goes places without *me* . . . . She didn't say anything about the dress. She said, "Leave me and Jimmy alone."
K: Why'd she say that?
A: She doesn't love me.

Gottman developed a temporal theory of friendship formation that indexes how children manage their social relations in ways that promote the development of friendships. Three social processes are seen to be important, play, self-exploration, and social repair, as are two affective states, amity (friendliness) and conflict. Gottman found that children use the processes, such as play, to orchestrate other elements of the social interaction. For example, when play is turned to something like coloring side by side (compare to Parten's concept of parallel play), there is little risk of conflict because there is little true interaction—but of course there is little chance for amity or other aspects of friendship interchange.

It is interesting to note that Gottman found little to indicate that the sex of the children had much influence on friendship formation among 3- to 9-year-old children of the ages he studied, as others have also found for younger children (Jacklin & Maccoby, 1978). There was some tendency for children to show greater dexterity in some of the processes facilitating friendship formation (such as exchanging information, or resolving conflicts) as they grew older, but these age differences were not particularly remarkable.

In general, Gottman's analysis of the friendship formation process is consistent with the notion that children develop a repertoire of social skills. These skills apply not only to everyday interaction with new acquaintances but they also play an important role in the development of close relationships—friendships—among young children.

Family and Peer Influences on Development

Put most simply, the family provides the foundation from which peer interactions initially develop. Infants and toddlers whose attachment to their mother is judged to be secure and who can comfortably spend time exploring a new environment at a distance from their mother, are more likely to engage in peer interactions than those whose attachments are rated insecure or who consistently maintain proximity to their mothers (Easterbrooks & Lamb, 1979; Lieberman, 1977). In addition, estimates of the security of attachment in older infants (15 months of age) have been found to predict the quality of social interactions toward the end of the preschool years (Waters et al., 1979). It is found that security of earlier family attachments is related to more competent peer relations, including the tendency to express sympathy to peers in distress, to show greater levels of social activity and responsiveness to peer overtures, and to be sought out by peers for social interaction. Although there have been some reports of family versus peer "cross pressures," especially during adolescence (Brittain, 1963), this does not contradict the general conclusion that the overall quality and supportiveness of family relations, especially during the early years, promotes competent and productive peer relations. We will discuss the role of the family more fully in a later chapter on the important social contexts for development.

The Impact of Peers

Interactions with Peers of Different Ages

While the term peer is generally reserved for individuals of approximately the same age or behavioral complexity, it has also proved to be the best descriptor for individuals slightly older or younger than one another. Descriptively, interaction between children who are not precisely the same age is of interest because it occurs often in the natural environment: neighborhoods, playgrounds, and day care centers typically have children of mixed ages, and even within the same school classroom children may differ by both age and behavioral competence, although to a lesser degree. Older children often interact with younger children in a caretaking role, and through contact with brothers and sisters or other youngsters in a neighborhood, children may be confronted with periodic or even extensive interactions with peers either younger or older than themselves, or both (Allen, 1976; Barker & Wright, 1955). The consequences of these interactions have only recently begun to be studied, but the findings are of particular interest.

The clearest generalization that can be made about cross-age peer interactions is that peers of different ages adapt their behavior to each other. This mutual adaptation is apparently something automatic and largely independent of skills relating to understanding the position of another person or role taking. Shatz and Gelman (1973) found that 4-year-old children who were egocentric when tested were nevertheless sensitive to the age of a peer with whom they were talking. This was clearly revealed when they adjusted their speech so that it more closely matched the communication capabilities of the child to whom they spoke. When 4-year-olds talk to one another, their speech is generally unregulated and its complexity is about the same as when they talk with adults. However, Shatz and Gelman found that when 4-year-olds were talking to 2-year-olds, they shortened and simplified their utterances and tended to say or phrase things to maintain the younger child's attention. The adjustment in speech was greater when the 4-year-olds were talking to the younger 2-year-olds than it was for the older 2-year-olds. When these investigators checked to see whether this pattern of adjustment might be due to consistent practice at home—which 4-year-olds with younger siblings would have—they found that the presence of a younger sibling in the family made no difference in older children's tendency to adapt their communication to the capability level of the listener.

With respect to social interaction, children also adjust their actions to the actions of others in cross-age peer dyads. Lougee, Grueneich, and Hartup (1977) studied nursery school children who differed in age by 16 months or who were age mates. Both older and younger children clearly regulated their social responses. Older children confronted with a younger peer decreased the vigor of their social responding relative to the activity level they showed when they were with an age mate; similarly, younger children showed an increased vigor in their interactions when their peer was older than they were.

Mutual regulation clearly has implications for the role of peer interactions in development. As the more mature members of mixed-age peer groups adapt their behavior so that its maturity or complexity level is not so far removed from the competencies of their peers, it is more likely that mature members will have an upgrading or socializing impact on the younger members. If the behavior that is expected or modeled by a socializing agent is significantly beyond the capabilities of the child, not only will the child have difficulty adopting the behavior, but there may be problems in simply understanding it. Sometimes this accommodation children make to the current development level of the individual being socialized is of the utmost importance, perhaps most especially so when the other person is someone whose current developmental level is retarded (inappropriate for their chronological age) because of some inadequacies of prior socialization.

The role that peers may play in developmental or remedial socialization was first explored in studies with primates, because deficiencies in social development could be experimentally manipulated. Rhesus monkeys who were deprived of social contact during the first few months of life developed severe problems in their behavior patterns, coming to show self-directed

451

behaviors such as self-clasping, self-mouthing, huddling, and stereotypic rocking rather than the social behavior characteristic of normally reared monkeys of the same age (Harlow & Harlow, 1977). When monkeys with these behavioral deficits are given the opportunity for social contact with other monkeys of the same age, they are unresponsive and continue to exhibit bizarre behaviors with few changes up through maturity, even after long exposures to peers (Gluck & Sackett, 1976; Harlow & Harlow, 1977; Harlow, Harlow, Dodsworth, & Arling, 1966).

It was discovered, however, that when monkeys who had been isolated for the first six months of life interacted with monkeys who were only three months of age, the isolated monkeys showed many fewer self-directed behaviors and more interactive behaviors (Suomi & Harlow, 1972). Apparently, the younger monkeys required fewer adaptations for effective social interaction than same-age monkeys did; consequently, the socially deprived monkeys' capabilities were more in line with the social demands of the younger peers. Using this finding as a clue, Novak and Harlow (1975) attempted to improve the social skills of monkeys who were severely lacking in social skills, because they had been reared without social contact for the entire first year of their lives. Using 3-month-old peer monkeys as "therapists" for these socially deprived older monkeys, resulted in striking improvements. In fact, after six months of play and interaction with younger peers, the formerly isolated monkeys actually approximated the normal behavior of their peers.

Is this insight about the value of playing with younger peers applicable to the case of human children who lack social skills? To test this possibility, Furman, Rahe, and Hartup (1979) worked with a group of 24 preschool children, ranging in age from 4 years to 5½ years. None of the children was mentally retarded or emotionally disturbed, but all were observed to be noticeably lower in social interaction than other children in their day care centers. Furman et al. paired 8 of these children with another child who was 12 to 20 months younger and arranged for each pair to play together for 20 minutes each day over a period of 4 to 6 weeks. For eight of the remaining children, similar play sessions were arranged with peers of the same age. The third group of eight were not given "therapy" with peers and served in the study as a control group.

At the end of the four to six week period, all children were again observed in free-play sessions at the day care centers. Figure 13-2 shows that the children who had been paired with peers all improved in peer interactions during free play between the pretreatment and post-treatment observation periods. Indeed, like the monkeys in the study by Novak and Harlow (1975), the children who were paired with younger peers improved in their typical rate of interactions with peers to the point that their behavior was similar to the average behavior of children in the day care centers. The behavior change consisted largely of an increase in positive interactions with other children: helping, giving, sharing, cooperating, and accepting suggestions. The eight socially withdrawn children who were not paired with peers changed little in their interactions with other children, however.

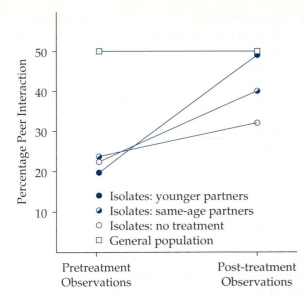

FIGURE 13-2

Peer interaction rates before and after mixed- and same-age socialization.

Source: from Furman, Rahe, & Hartup, 1979.

Group Pressures: Conformity

When individuals are in a position to know how others feel about a topic, for example, what judgments they make about the accuracy of a statement, the length of a line, or even the solution to a problem, there is likely to be some pressure to conform. After all, if everyone else agrees on a solution different from the one you have chosen, is it not likely you will feel you are "wrong?" If you disagree, is there not some threat of being accused of being "odd" or at least "marching to the beat of a different drummer?" Probably, but it is difficult to tell because such pressures, often indirect, are difficult to measure (for example, merely asking someone whether they feel some pressure may induce or incline some people to deny it and resist the pressure when they would not have done so otherwise). What *can* be done is to observe and record whether individuals succumb to peer pressure—that is, whether they conform or not by adapting their behavior to that of the group. The question of interest, then, becomes: "What are the factors that influence conformity to the peer group?"

Unfortunately, the answer to that question is complex. A variety of factors may influence conformity, ranging from the age and sex of the individual to the nature of the judgment or opinion or act to which the individual may be pressured to conform. In the standard investigation of conformity, a group of individuals are brought together and asked to make public judgments about something. The task may be one of perceptual judgment (for example, which of three lines is the longest) or it may be one of opinion (should people your age have a curfew time for weekend dates). One of the individuals in the group is the subject in the experiment, while the rest are confederates of the experimenter. The peer confederates are programmed to agree on their answers to various questions, and they agree on a response that is either incorrect (saying that the middle-length line is actually the longest) or per-

453

haps unpopular (16-year-olds like us should be in by 8:30 on weekends). They thus provide answers that the subjects would not be likely to give if making the judgments alone, and so the degree to which they agree with their peers provides an index of the degree to which they are motivated to conform to peer pressure.

The classic study of peer conformity (Berenda, 1950) is now almost 50 years old, but it continues to be cited heavily in any discussion of age changes in children's conformity to peers. In this experiment children made perceptual judgments about the length of lines. It was found that peer conformity decreased slightly with age when 7- to 10-year-old children were compared to those 10 to 13 years of age. In a study that examined children from ages 6 to 16, Allen and Newtson (1972) found a decrease between the ages of 6 years and 13 years in conformity for both perceptual and opinion judgments, at least up to age 13. This decrease in conformity with age seems to be limited, however, to judgments for which the truly accurate or popular answer is reasonably obvious. In a different study, Hoving, Hamm, and Galvin (1969) utilized a task that was more difficult in that the correct answer was not immediately clear. Children were shown two slides containing a large number of dots and asked to judge which slide had more. For a nonambiguous problem, the number of dots differed significantly, whereas for an ambiguous problem the number was the same on both slides. Hoving et al. found that for the ambiguous problems conformity *in*creased with age (up to age 14), whereas for the nonambiguous problems conformity decreased with age. Berenda (1950) also found increased conformity on more difficult (that is, more ambiguous) problems. With increasing age, it appears that the peer group becomes more trusted as a source of information, producing conformity when arbitrary or ambiguous choices exist for behavior (for example, clothing styles may be seen as an "arbitrary" behavioral choice often influenced by peers, even into adulthood). At the same time, the capacity for independence may increase, producing a *de*creasing amount of conformity when a violation of firmly held standards or clear knowledge of the accurate response or choice would be required.

It is probably most reasonable to view conformity as a behavior pattern that is a means rather than an end and which will occur if the outcome is compatible with the goals of the individual. The age effects that have been observed would indicate that the goal of accuracy becomes more potent with age and that children will be true to their own opinions when they are relatively confident of their accuracy but will conform in the face of ambiguity or difficulty.

Other research has highlighted different goals that may be served or interfered with by conformity and thus produce increased or decreased reliance on peers. For example, the prestige or status of one's peers, plus the degree to which a child aspires to that prestige or status may elicit increased conformity with age (Harvey & Rutherford, 1960). In a study of delinquent boys, Harvey and Consalvi (1960) found that peer conformity was maximal among middle-status adolescents: high-status boys (those who were popular or admired) apparently had little motivation to conform and perhaps expected others to conform to *them.* Low-status boys also failed to conform to any great degree, and, perhaps in their case, low status was in part due to that failure to conform. Compatible with these interpretations is the possibility that the medium-status boys were more highly motivated to conform because it served to improve their status within their peer group.

Conformity among peers is actually influenced by many different factors, from the age of the child who has the opportunity to conform to the nature of the situation in which pressure for conformity exists. An interesting study (Berndt, McCartney, Caparulo, & Moore, 1983–1984) illustrates how a number of different factors may interact simultaneously. In this study, third- and sixth-grade children who were friends were assembled in same-sex groups. They were then given the opportunity to discuss moral dilemmas that concerned either a choice between altruistic or self-interested behavior or a choice between honesty and dishonesty. For example, one dilemma went as follows:

> Joe went to the drugstore after school to buy some candy. The store was crowded, and the saleslady was very grouchy. She told the kids not to touch anything they weren't going to buy. She also waited on all the adults first, instead of giving everyone their turn in order. Finally it was Joe's turn. He paid for his candy quickly and left. On the way home Joe noticed that the saleslady had given him too much change—50 cents more than he was supposed to have.
>
> What do you think Joe should do, go back to the store and return the change, or keep the change and forget about it? (Berndt et al, 1980, pp. 347–348).

While children discussed these dilemmas, attempting to reach a group consensus on the proper course of action for each one, their discussions were videotaped and later analyzed for how often individual children stated opinions in favor of one solution or another, how often reasons were given, and other aspects of group interaction such as incidences of verbal aggression. Most of the time the groups reached agreement in a broad, mutual fashion rather than through the vociferous opinions of a few group members. The number of different reasons given by various group members for a particular outcome was related to whether or not it was chosen. The more reasons that were given, the more likely a given outcome would be endorsed by the whole group. Interestingly, however, reasons were given more frequently for socially *un*desirable alternatives (for example, dishonesty) and so these frequently tended to be the group consensus.

It was also found that elements of the group interaction influenced which alternatives were eventually chosen. Those groups in which there was more verbal aggression, for example, tended more often to select dishonest solutions to the dilemmas, and groups in which social interaction was more cordial (for example, taking turns in the discussion itself) tended to endorse altruistic solutions. This study illustrates some of the various situational or contextual factors that influence the extent to which peer judgments and decisions are likely to conform to one another.

455

The most reasonable generalization regarding peer conformity is that it is one of the ways that the peer group may affect children's behavior, in this case by inducing children to adopt judgments, opinions, or behaviors that are held by others at or close to one's age. The factors affecting conformity are many, and depending upon a child's age, sex, contextual factors (such as the difficulty of the task or its relation to the child's own goals and standards), or the nature of a group discussion, the peer group will have a varying impact on a given child's thinking or behavior.

Group Pressures: Cohesiveness and Conflict

There is one primary prerequisite for the formation of a group: some sort of underlying commonality that unites the members and sets them apart—perhaps at odds—from other groups. The commonality most often nominated as a prime mover of group formation is that of shared values, goals, or norms. It is only when children are able to share values or norms that cohesive groups are likely to form. While children play *in* groups in nursery school, they seldom play *as* a group. Although some children may emerge as leaders, and behavior does conform to rules, leaders are likely to be simply more assertive or socially skilled children, and the rules are usually generated not by the group of children but rather by their caretakers.

In later childhood and certainly in adolescence, children begin to form groups that are truly groups. The group may be a club, with a specific shared interest in an activity or joint accomplishment, or a short-lived ad hoc camaraderie of cowboys or Indians ranging the neighborhood. The clearest and most intriguing investigation of group processes as they influence children's behavior is a single field study that has become a classic: The Robbers' Cave Experiment (Sherif & Sherif, 1953; Sherif, Harvey, White, Hood, & Sherif, 1961).

In these experiments, fifth grade boys were studied in a summer camp. The boys were divided into two groups and stationed at different parts of the camp area; each set was unaware of the other's existence. During the course of the camp, the investigators observed each set of boys become a cohesive group, a process of "naive" group formation. Following this, the two groups became one single group; this merging caused a period of antagonism with one another followed by a process of group formation involving amalgamation after conflict. We will describe this marvelous experiment in some detail because it provides a richness of information on this topic, unrivaled by any other investigation. It also illustrates a fruitful combination of both the observational and experimental methods. The original group formation was only partly manipulated by the experimenters, who simply described its natural evolution. In subsequent experiments, the principles governing the creation and resolution of intergroup conflict were clarified by intentionally manipulating factors that might increase conflict or facilitate resolution.

In the first experiment (Sherif & Sherif, 1953), the groundwork was laid for the actual Robbers' Cave Experiment (Sherif et al., 1961). In this study, during an initial stage the two groups of boys lived apart from one another and friendships within each group began to emerge. After three days, these groups were dissolved and the boys were recombined into two new ones. Friendship combinations were broken up, and every attempt was made to match the new groups of boys for ability and personality characteristics so the groups were relatively equal. The new groups had their own separate areas and activity schedules and did not interact with one another.

Five days were allowed for spontaneous groups to form. A friendship hierarchy emerged, first with the top and bottom ranks (those liked most and least) and then gradually a full hierarchical ordering. Group names were chosen, one set became the Bull Dogs and the other the Red Devils. The internal group structures for the two groups differed: The Bull Dogs were more cohesive than the Red Devils. Norms also emerged, with rules for behavior and sanctions for those who disobeyed. Each group had a mildly competitive attitude toward the other, although no direct competition had yet occurred.

Direct competition was then engineered by the experimenters (who served as the camp staff) by planning some contests that pitted the groups against one another. Although the experimenters had not foreseen it, one group consistently lost and the other consistently won. Eventually, the intergroup hostility became almost violent, especially after a particularly frustrating experience for the losing group, and the intergroup antagonism included not only drawing malicious posters (see Figures 13-3 and 13-4), but vandalism. The experiment concluded after a relatively unsuccessful attempt by the staff to quell the hostility.

FIGURE 13-3

Competition between groups: a tug-of-war between the Bull Dogs and the Red Devils.

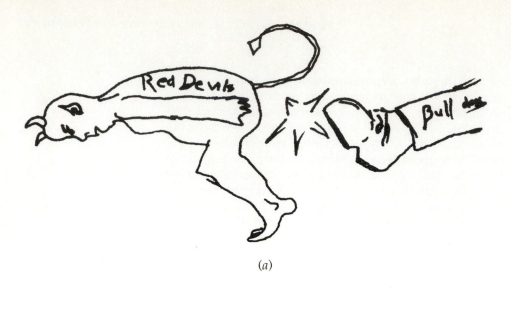

(a)

(b)

FIGURE 13-4

Two posters made by the Bull Dogs, illustrating their rivalry with the Red Devils.

Source: from Sherif & Sherif, 1966.

Sherif and his colleagues (Sherif et al., 1961) then undertook the classic Robbers' Cave Experiment to replicate the findings of the original experiment and to extend them through experimental controls and manipulations suggested by the initial study. In the Robbers' Cave Experiment, the two groups of boys were kept totally separate from the beginning, each being unaware of the other's presence. After a while, norms and status/friendship hierarchies emerged. When the two groups accidentally discovered the others' existence, group norms blossomed, and signs of in-group solidarity appeared. At this point the Rattlers and the Eagles were born.

Care was taken to ensure that competition between the groups, when allowed as part of the experiment, produced balanced outcomes and no single group accrued too heavy a load of successes or failures. Regardless of outcome, competition clearly enhanced intergroup hostility and increased solidarity within each group. The emergent solidarity had a different structure from before, however, with leaders now being those boys who were most vital for and did best in the competitions.

At this point the most difficult manipulation of the experiment was carried out. A prime intent of the study was to test some alternative procedures involving group contact that would lessen antagonism and perhaps even cause the groups to coalesce into a single superordinate one. The first attempt by the experimenters involved arranging noncompetitive group contacts that they thought might reduce friction between the warring factions. For example, both groups were invited to see a film and had to wait with one another outside the building where the film was to be shown for 15 minutes while the projector was being "fixed." In another situation, both groups were scheduled to eat in the mess hall at the same time (something that had not been done before). These contacts were to no avail: noncompetitive contact with no overriding goal that could be shared by the groups did nothing for their coalescence. In fact, the joint eating schedules produced a garbage fight.

In a second attempt to meld the two groups, an apparent "emergency" was staged that involved the entire camp. Furthermore, a *superordinate goal* was included that required the *cooperation* of the two groups. The camp was served entirely by a single water tank, up on a mountain. Late one day, at a time when the boys would not have much water in their canteens, the water was turned off at the tank. When the announcement was made to both groups of boys assembled that there was no water, it was mentioned that about 25 people were needed. There were 20 boys in both groups combined. Members of both groups immediately volunteered, but stayed in small groups of all Eagles or all Rattlers. When the boys reached the tank, there was a minor comingling of group members, but little interaction. However, as the problem narrowed toward a solution and the valve that had been plugged was discovered, intergroup participation was more common. Soon, boys were working or giving advice with no notice of who was directing their work or to whom they were giving directions, Rattler or Eagle.

Subsequently, other superordinate goals and problems were introduced to the groups. These included securing a movie that was to be shown to every-

459

one, pulling the camp food truck when it became inoperative, or pitching individual group tents when the various parts had "accidentally" been distributed across members of *both* groups. Overall, there were eight such tasks, and the final outcome was the near total dissolution of the two groups. When the boys were on a final outing, a stop for cool drinks at a soda fountain found them sitting at small tables with no clear groupings of all Rattlers or Eagles at a single table. In fact, the two groups finally voted to return home on a single bus. During that trip, again at a soda fountain, a $5.00 prize that had been awarded the Rattlers in a bean bag competition was used, at the suggestion of (former) Rattlers, to purchase malts for all 20 boys, an amount that exactly covered the bill.

There are many lessons in this research for our understanding of group tensions in society, as well as for the design of efforts to reduce such tensions. In addition, it illustrates well how naturalistic research may still lead to formal conclusions that advance basic knowledge and theory. In this case, the Sherifs formulated some very specific principles of group interaction and the resolution of intergroup conflict:

1. When individuals interact in a series of situations toward goals with common appeal that require interdependent activity for their attainment, definite group structures arise;
2. These structures involve status hierarchies and group norms that regulate the behavior and experience of individual group members;
3. When two groups meet in competitive and reciprocally frustrating engagements, in-group solidarity and cooperativeness increase; and finally,
4. When groups in a state of conflict are brought into contact under conditions embodying superordinate goals, and the attainment of these goals is important to all but cannot be achieved by the efforts of one group alone, the groups will cooperate toward the common goal and previous group boundaries are erased.

Social Acceptance and Popularity

Within any group of children, not all members are equally accepted or liked. Some children, the "popular" ones, are more liked and have more frequent interactions with other members of the group. Similarly, others are much less likely to be selected as a friend and will be generally isolated in their play or activities from the other members of the group.

In studying peer acceptance, there have been two basic methods for determining an acceptance hierarchy or "popularity scale" for a given group of children. First, it should be noted that acceptance and popularity are two terms that generally apply only to a given child interacting with members of a given reference group. Acceptance is not necessarily acceptability. It is a property of a group as it responds toward a given individual and not a characteristic of that individual. Although it may be the case that popular children in one group achieve popularity because of social skills that would cause them to surface as popular children in a totally new group of peers, this has not been firmly demonstrated, and all the causes of popularity are not well understood. Although some investigators have reported a considerable degree of stability for an individual child's acceptance across groups (Wytryol & Thompson, 1955), generally, the questions asked have been whether a child's acceptance or popularity in a group can be determined and, if so, what the qualities or outcomes of such popularity appear to be.

The first problem facing an investigator lies in the determination of popularity or acceptance. Two techniques have generally been used, one attitudinal and one behavioral. Most often, an attitudinal measure uses peer nominations: Whom do you like the most? Whom do you dislike? Whom would you like best to play with? These questions may be asked directly of a child, but more often than not an array of pictures of all the children in a given group (usually a class) will be shown to a child, who then points to the individuals chosen for acceptance or rejection. Another technique, termed the "moving sociometric technique" (Marshall & McCandless, 1957), involves behavioral observations. For this instrument, children's actual interactions in the group setting are observed and tallied, and an index of acceptance is derived.

However acceptance is measured, it is used to study peer group processes in two ways. The simplest way is to isolate extreme subsets of children—the ones generally nominated as friends by many of their peers and the ones generally nominated as enemies or someone to be avoided—and then to contrast them with one another or simply characterize them on various dimensions (for example, their level of moral reasoning or the degree to which they are compliant to adult requests).

We have already given some attention to popularity when discussing the ramifications of peer reinforcement. In the study by Furman and Masters (1980) it was found that neutral interactions with peers were associated with peer acceptance, more than either negative or positive interactions. In addition to specific types of behavior, numerous characteristics of children have been linked to social acceptance. These are represented in Table 13-2. In general, the correlates of popularity tend to be positive virtues by either peer or adult standards.

TABLE 13-2

Correlates of peer acceptance

Attribute
Much "friendly approach" and "associative" behavior
Nurturant to other peers
Friendly and outgoing
Kind
Succorant (responding positively to dependent behavior by peer)
Willing to share
Helpful
Conforming to group rules
Accepting others
High level of moral judgment

461

One particularly interesting characteristic of peer acceptance is physical attractiveness. Popular children are rated more physically attractive by both adults and peers (Dion, 1973; Dion & Berscheid, 1974). With respect to body types, rather than general attractiveness, there are stereotypes regarding the characteristics expected to be associated with them. Research on body types has been limited to boys, and thus the findings are almost certainly relevant for boys alone. When body types are rated alone, without reference to a specific child, it is clear that at least in the United States the mesomorphic build (muscular) is by far the most attractive for boys, and stereotypes exist that imply that individuals with such a build have a number of positive social and cognitive characteristics, from happiness to intelligence (Lerner, 1969; Staffieri, 1967). In the group setting, sociometric analysis has also indicated that mesomorphic boys are more likely to be nominated as best friends than those who are more lanky (ectomorphic) or chubby (endomorphic). Table 13-3 lists some of the stereotypes that are assigned to boys with different types of body builds.

Developmentally, physical attractiveness may be related to a child's age because of the physical changes that occur at different points. One of the prime periods when this can affect acceptance is during puberty, and thus for older, preadolescent children, physical attractiveness and social acceptance may vary as a function of the degree to which pubertal changes have begun to occur. This has been studied by examining the social acceptance and other personal characteristics of children who are early maturers or late maturers relative to most of their peers: early maturing children possess adult physical characteristics when most of their peers do not, while later maturers remain more child-like in their appearance.

For boys, it is clear that late sexual maturation and its attendant changes in build and appearance are associated with judgments of lesser physical attractiveness (Jones & Bayley, 1950). In addition, boys judge peers who are late maturers to have a number of negative social characteristics and late maturing boys are less likely to be elected to positions in school politics, a particularly direct measure of popularity.

By contrast, for girls, the social blessing falls upon those who are late maturers, but the blessing may be a mixed one depending upon the age of the girl. The late maturing girl is indeed more likely to be accepted by her peers during the early part of the pubertal period (12 to 15 years), when early maturers have already begun to undergo physical changes. By the end of this period, when most of her peers have matured but the late maturing girl is only beginning to do so, her initially high social acceptance has seriously eroded, and girls whose maturation is now complete and whose interests and activities have now come to include boys are gaining enhanced prestige and popularity among their female peers.

For young children, then, general physical attractiveness is related to peer acceptance for children of both sexes. During the transition from preadolescence to adolescence, sexual maturation and its physical changes have different effects on the peer acceptance of boys and girls. For boys, it is advantageous to be an early maturer while for girls it is advantageous in terms of

TABLE 13-3
Attributes children assign to boys with different types of body build

| | Descriptive Adjectives | |
Mesomorphic Build	*Ectomorphic Build*	*Endomorphic Build*
Strong	Quiet	Fights
Best friend	Worries	Cheats
Clean	Nervous	Worries
Lots of friends	Remembers	Nervous
Happy	Lonely	Argues
Helps others	Sick	Forgets
Polite	Sneaky	Lazy
Remembers	Afraid	Lies
Healthy	Sad	Sloppy
Honest	Tired	Naughty
Brave	Weak	Mean
Good looking	Fights	Ugly
Smart		Dirty
Neat		Tired
		Stupid
		Clean

| | Descriptive Phrases | |
Mesomorphic Build	*Ectomorphic Build*	*Endomorphic Build*
Assumes leadership	Eats the least	Poorest athlete
Has many friends	Needs friends	Drinks the most
Does not smoke at all	Has few friends	Needs friends
Is most aggressive	Least preferred	Eats the most
Serves own interests	Eats least often	Has few friends
Endures pain best	Makes a poor father	Least preferred
Best athlete	Smokes a lot	Makes a poor father
Best soldier	Not aggressive	Not a leader
Likely leaders	Can't endure pain	Not aggressive
No nervous breakdown	Have nervous breakdown	Can't endure pain
Most wanted as friend		Worst soldier

SOURCE: Staffieri, 1977, p. 102; Lerner, 1969, p. 140.

peer acceptance to be a late maturer. The findings for boys are bolstered by other results indicating that the social characteristics ascribed to early and late maturing boys, which are also linked to peer acceptance, are still used to characterize the individuals in early and middle adulthood, and some psychological differences persist as well, even though at that age there are no differences in the physical appearances of men who matured early or later (Jones, 1957). Table 13-4 lists some illustrative comparisons between physical and psychological characteristics of adult men who were early or late maturing as boys. For girls, there has thus far been no indication that age of sexual maturation has any relation to adult physical, social, or personality characteristics.

463

TABLE 13-4

Selected physical characteristics of early and late maturing boys in adolescence and adulthood

| | Adolescence (age 14) | | Adulthood (age 33) | |
	Early	Late	Early	Late
Height	5'8"	5'0"	5'10"	5'9½"
Weight	126.9 lb.	93.2 lb.	172.0 lb.	165.0 lb.
Endomorphism*	2.6	3.1	3.1	3.3
Mesomorphism	4.5	3.9	4.6	4.3
Ectomorphism	3.4	3.7	3.4	3.7

Selected psychological characteristics that differentiate early and late maturing boys after they have reached adulthood

	Early Maturers	Late Maturers
Good Impression[†]	25.6	15.7
Delinquency[‡]	13.9	20.3
Impulsivity	17.1	23.4
Responsibility	32.9	30.0
Dominance	19.4	12.6
Succorance[xx]	7.1	12.4

* = Measured on a 7-point scale, where 7 is high for a particular build.
† = Except for delinquency, a high score indicates a greater level of the trait.
‡ = For delinquency, a low score indicates better socialization.
xx = Succorance is the willingness to give help or aid.
SOURCE: Jones, 1957, pp. 113–128.

The data on physical attractiveness and maturation and their relation to social acceptance do not provide information about the reasons for the correlation between the two or the processes by which individual children are affected. It would be a mistake, for example, to conclude automatically that physical attractiveness directly promotes acceptance and unattractiveness undermines it. That may well be the case, of course, if stereotypes regarding negative social characteristics of persons judged unattractive are so ingrained that actual social behavior cannot alter peer perceptions and subsequent acceptance. If unattractive peers are believed to be sullen and withdrawn, they may discount or forget instances of positive social interaction while they dwell on examples of discord or isolation.

On the other hand, a mechanism such as this might be at the bottom of these results but in quite a different way: If children judge *themselves* to be unattractive and unaccepted, they may withdraw or behave in a manner consistent with the stereotype they hold of themselves. Another possibility would be that physical attractiveness is to some extent judged from behavior, and withdrawn, sullen children are not judged as attractive as happy, enthusiastic ones. Finally, children may be accepted or rejected largely because of the ways in which they behave, not the way they appear, but accepted children may tend to become enthusiastic and happy because of numerous

RESEARCH FOCUS 13-3

The Role of Physical Attractiveness in Peer Relations

It would be pleasant to learn that physical attractiveness bore no relation to children's peer interactions or choices of friends. Unfortunately, this is not the case. Both children and adults judge the attractiveness of children, and these judgments influence their thinking about them and behavior toward them. Dion (1973) found that children as young as 3 to 5 years of age can choose the "prettier" or "cuter" of two photographs and make the same choices as do adults. In addition, to be "prettier," "cuter," or simply more physically attractive is generally an advantage. Children hold different stereotypes about attractive versus unattractive peers, attributing to attractive ones such characteristics as greater intelligence or better overall social skills (Langlois & Stephan, 1977). There is also evidence that differing stereotypes literally begin to be applied while babies are still in the crib. Corter et al. (1978) found that nurses rated the intelligence of preterm infants higher as a function of the infant's attractiveness. In addition, stereotyped expectancies pervade some of the most important environments in which children spend their time. Styczynski and Langlois (1980) found that teachers perceive attractive children in their classrooms to be better achievers, better adjusted to the classroom, more intellectually and emotionally adjusted, and more competent in their social behavior. Children of all ages, from preschool to adolescence, want attractive children as friends (Cavior & Dokecki, 1973; Dion, 1973; Langlois & Stephan, 1977). There is also some evidence that physically attractive children behave differently from unattractive ones as they grow older. For example, in one study attractive preschool children did not behave much differently from unattractive ones, but among older children unattractive peers were more aggressive toward their companions (Langlois & Downs, 1979). It has also been found that attractive children obtain higher scores on achievement tests (Styczynski & Langlois, 1980) and engage in more positive interactions with teachers (Algozzine, 1977). The possibility, therefore, exists that stereotypes about the behavior of attractive and unattractive children become self-fulfilling prophesies, inclining others to treat children differently as a function of their physical attractiveness and, through this differential treatment, encourage the development of expected differences in behavior.

The most important question concerns the origins of both the stereotypes and the cognitive and behavioral differences that have been observed with respect to attractive and unattractive children. The strongest hypothesis is that, in Western cultures, at least, judgments of physical attractiveness are commonly made and lead others to treat differently children who become labeled as attractive or not. There is no clear evidence that this occurs and is continued as the child grows older, but there is certainly no evidence to the contrary—and the existence of stereotypes about children's intellectual and social competencies that differ according to physical attractiveness imply strongly that they may lead to differential treatment. Research on this issue is of particular importance if steps are to be taken toward removing the impact of this one dimension of stigma on children's development. ❧

---

and enjoyable peer interactions, while rejected children withdraw and appear unhappy or sullen because they are socially isolated. Certainly the answer does not lie in any single one of these possibilities, some of which are clearly less viable than others as possible explanations for the observed relation between attractiveness and peer acceptance (studies, for example, in which attractiveness is rated by adults who do not know a child and who complete their ratings from pictures and cannot infer unattractiveness from knowledge of a child's behavior report findings that indicate a relation between culturally defined physical attractiveness and observed peer acceptance, but this does not mean that the relation is not mediated by the unattractive child's social behavior).

Another characteristic of a child that appears to be related to social acceptance is the child's name. In an intriguing study, McDavid and Harari (1966) asked 10- to 12-year-old children to rate the desirability of each of the first names of children in their social group at a community center. The

RESEARCH FOCUS 13-4

The Role of Physical and Intellectual Handicaps in Peer Relations

Recent developments in American society and social policy have had an important impact on the development of handicapped children. Following the broad principal that everyone should have a minimally restrictive environment, there have been efforts to increase the freedom of movement and access for all handicapped individuals. For children, this has had the greatest effect in the area of schooling, with Public Law 94–142, in particular, promoting the inclusion of handicapped children in the general classroom ("mainstreaming") to the extent that it can be done and benefit the child. One consequence of this has been to provide many handicapped children with far more extensive peer relations than they might otherwise have had and, conversely, to enrich the peer experiences of nonhandicapped children.

Because these changes are recent, there is relatively little information available about the role of handicapping conditions in peer interaction. Children with intellectual handicaps (learning disabilities and mild mental retardation) are less well accepted in the classroom or occupy a lower social status than do their nonhandicapped peers (Bryan, 1974, 1976; Bruininks, 1978; Gottlieb, 1975). Handicapping conditions seem to be associated with behavior that does not facilitate peer interactions, such as lowered communication effectiveness or constructive play (Guralnick, 1981), antisocial behavior (McMichael, 1980), and aggression (Campbell & Levine, 1980; Schleifer et al., 1975).

Certainly it is important to learn the degree to which the behavior of the handicapped lead to poor peer relations or, more plausibly, the degree to which the handicap leads to different behavior by the handicapped child's peers, which then leads to the development of socially maladaptive behaviors by the handicapped children themselves. These possibilities are not mutually exclusive. For example, many handicapped children (particularly those with multiple or orthopedic handicaps) may have very different and impoverished social experiences with peers prior to the school years and thus come to the school environment with a deficit of social skills needed for the development of good peer relations. At the same time, nonhandicapped children may notice the handicap, judge that there is something "different" about the handicapped child (Gerber, 1977), and then behave differently toward the child or even tend to avoid contact (Richardson, Goodman, Hestorf, & Dornbusch, 1961). It may also be the case that changing social policies, as in the United States, will lead to different findings about handicaps as contact with handicapped children becomes more common, occurs more often in the preschool setting, and as children who have themselves had more contact with handicapped peers grow up to be parents and teachers. ❧

children also rated the desirability of first names of children whom they did not know (from another center). Popularity was then assessed by a socio-metric technique. The relationship between children's ratings of the desira-bility of their peers' names and the popularity of those peers ($r = .63$) was particularly strong. This, of course, could indicate that children's popularity influenced their peers' judgments of the desirability of their first name, or

RESEARCH FOCUS 13-5

Race and Ethnicity in Peer Relations

Even before entering school (at 4 years of age), children are aware of racial differences (Clark & Clark, 1939). This is true of children who are black, white, or Hispanic (Werner & Evans, 1968). And, on the foundation of an awareness of race or ethnic background, children develop attitudes, preferences, and patterns of interaction that distinguish children from each other by race. Early attitudes and preferences tend to favor white children. For example, when given the op-portunity to select a black or white doll or to choose a family that one might live with, pref-erences tend to favor white dolls or families. Most studies have been conducted on American children, but a tendency to prefer lighter skin color has been found among children in Europe and Japan (Best, Field, & Williams, 1976; Best, Naylor, & Wilham, 1975; Iwawaki, Sonoo, Wil-liams, & Best, 1978). Interestingly, a bias toward whites is frequently found among black children as well as white, though it is somewhat weaker among black children (Williams & Moreland, 1976). This result is interpreted to be influenced by a tendency in multiracial societies for white individuals to enjoy a more privileged station in life (Hartup, 1983). Interestingly, when children's level of cognitive development is taken into ac-count, it is found that a bias toward whites is significantly lower among children with higher levels of cognitive development, at least when the person inquiring about preferences is black (Clark, Hocevar, & Dembo, 1980).

It is important to note that racial preferences tend to follow gradations in color and are thus not directly indicative of racial biases that dis-criminate one race versus another. For example,

in studies that use pictures or other stimuli that vary continuously in shades of lightness or dark-ness of skin, preferences change gradually, as relative whiteness or blackness varies (Hartup, 1983). It has also been found that among black children, those who are darker show a greater preference for black dolls than do black children whose skin is lighter (Clark & Clark, 1958). This indicates that the relative lightness or darkness of one's *own* skin contributes to attitudes and preferences. Peer interaction also occurs more frequently among same-race children than on a cross-race basis, and this changes very little through childhood to early adolescence (Mc-Candless & Hoyt, 1961; Sagar, Schofield, & Sny-der, 1983; Schofield & Sagar, 1977). However, when cross-race interactions are examined, it has been found that black children are more than twice as likely to initiate such interactions than are white children (Sagar et al., 1983). If any-thing, there is some longitudinal evidence that racial identification and within-race peer prefer-ences may increase slightly with age, up to the sixth grade (Singleton & Asher, 1979). It is also found that the frequency of cross-race friend-ships declines during the elementary school years, and abruptly so on entrance to high school (Jelenek & Brittan, 1975). Why these age changes are noted is not clearly understood and merits further attention. In addition, there has been lit-tle examination of changes in children's cross-racial preferences and interactions with the pas-sage of time, as social changes are implemented to reduce discrimination at the societal level (such as desegregation). ❧

that the desirability of their first names contributed to their social popularity—or both. The more accurate test came, however, when desirability ratings of names were made by children who did *not* know the children who had these names; when these results were correlated with children's popularity, the correlation remained high ($r = .49$). This independent assessment of name desirability strengthens the conclusion that children's names influence the degree to which they became socially popular. However, as was the case for physical attractiveness, the mechanisms mediating any effect of name desirability on popularity are still unclear. Do children initially avoid other children whose names are difficult to learn, pronounce, or spell, in this way starting a pattern of social rejection that then continues? Do teachers give less attention to children with difficult names for similar reasons? Are children with common names more likely to be hailed and thus brought into the group? There is little knowledge about the reasons why one unusual name might be considered attractive, whereas another is not.

Infrequently used names—which, of course may be quite attractive—do not invariably impose a stereotype on a child or cause differential treatment that may stem from such stereotypes. In addition, even though it makes sense that the desirability of a name, more than its frequency, should be a major factor in determining how a child's name comes to have an effect on achievement or behavior, still more obvious factors in stereotyping and discrimination, such as race or ethnicity, are of greater importance. When these factors are taken into account, a child's name has little effect (Ford, Miura, & Masters, 1984).

This may be a particularly interesting and important time to investigate the influence of stereotypes since many are changing or being eliminated. Indeed, popular athletes and books have drawn attention to unusual names such as those drawn from the Muslim heritage (Ali, Abdul, Karim) or African cultures. Today's vital statistics in the newspaper stand as evidence to an incoming generation of children with distinctly different names. The current findings of the relation of infrequent names and their social development may someday stand as testimony to important changes in society.

Summary

We live and develop in a social world, one that is initially populated by older people, and later also populated by others younger than ourselves; throughout, however, this world is populated by our peers. Although it is perhaps most common to view socialization as a "downward" process, with those older, wiser, more skilled, or in positions of authority influencing the development of younger and less mature individuals, this avenue of socialization is paralleled by socialization influences stemming from peer interactions. In addition, the peer group comprises an important context for development, including the practice and implementation of skills and abilities and the development of needs and desires.

Unlike other domains of development, it is probably fair to say that peer influences do not have any specific origins. Peer interactions and the developmental influences from those interactions originate during infancy, to the extent that infants have the opportunity to interact with infants their age. This interaction is becoming increasingly common as social institutions such as group day care come to be more available, acceptable, and used by parents and caretakers of infants.

Several threads comprise the fabric of the developmental course for peer interactions and influences on development. Initially, in infancy, interactions are only technically social as infants treat one another as social "objects." Gradually they come to play with one another, treating each other as individuals and eventually interacting in ways that are cooperative and reciprocal. Later at least some peer interactions take on an affective character, and friendships develop that provide an additional context for socialization influences beyond that deriving from more cursory play- or activity-oriented interactions with less familiar or liked peers. Finally, while peer interactions initially are nested within the superordinate context of the family, and subsequently the school, as the child matures the influence of peers on behavior and development becomes more predominant.

To some extent, like other contexts of development, the peer group *is* an environment. However, peer interactions themselves occur within other contexts such as family, school, and eventually work place, that lend further environmental effects. As an environment, peers act as models for standards and patterns of behavior, socializing agents who reward and punish, comrades with whom children cohere and competitors whom they assail, and groups of individuals, some who accept the children, others who reject them, and still others who ignore them.

Peers and peer influences are interrelated with many domains of a child's development. The peer group itself typically provides the context for maladaptive, antisocial behavior and the maladjusted social cognitions that may foster such behavior. At the same time, prosocial behaviors toward peers will be targeted.

Physical development, particularly during preadolescence, may have consequences for social and emotional development because of children's appearance or level of physical maturity relative to age mates. In general, it is difficult to imagine how all aspects of development could fail to be influenced, at least to some small degree, by children's experiences with their peers.

Suggested Readings

BERNDT, T. J., & LADD, G. W. (1989). *Peer relationships in child development*. New York: Wiley.

HARTUP, W. W. (1983). Peer relations. In E. M. Hetherington (Ed.), P. Mussen (Series Ed.), *Handbook of Child Psychology: Vol. 4. Socialization, Personality, and Social Development* (pp. 103–196). New York: Wiley.

HARTUP, W. W. (1989). Social relationships and their developmental significance. *American Psychologist, 44*, 120–126.

YOUNISS, J. (1980). *Parents and peers in social development: A Sullivan-Piaget perspective.* Chicago: University of Chicago Press.

CHAPTER FOURTEEN

Gender and the Development of Gender Roles

Introduction

Human beings are distinctive individuals as a result of the complex interplay of genetic endowment, capabilities and competencies that emerge as they develop, and social and cultural influences that other persons and social institutions provide as persons interact with them. In the previous five chapters, the focus has been on the processes by which this interplay takes place. At different times we have addressed the origins of significant patterns of social behavior, the developmental course that most individuals follow in acquiring a repertoire of behaviors that are necessary in social life, and the environmental contexts and influences that contribute to the acquisition and performance of those behaviors. We also have considered interrelations among the cognitive, emotional, and social aspects of individual functioning across age periods.

In this chapter and the next, we will shift the focus to the products of developmental processes. We will focus particularly on two aspects of development that are viewed as especially significant in forming personality—that is, in establishing differences among individuals. In this chapter we discuss differences attributed to being male or female. Of particular interest are the social expectations and direct and indirect socialization pressures for males and females to behave differently from one another. The other, which we will address in Chapter 15, concerns the capacity for self-regulation. The degree to which individuals manage their own behaviors and mesh them with the expectations and actions of others marks them in ways that are socially meaningful. With respect to both sex differences and self-regulation, the emergence of individuality is channeled to some extent by common patterns of change from one age period to another. Accordingly, an important focus will be the role of developmental changes in how differences between persons manifest themselves.

We now turn to the topic of differences between males and females. We will first describe some of these differences and possible explanations for them. We will then consider the nature and course of development with respect to social expectations about male–female differences and the development of children's knowledge about these expectations. Next we will examine the acquisition of behaviors that are expected either of males or females and the pertinent influences that encourage different patterns of behaviors for the two sexes. Finally, we will briefly discuss sexual orientation and its relation to socialization influences.

Sex Differences in Behavior and the Processes of Gender-Role Development

As a first step, we should consider the basic question: *Are* there psychological sex differences in behavior and cognition? The answer is almost undoubtedly yes. What general characteristics seem commonly to characterize children of one gender or the other? With respect to personality characteristics and social behaviors, in general, boys seem more likely to become more active, aggressive, demanding, and risk-taking, whereas girls are more likely to be socially responsive and accommodating and to experience emotions (both positive and negative) more intensely (DiPietro, 1981; Eaton & Keats, 1982; Ginsburg & Miller, 1982; Gunnar & Donahue, 1980; Maccoby, 1980; Martin, 1980; Phillips, King, & Dubois, 1978). Despite their generally better performance, girls show more negative self-evaluations of their academic performance than boys (Dweck & Gilliard, 1975) and tend to "internalize" failure by attributing it to a lack of ability (as opposed to luck, difficulty of the material, and so on) (Frey & Ruble, 1987).

Several qualifications need to be kept in mind. First, except for case studies (which clearly apply only to the individual studied), research on sex differences involves studying *groups* of girls and boys, and the results, that may be reliable and valid for groups, may well not apply to some individual children, perhaps even a large number of them. Second, where personality and social behaviors and even cognitions are concerned, there may well be cultural or subcultural differences in the sex typing that children acquire so that a sex difference in a given culture would not represent a universal one, even with respect to group data. Children in an extremely docile and passive society, for example, might show very little aggressive behavior, with no sex differences in that which is shown. Third, although there are many cognitive and behavioral differences between the sexes, these are certainly outweighed by the similarities. A scientific interest in sex differences does not imply a value judgment that such differences are frequent, of special significance, or that the patterns of behavior and cognition characterizing children of one sex are more adaptive or somehow "better" than those pertaining to the other. Finally, whatever sex differences there may be, or however parents and peers treat children of the two genders differently, it is not always clear what judgments should be made about the exact nature of these differences and what value they might have for adaptive, healthy development.

To what degree are sex differences in social behavior and cognition a product of biological sex differences? Males and females are chromosomally different,

Biological Sex Differences

with males bearing an XY combination and females an XX, and there are hormonal differences as well (androgen versus estrogen). In terms of tissues and organs, the two sexes also differ, both in terms of internal organs and in terms of those external organs that can have direct social and psychological as well as physiological meanings. There are also differences in musculature, size, and appearance that are not related to actual reproduction but that still differentiate the sexes.

From a biological perspective, one may ask whether there are any direct influences of biological factors on behavior that may constitute or lead to sex differences in behavior and cognition that arise during development. In this vein, attention has been given primarily to biologically sex-linked characteristics in behavior that appear at or around the time of birth. For example, it has been found that male infants tend to sleep less, be more active, show a lower sensitivity to pain, and exhibit more crying, irritability, and resistance to being comforted than infant girls (e.g., Bell, Weller & Waldrip, 1971; Maccoby, 1980). It is possible that these differences between male and female infants contribute to different experiences in later childhood. That is, the lower tractability implied by boys' generally higher activity level, lower sensitivity to pain, and greater resistance to being comforted could increase the likelihood that boys would, on the average, be more assertive and independent than girls. The general assumption is that sex differences in behavior or receptiveness *before* socialization could have played a role that may be ascribed to biological factors (even if the exact factors cannot be pinpointed), but that the most important role of biological factors is providing the foundation for differential treatment and experiences that can compound them into broader and much more significant types of sex differences at later periods of development.

This is not to say that physiological factors do not play an important role, but this role is not well understood and seems guaranteed to be indirect and not as powerful as a person might at first think. For example, while prenatal injections of male hormones such as testosterone may induce high activity levels and promote aggressive responding in other species (Young, Goy, & Phoenix, 1964), measuring the level of such hormones as they occur naturally in children of different ages will not predict individual differences in aggressive responding with any degree of accuracy. In short, cognitive and behavioral sexual differentiation appear to be largely the result of psychological and social aspects of development, and not physical aspects.

A Model of the Gender-Role Development

In general, contemporary approaches to the study of sex typing are frequently not established principles and often represent an apparent amalgamation of concepts. Most theories of social and personality development, however, identify at least some components that are likely to be important. Psychodynamic theories call attention to the importance of early development and the role of parents. Cognitive developmental theory stresses the importance of taking into account how the child understands the world, including his or her own gender, as both an aspect of gender-role development and a filter

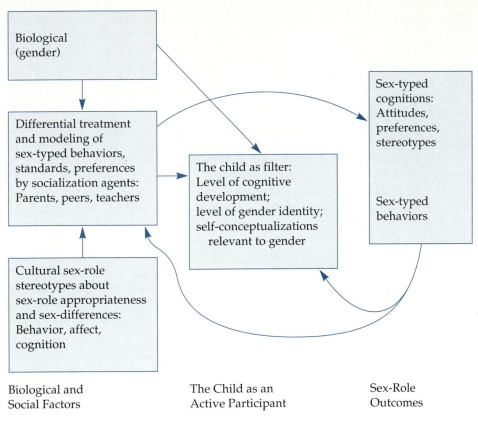

Biological
(gender)

Differential treatment
and modeling of
sex-typed behaviors,
standards, preferences
by socialization agents:
Parents, peers, teachers

Cultural sex-role
stereotypes about
sex-role appropriateness
and sex-differences:
Behavior, affect,
cognition

The child as filter:
Level of cognitive
development;
level of gender identity;
self-conceptualizations
    relevant to gender

Sex-typed
cognitions:
Attitudes,
preferences,
stereotypes

Sex-typed
behaviors

Biological and
Social Factors

The Child as an
Active Participant

Sex-Role
Outcomes

FIGURE 14-1

Schematic representation of major factors in gender-role development and the relations between them.

for the impact of social experience. Finally, social learning theory identifies
some of the processes by which social experiences with peers and adults
promote the acquisition of gender-role standards, expectancies, and behavior.

Figure 14-1 presents a schematic representation of some of the major factors
entering into gender-role development and outlines some of the relations
between them. A person's biological gender is a cornerstone of their acquisition of a gender role, providing two kinds of influence, physiological (e.g.,
hormonal) and psychological (e.g., people's own recognition of their physical
gender and others' recognition of it). Those who populate the child's social
world, predominantly parents, peers, and teachers, are influenced by cultural
beliefs about gender roles, their recognition of the child's gender, and their
own sex typing as they verbalize gender-role appropriate standards of conduct, model behaviors culturally sex typed as appropriate for their own
gender, or treat the child differently as a function of the child's gender (e.g.,
reinforce gender-role appropriate behaviors and punish or ignore inappro-

475

priate ones). Children themselves are both "targets" of these influences and filters, in the sense that factors such as current level of cognitive development or degree of sex typing will affect how they are influenced (for example, a girl may become more and more attentive to—and influenced by—female models as she comes to perceive herself clearly to be a girl who will become a woman). The outcome—gender role, the roster of sex-appropriate cognitions and behaviors that children adopt—is also an influence, feeding back to the children themselves through self-monitoring, and to socialization agents as they react to sex-appropriate (and inappropriate) behaviors that the children display or cognitions (for example, preferences) that they verbalize or in some other way make apparent.

Now we will consider the other aspects of Figure 14-1 relevant to gender-role development. We begin with a review of some of what we know about the development of gender-role stereotypes and expectations influencing sex differences in behavior. Periodically, it may be helpful to refer to Figure 14-1 as a guide to the particular domain of influence under discussion and how it may be related to other factors.

Gender-Role Expectations and Knowledge

Social and Cultural Expectations Related to Gender

Rightly or wrongly, it is almost always the case that societies hold belief systems relating to various classes of individuals, either within that society or in other cultural groups. Such beliefs may be developed about tall people, short people, athletic ones, sedentary ones or, more unfortunately, about black people, white people, male or female people. Beliefs of this sort, which include common inferences and expectations about individuals who may be labeled as belonging to a certain class, are frequently termed *stereotypes*. It is not within the purpose of this book to assess the validity of particular beliefs but rather to discuss their development and implications. Indeed, it is not all that necessary for the existence of a stereotype that it be accurate, and to the extent that we are all individual people, no stereotype can go very far toward providing a complete description of any one person's characteristics or behavior.

There are two primary reasons to be concerned about gender-role stereotypes. First, to the extent that they exist among peers or adults, such stereotypes may shape how a child is treated by others and, through such socialization experiences, become self-fulfilling prophecies by shaping the child's behavior and thought to be consistent with them. Second, the acquisition of such stereotypes is itself a part of gender-role development. Children learn the typical expectations held by other members of the society both for persons of the same gender and for persons of the opposite gender.

476

RESEARCH FOCUS 14-1

Gender-Role Stereotypes and Methods of Studying Gender-Role Development

Given that there are strong beliefs, myths or otherwise, about gender differences, and given that boys and girls, women and men, frequently find themselves in different contexts for reasons that may or may not be justified only by gender (for example, conscripted for war, accepted to positions of leadership, or placed in deferential positions), the differences observed may be influenced by the contexts in which they are observed or the measures used to define them. Let us elaborate.

First, it should be noted that even theories of sex typing, from which measures are derived, have been criticized as biased with respect to sex differences. Kohlberg's theory in particular has been intensely criticized from both a theoretical and methodological perspective (Gilligan, 1977, 1979, 1982a, 1982b). Theoretically it has been contended that Kohlberg's general theory of moral development is "androcentric" in identifying masculine sex-typed characteristics (for example, individuality and detachment) as characteristic of "higher" moral developmental stages and other characteristics that may be more "feminine" (for example, adherence to responsibility, valuing interpersonal relationships) to lower ones, something that Kohlberg in fact defended (Kohlberg, 1981). Methodologically, it has been pointed out that the longitudinal data from which the stage sequence was constructed were data comprised totally of men (Colby et al., 1983) and the assessment instrument consists of moral dilemmas that include primarily men as the major actors. Although controversy remains regarding the sex-neutral character of Kohlberg's theory or the general finding that there are no sex differences in moral reasoning (Baumrind, 1986; Walker, 1984, 1986), the point is to illustrate how a bias *might* be present in a theory or associated methodology, which could produce consistent but erroneous research findings suggestive of a sex difference (or lack thereof).

It is also possible that sex differences are context sensitive, which would mean that even if they do exist in certain contexts they should not be generalized. In short, they would be a function of the interaction between a child's sex and a given context. One study illustrates this possibility well (Huston, Carpenter, Atwater, & Johnson, 1986). Children were observed in two different activity settings, one with high structure in which adults provided rules, guidelines, suggestions, and modeling, and one in which the adults were less constraining or leading. When given the option, girls tended to spend more time in activities where there was high structure and boys opted more frequently for ones with low structure. However, while engaged in high structure activities, there were no gender differences in children's social behavior toward the adults. Both girls and boys tended to make many bids for adult attention, showed less peer interaction, were equally compliant and equal in their attempts to exert leadership. In low structure activities children were more peer oriented, primarily toward same-sex peers. These results suggest that sex differences, and other gender-role related behavior such as a focus on same-sex peer interactions, are not as general as they might blindly be interpreted to be, even though the behavior is shown in a multitude of findings. Also the results indicate that sex differences, as well as similarities, should be interpreted with attention to the context as well as a child's physical gender, age, or other factors that are more commonly recognized as playing a part in gender-role development.

The existence of gender-role stereotypes among children as well as adults has ramifications for *how* one might best study sex role development as well as for *what* differences there may be in gender roles and the developmental course for children's adoption of them. One group of investigators (Zarbatany, Hartmann, Gelfand, & Vinciguerra, 1985) called into question the frequent observation (and experimental finding) that girls are more generous or altruistic than boys (Hartshorne, May & Maller, 1929; Shigetomi, Hartmann, & Gelfand, 1981). They noted that a given child's altruism is variable and often specific to a context (for example, children may only be generous or helpful when there are ample rewards to share or help is clearly needed), suggesting that if the context is sex typed, sex differences in behavior may be elicited that are actually a function of the context and not the character or personality of a given child.

Generosity itself is generally sex typed as more feminine than masculine. To test the hypothesis that sex differences in altruism favoring girls may reflect a sex typing of the opportunities to be generous, Zarbatany and her colleagues developed a "gender fair" assessment of altruistic reputation that included "masculine" contexts for altruistic behavior (for example, helping "get another kid's cat out of a tree"), "feminine" ones (for example, consoling a child who had slipped and fallen), as well as neutral ones (for example, sharing a school utensil, such as a crayon). While there was a tendency for preadolescent children (fifth graders) of both sexes to see girls as more likely to engage in prosocial, altruistic behavior, confirming the general stereotype, boys were perceived to be more altruistic for masculine sex-typed contexts and opportunities, while girls were seen to be more altruistic in feminine or neutral contexts. This suggests that while the gender-role socialization of girls may press for altruistic behavior a bit more than that for boys, in a sex-appropriate context boys are seen to be quite capable of prosocial behavior and are even expected to be more likely to behave that way than are girls. It is to be noted, however, that this study actually reveals the gender-role stereotyping of *expectations,* and it remains for other research (for example, an observational study) to confirm whether boys' and girls' altruistic behavior really is differentiated not in overall frequency but simply by the sex-typed nature of opportunities to behave that way. ❧

One powerful dimension of stereotyping is an individual's sex. Consider Roger Brown's characterization of American stereotypes about the characteristics, cognitive, affective, and behavioral, of boys and girls:

> In the United States a *real* boy climbs trees, disdains girls, dirties his knees, plays with soldiers, and takes blue for his favorite color. A real girl dresses dolls, jumps rope, plays hopscotch, and takes pink for her favorite color. When they go to school, real girls like English and music and "auditorium"; real boys prefer manual training, gym, and arithmetic. In college the boys smoke pipes, drink beer, and major in engineering or physics; the girls chew Juicy Fruit gum, drink cherry Cokes, and major in fine arts. The real boy matures into a "man's man" who plays poker, goes hunting, drinks brandy, and dies in the war; the real girl becomes a "feminine" woman who loves children, embroiders handkerchiefs, drinks weak tea, and "succumbs" to consumption (Roger Brown, 1965, p. 161).

Thus, it is generally not difficult to develop a set of broad dimensions that describe societal "standards" for behavior related to a person's sex: "real" boys climb trees and so forth, while "real" girls surely value playing with dolls and other "ladylike" activities. Stereotypes about sex roles are important for several reasons. To the extent that they characterize the beliefs of people

478

who act as socializing agents, they may incline people to treat children differently as a function of their sex, thus possibly causing the stereotypes to emerge by influencing the behavior of others to conform to the stereotypes. In addition, if sex-role beliefs abound, then it is important to understand how they are acquired and the how, once acquired, they affect behavior.

Within Western culture, role beliefs are common and are often shared by large groups of people. Traditional sex-role beliefs may be found readily within modern society even though recent years have seen increased latitude in the range of sex-typed behaviors allowed for people (Broverman, Vogel, Clarkson, & Rosenkrantz, 1972; Huston, 1983). Even more unfortunately, it also seems that the social value of different stereotypes is not equal for the two sexes. Stereotypes relating to women or girls are not as positive as those relating to presumably male-appropriate behaviors and may even filter into people's interpretation of a given person's behavior. For example, a part of the male stereotype is that men are more intellectually capable and adventurous than women, who are stereotypically dependent, passive, and often illogical (Broverman et al., 1972; Kohlberg, 1966).

When behavior counter to a stereotype is observed, it may be interpreted differently than when this behavior is shown by a person for whose sex it is "appropriate." Thus, when women succeed at a task, the success is devalued and, as it has been said: "What is skill for the male is luck for the female" (Deaux & Emswiller, 1974). Similarly, even professional people may find themselves showing judgments that are obviously influenced by stereotypes in ways that they themselves are not aware. One study showed that a standard for good mental health proposed by a group of clinical psychologists very closely matched their conceptualization for the mentally healthy male, while there were significant differences between the broad mental health standard and the concept of what comprised a healthy female (Broverman, Broverman, Clarkson, Rosenkrants, & Vogel, 1970). It is lamentable that our society contains stereotypes of these sorts, but this underscores both the social and psychological importance of understanding factors influencing the development of sex-role stereotypes and the role such beliefs may play in the organization of behavior.

Children's knowledge about sex or gender as a personal characteristic develops quite early, and children can correctly identify another child's sex easily by 3 years of age (Thompson, 1975). Sex-role expectations have also developed by this time. Children show preferences for toys that are typed appropriately for their sex (Nadelman, 1974; Thompson, 1975). They have also learned that there are activities and responsibilities that are deemed appropriate for one sex or another (Kohlberg, 1966). Indeed, sex-typed preferences in toys are evident very early. In one study (O'Brien & Huston, 1985), toddlers aged 14 to 35 months showed distinct preferences for toys that were sex-stereotyped as appropriate for their own gender. In this study, the toddlers were then followed over a 14 month period to track any changes in sex-typed toy preferences. It was found that girls' attraction to "feminine" toys increased, but boys' preferences for "masculine" toys did not. Interest-

Development of Gender-Role Knowledge and Stereotypes

Imitating the behavior of same-sex adults is an important part of the transmission of gender roles.

ingly, this seems to reflect a tendency for boys to show a strong preference for "masculine" toys very early, choosing male sex-typed toys with such frequency that there is little room for those preferences to show any increase.

There is evidence (Flerx, Fidler, & Rogers, 1976) that young children's sex-role stereotypes also extend to judgments regarding cognitive abilities such as intelligence, the expression of emotion, and various play and work activities. Four and 5-year-old children show a greater degree of stereotyped judgments than 3-year-olds. Findings like these indicate that the significant socialization of sex-role stereotypes may begin during the toddler years, with stereotype judgments showing signficant increases between 3 and 5 years. Other studies have indicated that stereotypic judgments made by 4-year-old children may already correspond quite closely to those of adults in the society.

In one experiment (Masters & Wilkinson, 1976), 4-year-old children, 8-year-old children, and adults were asked to judge whether a large group of toys was appropriate for boys or girls. The youngest children already showed a great degree of stereotyping, and by 8 years of age the children produced judgments that were essentially identical to those produced by adults. The child's own sex was also found to have an effect, with children (primarily the youngest) showing less stereotyping for their own sex than for the opposite sex. Among adults, it was found that parents having children of one sex were likely to show less stereotyping for children of that sex than were parents of children of the other sex. These last findings indicate that, in addition to socialization determinants of sex stereotypes, an individual's own experience enters in: parents of boys were likely to characterize a wide variety of toys as being appropriate for boys, while parents of girls were likely to have a much expanded category of toys that were appropriate for girls. In this way, the experience of parenting influences parents themselves, and their beliefs about behaviors that are appropriate for some children (who are the same sex as their own) are likely to be less rigid.

Gender Stereotypes Held By Children. It is reasonable also to ask what sorts of experiences initiate stereotypes in *children* and what sorts of experiences might lead to changes in these stereotypes—for example, a liberalization of sex-role conceptualizations that does not place heavy constraints on the variety of behaviors that are expected and deemed appropriate for people as a function of their physiological gender. The major processes involved are likely to include those already discussed: praise and reinforcement by parents and other socialization agents for sex-appropriate behaviors, punishment for inappropriate behaviors, and selective exposure to models who demonstrate behaviors that are deemed sex appropriate. In addition, consistent exposure to symbolic models demonstrating traditionally sex-typed behaviors—heroes and heroines of stories, movies, and TV shows—may have an enduring influence on the adoption of sex-appropriate behaviors as well as the emergence of beliefs regarding the appropriateness of various categories of behavior, activities, and toys or equipment for one sex or another.

Along this line, extensive surveys of children's literature indicate that by far the majority of these books depict men and women in quite traditional, stereotyped manners (Weitzman, Eiffer, Hokada, & Ross, 1972). Women are clearly in the minority as leading characters and are far outnumbered by men overall. When included in a story, women are frequently cast in passive and dependent roles relative to the men, often being rescued by the men. Among the books that won a medal given annually for the outstanding children's book for the entire 30-year period from 1941 to 1971 there is not a single book in which a woman is allowed a role that puts her in a job or profession.

Judgments About Gender Appropriateness. One corollary of general stereotypes about gender-role appropriateness is that they will be used to judge behavior, preferences, and appearances, both of others and in oneself. This is a more complex issue than it might seem at first because the judgment process is not merely one in which a given behavior is gauged to be appropriate or inappropriate. Consider the case where a behavior is judged to be inappropriate: *How* inappropriate might it be? How *serious* is this transgression from the "norm" of gender-role appropriate behavior? By what *criteria* would this seriousness be judged? In this sense, the application of gender-role stereotypes is a judgment process much like that of moral judgment, in which the transgression violates an implicit rule of conduct.

Although it depends somewhat on what is being judged (behavior, appearance, preference), generally transgressions in sex-appropriate behavior are judged more harshly by preschool children and by adolescents than by children during the middle school years (e.g., Stoddart & Turiel, 1985). This appears to reflect the degree to which children understand the variety of forms that "rules" can take. Rules are sometimes absolute, based on reasoning that is not arbitrary and is unquestioned: You don't run out into the street because you might get hit by a car. Other rules take the form of conventions, arbitrary in nature but generally agreed upon: You don't eat with your fingers, especially at someone else's house. Younger children are more likely to consider rules, any rules, to be absolute and nonarbitrary and only later consider the possibility that they are flexible because they reflect conventions rather than absolutes. It appears that gender-role stereotypes may be treated differently by children of different ages (or of different genders), either as absolute rules of appropriate conduct or as conventions.

Stoddart and Turiel (1985) interviewed kindergarten through eighth grade children about many sorts of transgressions, including those that violated gender-role stereotypes. They found that kindergarten and adolescent children were more inflexible and harsh in their judgments of such transgressions than were children of intermediate age. Interestingly, children gave different sorts of reasons for their judgments. The youngest children argued that sex-inappropriate behavior was wrong because it was inappropriate to one's biological gender, and it was an inviolable rule that behavior and gender should match. This sort of judgment may reflect both a difficulty in considering apparent rules as conventions rather than dogmatic prescriptions and a not-yet-solidified overall sense of gender identity (for example, one reason sex-inappropriate behavior would be intolerable is that it might alter one's biological gender). Slightly older children treated the sex appropriateness of behavior as a convention, one that most people might agree to adhere to but which was nevertheless arbitrary, with violations not judged as that serious. Adolescents, on the other hand, reasoned that sex-inappropriate behavior might reflect (or cause) problems in one's psychological gender identity—sexual orientation—and found it particularly unacceptable on those grounds. Thus, despite their cognitive ability to treat rules as conventions, adolescents chose to treat sex inappropriateness as an absolute sort of transgression because of a strong distaste for the inference they drew from it regarding a person's sexual orientation.

In short, the way that gender-role stereotypes are interpreted and the ways they may influence judgment and behavior are themselves influenced by other factors. The research just discussed illustrates two of them, the child's ability to reason about rules (an aspect of social cognitive development) and the values that have been acquired during the process of socialization. Several investigators have attempted to alter already acquired sex-role stereotypes of preschool children by intervention procedures that involved exposure to egalitarian children's literature or films that present men and women in equivalent roles. The results have been mixed. Initially, boys often demonstrate more stereotyped beliefs than do girls, and, in one study the influence of egalitarian literature was more effective for girls than for boys (Flerx et al., 1976). In another study, a program of reading egalitarian stories to nursery school children over a 4-week period produced no change in girl's stereotypes and *in*creased the stereotyped beliefs shown by boys: the possibility of sensitization by overly egalitarian experiences must be considered, especially when stereotypes have already been acquired and are fairly strong (Pingree, 1978). When films have been used in an attempt to combat children's stereotypes (Flerx et al., 1976), changes in children's attitudes regarding the sex appropriateness of intellectual abilities and emotional expressiveness were somewhat more enduring than those established by exposure to literature.

482

Also, older children, even though they have presumably held the stereotyped beliefs for a longer time, were more likely to be influenced by the liberalizing intervention.

In essentially every society, children of one sex are treated differently from children of the other, although some societies exert more marked differential treatment than do others (Mead, 1935). The process of sex typing through socialization often begins at birth, with pink or blue labels on bassinets at hospitals and differential treatment by parents that ranges from selecting clothing of different colors or style to outfitting the child's room in the home with significantly sex-typed furniture, toys, and other items (Rheingold & Cook, 1975). Within American society, stereotypes abound regarding appropriate behavior (and thoughts and feelings) for boys and girls and men and women, and these stereotypes often lead to actions that promote the expected or approved behavior in children.

The most recent theoretical and experimental work on sex-typing has focused on social learning factors, rather than on hormonal or heritable factors influencing behavior. While there are obvious physical and hormonal differences between the sexes, their effects upon behavioral development are likely to be indirect. For example, a child's physiological sex has strong stimulus value for adults, generating expectancies in them regarding sex-appropriate behavior and inclining them to treat girls and boys differently (Fagot & Patterson, 1969). However, while the power of environmental as opposed to physiological factors influencing common behavioral and cognitive sex differences is impressive, physiological factors cannot and should not be dismissed out of hand, both in terms of any direct effects they may have and in terms of the way they may provide the stage for psychological factors to come into play.

Parental and Peer Influences. Parents tend to reinforce sex-appropriate behaviors in their children, fathers to some extent more than mothers (Fagot, 1978; Langlois & Downs, 1980). As early as the preschool years, peers are also clear in their reactions to sex-appropriate and sex-inappropriate behaviors and verbalizations, tending to focus more on punishment (ridicule, disapproval) of sex-inconsistent behaviors while showing acceptance (but not overwhelmingly positive reinforcement) for sex-consistent ones.

In some ways it can be surprising how much more powerful socialization factors are compared to biological ones in gender-role development. The work of John Money and his colleagues underscores the degree to which social treatment may be a major determinant in the development of sex differences. The socialization period prior to age 3 or 4 appears to be of primary importance. One study examined the sex-role adjustment of hermaphrodites (individuals whose external genitalia may not be indicative of their hormonal or internally determined sexual status). As children, hermaphrodites are occasionally assumed by physicians as well as parents to be of one sex when their internal characteristics are actually the opposite. When such "assignment errors" are detected early, prior to age 3 or 4, children

The Acquisition of
Sex-Typed Behavior

483

who are then reassigned from being one sex to the other, and who are then treated like members of the other sex will develop sex-role behavior appropriate for their reassigned sex. When such sexual reassignment takes place after age 3 or 4, a likely consequence is severe maladjustment in later sex role development (Money, Hampson, & Hampson, 1957). Other research has shown the power of social experiences to establish an enduring sex role that is in conflict with one's "true" sex. Genetic or physiological males whose external genitalia leads others to mistakenly assume them to be girls will develop a sex role and overall patterns of behavior consistent with being female even though actually they are not (Money, 1965a, b).

A major question regarding the effects of social experience on sex-role development concerns the nature of social experiences, especially those that promote the establishment of enduring behavior patterns. Earlier we talked about expectancies a child's assumed sex may generate in caretakers, who then influence the child to behave in a manner consistent with cultural stereotypes for sex-appropriate behavior. Money and Ehrhardt (1972) reported the case of identical twin boys, one of whom suffered an unfortunate accident. In infancy, during circumcision by electrical cauterization, the current was too high and one boy's penis was damaged totally beyond repair. Treatment involved reassigning this child to be a girl by surgically establishing a vagina and psychologically counseling the parents. Here is a description of what the mother said about her children several years later, including the children's behavior and the way she and her husband treated them:

> The mother stated that her daughter (formerly her son) by four and half years of age was much neater than her brother, and in contrast with him, disliked to be dirty: She likes for me to wipe her face. She doesn't like to be dirty, and yet my son is quite different. I can't wash his face for anything. . . . She seems to be daintier. Maybe it's because I encourage it: Elsewhere in this same recorded interview, the mother said: One thing that really amazes me is that she is so feminine. I've never seen a little girl so neat and tidy as she can be when she wants to be. . . . She is very proud of herself, when she puts on a new dress, or I set her hair. She just loves to have her hair set; she could sit under the drier all day long to have her hair set. She just loves it (Money & Erhardt, 1972, pp. 119–20).

The findings of one early study demonstrate quite clearly how the assumed sex of a child may change the response of a caretaker to a given behavior. Rothbart and Maccoby (1966) allowed parents to listen to tape recorded statements made by a 4-year-old child whose voice did not indicate clearly whether s/he was a boy or a girl. Parents were told that the child was a boy *or* that it was a girl and then asked to respond to the child's remarks as they would in their own home (for example, if the child said "You're bad! I hate you!" they were asked to indicate whether such verbal aggression would be punished). On the tape the child made bids for attention, pleas for approval and comfort, plus statements that were clearly aggressive or dependent. Mothers and fathers responded that they would treat boys and girls differ-

484

ently for several behaviors and the type of differential treatment was different for mothers than for fathers. For example, mothers were more permissive of comfort seeking and dependency if they thought the child was a boy, while fathers were more tolerant if they thought it had been a girl speaking. On the other hand, mothers also tolerated more aggression from boys while fathers tolerated less from boys and more from girls. These findings illustrate how children's assumed sex and not the way they actually behave may determine the reactions of others. These reactions include many of the socialization practices that may then shape children's behavior and produce actual differences between the sexes.

There is ample evidence that parents treat boys and girls differently in many facets of daily life. Household chores are assigned differently to boys and girls (Duncan, Schuman, & Duncan, 1973). Mothers who are employed are more likely to leave sons unsupervised after school than they are daughters (Gold & Andres, 1978b) and in general to chaperone daughters more (Newson & Newson, 1976). It is consistently found that in teaching their child to do something parents of preschool children have higher expectancies and demand more independent task performance from boys, while they are quick to provide help to girls (Golden & Birns, 1975; Rothbart, 1971; Rothbart & Rothbart, 1976). Across cultures both parents and children report that boys encounter pressures to compete, suppress feelings, conform socially, and not to cry (Block, 1978).

In addition to the role of adult and peer reactions in the development of sex typing, modeling processes also contribute to the acquisition and maintenance of sex-typed behavior in children. As they develop, children show a growing tendency for selective attention to same-sex models (Ruble et al., 1981). Within any culture a child is surrounded by adults who display the patterns of behavior that we characteristically assigned to one sex or the other, including both stylistic behaviors (patterns of dress) and more complex roles (which are often stereotypes but nevertheless likely to be statistically accurate, for example, in our society more men provide the primary wage earning in a family than do women while more women provide nursing care than do men). The media (television, in particular) present remarkably sex-typed models of behavior (Huston, 1983). In addition, children are surrounded by peers of each sex who display sex-appropriate behaviors as well as reinforce them (Fabot & Patterson, 1969).

Clearly, the cognitive aspects of gender-role differences, such as expectations, are distinct from actual behavioral differences, but they may interact. In an observational study of nursery school children, Fagot (1985) recorded teacher and peer reinforcement of behaviors that were stereotyped as masculine or feminine. The basic question was, what factors influenced the reinforcement of those behaviors in the nursery school children? For example, was it simple and obvious: girls are reinforced for feminine behaviors and boys for masculine? No, it was neither simple nor, in all cases, obvious. Teachers reinforced female-typed behaviors more frequently *regardless of the sex of the child*. This was perhaps because masculine-typed behaviors are more disruptive to smoother group functioning, including rough and tumble play

485

RESEARCH FOCUS 14-2

Sex Differences in Sex Differences

Gender-role stereotypes differ in more ways than simply enumerating one set of behaviors, attitudes, appearances, and preferences as appropriate for girls and another for boys. The rigidity or flexibility of gender roles also varies, and not surprisingly, at least in the North American culture, the male gender role seems to be held more tenaciously and boys are more constrained than girls against displaying behavior, preference, or assuming any appearance not "on the approved list" as stereotypically male. What are the findings that suggest this conclusion?

For one thing, although parents tend to provide sex-typed toys for their children (of both genders), as toddlers boys show a high frequency of play with masculine toys, so high that during the toddler months (1½ to 3 years of age) they show little increase in sex typing. O'Brien and Huston (1985) followed a group of toddlers for 14 months, from when they were approximately 19 months of age until they were approximately 33 months old. They found that girls' play with feminine toys increased significantly over this period but boys' did not, primarily because boys showed a high frequency of play with masculine toys from the very beginning.

The consequences for sex-inappropriate behavior also appear to be stronger or more negative for boys than for girls (Fagot, 1977; Langlois & Downs, 1980). In an interview study, Smetana (1986) asked preschool children about gender-role "transgressions," the performance of sex-inappropriate behaviors (for example, a boy coming to nursery school wearing nail polish). She found that children of both genders felt less strongly about girls' avoiding any transgression of female-appropriate behaviors than they did about boys' avoiding transgressions of male appropriateness. Interestingly, boys considered transgressions involving appearance (for example, nail polish) more serious than those involving activities (for example, playing with dolls). Findings of this sort suggest that even if male-

typed behaviors are of high frequency to begin with, an additional factor influencing their stringent adoption or retention by boys may be the particularly strong negative consequences for alternative behaviors.

Another domain in which boys may be seen to remain consistent, while girls change, is with respect to aggressive responding. Fagot, Leinbach, and Hagan (1986) found that among children who appeared not to have attained a sense of gender identity, there was no sex difference in aggressive behavior. However, among children who were judged to have attained gender identity, boys still showed a high rate of aggression while girls were significantly less aggressive. It should be remembered that aggressive behaviors in general are discouraged by socialization agents, and the ones identified in this study included hitting, pushing, shoving, taking objects, and yelling or calling names. These findings suggest that some behaviors eventually sex typed as masculine, but which initially characterize children of both sexes, are maintained by boys, perhaps in the face of negative socialization pressures, while girls discard those patterns of behavior.

During the later preschool years, from 3 to 5, boys' behavior also tends to be more consistent with gender-role stereotypes than does girls' (Carter & Levy, 1988). Among older children, boys are assumed by their peers to limit their behavior to sex-appropriate acts more than girls. For instance, Zarbatany, Hartmann, Gelfand, and Vinciguerra (1985) asked fifth graders to nominate classmates or simply to indicate whether boys or girls would be more likely to engage in a variety of altruistic behaviors. In assembling the list of altruistic acts (helping, behaving generously, and so on), these investigators were careful to include ones that were masculine, feminine, as well as neutral in sex appropriateness (without this precaution it is likely that the list of altruistic behaviors would have been primarily feminine sex typed). It was found that boys were nominated more often as likely to engage in the masculine altruistic behaviors, while girls were nominated as more likely to engage in feminine *and* neutral types of altruisim. Although this study does not necessarily indicate that children would actually behave this way, it does show that the stereotypes children cast on others are more limiting for masculine behaviors while providing some flexibility, including both feminine and neutral behaviors, for girls.

Finally, in an observational study, Fagot (1985) defined sex appropriateness in terms of whether particular behaviors were generally preferred by boys, girls, or engaged in by children of both genders with no apparent preference. She found that boys consistently displayed masculine sex-typed behaviors even though teachers responded positively to feminine or neutral behaviors (by children of both genders) but were infrequently positive towards behaviors that were male sex typed. Within the peer group, girls tended to react positively to other girls, regardless of the sex appropriateness (masculine, feminine, or neutral) of the behavior, but boys were more positive to other boys primarily when the behavior involved was masculine. Furthermore, when the effects of negative responses were examined, it was found that the frequency of masculine-typed behavior by boys was unaffected when it met with negative reactions from teachers or girls. On the other hand, negative reactions from one boy to another were effective in altering all types of behavior, male-appropriate, neutral, or female-appropriate behaviors.

Taken together, these results suggest that boys display at least some masculine sex-typed behaviors very early and that they persist in this early sex-typed behavior. No studies report any early adoption of sex-appropriate behaviors by girls, but several reveal girls' "flexibility" in moving from behaviors that come to be male sex typed to ones that are female. Girls are perceived by others as having somewhat more flexibility in their behavior, whereas boys are expected to engage in behavior that is more consistently typed as male appropriate. Finally, it appears that boys may be relatively inflexible in their adoption of sex-appropriate behaviors, bending only to socialization pressures from other boys. This general picture may reflect a general societal tolerance for greater flexibility of sex-typed behaviors for females than for males (for example, the acceptability of "tom-boy" behaviors by girls versus effeminacy in boys). Nevertheless even very young boys appear to be highly focused on sex-appropriate behaviors, maintaining them consistently, and being relatively unaffected by negative pressures . . . except by other boys. ❧

---

or the manipulation of large blocks. Among the children themselves, boys did have a sex-typed focus to their reinforcement of other boys, responding positively to them most when they were engaged in masculine activities. However, girls responded positively more to girls than to boys and did so without regard to whether the girls were engaged in feminine sex-typed behaviors.

On the other hand, there may be some aspects of social interaction that contain implicit reinforcement processes for sex-typed behavior. Fagot (1985) also found that boys received more positive reinforcement and feedback when they were playing with boys, and the same was true for girls when they were playing with girls. Because children are more likely to engage in sex-typed behaviors when playing with same-sexed peers, the frequency of reinforcement for appropriate sex-typed behaviors may still be significantly and effectively focused on behaviors linked to gender-role stereotypes.

Feedback from teachers about schoolwork may also convey information about the way society has different expectations for intellectual performance from boys than from girls.

The development of sex differences is complex, and it is clear that there is more at work in the development of those differences that characterize boys and girls than can be accounted for by simple differential reinforcement by adults and peers. The complexity in this development has not been totally unravelled, but is probably responsible for the attempt to combine biological, social learning, and cognitive developmental factors in attempting to understand the sex-typing process during childhood. Although parents do show differential reinforcement for some sex-typed behaviors, this is not totally uniform. For example, mothers may be observed to reward sons for playing with masculine *or* feminine toys (Langlois & Downs, 1980). Results such as these have led to an apparent mixing of theories in contemporary research on typical gender-role development, where biology (physical gender) is recognized as the starting point and the child's cognitive development then interacts with social experience to influence the adoption of gender-role behaviors and cognition.

Schools and Sex-Role Development. We give broader attention elsewhere to schools as a context for development, but there has been a significant amount of research on children's experiences in school and its influence on their sex-role development, which merits specific consideration here. It would not be appropriate to say that schools are a context that provide a primary influence on children's sex-role development, but children's experiences in school may contribute to their conceptualizations of sex roles and to their actual sex-role behavior (Minuchin & Shapiro, 1983). Differential treatment of children as a function of their sex clearly occurs in the school context. Fagot & Patterson (1969) recorded preschool children's behaviors in a nursery school setting and then examined the way children of each sex were treated by their peers.

488

Peers essentially never reinforced one another for behavior that was appropriate for the opposite sex, implying that in the school setting sex-typed responding is influenced heavily by peer interactions. There were clearly different behavior preferences in the two sexes, as summarized in Table 14-1.

School experiences provide many informal opportunities to learn about appropriate sex roles and, thereby, potential biases and stereotypes about sex-appropriate behavior (Weinraub & Brown, 1983). Teachers also spend their time interacting with children, and the opportunity arises to treat children of one sex quite different from those of another or hold very different expectations for them (Fagot & Patterson, 1969; Gaite, 1977).

There is no question that teachers treat boys and girls differently. Boys' behavior is much more likely than girls' to be subject to disapproval by teachers, although they also receive more attention, overall, from teachers than girls do (Meyer and Thompson, 1956). In the school setting, "feminine" behavior (quietness, obedience, task orientation) is more desired, and is much more likely to be reinforced by teachers (Fagot & Patterson, 1969; Biber, Miller, & Dyer, 1972; Etaugh, Collins, & Gerson, 1975; Fagot, 1973, 1977a, 1977b). This is interesting since such reinforcement tendencies do not tend to shift boys' behavior to be more feminine, suggesting that peer-reinforcement contingencies are important as well (Fagot & Patterson, 1969).

It is also the case that teachers respond differently to the same behaviors if they come from boys as opposed to from girls. For example, teachers are more responsive to boys when they are disruptive and their reprimands tend to be more forceful (Serbin, O'Leary, Kent, & Tonick, 1973). There seems to be a tendency for teachers to expect boys to find it difficult to attend to tasks, and when they do, the teachers give them more attention than they do to girls who are having similar problems.

With respect to math ability, by junior high school, girls are generally more talented than boys in computation, but boys are likely to do better on tasks requiring mathematical reasoning. There are several possible reasons for this. One is that fathers are more likely to be the parent with a positive attitude toward mathematics or to help with math homework (Fennema & Sherman, 1977), thus emphasizing the "masculine" nature of mathematics. This could

TABLE 14-1

Behavior preferences for preschool boys and girls

Behaviors Significantly Preferred by Boys	Behaviors Significantly Preferred by Girls
Building blocks	Painting
Transportation toys	Art work
Climbing	Doll house
Sand box	Play dolls
Ride trikes	Clay play
	Listen to stories
	Kitchen

SOURCE: Fagot & Patterson, 1969.

RESEARCH FOCUS 14-3

The School as a Feminine Institution

An interesting point has been made regarding the school context: In terms of sex-typing, it is basically a feminine institution (Minuchin & Shapiro, 1983). Girls are viewed as quiet, task oriented, and academically successful, and expected to behave that way without help or encouragement while boys are seen as requiring support. Then, even though boys are intellectually less successful and are pressured to treat academic tasks more seriously, they maintain their boyish behavior and self-esteem. Girls, meanwhile, are more successful and seem more upset with their failures. Dweck and her colleagues have focused on the attributions girls and boys make for their successes and failures in the school setting. She finds that girls tend to attribute failure in the school context to deficits in their own ability, while boys simply attribute failure (with potentially a sense of pride) to lack of effort

(Dweck & Bush, 1976). Indeed, teachers do treat boys and girls similarly in terms of giving feedback about the correctness of their answer, but in terms of the "intellectual quality" of the work, boys are given more positive feedback than girls (Dweck, Davidson, Nelson, & Enna, 1978). Teachers appear to give more positive feedback to boys for achievement, perhaps because they do not expect boys to do well, so when they do, teachers give boys more reinforcement. Dweck also found that boys, not surprisingly, were punished more for failing to obey the rules, as one might expect from a cognitive expectancy for boys to be "exuberant," but in terms of intellectual behavior they received some degree of leniency due to their exuberance. Girls, on the other hand, were not expected to be so exuberant and were not excused whenever their performance did not pass muster. ❧

be an effect of the sex difference in ability rather than a cause, of course. Fathers could, for example, be more positive in their attitude toward math or more likely to help with math homework because they are better at it. However, in a study of verbally and mathematically talented youth, Raymond and Benbow (1986) found no indication that facility in math was related to differential parenting or a youth's own level of sex typing (the degree to which the individual demonstrates behavior or cognitions in keeping with a society's stereotypes about masculinity or femininity). Although this result could be due to a failure to measure the most relevant aspects of parenting or sex typing, the failure to find that parents or stereotypes account for sex differences, especially in abilities, leaves physiological differences between the sexes as a possible cause. In short, physiological factors should not be discounted totally, but in many instances they are inferred to be at work when psychological factors are difficult to find.

While boys and girls may bring different behavior to the school context, they also receive different responses as a function of their sex. The school context thus interacts with already established sex-role development in shaping future cognitive and behavioral aspects of sex typing and continuing sex-role development.

In addition to actually being treated differently as a function of their gender, through simple observation children develop an image of sex-typed

Knowledge of adult gender-role behaviors may be acquired at an early age.

behavior that includes those behaviors labeled as appropriate for both sexes, not just their own (Huston, 1983). There is some evidence that children develop different sensitivities to same-sex models and the behavior they display as part of sex-role socialization, and this sensitivity may enhance the role of modeling in sex typing. For example, children may pay particular attention to models of their own sex, especially when a model's behavior is sex appropriate. Consider a study designed to explore the effects of a child's similarity to a model (Maccoby & Wilson, 1957). These investigators assessed children's attention to models of the same and opposite sex as well as the degree to which children learned and remembered the model's behaviors. Children recalled the actions and verbalizations of a same-sex model better and were also responsive to the sex appropriateness of the model's behavior for the model's own sex. For example, boys remembered *aggressive* behaviors better if the model had been a *boy,* while girls recalled behaviors related to *boy-girl* interactions (feminine-preferred content) if it were a *girl* who was displaying the behavior. The role of modeling in sex typing is thus not a simple one and its influence on ongoing sex typing is to some extent the end product of past sex typing. Finally, a child's own understanding of gender may facilitate the impact of other socialization factors.

Kohlberg's View. Cognitive–developmental theory, it will be recalled, proposes that personality and social development will reflect the cognitive development of the child at any given point in time. The child's cognitive level represents a readiness to respond to experience in terms of how it is understood, much like a filter through which external socialization pressures must pass before having an effect on the individual. Lawrence Kohlberg proposed a theory of gender-role development that focuses on three stages of under-

Effects of Gender–Role Concepts and Knowledge

491

standing that children gradually achieve regarding the characteristics of gender, their own or that of another.

1. The first stage is children's appreciation that they have a *basic gender identity,* male or female. In effect, the social world, including the self, becomes dividable into two parts. Kohlberg proposed that children attained this recognition by the age of three. At the same time, he believed that children of this age were generally unaware that gender is an *unchanging* attribute. For example, in a study of 21- to 25-month old children, psychologist Beverly Fagot (1985) reported such remarks as "you're silly, that's for girls" and (from a small boy) "now you're a girl." Kohlberg would probably propose that the first child was indicating awareness of the difference between male and female preferred toys and activities. He also would see the second child's remarks as evidence that the child's concept of gender was fluid, although many other experts would view this as an early example of word play and teasing. It should be noted that most researchers now report that children make gender-specific comments as early as age 2 (Huston, 1983).

2. A second cognitive developmental stage within sex role development is attained when children conclude that gender is stable over time: *gender stability.* Boys are seen to become men and girls women. Note how the attainment of this stage could have implications for children's modeling their behavior after that of an adult of the same gender since it implies a recognition that they will become an adult of a particular gender (so that what that adult does is potentially meaningful for the self). The implication of cognitive developmental theory, in that case, would be that the active, intentional modeling of gender appropriate behaviors from adults could not occur prior to the attainment of this stage.

3. But simply because gender is seen to be stable in the sense of not changing capriciously does not mean that changes in situations or appearances cannot have an influence. Women who drive buses might be seen as men, and men who let their hair grow long, do housework, or wear a caftan might be seen as women. Kohlberg thus proposed that by the age of 6 or 7 children attain *gender consistency,* concluding that gender is stable across time and across situations or changes in behavior that may violate a sex role stereotype in the child's mind. At this point, then, the child becomes able to appreciate the possibility of sex *in*appropriate behavior (which requires that the behavior and the underlying gender not be consistent).

The cognitive–developmental approach to gender-role development can be characterized as an active one in the sense that the child is an actor in the socialization process, not merely a passive target of experiences or pressures from parents or peers. Kohlberg's contention is that as children assume a mature gender identity (i.e., acquire the three perspectives on gender represented in the three stages), they will pursue sex appropriate behaviors because these behaviors are consistent with their self-concept, and they will be more responsive to the behavior of others, peers or adults, of their own gender. There is also evidence that the overall recognition that gender is constant and unchanging is also acquired at a different rate for the self versus others: It is first recognized that one's own gender is unchanging, then this assumed constancy is applied to others of the same sex, and finally to members of the opposite sex. Although the theory can be criticized on grounds that children show many signs of sex typing before the age of 6 or 7, there is evidence that children acquire these gender perspectives in the order proposed and that, having attained them, they are more likely to pay attention to same sex models (Ruble et al., 1981; Slaby & Frey, 1975).

Knowledge and Gender-Role Behavior.   There is evidence that cognitive factors influence the adoption of sex-typed behavior patterns in ways that are easily understandable. A consideration of cognitive–developmental theory suggests that even if children understand gender-role stereotypes (e.g., boys are more aggressive) or observe gender-role socialization in action (for example, they see aggression punished in girls but not in boys or observe older boys to be more aggressive than older girls), their own behavior may not be influenced if they have not attained gender identity, the recognition that they themselves are a girl or a boy. Fagot, Leinbach, and Hagan (1986) assessed young (21 to 40 months of age) children's ability to apply accurate gender labels to pictures of male and female children and adults. This was taken as a conservative index of the child's own sense of gender identity since children's cognitive understanding of gender is typically more advanced with respect to themselves than it is for others. The investigators proposed that only children

Expectations about appropriate occupations are part of gender-role learning.

493

who demonstrated gender identity would show sex differences in behavior or tend to associate with playmates of the same sex.

Both predictions were confirmed. Specifically, it was found that, among children who did not demonstrate an understanding of gender identity, there was no sex difference in aggression. Boys who showed a sense of gender identity showed about the same level of aggression as those who did not, but girls who had attained gender identity showed a markedly reduced level of aggression, less than one-tenth as much as boys. The finding that children with a sense of gender identity show an increased preference for same-sex peers is particularly interesting in that it suggests some of the social learning processes that may enhance the influence of gender identity on sex typing. First, same-sex play choices increase children's exposure to same-sex models who may display sex-appropriate behaviors that they have not yet acquired. Furthermore, since same-sex peers tend to respond positively to sex-appropriate behaviors and treat sex-inappropriate behaviors as a transgression especially for boys (Fagot, 1985; Smetana, 1986), choosing same-sex playmates increase children's interactions with peers who are more likely to reinforce appropriate sex-typed behavior and punish or disapprove of behavior that is inappropriate to the child's sex.

Gender-Role Development and Sexual Orientation

In the text of this chapter we have focused on *gender-role* development, the adoption of behaviors, attitudes, and preferences for activities or objects (for example, toys) that match cultural stereotypes about masculine or feminine characteristics. Another facet of gender-role development is the development of truly sexual feelings and the adoption of preferences for members of the opposite or same sex as sexual partners. Little is known about factors influencing the development of sexual orientation, perhaps because this aspect of development is particularly difficult to study.

However, with increasing social interest in the topic of sexual orientation, including the relatively recent movement within clinical psychology and psychiatry to declassify a homosexual orientation as automatically indicative of disturbance, it seems reasonable to give some consideration to what is known about developmental paths to sexual orientation and how this question is studied. In many ways, the development of a heterosexual orientation may be seen as so "natural" or "automatic" that it has been treated as a given, not as a consequence of development.

Put most simply, it appears that the acquisition of a typical repertoire of sex-appropriate, stereotypic cognitions and behavior precedes an eventual heterosexual orientation. This is a descriptive statement that heterosexual adults, as children, typically showed little out of the ordinary in their early

494

adoption of stereotyped gender-role behaviors culturally defined as appropriate for their gender, but it suggests little as to the processes that may underlie the development of sexual orientation.

Research is accumulating, however, regarding antecedents of a homosexual orientation, although knowledge cannot yet be said to be very great. In

RESEARCH FOCUS 14-4

The Development of Gender Identity

A major distinction in current theory and research on sex typing is that between gender *role* and gender *identity*. Gender role refers to the typical or socially defined appropriate behavior for males and females in a given society. The term gender *identity* is reserved for the individual's beliefs, understanding, or self-awareness of his or her own sexual status. This understanding is generally private and may change with age as people learn more about themselves through self-observation and as cognitive development provides the capacity for different levels of understanding.

While gender role and identity are conceptually distinct, they may interact with one another. After children have developed clear pictures of themselves as male or female, they may carefully watch the behavior of others whom they can identify as male or female in order to determine the behaviors that fit male and female roles. They may also seek out and attend to the behavior of models of the same sex, thus enhancing their own adoption of an appropriate sex role.

One of the most interesting aspects of gender role development is the way it mirrors more general cognitive development. Theorists such as Kohlberg (1966) hypothesize that several aspects of personality development, such as moral or sex-role development, reflect basic cognitive developmental milestones. It has been proposed that the child's understanding of his own gender proceeds through four stages (Eaton & Von Bargen, 1981). First children are able to label themselves as girls or boys. This label, however, is more superficial than it might seem. For example, if

you ask a very young boy whether he would still be a boy if dressed in girls' clothes he may very well tell you that he would then be a girl. The next development is children's understanding that their own gender is stable, that it does not change with time. In this case, a little girl would be able to tell you that when she grew up she would be a woman. The next two stages are related. One deals with motives: the children come to understand that their gender is invariant in that it could not be changed even if they wished. Children also develop a concept of gender constancy, that their sex is an attribute of the person and not affected by changes in behavior or dress (or appearance in general).

Although developmental changes in the ways children seem to understand gender do seem to mirror cognitive development, it is not clear that children's actual sexual identity is developing or, rather, the way that they understand it or express it to others is developing. Cognitive–developmental theory would predict that gender identity is malleable up into middle childhood at which time children recognize its constancy. The research of Money (Money & Ehrhardt, 1972), however, suggests that malleability to the point of being able to reassign children from one sex to another is present up to about age 2, but not thereafter. Although the distinction has not been proposed in the research literature, discrepancies such as this may indicate that children's *understanding* of gender roles and identity is separate from their *adoption* of those roles or their own gender identity. ❧

almost every instance the research includes men, rather than women, as subjects and is frequently retrospective (adults are asked to recall aspects of their childhood). Studies of practicing homosexuals (Bell, Weinberg, & Hammersmith, 1981; Harry, 1982; Saghir & Robins, 1973; Whitam, 1986), male transvestites (Saghir & Robins, 1973), or transsexuals (individuals who wish to change their physiological sex) (Benjamin, 1966; Green, 1974; Green & Money, 1969; Stoller, 1968) consistently found that these individuals reported early behavior or thoughts inconsistent with appropriate gender–role stereotypes. For example, they recall role playing and preferring the dress of persons of the opposite sex, little involvement with same-sex playmates or appropriate sex-typed toys and games, and in some instances specific wishes to be a person of the opposite sex. As already noted, this is largely descriptive information that might indicate simply that factors leading to the eventual development of a homosexual orientation were also affecting gender–role behaviors and attitudes in childhood, leaving the factors still unspecified.

How might one look for those factors? Given that sexual orientation can generally be assessed only in adulthood, if actual sexual preference and behavior are used as the index, is it possible to conduct research without reliance on retrospective data? A recent study by Roberts, Green, Williams, and Goodman (1987) illustrated how this could be done.

These investigators began to study (boys') gender-role development in the early 1970s. Their subjects were children whose parents contacted a clinic with a concern that their son, aged 4 to 12 at the time, was displaying feminine behavior. There was also a comparison group of boys from families with similar demographic and socioeconomic characteristics (level of parent education, income, presence of the father in the family, and so on) who did not show any unusual incidence of feminine behavior. Data included interviews and questionnaire responses from the parents as well as behavior descriptions of the boys—all gathered at that time, that is, not retrospectively. Fifteen years later, followup contacts with approximately two-thirds of the boys allowed the investigators to evaluate the degree to which the boys referred for early feminine behaviors were likely to develop nonheterosexual orientations (homosexual or bisexual). It was found that 80% were either bisexual or homosexual, whereas all of the boys in the comparison group were heterosexual (Green, 1987). Thus, this could be considered a prospective study, with early data on the behavior and families of boys, most of whom *subsequently* developed a nonheterosexual orientation.

Not surprisingly, the two groups of boys themselves were very different on a number of behavioral and attitudinal variables as reported by their parents. Parents of "feminine" boys reported that they were more likely (than comparison boys) to have worn an article of feminine clothing at some time, stated a wish to be a girl, shown some degree of interest in women's clothing, and shown some preference for playing with dolls, and that they were less likely to engage in rough-and-tumble play or express a desire to grow up to be like their father. These boys were also reported to be more feminine in appearance. Both the fathers and mothers of "feminine" boys reported spending less time with their sons, and the sons were also more

496

likely to have been ill or hospitalized than comparison boys. Although the results from a single study cannot be considered conclusive, the authors suggest that opportunities to be with parents of both sexes and the degree to which a young child is "masculine" or "feminine" in appearance are among the factors influencing eventual sexual orientation.

It should perhaps be noted that there were many variables that did *not* differentiate feminine from comparison boys. Their fathers were not less masculine, their parents had not wanted a girl during the pregnancy, their mothers were not overly protective (more concerned about their welfare as infants) or more dominant. Finally, parents of both groups of boys were not different in their marital satisfaction or attitudes toward sexuality. These findings call into question some common speculations about factors leading to atypical gender–role development in boys (for example, the dominant, overprotective mother).

Do these findings suggest that factors leading to femininity in boys are the precursors of an eventual homosexual orientation? This is not necessarily true. In addition to analyses comparing "feminine" to comparison boys, the investigators also examined factors that related to degrees of femininity shown by boys *within the comparison group.* Boys who were smaller, perceived as infants to be less aggressive, husky, or plain (for example, were seen as cuddly, pretty) showed more feminine characteristics. These variables were

Toddlers may not categorize items of clothing as being either "male" or "female," but they will quickly learn these connotations when they reach early childhood.

497

not related to the *degree* of femininity shown by the boys in the "feminine" group. The degree of femininity within a given sexual orientation appears to be influenced by factors different from those influencing the development of the orientation, and thus these may be two separate aspects of gender-role development.

These findings are of great interest and lead to some intriguing speculations about different aspects of gender-role development. It should be noted, however, that the study focused on only "feminine" boys whose parents sought clinical treatment, a group that may not be representative of individuals eventually adopting a homosexual orientation, but whose early behavior was not considered by parents (or others) to be problematic. It also included only boys. However, it illustrates how research on this difficult topic can proceed and suggests that the time is at hand when developmental psychology should include sexual orientation as an aspect of gender-role development that merits greater attention and understanding.

Summary

Sex-role development is broad; it has both behavioral and cognitive dimensions that merit consideration. Sex-role development can be looked at both from the perspective of socialization agents whose behavior influences the child and from the perspective of the children themselves in terms of the developing knowledge and behavior patterns that match the cultural norms for their sex. Cognitive factors such as the beliefs and behavioral standards held by individuals of one sex or the other influence the behavior of socialization agents in ways that promote the transmission of these standards to new generations, both as standards by which their own behavior and the behavior of others may be judged as sex appropriate, inappropriate, or characteristic behavior patterns or beliefs (such as stereotypes).

A consideration of the origins of gender roles, particular gender differences in behavior, blends biological and environmental factors. This is perhaps more true for this domain of development than for any other. Although children's actual physical gender is determined biologically (except in cases of gender reassignment), the role of biological factors in behavioral development is primarily indirect. As noted previously, although a person's biological gender provides a foundation, or at least a cornerstone, for the development of behaviors and interests pertinent to a given gender role, environmental factors related to the overall socialization process are of particular importance and have been the focus of by far the majority of research on this topic. Gender-appropriate behavior is especially acquired by a child's observation of how others of similar gender tend to behave. Of course, the child's cognitive capabilities and cognitions about gender-appropriate behavior may operate as a filter for environmental influences or guide the child's active participation in the socialization process.

Gender roles develop largely as a function of the gender-differentiated socialization pressures a child experiences and the internalization of this knowledge, expectations, and stereotypes about behavior that is gender appropriate for the culture in which the child lives. The course of development will be influenced by age-related exposure to different contexts so that, for example, parents and other caretakers necessarily play a greater role than teachers or peers during the preschool years. The course of development is relatively gradual, although gender differences in behavior may be clearly seen well before the end of the preschool years.

Finally, gender-role development is closely tied to other domains of development. It is influenced by the child's own cognitive maturation. Socialization pressures ebb and flow as children find themselves in the various contexts of development. To the extent that differential treatment is influenced by others' perception of a child's gender and apparent masculinity and femininity, physical development that affects the child's appearance will indirectly play a role as it evokes expectations in others about a child's gender-appropriate behavior and leads them to respond to it in different ways.

Suggested Readings

BLOCK, J. H. (1983). Differential premises arising from differential socialization of the sexes: Some conjectures. *Child Development, 54,* 1335–1354.

CHODOROW, N. (1978). *The Reproduction of Mothering: Psychoanalysis and the Sociology of Gender.* Berkeley, CA: University of California Press.

FEINGOLD, A. (1988). Cognitive gender differences are disappearing. *American Psychologist, 43,* 95–103.

HUSTON, A. C. (1983). Sex-typing. In E. M. Hetherington (Ed.), P. Mussen (Series Ed.), *Handbook of Child Psychology: Vol. 4. Socialization, Personality, and Social Development* (pp. 387–467). New York: Wiley.

JACKLIN, C. N. (1989). Female and Male: Issues of gender. *American Psychologist, 44,* 127–133.

MACCOBY, E. E., & JACKLIN, C. N. (1974). *The Psychology of Sex Differences.* Stanford, CA: Stanford University Press.

CHAPTER FIFTEEN

Self-Regulation: The Development and Control of Prosocial and Antisocial Behavior

501

Introduction

The implicit goal of socialization is to render individuals capable of regulating their own actions in a way that will be acceptable to the society. In earlier chapters we have noted repeatedly how persons differ in their self-regulatory abilities, although the precise term "self-regulation" has not always been used. Some of these differences are the result of developmental status. Young, immature persons are generally less able to inhibit inappropriate actions and to direct behavior in socially desirable ways than are more mature individuals. But in every age group there are also easily recognizable differences among persons in these abilities (Block & Block, 1980). This poses two important questions for personality and social development: What are the factors that contribute to differences in self-regulation, and what do they tell us about the nature and course of development in self-regulatory abilities?

To address these questions, developmental psychologists have focused on several categories of behavior that involve the regulation of cognitions, emotions, and behaviors. One category involves the inhibition of behaviors either to gain greater benefits later on or to avoid aversive consequences for inappropriate or forbidden behavior. A second category is typically referred to as prosocial behavior, but might better be termed the exercise of social responsibility, including generosity toward others, altruism, and helping others in distress. A third category, aggression, essentially involves a failure of self-regulation that leads to antisocial behavior. Clearly, self-regulation touches on many interrelated aspects of human behavior and ability.

In this chapter we discuss these three categories of self-regulation. As in other chapters, we will consider the origins of the behaviors in each category, the course of development of each, the environmental influences that are particularly significant in the acquisition and performance of the behaviors, and the interrelations among self-regulatory behaviors and other aspects of personality and social development.

Prosocial Behavior and Self-Regulation

Prosocial behavior and self-regulation are two components of what is frequently termed moral development. Described most broadly, moral development includes children's gradual internalization of behavioral codes and values that are characteristic of the society, family, and peer groups with which they have contact. Other aspects of individual development also play a role, including factors such as developing cognitive capabilities or the accrual of experience and knowledge about appropriate and inappropriate behavior. These factors may foster prosocial development or may limit children's ability to implement moral judgment or behavior. Some aspects of the topic, those dealing with children's moral judgments about the legitimacy of behavior in certain situations, are an important focus of social cognition, and we dealt with that in Chapter 10. Here we will focus on four aspects of prosocial self-regulatory skills: (1) the ability to delay gratification; (2) resisting temptation; (3) honesty; and (4) the exercise of social responsibility, such as sharing (generosity) or helping others in distress. These are patterns of behavior that implement the most common codes of behavior and values that are part of socialization in many different cultures.

The ability to delay gratification is a self-regulatory skill that provides a foundation for prosocial development. The necessity to delay immediate gratification in favor of long-term outcomes that are of greater importance is a cornerstone of rational behavior that maximizes eventual positive outcomes. Prosocial behaviors like sharing that are of benefit to others also frequently require delaying immediate or sometimes any eventual personal gain. For reasons such as these, one of the goals of socialization in most cultures is to enhance children's abilities to control pleasure seeking.

Delay of Gratification

Early research on delaying behavior concentrated on contextual and personality factors that affect the ability to postpone gratification. In this research a child was often given a series of choices between a small immediate reward (for example, 1 stick of gum now) or a larger delayed one (for example, 3 sticks of gum 1 week from now) (Mischel, 1958). Not surprisingly, if children expect that delayed rewards may not be forthcoming ("A bird in the hand" [immediate] is worth two in the bush [delayed]."), they may elect to receive a small but immediate reward. Because an expectancy may be specific to a given situation, children's choices in one instance may be for an immediate gratification while in another they may choose a larger, delayed outcome.

Children's delaying behaviors depend heavily on emotional and cognitive factors. One factor of particular interest has been a child's emotional state. Positive states, such as those induced by success or simply reminiscing about pleasant events, increase children's tendency toward immediate self-gratification (Mischel, Coates, & Raskoff, 1968; Mischel, Ebbesen, & Zeiss, 1972; Underwood, Moore, & Rosenhan, 1973). Furthermore, as the delay period becomes extremely long, children also tend to prefer the more immediate gratification, probably because the delay period is inherently frustrating and the longer the delay, the more likely the reward will eventually *not* be forthcoming. Social factors are important, as well. If children are exposed to models who consistently make immediate or delayed choices and justify them (for example, "I'll take the small one right now—it looks like a fun toy and you miss so much in life if you are always waiting for the things you want."), they are likely to adopt the immediacy or delay preference shown by the model.

These findings do not touch very directly on the basic psychological processes by which children learn to initiate delay periods and, perhaps more

503

importantly, by which they learn how to wait successfully until the delay period has passed. Some of the most important factors influencing the ability to delay are the thoughts and anticipations that a child engages in during a delay period. Consider what the child might do. One possibility would be to think about the valuable, delayed reward in an attempt, perhaps, to achieve some sort of symbolic or *vicarious gratification* during a waiting period (Freud, 1911; Rappaport, 1967). On the other hand, thoughts could be directed toward things other than the delayed reward, providing a *distraction* from the frustration of waiting.

In a series of studies, Walter Mischel (1984) demonstrated the role of cognitive factors such as attention and imagery in effective delay of gratification. In these experiments, preschool children are given a choice between a small reward that they can have immediately or a larger reward that they may achieve by enduring a relatively long waiting period (15 minutes). They must wait in a room by themselves, and if they choose not to wait for the entire delay period, they may call the experimenter back—by doing so, however, they lose the larger, delayed reward. The question Mischel and his colleagues asked was simple: How might attentional and cognitive activities during the delay period influence children's capabilities to delay?

In some of the first studies on this issue, the focus was on situational or contextual factors related to a child's attention to the gratification in question. For example, what is the effect of being able to *see* (and thus think about) the reward during the delay period? As noted above, watching the reward might provide symbolic gratification or perhaps an *incentive* to wait (a constant reminder of the valued eventual outcome or the small immediate one). To answer this question, children were allowed to wait in a room that contained both the large (delayed) and small (immediate) rewards, the delayed one only or the immediate one only, or neither. Only when the rewards were totally absent could children wait effectively. When *either* the delayed or immediate (smaller) reward was actually present, children could delay only a moderate period of time, and when both rewards were present, delay behavior was minimal (Mischel & Ebbesen, 1970). This suggests that attention to rewards makes it difficult to postpone them.

Most of the research on delay of gratification has included preschool and early school age children as subjects. What about the delay behavior of even younger children? Are the strategies and conditions promoting effective delay applicable to them? It might be argued that a minimum level of cognitive development and the ability to focus attention would be prerequisites to some of the factors that have been found to be important. Although it has not been investigated thoroughly, it appears that at least some of the factors influencing delay are operative in 2-year olds (Vaughn, Kopp, Krakow, Johnson, & Schwartz, 1986). During a task requiring self-control and the ability to wait or persist at the task to achieve a desirable goal, behaviors that brought the goal into a child's attention seriously reduced toddlers' ability to delay, whereas strategies that deflected attention from the goal signficantly increased delay time. Thus, temptation appears to be a similar evil regardless of age, and the distraction of attention away from tempting aspects of a goal or desired outcome is an effective strategy to achieve it.

504

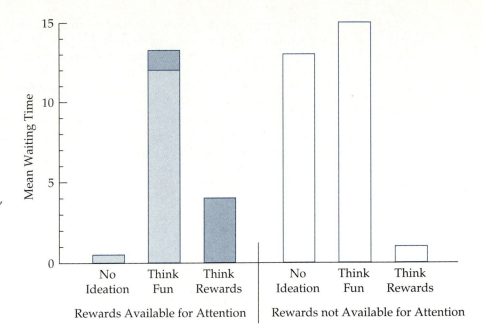

FIGURE 15-1

Mean number of minutes of voluntary waiting time, comparing children who received different ideational instructions in the presence or absence of material rewards.

Source: from Mischel, Ebbesen, & Zeiss, 1972.

Other cognitive variables besides attention are also important in understanding delay of gratification. For example, one experiment (Mischel, Ebbesen, & Zeiss, 1972) examined the effects of fantasy or ideational processes. In this study, children were left alone without the rewards being present but were given instructions either to think about the rewards (fantasy gratification), to think fun thoughts (a cognitive distraction), or they were given no instructions about what to think during the delay period. Figure 15-1 presents the results from this study. Perhaps because the rewards were not available for attention, and thus there was nothing to be distracted from, a cognitive "distractor" (thinking fun thoughts) was no more effective than whatever the children thought about when given no instructions. However, thinking about the rewards did not facilitate waiting any more than actually looking at them in other studies. In fact, the fantasy gratification instructions seriously reduced the ability to delay, implying that thinking about the rewards is essentially tantamount to actually having them present as temptations.

As first it might seem from these findings that ideation during a delay period either had no effect or perhaps even interfered with the ability to delay gratification. This conclusion does not, however, take into account all the ways that the *content* of one's thinking during a delay period might reduce the frustration of delaying or enhance the motivation to continue to delay. To address this issue (Mischel & Baker, 1973), children were given the opportunity to delay in order to get some pretzels or marshmallows as a treat but given different ways to think about them during the delay period. In this study, therefore, one group of children was told to think about the treats in a way that would emphasize their delicious ("consummatory") qualities: the crunchy, salty taste of a pretzel, the chewy, sweet taste of a

505

marshmallow. Notice how attention to this aspect of a reward might *increase* the frustrating nature of waiting for it.

Another group was told to concentrate on other aspects of the rewards, such as those related to their appearance ("nonconsummatory"): they were to think of pretzels as long, thin brown *logs* or marshmallows as white, puffy *clouds*. Here, even though color or shape are characteristics of the rewards, notice how they illustrate that attention to rewards may still be directed away from aspects that would enhance frustration and reduce the ability to delay. Notice also that in this study, even though children were confronted with the rewards themselves during the delay period and were also told to think about them, it was found that children who were given instructions to think about nonconsummatory aspects were able to endure a much longer delay period than children who focused on consummatory aspects of the rewards. Thus, subtle aspects of cognitive activity during a delay period may have major consequences for the way these factors influence behavior, and it may help *or* hinder the ability to delay.

Research such as this underscores the important role of cognitive factors in personality, and it illustrates vividly how cognitive processes may have both facilitative and debilitating effects. In the following sections on other aspects of prosocial development the important roles of thinking and reasoning will become even clearer. (You may also wish to review Chapter 10 where we discussed thinking and reasoning about the social world.)

Resisting Temptation: Obeying Social Prohibitions

Another aspect of moral development, which may be related to the delay of gratification, is children's ability to resist temptation. Although there is often a delay period inherent in resisting temptation, the concept of resistance to temptation or resistance to *deviation*, as it is sometimes called, typically refers to children's obedient *compliance*, that is, not doing something that is enjoyable or otherwise tempting because they have been told not to. The term *resistance to deviation* suggests that obeying a prohibition against performing an attractive behavior or manipulating an attractive object (for example, playing with a forbidden toy) involves withstanding the temptation to move away from socially prescribed patterns of behavior.

Much research has dealt with the role of punishment for transgressions in enhancing resistance to temptation. In general, if children were punished early in the sequence of a prohibited act, for example, as they simply reached for a prohibited toy rather than after they had played with it for awhile, they were subsequently more likely to resist that temptation to play with the toys in the absence of the socialization agent (experimenter) who made the prohibition and punished them for transgression (Walters, Parke, & Cane, 1965). This effect was interpreted to be due to attaching anxiety from the punishment to early components of a transgression response, alerting children so they can more readily inhibit the behavior before the prohibited item is in hand (when it would be harder to stop) or the prohibited deed is done. This finding illustrates how aspects of the way punishment is delivered, such as timing, may enhance its effectiveness. It also suggests at least one reason why punishment may sometimes be ineffective: when a temptation is very great, punishment that is not early in the transgression episode may be ineffective because it is outweighed by the attractiveness of the temptation.

Subsequent research has focused on more cognitive components of the processes that underlie resistance to temptation. For example, consider the impact of reasoning on children's behavior. When children are given a reason or a rationale for resisting temptation, timing becomes less important as a determinant of the effect of the punishment. Either early or late punishment is equally effective when reasoning is combined with punishment (Aronfreed, 1965; Cheyne & Walters, 1969; Parke, 1969). Furthermore, although more severe punishment usually enhances future resistance to deviation, this effect vanishes when reasons are provided for nontransgression. In other words, with reasoning, even minimal punishment may be quite effective. There are several processes by which rationales may alter the effects of punishment. One is that rationales heighten the informative functions of punishment. Reasons for complying with a prohibition frequently include information and expectancies regarding future punishment and thus generate expectancies. When told that a toy must be left alone because "your turn is over" or "it belongs to ——————," the child may infer that disobedience will provoke punishment because a rule set forth by the agent would be broken. Second, rationales may give rise to internal, self-generated reprimands if children feel they are violating a general rule of good conduct (for example, "always take turns"). Finally, a rationale may enhance effectiveness if it reminds the child of the rewards for obedient behavior by invoking prior positive socialization experiences, for example, memories of rewarded interactions such as being praised for taking turns or carefully avoiding someone else's property.

All rationales are not alike, and interesting questions may be raised about the types of reasoning that children of different ages are most responsive to. In one experiment (Parke, 1973), 3- and 5-year-old children were prohibited from playing with some attractive toys. When the children were told of the prohibition, they were also given one of two rationales: (1) that the toys were "fragile and might break" (an *object oriented rationale* that focuses on the possible damage to the toys), or (2) that the toys belonged to another child (a *property oriented rationale*).

For younger children the object rationale was more effective, while older children were more responsive to rationales stressing property rights of others. This is compatible with observations that young children frequently base moral judgments on criteria related to objects rather than to a social or personal dimension (for example, breaking five cups by accident is deemed a worse act than breaking one cup on purpose), whereas older children have a more abstract understanding of motivational standards for appropriate behavior and use this to shape their moral judgments (Kohlberg, 1964). Findings regarding the effects of different types of rationales on children of different ages, therefore, illustrate a connection between moral judgments of the child and the reasoning that children of various ages respond to in directing their own behavior.

Still other factors may be shown to alter the influence of rationales, even to the point of reversing their effects. For example, Parke (1973) studied the role of the peer group in the effectiveness of property- or object-oriented rationales. When a peer endorsement was added ("The other children do not *want* you to play with these toys because. . . .") to the property- or object-oriented rationales, the object-oriented rationale was as effective as property-oriented reasoning. Furthermore, children of both ages resisted the temptation to play with the prohibited toys. Thus, the effectiveness of reasoning was influenced by sensitivity to peer pressure. (You may wish to review Chapter 13 for a more complete discussion of conformity to peers.)

In summary, obedience to a prohibition—resistance to deviation—is not merely an ability that comes with age and maturation. Some aspects of socialization, such as punishment for misbehavior, interact with cognitive elements such as reasoning and aspects of social development such as a sensitivity to the wishes of peers. Also note that resistance to deviation frequently contains an implicit requirement to delay gratification, and factors influencing the capacity for effective delay should also influence effective resistance to deviation. Therefore, in addition to previous social learning, the level of cognitive development, and the possible role of the peer group, acquired self-regulation skills, such as the ability to delay gratification should also combine to influence a child's ability to obey a prohibition and resist the temptation to deviate.

Honesty

In many ways, honesty can be seen as a prime example of moral behavior. Perhaps because of this, questions relating to honesty and cheating have one of the longest histories of interest in developmental psychology. What seems to be at issue is not honesty in the sense of reporting something accurately or cheating when there is no advantage from doing so. Rather, it is "honesty under duress": telling the truth or resisting the temptation to cheat when the truth would hurt or failure to cheat would put some desired outcome at risk. In other words, it is honesty under conditions when self-control is required and when there is the need to resist some temptation, either to avoid punishment or to gain a desired outcome.

A recurring question in studying honesty concerns the degree to which honesty can be considered a generalized trait, so that a given child might be looked upon as becoming or having become a basically honest or dishonest person. Some of the very first studies relating to the consistency of honest behavior come from a series of related investigations by Hartshorne and May (1928). These investigators examined children's cheating or deception in a wide variety of settings and with respect to a large number of tasks. A major conclusion was that when dishonesty was assessed within the same context (for example, a single teacher's room) or when the same form of dishonesty was examined (for example, copying on a test), there was a modest tendency for a child who cheated on one type of test or cheated in a given way to do so repeatedly. When the situation changed, individual differences among children came into play, and honest or dishonest behavior in one context was not necessarily related to that in another. A given child, for example,

508

might cheat on one test (English) but not another (math), or might cheat in one teacher's classroom but not another. Not surprisingly, then, most research on this aspect of moral development has focused on factors that influence honest and dishonest behavior.

With respect to personality and intellectual factors that might influence dishonest behavior, several factors have been found to foster a motivation to cheat. These include fear of failure, the need to succeed, or a reduced tendency (or reduced skills) to delay gratification. These sorts of results suggest that honest behavior is more than a mere failure to be able to resist temptation and includes factors that enhance temptation or engender anxiety as well.

Fear of failure and the motive to succeed often interact in the determination of cheating. For example, two studies suggest that cheating is especially likely when an individual is not only highly positively motivated to succeed, but also fears failure (Gilligan, 1963; Shelton & Hill, 1969). The ability or preference to delay gratification also plays a role. Mischel and Gilligan (1964) found a modest relationship between sixth grade boys' tendencies to delay gratification and cheating on a competitive game, with preferences for delayed gratification being associated with reduced cheating. These findings suggest the important role of self-regulatory skills, such as cognitive factors, including those that enhance the ability to delay gratification (cf., Mischel, 1984), as determinants of dishonesty in children and adults.

Probably the characteristic that has been found to relate most strongly to aspects of honesty is intelligence. Correlations between IQ and honesty have been found as high as .60 (with age controlled) (Hartshorne & May, 1928), and this relationship is reported consistently by different investigators in this area who have assessed intelligence in their studies (Kanfer & Duerfeldt, 1968; Nelsen, Grinder, & Mutterer, 1969). It should be noted that this relationship applies primarily to cheating on tests or tasks for which the individ-

Resisting the temptation to copy another student's work is an example of honesty, a prime exemplar of moral behavior.

ual child can tell how well he or she is doing and on which there is a history of past success or failure. That is, children are more likely to cheat when the task is one in which they failed in the past and are presently doing poorly; thus, their only hope of success depends on cheating (Hartshorne & May, 1928). This is true both for children who score high on IQ tests and those who score low. Thus, it is probably not intelligence *per se* that is related to cheating but, rather, children's expectancies for success through honest effort.

A very small tendency has been found for dishonesty to increase with age (Hartshorne & May, 1928; Kanfer & Duerfeldt, 1968). No reliable differences have been established for boys versus girls, however. Some studies conclude that boys cheat more than girls (Parke, 1967; Sears, Rau, & Alpert, 1965); others find that girls are more dishonest (Burton, 1971; Hartshorne & May, 1928); still others have reported mixed results (Krebs, 1969) or no sex differences (Rest, 1983).

Practicing Social Responsibility

Prosocial development also concerns the acquisition of social responsibility—patterns of behavior to benefit others. This category of behavior includes altruism (generosity and sharing), helping others in distress or need of aid, and acquiring the norms of social responsibility (knowing those common, desirable behaviors and the conditions that demand them).

Generosity and Altruism.   Children's altruism and sharing are relatively complex behavior patterns. Children generally become more generous and helpful as they grow older and increasingly internalize general norms regarding the social value and appropriateness of these behaviors. They also become more sensitive to aspects of situations that may determine whether some form of prosocial behavior is appropriate or needed (Radke-Yarrow, Zahn-Waxler, & Chapman, 1983).

Social learning factors influence generosity and altruism much as they do other aspects of social behavior. Children's generosity was found to be enhanced by exposure to peer and adult models who share or donate rewards (Harris, 1967; Harris, 1970; Hartup & Coates, 1967; Rosenhan & White, 1967). Also important are direct encouragement and reinforcement for this type of behavior from parents, peers, and other socialization agents (Doland & Adelberg, 1967). When modeling and direct encouragement were compared, interesting contrasts of "preaching versus practicing" occurred.

The most effective socialization technique for generosity seems to be to model behaviors you want children to acquire (Bryan & Walbek, 1970).

The most stringent test of generosity involves giving to others even when it requires self-sacrifice. It is almost always the case, for example, that the rewards a person shares or gives away could otherwise have been kept for personal consumption and enjoyment. The rewards are also often themselves the consequence of hard work and sacrifice. A clever study by Midlarsky and Bryan (1967) demonstrated how the pleasure shown by those to whom one is generous can influence both the degree of self-sacrifice in obtaining

510

rewards and in subsequent generosity in sharing those rewards. Children played a game that involved two levers. One produced candy when pushed and the other simply turned on a red light that could only be seen by another person participating in the game. When children played the game with a warm and friendly adult, one who displayed a great deal of pleasure over the illumination of the light, they frequently responded by pressing the lever that turned on the light, thus sacrificing opportunities to get rewards for themselves in favor of promoting someone else's pleasure. It was also found that when children were subsequently given the opportunity for the *anonymous* donation of some of their candy, those who were most self-sacrificing in order to please the adult were also most willing to donate some of their rewards to "needy children whose parents can't afford to buy them candy." Thus, self-sacrifice, which may initially occur publicly, in a social situation, because children can see that it enhances another's pleasure, generalizes to conditions of private donation for which there is no possibility that the recipient could express his or her pleasure. This suggests that early self-sacrifice or generosity, which is reinforced by the obvious pleasure it brings to another (including thank-yous or more tangible rewards as well), may be the foundation for altruism that is personally pleasing and its own best reward.

During the course of socialization children learn rules that appear to govern social interactions, and they come to use these norms to direct their own behavior. Thus, for helping behavior—coming to the aid of another—the rule or norm of social responsibility is that it is appropriate, good, and perhaps even imperative to help those who ask for help and especially those who are less fortunate than you. Another norm, the norm of *reciprocity*, refers to the belief that, when someone is generous or helpful to you, you should behave in kind, or reciprocate (the Golden Rule).

These two norms may sometimes imply different courses of action. For example, one norm may call for prosocial behavior (for example, responding when someone asks for help) in contexts where the other does not (for example, refusing to help a person who has not helped you in the past). Furthermore, although children probably learn both norms, applicability of the norms may vary from one age period to another. Older children, for example, are guided more by the norm of social responsibility and are more likely than younger children to offer help to others who need their aid (Gelfand et al. 1974; Harris, 1967; Midlarsky & Bryan, 1967; Ugurell-Semin, 1952). This developmental trend is also apparent in children's judgments of altruistic behavior (Hartmann, Peterson, & Gelfand, 1977). When an altruistic or helpful act was described to them, children of all ages judged helping someone in need (social responsibility) more praiseworthy than helping or sharing with someone who had been helpful or altruistic in the past (reciprocity). Older children, however, felt that socially responsible altruism was much more praiseworthy than reciprocal altruism, whereas younger children did not see as great a difference.

The impact of prosocial norms of behavior in determining children's actions is apparent in an experiment by Peterson, Hartmann, and Gelfand, (1977).

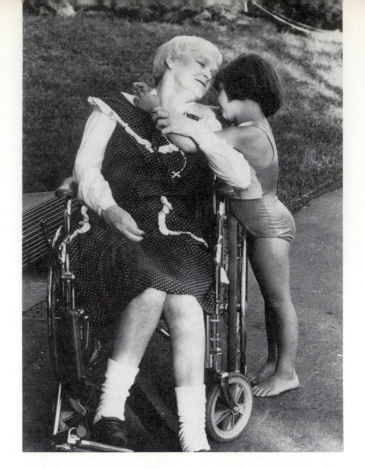

Developing a sense of social responsibility includes learning to show concern for others in special circumstances.

Children of various ages played a game in which marbles repeatedly became stuck and took a long time to free themselves. It was supposedly possible for a (fictitious) child in the next room to press a button and free the marble, but whether assistance was given was actually under the control of the experimenter. Over the course of a large number of turns, the marble often became lodged in the machine and was either quickly freed, purportedly by the other child, or remained stuck for 30 seconds before apparently becoming dislodged on its own. When children were later given the opportunity to donate rewards to the unseen peer, they were noticeably less generous toward peers who had not been perceived as helpful. Although this is consistent with a norm of reciprocity, it also illustrates a different sort of norm that may be seen as part of reciprocity, namely a norm of *retaliation* (Staub, 1972; Wolosin, Sherman, & Mynatt, 1975). In this instance, the reduction in generosity toward nonhelpful peers was greatest for the youngest children (kindergarten age), confirming other findings that reciprocity norms—or retaliatory ones, as in the present case—are more attractive to younger children than to older ones.

Helping Others in Distress. One of the moral imperatives typically instilled during the process of socialization is the responsibility to help others who need assistance. In some countries, the USSR for example, the social responsibility to help others is indeed imperative, being written directly into their legal code so that *not* helping others in need is a punishable offense.

512

Conflicting norms regarding "appropriate" behavior may be particularly problematic when they involve helping another in distress. Consider the case of helping another in distress when no one is around to sanction the independent action a child might need to undertake in order to provide help. For example, children are generally taught to be obedient, not to be nosey, to mind their own business (as much as they can), and not to do things unless they have been told it is "OK." These constraints comprise a broad norm of *not* doing anything if not specifically told to. The norm of helping, however, often requires children to behave in certain ways without being told (for example, opening doors for others, not forgetting to say please and thank you, or making a bed in the morning). The influence of conflicting norms was examined in a series of experiments by Staub (1970, 1971). In this research, children came to an experimental room and were explicitly instructed to perform a task such as coloring or completing a questionnaire. The experimenter then left for a while, and shortly afterwards the children heard distress sounds from behind a closed door. For example, the children heard a loud crash, followed by some whimpering and calls to "help me—I've fallen off a ladder and my foot is caught," apparently from another child the same age.

At issue is whether and how quickly the subject child goes to investigate—and potentially provides aid. A social norm for helping others in distress should motivate the child to go into the next room, but norms for obedience (staying and finishing the task) and norms against prying, nosiness, or going where one has not expressly been invited by an adult should interfere with helping.

Staub (1970) found that helpfulness increased from about ages 5 to 7, but then decreased between ages 7 and 11. These findings implied that norms regarding privacy, staying out of places that one has not been invited into, and so on may be learned later in childhood and, thus, only reduce children's tendencies to help in this older age period. In a subsequent study (Staub, 1971), Staub demonstrated that 12-year-olds were indeed reluctant to enter a strange room to give help, unless they had received some indication from an adult experimenter that it was permissible to do so. Lest this picture of timorous helpfulness in childhood be taken too negatively, it should be noted that in young adulthood (ages 18 to 28), Staub (1971) found greater concern with another person's need for help than with norms that favored doing only what one has been given permission to do.

There is evidence that willingness to help someone else in need is related to aspects of children's moral reasoning and empathy. Eisenberg and her colleagues (Eisenberg et al., 1987) assessed 9- to 12-year-old children's responses to several moral dilemmas and also their empathy for others. They found that children's willingness to help was positively related to children's tendency to emphasize the needs to the protagonist in reasoning about moral dilemmas and negatively related to their tendency to use hedonistic reasoning that emphasized gain to the self rather than the other. Higher degrees of empathy were related to more prosocial helping only for older subjects, suggesting that the ability to empathize with another's predicament is a later-emerging factor in helping behavior than is reasoning about the worthiness of coming to the assistance of others in need.

Learning Norms of Helping. The research described so far illustrates factors influencing children's behaviors: their willingness to try to help another in distress. It is also important to understand the factors that influence learning norms that influence socially responsible behavior such as helping. One factor influencing the acquisition of a norm of helpfulness was inadvertently demonstrated in a study (Staub, 1971) in which children were being trained to be helpful by attending to someone else's needs. For the training to take place, other children were enlisted as confederates who at different times pretended to need help (such as in reaching for something too high for them or falling from a chair). After the training was completed, children were given opportunities to share and to help someone in distress, and the experimenters gave these opportunities to the confederates as well as to the children being trained to help others. Surprisingly, the *confederates* showed more helpfulness than the children who had supposedly been trained. In fact, confederate children often verbalized a broad but clear norm for helping: One *ought* to help others. Thus, one source for learning helpfulness may be a child's own experiences of having needed assistance and then having been helped. Those who come to a child's assistance act as helpful models, and across different occurrences this may demonstrate both helpful behavior as well as the implicit norm for helping others.

Indeed, there is little question that observing helpful behavior by others is an important determinant of helpfulness, even when the help rendered is not to the child himself. In addition, there are other factors that may enhance the effectiveness of models. Yarrow, Scott, and Waxler (1973) examined how the warmth or the nurturance of a socialization agent may facilitate the acquisition of helpful and sympathetic behavior in children. In two separate experiments, preschool children were given experiences likely to promote the development of helpful behavior; these experiences involved an adult female who had been either highly nurturant toward the child or generally neutral in her demeanor.

The nurturant adult interacted with the child in three types of settings. One type involved dioramas, small three-dimensional models of situations in which help or sharing was needed. For example, one depicted a monkey in a cage trying to get a banana that was out of reach, while another showed several children at a table, all but one with a cupcake. The adult presented the diorama, described the distress of one member in the scene, and then rectified the problem, noting his or her sympathy for the unfortunate person or animal and how relieved he or she was now that the individual was happier. A second aspect of training involved pictures (two-dimensional) that illustrated scenes requiring help: The child was asked to identify what was happening and what he or she would do if he or she were actually there. Third, children encountered some actual incidents in which a real person or animal needed comfort or aid and the socializing agent responded appropriately. In one incident, another adult was in the room with the child and the agent and, while picking up something from the floor, the child banged her head severely on the table. The first adult then asked her if she were hurt and warmly suggested that she sit down a moment to recover. In another incident a kitten was in the room but its food dish was covered, preventing it from eating. The adult nurturantly helped the kitten get its food. In short, the study involved providing true, behavioral examples (models) for help-fulness or sympathy in situations that were quite real.

The investigators also tested the effects of those experiences on children's helpfulness in "real life" settings. Two weeks following the interactions with the adult model, children visited a house adjacent to their nursery school where a mother and her baby were supposedly visiting. While the child was there, a basket of spools and buttons "accidentally" fell off of a table. Next, the mother asked the child to stay with the baby for a moment, and there were a number of baby toys just outside the infant's play pen and beyond reach. More than 80% of the children whose training had come from a nurturant adult gave help in this realistic situation, and more than half of them expressed sympathy. By contrast, few children who had received no training or whose training had not involved a nurturant adult either helped or expressed sympathy in these instances. The results of this study indicate the potential impact of nurturant models in the socialization of helpfulness.

Antisocial Behavior: Aggression

Understanding antisocial and aggressive behavior has long posed a formal problem for moralists, philosophers, and psychologists and a practical one for parents and concerned members of all societies. This breadth of interest and importance has made it one of the central areas of concern within the field of personality development. The concept of aggression is particularly broad, and arguments have developed concerning the degree to which particular behaviors in children and adults, animals and man actually constitute aggression. We will briefly consider some of the factors that have been proposed to identify and characterize aggressive behavior and then proceed to examine research on developmental factors influencing the broad range of behavior that is covered by most definitions of aggression.

Essentially all societies tend to devalue and to regulate antisocial behavior toward other members of one's own social group. In the family and school contexts, and perhaps to a lesser extent in the peer context, the socialization of aggression involves attempts to prevent its occurrence by sanctions against it and, to a lesser extent, the promotion of skills at suppressing or avoiding aggressive encounters. Thus, the development and display of antisocial behavior is typically seen as a *failure* of self-regulation. Some types of antisocial or nonmoral behavior (for example, dishonesty or cheating) have already been discussed as failures of prosocial responding. However, perhaps the prime example of antisocial behavior in terms of negative consequences to others (injury, pain) or the disruption of productive social interaction is aggressive responding. We now turn our attention to what is known about the development and control of aggression, beginning with a consideration of how best to define this class of behavior.

The Definition of Aggression

The term aggression is used to refer to a diverse category of behaviors that cause harm or damage to persons or their property. The most common usage of the term implies that the harmful acts were intended to cause injury of some kind (Dollard, Doob, Miller, Mowrer, & Sears, 1939). Indeed, *intent* is a key element in legal definitions of antisocial behavior. Including the words "intent to injure" in the definition of aggression, however, excludes many behaviors that would be considered by many people to be aggressive, even though these behaviors may not include an intent to injure. For example, it is common for adults to think a child is being aggressive when he or she pushes or inadvertently injures another child to retrieve a toy or obtain some other valued goal that was blocked by another child.

This diversity in everyday definitions of aggression has led to the proposal that we think in terms of two basic "types" of aggression: *hostile* aggression, for which the end result is indeed the injury of another, and *instrumental* aggression, for which any injury is inadvertent but the aggressive act is instrumental in securing some other goal (such as the toy in the aforementioned example). The range of behaviors accepted as "aggressive" is thus quite wide when both definitions are used. Hostile aggression would include behaviors that were intended to injure someone even if they failed to do so. Instrumental aggression would include behaviors that injured people even if they were not intended to do so. This general type of definition combines "person" and "social" determinants or factors influencing aggression that are "internal" and "external" to the individual. Internal factors include goals, intentions, cognitions, and emotions. External factors include the actions of others and the conditions under which they occur.

The Development of Aggressive Behavior

As children mature, their aggressive behavior changes, with some categories of aggressive action becoming more common and some less common from one age to the next. In general, the incidence of aggressive behavior appears to increase during the preschool years, although some specific types of aggressive interchanges appear to decrease. Thus, the frequency of *conflicts or quarrels* has been reported to decrease with age (Jersild & Markey, 1935; Dawe, 1934), whereas grabbing objects and making verbal demands have been found to increase (Muste & Sharpe, 1947; Walters, Pearce, & Dahms, 1957).

The most extensive descriptive study of aggressive development (Goodenough, 1931) provides a good example of the principle that different aggressive behaviors followed different patterns of development. Goodenough found that *retaliatory* aggression, physical or verbal, increased with age, especially after 3 years of age. On the other hand, undifferentiated, aggressive *outbursts* (flailing or screeching) decreased with age, gradually at first and then sharply after age 4. The occurrence of coordinated, controlled aggression was correlated with the development of skilled social behavior in general, including positive interactions like cooperation. Other investigators have also reported a positive relationship between the frequencies of aggression and other, specific prosocial behaviors such as sharing (Muste & Sharpe, 1947). Findings like this imply that in very young children the general acquisition of social skills includes skills for both antisocial and prosocial behavior.

The *antecedents* of aggression, the situations, experiences, or emotional states that may precede children's antisocial behavior also change from one age to the next. Such changes seem to be related to the natural pressures of the different types of social encounters that occur at different ages. For example, it has been reported that around age 2 or 3 aggressive outbursts are likely to follow parents' attempts to direct children's behavior, such as efforts toward toilet training or the promotion of self-help skills. In the preschool and elementary school years as peer interaction becomes more common, disagreements, intrusions, and frustrations in social encounters become more common factors leading to aggression.

A complementary question regarding the development of aggression concerns the *stability* of aggressive responses in children across long periods of time, especially when other patterns of behavior may be changing radically. If children appear to be quite aggressive at one age, compared to other children, will they continue to be unusually aggressive as they grow older? The answer is that it depends: The stability of aggression varies as a function of many factors. In one longitudinal study (Kagan & Moss, 1962) children's aggressive behavior was examined at several points during childhood. During the first 10 years, physical aggression toward peers was only moderately stable, but there was very high stability during the first 3 years. The stability of aggressive behavior is also different for various types and targets of aggression. Kagan and Moss found that aggression toward the mother is erratic and achieves only moderate stability towards the end of childhood. In older children (10 to 14 years) new types of aggressive behavior are available, such as dominance or competitiveness (if one wants to label these behaviors aggressive), and stability for these types of aggression is reasonably high during the preadolescent and early adolescent years.

One reason antisocial behavior may change with age is that new behaviors are likely to be adopted that are age appropriate or more acceptable (less unacceptable) to socialization agents, but that achieve the same ends as earlier behaviors did. For example, biting or pinching are virtually never tolerated as retaliatory gestures. Infants and toddlers are likely to show such behaviors, but only briefly because they are immediately and almost invariably punished. These behaviors may be replaced by pushing, hitting, or, eventually, name-calling as verbal skills are developed.

Origins of Aggression

Aggression is an aspect of behavior about which the nature-nurture debate has been especially fierce. One line of argument is that aggression is a natural defensive response to threat (e.g., Lorenz, 1966; Wilson, 1975). In general, however, most experts agree that specific behavior patterns such as aggression are also strongly influenced by environmental experiences. In a classic series of experiments with kittens, the Chinese psychologist Z. Y. Kuo (1930) provided one test of the importance of species membership versus specific rearing experiences with respect to aggressive behavior. The focus of Kuo's study was a behavior that is often assumed to be "natural" for cats: killing rats. Three rearing experiences were contrasted: being reared alone (in isolation), with rats for companions and playmates, or with mothers who were adept at killing rats. Then, at maturity, the kittens (now cats) were given the opportunity to attack, kill, and eat rats.

The different rearing conditions produced striking effects on the aggressive, predatory behavior of the cats. Nearly all of the cats who had been reared by a rat-killing mother became rat killers themselves. On the other hand, the cats who had been reared with rats rarely showed aggression toward them and even appeared to have formed an attachment. Slightly less than 50% of the cats reared alone showed any tendencies toward killing rats and much less aggression than that shown by the cats raised with rat-killing mothers, but they showed more aggression than those cats reared together with rats.

Additional evidence was provided by Kuo that social experiences influence aggression. This was accomplished by examining separately the frequency of rat *killing* and rat *eating*. Half of the kittens in each rearing condition were brought up on a vegetarian diet, while the other half were given meat. There were no effects of diet on killing behavior, but vegetarian diets led to a reduced frequency of eating captured rats. If aggression and attacking prey (predation) are considered separate, it is apparent that social factors influence aggression but not predation. The reverse is true for dietary experiences, however. In both cases, experience was a powerful determinant influence, and the importance of *social* antecedents of aggression were clearly demonstrated.

One type of social antecedent, reinforcement of aggressive behavior, can be shown to lead to an increase in aggressive actions, even when the aggressive behavior involved includes no actual intent to injure others (Walters & Brown, 1963). Paradoxically, the act of punishing aggression may also comprise a model of aggression, containing elements that could both enhance (the agent models punishment, an aggressive sort of behavior) and deter (as a consequence of contingent punishment) aggressive responding in the child. This amounts to a conflict, one that may be resolved by a twofold change in aggression: less is expressed towards the person administering punishment or in the setting where punishment occurred, but aggression may continue or even increase in other settings or toward other targets. Bandura and Walters (1959), for example, found that the parents of highly aggressive young adolescent boys were often highly punitive of aggression, specifically, of aggression against the parents themselves. At the same time, however, they *approved* of aggression against peers, especially when it could be construed as indicative of righteous self-defense, manliness, independent assertion, or some other valued trait. The result of this pattern of training was the entrenchment of aggressive interaction with peers but a conspicuous absence of aggression in the home.

Cooperative play and the regulation of aggression are two aspects of the development of social competence in childhood.

Many learning experiences that affect the development of aggressive behavior involve the experience of "victimization" (being the victim or target of another person's aggressive attack). Interestingly, the processes influencing the development of aggression following victimization include more than simple modeling or observational learning. Gerald Patterson and his colleagues (Patterson, Littman, & Bricker, 1967) documented the development of aggression in children who were initially passive and often the victims of aggressive peers in nursery school. Specifically, these investigators observed how children responded when they were the targets of peer aggression and noted how these responses to victimization affected the development of aggressive behavior by the victimized child. Initially passive children who experienced frequent victimization and whose retaliatory aggression was successful ceased being passive and themselves became active aggressors against their peers. Thus, being a victim may actually lead to becoming the aggressor if it leads the individual to attempt aggressive behavior that is then reinforced by its own success. By contrast, some children did not become more aggressive. These were passive children who were rarely victimized (and hence had had little opportunity to attempt retaliatory counteraggression) or those who retaliated but were unsuccessful in overcoming the aggressive attack (for example, by driving off the aggressor, retaining a toy the aggressor was after, and so on).

Let us now consider how children's aggression, once it has become part of their characteristic patterns of social behavior, may be altered. Patterson and his colleagues' (1967) findings that aggression may be developed and maintained when it is socially successful suggests that much aggression, especially instrumental aggression, may be self-maintaining. Given that aggression has some drawbacks (e.g., it is likely to elicit counter aggression from others or negative sanctions from adults), one possible factor in changing it would be the availability of alternative behaviors that could achieve similar goals in a more socially acceptable or prosocial fashion. In a very early study, Chittenden (1942) demonstrated how aggressive children may quickly learn and implement alternative social behavior. Chittenden examined the degree to which modeling *cooperative* solutions to common social problems could alter the aggressive behavior of children who were hyperactive and domineering toward other children.

After first observing these children's aggressive behavior, Chittenden gave them the opportunity to watch vignettes in which two dolls illustrated both aggressive and cooperative solutions to conflicts with others. These vignettes included content that showed how aggression often produced unpleasant consequences for all involved and how cooperative behavior was likely to be rewarding. For example, two boys argue over a wagon and, while fighting to see who gets to play with it, break the wagon. An alternative cooperative ending was also supplied in which the two boys took turns with the wagon and had a good time. As a result of this training, aggression was greatly reduced in frequency, and cooperation increased. These changes were still evident when children were observed 1 month later. Although this training experiment is often interpreted to confirm the influence of modeling influences on aggression, it also illustrates the impact of *information* about alternative constructive responses to conflict.

Peer and Peer Determinants of Children's Aggression. Much of the everyday modeling of aggression and constructive alternatives to conflict takes place in interactions with family members and peers. What characteristics of these social contexts have been found to be especially important in influencing aggressive behavior, rather than more constructive responses? One major dimension of parental behavior that may be related to children's aggression is that of permissiveness–restrictiveness and the warm or cool (hostile) nature of the family context. It has consistently been found that within a hostile environment (characterized by a high frequency of punishment and other indications that a child was often rejected by his parents), parental permissiveness for aggression is likely to be related to a high frequency of aggression in the child (Feshbach, 1970; Glueck & Glueck, 1950). Other research suggests that aggression is fostered when there are few specific expectancies for obedience or little consistency in exercising restrictive control (McCord, McCord, & Howard, 1961). By contrast, within a nurturant or warm family context, children of permissive parents are likely to be seen as outgoing and friendly, with aggression being limited to assertive, instrumental acts that would not generally be characterized as inappropriate (Baldwin, 1949; Feshbach, 1970).

TABLE 15-1

Backgrounds of aggressive, assertive, and nonaggressive boys

Environmental Conditions	Aggressive Boys	Assertive Boys	Nonaggressive Boys
Parents' emotional relationship with the boy	Rejecting Punitive Frequent use of threats	Affectionate Relatively punitive* Infrequent use of threats	Affectionate Nonpunitive Little use of threats
Instillation of direct controls	Overcontrolled or subnormally controlled by mothers	Normally or subnormally controlled by mothers	Normally or overcontrolled by mothers
	Low demands on the child	Low demands	High demands
	Lack of supervision	Relatively little supervision of the child*	Firm supervision of the child
	Inconsistency in discipline	Relatively inconsistent in discipline*	Consistent in discipline
Parental model	Socially deviant	Relatively deviant*	Socially conformist
Parental relationship to each other	A high degree of general conflict	High degree of general conflict	Low degree of general conflict
	Lack of mutual esteem	Relatively low mutual esteem*	High mutual esteem
	Dissatisfaction with role in life	Relatively dissatisfied with role*	Satisfied with role
	Unaffectionate	Affectionate	Affectionate

* In comparison to the background of nonaggressive boys.
SOURCE: From McCord, McCord, & Howard, 1961.

Some generalizations regarding the backgrounds of aggressive, assertive, and nonaggressive boys are noted in Table 15-1.

There has been relatively little attention to peer influences on children's aggression. It is clear that aggressive behaviors may be acquired by modeling (Hicks, 1965) as children observe effective aggressive behavior by others. The study by Patterson and his colleagues discussed previously (Patterson, Littman, & Bricker, 1967) indicates that increased aggression may be inspired when one is the victim of aggression by a peer. Recall how Patterson and his colleagues found that when victims remained passive, took a defensive posture, or cried, these reactions acted as reinforcers and the aggressor was more likely to behave aggressively in the future. In a separate study, Buehler, Patterson and Furniss (1966) examined peer reinforcement factors that maintained deviant behavior in older, delinquent girls. The girls' peers selectively reinforced hostility and punished social behavior more often than they reinforced it, while adults attempted to reinforce social behavior and at least to some extent punish hostility. Although it is not clear that the peers' behavior was maintaining aggressive, hostile behavior in these girls, this seems likely and it is noteworthy that this behavior was being maintained despite reinforcement contingencies from adults to the contrary.

Sex Differences in Aggressive Responding. A child's gender may influence aggressive behavior, but a simple generalization, such as "boys are more aggressive than girls," does not do justice to the complex determinants of aggressive responding. There is little evidence that hormonal differences between the sexes influence the degree of aggressive response in humans. Although studies with animals indicate that the administration of male hormones (testosterone) to young or unborn female rats and monkeys may influence the degree to which they subsequently display aggressive behaviors (e.g., Young, Goy, & Phoenix, 1964), these studies do not mirror the variations in hormonal makeup that characterize boys and girls during normal development. Although it may be true, when all the findings are totalled in a "box-score" fashion, that boys *are* more likely to be aggressive than girls (Maccoby & Jacklin, 1974, 1980), a more discriminating approach is to inquire about the conditions under which this is true, when there may be no sex differences, and when sex differences might even be reversed.

In general, boys in U. S. culture have been thought to be more likely to show stability in their levels of aggression from one age to the next, whereas girls have been thought to become less aggressive with age because of stereotypes against aggression for females relative to males (Kagan & Moss, 1962). Recently, however, a longitudinal study of 600 men and women over the age of 22 years found that aggressive tendencies such as criminal behavior, spouse abuse, and self-reported physical aggression could be predicted for both men and women from measures of aggression taken when the individuals were 8 years of age (Huesman, Eron, Lefkowitz, & Walder, 1984). This finding may indicate a change over the past few decades in the degree to which aggressiveness is likely to persist in the behavior of females. When gender is investigated as a factor influencing the learning or acquisition of various types of aggressive behavior moreover, there appear to be no sex differences in learning *how* to behave aggressively, even though children of one sex may actually show more aggression. For example, in an early study of the learning of aggression through modeling, Bandura (1965) argued persuasively for examining acquisition and performance as distinctly separate factors in social learning and behavior. In a study Bandura reports about, children observed an aggressive child who was either rewarded, punished, or received no consequences for his aggressive behavior. Although boys spontaneously displayed more aggressive behavior than girls, when given an incentive to do so, boys and girls were equally able to reproduce the model's aggressive behavior. Several other studies have indicated that girls tend to acquire greater inhibitions aginst behaving aggressively than do boys, but they still attend to and learn about aggression by observing the aggressive behavior of others (Dubanoski & Parten, 1971; Madsen, 1968).

There are also indications that boys may show different *kinds* of aggressive behavior than girls. For example, in one study (Darville & Cheyne, 1981), boys were only 26% more likely to initiate attacks than were girls, but boys were more than twice as likely to retaliate to an attack on themselves. Because retaliated aggression may be more noticed by others ("It takes two to tangle"), this may lead to an inaccurate impression that boys are much more aggressive than girls.

In fact, if the generalization about boys being more aggressive than girls is examined more carefully (Hoffman, 1970), it appears to hold primarily for physical aggression. For "indirect" or nonphysical aggression (for example, verbal aggression), the results are more inconsistent, and there is some evidence that girls are more inclined to use indirect forms of aggression more than are boys (Feshbach, 1965). Again, this may reflect socialization that is consistent with sex-role stereotypes about acceptable types of antisocial behavior.

The safest generalization is that the best recognized or assumed sex differences in human aggression are primarily the product of differential socialization pressures brought to bear on boys and girls. In societies where boys and girls are expected and encouraged to behave differently in certain ways—for example, for boys to engage in rough and tumble play, and to react physically to frustration or retaliate aggression shown by others, and for girls to be indirectly or verbally aggressive—sex differences are likely to develop.

Aggressive Effects of Mass Media on Children. In addition to direct experiences of aggression in interactions with family members and peers, children are also exposed to vicarious aggressive experiences in the mass media. We have already given extensive consideration to the role of mass media as an influence on development (see Chapter 12), including effects on aggressive, violent, or other forms of antisocial behavior. It might be helpful to review this material (especially pages 423–428) before reading further in the present chapter.

The media, particularly television, is replete with actors, plots, depicted or diguised motives, and tempos of action that are effective models for aggressive, high-magnitude, impulsive, and to a large extent *un*regulated, antisocial behavior. The media provide a poor source for children to learn either the motives or the mechanisms for the self-regulation of antisocial tendencies. Because exposure to the media is so extensive in the United States and other highly technological societies, this becomes a powerful and pervasive influence on the development of antisocial behavior, which may then continue into adulthood (Eron, 1963; Eron, Huesmann, Lefkowitz, & Walder, 1972).

A recurring hypothesis about the effects of media violence deserves brief notice in this discussion of aggression. It has frequently been suggested that viewing antisocial behavior, as opposed to actively engaging in it, may actually provide a means of reducing aggressiveness in mass-media viewers. This idea is referred to as the *catharsis hypothesis*. The principle underlying this hypothesis is that a viewer's aggressive impulses can be depleted, or drained, by watching someone else performing an aggressive act. In general, when the hypothesis is tested experimentally, the findings indicate that observing aggression either increases it in the observer or maintains aggressive responding at its current levels (Parke et al., 1972; Ellis & Sekyra, 1972; Liebert & Baron, 1972). Figure 15-2 illustrates a measure of children's willingness to hurt another child after watching a television program that was either aggressive or nonaggressive in nature (Liebert & Baron, 1972).

523

Mean Total Duration (Transformed) of Aggressive Responses in All Groups

Program shown	5-to-6-year-olds		8-to-9-year-olds	
	Boys	Girls	Boys	Girls
Aggressive	9.65	8.98	12.50	8.53
N	15	18	20	17
Nonaggressive	6.86	6.50	8.50	6.27
N	15	17	18	16

(a)

Mean Number of Time-Sampled Aggressive Play Responses in All Groups

Program shown	5-to-6-year-olds		8-to-9-year-olds	
	Boys	Girls	Boys	Girls
Aggressive	7.13	2.94	5.65	3.00
Nonaggressive	3.33	2.65	5.39	2.63

(b)

Note—The number of subjects for each cell in this analysis is the same as that shown in (a).

FIGURE 15-2

Children's aggressive behavior observed in laboratory tasks and in the natural environment following viewing of aggressive and nonaggressive television programs.

Source: from Liebert & Baron, 1972.

Antisocial Behavior and Aggression: A Social–Cognitive Approach

Much of the research we have discussed so far in this chapter is historical. It is old, but not dated, because much of both theory and research on aggression were clustered in the 1930s and 1960s, possibly for a number of reasons. The decade of the thirties followed World War I and contained the seeds of World War II. A concern with global violence may well have sensitized individuals, including behavioral scientists, to issues related to aggression—even in children. The sixties followed the Korean conflict and saw the escalation of the United States' involvement in Vietnam, coupled with intense public concern. In addition, television had become a ubiquitous feature of households across the country, an early aspect of the electronic revolution that coincided with the beginning of theory and research on observational learning (modeling) and helped focus interest on the role of modeling and the media in the development of aggressive responding. The flurry of research during these decades in many ways fully explored the questions related to aggressive development that could be gleaned from the theories of personality and social development that were predominant at the time.

More recently, with increasing attention to the role of social cognition, theorists and investigators have begun to study how children's interpretation and understanding of the social world influence their reactions to others. One aspect of social competence would seem to be children's acquired skills to process social information accurately, to understand and correctly infer the causes and consequences of their own behavior or the behavior of others from available information. But judging a child's social competence is itself an inference that others, such as parents, teachers, or therapists, make by observing children's apparent social skills. Since these others may judge children's competence incorrectly, and since they are likely to act on judgments that may or may not be accurate, the concept of social competence is distinct from children's precise roster of social skills. If many of those with whom children interact hold similar views of the children's competence, it becomes, bluntly put, children's *reputation* for having good or poor social skills. Thus, the proposal has been made that social skills and social competence should be treated separately, with social skills referring to those skills that children actually demonstrate and social competence reflecting how others judge those skills or the expectancies they have about children's likely social behavior (McFall, 1982; McFall & Dodge, 1982).

These two concepts may be distinct, but they also are likely to be interactive. One would expect children's actual social skills, at least eventually, to lead others to an accurate judgment of their social competence. Similarly, adults' and peers' reactions to children may be based on estimates of social competence and thus actually help shape or maintain the good or poor roster of social skills that children display. This distinction is illustrated in research testing the relationship between children's skills at social information processing and their aggressive behavior.

One of the most interesting areas of concern has been children's inferences of hostile motives to others as a possible antecedent of their own aggressive (retaliatory) behavior. Another focus has been on children's social problem-solving skills. Much in the manner of Chittenden's (1942) analysis, the question has been whether children who do not approach a social problem (for example, a conflict over a toy) with alternative ways of understanding the situation (for example, "he's trying to take my ball just to be mean" versus "he wants to play with the ball, too") and alternative ways of responding (for example, "I'll teach him!" versus "We could toss it back and forth.") are prone to poor solutions, aggressive ones if they are likely to attribute hostile intent and can think of few ways to respond other than with hostility of their own.

One approach to understanding the role of social cognitions and skills in aggressive, antisocial behavior is to contrast aggressive children with peers who are not consistently aggressive. One would expect aggressive children to have a tendency to overinterpret hostile intent to others, to misinterpret cues that need not indicate hostility, and to have skill deficits in effective social problem solving. And this appears to be the case.

Consider the following incident that was observed by Kenneth Dodge:

> The bell rang, signaling the end of classes, and the children ran out of the door from their second grade classroom. A number of the boys headed straight for the water fountain, led by Derek. As he began to drink, Joshua, who was next in line, accidentally bumped him and the stream of water splashed in Derek's face. The other boys thought this was funny and Derek, hearing them giggle, turned abruptly and hit Joshua in the face, shouting, "You can't make fun of me!" A fight erupted between the two boys, who had to be separated by a teacher. In exasperation, the teacher told Derek: "Honestly, I just don't know what I'm going to do with you. You're always picking fights with other boys."

If we were to crawl into Derek's mind, we might find the following: an assumption that Joshua had pushed him on purpose (hostile intent), embarrassment and anger (emotional reactions), and an inability to think of any way to respond other than by fighting (a deficit in social skills). While this

525

makes clinical sense, what evidence is there that this may indeed summarize the psychological factors influencing Derek's behavior in this and other situations where he behaved aggressively?

Dodge (1980) studied aggressive and nonaggressive boys' reactions when a puzzle they had partially completed was supposedly disassembled by another boy. Completing the puzzle would achieve a prize. While subject children were taking a break from working on the puzzle, they overheard a fictitious conversation between another child and a second experimenter who were presumably in the room with the subject's partially completed puzzle. In all cases this conversation ended with a crash, signifying that the other boy had dropped the subject's puzzle and it had fallen apart, but the apparent intent of the boy was varied. In one condition, the other boy was heard to mouth hostile intent, saying "Well, I don't like it. I don't want him to win that dumb prize, so there. I'll mess it up. [crash]" In another condition, where hostile intent was to be absent, the overheard conversation went as follows: "I think I'll help him put some more pieces together. Hey, there's one. I'll put it here. [crash] Oh, no, hey, I didn't mean to drop it. I didn't mean it." After overhearing this conversation, children were taken to a room into which the experimenter brought both puzzles, the subject child's (in pieces) and the fictitious other child's (partially complete). The experimenter then left and the subject's behavior was videotaped for the next several minutes.

Victimization may lead to retaliatory aggression.

In some ways aggressive and nonaggressive children were similar to one another in the ways they responded to these two scenarios. When their puzzle had been destroyed with hostile intent, children were likely to disassemble the other boy's puzzle and express verbal hostility, but when there had actually been a benevolent intent children sometimes helped the fictitious boy by adding some pieces to his puzzle. When the other child acted in a hostile manner, aggressive boys did display more verbal hostility than nonaggressive boys. Overall, these results suggest that when the cues are clear and there is little question about hostile intent, aggressive boys may not behave much differently from boys who are typically nonaggressive. What, then, makes them more likely to be aggressive?

One possibility is that when there is no reason to infer a hostile intent behind a disruptive or unpleasant act, but also no reason to infer good intentions, aggressive boys will infer a hostile intent, which then might lead them to behave aggressively in retaliation. In a second study as part of this research, Dodge (1980) read aggressive and nonaggressive boys stories that supposedly represented occurrences involving some of their peers. In each story, something unfortunate happened (for example, the peer spilled a carton of milk on someone else) but no information was provided that could justify any hostile intent. Aggressive boys nevertheless attributed a hostile intent 50% more often than did nonaggressive boys. Aggressive boys also said that they expected the peer in the story to behave aggressively in the future and said that they did not trust him more often than did nonaggressive boys.

The finding that aggressive boys are biased in favor of inferring hostile intent to others is found repeatedly (e.g., Dodge & Tomlin, 1987). There is some evidence that such boys are not careful in processing information that would help decide hostile or benign intent in that they leap to conclusions more quickly than nonaggressive boys, while paying less attention to information that would help them reach a more accurate inference about someone else's motives. Also, they are more likely to infer hostile intent when they come to conclusions quickly (Dodge & Newman, 1981). Finally, despite the caution we have urged in concluding there to be broad sex differences in aggression, it remains the case that boys comprise the majority by far among children who could be characterized as highly aggressive.

Given that the subjects in all of the studies we have discussed so far were boys, does this mean that the cognitive bias to infer hostile intent characterizes only aggressive boys? Apparently not, because at least one study of aggressive adolescents (Steinberg & Dodge, 1983) included girls as well as boys and found a significant hostile bias for both, although there was a slight tendency for boys to make hostile attributions more frequently than girls. Other research has found cognitive biases to characterize the social problem solving of adolescent boys and girls alike. Slaby and Guerra (1988) examined cognitive mediators of aggression in adolescents who were incarcerated for delinquent offenses, comparing them to nonaggressive high school students. The aggressive, delinquent youth were likely to approach a problematic social situation (for example, asking to borrow something and being refused) by

527

RESEARCH FOCUS 15-1

Skills for Processing Social Information and the Regulation of Aggressive Behavior

Given the conceptualization of the relationship between social cognition and behavior, it is not surprising that a recent focus of research on antisocial behavior has been on the way children impute motives to others and how such social inferences may then affect how they behave. The complexity of social situations increases as children grow older, both in terms of the variety of settings in which children find themselves and in terms of the increasing sophistication of goals, motives, and intentions that children have and which they infer others to have. Often, effective interaction in a difficult situation calls for effective social problem solving and the ability to interpret the behavior of others accurately. Thus, a more contemporary approach to factors involved in changing aggressive behavior, especially in older children and adolescents, emphasizes skills for effective social problem solving (Dodge, 1980; Dodge, 1985; Dodge & Frame, 1982).

If aggressive children misinterpret the intentions of others in ways that incline them to retaliate aggressively when there may really have been no hostile provocation, can they learn new ways to process social information that might increase the validity of their inferences and, in the process, reduce their aggressive responding? Similarly, if understanding the world accurately provides a foundation for the ability to behave appropriately, do skills in determining appropriate behavior also play a role? Recent research on children's social information-processing skills suggest this to be the case.

Finding that aggressive children have biases in the way they process social information, such as inferring that accidental damage was actually intended, suggests that inadequate social cognitive skills may be at the root of the behavioral problem, but this is far from conclusive. Because their antisocial behavior limits peer relations, it might be argued that aggressive children fail to develop good social problem solving skills *because* of their antisocial behavior. As for most psychological research, an inference of causality is strongest when it can be shown that experimentally manipulating one variable then leads to a change in another. In this case, one might ask whether training in effective skills for social information processing might lead to a reduction in aggressive behavior among antisocial children. This appears to be the case.

Brown and Dodge (1988) identified 43 children, through teacher referral, who were felt to have poor peer relationships and showed an undue amount of antisocial behavior. These children constituted the bottom 2% of those in the entire school system in terms of effective social functioning. Two intervention or "treatment" programs were developed, and children received one or the other. In one, termed *peer pairing*, antisocial children were given 32 half-hour sessions in which they received 10 minutes of instructions and discussion about relationship skills (cooperation with others, effective communication, and so on), following which they had an opportunity to practice these skills during 20-minute play sessions with a same-age peer. During the second intervention, *social information skills processing*, children also received 32 half-hour sessions divided into three segments. The first segment taught children to analyze any problematic social situations they found themselves in by asking three questions. The children first asked: "What's going on?"—designed to focus their attention on the behavior of others, think about what was happening and what it meant, and think about what they would like to *have* had happen in that situation. Then, they were to ask: "What's the best thing *I* can do?" This question was designed to encourage children to think of several alternative ways that they might behave, evaluate the alternatives by considering the consequences for each, choose one, and enact it. Finally, the child was to ask: "Is it working?" The purpose of this question was two-fold: (1) to keep children thinking about the social situation and (2) to force an assessment of whether their behavior was generating the desired consequences. If the consequences were not what was desired, the child was to begin asking the questions all over again.

After approximately ten sessions of analytic training, children were taught to apply these questions to specific types of social situations likely to be problematic for antisocial children. These situations included such "social problems" as successful peer group entry (joining other children already at play), responding to a provocation, asking for help, or apologizing. Finally, there were sessions devoted to actual problems the children themselves were encountering, and children had the opportunity to practice effective information processing by role playing responses to problem situations that were real to them.

Before, and then again following training, the investigators performed two types of assessments. First, they attempted to assess children's social problem-solving skills by presenting them with videotaped scenes depicting peer group entry or children responding to provocation; they were asked questions about the behavior of children in the scenes. Children also were asked to role play how they might respond to a provocation or attempt to get another child to play with them. Second, they collected an hour's worth of observations of children's actual social behavior in the school situation by having trained observers record children's peer entry and provocation-related behaviors in six 10-minute observation periods (during which the children were not necessarily aware they were being observed). Estimates of children's social competence (their perceived social skillfulness) were made by asking teachers to rate children's aggression, ability to respond effectively to provocation, and skills at peer entry; peers completed sociometric ratings.

Both types of intervention were found to be effective in enhancing children's social problem-solving skills and reducing the level of aggressive responding. Following training, children were better at interpreting social situations, generating alternative behaviors, and evaluating the success of the behavior selected. Behaviorally, while they showed no improvement in abilities to gain peer group entry, there was a significant reduction in their aggressive behavior toward peers, and the degree of improvement in social-processing skills was correlated with the degree to which aggressive behavior was reduced. Finally, even though there was a change in the children's actual behavior, there were no significant changes in teacher or peer estimates of children's social competence.

These results indicate that changes in children's social problem-solving skills do relate to improvements in antisocial behavior, supporting the hypothesis that such skills underlie effective social adjustment and that social cognition does influence social behavior. Since both the peer pairing and social information-processing training interventions were effective, there is the further suggestion that opportunities for peer interaction in which nascent social interaction skills can be practiced (the peer pairing intervention) provide "natural" learning experiences for social problem-solving skills, and it is presumably in this context that most children learn them. It is impressive, nevertheless, that such experiences can also be effective for antisocial children such as those in the present study who have *not* learned such skills although most of their peers have. Finally, the finding that estimates of social competence were not influenced by the intervention suggests that effective cognitive and behavior change for antisocial children might well be accompanied by separate interventions designed to change others' estimates of the children's social competence so that continued expectations for antisocial behavior do not become a self-fulfilling prophecy and undermine any gains these children may have made in the capacity for skillful social interaction.

establishing hostile goals, considering few alternative ways of behaving, and anticipating few consequences for an aggressive response. They also sought little additional information about the situation and generally defined the problem in a hostile way (for example, that retaliation rather than some other way to get the needed object was the preferred way to proceed).

The research discussed so far illustrates the recently revived interest in aggression, due in large part to new approaches sparked by a social–cognitive perspective. Interest is also turning to the role of emotion in aggression, particularly the anger that can be generated by a given experience or, as in the research described earlier, by the cognitive interpretation of that experience (Berkowitz, 1989). However, it was also proposed earlier that one factor influencing the development of aggressive responding may be a deficit in social skills for problem solving, particularly if the individual has learned

FIGURE 15-3

Interrelations of constitutional, environmental, cognitive, and interpersonal determinants of aggressiveness toward peers and the possible long-term outcomes.

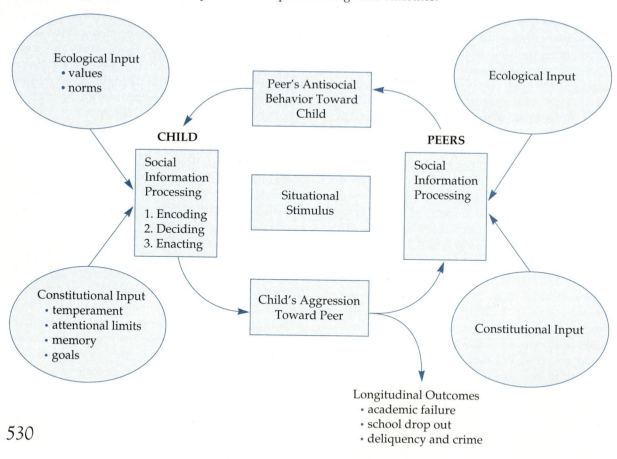

few alternative ways to respond to a situation (cf. Chittenden, 1942). The research we have described suggests, by inference, that aggressive children may have such deficits because they are so likely to react aggressively rather than in some other, more adaptive fashion but in many ways this is circular (that is, Why do they respond aggressively? Because they have no other way to respond. How do you know they have no other way to respond? Because they respond aggressively.). However, recall the Chittenden (1942) study described earlier. That study, and more recent research on interventions to teach social problem-solving skills to aggressive children reveals that providing those skills produces a reduction in their aggressive behavior, suggesting that a more general aspect of social development, learning effective skills to deal with difficult social situations, is also a factor influencing the degree to which aggression may become a characteristic pattern of behavior.

Figure 15-3 depicts one way to conceptualize a social–cognitive approach to antisocial behavior during childhood in relation to an appreciation of other factors likely to influence thinking and behavior, peer relations, and ultimately long-term results (Dodge, 1983). Both a child and his peers, who are also children, are affected by the values, standards of conduct, expectancies of others, and other aspects that might be termed their social background or part of a child's social ecology. Similarly, although this is largely a cognitive model, personality and constitutional factors may play a role, especially those that influence aspects of social problem solving such as the ability to attend to a situation, choosing a goal (desired outcome), or recalling what behavior has worked in the past or has been seen to work for others (see Research Focus 15-1). These contribute to how both the child and his peers understand a situation and how they choose to act toward one another. If this becomes a cycle of repeated aggressive, antisocial relations, some unfortunately long-term outcomes have already been identified, including academic failure, dropping out of school, and unlawful behavior (Parker & Asher, 1987).

Summary

The concept of self-regulation subsumes a broad range of behaviors that, on the surface, might appear to bear little relationship to one another or even to be antithetical. Indeed, it would probably strike the casual reader as unusal or even absurd to link prosocial behaviors such as altruism, helping, or honesty to antisocial acts like aggression, sandwiching in behaviors that seem more private than social such as resistance to temptation or delay of gratification. All of these classes of behavior have in common the effective implementation or the failure of self-regulation.

The capacity for effective self-regulation is clearly a product of socialization. Children are exposed to exhibited and verbalized standards of conduct, rewards and punishment for behavior that does or does not meet those standards, models of socially valued behavior, and reasoning (about the social

531

world) that leads to inferences likely to motivate prosocial behavior and disincline, or at least not to motivate, antisocial acts. Unfortunately, antisocial and unregulated behavior is also sometimes exhibited, verbalized, rewarded (or merely successful), or uncorrected so that socialization experiences can also lead to a failure to develop effective self-regulation.

The development of self-regulation follows a familiar course. Initially regulation is likely to be external. Children are restrained from temptations that might be harmful, reasoned *to* about standards of conduct or social motives of others or themselves, but their behavior and exposure to temptations remains largely under the control of others. Through a variety of processes and experiences the capability for *self*-regulation increases, behavior becomes more and more guided by internalized standards, accurate (or at least benign) interpretations of the world, the strategies that enhance their ability to restrain themselves from the immediate gratifications or prohibited temptations that they occasionally confront. The best conceptualization, we would argue, is one of increasing *capability* for self-regulation. Although in some instances it could be said that children move from socially devalued ways of behaving (for example, yielding to temptation or immediate gratification or failing to help others in distress) toward more socially valued ones, this is not always true (for example, children are not uniformly dishonest or aggressive until socialized to behave otherwise). The common thread is simply the ability to regulate all sorts of behavior, prosocial and antisocial alike.

Environmental factors play several different roles in affecting the development of self-regulation. Socialization is a product of the social environment. The family, peer, school, and media environments, therefore, are certainly important. Temptations, opportunities for gratification, either immediate or gained dishonestly, and occasions to help another in distress, to share, or otherwise behave generously are aspects of the environment that provide the occasions that call for self-regulation. The experience of being a target or victim of aggression is a function of the sorts of social environments a given child may encounter and may influence the development of antisocial patterns of behavior. In short, the social environment, and to a lesser extent aspects of the physical environment (such as temptations), play a major role in the development and exercise of self-regulation, though their influence is consistently filtered by cognitive factors: internalized standards of conduct, strategies, and skills for self-regulation, as well as interpretations of the social world.

This last point illustrates as well the relation between the development of self-regulation and other domains of development. The primary domain intersected is that of cognition. Most important, perhaps, is social cognition in terms of the child's interpretations and predictions about the thoughts, motives and behaviors of others. Nevertheless, other cognitive factors such as the way children symbolically construe tempting items or their consumption provide avenues to effective self-regulation.

Suggested Readings

LIEBERT, R. M., & SPRAFKIN, J. (1988). *The early window: Effects of television on children and youth*. New York: Pergamon Press.

OLWEUS, D., BLOCK, J., & RADKEY-YARROW, M. (Eds.) (1986). *Development of antisocial and prosocial behavior: Research, theories, and issues*. New York: Academic Press.

PARKE, R. D., & SLABY, R. G. (1983). The development of aggression. In E. M. Hetherington (Ed.), P. Mussen (Series Ed.), *Handbook of child psychology: Vol. 4. Socialization, personality, and social development* (pp. 547–641). New York: Wiley.

PATTERSON, G. R., DeBARSYSHE, B. D., & RAMSEY, E. (1989). A developmental perspective on antisocial behavior. *American Psychologist, 44*, 329–335.

RADKE-YARROW, M., ZAHN-WAXLER, C., & CHAPMAN, M. (1983). Children's prosocial dispositions and behavior. In E. M. Hetherington (Ed.), P. Mussen (Series Ed.), *Handbook of child psychology: Vol. 4. Socialization, personality, and social development* (pp. 469–545). New York: Wiley.

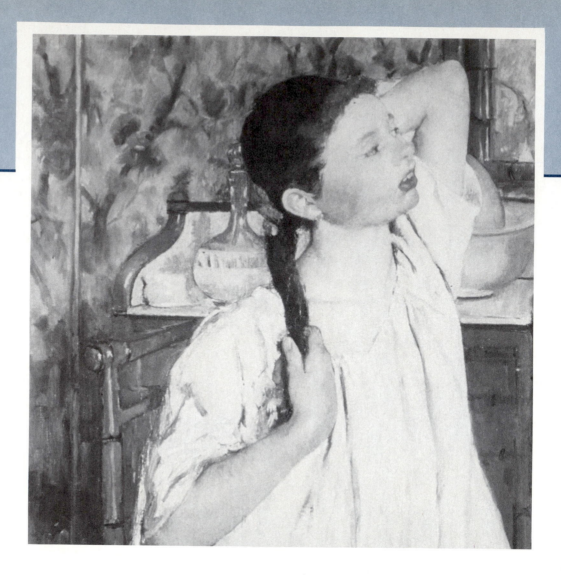

Adolescence is a period of life that continues the developmental patterns of the childhood years, but nevertheless seems to many people to be a time of very different behaviors, thoughts, and experiences. One reason for this impression is that puberty is the most dramatic biological change that occurs in the first two decades of life. Another reason is that the expectations of others seem to put new pressures on young people who have just experienced, or are about to undergo, the changes of puberty. Like infancy, adolescence has often been set apart for scientific study because of the opportunity to examine closely the effects of both biological change and environmental pressures.

PART FIVE

Beyond Childhood: Development During Adolescence

Because adolescence often receives special attention, Part Five is devoted to examining information about how this time appears to be different from earlier periods of development. Chapter 16 begins with an overview of the physical changes of adolescence. For adolescents themselves, these changes often require considerable psychological adjustments that affect behavior, thought, and emotions. Chapter 17 examines the common belief that social relationships change and behavior and emotional problems multiply during adolescence. In both chapters, the linking of adolescent development to the processes outlined in previous chapters illustrates the continuous operation of developmental principles as children mature.

535

CHAPTER SIXTEEN

The Transition to Adolescence: Physical Growth and Psychological Change

Introduction

Adolescence comprises the transitional period between childhood and adulthood. Adolescence has only recently been seen as different from adulthood (see Chapter 1), largely because the economic demands and social organization of earlier eras required that adolescents work as adults to support themselves or their families. In Western cultures today, however, child labor laws, the skills required for work in technologically advanced industrialized economies, and compulsory education mean that the adolescent years ordinarily extend the shift from childhood to the prerogatives and role responsibilities of adulthood over a 10- to 15-year period—one-fifth of the lifespan of the average person. As a consequence, adolescence has come to be viewed as a distinct period of life—and a uniquely difficult phase of psychological development.

In the 1980s, the distinctive characteristics and experiences of adolescents have become increasingly visible in connection with a number of practical social and political problems in the United States and other industrialized nations. The most frequently mentioned of these are a rapidly rising drug problem with attendant increases in delinquent gang activity and crime rates, a high incidence of teenage pregnancy and childbearing that pose short- and long-term risks for mothers and their children, and a high rate of educational failure in middle schools and high schools (Carnegie Council on Adolescence, 1989). Concerns about these problems are one reason that psychologists and other behavioral, social, and medical scientists are devoting more attention to development during adolescence, including the preadolescent years during which many of the problems begin. Whereas the first decade of life has dominated research throughout most of the history of developmental psychology, a great deal of new knowledge is now appearing about the second decade of growth and development.

Because of the burgeoning knowledge about the years from age 10 to age 20, we have taken the somewhat unusual step of devoting two chapters to development during adolescence. The underlying questions in both chapters are: What are the characteristics of the second decade of life that set it apart from earlier and later periods of development? What are the implications of this period for the development of individuals and their later lives? Using many themes from earlier chapters as a reference point, we will note the contrasts between childhood growth patterns and behavior and the growth and behavior of adolescents. At the same time, we want to make clear how development during adolescence follows principles and repeats and extends patterns that we saw during the earlier years of life. After all, the biological makeup and history of social experiences of infancy and early and middle childhood years are the basis from which further growth and development proceed. When trying to understand the course of adolescent development, consequently, we must consider the history of family relationships, previous school experiences, and community expectations and resources.

These two related themes of distinctiveness and continuity will be apparent in both Chapters 16 and 17. In an effort to make the complex subject of adolescent development as understandable as possible, however, we will use Chapter 16 to emphasize some of the ways in which adolescence seems to be different from childhood and Chapter 17 to show how continuing influences such as the family, peers, and schools are affected by the distinctive characteristics of adolescence.

The Nature of Adolescent Development

Three categories of changes are particularly important for understanding the apparent *differences* or contrasts between adolescence and earlier phases of development:

Changes in Physical Characteristics Resulting from Puberty.   Alterations in appearance and other physical characteristics—in size and shape, in the advent of primary and secondary sex characteristics, in physical strength and capacity—occur during adolescence, sometimes radically altering children's perceptions of themselves, as well as their actual physical capabilities.

Differing Responses and Demands from Others.   In cultures throughout the world, adults expect different behaviors from adolescents than from children. Often, these expectations demand skills and knowledge for which there was little preparation in childhood: consequently, new skills and behavioral routines must be mastered.

More Complex Thinking and Reasoning Abilities.   The intellectual skills of adolescents are more conducive to speculative, complex thinking and problem solving than are the cognitive patterns of childhood. These advanced skills are valuable in facing the more difficult intellectual and social problems of adolescence; they also give rise to views of the self, others, and others' reactions that may indeed make adolescence an emotionally difficult time. Because self and social relations are so central to common definitions of adolescence, we will give particular attention to these implications of cognitive changes.

In general, behavioral scientists have tended to propose possible causes of such differences that are too simple for the complexities of the changes involved. Most views have been divided into either *maturationist* or *environmentalist* explanations. The earliest and most historically influential views were the *maturationist* ideas put forth by such theorists as G. Stanley Hall and Sigmund Freud and elaborated by Anna Freud (1969). In the Freuds'

Explanations of Adolescent Development

539

view, individuals must develop new psychological defenses to cope with the strong sexual impulses associated with puberty; as a consequence, adolescence would inevitably be a period of *psychological* turbulence and turmoil. Maturationist views emphasize the psychological ramifications of puberty.

In environmentalist views, the nature of adolescence depends on the nature of the expectations and demands placed on adolescents by the society or culture of which they are a part and the modes of training provided to help them meet those expectations. Emphasizing the social changes to which young persons must adjust in the second decade of life, environmentalists see adolescent development as a matter of acquiring the behavior patterns, attitudes, values, and general social knowledge that is required for adult roles in a particular society or culture. The reasons for difficulty are the necessities of "unlearning" childhood behavior patterns and learning new patterns of behavior appropriate for later periods of life (Bandura, 1964). If there has been gradual preparation for adult roles during childhood, then adolescence need not be a difficult and turbulent time. However, if a community or society expects very different behavior of adolescents than of children, or if the expectations for adolescents are unclear (e.g., Lewin 1939), then the second decade of life may be a very difficult time indeed.

Clearly, the unique qualities of adolescence are not caused either by the individual alone or by society alone. Indeed, it has been said that adolescence begins in biology, and ends in culture. In recent years, in cultures throughout the world, it has become increasingly apparent that the usual problems faced by adolescents are complicated further by the need to adjust to rapidly changing expectations and demands of the society and culture in which they live. Take, for example, an adolescent girl who is considered old enough to take a fast-food restaurant job, although even a year earlier she would have been too young to be hired. Imagine an adolescent boy whose newly attained height and muscularity suddenly give him an advantage in sports over other boys his age. For both, social opportunities and pressures change significantly in a fairly short time. In most cases, age or physical appearance substitutes for more subtle indicators of maturity in determining what kinds of experiences young people have.

Psychologist John Hill (1980) has proposed a *transactionalist* view of adolescent development that is different from both maturationist and environmentalist views. The basis for transactionalist ideas is that changes in the individual are assumed to trigger new expectations and altered reactions from other persons, which in turn influence further changes in the individual. In a transactionalist perspective, once young persons begin to look more like adults, parents, teachers, and even strangers begin to expect behavior from them that is more like the behavior of adults; and parents and teachers may also permit behavior that is ordinarily permissible only for adults. These new standards and opportunities mean that adolescents' experiences are different in important ways from those of children. New patterns of behavior and thought emerge as a result of these experiences, and these new patterns then lead to distinctive opportunities and demands for the young person. An important question suggested by the transactionalist view, but not by the maturationist or environmentalist perspectives is: How do common adolescent changes affect those individuals who are not physically, emotionally, or socially ready to meet the opportunities and pressures foisted upon them by age or physical maturity?

Figure 16-1 shows a diagram of Hill's framework. This diagram is not intended to represent the personality of an individual adolescent, but to indicate the interrelationships of individual and social factors and their joint contributions to development of adolescents generally. Notice first that the framework identifies several *primary changes*—changes that happen to everyone and that influence further development. The primary changes listed by Hill correspond to the three aspects of change outlined earlier in this section: pubertal maturation, altered responses and demands from others, and increasingly complex thinking and reasoning abilities. Children encounter changes in social expectations during the transition to adolescence. In the terminology of Chapter 1, primary changes emphasize the *origins* of the differences between adolescence and other periods of development.

Second, the framework includes several *settings* or *conditions* within which primary changes are especially likely to be manifested and to which primary changes require special adjustments. Family relationships, interactions with peers, and demands and expectations encountered in school are examples

FIGURE 16-1
During adolescence, biological and psychological changes and altered social expectations are manifested in family, peer, and school settings to produce changes in varied aspects of individual and interpersonal development.

Source: from Hill, 1980.

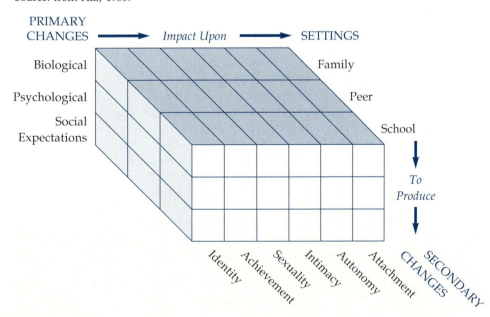

541

of settings and conditions. These significant *environmental influences* will be discussed primarily in Chapter 17.

Finally, *secondary changes* refer to aspects of behavior that seem to be especially affected by the primary changes of adolescence and the interplay of these primary changes with the influential settings and conditions of adolescents' lives. These include changes in relationships with parents and siblings (attachment and autonomy), the formation of intimate relationships outside of the family, sexuality and its expression, mastery of skills and roles required for adult life (achievement), and a sense of oneself that integrates the feelings and roles of childhood with the demands and opportunities of adulthood. In the perspective of Chapter 1, these secondary changes refer to the *course* of development for individual adolescents and the interrelations of different aspects of individual growth and change. Consequently, we will consider them throughout both Chapters 16 and 17.

The Role of Society and Culture

In cultures throughout the world, the age of 12 or 13 is considered a major marker between childhood and adulthood. A change in behavior is expected when children reach this age, regardless of whether the society is a traditional tribe or a technologically sophisticated modern nation (Rogoff, Sellers, Pirrotta, Fox & White, 1975). The particular behaviors expected are quite different from one culture to another, of course; after all, adults in these different cultures behave in quite different ways, as well. Common to all, however, is the expectation that young adolescents will engage in more adult-like behavior.

In some societies, these expectations represent a smooth continuation of childhood patterns of behavior that lead into adult roles. For example, the Samoan society studied by Margaret Mead in the 1920s (Mead, 1961) imposed few and simple social expectations on adolescents. The youths were assigned roles in the village society that matched their abilities and otherwise were allowed considerable freedom in peer group and family relationships and activities. As a result, Mead concluded, adolescents appeared to experience fewer stresses than are typical in more demanding societies. Although Mead's descriptions have recently been criticized as presenting too idyllic a picture of Samoan adolescence, her view that cultural norms and expectations help make adolescence a more or less stressful time has been widely supported by studies in varied cultures (Levy, 1983).

What societal differences make adolescence more or less psychologically difficult? First, the length of the transition from childhood to adulthood contributes to its difficulty. The transition is longer in highly developed societies such as those of the Western nations than in some primitive tribes. In these primitive societies, the time between child status and adult status may last only a few months, weeks, or days; instead of leaving their adoles-

Formal rites of passage, like the bar mitzvah, help to mark the distinction between childhood and adolescence.

cents to grope toward adult patterns of behavior and responsibility, these societies aid the transition by requiring youths to undergo rather severe rites of initiation (rites de passage) into adulthood. Often, periods of intensive training teach initiates the facts of adult life in the society. Consequently, children may be assigned "children's jobs," such as herding cattle, on one day and then only a few weeks later be given adult jobs, such as trading for the village (LeVine & LeVine, 1967).

When the transition period stretches into years—in the United States, to more than a decade—entry into adulthood is not marked by a single event. Rather, moving out of the roles required of children into those reserved for adults involves exploration and experimentation that sometimes leaves individuals in a state of psychological limbo. Psychologist Kurt Lewin (1939) has consequently referred to adolescents as *marginal* persons in the society because they belong to neither child nor adult social groups. Other observers have argued that adolescents are marginal because they are assigned no meaningful roles in United States society (Csikszentmihalyi & Larson, 1984; Friedenberg, 1965; Goodman, 1956). It may be that, despite prolonged adolescence, young people in other societies do not feel marginal because many years of education are considered a laudable investment of time in the future.

The accompanying research focus describes how differing economic circumstances determined both the degree to which adolescents experienced marginal status and the resulting implications for their preparation for adult roles and challenges.

Second, as environmentalist theories remind us, the difficulty of the transition—regardless of its length—depends on the amount of unlearning and relearning of behaviors, attitudes, and values required to fill adult roles.

543

RESEARCH FOCUS 16-1

Historical Variations in the Effects of Adolescent Development

Psychological development results from unique combinations of biological and cognitive changes in the individual and the impact of significant settings in adolescents' lives. One example of this complex process comes from sociologist Glen Elder's studies of individuals who were adolescents during the Great Depression of the 1930s (Elder, 1974; Elder, Caspi, & Burton, 1988).

Some of the families of these adolescents suffered more economic disadvantage during the depression than others, and Elder found that the amount of income loss a family suffered affected adolescent experiences and long-term outcomes for their children. Compared to adolescents whose families were not severely affected by the depression, those whose families were most economically hard pressed were more likely to help out by taking on some adult tasks in the family, to aspire to be a "grownup," and to marry and to fill adult jobs at an early age. Compared to the more fortunate adolescents, the more deprived group also showed more self-consciousness, emotional vulnerability, and desire for social acceptance.

Girls and boys were affected differently in several respects, however. Girls from more deprived families later remembered adolescence as the worst stage of their lives. One reason for their dissatisfaction was that they were often required to take on many household responsibilities because their mothers had to take outside jobs to help support the family. These girls also worried that they were less well dressed in school than other girls and often they felt excluded from social activities. Nevertheless, family caretaking roles in adolescence seemed to affect the later lives of Depression-era adolescent girls very strongly. Compared to less-deprived girls, those from "hardship" families more strongly favored marriage and family over a career, tended to marry at an earlier age, and frequently dropped out of the work force after marriage or before the birth of their first child. These differences were true regardless of whether the girls had attained a high education level or social position.

The increasing discord and tension over the family's economic problems may have affected girls more than boys from deprived families, who more often sought jobs outside the home and helped provide extra income. For Depression-era adolescent boys, those who came from more deprived families had more clear occupational goals as young adults and eventually ended up at higher occupational levels than sons of families that had not experienced such hard times. The more deprived group were also more likely to stress family values and to place a high value on children and the parental role.

Elder points out that the self-confidence and success of depression adolescent boys may partly reflect experiences before and after their adolescent years. Born in 1920–21, these individuals were children during the prosperous 1920s; consequently, they had had a period of family life that was relatively free of the difficulties they later experienced as adolescents. Furthermore, as they entered adulthood, the males were faced with military service in World War II. Although war is not a pleasant experience, military service brought with it educational and occupational-training benefits; afterward, servicemen were eligible for funds for college education through the G.I. Bill. Men who had experienced economic hardships during the depression seemed especially ready to take advantage of these benefits. In other words, the experiences of adolescence may affect readiness to benefit from experiences of later life periods, as well.

The historical period during which a young person experiences adolescence may give a unique flavor to the adolescent years themselves and, in turn, to the person's later life. Elder warns against generalizing about what "adolescents" are like on the basis of studies conducted with only one cohort, because we may be seeing only what adolescents were like at one particular point in history. Although we see this especially clearly for depression youths, other historical periods may also have distinctive effects. For example, high school and college studies in the era of the Vietnam War and the Civil Rights Movement are thought to have experienced adolescence very differently from the relatively apathetic cohorts who were adolescents in the 1950s. Similarly, individuals born from 1962–72—during the height of protest and the drug culture—are now experiencing adolescence in a period that is thought to put relatively greater emphasis on material success and a career orientation than the cohorts of the decades just preceding them. Like cultural expectations about what young people are expected to be and do, the unique opportunities, constraints, and demands of a historical period shape what adolescence is and what it means to the course of human development. 🐛

According to the social anthropologist Ruth Benedict (1954), some societies provide continuous socialization for adult roles; children are taught roles and responsibilities that are compatible with the roles and responsibilities they will have as adults. More often, particularly in Western industrialized nations, socialization is discontinuous: Certain roles exist for children, others for adults; and learning the adult roles often first requires unlearning the patterns of behavior and attitudes that were appropriate for children. For example, while adults ordinarily are expected to be sexually active when they are married, children and adolescents are generally expected to refrain from sexual experimentation; and the childhood training that inhibits sexual feelings may often make it difficult to become sexually responsive in adulthood. Similarly, children are sometimes given little responsibility and are expected to be dependent on their elders; yet as adults they are expected to know how to assume responsibility and to act independently. Benedict speculated that adolescence is more difficult in a society with many discontinuities in socialization. Her prediction is probably especially true in societies where the unlearning–relearning process is left largely to trial-and-error, as is frequently the case for American adolescents.

Physical Changes and Psychological Effects

The second origin of differences between adolescence and other life periods is a biological one. The most fundamental of these biological changes, from a physiological point of view, is achieving reproductive, or sexual, maturity. Psychologically, however, the aspects of physical change that may affect adolescents involve far more than reproductive capacity.

Adolescent physical changes begin when the hypothalamus, an area at the base of the brain, stimulates the anterior pituitary gland to secrete hormones that cause the gonads and the adrenal cortex to produce rapid growth and

Pubescence and Puberty

545

the appearance and reproductive capabilities of adults. The process by which these changes then produce the characteristic patterns of growth at puberty is similar to self-regulating mechanical systems, like automatic furnaces. In furnaces, thermostats, or heat sensors, trigger heat production when the temperature of a room falls below a predetermined level. In puberty, sensors in the body monitor the concentration of growth-producing hormones and either increase or decrease further hormonal secretions to maintain a proper level.

The system seems to operate as follows: The hypothalamus, which acts as the sensor, initiates secretion of adrenocorticotropic hormones, known as ACTH, which stimulate the adrenal cortex, and gonadotropic hormones, which stimulate the ovaries (in females) and the testes (in males). ACTH and the gonadotropic hormones cause the receptor organs to enlarge and begin to secrete their own hormones, and these in turn stimulate growth generally. In particular, testosterone, estrogen, and progesterone stimulate the maturation of the reproductive system and the development of secondary sex characteristics (Katchadourian, 1977). When certain concentrations of hormones are reached, growth begins to slow, and the growing ends of long bones (for example, in the legs and the arms) begin to close, or harden. Thus, the growth spurt is set into motion and also ended by a self-regulating hormonal system (Katchadourian, 1977). This process of hormonal regulation is diagrammed in Figure 16-2.

Note that the same hormones are involved in normal development in both males and females; sex differences result from different concentrations of the hormones produced by the gonads. Males have much higher concentrations of testosterone than females, and females have higher levels of estrogen and progesterone than males. These different concentrations produce the internal and external changes that cause male and female bodies to develop differently.

Figure 16-3 shows the rapid acceleration in height during puberty, which is known as the adolescent growth spurt. The rate of increase in height almost doubles for both boys and girls during this rapid growth. At its most rapid, growth rate averages about 10.5 centimeters a year in boys and 9.0 centimeters a year in girls. Notice that the growth spurt occurs about 2 years earlier for girls than for boys. In most cases, even after everyone in an age group has experienced the growth spurt, a particular adolescent is shorter than other persons who were taller before the growth spurt and taller than others who were previously shorter. Nevertheless, in about 30% of cases, the growth spurt produces such dramatic changes that, afterward, the adolescents are taller than you would have expected from their heights before puberty (Tanner, Whitehouse, & Takaishi, 1966).

An adolescent's growth spurt means that he or she has reached *pubescence,* the period of physical changes that lead to reproductive maturity. Pubescence culminates in puberty, the point at which reproductive maturity is reached. Before that point, however, several sex-related characteristics emerge that affect adolescents' appearances. *Primary sex characteristics* (in males, the penis; in females, the vulva) change in size and appearance. *Secondary sex character-*

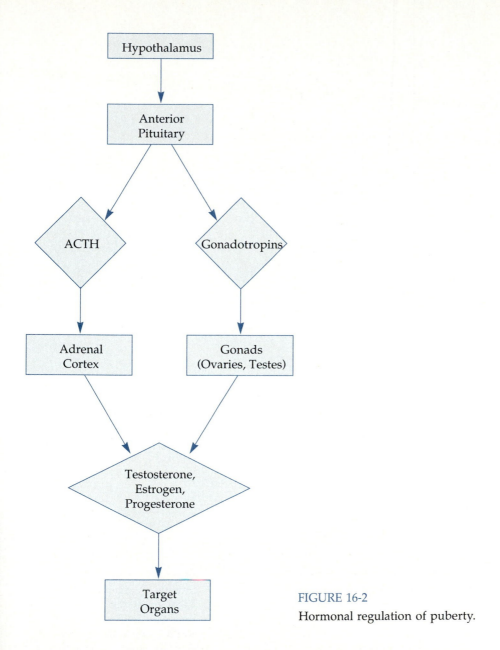

FIGURE 16-2

Hormonal regulation of puberty.

istics, which denote sexual maturity, but are not essential to sexual functioning, also appear; they include auxilliary and pubic hair, male facial hair, and female breasts. Although ages at which these characteristics change vary widely, the sequence of their occurrence is highly predictable. Table 16-1 lists these changes and their usual sequence during pubescence.

Reproductive maturity comes rather late in the sequence. For girls, who may have been pubescent since age 10 or so, the average age of puberty is about 12. It is signaled by menarche, the first menstrual flow. Boys ordinarily

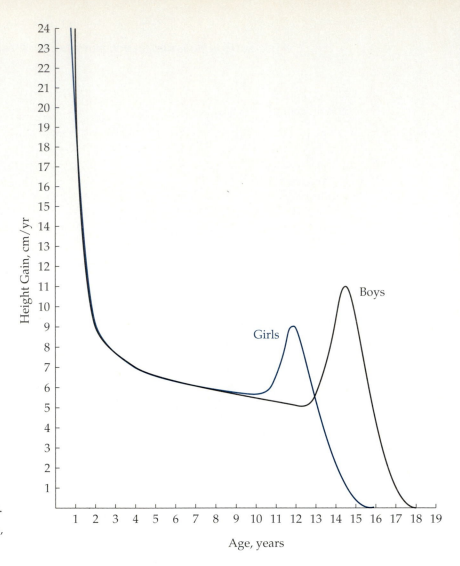

FIGURE 16-3

Growth rates for height for boys and girls during puberty.

Source: from Tanner, Whitehouse, & Takaishi, 1966.

TABLE 16-1

Sequence of pubescent changes*

Girls	Boys
Initial enlargement of breasts	Beginning growth of testes
Straight, pigmented pubic hair	Straight, pigmented pubic hair
	Early voice changes
	First ejaculation of semen
Kinky pubic hair	Kinky pubic hair
Age of maximum growth	Age of maximum growth
Menarche	
Growth of auxilliary hair	
	Growth of auxilliary hair
	Marked voice changes
	Development of the beard

* Although the *timing* of pubescent physical changes varies from person to person, they seem to occur in the same *sequence* across individuals. These lists show the order in which some standard physical signs of pubescence can be expected to appear for both boys and girls. SOURCE: Adapted from Ausubel, 1954, p. 94.

do not begin pubescent changes until age 11 or so, on the average. They also reach puberty later (on the average, at 13 to 14). In general, information about timing of puberty for boys is less satisfactory than information about girls, because the most reliable indicator of boys' reproductive maturity—the presence of live spermatozoa in a sample of urine—must be assessed in the laboratory.

As Figure 16-4 shows, the indicators of sexual maturity appear at strikingly different times for boys and girls. Although girls (top chart) typically reach puberty earlier than boys do, boys and girls alike show wide variability

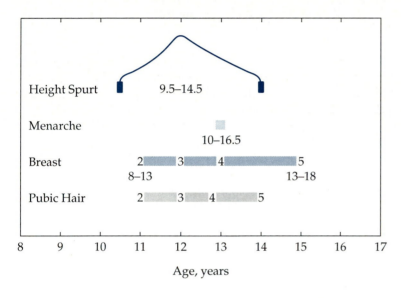

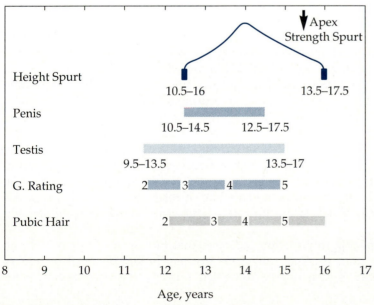

FIGURE 16-4

The indicators of sexual maturity appear at strikingly different times. Girls (top chart) mature earlier than boys do, on the average; but both boys and girls show wide variability around the averages for their sex. For example, penis growth accelerates at about age 12½ for most boys and growth is completed by age 14½. Penile development may begin as early as 10½; and in a few boys, changes may begin as late as age 14½ and are not complete until age 16½.

Source: from Marshall & Tanner, 1970.

around the averages for their sex. For example, penis growth accelerates at about age 12 for most boys, and growth is completed by age 14. But penile development may begin as early as 10; and for some few boys, changes in this primary sex characteristic begin as late as age 14 and are not complete until 16. Tanner, who bases these averages on his studies of British adolescents, says: "At age thirteen, fourteen, and fifteen there is an enormous variability among any group of boys, who range all the way from practically complete maturity to absolute preadolescence. The same is true of girls aged eleven, twelve, and thirteen" (Marshall & Tanner, 1974, p. 13). Variations in the timing of puberty appear to be determined largely by heredity. In extreme cases, malnutrition or disease may also affect pubertal time and reproductive maturity (Katchadourian, 1975).

Interrelations of Puberty and Psychological Effects

Pubescence and emergent sexuality are universal physical experiences, but their psychological impact varies from one adolescent to another. For example, adolescents who do not conform to others' expectations of physical and sexual maturity for their age may become acutely aware of being different, and this perception may cause self-consciousness or lowered self-esteem. Differences in appearance may also cause adults to have different expectations for some adolescents than they do for others, and these may create new uncertainties and stresses.

There is little evidence that the hormonal changes of puberty directly affect psychological functioning. Although it has been widely supposed that differences in gonadal hormones at puberty would produce differences between adolescents in cognitive skills and emotionality, most research findings indicate that differences in hormone levels between one person and another do not correspond to measures of intellectual skill, emotional stage, or behavior patterns (e.g. Newcombe & Dubas, 1987; Petersen & Taylor, 1980; Brooks-Gunn, Petersen, & Eichorn, 1985). In other words, biological measures, such as measures of gonadal hormones, cannot ordinarily tell us whether an adolescent will be depressed or rebellious. Very recently, however, researchers have used very detailed analyses of hormone levels in the bloodstream to examine this possibility more closely (Inoff-Germain et al., 1988; Susman et al., 1987; Udry & Talbert, 1988). Their findings generally indicate that levels of certain pubertal hormones may be correlated with emotions and behavior in early adolescents. The specific links between hormones and particular types of responses (for example, anger, acting out, attempts to dominate and control in parent–child interactions) seem to vary a great deal, however. In some cases, variation in hormonal level seems to be related to differences in boys' behavior, but not girls; in other cases, girls, but not boys, show a connection. This line of research is in its infancy, but may eventually help to clarify the role of pubertal hormones in adolescent changes.

Currently available information indicates that biological changes have an indirect, rather than a direct, effect on the psychological development of adolescents. That is, the degree to which puberty creates difficulties for adolescents appears to be strongly linked to the social significance of changes in adolescents' bodies. Four areas of research in particular show this indirect linkage: studies of the effects of menarche on girls' attitudes and self-perceptions; studies of the timing of puberty; studies of physical appearance and satisfaction with one's body; and the emergence of sexuality.

Attitudinal Effects of Menarche.   Menarche is a particularly salient biological change. Some theorists have viewed menarche as traumatic and negative, while others have emphasized the stronger sense of self that may emerge from the distinctive experience of maturity (Greif & Ulman, 1982). In recent years, partly in response to increased interest in the psychological development of women, many researchers have begun to study the experience of menarche. Most often, comparisons are made between girls who have not yet experienced menarche (premenarcheal) and those who have recently experienced it (postmenarcheal).

These studies indicate that the biological event of menarche elicits different reactions from adolescent females, depending on the understanding and significance of menarche to which they have been exposed. For example, girls from families with negative, secretive attitudes toward sexuality often experienced menarche more negatively than girls from families with more positive, open attitudes. If girls had little or no information about their bodies and the nature and significance of menarche, they were more likely to respond with more fear and distaste than those who were better prepared (Brooks-Gunn & Ruble, 1982, 1983; Rierdan & Koff, 1985). Girls who experienced menarche very early were more likely to find it fearsome and negative than those who were on time or late, perhaps because early maturers were less likely to have been given adequate information about what to expect (Ruble & Brooks-Gunn, 1982). Thus, depending on social influences, menarche may be experienced as a joyous, happy event or as a negative, shameful one.

Much more information is needed about the experience of menarche and the psychological effects of other major physical changes in adolescence. One difficulty in studying both the negative and the potentially positive effects of menarche is that, so far, most of the available information comes from the self-reports of adolescents and adult women. Objective behavioral observations of adolescents at different stages of pubertal development would give us more confidence about differences between pre-menarcheal and post-menarcheal girls. Another difficulty is that, at present, most of our findings come from studies of white middle-class girls. Because menarche may be experienced differently by girls in other subcultural groups, studying a wider range of girls would help us to better understand the role of cultural beliefs, attitudes, and expectations in mediating the effects of biological changes such as menarche.

Little is known about how boys are affected by signs that they are sexually mature. Boys may be less consciously aware of changes in their bodies, which occur more gradually and less obviously than menarche does. For both boys

551

and girls, however, coming of age sexually is almost certainly accompanied by feelings that make a difference in how young persons view themselves and respond to others during early adolescence.

Social Impact of Pubertal Timing. A second example of the role of social significance in the psychological effects of puberty comes from studies of adolescents who are either notably ahead of or behind their peers in reaching puberty (Mussen & Jones, 1957, 1958a, 1958b). Early-maturing boys—those who attain physical maturity well ahead of their peers—seem to have an advantage over boys of the same age who mature at a slower than average rate. Longitudinal studies of males from preadolescence to adulthood show that early maturers were consistently judged by adults and peers to be more attractive and competent during adolescence than late maturers; furthermore, at age 33, early maturers had attained greater success in their careers and higher social status than late maturers (Jones, 1957).

Why should early maturity make such a difference in males' social success? One reason may be that the pubescent growth spurt affects physical strength and endurance such as heart and lung capacity that influence adolescent boys' success in athletics. Because athletic success is a major ingredient in boys' prestige and social success in the American high school (Coleman, 1961), early maturers are more likely than late maturers to be successful in athletics and, thus, to be socially successful in high school society. In addition, the sense that they are approaching the prerogatives of young adulthood seems to increase boys' positive feelings about the changes in their own bodies (Tobin-Richards, Boxer, & Petersen, 1983).

Girls also experience some advantages of early maturing, but the benefits are less clear-cut for girls than for boys. Girls who develop breasts and curvaceous figures earlier than their agemates may, at first, be less popular with other girls than girls who have not yet reached puberty. There are several possible reasons for this. Early-maturing girls may be seen as sexually precocious by both adults and other girls. Furthermore, their larger size may make them seem physically unattractive and less feminine than on-time and late-maturing girls, particularly in a culture in which lithe, trim bodies are favored (Simmons, Blyth, & McKinney, 1983). However, by the time the majority of girls in an age group have matured physically, girls who matured early are often among the most popular members of the girls' crowd (Faust, 1960). As adults, early-maturing girls eventually enjoy greater social benefits than girls who matured more slowly (Livson & Peskin, 1980).

By comparison, late-maturing males may be more tense, anxious, and eager then the average teenager (Jones, 1957). Late physical maturation may ultimately benefit psychological development, however. Late-maturing male adolescents often seem to have learned more flexibility in dealing with life problems than early maturers (Livson & Peskin, 1980; Peskin, 1967; Weatherly, 1964). Perhaps because late maturers fit less readily than early maturers into social activities, such as sports and dating, late-maturing males may develop a variety of alternative strategies for social rewards. For example, late-maturing males may develop more skills in solving interpersonal problems than early-maturing males, for whom social interactions are generally easier; and late-maturing males may learn to find bases for relationships that do not depend on physical appearance or social status. These skills may be one reason that, in follow-up studies, late-maturing males at age 33 had more successful marriages than early-maturing males (Livson & Peskin, 1980).

Appearance. The appearance of pubescent youngsters often includes some usually transitory, but painful, conditions that illustrate the psychological impact of adolescent physical changes. One notorious example is acne (Schachter, Pantel, Glassman & Zweibelson, 1971). During pubescence, oil secretion from the sebaceous glands of the skin increases, sometimes clogging pores and causing them to become inflamed. Aggravated by the eating habits of teenagers and the social anxieties and tensions of adolescence, disfiguring blemishes that are difficult to control can result. To a self-conscious boy or girl, this can further compound the social anxieties of adolescence.

Physical awkwardness is another example of an apparently physical problem that is often the result of physical change and social factors working together. The unevenness of growth rates of different body parts may make it more difficult to coordinate actions smoothly. But the legendary clumsiness of adolescents may also result from uncertainty in new and unusual situations during this transitional age period. Body changes undoubtedly contribute to that uncertainty, but are almost surely not the only source of it.

Girls' psychological reactions to the bodily changes of puberty are particularly affected by their perceptions of and satisfaction with their weight. The current ideal body image in the United States emphasizes thinness, and girls who perceive themselves as overweight are likely to have more negative self-

Variations in physical characteristics may become more psychologically significant during adolescence.

553

images than other girls (Tobin-Richards, Boxer, & Petersen, 1983). Early-maturing adolescent girls are especially likely to be dissatisfied with their weight (Duncan, Ritter, Dornbusch, Gross, & Carlsmith, 1985). Erroneous perceptions of oneself as overweight are commonly noted as symptoms in two widely publicized eating disorders of adolescence: anorexia nervosa and bulimia. Recent findings from research into these two disorders are described in Research Focus 16-2.

A Sociocultural View of Effects of Physical Change.   Psychologists Anne Petersen and Brandon Taylor (1980) have recently suggested that the impact of biological changes on psychological development partly results from sociocultural norms and the expectations of other persons with whom adolescents interact. As Figure 16-5 shows, adolescents' own expectations about their appearances and the expectations that others communicate to them affect their body image, self-image, self-esteem, and gender identity. These per-

FIGURE 16-5

Directions of influence between pubertal changes and psychological responses, according to the biological approach to adolescence.

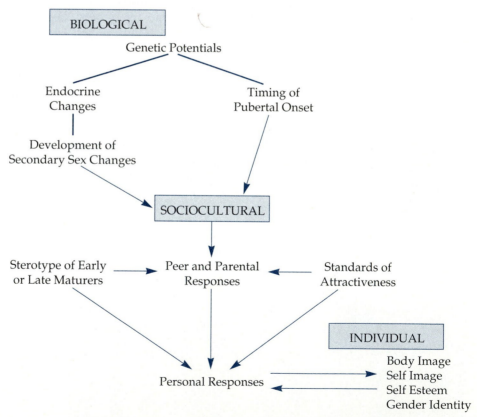

sonal and emotional states in turn determine how successfully individuals adapt to pubertal changes.

The joint effects of physical and social change in adolescence are illustrated by findings from a large longitudinal study of self-concept and self-esteem among early adolescents. Sociologists Roberta Simmons and Dale Blyth and their colleagues (Simmons & Blyth, 1987; Simmons, Blyth, Van Cleave, & Bush, 1979) were particularly interested in two influences on the adolescents' self-esteem or positive feelings about themselves: (1) the physical changes of puberty and (2) changes in organization of the school settings in which the young people participate.

To examine these influences, the researchers compared the self-esteem of adolescents in two different settings: schools in which elementary school children are grouped together with early adolescents in a building that houses grades 1 through 8; and (2) schools in which grades 1 through 6 are put in a separate building from the early adolescents in grades 7 and 8 who, in turn, are placed with some or all of grades 9 through 12. In the latter case, adolescents are obliged to change to a new school with older peers at about the same time that they are also coping with the physical and social changes of puberty. The adolescents were between ages 10 and 15 and were from different socioeconomic backgrounds. Adolescents who were undergoing pubertal changes at the same time that they had to transfer from their lower school to a different school showed significant decreases in positive feelings about themselves (self-esteem). As can be seen in Figure 16-6, this was particularly true for females who were experiencing several changes simultaneously: (1) greater sexual maturity, (2) more attention from males, and (3) the transition to a new school setting. Both females and males who remained in the same school until they were in grade 8 showed considerably less decline in self-esteem during puberty than those who changed schools earlier.

The effects may have greater impact on girls than boys because socialization in American society often encourages girls to be more concerned about personal appearance than boys are. Girls may be especially susceptible to the unclear social expectations that accompany both pubertal changes and new social settings. These findings support Petersen and Taylor's (1980) view that an individual adolescent's experience is not merely the result of internal changes or of external pressures. Psychologically, adolescence involves a unique combination of changes in both within a short period of time.

The Emergence of Sexuality.   The effects of social context on adolescent sexuality is another instance of the importance of the sociocultural model for understanding the impact of puberty in adolescent development. The most obvious effect of puberty is that it becomes physiologically possible for adolescents to beget children. However, changes in sexuality, or interpersonal emotions pertinent to sexual relationships, are not the result of physiological development at puberty. The bases for physiological sexual responses are laid down either before or immediately after birth through the action of hormones such as the androgens and progesterones. At puberty, only the absolute level of androgens changes, affecting the frequency and intensity

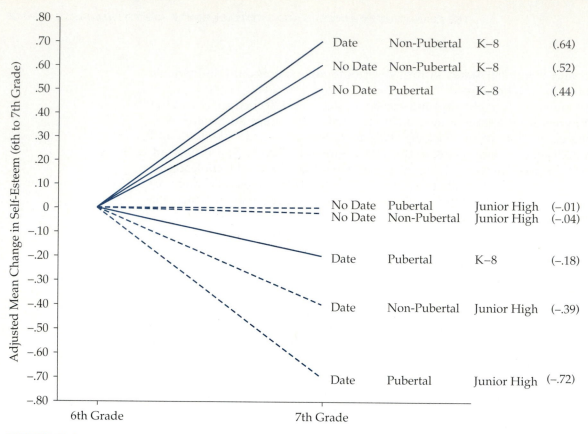

FIGURE 16-6

Changes in girls' self-esteem between sixth and seventh grades as a function of puberty, dating behavior, and type of school.

Source: from Simmons, Blyth, Van Cleave, & Bush, 1979.

of sexual arousal in both males and females. The other major significant pubertal event for adult sexuality is that males become capable of ejaculation (Katchadourian, 1975; Money & Clopper, 1974).

The emergence of sexuality involves a very wide range of social experiences, social learning, and social roles within which adolescents move toward adulthood. Many of the most pronounced sex differences in sexuality are even social rather than physiological. In a classic study, Ford and Beach (1951) found great variation from culture to culture, supporting the idea that sexual practices are largely the result of social and cultural transmission, rather than the increased frequency and intensity of arousal associated with hormonal changes at puberty. William Simon and John Gagnon (1969; Gagnon, 1974), leading authorities on sexuality, refer to sex as a socially scripted activity, because sexual behavior is so heavily determined by the expectations and social significance associated with patterns of sexual activity. For example, males' sexual behavior, like their cultural sex roles, tends to be instrumental and goal directed; in the case of lower-class males particularly, premarital sexual behavior is important to status in the male peer group. By contrast, females are more likely to subordinate sexual activity to the goals of expressiveness and sensitivity that characterize females' culturally prescribed gender role (Simon & Gagnon, 1969). For both males and females, the perceived social importance of dating is likely to be a major factor in becoming involved with members of the opposite sex (Newcomb, Huba, & Bentler, 1986).

The importance of age-specific social expectations to the emergence of sexual behavior is illustrated by findings about the time at which U.S. adolescents begin to date.

Beginning to Date.   Starting to date is a behavioral transition that has usually been linked to pubertal change. Sanford Dornbusch and his colleagues used information from the U.S. National Health Examination Survey of 12- to 17-year-olds to sort out the effects of pubertal status versus social variables on whether young people had yet dated. Pubertal status was assessed by physicians. The puberty measure predicted less than 1% of the differences among adolescents in dating behavior. Among adolescents between 12 and 15, all of whom were at the middle stage of pubertal development, the percentage of those who had ever dated increased steadily across ages. We still need evidence on how either general norms for behavior or the expectations of friends and family may encourage adolescents to begin to date, but these findings imply that these social factors, rather than physical maturity status, are probably the instigating influence. Dornbusch's analysis reminds us that, although physical maturation is a change of unquestionable relevance to the development of sexuality, many concomitants of social roles and behaviors associated with sexuality are linked to environmental influences that stem from a person's membership in the adolescent age group.

RESEARCH FOCUS 16-2

Thin at Any Cost

For thousands of teenagers and young adults in the United States, coping with the stresses of the transition to adulthood also means struggling with the ordinary matters of food and eating. Two types of adolescent eating disorders have recently received widespread attention: anorexia nervosa, which is characterized by marked weight loss and an intense desire for thinness, and bulimia, or binge eating (Russell, 1985). Most often, the victims of these disorders are adolescent females. In the case of anorexia, girls are 10 times more likely than boys to develop the disorder; it is estimated that as many as 1% of the population of adolescent girls in the United States is anorexic. Less is known about the incidence of bulimia, because it has been considered a separate problem from anorexia for only a short time (Russell, 1985). From what is known at pres-

ent, however, both disorders seem primarily to affect girls from middle- and upper-middle-class white families; and it is rare to find the symptoms until after puberty.

What causes the sudden emergence in adolescence of the extreme and sometimes life-threatening symptoms of these disorders? Several ideas have been suggested, mostly on the basis of clinical studies of affected girls.

One idea is that the natural effects of puberty conflict with cultural ideas of beauty in U.S. society, causing an overreaction to the threat of gaining weight (Graham & Rutter, 1985). Recall that in females, pubescent changes include increases in fat deposits. In cultures that place great stress on thinness for females, the signs of fat may cause some girls to diet severely or to go on secretive binges, perhaps followed by self-in-

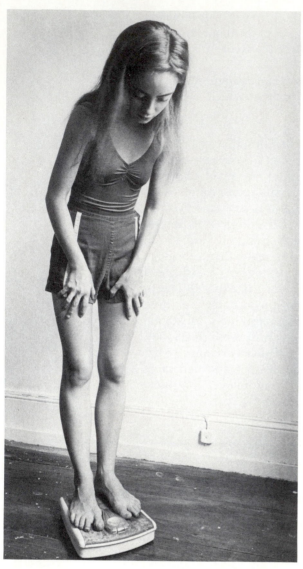

Eating disorders, such as anorexia nervosa, sometimes emerge from the physical changes and psychological issues facing adolescents.

duced vomiting to avoid gaining weight. The effect of cultural ideals about body size and shape is apparent even for girls who are not anorexic or bulimic. For example, in a recent study, about one-half of girls in grades six and seven mistakenly perceived themselves as being either under- or overweight (Forehand, Faust, & Baum, 1985).

A second idea is that anorexia and bulimia are attempts to gain control over one's body. Anorexic girls are often high achievers who may also come from families in which perfection and self-control have been highly valued. By refusing to eat, girls may feel they are showing self-control, assuring themselves of social success, or improving their chances of achievement in sports or the arts. Patients with both disorders typically show fear and self-disgust over loss of control.

A third possibility is that anorexia is an extreme reaction to menarche and to anxiety about sexuality. By remaining "unwomanly" in body function and appearance, girls may be responding to fears about being sexually active or avoiding pressures to become sexually attractive. A related idea is that the cause is actually anxiety over impending separation from parents. The weight losses associated with anorexia make adolescents look more like "little girls" who need to remain with their parents.

Both anorexia and bulimia are typically accompanied by depression and poor self-concept. It is impossible to tell whether these emotional difficulties cause girls to misperceive their weight and to react in this extreme way or the other way around (Forehand, Faust, & Baum, 1985). However, the self-perceptions and behaviors that accompany anorexia and bulimia are so extreme that multiple cognitive and emotional factors may be at work.

Statistics indicate that large numbers of adolescents in the United States are sexually active. In a national sample of U. S. teenagers in 1986, 61% of boys and 53% of girls reported having experienced sexual intercourse (Harris, 1986). Although it is difficult to collect information about the sexual lives of very young adolescents, the most reliable study available indicates that about 1 in 10 adolescents under the age of 15 has experienced sexual intercourse. Early adolescents in some subgroups in the population may be more likely to have become sexually active than those in other groups (Chilman, 1986; Miller & Simon, 1980; Udry, 1983).

Relatively small proportions of sexually active adolescents practice contraception regularly, although birth control devices are more readily available and more frequently used today than in the past. The reasons for this significant failure are difficult to identify, as Research Focus 16-3 makes clear, but the consequences are readily apparent. Failing to practice contraception or practicing it only sporadically, has resulted in more than a million teenagers' pregnancies each year in the United States. More than 800,000 of these pregnant adolescents are unmarried. The rate of teenage pregnancy in the United States is one of the highest in the world, and black teenagers in the United States have the highest fertility rate of any teenage population worldwide (Wallis, 1986). However, even though the rate of pregnancy in unmarried black teenagers is alarmingly high and receives a great deal of media attention, it is important to remember that this group does not represent the majority of teenage mothers. In absolute numbers there are more births to teenagers from other groups than from the poor, urban, black group (Brooks-Gunn, & Furstenberg, 1986).

The consequences of unmarried parenthood are likely to be serious for both mother and child. Young mothers are more likely than older women to have difficult pregnancies and deliveries, with higher rates of toxemia and related anemia, irregular size or position of infant to the pelvic structure of

The emergence of heterosexual relations in adolescence results from social expectations, as well as from pubertal maturation.

559

RESEARCH FOCUS 16-3

Contraception: Ignorance, Superstition, and Choice

Relatively small proportions of sexually active adolescents practice contraception regularly, although birth control devices are more readily available and more frequently used today than in the past. One reason appears to be ignorance about conception and contraception. Although adolescents of all ages know about contraception itself, their knowledge of methods and when and how to use them is limited (Morrison, 1985). In a national sample of 15- to 19-year-old women, 40% believed that fertility does not begin with menarche (Zelnik & Kanter, 1979). Many early adolescents also believe that "if a girl does not truly want a baby, she won't get pregnant" (Morrison, 1985; Sorenson, 1973).

A second reason is that large numbers of adolescents express negative or mixed attitudes about contraceptives. Many believe birth control methods frequently "don't work anyway," consider them inconvenient or "messy," or worry about side effects (Morrison, 1985). Others express concerns that using contraception makes it seem as though intercourse was planned or interferes with spontaneity, or they fear that others will find out that they are using contraceptives. Said an 18-year-old mother: "I chickened out. I just never went back . . . for the pills." Some experts believe these feelings reflect social scripts about the inappropriateness of sexual feelings and behaviors.

Some experts suggest that adolescents often lack the cognitive maturity to understand the implications of failing to practice contraception. One view is that they often fail to comprehend the chance of conception in each act of unprotected intercourse (Cvetkovich & Grote, 1981; Oskamp & Mindick, 1983). Researchers report that about 15% of adolescents believe that if a girl has had unprotected intercourse over a period of a month without becoming pregnant, she is unlikely to get pregnant very soon (Oskamp & Mindick, 1983). A related common belief is that a girl cannot become pregnant the first time she has intercourse (Cvetkovich & Grote, 1983).

Several characteristics of individual adolescents and their environments also correlate with contraceptive use. Women who use contraceptives tend to have higher self-esteem and a stronger sense of control over what happens to them than those who do not use contraceptives or use them unreliably (Herold, Goodwin, & Lero, 1979; Lundy, 1972; Steinlauf, 1979). Adolescents from families in which the father works at a blue collar job and earns a relatively low income are statistically less likely to know about

Failing to practice contraception puts both adolescent mothers and their children at risk for continuing problems.

and use contraception than teenagers from high-income, white collar families. If females perceive that their families would approve of their sexual behavior, they are more likely to use contraceptives than if they think their families would not approve; but there is some indication that males who perceive family approval are somewhat less likely to use contraception than those who do not (Furstenberg, 1976; Garris, Steckler, & McIntire, 1976; Herold & Samson, 1980; Hornick, Doran, & Crawford, 1979).

Most experts believe that sex education programs are likely to be the most effective means of getting teenagers to practice contraception. Research findings indicate that sex education programs are an important supplement to parental teaching about responsible sexual behavior. Sociologist Frank Furstenberg, Jr., and his cowork-

ers (Furstenberg, Herceg-Baron, Shea, & Webb, 1985) conducted a survey of a sample of 15- and 16-year-olds across the United States. They questioned these teenagers confidentially about their sexual behavior, how much information they had gotten about sex, and from what sources. Of this group, 31% of those who had not gotten information about sex from either parents or sex education programs were sexually active; of those who had talked with parents, but had not had sex education, 21% were active. However, only 17% of those who had had sex education courses reported having had intercourse. Having an opportunity for sex education at home and at school is highly desirable, but for those who do not have parental guidance, sex education appears to be valuable. 🐚

---

the mother and prolonged labor (McKenry, Walters, & Johnson 1979). The number of teenage mothers who attempt suicide is seven times greater than the number of teenage girls without children who attempt suicide. Fewer than half of the females who become pregnant between the ages of 13 and 15 complete high school. Adolescents who give birth are less likely than women who give birth later to find stable employment, marry, or be self-supporting (Chilman, 1983; Furstenberg, Lincoln, & Menken, 1981; Moore & Burt, 1982). Many teenage mothers are surprised by the impact of the baby on their lives. In the words of one 15-year-old with a 6-week-old son: "Last night I couldn't get my homework done. I kept feeding him and feeding him. Whenever you lay him down, he wants to get picked up. Babies are a big step. I should have thought more about it." Said another: "It has been a long, long while since I had a good time." (Wallis, 1985, pp. 78–79). For adolescents who experience pregnancy and birth early in their lives, the disruption to psychological development is enormous.

Death rates for babies born to mothers under age 15 are greater than death rates for those born to 15- to 19-year-olds and more than twice the rates for babies born to mothers age 20 to 34. Even when they survive, babies born to mothers under age 20 show a higher rate of mental retardation, birth defects, epilepsy, and birth injuries. The problems of these babies seem to increase as they grow into childhood and adolescence. Across a number of studies, behavior problems and poor school performance have been found to be more common in these children of unmarried teenage mothers than other children. The impact is especially noticeable for boys (Brooks-Gunn & Furstenberg, 1986). The ever-growing population of children born in these circumstances constitutes a group for whom social services will be necessary to try to compensate for deficient early experiences (Moore & Burt, 1982).

561

Misperceptions About Teenage Sexuality and Parenthood

J. Brooks-Gunn and Lindsay Chase-Lansdale

1. *"Sex Education Increases Sexual Activity."* Even though three-quarters of all adolescents today report having had some sex education and three-quarters of all school districts report offering sex education, many still believe that sex education increases early sexual activity. If teenagers have not learned about sex, the argument goes, then they will not engage in it. Large-scale evaluations suggest that sex education does not promote early sexuality (Furstenberg, Moore, & Peterson, 1986; Zelnik & Kim, 1982). Instead, knowledge about reproduction increases after such programs, especially in younger adolescents. Such

programs may promote contraceptive use in sexually active teens, although few large-scale evaluations have been conducted (Kirby, 1984).

In Western Europe, where much more extensive education is provided to youth, rates of sexual activity are no higher than those in the United States; moreover, rates of contraceptive use are significantly higher, and rates of teenage pregnancy are much lower in Europe than in the United States (Jones et al., 1985).

2. *"Early Sexuality Is Only Seen in Disadvantaged Groups."* Although it is true that minority youth

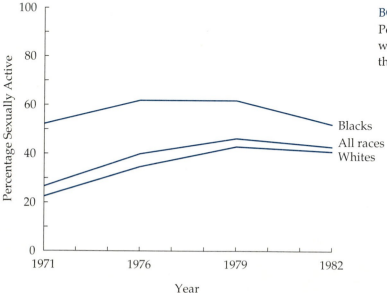

BOX FIGURE 16-1
Percentage of girls aged 15 to 19 who were sexually active between the years 1971 and 1982 (by race).

are more likely to have had intercourse as teenagers than are nonminority youth, the differences between the two have narrowed considerably in recent years. Teenage sexuality trends for girls have been carefully documented in the 1970s and 1980s. The proportion of all never-married girls ages 15 to 19 who have made their sexual debut are illustrated in Box Figure 16-1 by race and by time (1971 to 1982). Large increases occurred between 1971 and 1979, after which time the percentage of sexually active girls remained stable or perhaps even declined. Black girls had significantly higher rates of intercourse than white girls at all time points, although the difference had dropped to *only 13 percentage points* by 1982. While directly comparable data do not exist for Hispanics, estimates from other nationally based studies suggest that their rates of teenage intercourse are similar to those of white adolescent girls.

Additionally, the proportion of teenagers, whether Hispanic, white, or black, having intercourse is significant. Cumulative percentages by age of initiation, sex, and race in 1983 tells the story. Sixty percent of white male teens had made their sexual debut by age 18 and 60% of white girls just a year later, by age 19. Sixty percent of black males had had intercourse by age 16, and 60% of black females two years later, by age 18.

Another way to explore the premise that teenage sexuality differs for minority and nonminority youth involves an examination of the antecedents of teenage sexual activity. In general, these antecedents are similar for blacks and whites. They include such factors as poor academic achievement, poverty, attendance at schools where early sexual activity is the norm, and poor parent–child communication (Brooks-Gunn & Furstenberg, 1988; Hoffeth & Hayes, 1987).

3. *"It Is Impossible to Alter Teenagers' Sexual Behavior or Contraceptive Use."* Clearly, the experience in Western Europe suggests just the opposite. Pregnancy rates of European youths are much lower than those in the United States, while the rates of sexual activity are the same.

Closer to home, several clinic programs, particularly those based in schools or close to schools, have had the effect of changing behaviors related to sexuality. The most well known, and perhaps the earliest school-based clinic program, may be that in St. Paul, Minnesota. In a preprogram–postprogram comparison, fertility rates dropped from 79 per thousand to 26 per thousand from 1973 to 1984; continuation rates from contraceptive use was high (over 80% over a 2-year period); dropout rates for girls with babies had declined from 45% to 10% from 1973 to 1976–77 (Edwards et al., 1980).

Another innovative program has recently been evaluated in Baltimore, Maryland, where a health clinic was opened adjacent to a junior high and a high school. Using a pre–post, comparison treatment design, first intercourse was delayed by 7 months by girls who were exposed to the program for 3 years; clinic attendance increased by girls prior to sexual initiation; and many boys attended the clinic. Most impressively, conceptions dropped in the program schools over a 3-year period, while conceptions increased in the comparison schools (Zabin et al., 1986).

4. *"Parents Will not Accept Sex Education Outside the Home."* Parents are very concerned that their offspring become responsible sexual citizens. Parents are often very uncomfortable talking about reproductive and sexual issues with their children (Brooks-Gunn, 1987).

Indeed, once believed to be the province of the family, in reality the responsibility for sex education has shifted in part to the school. A vast majority of parents, other adults, and adolescents support sex education in the schools. In the early 1980s, three-quarters of all school districts provided some sex education. Only one state currently prohibits instruction in reproductive topics. The spectre of HIV infection may increase the already high proportion of parents wishing to have sex education in the schools. In a recent national survey by Harris, virtually all parents wanted AIDS education in the schools (94%).

5. *"Welfare Causes Early Childbearing."* Several policy analyses have advanced the notion that the growing availability of welfare to young mothers has contributed to the decline of marriage and the rise of single parenthood.

Two arguments have been made to support this claim. Specifically, people argue that pregnancy rates have increased since the 1960s, and that these pregnancies are desired by girls (in the hopes of obtaining welfare). However, first of all, most teens do not deliberately plan to become pregnant when they do. Indeed, if teens had to take a pill to *become* pregnant, relatively few would elect to do so. Most teens become pregnant because they are having sex and are insufficiently adept and motivated to use contraception effectively (Brooks-Gunn & Furstenberg, 1988). For example, less than one-fifth of all teens intend to get pregnant.

Second, teenage birth rates, while increasing during the 1960s and early 1970s, have been decreasing since then. The increases were due to the earlier ages of sexual activity as well as the sporadic use of contraception. The decreases have been due to the fact that approximately 40% of pregnancies to teenagers end in abortions (Hayes, 1987), with approximately 400,000 abortions occurring annually. This finding substantiates reports about the fact that most teenage pregnancies are not planned.

What has changed is that births to teenage mothers increasingly are out of wedlock. Today, the vast majority of teenage mothers are unmarried. By the early 1980s, close to two-thirds of all white teen mothers (delivering first births) were unmarried when they became pregnant, and almost all blacks (97%) were single. One explanation for this change locates the historical rise in out-of-wedlock childbearing in the shrinking job opportunities for young males, especially blacks (Wilson, 1987). In urban areas, particularly Northern and Midwestern cities where the loss of high-paying industrial jobs has been acute, black teenage unemployment has reached epidemic proportions. In 1984, only 34% of black males 18- to 19-year-olds and 58% of 20- to 24-year-olds were employed in these communities. Wilson argues that male joblessness is causally associated with female-headed households in out of wedlock births.

To return to the welfare causes of early childbearing argument, the decline in marriage among pregnant teens preceded the rise in welfare, especially among blacks, and has continued into the 1970s and early 1980s despite a fall-off in real welfare benefits (Jencks, 1985).

6. *"Contraceptive Use Is a Female Matter."* All societies attempt to manage sexuality in order to regulate fertility. Typically, efforts to control fertility and sexual arousal emerge during puberty, with the focus usually being on the adolescent girls' sexuality prior to marriage.

Efforts to help teenagers manage sexuality are limited by a focus on female fertility, as though fertility were a gender specific issue. However, fertility is not gender specific, and males do take responsibility for contraceptive use (although perhaps not as much as many people would like). About one-half of all teenagers do not use contraceptives the first time they have sexual relations. Of those who use any method, male methods seems to be the overwhelming choice, as reported by both males and females, blacks and whites. For example, two-thirds to three-quarters of all white teenagers and black teenage boys report using a male method. Among both boys and girls, those who planned first intercourse were much more likely to have used contraceptives than those who did not: The females were more likely to have used the female prescription methods than the male was likely to have used the male contraception method (Hofferth & Hayes, 1987; Zelnik & Shah, 1983).

However, we know very little about males' attitudes about contraceptive use, even though 40% of females depend on male methods or in what may be called the "vigilance of males."

7. *"Having a Child as a Teenager Renders a Young Girl Destined to a Lifetime of Failure."* It is the case

that in the short term (1 to 5 years after the birth of the child), adolescent mothers are more likely to drop out of school, to have difficulties obtaining employment, and to become reliant on government assistance than teens who do not become young mothers. However, even in the short term, there is significant variation in the outcomes of early parenthood (Brooks-Gunn & Furstenberg, 1987). Over the long term, this variation becomes especially pronounced. In the 17-year followup of early childbearers in the Baltimore Study, a significant proportion of teen mothers by age 35 had improved their life chances: 33% of those who had not graduated in the short term had completed high school, 30% had received some postsecondary education; 5% had completed college; 60% had been employed in the previous 5 years; 25% were earning middle-class incomes; and only 13% were on welfare (Furstenberg, Brooks-Gunn, & Morgan, 1987). Despite the tremendous diversity in outcomes, the adolescent mothers by age 35 remained at a disadvantage in terms of economic success and marital stability compared to women who postponed childbearing until their twenties. The important conclusion here is that the popular conception of teenage mothers perpetually on welfare, surrounded by many children, facing a lifetime of poverty, is a stereotype.

8. *"There Is a Much Higher Incidence of Child Abuse, Learning Disabilities, and Delinquency Among Children of Teen Mothers Than Those of Older Mothers."* These problems have not been documented by research. Moreover, we know very little about the parenting competence and practices of adolescent mothers. In general, there are surprisingly few studies of the children of teenage mothers. Furthermore, most of the studies have focused on infants. The available studies indicate that infants and preschoolers of adolescent mothers show more small but consistent decrements in cognitive functioning than children of older mothers (Brooks-Gunn & Furstenberg, 1986). In addition, children of teen mothers seem to have more behavior problems, for example, keeping aggression under control. Differences between offspring of teen and older mothers become more pronounced as children grow older. Grade failure in adolescence is a particular problem for children of teen mothers (Furstenberg, Brooks-Gunn, & Morgan, 1987). Boys are more negatively affected in all domains than girls.

The reasons for these negative outcomes are not yet well understood. The strongest empirical evidence involves the adverse consequences of the socioeconomic status of the teen mother. To the extent that teenage parenthood is associated with poverty, lower maternal education, disadvantaged neighborhoods, poor quality schools, and high rates of family instability, child development will be negatively affected. Age and maturity of the mother may also be important factors (Brooks-Gunn & Furstenberg, 1986).

Dr. Brooks-Gunn is Senior Research Scientist in the Division of Educational Policy Research at Educational Testing Service. In addition, she is the Director of the Adolescent Study Program at Educational Testing Service and the St. Luke's-Roosevelt Hospital Center in New York City, and Adjunct Associate Professor of Pediatrics at the University of Pennsylvania.

Lindsay Chase-Lansdale is currently Senior Program Associate for Development and Family Research at the Chapin Hall Center for Children, The University of Chicago. She also serves on the board of directors of the Foundation for Child Development, as Chair of the Committee on Social Policy of the Society for Research on Adolescence, and on the Technical Advisory Board for the National Longitudinal Surveys on Labor Market Experience.

Changes in Thinking and Reasoning

A third origin of differences between adolescents and people in other life periods is the nature and patterns of change affecting cognitive capabilities and performance. As we saw in Chapters 7 and 8, children in middle childhood think and reason primarily in "the here-and-now." By contrast, adolescents and adults can more readily deal in the "world of pure possibility," imagining what might be as well as what is (Flavell, 1963, 1985). This intellectual capability enables—perhaps obliges—adolescents to deal not only with knowledge of themselves from the past and present, but with what they can imagine about themselves in the future. In addition, the more complex thinking and reasoning that emerge in the second decade of life increase adolescents' awareness of others, of self, and of social relationships and obligations.

Formal Thought: Piaget's Description of Adolescent Thought

Adolescent cognitive skills are usually described with the term, formal thought, because they more nearly follow the rules of formal logic than does thought in childhood. This logic is called formal operations in the final stage in the developmental sequence described by Piaget (see Chapter 7). Although most experts now believe that Piaget's explanation for the changes in thought between childhood and adolescence is incomplete, his ideas were very important in providing a general description of aspects of adolescent thought that are different from typical childhood capabilities for thinking and reasoning. Generally speaking, formal thought can be contrasted to the thought of younger children in the following four areas (Flavell, 1985; Keating, 1980): complexity of concepts and reasoning, foreseeing possibilities, methods of solving problems, and abilities for inferring the perspectives of others.

Complexity.   Adolescent thinking is typically more complex than the thought of younger children. For example, adolescents can consider more elements (such as objects, events, or ideas) simultaneously. Pre-formal children operate most efficiently with no more than two elements in combination, but adolescents can operate effectively with four, five, or six elements (Inhelder & Piaget, 1958). Furthermore, adolescents' mental operations with this larger number of elements are likely to be systematic and exhaustive. Researchers have demonstrated this characteristic of adolescent thought in the following way: Ask 7-year-old Jim and 14-year-old Kevin to show you all the ways four differently-colored blocks can be put together. Jim will probably put together two blocks at a time and may not exhaust all the possible combinations of two blocks. By contrast, Kevin will most likely march through most, if not all, the 20 possible arrangements, or permutations, of the four blocks (Elkind,

566

1968). In everyday experience, a similar difference might be seen as children and adolescents try to figure out how best to combine a variety of resources to meet a group goal.

Thinking About Possibilities. Adolescents' thinking capacities also permit more abstract thought than the typical thinking of younger children. In the example above, Kevin probably imagines a scheme in which each of the differently colored blocks can potentially be first in a sequence, followed in varying order by the other three. This mental scheme of possibilities guides Kevin's systematic solution. Moreover, while younger children think primarily in terms of objects and events that they have experienced in one way or another, adolescents think also in terms of thought itself—they "think about thinking" (Flavell, 1985; Keating, 1980; Miller, Kessel, & Flavell, 1970).

One implication of the ability to imagine possibilities is an increased tendency to think further into one's own future and to speculate about possible long-term outcomes of current or anticipated events. For example, students who achieve in school work tend to think about the future in terms of longer time periods than those whose grades are poorer—for example, 5 to 10 years rather than 2 to 3 years—even when intellectual aptitude is the same (DeVolder & Lens, 1982).

Cognitive development in adolescence involves greater capacity for reasoning and problem-solving.

Solving Problems.   Because these generally more complex, abstract intellectual capabilities are available to them, adolescents think and reason more flexibly and speculatively than children typically do. For adolescents, reality is a subset of possibility (Flavell, 1985). Younger children deal with what they can see or have seen in the past; what they can perceive defines reality for them. But formal thinkers more often recognize that what they perceive is only one possibility among many; things might be different than they are. For example, when Piaget asked adolescents to find the combination of five colorless chemicals that would produce a colored solution, the adolescents seemed to know immediately that the right answer was one of the logically possible combinations of the solutions. In the typical solution, adolescents proceeded to solve the problem by systematically trying each possible combination in turn until the right one emerged (Inhelder & Piaget, 1958). By contrast, younger children did not typically conceive of the possible combinations of so many liquids, nor did they proceed step-by-step through them in search of the correct one.

Perspective-Taking Ability.   Adolescents, more than children, recognize that their own perspective on a situation is only one of a number of different views (Elkind, 1967; Piaget & Inhelder, 1956). Young children tend to confuse their perspectives with others' points of view. In Piaget's famous Three-Mountain task, described in Chapter 10, young children typically thought others' views of a model mountainous terrain were the same as their own. Older children, however, recognized that others' views were different and gradually improved at inferring what those views were. This perceptual–perspective task shows the young child's egocentricism and its gradual decline with age.

How might taking the perspective of others work in everyday experience? In a study by Chandler and Greenspan (1972), children and adolescents saw cartoons showing a child losing some money and becoming very upset about it. The last picture of the sequence showed a new character walking up to the child, and the participants were asked to explain what this newcomer would think about what was happening. Preschool and elementary school children often confused their own knowledge of the situation with the newcomer's. They acted as though the new character would know what had happened in the early frames of the cartoon story, even though the character presumably had come into the action at a later point and, thus, could not know the reason for the cartoon child's distress. They confused their own knowledge of the situation with the newcomer's. By contrast, 11-year-old and older participants clearly seemed aware of the difference between their knowledge of the situation and the newcomer's. Everyday social interaction often requires recognizing the different perspectives of others and using that knowledge to respond appropriately.

Because adolescent thought is more abstract, flexible, and speculative, adolescents have the capacity to solve problems involving more complex elements and also to consider the possibilities inherent in such situations. This skill allows adolescents to speculate and to think of new possible ways to approach problems in social relationships, including their own.

An alternative view of cognitive change between childhood and adolescence comes from information-processing theories. The information-processing approach (see Chapter 8) pictures the human mind as a complex system for taking in, storing, and using information, analogous to computers. As children mature into adolescents, the capacity of this information-processing system appears to increase; and many psychologists believe that adolescents' thought is more complex and sophisticated than children's thought because of greater knowledge and skill in handling information, rather than because of more complex cognitive structures (Case, 1985; Flavell, 1985; Sternberg & Powell, 1983).

At least three aspects of information processing appear to contribute to these changes: increases in knowledge, more sophisticated control processes, and more rapid, automatic processing.

Increases in Knowledge.   Knowledge increases the efficiency and rapidity with which problems can be solved and new knowledge acquired (Brown, Bransford, Ferrara & Campione, 1983). For example, individuals who know the rules and conventions of chess are better able to see possible strategies for winning the game than novice players are. Adolescents have had more time to accumulate relevant knowledge than have children, and this gives them an advantage over children in many problem-solving tasks.

More Sophisticated Control Processes.   Adolescents are also more likely than children to develop effective plans for solving problems. As we noted earlier, adolescents are more likely than children to have strategies for getting and using the information needed to solve problems. For example, adolescents' greater abilities for "thinking about thought" enable them to assess what additional information may be needed to solve a problem. If you tell a group of 8-year-olds and a group of 15-year-olds to go over a list of words until they know them, the 8-year-olds are likely to study for a while and claim to know the material, even though they do not know it very well. The adolescents are more likely to know whether they have learned the material or not. A second example is that adolescents are likely to be more adept at devising specific techniques for learning material or solving problems. Compared to elementary school children, adolescents are more likely to write things down or use special mnemonics or other devices to help themselves solve a problem (Butterfield & Belmont, 1977). In one study of fourth, sixth, eighth, and tenth graders' comprehension of a brief written passage, students were told they could look back at the text in answering a series of written questions. Nevertheless, there was an increase across the four grade levels in how frequently they looked back at the material, with each group showing much more rereading than the just-younger group (Garner & Haynes, 1982; cited in Flavell, 1985). It may be possible to use knowledge about control processes to devise ways to teach children and adolescents to do cognitive tasks efficiently and well (Brown et al., 1983; Flavell, 1985).

Information-Processing Perspectives on Adolescent Thought

569

More Rapid, Automatic Processing. During childhood and adolescence, steps in thinking and acting that originally required voluntary, concerted attention and effort begin to be done more automatically. Thus, we can do more mental steps in a shorter period of time and sometimes can do several of them simultaneously. Consequently, more items of information can be learned in each unit of time (Brown et al., 1983; Flavell, 1985).

Although much still needs to be understood about developmental changes in information-processing capacities, knowledge, control processes, and automaticity in information processing, all appear to play a role in the cognitive shift between childhood and adolescence.

Individual Differences in Mental Abilities

The concept of formal thought emphasizes developmental differences in thinking and reasoning between childhood and adolescence, and information-processing approaches provide some alternative ways of understanding this general change in the cognitive capabilities. As in other periods (see Chapter 8), however, individual adolescents vary considerably in intellectual aptitude and achievement. The standard techniques for assessing individual differences are mental abilities tests, also known as IQ tests, and similar tests for assessing particular types of intellectual skills, such as creativity.

Individual Differences in Solving Intellectual Problems. Scores on standardized tests indicate ability relative to a comparison group of young people of the same age or school grade. Thus, the results of school achievement tests for Rob, an eighth grader, are reported in terms of the percentage of eighth graders nationally whose scores fell below Rob's score. In general, such test scores should also be regarded as indicators of the kinds of abilities needed for school and school-like tasks (Sternberg & Powell, 1983; Tyler, 1963). The culture specificity of most abilities tests may result in underestimation of the academic aptitude of an adolescent from a different cultural background than the test makers assumed (see Chapter 8).

Standard ability tests and techniques such as Piaget's for examining qualitative differences in thinking and reasoning both address basic characteristics of cognitive growth in adolescence. Experts now believe that the two methods of assessment tap closely related aspects of thinking and reasoning, but give different types of information about them. For example, adolescents who score high on mental abilities tests are typically found to be more developmentally advanced in performance on tasks that require formal thought, such as Inhelder and Piaget's balance-beam or colorless-liquids problems (Keating, 1980; Sternberg & Powell, 1983). Both mental abilities tests and tests of formal reasoning have been found to be correlated with achievement in algebra in a sample of eighth graders (Belli & Gatewood, 1987).

One type of information about adolescent cognitive development from mental abilities tests concerns the age differentiation in test scores during the second decade of life. We have previously discussed the issue of whether ability scores represented a single, global ability or a configuration of different intellectual strengths on particular types of intellectual tasks. Before adolescence, it is difficult to specify what a child's particular pattern of strengths and weaknesses might be. Generally, children's aptitude is described in terms of a verbal skill score and a quantitative skill score. In adolescence, however, intellectual strength can be assessed in relatively specific areas such as verbal ability, inductive reasoning, deductive reasoning, numerical facility, mathematics achievement, and arithmetic reasoning. Thus, it becomes increasingly possible to interpret the results of standardized tests in terms of the types of cognitive tasks on which an adolescent might do particularly well (Dye & Very, 1968).

Differences in Thinking Creatively. Because mental abilities tests primarily address skills for answering certain types of questions correctly, they do not tap the possible range of cognitive skills that may be relevant to the interests and opportunities open to adolescents. Creativity tests tap another area of cognitive skills; and studies indicate that these tests provide information that helps us to understand some of the stresses experienced by adolescents in school and in other achievement settings. In a class study, psychologists Michael Wallach and Nathan Kogan (1965) compared early adolescents who were high on both creativity and mental abilities test scores, those who were low on both, and those who were high on one but not the other. They found that school adjustment was most satisfactory for the high mental abilities students, regardless of creativity scores. Students who were high on creativity, but low on mental abilities tests, tended to be frustated and unhappy in school. Thus, patterns of abilities, as well as their absolute level, may be an important key to individuals' adjustment during the rapid cognitive changes of adolescence.

Maturing intellectual skills may often produce understanding and interpretations of social experiences and relationships that would be unlikely for younger children. Psychologists recently have begun to view some of the classic problems of adolescent development in terms of changing cognitive skills. Decisions may become more complicated and bothersome for adolescents because they now recognize that choices often carry more ramifications than they might previously have realized. Going to a movie with friends can be simultaneously viewed as an opportunity to see an amusing film, a chance to see and be seen by members of the peer group, an alternative to a planned family activity, and a competitor for time that needs to be spent studying. Younger children would be less likely to consider the various implications of an event, as adolescents are likely to do.

Social Cognition

Three characteristics of adolescents' thinking about persons, social relationships, and situations seem especially important to development during the transition into adolescence: awareness of discrepancies between ideal and real circumstances, more complex concepts of others and self, and enhanced role-taking skills.

Awareness of Discrepancies Between the Ideal and the Real. Adolescents are capable of realizing that a particular relationship between persons is only one instance of the possible relationships that could exist. This realization

571

probably affects responses to many social situations, including some of great personal significance. This possibility was first suggested by David Elkind (1967), who pointed out that adolescents often feel the "grass is greener" because they understand that things could be different. Younger children, on the other hand, are less likely to have this intuition and, consequently, may more readily accept things as they are. For example, 8-year-old Maria may be unhappy in an authoritarian family, but because she does not recognize that families can be different than hers, she accepts the situation with more equanimity than her 15-year-old sister does. Elkind attributes some of adolescents' stereotypical melancholia and rebelliousness to this cognitive process.

More Complex Concepts of Others and Self. Adolescents also tend to think more abstractly than children about other people's characteristics. Young children, for example, are likely to emphasize appearance or activity in their descriptions of others: "She has brown hair," "He plays hockey," or "They live in Sundance Court." Adolescents more typically talk about personal traits or dispositions that summarize or explain overt, observable actions: "She is neat and concerned about her appearance," "He is the athletic type—enjoys physical activities." Such characterizations of others frequently require inferences about traits that may underlie many, sometimes diverse behaviors. In such cases, adolescents' more mature cognitive abilities are often apparent in their qualified, complex descriptions of others (Barenboim, 1981; Gollin, 1958; Livesley & Bromley, 1973; Shantz, 1983). (See also Chapter 10.)

Finally, adolescents typically describe others more objectively than younger children, who often characterize people in terms of the activities they share with them (Peevers & Secord, 1973). Adolescents are more likely to surprise adults by speaking as though they were detached observers, even when describing close friends. For example, Meara described Kari this way: "She's a sort of romantic person. Like, she likes to read novels about romance, and she dreams about her wedding a lot." Such objectivity may be possible because adolescents recognize the existence of perspectives other than their own and sense that a neutral perspective makes the description more understandable to others.

It may be more difficult to be objective in describing oneself than in describing others, but during adolescence self-descriptions do seem to show more reflection about the self. For example, as in their descriptions of others, adolescents tend to attach qualifiers to the statements they make about themselves: "I like to have a good time, but I don't want to get rowdy." Adolescents' descriptions of themselves have many other characteristics of their statements about others, as well. If you ask adolescents to describe themselves, they mention more general and psychological characteristics and proportionally fewer concrete details about appearance and activities than children do. Jenny, age 17, described herself as follows:

> I was always shy with boys—you know, if a boy looked at me, and I saw him looking at me, I thought, it was an insult because I thought he was looking at

me—or making fun of me—usually I thought he was making fun of me, you know—look at that funny looking girl—but after I had some self-confidence— when one did look at me I took it as a compliment (Secord & Peevers, 1974).

Self-understanding also changes in adolescence. Damon and Hart (1982, 1988; Hart, 1988) have pointed out that adolescents' sense of themselves as distinctive, coherent individuals becomes increasingly linked to their aware- ness of the internal experiences that make a person different from others, but able to live and work successfully. These include adolescents' recognition that their private thoughts and feelings may make them different from others. In addition, adolescents—unlike children—are aware that we are affected both by conscious and unconscious thoughts and feelings, but that we can exercise some degree of control over these internal states.

Enhanced Role-Taking Skills. Understanding the perspective of others about most social situations is probably a great deal more complicated than the simple perceptual perspective taking required in the Three-Mountain Task. Role taking (Feffer 1959; Flavell 1966), defined as the ability to infer another person's perception of and reaction to a personal or social situation, enables a person to adjust interactions with others to make them more appropriate. For example, recognizing that another person does not know about you and your experiences can help you describe your events and feelings more fully to make conversations proceed more smoothly. The ability to take account of others' thoughts and perspectives has been called "the central element" of adolescent cognitive growth that most sharply distinguishes the social reasoning of adolescents from that of younger children (Elkind, 1967).

Although most adolescents realize that others' perspectives are different from their own, however, they still make the partial error of assuming that they themselves are the object about which others are thinking (Elkind, 1967; Elkind & Bowen, 1979; Gray & Hudson, 1984; Goossens, 1984). Psychologist David Elkind used the term, the Imaginary Audience, for this aspect of "adolescent egocentrism" because adolescents appear to believe that they are the focus of everyone's attention. Elkind has suggested that this adoles- cent egocentrism accounts for the self-consciousness that is so much a part of the stereotype of adolescents. Although researchers have been unable to document the connection between adolescent self-consciousness and the shift into formal operations, the importance of role taking in adolescents' devel- oping understanding of themselves in relationship to others is clearly appar- ent (Lapsley, Milstead, Quintana, Flannery, & Buss, 1986). As adolescents become better able to coordinate their own perspectives with the viewpoints of a variety of others, it becomes easier for them to test how realistic their own perceptions actually are.

As adolescents develop the skills to recognize and interpret the perspectives of others, their understanding and judgments of such important social con- ditions as fairness, justice, and responsibility may change. As we saw in Chapter 10, cognitive skills increasingly affect evaluations of right and wrong

Interrelations with the Social Lives of Adolescents

573

and of good and bad behavior and concepts of the society in which adolescents will soon assume adult roles (Colby, Kohlberg, Gibbs, & Lieberman, 1983; Rest, Davison, & Robbins, 1978). A significant problem for some adolescents may emerge during the development of moral judgments. Adolescents may reach the conclusion that absolute moral principles are too rigid and cannot possibly apply in every case; as a result they may temporarily come to assume that what is right and wrong, good and bad, depends largely on the situation at hand. This conclusion is called *relativism,* meaning that a person feels that moral judgments can never be absolute, but must be reached relative to the situation (Kohlberg, 1969; Kohlberg & Kramer, 1969). Studies by Kohlberg and his colleagues indicate that relativism in moral judgments occurs in transitions between stages when there has been "a breakdown of faith in the currently held moral frame of reference with no substitution of a more adequate system" (Colby, Kohlberg, Gibbs, & Lieberman, 1983, p. 73). Extreme relativism, or the conviction that no general moral principles exist, may make it difficult for adolescents to resolve the complex uncertainties or crises associated with achieving a mature identity (Kohlberg & Gilligan, 1971). One aspect of development during adolescence is deriving a complex, varied, and flexible understanding of moral standards and principles that are acceptable both to other members of the society and to one's own individually held values (Erikson, 1968).

A second example of how the more mature reasoning abilities of adolescents can affect social development comes from research on children's and adolescents' concepts of society, government, and law (Adelson & O'Neil, 1966; Adelson, Green, & O'Neil, 1969). Adolescents are more likely than children to recognize that individuals coexist in communities and use social institutions such as government and law to serve the needs of the community. Such realizations are important in their own right, because we all must make choices in our personal lives and in our roles as citizens and members of social groups. For example, complex reasoning abilities undoubtedly affect an individual's decisions about which candidates to choose in political campaigns and how to vote on public issues.

In addition, social reasoning affects everyday interactions, such as, resolving an argument with a classmate or family member or whether or not an adolescent will engage in antisocial behaviors. Children and adolescents who behave antisocially typically have poor social–cognitive abilities. In experimental studies of cheating, the higher a child's social–cognitive level, the lower the likelihood of cheating (Hoffman, 1970; Rest, 1983). Connections have also been documented between social–cognitive skills and social competence of adolescents in schools. Psychologist Martin Ford (1982) found that ninth and twelfth grade students' overall scores on social–cognitive tasks were highly correlated with ratings of social competence by teachers, peers, and an adult observer previously unacquainted with the adolescents. Students who were able to infer the feelings of others, who considered the consequences of different actions, and who could foresee different strategies for achieving goals were also seen as more socially competent than those who were rated lower on social–cognitive skills.

574

Participation in group activities provides opportunities for adolescents to learn about the similarities and differences between themselves and others.

One skill that may contribute to social competence, effective strategies for negotiating resolutions to conflict, appears to be related to social–cognitive maturity. Robert Selman and his coworkers (Selman, Beardslee, Schultz, Krupa, & Podorefsky, 1986) devised stories about situations in which fictional characters were pressured by others to do something they did not wish to do. For example, one story featured repeated last-minute requests from a boss to work late on Friday nights; another featured pressure from a mother to go on a picnic with her friend's daughter (or son) whom the adolescent does not like; and another involved pressure from a girl (or boy) friend not to date others. The researchers presented eight such situations to adolescents who were either 11 to 13, 14 to 16, or 17 to 19 years of age. In each case, they asked the adolescents to describe the problem, to propose a good way for the fictional character to deal with it, and to guess what the consequences of that action might be. They found that more than half of the 14- to 16- and 17- to 19-year-olds proposed solutions based on the reciprocal needs of both parties, emphasizing persuasion, making deals, and trading. In the 11- to 13-year-old group, about one-fourth proposed solutions that depended on reciprocity. As we saw in Chapter 10, awareness of reciprocal needs is associated with Stage 2 in Selman's model of the development of interpersonal understanding (see pp. 330–331). Few adolescents in any of the age groups proposed solutions based on collaborative discussions and mutual perspective taking, which is Stage 3 of interpersonal understanding. Consequently, Selman concluded that although differences in maturity of perspective taking affects the kinds of negotiation strategies adolescents use, adolescence is a period of continuing development in the application of social–cognitive skills to interpersonal conflicts.

575

Research Focus 16-4 describes the effects of cognitive changes in adolescents' reasoning about common decisions at different ages and discusses the implications of those changes. Studies such as these indicate that social–cognitive skills may be an important foundation for the social actions of adolescents. However, a great deal more information is needed about the strength of the relation between cognitive abilities and behavior, as well as about the conditions under which cognitive abilities are especially important to adolescent development.

We have now reached the end of our overview of the most important *origins* of differences between adolescence and other periods of life and some of their ramifications for the *course* of development for individual adolescents. In Chapter 17, we turn to a more detailed discussion of environmental settings and influences that act upon individuals who are experiencing the physical changes, cognitive growth, and altered social expectations of the adolescent years.

RESEARCH FOCUS 16-4

Tackling Decisions: Practical Implications of Cognitive Growth

The cognitive shift associated with adolescence is most often discussed in connection with solving problems that are more typical of the laboratory or the classroom than of the real world. If the descriptions of adolescent thought from these tasks are valid, however, it should be apparent in the emerging maturity of reasoning and judgments that adolescents are required to face in their own society. In a recent study Lois Weithorn and Susan Campbell (1982) examined the competency of children and adolescents to make informed decisions about whether to undergo medical treatment. Such decisions are often left to parents and guardians because young people are not presumed to be legally competent to decide for themselves.

Weithorn and Campbell tested 9-, 14-, 18-, and 21-year-olds (12 males and 12 females at each age). They first described four hypothetical cases: two (epilepsy and diabetes) in which decisions about medical treatment would have to made, and two (depression and enuresis, or bed-wetting) in which psychological treatment was being considered. Each case description included information about the nature of the problem, alter-native treatments, expected benefits of treatments, possible risks, discomforts, and side effects, and consequences of failure to be treated at all. For example, in the depression dilemma, the interview described Tom:

(He) has been feeling sad and down much of the time for several weeks. . . . He refuses to come out of his room or to go to school or to talk to anyone in the family. He has lost his appetite and has had trouble sleeping at night. No one is sure what is going on with Tom, but they think that it is not a physical problem.

Tom's doctor suggested that he see a psychotherapist . . . a person whose job it is to talk with people who are upset about things on their mind. . . . The psychotherapist . . . said she thought Tom could do either of two things for the depression.

One choice would be . . . to set up regular appointments with the psychotherapist in (her) office. Each . . . would last about an hour. Once a week, Tom would meet with the psychotherapist alone, and they would talk about whatever was on Tom's mind, or about some subjects the psychotherapist might suggest. On another day during the week, the psychotherapist would meet with Tom and his entire family for an hour. During these meetings, they all would talk about things which were important to them as a family. If Tom and his family kept their regular appointments for several months, it is possible that Tom would be able to get back to a normal routine, although there is no guarantee that the appointments will help the problem.

A second choice . . . is to be admitted to a . . . special hospital for people with problems with their emotions. Some patients there might be depressed, like Tom, whereas others might have different problems. While there, Tom would share a hospital room with another patient, and would take a part in certain daily activities, like art and music. He would meet with the psychotherapist at the hospital twice a week alone, and the entire family would come in for an appointment with Tom and the psychotherapist at the hospital. Tom would also take part in group psychotherapy with other patients, where they all would talk together with the psychotherapist about their problems.

While in the hospital, Tom would be away from his family, friends, and home. He would miss school, although he could arrange to have work brought to him so that he could try to keep up with his studies. He would need to obey certain regulations, such as when to go to bed, and that he could not leave the hospital without permission. If Tom stayed in the hospital for several weeks, and then continued to see the psychotherapist for weekly appointments afterwards, it is possible that he would be able to get back to a normal routine, although there is no guarantee that the hospital will help the problem.

In Tom's case, he has three choices. He can decide to wait and hope the depression gets better on its own; he can see the psychotherapist in her office for regular appointments; or he can be admitted to the mental hospital. If you were in Tom's situation, and had to decide among these choices, what do you think you might decide to do?

Following each case description, the researchers asked detailed questions about the participants' reactions. To be sure that everyone understood the case, they asked some specific questions about the basic facts (for example, "What is a psychotherapist?") and about the implications of the facts (for example, "Using your imagination, name at least two subjects which you think a person might discuss in psychotherapy.") They also asked which treatment alternative the participant would prefer and probed to find out whether the participant had considered the essential issues in the case in making a decision (for example, that depression might improve without treatment, that severe depression interferes with essential activities, that treatment might not resolve the problem, and so forth). These questions are usually important to legal decisions about the competency of young persons to make choices.

Were children and adolescents as mature in their responses to these dilemmas as young adults? Could a 14-year-old be considered competent to decide such issues for herself or himself? These researchers found that 14-year-olds showed understanding of the cases equivalent to that shown by 18- and 21-year-olds, but 9-year-olds' understanding was not as mature as the other age groups'. Although 9-year-olds expressed certain treatment preferences, just as the older groups did, they showed less evidence of considering the essential issues in the cases than 14-, 18-, and 21-year olds. Again, 14-year-olds performed at the same level as the young adult groups on consideration of the rational reasons for choosing one treatment over another. The authors conclude that 14-year-olds are cognitively capable of making well considered, competent decisions about medical treatment.

It is interesting that some earlier studies had indicated that adolescents' decision making about health issues reached maturity more slowly than these findings indicate. In one study, for example, psychologist Catherine Lewis (1981) concluded that even by age 16, most adolescents lack the necessary skills for making a competent decision. The differences in findings may be due partly to the researchers' methods for judging competence. Lewis's study assessed competence on the basis of spontaneous answers to questions about what kind of advice adolescents would give to peers facing difficult decisions. As in much research on cognitive development, this method makes it difficult to tell whether young adolescents lack competence in judgment or simply have difficulty putting into words all of the things they are thinking about. Older adolescents may find it easier to verbalize their reasoning. By contrast, Weithorn and Campbell's method did not rely entirely on participants' abilities to put their thoughts into words. These authors combined interviews about the participants' own ideas with specific questions that allowed children and adolescents to respond without having to rely so much on their own verbal skills.

These studies are among the few sources of information available regarding adolescent reasoning and thinking about real life problems. Such decision making is pertinent to issues of adolescent sexual involvement and the risk of unmarried pregnancies among adolescents and to issues relating to career choice. Undoubtedly many other decisions that affect adolescents and society also involve the extent to which adolescents have reached a level of cognitive competence that permits adequate reasoning and thinking about complex, problematic situations. 🐦

Summary

Adolescence is said to begin in biology and end in culture. This statement implies that the *origins* of the differences between adolescence and other periods of life lie both in adolescents' changing physiology and in cultural demands and social pressures that determine the difficulty of the transitions toward adult roles. At the same time, these demands and pressures are triggered in most societies by puberty, which in turn elicits different expectations from others than were characteristic of children's prepubertal experiences. In the transactional view outlined in this chapter, therefore, the origins of distinctiveness in the adolescent period come from a complex interplay of physical changes and social expectations associated with age.

This interplay is visible in the study of adolescent behavior partly because pubescence, or the period of physiological changes leading to reproductive maturity, varies greatly in timing from one individual to another. Early-maturing boys show marked social advantages over late maturers, but for girls early maturation may initially be a disadvantage socially. Both early-maturing girls and late-maturing boys may have some psychosocial advantages that permit more flexible adaptation to problems and situations in adulthood, however.

Another indication that pubertal and environmental forces combine to determine the distinctive characteristics of adolescence can be seen in the emergence of sexuality. Although concern about sexuality is correlated with pubertal changes, most physiological bases for adult sexual functioning are established before puberty. Sexual behavior is believed to be more closely tied to social and cultural transmission of behavior patterns and attitudes related to sexual functioning than to increased physiological pressures resulting from puberty. Environmental factors are particularly significant in determining such "socially scripted" facets of adolescent sexuality as the initiation of sexual activity, contraception, and teenage childbearing.

A third *origin* of distinctive behavior in adolescence reflects cognitive capabilities during adolescence that affect the types of intellectual tasks individuals can perform well. In the theory of Jean Piaget, adolescence is the time of transition to formal thought, meaning that concepts and reasoning more nearly follow the rules of formal logic than in childhood. Formal thought enables adolescents to engage in cognitive processes involved in more complex problems, including thinking about possibilities, engaging in flexible, speculative reasoning, and understanding the implications of different perspectives of a problem or event. An alternative view to Piaget's theories is that cognitive growth in adolescence reflects changes in information-processing capacity. That is, the more abstract, flexible, and exhaustive mental processes shown by adolescents are thought to result from increases in knowledge, more sophisticated processes for using knowledge, and more rapid, automatic problem solving. Individual differences in cognitive abilities are usually assessed through standardized tests; and the results of such tests during adolescence provide more specific, detailed information about the areas of relative strength and weakness in intellectual skills than do the results of tests given during childhood. Special tests are needed to assess the degree to which individuals are creative; and adolescence may be a time when such tests can be used to understand the unique characteristics of a young person's cognitive functioning.

Cognitive changes during adolescence can also affect understanding of the self, others, and social relationships and events. Consequently, changes in cognitive abilities may be a factor in the array of new social behaviors and sensitivities that adolescents often show. The period of transition to more complex social concepts can result in adolescent egocentrism, in which young teenagers overestimate the degree of social attention directed toward them. These social–cognitive changes are *interrelated* with other distinctive characteristics of adolescence such as the occurrence of extreme relativism, or the belief that value judgments can only be made relative to a particular set of circumstances and thus that there are no general principles of morality, and the capacity for managing social relations effectively, including the capacity for resolving conflict through negotiation.

Suggested Readings

Adams, G. R., Montemayor, R., & Gullotta, T. P. (1989). *Biology of adolescent behavior and development.* Beverly Hills, CA: Sage.

Brooks-Gunn, J., & Furstenberg, F. F., Jr. (1989). Adolescent sexual behavior. *American Psychologist, 44,* 249–257.

Brooks-Gunn, J., & Petersen, A. C. (1983). *Girls at puberty: Biological and psychological perspectives.* New York: Plenum.

Furstenberg, F. F., Jr., Brooks-Gunn, J., & Chase-Lansdale, L. (1989). Teenaged pregnancy and childbearing. *American Psychologist, 44,* 313–320.

Simmons, R. G., & Blyth, D. A. (1987). *Moving into adolescence: The impact of pubertal change and school context.* New York: Aldine de Gruyter.

579

CHAPTER SEVENTEEN

Social Relationships and Behavior in Adolescence

Introduction

The physical, cognitive, and social changes of the transition to adolescence, which we discussed in Chapter 16, occur simultaneously with increased demands and opportunities presented by a rapidly widening social world. These distinctive environmental influences help to set adolescence apart from childhood as a period of development. For example, a larger proportion of time is spent outside of the home than in earlier years; and a larger proportion of that out-of-home time, in turn, is spent in situations with peers (Csikszentmihalyi & Larson, 1984; Rutter, Graham, Chadwick, & Yule, 1976). In junior high and high school the social field broadens to include the school as a whole, whereas the social field for the elementary school child is usually the self-contained classroom (Minuchin & Shapiro, 1983). Extracurricular activities and parttime work further change the environment in adolescence (Csikszentmihalyi & Larson, 1984). Adjusting to these changes can add considerably to the adaptations that adolescents are already making to physical and psychological maturation and to changing social expectations. In terms of the transactional model of adolescence described in Chapter 16, the combination of primary biological and cognitive changes with dramatic changes in settings can present significant challenges in individuals.

In this chapter, we will begin by considering the implications of this widening social world for a central task of adolescence: forming an identity, or a coherent sense of self that enables individuals to meet a variety of social and emotional challenges. Although a person's identity is being formed from the moment of birth, the special challenges of changes in the second decade of life are believed to force adolescents to face significant new identity issues. Next, we will consider the impact on identity development of two salient social settings of adolescence: relationships with family members and peers. Some of the questions we will address are: How are the influences and relationships of family and peers altered as individuals move from childhood into adolescence? What are the effects of these relationships on the development of identity? Finally, we will examine some problem behaviors that are particularly identified with the adolescent years. As in Chapter 16, the underlying focus is on how development in adolescence extends from development in childhood, but is different from it.

Identity Formation: The Central Task

The most important questions about psychological development in adolescence are concerned with how children achieve the skills, knowledge, and other aspects of maturity required for adult society. One famous view of this

Adolescence and Peer Relations

Adolescence is said to begin in biology and end in culture. Less apparent than the physical changes brought on by puberty are the cultural patterns and expectations that shape the way other members of a society react to individuals as they mature physically. In the United States, schools are the primary social arenas of adolescence. The junior high or middle school is the center of the social system for most young teenagers in the United States, as the high school is for older adolescents. At school, adolescents learn the norms of peer culture and define themselves through interactions and comparisons with others.

Extensive programs of extracurricular activities promote the development of skills. Classrooms, though scarcely the least important setting for the experiences of adolescents, nevertheless account for only a part of the learning environment of the contemporary secondary school.

process comes from Erik Erikson's (1968) description of psychological development. Erikson believes that development in adolescence involves achieving a sense of *identity*, which is an "internal, self-constructed, dynamic organization of drives, abilities, beliefs, and individual history" (Marcia, 1980). This characteristic organization of young people's personalities gives them a sense of continuity and stability about themselves from one period of development to another.

As adolescents change toward physical adulthood and become aware that others expect them to begin to fill or anticipate adult roles, they typically also begin to feel pressure to integrate, or bring into harmony, information and emotions about themselves and their experiences. The task of adolescence is, therefore, to achieve a sense of continuity between past, present, and future roles and concepts of self and to adjust to important parts of the social environment of adulthood.

Crisis and Commitment

The achievement of identity involves several processes, which have been outlined by James Marcia (1966, 1980). First, a crisis, or a struggle, occurs in which the individual feels pressure to achieve greater organization or coherence between personal history, feelings, abilities, current circumstances, and future personal and social issues that face him or her. Second, a commitment must eventually be made to some role or roles and to a set of beliefs. Both crisis and commitment must occur for true identity achievement, according to Erikson. Without crisis, commitment would be potentially superficial and short lived, instead of being a core aspect of one's self. Marcia (1966, 1980) sees four possible identity statuses for adolescents: *achievement, foreclosure, noratorium,* and *diffusion.* Figure 17-1 shows the relationship of these four stages to the two basic elements of *identity formation:* crisis and commitment.

In Marcia's interpretation of Erikson's ideas, adolescents who make a commitment to values and roles, perhaps to those of their parents or friends, without having considered the implications in a personal sense are said to have foreclosed on an identity. Individuals who are struggling with identity

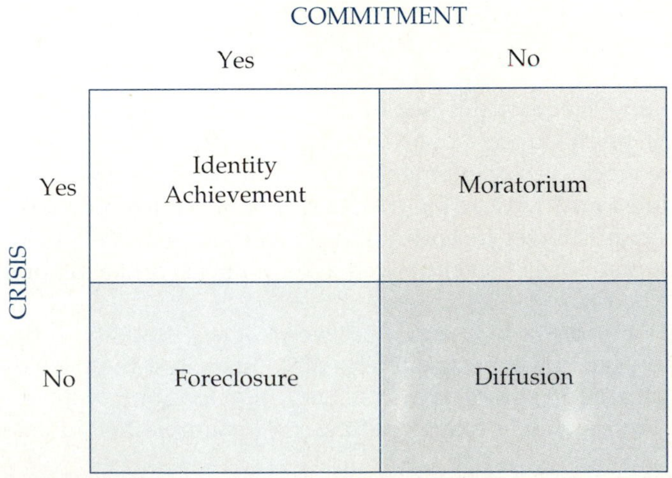

COMMITMENT

	Yes	No
Yes	Identity Achievement	Moratorium
No	Foreclosure	Diffusion

CRISIS

FIGURE 17-1

Marcia's four identity statuses, based on Erikson's theory, involve different combinations of crisis about identity issues and commitment to self-definition.

Source: from Marcia, 1986.

issues but have not yet committed themselves to roles and values are said to be experiencing a psychosocial moratorium, or a period of retreat for struggling with decisions. Failure to resolve the *identity crisis* results in a sense of *identity diffusion,* or the absence of a coherent, organized, and stable sense of self. Some scholars believe that Marcia's four identity statuses do not accurately reflect the full details of Erikson's view of identity in adolescence, especially his belief that social constraints and pressures play a central role in how difficult the process of identity achievement is for young persons (Cote & Levine, 1988). Most researchers, however, report substantial support for Marcia's statuses across a broad range of issues that adolescents face in achieving identity (Waterman, 1988).

Recurring Crises: Gradual Achievement of Identity

In the years since Erikson first described his view of identity crisis, much information has come to light indicating that identity formation occurs in a somewhat less dramatic and more complex way than Erikson first implied. One important point is that resolving personal crises involves a number of aspects of self in addition to the two that Erikson and his followers identified, that is, vocational choice and belief systems. Erikson refers to the beliefs and values one adopts as *ideology* and sees them as answering a fundamental need of every person to be able to show *fidelity,* or faithfulness to a set of principles, actions, and even to persons. Studies of identity formation among women have been especially important in calling researchers' attention to other fundamental issues that adolescents may face, such as sexual activity (Josselson 1980; Marcia 1980).

A second significant point about identity formation is that instead of a single major period of crisis, development consists of recurring small crises that, little by little, lead to adult commitment (e.g., Nawas, 1971; Waterman, 1985; Waterman & Waterman, 1970; Waterman, Geary, & Waterman, 1974). These gradual changes are apparent in studies of self-concept, which is one element of identity as Erikson described the term. For example, psychologists Jerome Dusek and John Flaherty (1981) recently examined self-concept changes in a longitudinal study of adolescents from early adolescence to graduation from high school (ages 11 to 18). They began with a questionnaire, on which adolescents rated themselves on a number of different personal characteristics. Dusek and Flaherty then submitted these ratings to factor analysis to determine whether ratings clustered into a few categories of characteristics. Dusek and Flaherty did not find enormous upheaval in the self-concept at any one point during adolescence. Rather, from one year to another during adolescence, the same dimensions or categories of characteristics were used by adolescents to describe themselves. The four dimensions of self were: sociability or interest in and ability to get along with others, leadership and achievement, aggressiveness and assertiveness, and a general sense of well being.

Dusek and Flaherty's findings did reveal, however, some instability in the self-concept. From one year to the next, adolescents often rated themselves on a particular characteristic in different ways. Large fluctuations were especially likely at certain predictable times of stress. For example, as adolescents approached graduation from a high school and faced the multiple changes that this event brings, young people seemed to rate themselves less positively. Such crisis points may occur at other times in an average person's life as well. The transition from elementary to junior high school involves a shift to a new and more complex setting that is accompanied by self-image "disturbances" such as greater self-consciousness and instability of self-image, lower self-esteem, and less confidence that their parents, teachers, and friends held favorable opinions of them (Simmons, Rosenberg, & Rosenberg, 1973; Simmons, Burgeson, & Reef, 1987).

Identity can be thought of as a feeling of confidence in, and comfort with, oneself and most of the world around one as adulthood approaches. In Chapter 16 we noted that one factor in this feeling of confidence may be the degree to which childhood experiences have prepared adolescents for mature roles. The more relevant and extensive this preparation, the easier it will be to resolve identity crises and overcome a sense of diffusion and confusion. Although the pressures to overcome these unsettled feelings affect most adolescents, the observation of comedienne Lily Tomlin must often seem appropriate: "We are all in this together—by ourselves." (*The Search for Signs of Intelligent Life in the Universe*, 1986).

In the next two sections of this chapter, we examine the implications of the most influential other persons in most adolescents' lives: their parents and their friends.

Family Relationships and Influences

Identity, as Erikson defined it, emerges from varied childhood experiences. Many aspects of a person's sense of self reflect experiences in the family. The more readily the roles, expectations, and self-perceptions experienced in family relationships can be integrated into the demands of adult roles, the smoother the transitions of adolescence. Consequently, how families meet the special circumstances and problems of the transition from childhood to adulthood is important to adolescent development.

Effects of Childrearing Patterns

Parents' childrearing practices have been found to be related to the extent of independence, competence, and sense of social responsibility that children show in every age period. In a large-scale study of more than 7,000 junior high and high school students, sociologist Glen Elder (1963) categorized adolescents' descriptions of their parents as either autocratic, democratic, or permissive. Elder believed the most important difference among these different types was how parents exercised their power within the family. In democratic families, parents legitimate their power by encouraging adolescents to "participate in discussing issues relevant to their behavior, although the final decision is always made or. approved by the parents" (p. 51). In autocratic families, parents do not "allow the adolescent to express his views

585

on subjects regarding his behavior nor permit him to regulate his own behavior in any way. . . ." (p. 51). Laissez-faire parents make few demands regarding their children's behavior. Elder's results showed that adolescents from democratic families were more self-confident and independent than were those from families in which parents used autocratic or laissez-faire childrearing methods. As we saw in Chapter 13, Diana Baumrind (1973) documented a similar link in her studies with young children.

In families of adolescents, a democratic atmosphere seems to foster the development of mature social–cognitive skills and a healthy ego identity. For example, psychologists Catherine Cooper and Harold Grotevant (Cooper, Grotevant, & Condon, 1984) recently observed a sample of parents and the eldest children in their families, all of whom were 17-years-old. The parents and adolescent from each family were asked to play a fictional 2-week vacation for which they had unlimited funds. This activity was designed to get all family members to express their opinions and reach a decision that all could agree upon. Cooper and Grotevant recorded the discussion and then analyzed them in terms of four characteristics of the family members' interactions: (1) self-assertion, or awareness of one's own point of view and responsibility for communicating it clearly, (2) separateness, or expressions of differences in view between self and other; (3) permeability, or responsiveness and openness to others' ideas, and (4) mutuality, or sensitivity and respect in relating to others. Notice that these characteristics are similar to the description of the democratic parenting style.

Cooper and Grotevant found that adolescents from families that were high on the four characteristics were more advanced than the offspring of other families on role-taking skills, that is, they were more likely to be able to recognize and coordinate others' viewpoints with their own perspectives. In other words, families that balance the four characteristics that Cooper and Grotevant identified provide challenges that stimulate the development of mature social–cognitive skills. In addition, these adolescents were more advanced in identity exploration than adolescents from families who were rated lower on Cooper and Grotevant's interaction measures. Using Marcia's interview method, these researchers found that adolescents who came from families where parents were open to the expression of others' ideas, even when those ideas were different from their own, were more likely to be actively considering a wide range of options for themselves. Cooper and Grotevant argued that family atmospheres that support both individuation, or the tolerance of differences from one person to another, and connectedness, or the warm, positive emotional ties between family members, are particularly conducive to a mature sense of self and commitments and abilities for understanding and accommodating to the perspectives of others. These fundamental aspects of adolescent development may, then, foster the greater self-reliance, self-control, exploration, and contentment of children from democratic families. Even in the most flexible, democratic families, however, adolescence brings changes in the interactions of parents and their children.

Family Conflict and Adolescent Influence. Most families experience a decrease in positive emotional expressions in their interactions during the early years of adolescence (Papini & Datan, 1983; Roberts, Block & Block, 1981). In addition, for the majority of families, disagreements and contentiousness increase between the ages of 10 and 13 and then decrease again between the ages of 16 and 18. Most of these episodes seem to concern rather mundane matters, such as chores and proper dress (Montemayor, 1983), but many parents find them distressing.

One implication of these changes in interactions has been documented in longitudinal studies (Hill, 1987; Steinberg, 1981). In the United States and most of Western Europe, it is widely expected that adolescents will take part in family decisions. Lawrence Steinberg (1981) studied the decision-making discussions of 27 families of adolescent boys before the boys had reached puberty. He then reexamined each family's decision making over the course of the year until most pubertal changes had been completed. As a result, he took samples of family interactions at three different points: before their sons had reached puberty, in the middle of pubertal changes, and after puberty was mostly completed.

Steinberg found that sons' influence in decision making increased over the course of his study, and this increase was correlated with their physical development. Before puberty, the mothers and fathers dominated the families' decision making; sons mostly deferred to their parents' opinions. At

Changes in Family Interactions

Clothing styles may often exaggerate differences between generations.

midpuberty, however, adolescent boys less often deferred to their parents, particularly their mothers. Sons challenged mothers' statements more often than they had previously, and mothers in turn took issue with their sons' statements more often. Both mother and son also interrupted each other more often and explained their opinions to each other less often. After pubertal changes were mostly completed, mothers and sons were more respectful to each other in family interaction. Mothers deferred to sons more often, showing more respect for their sons' opinion. At the same time, sons began to have increasingly more influence on the decisions that the family reached together. Although there are a number of possible reasons for this transformation, physical changes in the son and also the reaction of mothers to these changes appear to play a part. For example, it may be that the sons began to expect that they would be treated as more mature and adultlike, and these expectations affected their behaviors in family discussions.

For girls, changes in interactions with parents follow a somewhat different pattern. John Hill and his colleagues (Hill, Holmbeck, Marlow, Green, & Lynch, 1985; Hill, 1987) have conducted research with parents and their seventh grade daughters. The girls and their parents reported on whether menstruation (1) had not yet begun, (2) began within the past 6 months, (3) began within the past 12 months, and (4) began longer than 12 months ago. Girls who had experienced menarche within the past 6 months were experiencing difficulty in their family relationships. These girls were more likely than premenarcheal daughters to resist family rules and standards and to feel that their mothers did not accept them, and their mothers were more likely than the mothers of premenarcheal girls to feel that the daughters were not sufficiently involved in family activities. By contrast, girls who had experienced menarche between 6 and 12 months before the study seemed to have settled into a pattern of family relationships that was not greatly different from that of the premenarcheal girls. For these three groups, then, the pattern is similar to boys' pattern of disruption at about the time of extensive pubertal changes, but more harmonious interactions at other times. A complication arises, however. The group of girls who had begun to menstruate more than 12 months before the study showed a number of difficulties in their family interactions. Hill suggests that this group of seventh graders are early-maturing girls who may have joined an older group of peers and fallen into problem behaviors because of these associations. Difficulties in the family may result largely from tensions over these activities with peers that are not appropriate for girls of this age.

The information from studies of both boys and girls implies that perturbations in parent–adolescent interactions are relatively short lived. As time passes, most adolescents and their parents seem to devise new ways of reaching decisions that are appropriate to the adolescents' increasing physical and social maturity (Brooks-Gunn & Zahaykevich, 1989; Collins, 1990).

Cognitive Change and Parent–Adolescent Relationships.   In addition to changing interactions, families may also be affected by the changing capacity of adolescents to form concepts of parent–child relationships and their roles within them. Robert Selman, whose ideas we discussed in Chapter 10, has applied his analysis of the development of interpersonal understanding to concepts of parent–child relationships (see Table 17-1). He argues that the immature social thinker views parent–child relationships as a master–servant arrangement. At later stages of cognitive development adolescents increasingly recognize that children and parents owe mutual responsibilities to each other.

During adolescence, views of parents may also become less idealistic. Young children typically think of their parents as knowing virtually everything and as being powerful and competent enough to handle any situation, but adolescents gradually recognize that this is untrue. The psychoanalyst Peter Blos has used the term de-idealization for this dawning awareness that parents are fallible. Between grades 5 and 9, children's perceptions that parents are authorities in all matters generally declines and faith in the adolescents' own judgments increases (Steinberg & Silverberg, 1986; Youniss & Smollar, 1985). As one 13-year-old put it: "When I obey [my mother] now, it's not out of fear. I know when something is right now, not just because she says it's right."

Cognitive changes may affect adolescents' perceptions of the areas in which parents have legitimate authority over their activities. Psychologist Judith Smetana (1988) has demonstrated that parents and offspring often have different perceptions of whether parents should have authority over certain aspects of behavior. Smetana interviewed white middle-class young people in grades 5 through 10 and their parents about four categories of behavior: moral, or issues pertaining to the rights and welfare of others (for example, stealing pocket money from parents or hitting brothers and sisters); conventional, or behaviors that are judged on the basis of common agreement about whether they are appropriate or inappropriate (for example, doing assigned chores or keeping parents informed of their activities); personal, or issues that pertain only to the adolescent (for example, choice of friends or content of correspondence); and mixed issues that contain both personal and conventional elements (for example, dressing in a punk style, going out with friends instead of going to a family picnic, or not cleaning their rooms). She found that both parents and adolescents typically thought that parents had legitimate jurisdiction over conventional and moral issues. However, on the personal and mixed issues, parents were more likely than adolescents to see them as conventional, whereas adolescents were more likely to see them as

TABLE 17-1
Selman's Stages of Conceptions of Parent-Child Relations

Stage 0	Parent as boss
Stage 1	Parent as caretaker and helper for child
Stage 2	Parent as guidance counselor/need satisfier
Stage 3	Parent and child mutually show tolerance and respect
Stage 4	Parent–child relations change as circumstances, abilities, and needs of each change.

SOURCE: Adapted from Selman, 1980, pp. 147–152.

personal. In other words, parents and adolescents disagreed about whether parents should exert authority over matters such as keeping their rooms clean or dressing in a punk style, because they perceived these issues as falling into different categories of responsibility. This "mismatch" of perceptions about everyday events may be one reason conflicts seem especially common in the adolescent years.

"Family Development" and Changes in Parents.   Changes in family interactions may also partly indicate that parents are experiencing transitions in their own individual development. The adolescence of one's offspring constitutes a transition period in family life from a heavy emphasis on childrearing to an "empty nest" (Aldous, 1978). Parents, like adolescents themselves, are apt to be in a period of stress and questioning. These crises of adult development may affect some parents' abilities to respond constructively to the developmental challenges of their adolescent children (Aldous, 1978; Hill, 1980). For example, one study of parents' and adolescents' perceptions of family relationships indicated that parents and adolescents were in agreement about the degree to which there was stress in their lives, but they disagreed about the causes of the stress (Olson et al., 1983). Parents attributed their personal tensions and unhappiness to economic and work-related pressures, whereas adolescents attributed their stress to family conflicts and lack of communication. It may be that adolescents are unaware of the issues that their parents face, or they may simply concentrate on the impact of the resulting stress and tension on themselves. Parents may also be distracted by their problems and thus unaware of, or unresponsive to, their teenage children's concerns.

These parallel tracks may each influence the other in ways that are often difficult to comprehend. Recent findings (Silverberg, 1989; Silverberg & Steinberg, 1987) do indicate, however, that both mothers and fathers are affected by difficulties and increasing detachment from children when it occurs. Parents reported lowered feelings of life satisfaction and increased struggles with their own identity issues and self-esteem when they perceived increased distance in their relationships with their children.

In the next two sections, we will examine two issues of adolescent development to which family relationships are especially important: achieving independence and learning certain basic adult roles.

Independence: Disruption or Transformation?

The aforementioned changes in family interaction have been viewed as evidence that adolescence is a time of disruption in family relationships. However, drastic adolescent rebelliousness and rejection of adult values do not appear to be as common as people often think. Adolescents generally feel positive about their parents and become increasingly more positive over the course of adolescence (Bandura & Walters, 1959; Kandel & Lesser, 1972; Richardson, Galambos, Schulenberg, & Petersen, 1984). Evidence indicates that parent–adolescent differences are often exaggerated or misunderstood. Although adolescents' values often seem different from their parents' attitudes and opinions, many studies indicate that the differences lie in how extreme the attitudes and opinions are in the two age groups, rather than in the attitudes and opinions themselves (Hess & Goldblatt, 1957; Lerner, Karson, Meisels, & Knapp, 1975). For example, parents may believe in fair treatment, whereas their offspring may feel that fairness is so significant an issue that radical action should be taken to guarantee fairness to all. Furthermore, both parents and their adolescent children tend to overestimate the differences between them, and each side is also likely to underestimate the amount of positive feeling the other group has for them (Hess & Goldblatt, 1957). As an example, adolescents believe that parents have a general tendency to depreciate teenagers, and parents believe that teenagers generally undervalue adults. In one study, teenagers expected parents to view them negatively (for example, as untidy, frivolous, impulsive, and easily influenced), but parents were less extreme in their ratings than teenagers predicted. Similarly, parents expected teenagers to give them low marks on such characteristics as patience, cooperativeness, courtesy, and respectfulness, but teenagers' ratings were considerably more positive than parents' expected (Hess & Goldblatt, 1957).

It is also common to hear exaggerated statements of the degree to which teenagers break away from their families. Autonomy is a major issue for adolescents (Hill & Holmbeck, 1986; Steinberg & Silverberg, 1986), and young people do become less dependent on families for meeting their basic needs during these years than they were earlier in life. Most families, however, continue to have close emotional ties even when their children are grown (Gans, 1962; Offer & Offer, 1975; White, Speisman, & Costos, 1984). Although disruptions in these emotional ties can and do occur, for most young people, achieving independence means physically separating themselves from family and assuming responsibility for their own affairs; it does not mean rejecting or severing their emotional ties to their families. This finding has been reported in many studies from a number of different countries (Hill, 1980, 1986).

An illustration comes from the results of a survey of all 14- to 15-year-olds on the Isle of Wight in the English Channel (Rutter, Graham, Chadwick, & Yule, 1976). As Figure 17-2 shows, these adolescents reported overwhelmingly that they continued to go on outings with their families and that their parents approved of their friends; relatively few reported communication difficulties, rejection of mother, and physical withdrawal. The adolescents' parents answered similarly. However, the adolescents on the island who had been identified as having psychiatric or behavior problems reported problems with their families to a much larger extent than adolescents in the general population (see Figure 17-2). In a number of studies, reports of serious family difficulties come largely from the minority of cases in which adolescents have significant problems, including psythopathology (Montemayor, 1983).

Autonomy and the Quality of Family Relationships. Achieving autonomy depends partly on the extent to which relationships in families foster two somewhat contradictory psychological achievements: individuation, through which children acquire a sense of themselves as separate from the family, and connectedness, or a continuing connection of the individual with family (Cooper, Grotevant, & Condon, 1984). In families whose patterns are consis-

591

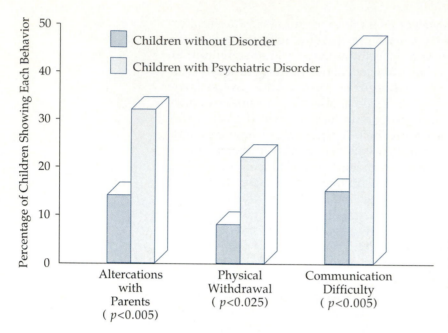

FIGURE 17-2

Parent-child alienation and psychiatric disorder at the age of 14 years.

Source: from Rutter et al., 1976.

tent with these goals, adolescent children show greater maturity on measures of ego development, identity, and social–cognitive skills for responding sensitively to others than in families with styles contradictory to individuation and integration (Grotevant & Cooper, 1985; Hauser et al., 1984). Psychiatrist Stuart Hauser and his colleagues (Hauser et al., 1984) have observed conversations between parents and their 16-year-old children. Their findings show that the more family members explained (rather than simply asserting) their views, showed acceptance of others' views, and showed empathy for one another, the more mature the adolescent's level of ego development was. In contrast, being judgmental, creating distractions in the conversation, and devaluing others' opinions appeared to limit self-expression and inhibit the development of mature ego.

In short, for most adolescents, family members continue to play a significant role in development. Psychologist Willard Hartup (1979) has suggested that families may provide a secure base for exploring the social world beyond the family much as the parents of toddlers serve as a secure base for the young child's explorations of the immediate physical environment (see Chapter 4). Reported closeness to parents and siblings is correlated with social competence during adolescence (Bell, Avery, Jenkins, Feld, & Schoenrock, 1985). For these reasons, we have referred to changes in family relationships as a transformation, rather than a disruption or a deterioration of relationships. In this view adolescent's striving for independence is a part of the natural flow of human development, similar to the increasing independence of toddlers from their parents and the transitions in some families in which elderly parents become dependent on their adult children for their basic needs (Hill & Holmbeck, 1986).

Independence Training.   Training for independence is an important aspect of preparing for adult roles. When parents' childrearing practices include training for independence, adolescents are better prepared for the tasks of transition to adulthood, autonomy, and responsibility. Such adolescents should experience less stress than those whose family training has not fostered independence.

In Denmark, for example, the democratic parenting style is more typical than in the United States (Lesser & Kandel, 1969). Danish parents exercise less tight control over their children's behavior than U.S. parents, but do typically involve them in discussions about their actions and about decisions involving them. Families emphasize training for independence from early childhood. Consequently, during adolescence, parents find it less necessary to restrict independent behavior; their sons and daughters have been prepared to be autonomous and to follow internalized standards rather than external constraints. By contrast, Lesser and Kandel found that families in the United States typically tried to exercise greater control over adolescents. The more authoritarian approach taken by parents in the United States provides fewer opportunities for teaching independence through explanations and inculcation of general principles and guidelines.

Cultural and social class differences in training for independence also occur among families in the United States. Sociologist George Psathas (1958) reported that different subcultural groups vary dramatically in the degree to which parents permit their children to determine their own activities. Families also differed in the types of activities in which autonomy is particularly restricted. At lower occupational and educational levels, adolescents were readily granted autonomy outside the home, but were expected to comply unquestioningly with parents' wishes inside the home. In middle- and upper-class families autonomy was restricted outside the family, but considerable attention was given to adolescents' opinions, judgments, and expectations within the family. These different patterns imply fundamental differences among parents in training for independence.

Value Autonomy.   One aspect of independence that is especially central to identity formation is value autonomy. Merely adopting the opinions and values of others is poorly suited to many adult roles (Douvan & Adelson, 1966). Erikson (1968) has pointed out that true autonomy involves reaching commitments to specific values—whether they are similar or dissimilar to the values of others—through individual reasoning and judgments. Otherwise, identity has not been truly achieved. Adoption of others' values and roles is a kind of dependence that may have serious consequences in adulthood. For example, a young adult may encounter fellow students or fellow employees at work whose values are dramatically different from those of the young person's family. Responding maturely and responsibly requires more than simply adhering rigidly to rules laid out by parents or easy conformity to contradictory values; rather, a reasoned response based on internally held principles is necessary.

593

Like other aspects of independence, autonomous reasoning about values requires training. Parents of the most independent, mature adolescents tend to be warm and supportive, to show respect for their children's opinions, and to take care to involve them in constructive discussions of issues (Dubow, Huesmann, & Eron, 1987; Elder, 1963; Grotevant & Cooper, 1985; Holstein, 1976). Both the positive emotional atmosphere in such families and the opportunity to hear mature reasoning about issues are probably reasons that many parents continue to influence their children in adolescence, despite the variety and number of competing forces outside the family (Elder, 1963; Holstein, 1976).

Role Learning and Identity

Becoming an adult also requires considerable learning about the behavior and roles that are expected in the society. Family relationships are an important context for learning basic features of adult behavior. A fundamental psychological process in role learning in the family is identification. As we saw in Chapter 9, identification involves knowing or wanting to learn another person's behaviors, values, and expectations. When adolescents can draw upon parents' examples to help them meet the novel situations and demands of impending adulthood, there is greater continuity between childhood experiences and adult roles than when parent models are inappropriate or unreliable guides. A particularly striking example is learning of gender roles, for which parental models are highly significant (see Chapter 14).

Family relations also influence learning that affects choice of, and success in, adult work roles. Adolescents' particular vocational preferences often reflect the degree of their identification with their parents. In one study, male college students' identification with both their fathers and mothers was assessed and compared to the students' profiles on a widely used test of vocational aptitude (Crites, 1962). Males who were strongly identified with their fathers were especially well suited to technical occupations; those who were strongly identified with their mothers showed great aptitude in linguistic–verbal categories. Mixed-sex identification, in which the young men were strongly identified with both mother and father, produced a blend of both technical and verbal vocational aptitudes—a pattern that is thought to be well suited to the social sciences and social services professions. In addition, relatively few students who showed strong identification with one or both parents reported difficulties in choosing a vocation. By contrast, students who were weakly identified with parents had experienced vocational choice difficulties that required them to seek counseling.

Identification with parents also affects eventual vocational success. Sociologist Alan Bell (1969) reported that boys who, at age 14, had considered their fathers to be positive role models were more satisfied and successful in their occupations at age 25 than boys whose early attitudes toward their fathers had been neutral or negative. Interestingly, successful, occupationally satisfied young adults reported that their current role models are not family members. Rather, these individuals chose as models someone in their profession, such as a successful employer or coworker, from whom valuable information about relevant roles could be acquired. Perhaps, warm identifi-

RESEARCH FOCUS 17-1

Adolescents at Work

Teenagers in the United States have joined the work force in ever larger numbers during the past two decades. Census figures show that in 1940 the proportion of all enrolled 14 to 15 year olds who worked was 1.7%. In 1970 the proportion had risen to 8.7% and, by 1978, 15.6% held a job. In one recent survey (Lewin-Epstein, 1981) of high school students, 42.1% of sophomores reported that they had worked during the week prior to the survey.

Among older adolescents (16- and 17-year-olds), the proportion is even higher—perhaps the highest in the world. In 1978–79, more than two-thirds of this age group held regular jobs. Among the industrialized nations for which information is available, these figures are extreme. For example, in 1978–79, the proportion of 16- to 17-year-olds in Canada who worked was 37%, in Sweden, 20%, and in Japan, less than 2%.

To Americans, who have traditionally valued work especially highly, these figures may seem a sign of extraordinary promise in the younger generation. Indeed, recent research does show valuable outcomes of part-time work for teens. Among the advantages are increased understanding of consumer and money matters; increased feelings of responsibility; increased self-reports of willingness to stick to a task and of enjoyment of doing a job well. For girls, particularly, those who worked reported greater feelings of self-reliance than those who did not hold a job.

Do these benefits outweigh the disadvantages of working—the extra time taken away from schoolwork, extracurricular activities, time with family, and so on? The leading researchers in this area, Ellen Greenberger and Laurence Steinberg, have shown that one important factor in balancing these costs of working with the advantages of work experience is the amount of time spent working. Teens who work 15 or fewer hours per week show the same advantages of working as those who spend more hours at work, but those

who work longer hours are more likely to show some significant disadvantages as well.

Greenberger and Steinberg have identified three disadvantages of working for the development of adolescents who devote long hours to their jobs:

1. *Decreased school performance.* Students who work long hours spend less time on homework and report that they enjoy school less than other students. On the average, they also have lower grade point averages than nonworking students or those who work fewer hours (Wirtz, Rohrbeck, Charner, & Fraser, 1988). While acknowledging that less capable students may elect to work longer hours than more academically able youth, Greenberger and Steinberg also note that working students themselves tend to report that their grades have declined since they began working. Of nonworking students, 41% say they do not work because working would take too much time away from studying and schoolwork.

This point is especially troublesome to those who are concerned about the comparative economic advantage of the United States. They believe that the overall decline in aptitude and achievement test scores of high school students in this country in the past two decades may be partially attributable to the increase in out-of-school employment that distracts students from academic endeavors.

2. *Less time spent with the family.* Working teenagers less often have dinner with their families, because dinner hour is prime working time for the types of jobs teenagers are likely to hold. Similarly, those who work long hours also report that they less often do things "for fun" with their families and—especially for girls—that they feel more distant from their families now that they work. Apparently, both quantity and quality of time spent with parents, brothers, and sisters goes down when a large amount of time is spent on the job. In the words of one psychologist:

While the family still has the primary moral

and legal responsibility for the character development of children, it often lacks the power or opportunity to do the job, primarily because parents and children no longer spend enough time together in those situations in which training is possible (Bronfenbrenner, 1970).

3. *Increased use of cigarettes, alcohol, and marijuana.* The longer hours young persons spend on the job, the more likely they are to use substances. Why this relationship between working and substance use? One possibility is that working youth are more likely to have money to spend on the substances. Greenberger and Steinberg found that, even when amount of money available was taken into account, more hours of work per week increased the risk of substance use.

Most likely, job stress contributes to this relationship. Like the jobs held by many adults, the jobs held by teenagers are often tedious and perceived to be meaningless. When Greenberger and Steinberg surveyed the most common types of employment situations for teenagers (for example, food service and retail sales), they found young people often working under poor environmental conditions, in an impersonal organization, with an autocratic supervisor, for low wages. Many young people, committed to spending a large proportion of their time in such conditions, may turn to substance use to relieve boredom and stress. Similarly, a peer culture undoubtedly builds up in many places of employment for teenagers, and this culture may encourage use of substances.

Greenberger and Steinberg (1982) have concluded that, while work experience may contribute positively to adolescent development, the overall benefits of work may depend on the type of employment setting and the amount of time devoted to work. They have argued eloquently that policies that permit increased work hours for adolescents under age 16 should be balanced against the costs of encouraging young people to devote less of their time to school and family experiences. ❧

---

cation with parents in adolescence facilitates later identification with adaptive role models.

In recent years, the effect of maternal employment on the attitudes of both adolescent boys and girls toward female work roles has become apparent. In general, daughters of working mothers have more favorable attitudes toward female employment and hold higher educational and vocational aspirations for themselves than do children of nonworking mothers (Etaugh, 1974; Hoffman, 1984; Huston, 1983).

In the past, families were influential in vocational training more directly, because many families operated income-producing ventures in which children and adolescents were expected to work. Today, most actual training for work roles goes on outside of the family, and this training sometimes conflicts with other aspects of adolescents' lives, including family relations and school performance. Research Focus 17-1 outlines some of the issues in teenage employment.

Does Parent Influence Mean Similarity?   Identification with parents does not mean that adolescent and adult children must be similar to their parents on all aspects of adult behaviors, preferences, and attitudes. Although similarity is one indicator of parents' influence, lack of similarity does not necessarily indicate that parents have no influence over their children. For example, several reports (e.g., Grotevant, Scarr, & Weinberg, 1977) have indicated that biologically related parents and children have more similar interests than do adoptive parents and their children. This finding shows that genetic factors may influence interests, but it does not indicate that adoptive parents have no influence on their children's interests. Rather, family influences may involve encouraging adolescents to recognize and act on their individual strengths and interests, whether they are the same as the parents' or not. The emotional bond between parents and children undoubtedly makes possible many different avenues to social role learning in the context of the family, not just identification.

In some cases, similarity may not be adaptive. Mindless adoption of parents' opinions and commitments may create problems when parents' attitudes, values, and behavior are inconsistent with the roles and responsibilities to which adolescents must adjust (as when the child of blue collar parents attempts to attain higher status). For the most part, however, continuity in socialization is greatest and the transition from childhood to adulthood easiest when adolescents are firmly identified with warm, nurturant parents who provide competent models for adult roles.

We now turn to the role of peers in adolescent development.

Peer Relationships and Influences

A prominent stereotype holds that adolescence is a time of negative influences from peers. However, peers contribute positively to the development of adolescents in ways that adults cannot (Hartup, 1979; 1983). In *Blooming,* her memoir of growing up in an Iowa community, Susan Allen Toth expressed it this way:

> Girlfriends were as essential as mothers. . . . A set of girlfriends provided a sense of security, as belonging to any group does. . . . What little we learned about living with another person in an equal relationship, outside our own families, we learned from our girlfriends. It certainly wasn't a full preparation for marriage, but it was the only one some of us ever got (Toth, 1981, p. 60).

In fact, it is as much a concern when teenagers seem isolated from others of their own age as when they seem to be overly influenced by peers (Hartup, 1983).

Peer relations change both in quantity and quality during adolescence. Peers make up a larger proportion of social experiences in adolescence than in childhood (Barker & Wright, 1955; Montemayor & Van Komen, 1980). In fact, adolescents spend more time with friends and classmates and also more time alone than they spend with their families (Csikszentmihalyi & Larson, 1984). Furthermore, relationships with peers and the role of peer interactions in adolescent development are different in adolescence than in childhood.

The Changing Nature of Peer Relationships

Social Groups in Adolescence.   Adolescent groups are better defined and more structured than the loosely organized groups of childhood. Childhood groups are formed for the purposes of play or the activity of the moment, whereas groups—like friendships—are formed on more stable bases in adolescence. Although the particular determinants of status in a group may change from time to time, adolescents adhere more rigidly to status rules in their groups than children do (Savin-Williams, 1979; 1987). Adolescents, both boys and girls, seem especially aware of their group identity and are eager to preserve it (Sones & Feshbach, 1971; Savin-Williams, 1979; 1987; Sherif & Sherif, 1969). An example comes from a recent longitudinal study in which the members of a seventh grade class were interviewed and observed to identify the social structure of their classroom (Cairns, Perrin, & Cairns, 1985). The students agreed that there were five clusters or groups in their classroom: two groups of males, and three of females. One year later in the eighth grade, the students still perceived themselves as being clustered in the same ways, although some consolidation of groups had occurred. Thus, adolescent groups can maintain their identity over long periods.

Social Acceptance and Rejection.   Predicting whether an individual will be thought of as a member of one social group or will be rejected by another is always difficult, but prediction is far easier in adolescence than in childhood. Socially accepted adolescents are usually physically attractive and engage in friendly, positive, competent behavior toward peers, whereas socially rejected individuals are often those that show negative behaviors, such as aggressiveness and insensitivity to others (Feltham, Doyle, Schwartzman, Serbin, & Ledingham, 1985). As at other age periods, however, it is difficult to find one single characteristic of a person that guarantees social acceptance or rejection (Hartup, 1983).

It is somewhat easier to predict popularity, or the degree to which one is actively sought out by others. Researchers have studied popularity for more than 25 years by interviewing adolescents themselves about what makes a teenager popular, and the answers have been surprisingly consistent (e.g., Coleman, 1961). For boys, popularity is usually associated with success as an athlete; for girls it's being in the "leading crowd" that matters. Other characteristics that are frequently mentioned for both boys and girls are being a leader in activities, getting good grades, and having a nice car.

Friendships.   In adolescence friends are seen as persons with whom you share common thoughts and feelings. These qualities are sharply different from the characteristics of childhood friendships. Before adolescence, friendships typically center around common activities. At age 8 Cathy described her current best friend as "the girl who plays with me all the time." In contrast, at 13, her best friend is someone who "thinks a lot like me, like about what it's fun to do and stuff." Adolescents behave differently toward their friends than toward nonfriends, whereas children don't make so sharp a distinction. For example, adolescents are more likely to share secrets with friends than with nonfriends, and they are also more likely to be empathic

In the high-school social system, popularity for boys is often linked to being a successful athlete.

toward friends. Adolescents also attribute less competitiveness and more equitable attitudes to their friends than to their nonfriends, whereas elementary school children make similar attributions to friends and to nonfriends (Berndt, 1985).

Changes in the qualities of relationships with friends are especially pronounced for girls. Adolescent boys focus on common activities more than on interpersonal sharing (Douvan & Adelson, 1966). Girls also appear to limit the size of their friendship groups more than do boys, but their groups are more likely to include new friends than boys' friendship groups (Berndt & Hoyle, 1985). Male friends tend to have known each other longer than do female friends in adolescence (Montemayor & Van Komen, 1985). One reasons for these sex differences may be that girls give greater attention to personal and interpersonal characteristics of others in forming and maintaining friendships. However, overall, girls do not seem to have more or less stable friendships than boys do (Berndt & Hoyle, 1985). For both boys and girls, the composition of friendship groups in high school depends partly on whether the groups occur in school or out of school. In school, groups tend to consist of relatively large numbers of adolescents of the same sex; whereas out-of-school friendship groups are typically smaller and include both boys and girls (Montemayor & Van Komen, 1985).

One reason adolescents' friendships may be different from those of children is the changing abilities of adolescents to think in terms of qualities of relationships and the nature of interpersonal bonds (Berndt, 1982). In Selman's theory of interpersonal perspective taking (Chapter 10), young children have very egocentric, or self-centered conceptions of individuals and their actions. During adolescence, however, more complex concepts of the self in relationship to other people develop (Selman, 1980) (see Table 17-2). The implications of this change in conceptual abilities for understanding peer relations were described in Chapter 10.

599

TABLE 17-2

Selman's Levels in Conceptions of Friendship

Level 0: Egocentric Perspective taking	Close friendship as momentary physical interaction: Friends are individuals who are close enough physically to play together and who engage in play without hurting people or things.
Level 1: Subjective Perspective taking	Close friendship as one-way assistance: Friends are people who do things which the other person wants done.
Level 2: Reciprocal Perspective taking	Close friendship as fair-weather cooperation: Friends meet personal needs for companionship, being liked, but these needs are thought of in terms of specific incidents or issues, rather than as an underlying system.
Level 3: Mutual Perspective taking	Close friendship as intimate and mutual sharing: Friendship is a relationship, rather than a focus on each individual separately. Basis of the relationship involves sharing intimate personal concerns and the efforts of each party to maintain the relationship.
Level 4: Societal–symbolic Perspective taking	Close friendships as autonomous interdependence: Friendships are seen as being in a constant process of formation and transformation, within which each individual is changing and growing. Thus, friendships partly serve the function of providing individuals with a sense of personal identity. The relationship depends on each person's understanding of this basic autonomy of two individuals, whose personalities are compatible, but who may grow out of the relations as further personal changes occur.

SOURCE: Adapted from Selman, 1980, pp. 136–142.

In adolescence the central themes of friendships are the personalities of friends and the ways in which they respond to each other. The emphasis is on loyalty, trustworthiness, and respect for confidence (Furman & Bierman, 1984). In short, intimacy is more central to friendship for adolescents than for children. The opportunity for intimacy is surely one of the reasons adolescents give so much time and importance to their friendships (Hunter, 1984, 1985a, 1985b; Youniss, 1980). Most experts view intimacy during preadolescence and adolescence as essential for the development of a capacity for healthy, mature interpersonal relationships in later life (Elkind, 1967; Erikson, 1968; Sullivan, 1954; Youniss, 1980).

The capacity for intimacy seems to grow during the adolescent years. In one study of fifth, seventh, ninth, and eleventh graders, adolescents rated the ways in which their friendships were intimate (Sharabany, Gershoni, & Hofman, 1981). Across these grades, friends increased in how much frankness, spontaneity, knowing, and sensitivity they showed toward each other. In the words of one adolescent, a sense emerges that you can "tell them what you feel and you can be yourself with them" (Youniss, 1980). However, trust and loyalty and taking and imposing were characteristics of friendship in preadolescence and adolescence alike. Psychologist Ruth Sharabany and her coworkers (1981) found that girls' friendships consistently involved more knowing and sensitivity, more giving and sharing, and also more taking and imposing than boys' friendships did. She also found that intimacy in opposite-sex friendship was only apparent among ninth and eleventh graders. Again, girls rated their friendships with boys as more intimate than boys rated their friendships with girls to be.

In summary, compared to the peer relations of children, adolescents' peer relations are based on the characteristics of individuals that contribute to their ability to enter into a mutual exchange of views and confidences or to engage in activities of common interest. At the same time, the status rules of schools and communities continue to affect who is chosen to be a friend or who is accepted or rejected for membership in a social group.

Peers play a variety of roles in the psychological development of adolescents: (1) as sources of knowledge about behavioral patterns, attitudes, and values and their consequences in different situations (informational influence) and (2) as sources of social pressure on adolescents to behave as others around

Functions of Peer Relations

Friendships become increasingly important sources of intimacy and social support during adolescence.

them behave (normative influence) (Deutsch & Gerard, 1955). Such influences play important roles in the development of a sense of one's self as a member of a social group, which is basic to identity formation.

Peer Influence. The influence of peers is especially strong in the early years of adolescence. A number of studies indicate that greatest conformity is likely to occur among 12- and 13-year-old young people. One example was done by Philip Costanzo (1970). In Costanzo's study adolescents sat in booths arranged in a semicircle, facing a screen on which a series of slides were shown. In each picture, there were four straight lines. One straight line was identified as the standard; the other three were comparison lines—one longer, one shorter, and one the same as the standard. The adolescents were asked to choose the line that was the same as the comparison line by pushing a button corresponding to the line that matched the standard. Although none of the adolescents could see the others who were supposed to be tested at the same time, each was told they would be able to tell which lines the other three adolescents had chosen by watching the panel of indicator lights in the booth. The lights on each person's panel were actually controlled by the experimenter, who made it appear as though the other three participants had chosen the wrong answer on 15 of the 20 choices. Costanzo tested 590 males ranging in age from 7 to 21 to see if the tendency to conform to group judgment was greater at some ages than others. As Figure 17-3 shows, the highest percentages of conformity occurred early in adolescence. Both elementary school children (ages 7 to 8) and young adults (ages 19 to 21) conformed less often to erroneous judgments than did 12- to 13-year-olds or 16- to 17-year-olds. This same pattern has been found in many other studies using a similar task.

Why are young adolescents especially susceptible to pressure to conform? Young adolescents may often misperceive the attention of others toward them, as in Elkind's (1967) concept of Imaginary Audience egocentrism that was discussed in Chapter 11. In Costanzo's study, young adolescents' sense of others' attention to their behavior may have caused them to conform to the erroneous judgments of others to avoid "standing out." At younger ages the cognitive skills necessary for Imaginary Audience thinking have not yet developed, so that individuals are more likely to follow their own judgments than the judgments of others. At older ages, the additional cognitive achievements that overcome the Imaginary Audience enable the adolescents to discount the judgments of others and to rely on their own judgment. Thus conformity, like other aspects of adolescents' social behavior, may partly reflect changing cognitive abilities and their effects on the adolescents' perceptions of others' attitudes toward them.

At the same time, adolescents' perceptions of peer pressures to engage in such activities as drinking, smoking, and sexual activity increase over the years from sixth grade to twelfth grade (Brown, Clasen & Eicher, 1986). This pattern may reflect increasingly more time spent with peers. It may also indicate that adolescents and their peers become more and more interested in activities that are perceived as adultlike as they approach adulthood them-

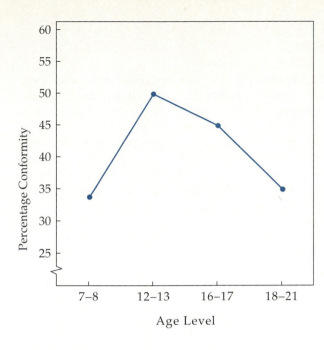

FIGURE 17-3

Percentage of conformity to the judgments of others as a function of age level.

Source: from Costanzo, 1970.

selves. Several studies indicate that, overall, males, rather than females, appear to be more willing to follow their peers in antisocial behavior (Berndt, 1979; Brown et al., 1986).

Several other characteristics of individuals make conformity more or less likely at every age. For example, a tendency to blame oneself for mistakes increases the likelihood of conformity (Costanzo, 1970). In addition, doubts about one's own competence to do a particular task and insecurity about one's status in the peer group tends to increase conformity to the judgments of others (Harvey & Consalvi, 1960; Landsbaum & Willis, 1971). A tendency to be especially concerned about approval from others, such as is characteristic of moral judgments in Stage 3 in Kohlberg's scheme (see Chapter 10), also increases the likelihood of conformity (Saltzstein, Diamond, & Belenky, 1972). Finally, adolescents who are struggling to form an identity are especially likely to conform (Marcia, 1980). In one study of young college women, those who were in *moratorium* or *diffusion*—those who had not yet achieved a sense of commitment to particular values and goals—were more likely to conform to erroneous judgments than their peers who were in the more stable *achievement* or *foreclosure* state (Toder & Marcia, 1973). Although bringing oneself into general accord with a social group may be one important part of the complex process involved in identity achievement, Erikson (1968) also considered it necessary to feel comfortable with some differences between one's self and the social group. Individuals in unstable statuses like moratorium and diffusion may use the social group to define themselves because they lack internally held standards or a coherent sense of self.

Peers and Individual Development. Erikson viewed peer relations as essential to normal, healthy development. He believed peer groups not only provided information to adolescents about important roles and their success in them,

603

he also believed that the peer group provided an important refuge or camouflage for adolescents during essential times of moratorium from the demands of adults and the prospects of adult roles. Other theorists, like Harry Stack Sullivan (1953), view peer relations as an essential aspect of managing pressures associated with the emergence of sexuality. In Sullivan's view, the experience of developing close relationships with same-age persons makes it possible for basic needs for intimacy and affiliation with others to be integrated successfully with needs for sexual gratification after puberty. Both of these views undoubtedly emphasize part of what is important about peer relations in psychological development.

Although it is impossible to describe fully the impact of peers in development, it is now well established that successful peer relations are important predictors of psychological adjustment in adulthood (Hartup, 1983; Parker & Asher, 1988; Reisman, 1985). For example, delinquency among adolescents and young adults has been shown to be closely tied to poor peer relations in childhood (Roff & Sells, 1970). Poor peer relations have also been found to predict a wide range of adult problems, including behavioral difficulties, occupational problems, and marital and sexual problems (Roff, Sells, & Golden, 1972). In one large-scale study of community mental health, the best predictor of mental health in adulthood was the rating individuals received from their peers in middle childhood. Adults who were listed in the mental health registers in this study were more than two and a half times as likely to have been rated as negative by their peers in the third grade than those who did not appear in the mental health register (Cowen, Pederson, Babigian, Izzo, & Prost, 1973).

It may be, of course, that poor peer relations do not cause later difficulties, but are simply an early symptom of many other problems that recur in different forms in later life periods. Adolescents who are withdrawn or notably aggressive have fewer friends, are rated lower on likeability, and have less mature conceptions of friendship than other adolescents. Without intervention, characteristics such as these can portend adult problems. On the other hand, having a supportive peer group has been found to be linked to positive developmental patterns, such as a positive self-concept (East, 1986), appropriate classroom behavior, and scholastic competence (Coleman, 1961). The capacity for relating to others, the development of social control, and the acquisition of social values all depend on interactions with other peers. Relationships with peers enable adolescents to work out problems together, rather than merely giving in to more powerful parents or teachers (Hartup, 1983).

Among the important areas of special influence by peers is that of sexuality. In addition, peers are repeatedly cited as the major source of information on which adolescents rely for information about sexual facts and sexual behavior (Miller & Simon, 1980; Roberts, Kline, & Gagnon, 1978). Although information from peers is frequently inaccurate or incomplete, the willingness of adolescents to accept information is a sign of the potential influence of peers on development.

Research findings indicate that peers play a complementary, rather than antagonistic, role to that of the family. For the most part, there seems to be considerable agreement between parents and children on values and attitudes, and more often than not parents approve of their children's choices of friends. When a conflict does occur, parents and peers appear to influence adolescents in different areas of activity (Hartup, 1983; Hill, 1986).

In a well-known study of parent–peer cross-pressure, sociologist Clay Brittain (1966) presented a group of hypothetical situations to girls in grades nine through eleven. The stories were presented twice, once with peers advocating certain alternatives and once with parents advocating those same alternatives. Brittain wanted to see if girls would change their opinions about which boy to go steady with, how to get selected for school honor, or how to dress for a football game or a party, depending on whether an alternative course of action was favored by a parent or by a peer. He found that the girls in his study were neither unusually oriented toward peers, nor unusually submissive to parents. Peers' influence was strongest for problems relevant to status in the peer group, while parents were more influential on life decisions, ethical and value judgments, and issues that were relevant to the reputation and status of the girls in the family and community. The reliance on parents for guidance in many aspects of adolescent life is especially strong when family relationships have been positive (Elder, 1986; Larson, 1972).

Adolescents engage in more different types of activities and interactions with peers than with parents. Time with parents often centers around work and tasks, while time with peers is more typically devoted to play and recreation (Montemayor, 1982). Adolescents perceive discussions with their parents as being more focused on the greater authority and expertise of the parent than on an interest in mutual understanding, whereas conversations with peers are seen as opportunities to share experiences and perceptions (Hunter, 1984; 1985a,b). However, adolescents continue to discuss a variety of personal and general topics with their parents (Hunter, 1985a).

Both parents and peers universally provide essential contexts for development of individuals from childhood to adolescence. Physical and cognitive changes interact with these important contexts to produce an individual identity appropriate to functioning as autonomous, responsible, competent individuals in adult society. In this chapter our main point has been that such development can only take place as a complex interaction between individual, interpersonal, and cultural factors. The important questions go beyond whether parents and peers are in conflict with each other to questions about how parents and peers together contribute to psychological development. One example, with both positive and negative aspects, appears in Research Focus 17-2.

Thus far, we have examined primary physical, psychological, and social–definitional changes during adolescence and the ways in which family and peer contexts affect, and are affected by, those changes. In the remaining sections of the chapter, we will consider several problems of emotional adjustment and behavioral transitions that occur for many adolescents.

Parent–Peer Cross-Pressures

RESEARCH FOCUS 17-2

Starting to Smoke: Cross-Pressures or Collaboration?

When adolescents adopt certain practices like smoking cigarettes or using drugs, adults are often tempted to blame the peer group. Kids wouldn't do such things, the assumption goes, unless their friends pressured them into it, since parents certainly would not favor such behavior in someone so young. Recent studies indicate, however, that family influences are very important indeed in determining whether young people begin to smoke. The National Institutes of Health have recently sponsored a number of studies of teenage smoking, and one of the main questions addressed is the respective roles of family and peers.

In one of these studies, psychologists Jon Krosnick and Charles Judd (1982) conducted a survey of 847 junior high students, ages 11 and 14. The questions concerned the young adolescents' own smoking habits and the smoking habits and attitudes of their parents and friends. For example, the participants were asked how often they smoked and, specifically, if they had smoked a cigarette "in the last month," "in the last week," and "yesterday." They were also asked how many of their "really good friends" smoked and whether and how often each of their parents smoked. Finally, they were asked what instructions parents had given them about smoking and what their parents' attitudes would be if the teenager smoked. Krosnick and Judd then tried to determine the effect of peer smoking or parental smoking and attitudes on teen and pre-teen smoking. Whether peers strongly affected smoking depended upon the age of the adolescent. Peer influence was weak among 11-year-olds, but was more important among 14-year-olds. Parents' own smoking and attitudes were important at both ages, however. If parents smoked or expressed relatively positive attitudes toward smoking, it was more likely that their children would smoke, too. In other words, parents do not lose influence as their children move into adolescence, but peer influence does increase.

How then do social influences contribute to adolescents' smoking? Judging from research findings, a large proportion of adolescents who began to smoke have parents or peers or both who also smoke and approve of the practice. To reduce the chances of adolescents' smoking, education and persuasion programs should be directed to both families and peers. ❦

Behavioral and Emotional Problems of Adolescents

Like the problem of teenage pregnancy discussed in Chapter 16, other personal and social problems of the adolescent years are linked to basic developmental processes affecting the formation of identity and the impact of family and peer relationships.

In this section, we briefly review four of the most common types of adolescent behavior problems: depression, including the increasingly frequent problem of suicides among adolescents, school adjustment and performance difficulties, chemical use and abuse, and antisocial behavior, or delinquency. The central theme is the importance of social relationships to these problems.

As we saw in Chapter 11, feelings of sadness, misery, and loneliness are common even in childhood, but depression becomes much more common among young people during the adolescent years. Between age 10 and age 14 and 15, the rate of reported depressive feelings has been found to increase from 10% of the general population to 40% (Rutter, 1979; Rutter & Garmezy, 1983).

Depression

Depression is more common among females than males in both adolescence and adulthood. This pattern is widely attributed to the typical socialization of females that can foster learned helplessness, or a sense that one has little control over the outcomes of one's efforts (Rutter, 1979; Seligman, 1975). Typical socialization for males in United States society appears to be less likely to induce learned helplessness. Depression in adolescent boys appears to be especially sensitive to pubertal change and the concomitant changes in expectations (see Chapter 11). In the longitudinal study reported by Rutter (1979, 1984), almost no prepubertal 14- and 15-year-old boys reported depressed feelings, while one-third of the postpubertal boys did so.

In both boys and girls, then, depression in adolescence may be related to the role expectations that become more pronounced as young people reach physical maturity and increasingly face the demands and choices of approaching adulthood. For example, lack of success in relationships with the opposite sex and uncertainty about future plans can lead to feelings of sadness and hopelessness. In addition, as we discussed in Chapters 6 and 11, adolescents are more focused on their own thoughts and feelings than children are, and they are generally more concerned with the significance of others' reactions to them. As in adults, the adolescents who suffer from chronic depression are likely to be those who show a "cognitive bias" toward expecting (1) that bad events will occur and (2) that they lack the power to avoid or deal with them (Seligman & Peterson, 1984). In a small minority of cases, depression is associated with endocrinological problems that may respond to medication (Rutter & Garmezy, 1983). Although one cannot dismiss adolescent depression as "normal" or "inevitable," the physical, cognitive, and social changes of the period clearly set the stage for feelings of unworthiness, inadequacy, and lack of power to determine the outcomes for oneself.

Compared to childhood depression, depression in adolescence is more often associated with thoughts of suicide (Rutter & Garmezy, 1983). Although suicidal thoughts occur in childhood, such thoughts become much more common about age 9 or 10 (Bolger, Downey, Walker, & Steininger, 1989). Statistics indicate that adolescents are responding more and more frequently to depressed feelings by attempting suicide. The rate of suicides in the 15- to 19-year-old age group has almost tripled since 1955 (Rutter & Garmezy, 1983; Weiner, 1980). The patterns of suicide attempts are similar to the patterns of depression in the population. Three times as many girls as boys *attempt* suicide, but three times as many boys as girls actually die as a result

607

of suicide. Stressful events, including family problems and difficulties in peer relations, may be precipitating events, although based on current evidence, they cannot be considered clear causes of adolescent suicides (Weiner, 1980).

Both suicidal tendencies and depression require sensitive intervention by parents and others. Professionals recommend that any talk of suicide be taken seriously and followed up with expert mental health counseling.

School Adjustment Problems

Adolescents spend a majority of their days in school. Consequently, it is not surprising that school-related problems are a focus of psychological difficulties. Two problems in particular receive a great deal of attention.

School Phobia. One is *school phobia,* or a fear of school that often leads to a refusal to attend. The evidence of school phobia rises rapidly during adolescence. The causes vary, but usually include some combination of emotions, such as fear of school, anxiety about performance, separation from family or friends, and so forth (Hersov & Berg, 1980; Rutter & Garmezy, 1983). Experts believe that, unlike separation anxiety or fear of new situations that are common in childhood, school phobia in adolescence is tied to heightened concerns with self and with the anticipated demands of the future. The concern is that this avoidant pattern may extend beyond school refusal to increasing social isolation and fearfulness (Weiner, 1980).

Underachievement. A second, more frequent problem is that of *underachievement,* or failing to perform at a level commensurate with one's ability. Unexpectedly poor performance in school occurs in an estimated one-fourth of all school children. In the United States, 20% of adolescents fail to complete high school despite the value placed on education in this society (Weiner, 1980). Some of these cases result from sociocultural factors that go counter to the prevailing belief in the importance of education. Minority, ethnic group, or disadvantaged youths often feel that school achievement is incompatible with sex role and other values in their cultures; often, such youth do not believe that education will lead to a better life, or they find the school environment insensitive or unsympathetic to their needs. In other cases of underachievement, specific learning disabilities, such as attentional or perceptual problems, interfere with performance on school tasks.

When underachievement appears to come primarily from lack of effort, two psychological and social relationship problems are often involved. One is resentment of, or hostility toward parents, usually for making heavy demands that young people feel they cannot meet or do not wish to meet. Since adolescence is a time of seeking some individuation from parents, resisting parents' academic goals may be a way to define one's separateness (Davids & Hainsworth, 1967; Janos, Sanfilippo, & Robinson, 1986). A second social factor may be concern about failing to measure up to the performance of parents, siblings, or peers. Another form of this social comparison problem is fear of success that might be interpreted as "standing out," "showing off," or attempting to make others look bad (Ishiyama & Chabassol, 1985). In both cases, sensitivity to social relationships and their importance to adolescents' personal and social concerns set the stage for underachievement.

Drug Use and Abuse

Perhaps the most commonly mentioned youth problem today is the widespread use of alcohol and other drugs. In the decade of the 1970s, both smoking and alcohol use increased among teenagers in the United States. While use of drugs such as marijuana, heroin, cocaine, and more arcane chemicals such as "angel dust" may seem less widespread than they were in the 1960s, large numbers of young people continue to use them throughout the second decade of life (Johnston, O'Malley, & Bachman, 1985).

Experts generally distinguish roughly two patterns of youth involvement with drugs (Proskauer & Rolland, 1973). In the first general category are young people who use chemicals because they are depressed or have chronic or severe personal problems from which they wish to escape. It is these individuals who are most likely to become "problem" drug users.

A more common type of drug use can be called social or experimental. In this type, drinking and using hallucinogenic substances are—at least initially—occasional and situational. Adolescents may drink or smoke marijuana to be with their friends who are doing so at a party. This occasional use may seem like a natural rite of passage and in the majority of cases may be so. In Erik Erikson's view, for example, drug use might be viewed as one aspect of the psychosocial moratorium for some adolescents. Nevertheless, the possibility of accidental death or injury while under the influence of these chemicals and the threat of addiction in some cases make this aspect of adolescent life risky (Baumrind, 1987).

Use of alcohol and other drugs may be either a part of peer-group relations during adolescence or a symptom of psychological problems.

The causes of social drug use again make clear the importance of both parents and peers to adolescent development. For example, in one study, adolescents' marijuana use was found to be more closely related to their friends' marijuana use than to their parents' use of psychotropic drugs. However, even when best friends used drugs, adolescents were somewhat less likely to use them if their parents did not use drugs than if they did (Kandel, 1973). Other researchers have found that mothers' own drug use was less related to their teenage children's use than was the teenagers' perceptions of the normativeness of drug use by adults. If the adolescents believed that drug use is fairly typical of adults, then they were more likely to use drugs themselves (Newcomb, Huba & Bentler, 1983). The relationship between parent and peer influences on adolescent drug use is also shown in Research Focus 17-3.

Parents' use of drugs may be less important than their general childrearing style in affecting their offsprings' use. Children of democratic parents have generally been found to be less likely to use drugs than those of parents who use authoritative or laissez-faire methods. However, researchers in this area are careful to note that if adolescents have a pattern of problem behavior and resistance to influence, their parents' childrearing methods may have less effect (Brooke, Whiteman, Gordon, & Cohen, 1986).

Juvenile Delinquency

Juvenile delinquency is a legal category, not a psychological concept or personal trait. We use the term to refer to patterns of antisocial behavior, including destruction of property, theft, violence, and a range of other antisocial actions, both major and minor. In the United States today, this large and diverse category of problem behaviors is an increasingly pressing social problem. The rate of criminal acts among adolescents, including preteen youngsters, is rising each year, and the severity of the crimes (for example, homicide) is increasing as well. Some aspects of this problem, such as aggression and moral behavior, were discussed in Chapter 15. In general, experts have found it useful to distinguish between delinquent behavior that is associated with membership in a particular social group, such as a juvenile gang or a criminal family, and antisocial acts that reflect psychological disturbance (Rutter & Garmezy, 1983). Although all criminal acts by adolescents cannot be cleanly divided into these two categories, the distinction helps us identify at least two patterns of cause for antisocial behavior in the adolescent years.

In both types of delinquency, however, major contributing influences come from the family and the peer group. Delinquents are more likely than non-delinquents to come from families with serious problems, such as a history of criminality, excessive drinking, poor work records, or serious parental personality disorder. Family discord is likely to be high in such families and may be one of the causative factors. Weak relationships with parents, including little time together, lack of parental warmth, and lack of intimate communication, also characterize delinquents' families. Parents of delinquents often have weak or inconsistent discipline and supervision practices, as well (Patterson, 1982).

Adolescent Drug Use: A Long View

Understanding the nature and causes of adolescent drug use presents a number of difficult problems for researchers. One is that it is difficult to follow the same adolescents over a period of time to get information about whether drug use was a short-term experiment or the beginning of a longer-term pattern of behavior. Another is that it is necessary not only to monitor drug use itself, but also to continue to gather information about the factors that seem to go along with drug use and abuse to learn about what fosters initial drug use and what maintains drug use across time.

Psychologists Judith Stein, Michael Newcomb, and P. M. Bentler (1987) have recently completed an extensive longitudinal study of drug use, in which they followed 654 adolescents from junior high school until they were several years beyond high school graduation age. As a group, the participants in the study were representative of young adults nationwide, as determined by the National Survey on Drug Abuse (Miller et al., 1983). Stein, Newcomb, and Bentler wanted to examine the relative importance of the individuals' own personality characteristics, the influence of peer and adult models, perceived community standards for drug use, and problems associated with family disruption in predicting (1) *changes* in drug use over the course of the study and (2) whether or not the participants were experiencing problematic drug use during young adulthood.

Their findings supported many of the conclusions drawn from other studies:

- Individuals who reported using drugs in junior high school were likely to be using drugs as young adults. However, there was greater stability of drug use from late adolescence (age 18 or 19) to young adulthood than from early adolescence to late adolescence. The specific drugs used by a young person may change, of course, but the tendency to use or not use drugs was remark-

ably consistent across the years. Drug use in adolescence did not necessarily presage *problem* drug use in young adulthood, however.

- Perceptions of drug use by parents and peers influenced drug use in adolescence and young adulthood alike to a greater extent than did perceptions of community behavior and standards. Adult and peer influence varied somewhat by the type of drug used. Perceptions of adult use particularly influenced alcohol use by young people, whereas perceptions of peer drug use influenced use of marijuana and hard drugs.

- Parental drug use and family disruption seemed to be intertwined in their influence on drug use during adolescence and young adulthood. For example, early exposure to alcohol use by adults was correlated with drug-related problems many years later. This may have been due to early modeling of drinking and drug use. Another possibility is that early exposure to drug use was associated with family disruption, and drug use may be one way in which adolescents have learned to cope with the stress of family problems.

- Personality characteristics associated with rebelliousness and low social conformity were linked to problem drug use in adolescence and in young adulthood. Lack of social conformity itself was strongly correlated with family disruption, implying that family disruption may be linked to drug-related problems via its effects on personality characteristics. As researchers frequently note, social factors (for example, peer and parent drug use) may influence whether or not a person uses alcohol and drugs, but personality characteristics and individual stressors determine whether or not that use attains problem dimensions.

When family problems like these are added to membership in a delinquent peer group, a pattern of antisocial behavior is often set that persists into adulthood. The conditions for this combination of factors has historically been especially likely among lower socioeconomic groups. However, more than in the past, middle-class youth today are more frequently recognized as being involved in antisocial behavior. This is partly because of changes in court record keeping and more judicial even-handedness in the cases of lower- and middle-class offenders (Rutter & Garmezy, 1983).

Summary

During adolescence, cognitive and physical maturation and changes in social expectations are *origins* of changes in individuals that, in turn, create new demands, opportunities, and constraints in social relations and in meeting the challenges of autonomy, achievement, intimacy, and sexuality roles. Erik Erikson has suggested that these numerous changes require adolescents to achieve a new sense of self, a task referred to as achieving an *identity*. Although Erikson's term *identity crisis* probably correctly captures some of the emotional turmoil experienced by most adolescents, the process of *identity formation* now appears to involve a series of adjustments that adolescents in Western societies must make over the course of the second decade of life.

The nature and degree of perturbation in the lives of adolesents is partly related to the number and extent of changes required to fill roles and master skills expected of adolescents and adults, but not of children. Several *environmental contexts* are significant in either easing the transition to new roles and behaviors or making it more difficult; the most important of these are family and peers.

Family influences help prepare adolescents for adult roles, such as those related to gender and to vocational choice and success. Although the effects of parents in adolescence may be largely an extension of earlier socialization, differences in parents' childrearing practices are associated with the degree to which adolescents show characteristics of independence, achievement orientation, and social responsibility. Certain transformations appear to occur in family interactions as adolescents become more adultlike, physically and cognitively, but there is little evidence that adolescence is inevitably a time of turmoil and disruption in family life.

Peer relations now appear to be complementary, rather than contradictory, to family influences. Peers are associated with socialization of sexual attitudes and behavior, control of aggression, and the development of social norms and behaviors necessary for smooth integration of adolescents into their social worlds. Compared to childhood peer relations, adolscents' groups have more readily identifiable normative and behavioral "rules"; in friendships, adolescents—especially females—emphasize commonality of interests and sharing of thoughts and feelings. Satisfactory peer relations in adolescence and childhood are important predictors of healthy adult functioning. In short, the social contexts of adolescence provide an opportunity for integration and expansion of skills and personal qualities necessary for adult life.

The changes that occur in adolescence are *interrelated* with a number of behavioral and emotional problems for many individuals. For example, the incidence of depression rises in adolescents. It is unclear whether these feelings are attributable to physical change or increased social expectations that emerge at about the same time. As compared with childhood depression, adolescent depression is more often associated with thoughts of suicide, a fact that is consistent with increases in suicide attempts during the adolescent years. Among the other problem behaviors especially associated with the adolescent years are school adjustment problems, drug use and abuse, and juvenile delinquency.

Suggested Readings

CSIKSZENTMIHALYI, M., & LARSON, R. (1984). *Being adolescent: Conflict and growth in the teenage years.* New York: Basic Books.

LERNER, R. M., & FOCH, T. T. (Eds.) (1987). *Biological-psychosocial interactions in early adolescence.* Hillsdale, NJ: Lawrence Erlbaum.

MONTEMAYOR, R., ADAMS, G. R., & GULLOTTA, T. P. (1990). *From childhood to adolescence: A transitional period?* Beverly Hills, CA: Sage.

NEWCOMB, M. D., & BENTLER, P. M. (1989). Substance use and abuse among children and teenagers. *American Psychologist, 44,* 242–248.

POWERS, S. I., HAUSER, S. T., & KILNER, L. A. (1989). Adolescent mental health. *American Psychologist, 44,* 200–208.

SAVIN-WILLIAMS, R. C. (1987). *Adolescence: An ethological perspective.* New York: Springer-Verlag.

Glossary

A not B error: The infant's tendency to look for an object in a place where it has previously been hidden (A), rather than where she has seen it most recently hidden (B).

Abstraction principle: The principle that anything can be counted.

Accommodation: The modification of existing knowledge to incorporate a new experience.

Adolescence: The transitional period between childhood and adulthood.

Adolescent growth spurt: The rapid acceleration in height during puberty.

Affective role-taking: The process of recognizing the emotions or feelings of another person.

Amniocentesis: The process by which amniotic fluid is withdrawn for biochemical and chromosomal analysis to discover the status of the fetus.

Amnion: The structure that contains the amniotic fluid that surrounds the embryo.

Amniotic fluid: Fluid that functions as both a support and a cushion for the embryo.

Amniotic sac: A protective cover that encloses the fetus and contains amniotic fluid.

Anorexia nervosa: An eating disorder found primarily in middle-class, adolescent females that is characterized by marked weight loss and an intense desire for thinness.

Anoxia: A shortage of oxygen that can lead to negative effects in infants if it occurs during birth.

Anxious attachment: An attachment wherein infants become angry and find it difficult to reestablish and maintain contact when their caregivers return after a separation.

Anxious avoidant attachment: An attachment wherein infants actively avoid their parents upon reunion after a separation.

Anxious resistant attachment: An attachment wherein infants both seek and resist physical contact and are difficult to comfort after separation from and reunion with the caregiver.

Apgar scale: A neonatal assessment device that checks an infant's heart rate, breathing, muscle tone, color, and reflexes at 1 minute and at 5 minutes after birth.

Apnea: A condition resulting in spontaneous interruptions of breathing.

Asphyxia: A loss of consciousness as a result of a shortage of oxygen (anoxia), accompanied by a build-up of carbon dioxide.

Assimilation: The process of interpreting the world in terms of existing knowledge.

Attachment: Strong affectionate ties with one's most intimate companions.

Authoritarian parents: Parents who are generally restrictive, emphasize rules, and expect their children to obey them unquestioningly.

Authoritative parents: Parents who set clear limits and standards for behavior, but enforce them with a combination of power and reasoning.

Authority relationships: Relationships in which one person has power over another by virtue of age or role.

Automatization: The increased efficiency of information processing that occurs as a task is performed over and over.

Autosomes: Chromosomes that are homologous, that is the members of a pair are similar to one another but different from all other pairs.

Babbling: Sound combinations produced by infants that may carry no real meaning.

Babbling drift: A hypothesis suggesting that infants restrict their later babbling to the sounds that occur in the language they hear.

Babinski reflex: Occurs when an infant's toes fan upward as the sole of its foot is stroked from heel to toe.

Basic gender identity: A developmental stage in which one realizes that he or she is either male or female.

Basic-level terms: Words that express an intermediate level in a category. For example "bear" is basic-level because mammal is too general and grizzly is too specific.

Behavioral genetics: The interaction between genotypes and environments to produce phenotypes.

Blastocyst: A developing zygote that begins to take nourishment from the uterine environment.

Bound morphemes: Units that are meaningful only when used in combination with free morphemes and that change the meaning of the free morphemes to which they are attached.

Brazelton Neonatal Behavioral Assessment Scale: A scale devised to measure a newborn's neurological functioning by checking 20 reflexes and responses 3 days after birth and again a few days later.

Breech birth: A birth in which the feet and buttocks, rather than the head, appear first; this occurs in about 10% of all births.

Bulimia: An eating disorder, common among middle-class, female adolescents, in which one engages in binge eating followed by the intentional expulsion of the food.

Cardinal principle: The last number used when one counts an array of objects is the cardinal number value of the array.

Categorical perception: The classification of individual sounds as phonemes.

Catharsis: The discharge of aggressive energy through action or experience.

Cathexis: A motive, in Freud's psychoanalytic theory, to approach, stay near, or in some other way behave positively toward an object.

Cell differentiation: The specialization of nerve cells upon reaching their final destination.

Cell migration: The migration of nerve cells from place to place within the neural tube, which gradually builds the brain from the inside out.

Cells: The basic building blocks of all living things that can exist in isolation or as members of a community.

Centered thought: The tendency to focus one's attention on a single feature of an object or situation rather than recognizing all potentially relevant features.

Cervix: The opening from the birth canal (vagina) into the uterus.

Chordamesoderm: Cells during the early stages of prenatal development that eventually form the brain.

Chromosomes: Units within the cell that contain all of the heritable information.

Chromotids: The two identical portions of a chromosome that are formed during the duplication of cells.

Class inclusion: The ability to simultaneously consider both the part and the whole of a class.

Classical conditioning: A learning theory that proposes that a particular stimulus is associated with and elicits a specific response.

Cognition: The mental abilities involved in the interpretation and organization of information.

Cognitive Developmental Theory: A theory that concentrates on the development of cognitive abilities and the ways in which a child's developmental level will influence how he or she interprets the world and his or her experiences in it.

Cognitive role-taking: The process of knowing what another person is likely to know, understand, or think about persons, situations, and events.

Cognitive Social Learning Theory: A learning theory that proposes that much of learning is under the control of the individual.

Conceptual tempo: The speed and accuracy with which individuals approach intellectual tasks.

Concordant traits: Traits that are present in each twin.

Concrete operational stage: Piaget's third stage in his cognitive developmental theory in which the child is able to solve class inclusion and conservation of liquid problems, but is still unable to think in abstract terms.

Conditional probabilities: The likelihood that, over many observed in-

617

stances, a given behavior will be followed by a particular response from another person.

Cones: Color receptors in the retina.

Connectedness: The continuing connection between the individual and the family.

Conscience: The part of the superego in Freud's psychoanalytic theory that contains the rules and regulations that define inappropriate or prohibited activity.

Content validity: The degree to which the items on a test are a representative sample of the items relevant to the ability being measured.

Contiguity learning: Learning that occurs when two events become associated with one another because of continued simultaneous presentation.

Continuous development: View stating that later development is predicted from and built directly on earlier development.

Control group: A group of subjects in an experiment which does not receive the experimental manipulation.

Conventional moral reasoning: A stage in Kohlberg's theory in which a child considers the attitudes and values of others and their probable reaction to the action being judged.

Convergent thought: Thought that focuses on a specific task or approach to a problem.

Cooperative learning: A method of classroom organization in which students work together on classroom assignments and prepare reports in common.

Cooperative play: Play in which there is true, reciprocal interaction.

Correlation coefficient: A statistic used to measure the strength and direction of the association between two variables in a correlation.

Correlational studies: Studies that address associations between variables.

Counterconditioning: The unlearning or replacement of a response by another one.

Creative generalizations: Errors that occur when children use a linguistic form in a novel context.

Crossing over: The exchange of chromosome segments by homologous pairs.

Cross-sectional research: Research based on samples of different groups tested at the same point in time.

Crystallized intelligence: The skills and information that an individual has accumulated during his or her life.

Decentered thought: The capacity to consider multiple aspects of a situation or problem.

Deep structure: The intended meaning of a sentence.

Deferred imitation: The ability to imitate the past actions of a model.

De-idealization: An adolescent's awareness that parents are fallible.

Denotative meaning: The use of a linguistic form to refer to something.

Dependent variable: The variable in an experiment that is not manipulated and is assumed to be affected.

Depth of focus: The distance that an object can be moved and still remain in focus without an accommodation change.

Depth perception: The capacity to perceive the dimensions of height, width, and distance.

Desensitization: The process of lessening anxiety over a person or situation by bringing the anxious person into closer and closer contact with the undesirable stimulus.

Development: Aspects of change that involve qualitative rather than quantitative growth.

Developmental quotient: The score arrived at by infant intelligence scales as these tests measure skills other than intelligence.

Deviation score: A score used in intelligence testing that records in some standard unit how far above or below the average for a given age a specific child scores.

Differentiation: The increase in the complexity and specialization of an individual's repertoire of skills and abilities across time.

Diploid number of chromosomes: The full set of chromosomes, including 22 pairs of autosomes plus one pair of sex chromosomes.

Discontinuous development: The view that the effects of earlier development can be overcome by later experiences.

Discordant traits: Traits that are present in one twin but not the other.

Discounting principle: The inability to determine the true cause of an event when several possible causes are present.

Divergent thought: Thought that is involved in perceiving multiple solutions to a problem.

Dizygotic twins: Fraternal twins that result when two separate ova are fertilized by two separate sperm.

Down's syndrome: An aberration caused by an extra chromosome, which results in mental retardation and specific physical anomalies.

Ectoderm: The layer of cells that will eventually yield cells to produce the skin, eyes, ears, nose, mouth, and central nervous system.

Ego: A psychic structure in Freud's psychoanalytic theory that coordinates behavior to mediate the conflicts that arise when the id strives to satisfy a need that is unacceptable to or in conflict with the superego.

Egocentrism: The tendency for children to center on their own experiences and perceptions, rather than recognizing that others have independent experiences and perceptions.

Ego control: The way in which an individual deals with impulses, desires, and wishes.

Ego ideal: The part of the superego in Freud's psychoanalytic theory that represents the acquired goals and aspirations for appropriate, socially desirable behavior.

Ego resiliency: The way in which control is exercised; "resilient" people flexibly express and inhibit affect depending on the situation, whereas "brittle" people do not.

Emotion: A person's feelings about a person or event and the visible signs of those feelings.

Empathy: The ability for one to experience the same emotion that another person is experiencing.

Empathy training project: A program designed to foster children's emotional responsiveness, ability to recognize others' emotions, and capacity to take the perspective of others.

Endoderm: The layer of cells that will result in such body organs as the liver, pancreas, thyroid gland, and lining of the intestinal tract.

Endogenous smiles: Smiles by infants that are not tied to external stimulation.

Environmental influences: External factors such as the family, day care, and school environments, which can affect the development of the child.

Environmental view of adolescent development: View in which development is seen as a matter of acquiring the behavior patterns, attitudes, values, and general social knowledge required for adult roles in a particular society or culture.

Epigenesis: The idea that stages fall in a particular order and individuals must pass through them in consecutive order.

Erikson's Theory of Psychosocial Development: A theory of psychological development that emphasizes the importance of early social experiences.

Ethology: The study of the characteristic behaviors of species, including their adaptation to the demands and opportunities presented by their typical environments.

Ethos: The academic values that characterize a school.

Executive behaviors: Behaviors used by an infant to achieve contact or overcome a separation.

Exogenous smiles: Smiles that are elicited by some external stimulus.

Experimental group: The group of subjects in an experiment that receive the experimental manipulation.

Experimental studies: Studies in which one variable is manipulated by the experimenter to assess its effects on another, unmanipulated variable.

Expressive children: Children who first tend to learn words that refer to personal desires or aspects of social interaction.

Extension of a word: The appropriate limits of the meaning of a word.

Factor analysis: An analysis that attempts to determine the relationship of items on a test.

Familial method: The comparison of the IQ scores of various family members to assess the effects of heredity on intelligence.

Family pedigree analysis: The examination of the frequency with which characteristics are passed from generation to generation within a family.

Fast mapping: The capacity to quickly make some reasonable guess about a novel word's meaning.

Fetal alcohol syndrome: A syndrome, caused by excessive drinking by the mother during pregnancy, which causes small heads and eyes, underdeveloped brains, and congenital heart disease.

Field dependency: The ability to perceive the entire visual stimulus as a whole to such an extent that the parts cannot be readily perceived.

Field experiment: An experimental condition in which the independent variable is manipulated, but it is done so in the subject's natural environment.

Field independency: The tendency to perceive the parts of something more readily than the whole.

Fixation: The likelihood that experiences during a particular psychosexual stage of psychoanalytic theory affect behavior in regular and characteristic ways in later life.

Fluid intelligence: The thought processes that make incidental learning possible, such as memory.

Formal operational thought: The final stage in Piaget's cognitive development theory in which the person has the ability to think in abstract terms.

Fovea: The area at the center of the retina where visual information is focused most clearly.

Free morphemes: Units that are meaningful when used in isolation.

Fricatives: Consonants such as "s" that are formed by the partial blocking of air flow during production.

G factor: A "general" intelligence factor assumed to be the most important factor of human intelligence on which all other aspects of intelligence were thought to depend.

Gender consistency: A developmental stage in which children understand gender is stable across time and across situations and that changes in behavior may violate sex role stereotypes.

Gender identity: An individual's beliefs, understanding, and self-awareness of his or her own sexual status.

Gender role: The socially defined appropriate behavior for each gender.

Gender stability: A developmental stage in which a child realizes that gender is stable over time.

General inheritance: The hereditary material necessary to make an organism a member of its species.

General nominals: Words that refer to both specific objects and classes of objects.

Genes: The part of chromosomes that stores all of the heritable information that is transmitted from generation to generation.

Genotype: The genetic make-up of an individual.

Germ cells: The mature ovum and sperm that contain the haploid number of chromosomes.

Goal-correction mechanism: A mechanism that activates attachment behavior patterns to reduce anxiety caused by a separation from the caregiver or the presence of a stranger.

Gradable contrasts: A type of lexical opposites that involves a comparison along some dimension, such as hot versus cold.

Group-difference studies: *See* mean-difference research.

Habituation: The process of becoming less responsive to a stimulus after repeated exposures to it.

621

Haploid number of chromosomes: Twenty-three chromosomes including 22 non-paired autosomes and 1 sex chromosome.

Haptic system: The system of an individual that is involved with the perception of touch.

High-magnitude theory of aggression: Theory of aggression in which any behavior that is perceived as being high in intensity is considered aggressive.

Holophrase: Single words that function as complete sentences.

Horizontal décalage: Piaget's term for the development of mastery of related content areas that occurred within a stage.

Hostile aggression: Aggression in which the goal of the aggressor is the injury of another person.

Hyaline membrane disease: A condition wherein the newborn's lungs are not properly coated with surfactin and it becomes difficult or impossible to breathe.

Id: A psychic structure in Freud's psychoanalytic theory that strives for the immediate satisfaction of any aroused need.

Identification: Knowing or wanting to learn another person's behaviors, values, and expectations.

Identity diffusion: The absence of a coherent, organized, and stable sense of self.

Imaginary audience: An aspect of adolescent egocentrism in which adolescents appear to believe that they are the focus of everyone's attention.

Imprinting: The tendency for young ducklings to follow the first and closest large moving object that they encounter.

Impulsive individuals: Individuals who make decisions quickly and often arrive at erroneous conclusions.

Independent variable: The variable that is manipulated by the experimenter in a hypothesis-testing situation.

Indiscriminate attachment: An attachment made between an infant and a person, regardless of the person's specific identity.

Individuation: The process through which children acquire a sense of themselves that is separate from the family.

Informational influence: Influence derived from knowledge about behavioral patterns, attitudes, and values, and their consequences in different situations.

Information processing approach: An approach to cognitive development that is concerned with determining the capacity of information processing systems and the speed and efficiency with which these systems process information.

Informed consent: The process whereby a subject must be provided with and consent to a fully understandable description of the research and the experiences to be encountered.

Innate releasing mechanisms (Fixed-action patterns): Behaviors, similar to reflexes, which are automatically elicited by particular types of stimuli.

Instrumental aggression: Aggression in which any injury is inadvertent, but the aggressive act is instrumental in securing some other goal.

622

Instrumental learning (operant conditioning): The acquisition and maintenance of patterns of behavior that result from experiencing a reinforcing or punishing consequence.

Integration: The coordination of specific skills and abilities into broader and more effective patterns of thought and action.

Intelligence quotient: Mental age divided by chronological age times one hundred.

Intension of a word: The actual meaning of a word.

Invariant cognitive functions: Functions, such as accommodation and assimilation, which are assumed to be present at birth and retained throughout the lifespan.

Inventory approach to parenting: A pattern of parenting in which the parents' behavior can range in permissiveness and warmth.

Juvenile delinquency: A legal category referring to patterns of antisocial behavior in a juvenile.

Kinetochore: The small structure that connects two identical chromotids.

Klinefelter's syndrome: A nondisjunction caused by one too many X chromosomes, resulting in a sterile individual with male characteristics.

Kohlberg's stage theory of moral development: A typology of the considerations people make when judging the rightness or wrongness of other persons and their actions.

Kohlberg's theory of gender-role development: A framework of the development of gender-role understanding. Children go through three stages of understanding: gender identity, gender stability, and gender consistency.

Language: In humans it is a symbolic, rule-governed system that is both abstract and productive, a system that enables its speakers to produce and comprehend a wide range of utterances.

Language Acquisition Device (LAD): The innate mechanisms hypothesized by Chomsky to explain language acquisition.

Latchkey child: The term for a child who spends time alone at home after school, before his or her parents get home from work.

Latency: A temporary domination of strong libidinal influences on behavior in psychoanalytic theory.

Learned helplessness: The sense that one has little control over the outcomes of one's efforts.

Lens: The part of the eye that adjusts our focus on objects at various distances from us.

Level I intelligence: The ability to form associations.

Level II intelligence: Sophisticated cognitive abilities, such as abstract reasoning.

Lexical opposites: Terms that express opposite sides of a dimension, such as good versus bad.

Libido: The internal psychic energy assumed to motivate all action in psychoanalytic theory.

Linear perspective: A pictorial depth cue that suggests that when two parallel lines appear to be converging, the closer together the lines appear to be, the farther away that part of the surface is.

Longitudinal research: Research based on the same sample tested over a period of time.

Looming: The expansion of the size of the retinal image as an object moves closer to the observer.

Mainstreaming: The placement of a retarded child in a normal school setting.

Marginal persons: Term applied to adolescents because they typically belong to neither child nor adult social groups in the United States.

Maturationist view of adolescent development: A psychoanalytic explanation for adolescent development that emphasizes the psychological ramifications of puberty.

Mean: The arithmetic average of all of the scores within a set of scores.

Mean-difference research: Research that looks at the statistical differences between groups of individuals to see if there is a meaningful correlation.

Median: The score in the center of the distribution of a set of scores.

Meiosis: The reproduction of cells with the haploid number of chromosomes, such as the sperm and ovum.

Mental representation: The capacity to mentally represent the world.

Mental retardation: The generalized difficulty in dealing with cognitive problems in children and adults.

Mesoderm: The layer of cells that will produce the circulatory, muscular, and skeletal systems.

Metacognition: The knowledge of one's own thinking.

Metamemory: The knowledge of one's own memory.

Microvilla: Tiny hairlike structures on an ovum that embrace and may assist a present sperm to penetrate the ovum.

Minimal brain dysfunction (MBD): The great difficulty in one or more learning situations experienced by individuals who have average or above average scores on standardized intelligence tests.

Mitosis: The reproduction of cells with the diploid number of chromosomes.

Mnemonic mediational deficiency: The use of a mnemonic strategy that does not improve memory.

Mnemonic production deficiency: The failure to use a mnemonic strategy even though the capability to do so is present.

Mnemonic strategies: Behaviors, such as verbal rehearsal, which are used to aid memory.

Mode: The most frequently occurring score in a set of scores.

Modeling: *See* observational learning.

Moderately discrepant events: Events that are both familiar and novel. Piaget considered them to yield the most cognitive growth.

Monozygotic twins: Identical twins that occur when one ovum divides after it has been fertilized by a sperm.

Mood: A short-term emotional state.

Moral development: The gradual internalization of behavioral codes and values that are characteristic of the society, family, and peer groups with which one has contact.

624

Moro reflex: Upon hearing a loud sound or being suddenly lowered, a baby will throw his or her arms apart and then quickly bring them toward each other.

Morphemes: The smallest meaningful unit in a language.

Moving sociometric technique: A technique of assessing popularity by making behavioral observations on the actual number of interactions a child has in a group setting.

Myelin sheath: A sheath around the axon of nerve cells that is involved in the effective transmission of information in the nervous system.

Myelinization: The formation of the myelin sheath around the axon of nerve cells.

Nativists: Scholars who believe that heredity determines development.

Natural experiment: An experimental condition in which the independent variable is manipulated through the non-random selection of subjects.

Naturalistic observation: Observational research that is done in a "real world," uncontrolled setting.

Nature-nurture controversy: A debate regarding the relative importance of heredity and environment on development.

Neonatal period: The period between birth and 28 days of age.

Neonate (newborn): An infant under one month of age.

Neonatology: The subspecialty of pediatrics that studies and treats high-risk newborns.

Nondisjunction: An aberration that occurs when either the homologous chromosomes do not separate in the first division or the chromatids do not separate in the second division.

Norm of reciprocity: The feeling of the need to reciprocate when someone is generous or helpful.

Normative influence: Influence derived from the social pressure for one to behave as others behave.

Nucleus: The control center of the cell, which contains all of the hereditary information necessary for the cell to reproduce itself.

Nurturists: Scholars who argue that the environment determines development.

Object permanence: The knowledge that objects continue to exist even if they are no longer in our presence.

Observational learning: Learning that occurs as a result of observing the behavior of others without the need for repeated trial and error.

Occlusion: A pictoral depth cue that occurs when one object is partially hidden behind another.

Oedipus/Electra complex: Part of Freud's psychoanalytic theory in which internal conflicts arise when the libidinal cathexis shifts to the genitals and results in sexual motives and desires for the opposite-sexed parent.

One-one principle: In counting, one counts each item once and only once, using a different number for each item.

Oogenesis: The process of the production of ova.

Operant conditioning: *See* instrumental learning.

625

Operating space: The amount of space available for operating on information in information processing theories.

Optic nerve: The nerve that transmits nerve impulses from the retina to the brain.

Order-irrelevance principle: The order in which objects are counted does not matter.

Organismic-developmental theory: Werner's theory of development that states that children follow the principles of differentiation and integration in psychological, physical, motor, and sensory development.

Overextensions: Errors in which children use a term to refer to too many objects.

Overregularizations: Errors that occur when children apply a regular rule to irregular words.

Ovum: The female germ cell.

Parallel play: Children play side by side, doing similar things, but not really playing with one another.

Peer: Agemates or people who show similar levels of capability or development to one another.

Peer socialization: Interactions among peers that contribute to the social development of all participating children.

Perception: The brain's interpretation of a sensory organ's response to a presented stimulus.

Perceptual role taking: The process of inferring what another person sees and experiences when observing a scene or event from the other's own physical perspective.

Permissive parents: Parents who generally allow children to play a role in establishing standards of conduct and make relatively few demands on them.

Phenotype: The outward appearance of an individual.

Phenylketonuria (PKU): An organic problem due to an enzyme deficiency and resulting in mental retardation.

Phoneme: A class of sounds that are not physically identical to one another but that speakers of a language treat as equivalent.

Phonology: The study of the perception and production of sounds.

Pictorial depth cues: Monocular vision cues that allow depth perception.

Placenta: A protective but permeable barrier that surrounds the amnion and allows nutrients to reach the embryo and waste products to pass into the mother's bloodstream.

Pleasure principle: A behavioral pattern in Freud's psychoanalytic theory that dictates that the satisfaction of needs is to be achieved immediately in the most direct fashion possible, regardless of the possibility of punishment or other dangers.

Polydactyly: A condition in which a child is born with six fingers on each hand and six toes on each foot.

Popularity: The degree to which one is actively sought out by others.

Postmature babies: Babies born after the 43rd week of pregnancy.

Postterm births: Births that occur after the 43rd week of pregnancy.

Prechtl scale: A scale used to assess the soundness of the newborn's nervous system.

Predictive validity: The degree to which scores on a test are capable of accurately predicting some relevant criterion.

Premature babies: Babies born before the 37th week of pregnancy.

Pre-moral stage of morality: A stage of Kohlberg's model in which a child judges the morality of another person in terms of the extent to which the other person conforms to the demands of authority figures and avoids punishment.

Prenatal development: Development from conception to birth.

Preoperational stage: The second stage in Piaget's cognitive development theory in which the major accomplishment is the emergence and organization of mental operations.

Preterm births: Births that occur before the 37th week of pregnancy.

Primary changes: Changes that happen to everyone and that influence further development.

Primary circular reaction: A reaction that occurs when an infant accidentally performs some action that produces an interesting effect involving her own body. She then attempts to reproduce the action to again experience the result.

Primary oocytes: The cells at the beginning of oogenesis.

Primary spermatocytes: The cells at the beginning of spermatogenesis.

Primitive emotions: Certain core emotions (joy, fear, anger) that are present throughout life.

Primordial gonadal streak: The cells during the early stages of prenatal development that eventually turn into external sex genetalia.

Principled moral reasoning: A stage in Kohlberg's model in which the child considers abstract principles or values in determining the morality of an action.

Processes: Causal mechanisms underlying developmental change.

Productive word blend: An error that occurs when children combine the phonological patterns of two words to form a novel lexical item.

Psychoanalytic theory: Theory proposed by Freud arguing that a person's thoughts and actions are motivated by known and unknown internal psychological structures.

Psychodynamic behavior theory: A reinterpretation of Freud's psychoanalytic theory that emphasizes that aspects of personality and social development are learned during the course of socialization.

Psychometric approach: An approach to intelligence that assumes intelligence has factors and these factors can be measured by standardized tests.

Psychosexual stages: In Freud's psychoanalytic theory, the stages are distinct developmental periods during which experiences have different consequences for a person's eventual personality and interpersonal relations.

Psychosocial moratorium: A period of retreat from struggling with decisions, often involved with identity crisis issues.

627

Puberty: The point at which reproductive maturity is reached.

Pubescence: The period of physical changes that leads to reproductive maturity.

Punishment: The experience of an aversive event, either because something negative happens or because a positive condition is withdrawn.

Pupillary reflex: The reflex that controls the amount of light entering the eye.

Reality principle: A principle in Freud's psychoanalytic theory that suggests that the ego is governed by reality demands.

Recast: A response to a child's ungrammatical sentence that has different syntactic form but similar semantic content to the child's utterance.

Recursive thinking: Thinking about people thinking about something else.

Referential children: Children who first learn words that refer to objects.

Reflective individuals: Individuals who approach intellectual tasks in a deliberate and time-consuming fashion.

Reflexes: Involuntary responses to stimulation.

Regression: Part of the psychoanalytic theory in which a person returns to earlier modes of gratification during periods of stress or frustration in later life.

Relativism: The feeling that moral judgments can never be absolute, but must be reached relative to the situation.

Reliability: A measure of the ability of a test to obtain the same results on subsequent testing.

REM: A period of sleep during which a person experiences rapid eye movements, changes in heart rate and blood pressure, and, in adults, dreams.

Resistance to deviation (temptation): A child's obedient compliance in terms of not doing something that is enjoyable because he or she has been told not to.

Retaliation: The decrease in generosity toward one who has not been helpful to you.

Retina: The part of the eye that transforms light into signals that are transmitted to the brain.

Role-taking: The ability of an individual to infer another person's perception of and reaction to a personal or social situation.

Rooting reflex: When infants' cheeks are stroked, they will turn their heads in that direction and open their mouths.

Saccade: A smooth, rapid eye motion that moves a visual image to the center of the field of vision where it can be seen more clearly.

School phobia: A fear of school that can lead to a refusal to attend.

Secondary changes: The aspects of behavior that seem to be especially affected by the primary changes of adolescence, and the interplay of these primary changes with the influential settings and conditions of adolescents' lives.

Secondary circular reactions: A reaction that occurs when an infant performs a chance action that produces an interesting result in the external world. The infant then repeats the action to achieve the same result again.

Secondary oocyte: The one large cell that is formed after the division of the primary oocyte during oogenesis.

Secondary sex characteristics: Characteristics that denote sexual maturity but are not essential to sexual functioning, such as male facial hair and female breasts.

Secondary spermatocytes: Cells resulting from the division of primary spermatocytes during spermatogenesis.

Semantics: The study of the attachment of meaning to linguistic forms.

Sensation: A sensory organ's response to some stimulus.

Sensitive periods: Periods during which a developing organism seems to be particularly susceptible to specific forms of experience.

Sensorimotor thought stage: Piaget's first cognitive development stage in which the infant actively searches for sensory and motor experiences.

Shape constancy: The ability to recognize the true shape of an object despite changes in the object's orientation.

Signaling behaviors: Behaviors that maintain contact across a distance and alert caregivers to the infant's location or need for help.

Size constancy: The ability to recognize the actual size of an object despite changes in the size of the retinal image.

Smooth pursuit eye movements: Eye movements that are slower than saccades and allow adults to fixate on and visually follow moving objects.

Social conventions: The formal and informal practices and rules that are set up to govern the day-to-day operations of communities and organizations.

Social referencing: The effect of another person's behavior on the ability of a child to organize his or her behavior in unfamiliar settings.

Social role-taking: The process of making inferences about the internal states of others.

Socially scripted behavior: Behavior that is heavily determined by social expectations and social significance.

Sociometric status: A measurement of acceptance by peers.

Solitary play: Play in which children merely look at one another rather than truly play.

Specific attachment: An attachment between an infant and a particular person or persons.

Specific factors: Factors of intelligence assumed to be pertinent to only one specific type of intellectual task.

Specific inheritance: The hereditary material that differentiates each member from the other members of its species.

Specific nominals: Words that refer to only specific objects or indiviuals.

Speech stream: An undifferentiated series of speech sounds.

Sperm: The male germ cell.

Spermatogenesis: The process of sperm production.

Spermatogonia: Cells within the human male's testes, each of which contains the diploid number of chromosomes.

629

Stable order principle: The principle that states that the order in which one counts should always be the same.

Stage: A relatively discrete period of time in which the development of one particular capability or behavior pattern predominates.

Statistical significance: A measure of the degree to which a finding is expected to occur if the study were repeated, and the degree to which the finding is not due to chance.

Stereotype: The attribution of specific, often unjustified, characteristics and expectations to all members of a group.

Stimulus: Any form of physical energy to which an organism is capable of responding.

Stop consonants: Consonants such as "p" that are formed by the complete blockage of air flow during production.

Storage space: The amount of space available for storing information in memory in information processing theories.

Strange situation: An experimental technique used to study the different kinds of attachments infants have.

Strategies (executive maneuvers): Strategies used in learning material or solving problems, such as writing things down or the use of mnemonic devices.

Structured observation: Observational research that is done in a structured setting, thereby controlling some independent variables.

Sucking reflex: When an object is placed in an infant's mouth, the infant will automatically suck.

Sudden infant death syndrome (SIDS): The unexplained death of an infant while sleeping. It is also called crib death.

Superego: A component of Freud's psychoanalytic theory that functions to place limitations on impulses of the id through societal ideals.

Surface structure: The actual spoken sentence.

Syntax: The manner in which words and bound morphemes are ordered relative to one another to produce acceptable and comprehensible sentences.

Tabula rasa: Locke's view of the mind—a blank slate on which experience imposes content and structure.

Telegraphic speech: Two-word speech in which children use only the most important words.

Temperament: The indiviual tendency toward the expression of emotion and responsiveness to stimulation that influence both the internal and interpersonal life of persons.

Teratogens: Environmental agents that may harm a developing organism.

Tertiary circular reactions: Actions that an infant performs to achieve a variation in the results of her actions.

Test norms: Some objective standard of comparison relating a given individual's performance to that of a specified comparison group.

Test-retest stability: The degree of correlation of scores between a first and a later testing session.

Testosterone: The hormone secreted by the testes that results in the formation of the testicles and penis.

Texture gradients: A pictorial depth cue referring to the fact that the texture of near surfaces appears to be more finely grained than does the texture of far surfaces.

Thalidomide: A drug once prescribed to pregnant women to alleviate morning sickness that caused various types of deformities among their newborn infants.

Transactionalist view of adolescent development: View in which changes in the individual are assumed to trigger new expectations and altered reactions from other persons, which in turn influence changes in the individual.

Trophoblast: The protective layer of cells around the inner cell mass that provides the cellular basis for the developing organism.

Turner's syndrome: An aberration caused by the absence of a chromosome, leaving the individual with only one X chromosome and resulting in female characteristics but nonfunctional sexual organs.

Typology approach to parenting: An approach to the pattern of parenting in which three types of parents are identified: authoritarian, permissive, and authoritative.

Ultrasound: A technique using sounds to create an image of a developing organism in the prenatal environment.

Umbilical cord: A structure that links the embryo to the placenta.

Underachievement: The failure to perform at a level commensurate with one's abilities.

Underextensions: Errors in which children use a term in an overly narrow sense.

Ungradable contrasts: A type of lexical opposite that involves absolute complementary subsets, such as male versus female.

Vagina (birth canal): The passage leading from the vulva to the uterus.

Variable: The behavior of interest in a hypothesis-testing situation.

Verbal rehearsal: The verbal repetition of material that is to be remembered.

Vicarious catharsis: The lessening of aggressive energy by viewing, or in some other fashion experiencing, aggressive behavior indirectly through the behavior of someone else.

Visual accommodation: The ability to shift one's focus from one distance to another.

Visual acuity: The ability to detect differences in visual patterns.

Visual cortex: The part of the brain involved in visual development.

Visual screening: Eye movement for the purpose of inspecting objects.

Visual tracking: Eye movements to follow the movement of objects.

Vocal tract: Tract comprised of the oral and nasal cavities through which air is expelled in the production of sound.

Zygote: The fertilized ovum.

Bibliography

Abel, E. L. (1981). Behavioral teratology of alcohol. *Psychological Bulletin, 90*, 564–581.

Abramov, I., Gordon, J., Hendrickson, A., Hainline, L., Dobson, V., & LaBossiere, E. (1982). The retina of the newborn infant. *Science, 217*, 265–267.

Abravanel, E. & Gingold, H. (1985). Learning via observation during the second year of life. *Developmental Psychology, 21*, 614–623.

Abravanel, E., & Sigafoos, A. (1984). Exploring the presence of imitation during early infancy. *Child Development, 55*, 381–392.

Adams, R., Maurer, D., & Davis, M. (1986). Newborn's discrimination of chromatic from achromatic stimuli. *Journal of Experimental Child Psychology, 41*, 267–281.

Adams, R. L., & Phillips, B. N. (1972). Motivational and achievement differences among children of various ordinal birth positions. *Child Development, 43*, 155–164.

Adamsons, K. (1975). Obstetric considerations in the prevention of perinatal asphyxia. In K. Adamsons & H. Fox (Eds.), *Progress in clinical and biological research* (Vol. 2). New York: Alan R. Liss.

Adelson, J. (1971). The political imagination of the young adolescent. In J. Kagan & R. Coles (Eds.), Twelve to sixteen: Early adolescence (pp. 1013–1050). New York: Norton.

Adelson, J., Green, B., & O'Neil, R. (1969). The growth of the idea of law in adolescence. *Developmental Psychology, 1*, 327–332.

Adelson, J., & O'Neil, R. (1966). Growth of political ideas in adolescence: The sense of community. *Journal of Personality and Social Psychology, 4*, 295–306.

Adler, R. P., Lesser, G. S., Meringoff, L., Robertson, T. S., Rossiter, J. R., & Ward, S. (1980). *The effects of television advertising on children*. Lexington, MA: Lexington Books.

Ainsworth, M., Blehar, M., Waters, E., & Wall, S. (1978). *Patterns of Attachment*. Hillsdale, NJ: Erlbaum.

Ainsworth, M., & Wittig, B. (1969). Attachment and exploratory behavior of one-year-olds in a strange situation. In B. Foss (Ed.), *Determinants of infant behavior* (Vol. 4). New York: Wiley.

Aldous, J. (1978). *Family careers: Developmental changes in families*. New York: Wiley.

Alegria, J., & Noirot, E. (1978). Neonate orientation behaviour towards the human voice. *International Journal of Behavioural Development, 1*, 291–312.

Algozzine, O. (1977). Perceived attractiveness and classroom interactions. *Journal of Experimental Education, 46*, 63–66.

Allen, J. (1978). *Visual acuity development in human infants up to 6 months of age*. Unpublished doctoral dissertation, University of Washington, Seattle.

Allen, T. (1982, March). *Oral-oral and oral-visual object discrimination*. Paper presented at the meeting of the International Conference on Infant Studies, Austin, TX.

Allen, V. L. (1976). *Children as teachers: Theory and research on tutoring*. New York: Academic Press.

Allen, V. L., & Newtson, D. (1972). Development of

conformity and independence. *Journal of Personality and Social Psychology, 22,* 18–30.

Allender, J. (1982). Affective education. In H. E. Mitzel (Ed.), *Encyclopedia of educational research* (5th ed.). New York: Free Press.

Allport, G. W. (1954). The historical background of modern social psychology. In G. Lindzey (Ed.), *Handbook of social psychology* (Vol. 2). Cambridge, MA: Addison-Wesley.

American Humane Association. (1984). *Trends in child abuse and neglect: A national perspective.* Denver, CO: American Humane Association.

Amir, Y. (1976). The role of intergroup contact in change of prejudice and ethnic relations. In P. Katz (Ed.), *Towards the elimination of racism.* New York: Pergamon.

Anastasi, A. (1988). *Psychological testing* (6th ed.). New York: Macmillan.

Anderson, D. R., & Collins, P. A. (1988). The impact on children's education: Television's influence on cognitive development. Washington, DC: U.S. Office of Education.

Anglin, J. (1977). *Word, object, and conceptual development.* New York: Norton.

Angoff, W. H. (1988). The nature-nurture debate, aptitudes, and group differences. *American Psychologist, 43,* 713–720.

Aoki, C., & Siekevitz, P. (1988). Plasticity and brain development. *Scientific American, 259,* 56–64.

Apgar, V. (1953). Proposal for a new method of evaluation of newborn infants. *Current Researches in Anesthesia and Analgesia, 32,* 260–267.

Apgar, V., & Beck, J. (1974). *Is my baby all right?* New York: Pocket Books.

Appleton, T., Clifton, R., & Goldberg, S. (1975). The development of behavioral competence in infancy. In F. Horowitz (Ed.), *Review of Child Development Research, 4,* 101–186. Chicago: University of Chicago Press.

Arbuthnot, J. (1975). Modification of moral judgment through role playing. *Developmental Psychology, 11,* 319–324.

Arend, R., Gove, F., & Sroufe, L. A. (1979). Continuity of individual adaptation from infancy to kindergarten: A predictive study of ego-resiliency and curiosity in preschoolers. *Child Development, 50,* 950–959.

Aries, P. (1962). *Centuries of childhood.* New York: Knopf.

Aronfreed, J. (1965). *Punishment, learning, and internalization: Some parameters of reinforcement and cognition.* Paper presented at the biennial meeting of the So-

ciety for Research in Child Development, Minneapolis, MN.

Aronfreed, J. (1969). The concept of internalization. In D. A. Goslin (Ed.), *Handbook of socialization theory and research.* Chicago, IL: Rand McNally.

Aronfreed, J. (1976). Moral development from the standpoint of a general psychological theory. In T. Lickona (Ed.), *Moral development and behavior: Theory, research, and social issues* (pp. 54–69). New York: Holt, Rinehart & Winston.

Aronson, E., & Carlsmith, J. M. (1963). Effect of severity of threat on the devaluation of forbidden behavior. *Journal of Abnormal and Social Psychology, 66,* 584–588.

Arras, J. D. (1985). Toward an ethics of ambiguity. *Hastings Center Report, 14,* 25–33.

Aslin, R. (1981a). Development of smooth pursuit in human infants. In D. Fisher, R. Monty, & J. Senders (Eds.), *Eye movements: Cognition and visual perception.* Hillsdale, NJ: Erlbaum.

Aslin, R. (1981b). Experiential influences and sensitive periods in perceptual development. In R. Aslin, J. Alberts, & M. Petersen (Eds.), *Development of perception: Psychobiological perspectives: Vol. 2. The visual system.* New York: Academic Press.

Aslin, R. (1987). Visual and auditory development in infancy. In J. Osofsky (Ed.), *Handbook of Infant Development* (2nd ed.). New York: Wiley.

Aslin, R., Pisoni, D., & Jusczyk, P. (1983). Auditory development and speech perception in infancy. In P. H. Mussen, M. Haith, & J. J. Campos (Eds.), *Handbook of child psychology: Vol. 2. Infancy and developmental psychobiology* (4th ed., pp. 573–687). New York: Wiley.

Atkinson, J., & Braddick, O. (1981). Acuity, contrast sensitivity, and accommodation in infancy. In R. Aslin, J. Alberts, & M. Peterson (Eds.), *Development of perception: Vol. 1. Psychobiological perspective.* New York: Academic Press.

Atkinson, K., McWhinney, B., & Stoel, C. (1970). An experiment on the recognition of babbling. *Papers and Research in Child Language Development, 1,* 71–76.

Austin, V., Ruble, D., & Trabasso, T. (1976). Recall and order effects as factors in children's moral judgments. *Child Development, 48,* 470–474.

Babad, Y., Alexander, I., & Babad, E. (1983). Returning the smile of the stranger: Developmental patterns and socialization factors. *Monographs of the Society for Research in Child Development, 48*(5, Serial No. 203).

Bahrick, H., Bahrick, P., & Wittlinger, R. (1975). Fifty years of memory for names and faces: A cross-sectional approach. *Journal of Experimental Psychology: General*, *104*, 54–75.

Bahrick, L. (1983). Infants' perception of substance and temporal synchrony in multimodal events. *Infant Behavior and Development*, *6*, 429–451.

Bahrick, L., Walker, A., & Neisser, U. (1981). Selective looking by infants. *Cognitive Psychology*, *13*, 377–390.

Baillargen, R. (1987). Object permanence in $3\frac{1}{2}$- and $4\frac{1}{2}$-month-old infants. *Developmental Psychology*, *23*, 655–664.

Baillargen, R., Spelke, E., & Wasserman, S. (1985). Object permanence in five-month-old infants. *Cognition*, *20*, 191–208.

Bainum, C., Lounsbury, K., & Pollio, H. (1984). The development of smiling and laughing in nursery-school children. *Child Development*, *55*, 1946–1957.

Bakeman, R., & Brown, J. (1980). Early interactions: Consequences for social and mental development at three years. *Child Development*, *51*, 437–447.

Baker, R., Brown, K., & Gottfried, A. (1982, March). *Ontogeny of tactile visual cross-modal transfer*. Paper presented at the meeting of the International Conference on Infant Studies, Austin, TX.

Baldwin, A. L. (1949). The effect of home environment on nursery school behavior. *Child Development*, *20*, 49–62.

Baldwin, J. M. (1906). *Social and ethical interpretations of mental development*. New York: Macmillan.

Ball, W., & Tronick, E. (1971). Infant responses to impending collision: Optical and real. *Science*, *171*, 818–820.

Bandura, A. (1964). The stormy decade: Fact or fiction? *Psychology in the Schools*, *1*, 224–231.

Bandura, A. (1965). Influence of models' reinforcement contingencies on the acquisition of imitative responses. *Journal of Personality and Social Psychology*, *1*, 589–595.

Bandura, A. (1969). *Principles of behavior modification*. New York: Holt, Rinehart & Winston.

Bandura, A. (1977). *Social learning theory*. Englewood Cliffs, NJ: Prentice-Hall.

Bandura, A., & MacDonald, F. (1963). Influence of social reinforcement and the behavior of models in shaping children's moral judgments. *Journal of Abnormal and Social Psychology*, *67*, 274–281.

Bandura, A., & Menlove, F. L. (1968). Factors determining vicarious extinction of avoidance behavior through symbolic modeling. *Journal of Personality and Social Psychology*, *8*, 99–108.

Bandura, A., Ross, D., & Ross, S. A. (1963). Imitation of film-mediated aggressive models. *Journal of Abnormal and Social Psychology*, *66*, 3–11.

Bandura, A., & Walters, R. (1959). *Adolescent aggression*. New York: Ronald Press.

Bandura, A., & Walters, R. H. (1963). *Social learning and personality development* (Vol. 2). New York: Holt.

Banks, M. (1980). Infant refraction and accommodation. *International Ophthalmology Clinics*, *20*, 205–232.

Banks, M., & Salapatek, P. (1981). Infant pattern vision: A new approach based on the contrast sensitivity function. *Journal of Experimental Child Psychology*, *31*, 1–45.

Banks, M., & Salapatek, P. (1983). Infant visual perception. In P. H. Mussen, M. Haith, & J. Campos (Eds.), *Handbook of Child Psychology: Vol. 2. Infancy and developmental psychobiology* (4th ed., pp. 436–571). New York: Wiley.

Banks, M., Stephens, B., & Hartmann, E. (1985). The development of basic mechanisms of pattern vision: Spatial frequency channels. *Journal of Experimental Child Psychology*, *40*, 501–527.

Barcus, F. E. (1978). Commercial children's television on weekends and weekday afternoons. Newtonville, MA: Action for Children's Television.

Barenboim, C. (1977). Developmental changes in the interpersonal cognitive system from middle childhood to adolescence. *Child Development*, *48*, 1467–1474.

Barenboim, C. (1978). Development of recursive and nonrecursive thinking about persons. *Developmental Psychology*, *14*, 419–420.

Barenboim, C. (1981). The development of person perception in childhood and adolescence: From behavioral comparisons to psychological constructs to psychological comparisons. *Child Development*, *52*, 129–144.

Barker, R. G., & Gump, P. V. (1964). *Big school, small school: High school size and student behavior*. Stanford, CA: Stanford University Press.

Barker, R. G., & Wright, H. F. (1955a). *Midwest and its children*. New York: Harper & Row.

Barker, R. G., & Wright, H. F. (1955b). *One boy's day*. New York: Harper & Row.

Barnes, K. E. (1971). Preschool play norms: A replication. *Developmental Psychology*, *5*, 99–103.

Barnett, K., Darcie, G., Holland, C., & Kobasigawa, A. (1982). Children's cognitions about effective helping. *Developmental Psychology*, *18*, 267–277.

Barrera, M., Rosenbaum, P., & Cunningham, C. (1986). Early home intervention with low-birth-weight infants and their parents. *Child Development*, *57*, 20–33.

635

Barrett, D., & Yarrow, M. R. (1977). Prosocial behavior, social inferential ability, and assertiveness in children. *Child Development, 48,* 475–481.

Barrett, M. D. (1983, September). *Scripts, prototypes, and the early acquisition of word meaning.* Paper presented at the British Psychological Society Developmental Section Annual Conference, Oxford University, England.

Barrett, M. D. (1986). Early semantic representations and early word-usage. In S. Kuczaj & M. D. Barrett (Eds.), *The development of word meaning.* New York: Springer-Verlag.

Baskett, L. M. (1984). Ordinal position differences in children's family interactions. *Developmental Psychology, 20,* 1026–1031.

Bauer, P., & Mandler, J. (1989). One thing follows another: Effects of temporal structure on 1- to 2-year-old's recall of events. *Developmental Psychology, 25,* 197–206.

Baumrind, D. (1971). Current patterns of parental authority. *Developmental Psychology Monographs, 4,* No. 1, Pt. 2.

Baumrind, D. (1972). Socialization and instrumental competence in young children. In W. W. Hartup (Ed.), *The young child* (Vol. 2). Washington, DC: National Association for the Education of Young Children.

Baumrind, D. (1973). In A. D. Pick (Ed.), *Minnesota Symposia on Child Psychology.* (Vol. 7). Minneapolis: University of Minnesota Press.

Baumrind, D. (1986). Sex differences in moral reasoning: Response to Walker's (1984) conclusion that there are none. *Child Development, 57,* 511–521

Baumrind, D. (1987). A developmental perspective on adolescent risk taking in contemporary America. *New Directions in Child Development, 37,* 93–126.

Bayley, N. (1969). *The Bayley scales of infant development.* New York: Psychological Corporation.

Beasley, W. (1933). Visual pursuit in 109 white and 142 Negro newborn infants. *Child Development, 4,* 108–120.

Becker, J. A. (1982). Children's strategic use of requests to mark and manipulate social status. In S. Kuczaj (Ed.), *Language development: Vol. 2. Language, thought, and culture.* Hillsdale, NJ: Erlbaum.

Becker, J. A. (1989). Preschoolers' use of number words to denote one-to-one correspondence. *Child Development, 60,* 1147–1157.

Becker, W. C. (1964). Consequences of parental discipline. In M. L. Hoffman & L. W. Hoffman (Eds.), *Review of child development research* (Vol. 1). New York: Russell Sage.

Beckwith, L., & Parmelee, A., Jr. (1986). EEG patterns of preterm infants, home environment, and later IQ. *Child Development, 57,* 777–789.

Bee, H. L., Barnard, K. E., Eyres, S. J., Gray, C., Hammond, M. A., Spietz, A. L., Snyder, C., & Clark, B. (1982). Predictions of IQ and language skill from perinatal status, child performance, family characteristics, and mother-infant interacton. *Child Development, 53,* 1134–1156.

Bee, H. L., Disbrow, M. A., Johnson-Crowley, N., & Barnard, K. E. (1981). *Parent-child interactions during teaching in abusing and non-abusing families.* Paper presented at the meeting of the Society for Research in Child Development, Boston, MA.

Bell, A. (1969). Role modeling of fathers in adolescence and young adulthood. *Journal of Counseling Psychology, 16,* 30–35.

Bell, A., Weinberg, M., & Hammersmith, S. (1981). *Sexual preference: Its development in men and women.* Bloomington: Indiana University Press.

Bell, D. (Ed.). (1980). *Shades of brown: New perspectives on school desegregation.* New York: Teachers College Press.

Bell, H., Avery, A., Jenkins, D., Feld, J., & Schoenrock, C. (1985). Family relationships and social competence during late adolescence. *Journal of Youth and Adolescence, 14,* 109–119.

Bell, R. Q. (1968). A reinterpretation of the direction of effects in studies of socialization. *Psychological Review, 75,* 81–85.

Bell, R. Q., & Harper, L. V. (1977). *Child effects on adults.* Hillsdale, NJ: Erlbaum.

Bell, R. Q., Weller, G. M., & Waldrip, M. F. (1971). Newborn and preschooler: Organization of behavior and relations between periods. *Monographs of the Society for Research in Child Development, 36*(1–2, Serial No. 142).

Belli, G., & Gatewood, T. (1987). Readiness for formal learning in the middle grades: A study of predictors for success in eighth grade algebra. *Journal of Early Adolescence, 7,* 441–451.

Belsky, J. (1984). Two waves of day care research: Developmental effects and conditions of quality. In R. McAinslie (Ed.), *The child and the day care setting* (pp. 1–33). New York: Praeger.

Belsky, J., & Pensky, E. (1988). Developmental history, personality, and family relationships: Toward an emergent family system. In R. Hinde & J. Stevenson-

Hinde (Eds.), *Relationships within families* (pp. 193–217). Oxford: Oxford University Press.

Belsky, J., Rovine, M., & Fish, M. (1989). The developing family system. In M.Gunnar & E. Thelen (Eds.), *Minnesota Symposia on Child Psychology* (Vol. 22, pp. 119–166). Hillsdale, NJ: Erlbaum.

Belson, W. (1978). *Television violence and the adolescent boy*. Westmead, England: Saxon House, Teakfield.

Bench, J., Collyer, Y., Mentz, L., & Wilson, I. (1976). Studies in infant behavioural audiometry: I. Neonates. *Audiology, 15*, 85–105.

Benedict, R. (1954). Continuities and discontinuities in cultural conditioning. In W. E. Martin & C. B. Stendler (Eds.), *Readings in child development* (pp. 142–148). New York: Harcourt Brace.

Benjamin, H. (1966). *The transsexual phenomenon*. New York: Julian Press.

Benn, R. (1986). Factors promoting secure attachment relationships between employed mothers and their sons. *Child Development, 57*, 1224–1231.

Berenda, R. W. (1950). *The influence of the group on the judgments of children*. New York: King's Crown Press.

Berko, J., & Brown, R. (l960). Psycholinguistic research methods. In P. Mussen (Ed.), *Handbook of research methods in child development*. New York: Wiley.

Berkowitz, L. (1989). Frustration-aggression hypothesis: Examination and reformulation. *Psychological Bulletin, 106*(1), 59–73.

Berlyne, D. (1960). *Conflict, arousal, and curiosity*. New York: McGraw-Hill.

Bernard, J., & Sontag, L. (1947). Fetal reactivity to tonal stimulation: A preliminary report. *Journal of Genetic Psychology, 70*, 205–210.

Berndt, T. J. (1979). Developmental changes in conformity to peers and parents. *Developmental Psychology, 15*, 608–616.

Berndt, T. J. (1982). The features and effects of friendship in early adolescence. *Child Development, 53*, 1447–1460.

Berndt, T. (1985). Prosocial behavior between friends in middle childhood and early adolescence. *Journal of Early Adolescence, 5*, 307–317.

Berndt, T. J., & Berndt, E. (1975). Children's use of motives and intentionality in personal perception and moral judgment. *Child Development, 46*, 904–912.

Berndt, T. J., Caparulo, B. K., McCartney, K., & Moore, A. (1980). *Processes and outcomes of social influence in children's peer groups*. Unpublished manuscript, Yale University, New Haven, CT.

Berndt, T. J., & Hoyle, S. (1985). Stability and change

in childhood and adolescent friendships. *Developmental Psychology, 21*, 1007–1024.

Berndt, T. J., McCartney, K. A., Caparulo, B. K., & Moore, A. M. (1983–1984). The effects of group discussion on children's moral decisions. *Social Cognition, 2*, 343–360.

Bertenthal, B., Campos, J., & Barrett, K. (1984). Self produced locomotion: An organizer of emotional, cognitive, and social development in infancy. In R. Emde & R. Harmon (Eds.), *Continuities and discontinuities in development*. New York: Plenum.

Best, D. L., Field, J. T., & Williams, J. E. (1976). Color bias in a sample of young German children. *Psychological Reports, 38*, 1145–1146.

Best, D. L., Naylor, C. E., & Williams, J. E. (1975). Extension of color bias research to young French and Italian children. *Journal of Cross-cultural Psychology, 6*, 390–405.

Biber, H., Miller, L. B., & Dyer, J. L. (1972). Feminization in preschool. *Developmental Psychology, 7*, 86.

Bichard, S., Alden, L., Walker, L., & McMahon, R. (1988). Friendship understanding in socially accepted, rejected, and neglected children. *Merrill-Palmer Quarterly, 3*, 33–46.

Bigelow, B. J. (1977). Children's friendship expectations: A cognitive developmental study. *Child Development, 48*, 246–253.

Bigelow, B. J., & La Gaipa, J. J. (1975). Children's written descriptions of friendship: A multidimensional analysis. *Developmental Psychology, 11*, 857–858.

Binet, A., & Simon, T. (1905). Upon the necessity of establishing a scientific diagnosis of inferior states of intelligence. In A. Anastasi (Ed.), *Individual differences*. New York: Wiley, 1965. (Translated from *Annee Psychologique, 11*, 163–191.)

Binet, A., & Simon, T. (1908). The development of intelligence in the child. In A. Anastasi (Ed.), *Individual differences*. New York: Wiley, 1965. (Translated from *Annee Psychologique, 14*, 90.)

Bjork, E., & Cummings, E. (1983). Infant search errors: Stage of concept development or stage of memory development. *Memory and Cognition, 12*, 1–19.

Bjorklund, D. F. (1987). A note on neonatal imitation. *Developmental Review, 7*, 86–92.

Bjorklund, D. F. (1989). *Children's thinking*. Pacific Grove, CA: Brooks/Cole.

Bjorklund, D. F., & Curtiss, D. D. (1989). Cognitive

styles. In D. F. Bjorklund (Ed.), *Children's thinking*. Pacific Grove, CA: Brooks/Cole.

Bjorklund, D. F., & Frankel, M. T. (1989). Information processing approaches. In D. F. Bjorklund (Ed.), *Children's thinking*. Pacific Grove, CA: Brooks/Cole.

Blaney, P. (1986). Affect and memory: A review. *Psychological Bulletin, 99*, 229–246.

Blasi, A. (1980). Moral cognition and moral action. *Psychological Bulletin, 88*, 1–20.

Blass, E., Ganchrow, J., & Steiner, J. (1984). Classical conditioning in newborn humans 2–48 hours of age. *Infant Behavior and Development, 7*, 223–235.

Block, J. H. (1978). Another look at sex differentiation in the socialization behaviors of mothers and fathers. In J. Sherman & F. L. Denmark (Eds.). *The psychology of women: Future directions in research*. New York: Psychological Dimensions.

Block, J. H., & Block, J. (1980). The role of ego-control and ego-resiliency in the organization of behavior. In W. A. Collins (Ed.), *Minnesota Symposia on Child Psychology* (Vol. 13). Hillsdale, NJ: Erlbaum.

Bloom, B. S. (1964). *Stability and change in human characteristics*. New York: Wiley.

Bloom, L. M. (1973). *One word at a time: The use of single word utterances before syntax*. The Hague: Mouton.

Bloom, L. M., Lightbown, P., & Hood, L. (1975). Structure and variation in child language. *Monographs of the Society for Research in Child Development, 40*(2, Serial No. 160).

Bloom, L. M., Rocissano, L., & Hood, L. (1976). Adult-child discourse: Developmental interaction between information processing and linguistic knowledge. *Cognitive Psychology, 8*, 521-552.

Boismier, J. (1977). Visual stimulation and the wake-sleep behavior in human neonates. *Developmental Psychobiology, 10*, 219–227.

Bolger, N., Downey, G., Walker, E., & Steininger, P. (1989). The onset of suicidal ideation in childhood and adolescence. *Journal of Youth and Adolecence, 18*, 110–123.

Bolton, P. (1983). Drugs of abuse. In D. Hawkins (Ed.), *Drugs and pregnancy: Human teratogenesis and related problems*. Edinburgh: Churchill-Livingstone.

Borke, H. (1971). Interpersonal perception of young children: Egocentrism or empathy? *Developmental Psychology, 5*, 263–269.

Bornstein, M. H. (1975). Qualities of color vision in infancy. *Journal of Experimental Child Psychology, 19*, 401–419.

Bornstein, M. H. (1976). Infants are trichromats. *Journal of Experimental Child Psychology, 21*, 425–445.

Bornstein, M. H., Kessen, W., & Weiskopf, S. (1976). Color vision and hue categorization in young human infants. *Journal of Experimental Psychology, Human Perception and Performance, 2*, 115–129.

Bornstein, M. H., & Sigman, M. D. (1986). Continuity in mental development from infancy. *Child Development, 57*, 251–274.

Borstelmann, L. J. (1983). Children before psychology. In P. H. Mussen & W. Kessen (Eds.), *Handbook of child psychology: Vol. 1: History, theory, and methods* (4th ed., pp. 3–40). New York: Wiley.

Bouchard, T. J., Jr., & McGue, M. (1981). Familial studies of intelligence: A review. *Science, 212*, 1055–1059.

Bower, G. (1981). Mood and memory. *American Psychologist, 36*, 128–148.

Bower, T. (1971). The object in the world of the infant. *Scientific American, 225*, 30–38.

Bower, T. (1972). Object perception in infants. *Perception, 1*, 15–30.

Bower, T., Broughton, J., & Moore, M. (1970). Demonstration of intention in the reaching behavior of neonate infants. *Nature (London), 228*, 679–681.

Bower, T., Broughton, J., & Moore, M. (1971). Infant responses to approaching objects: An indicator of response to approaching objects. *Perception and Psychophysics, 9*, 193–196.

Bowlby, J. (1951). Maternal care and mental health. *World Health Oranization Monograph, 2*.

Bowlby, J. (1969). *Attachment and loss: Vol. 1. Attachment*. New York: Basic Books.

Bowlby, J. (1973). *Attachment and loss: Vol. 2. Separation*. New York: Basic Books.

Bowlby, J. (1980). *Attachment and loss: Vol. 3. Loss*. New York: Basic Books.

Boyer, E. L. (1983). *High school: A report on secondary education in American*. New York: Harper & Row.

Boysson-Bardies, B., de Sagart, L., & Durand, C. (1984). Discernable differences in the babbling of infants according to target language. *Journal of Child Language, 11*, 1–15.

Brackbill, Y. (1979). Obstetrical medication and infant behavior. In J. D. Osofsky (Ed.), *Handbook of infant development*. New York: Wiley.

Brackbill, Y., Fitzgerald, H., & Lintz, L. (1967). A developmental study of classical conditioning. *Monographs of the Society for Research in Child Development, 32*(Whole No. 116).

Bradley, R. H. (1968). Birth order and school-related behavior: A heuristic review. *Psychological Bulletin, 70*, 45–51.

Braine, M. D. S. (1971). The acquisition of language in

infant and child. In C. Reed (Ed.), *The learning of language*. New York: Appleton-Century-Crofts.

Braine, M. D. S. (1976). Children's first word combinations. *Monographs of the Society for Research in Child Development, 41*(1, Serial No. 164).

Brainerd, C. J., & Kingma, J. (1985). On the independence of short-term memory and working memory in cognitive development. *Cognitive Psychology, 17*, 210–247.

Brazelton, T. B. (1979). Behavioral competence of the newborn infant. *Seminars in Perinatology, 3*, 35–444.

Breger, L. (1974). *From instinct to identity: The development of personality*. Englewood Cliffs, NJ: Prentice-Hall.

Breland, H. M. (1974). Birth order, family configuration, and verbal achievement. *Child Development, 45*, 1011–1019.

Bretherton, I., & Bates, E. (1979). The emergence of intentional communication. In I. Uzgiris (Ed.), *Social interaction and communication during infancy*. San Francisco, CA: Jossey-Bass.

Bridges, L., Connell, J., & Belsky, J. (1988). Similarities and differences in infant-mother and infant-father interaction in the Strange Situation: A component process analysis. *Developmental Psychology, 24*, 92–100.

Brittain, C. V. (1963). Adolescent choices and parent-peer cross pressures. *American Sociological Review, 13*, 59–68.

Brittain, C. V. (1966). Age and sex of siblings and conformity toward parents versus peers in adolescence. *Child Development, 34*, 709–714.

Brody, E. B., & Brody, N. (1976). *Intelligence: Nature, determinants and consequences*. New York: Academic Press.

Brody, G. H., Pillegrini, A. D., & Sigel, I. E. (1986). Marital quality and mother-child and father-child interactions with school-aged children. *Developmental Psychology, 22*, 291–296.

Brokaw, D., & McLemore, C. (1983). Toward a more rigorous definition of social reinforcement: Some interpersonal clarifications. *Journal of Personality and Social Psychology, 44*, 1014–1020.

Bronfenbrenner, U. (1970). *Two worlds of childhood*. New York: Russell Sage.

Bronfenbrenner, U. (1986). Ecology of the family as a context for human development: Research perspectives. *Developmental Psychology, 22*, 723–742.

Bronson, G. (1972). Infants' reactions to unfamiliar persons and novel objects. *Monographs of the Society for Research in Child Development, 37* (3) Serial #148.

Bronson, W. C. (1974). Mother-toddler interaction: A perspective on studying the development of competence. *Merrill-Palmer Quarterly, 20*, 275–301.

Brook, J., Whiteman, M., Gordon, A., & Cohen, P. (1986). Some models and mechanisms for explaining the impact of maternal and adolescent characteristics on adolescent stage of drug use. *Developmental Psychology, 22*, 460–467.

Brookman, K. (1980). *Ocular accommodation in human infants*. Unpublished doctoral dissertation, Indiana University, Bloomington.

Brookover, W., Beady, C., Flood, P., Schweitzer, J., & Wisenbaker, J. (1979). *School social systems and student achievement: Schools can make a difference*. New York: Praeger.

Brooks-Gunn, J. (1987). Pubertal processes and girls' psychological adaptation. In R. Lerner & T. T. Foch (Eds.), *Biological-psychosocial interaction in early adolescence: A life-span perspective* (pp. 123–153). Hillsdale, NJ: Lawrence Erlbaum Associates.

Brooks-Gunn, J., & Furstenberg, F. F., Jr. (1986). The children of adolescent mothers: Physical, academic, and psychological outcomes. *Developmental Review, 6*, 224–251.

Brooks-Gunn, J., Petersen, A., & Eichorn, D. (1985). The study of maturational timing effects in adolescence. *Journal of Youth and Adolescence, 14*, 149–161.

Brooks-Gunn, J., & Ruble, D. (1982). The development of menstrual-related beliefs and behaviors during early adolescence. *Child Development, 53*, 1567–1577.

Brooks-Gunn, J., & Ruble, D. (1983). The experience of menarche from a developmental perspective. In J. Brooks-Gunn & A. Petersen (Eds.), *Girls at puberty: Biological and psychosocial perspectives*. New York: Plenum.

Brooks-Gunn, J., & Zahaykevich, M. (1989). Parent-daughter relationships in early adolescence: A developmental perspective. In K. Kreppner & R. M. Lerner (Eds.), *Family systems and life-span development* (pp. 223–246). Hillsdale, NJ: Erlbaum.

Brophy, J. (1986). Teacher influences on student achievement. *American Psychologist, 41*, 1069–1077.

Broverman, I. K., Broverman, D., Clarkson, F. E., Rosenkranz, P. S., & Vogel, S. R. (1970). Sex-role stereotypes and clinical judgments of mental health. *Journal of Consulting and Clinical Psychology, 34*, 1–7.

Broverman, I. K., Vogel, S. R., Broverman, D. M., Clarkson, F. E., & Rosenkrantz, P. S. (1972). Sex-role stereotypes: A current appraisal. *Journal of Social Issues, 28,* 59–78.

Brown, A. (1975). The development of memory: Knowing, knowing about knowing, and knowing how to know. In H. W. Reese (Ed.), *Advances in child development and behavior.* New York: Academic Press.

Brown, A. (1976). The construction of temporal succession by preoperational children. In A. Pick (Ed.), *Minnesota Symposia on Child Psychology* (Vol. 10). Minneapolis: University of Minnesota Press.

Brown, A., Bransford, J., Ferrara, R., & Campione, J. (1983). Learning, remembering, and understanding. In P. Mussen, J. H. Flavell & E. M. Markman (Eds.), *Handbook of child psychology: Vol. 3. Cognitive development* (4th ed., pp. 77–166). New York: Wiley.

Brown, A., & Campione, J. (1986). Psychological theory and the study of learning disabilities. *American Psychologist, 41,* 1059–1068.

Brown, A., & Scott, M. (1971). Recognition memory for pictures in preschool children. *Journal of Experimental Child Psychology, 11,* 401–412.

Brown, B., Clasen, D., & Eicher, S. (1986). Perceptions of peer pressure, peer conformity dispositions, and self-reported behavior among adolescents. *Developmental Psychology, 22,* 521–530.

Brown vs. Board of Education of Topeka, 98F Supp. 797 (1951), 347 U.S. 483 (1954), 349 U.S. 294 (1955).

Brown, M., & Dodge, K. A. (1984). *Observations of peer group entry behavior by socially rejected and popular children in a school setting.* Paper presented at the 8th biennial Conference on Human Development, Athens, GA.

Brown, R. W. (1958). How shall a thing be called? *Psychological Review, 65,* 14–21.

Brown, R. W. (1965). *Social psychology.* New York: Free Press.

Brown, R. W. (1973). *A first language: The early stages.* Cambridge, MA: Harvard University Press.

Brown, R. W., & Bellugi, U. (1964). Three processes in the child's acquisition of syntax. *Harvard Educational Review, 34,* 133–151.

Brown, R. W., Cazden, C. B., & Bellugi, U. (1969). The child's grammar from I to III. In J. P. Hill (Ed.), *Minnesota Symposia on Child Psychology* (Vol. 2). Minneapolis: University of Minnesota Press.

Brown, R. W., & Hanlon, C. (1970). Derivational complexity and order of acquisition. In J. R. Hayes (Ed.), *Cognition and the development of language.* New York: Wiley.

Browne, J., & Dixon, G. (1978). *Antenatal care.* Edinburgh: Churchill-Livingstone.

Bruininks, V. L. (1978). Actual and perceived peer status of learning-disabled students in mainstream programs. *Journal of Special Education, 12,* 51–58.

Brunk, M., & Henggeler, S. (1984). Child influences on adult controls: An experimental investigation. *Developmental Psychology, 20,* 1074–1081.

Bryan, J. H., & Walbek, N. J. (1970a). Preaching and practicing generosity: Children's actions and reactions. *Child Development, 41,* 329–353.

Bryan, J. H., & Walbek, N. J. (1970b). The impact of words and deeds concerning altruism upon children. *Child Development, 41,* 747–757.

Bryan, T. H. (1974). Peer popularity of learning disabled children. *Journal of Learning Disabilities, 7,* 621–625.

Bryan, T. H. (1976). Peer popularity of learning disabled children: A replication. *Journal of Learning Disabilities, 9,* 307–311.

Bryant, P., Bradley, L., Maclean, M., & Crossland, J. (1989). Nursery rhymes, phonological skills, and reading. *Journal of Child Language, 16,* 407–428.

Buehler, R. E., Patterson, G. R., & Furniss, J. M. (1966). The reinforcement of behavior in institutional settings. *Behavior Research and Therapy, 4,* 157–167.

Bugental, D. B., Blue, J., & Cruzcosa, M. (1989). Perceived control over caregiving outcomes: Implications for child abuse. *Developmental Psychology, 25,* 532–539.

Buhler, C. (1930). *The first year of life.* New York: John Day.

Burns, A., & Goodnow, J. J. (1985). *Children and families in Australia* (2nd ed.). Sydney, Australia: Allen & Unwin.

Burns, N., & Cavey, L. (1957). Age differences in empathic ability among children. *Canadian Journal of Psychology, 11,* 227–230.

Burton, R. V. (1971). Correspondence between behavioral and doll-play measures of conscience. *Developmental Psychology, 5,* 320–332.

Bushnell, I. (1982). Discrimination of faces by young infants. *Journal of Experimental Psychology, 43,* 289–293.

Bushnell, I., Gerry, G., & Burt, K. (1983). The externality effect in neonates. *Infant Behavior and Development, 6,* 151–156.

Buss, A. H. (1983). Social rewards and personality. *Journal of Personality and Social Psychology, 44,* 553–563.

Butler, N. (1974). Late postnatal consequences of fetal

malnutrition. In M. Winick (Ed.), Nutrition and fetal development. New York: Wiley.

Butterfield, E., & Belmont, J. (1977). Assessing and improving the executive cognitive functions of mentally retarded people. In I. Bialer & M. Sternlicht (Eds.), *Psychological issues in mental retardation*. Chicago: Aldine-Atherton.

Butterfield, E., & Siperstein, G. N. (1974). Influence of contingent auditory stimulation upon non-nutritional suckle. In J. Bosma (Ed.), *Oral sensation and perception: The mouth of the infant*. Springfield, IL: Charles C. Thomas.

Bybee, J. L., & Slobin, D. I. (1982). Rules and schemas in the development and use of the English past. *Language, 58*, 265–289.

Byrne, D. (1973). *The development of role-taking in adolescence*. Unpublished doctoral dissertation, Harvard Graduate School of Education, Cambridge, MA.

Cairns, R., Perrin, J., & Cairns, B. (1985). Social structure and social cognition in early adolescence: Affiliative patterns. *Journal of Early Adolescence, 5*, 339–355.

Callanan, M. (1989). Development of object categories and inclusion relations: Preschoolers' hypotheses about word meanings. *Developmental Psychology, 25*, 207–216.

Campagna, A., & Harter, S. (1975). Moral judgment in sociopathic and normal children. *Journal of Personality and Social Psychology, 31*, 199–205.

Campbell, S. B., & Levine, P. C. (1980, September). *Peer interactions of young "hyperactive" children in preschool*. Paper presented at the meeting of the American Psychological Association, Montreal, Canada.

Campos, J., Barrett, K., Lamb, M., Goldsmith, H., & Stenberg, C. (1983). Socioemotional development. In P. H. Mussen, M. Haith, & J. J. Campos (Eds.), *Handbook of child psychology: Vol. 2. Infancy and developmental psychobiology* (4th ed.). New York: Wiley.

Campos, J., Langer, A., & Krowitz, A. (1970). Cardiac responses on the visual cliff in prelocomotor human infants. *Science, 170*, 196–197.

Campos, J., & Stenberg, C. (1981). Perception, appraisal, and emotion: The onset of social referencing. In M. Lamb & L. Sherrod (Eds.), *Infant social cognition: Empirical and theoretical considerations*. Hillsdale, NJ: Erlbaum.

Carey, S. (1978). The child as a word learner. In M. Halle, J. Bresnan, & G. Miller (Eds.), *Linguistic theory and psychological reality*. Cambridge, MA: MIT Press.

Carey, S. (1985). *Conceptual change in childhood*. Cambridge, MA: MIT Press.

Carey, S., & Bartlett, E. (1978). Acquiring a single new word. *Papers and Reports on Child Language Development, 15*, 17–29.

Carithers, M. W. (1970). School desegregation and racial cleavage, 1954–1970: A review of the literature. *Journal of Social Issues, 26*, 25–47.

Carlsmith, J. M., Lepper, M., & Landauer, T. (1974). Children's obedience to adult requests: Interactive effects of anxiety arousal and apparent punitiveness of the adult. *Journal of Personality and Social Psychology, 30*, 822–828.

Carnegie Council on Adolescent Development. (1989). *Turning points: Preparing American youth for the 21st century*. New York: Carnegie Corporation.

Carroll, J. (1982). The measurement of intelligence. In R. Sternberg (Ed.), *Handbook of human intelligence*. Cambridge: Cambridge University Press.

Carroll, J., & Horn, J. (1981). On the scientific basis of ability testing. *American Psychologist, 36*, 1012–1020.

Carroll, J., & Steward, M. (1984). The role of cognitive development in children's understandings of their own feelings. *Child Development, 55*, 1486–1492.

Carter, D. B., & Levy, G. D. (1988). Cognitive aspects of early sex-role development: The influence of gender schemas on preschoolers' memories and preferences for sex-typed toys and activities. *Child Development, 59*, 782–792.

Case, R. (1974). Mental strategies, mental capacity, and instruction: A neo-Piagetian investigation. *Journal of Experimental Child Psychology, 18*, 382–392.

Case, R. (1984). The process of stage transition: A neo-Piagetian view. In R. J. Sternberg (Ed.), *Mechanisms of cognitive development*. New York: Freeman.

Case, R. (1985). Intellectual development: *Birth to adulthood*. New York: Academic Press.

Casler, L. (1965). The effects of extra tactile stimulation on a group of institutionalized infants. *Genetic Psychology Monographs, 71*, 137–175.

Cattell, P. (1950). *The measurement of intelligence in infants and young children*. New York: Psychological Corporation.

Cattell, R. B. (1963). Theory of fluid and crystallized intelligence: A critical experiment. *Journal of Educational Psychology, 54*, 1–22.

Cattell, R. B. (1971). *Abilities: Their structure, growth, and action*. Boston, MA: Houghton-Mifflin.

Cavior, N., & Dokecki, P. R. (1973). Physical attractiveness, perceived attitude similarity, and academic achievement as contributors to interpersonal attraction among adolescents. *Developmental Psychology, 44*, 44–54.

641

Cazden, C. (1965). *Environmental assistance to the child's acquisition of grammar*. Unpublished doctoral dissertation, Graduate School of Education, Harvard University, Cambridge, MA.

Cernoch, J., & Porter, R. (1985). Recognition of maternal axillary odors by infants. *Child Development, 56,* 1593–1598.

Chalkley, M. A. (1982). The emergence of language as a social skill. In S. Kuczaj (Ed.), *Language development: Vol. 2. Language, thought and culture*. Hillsdale, NJ: Erlbaum.

Challman, R. C. (1932). Factors influencing friendships among preschool children. *Child Development, 3,* 146–158.

Chandler, M. (1973). Egocentrism and antisocial behavior: The assessment and training of social perspective-taking skills. *Developmental Psychology, 9,* 326–332.

Chandler, M., & Greenspan, S. (1972). Ersatz egocentrism: A reply to H. Borke. *Developmental Psychology, 7,* 104–106.

Chandler, M., Greenspan, S., & Barenboim, C. (1973). Judgments of intentionality in response to videotaped and verbally presented moral dilemmas: The medium is the message. *Child Development, 44,* 315–320.

Chapman, A. J., Smith, J. R., Foot, H. C., & Pritchard, E. (1979). Behavioral and sociometric indices of friendship in children. In M. Cook & G. D. Wilson (Eds.). *Love and attraction*. Oxford: Pergamon.

Charlesworth, R., & Hartup, W. W. (1967). Positive social reinforcement in the nursery school peer group. *Child Development, 38,* 993–1002.

Charlesworth, W., & Kreutzer, M. (1973). Facial expressions of infants and children. In P. Ekman (Ed.), *Darwin and facial expression*. New York: Academic Press.

Chase, H. (1977). Time trends in low birth weight in the United States, 1950–1974. In D. Reed & F. Stanley (Eds.), *The epidemiology of prematurity*. Baltimore, MD: Urban & Schwarzenberg.

Cherlin, A. (Ed.). (1988). *The changing American family and public policy*. Washington, DC: The Urban Institute Press.

Cheyne, J. A., & Walters, R. H. (1969). Intensity of punishment, timing of punishment, and cognitive structure as determinants of response inhibition. Journal of Experimental Child Psychology, 7, 231–244.

Chi, M. (1978). Knowledge structures and memory development. In R. Siegler (Ed.), *Children's thinking: What develops?* Hillsdale, NJ: Erlbaum.

Chibucos, T., & Kail, P. (1981). Longitudinal examination of father-infant interaction and infant-father interaction. *Merrill-Palmer Quarterly, 27,* 81–96.

Chilman, C. (1983). *Adolescent sexuality in a changing American society* (2nd ed.). New York: Wiley.

Chittenden, G. E. (1942). An experimental study in measuring and modifying assertive behavior in young children. *Monographs of the Society for Research in Child Development, 7*(Serial No. 31).

Chomsky, N. (1957). *Syntactic structures*. The Hague: Mouton.

Chomsky, N. (1965). *Aspects of the theory of syntax*. Cambridge, MA: MIT Press.

Chomsky, N. (1972). *Language and mind*. New York: Harcourt Brace Jovanovich.

Chomsky, N. (1981). *Lectures on government and binding*. Dordrecht, Netherlands: Foris.

Chomsky, N. (1988). *Language and problems of knowledge: The Nicaraguan lectures*. Cambridge, MA: MIT Press.

Cicchetti, D. J. (1977). *Affective development in Down's syndrome infants: An organizational perspective*. Unpublished doctoral dissertation, University of Minnesota, Minneapolis.

Clark, A. D., Hocevar, D., & Dembo, M. H. (1980). The role of cognitive development in children's explanations and preferences for skin color. *Developmental Psychology, 16,* 332–339.

Clark, E. V. (1973). What's in a word? On the child's acquisition of semantics in his first language. In T. E. Moore (Ed.), *Cognitive development and the acquisition of language*. New York: Academic Press.

Clark, E. V. (1975). Knowledge, context, and strategy in the acquisition of meaning. In D. P. Dato (Ed.), *Georgetown University round table on languages and linguistics: Developmental psycholinguistics*. Washington, DC: Georgetown University Press.

Clark, H. H., & Clark, E. V. (1977). *Psychology and language: An introduction to psycholinguistics*. New York: Harcourt Brace Jovanovich.

Clark, K. B., & Clark, M. K. (1939). The development of consciousness of self and the emergence of racial identification in Negro preschool children. *Journal of Social Psychology, 10,* 591–599.

Clark, K. B., & Clark, M. R. (1958). Racial identification and preference in Negro children. In E. Maccoby, T. Newcomb, & E. C. Hartley (Eds.), *Readings in social psychology* (pp. 231–245). New York: Holt, Rinehart & Winston.

Clark, M. (1984). A distinction between two types of relationships and its implications for development. In J. Masters & K. Yarkin (Eds.), *Boundary areas in social and developmental psychology* (pp. 241–270). New York: Academic Press.

Clark, M., Milberg, S., & Erber, R. (1983). Arousal cues arousal-related material in memory: Implications for understanding effects of mood on memory. *Journal of Verbal Learning and Verbal Behavior, 22*(6), 633–649.

Clarke-Stewart, K. A. (1978). Recasting the lone stranger. In J. Glick & K. A. Stewart (Eds.), *The development of social understanding*. New York: Gardner Press.

Clarkson, M., & Berg, W. (1983). Cardia orienting and vowel discrimination in newborns: Crucial stimulus parameters. *Child Development, 54*, 162–171.

Clifton, R., Morrongiello, B., Kulig, J., & Dowd, J. (1981). Developmental changes in auditory localization in infancy. In R. Aslin, J. Alberts, & M. Petersen (Eds.), *Development of perception: Psychobiological perspectives, Vol. 1, Audition, somatic perception, and the chemical senses*. New York: Academic Press.

Clingempeel, W. G., Brand, C., & Sevoli, R. (1984). Stepparent-stepchild relationships in stepmother and stepfather families: A multimethod study. *Family Relations, 33*, 465–473.

Cohen, L., DeLoache, J., & Strauss, M. (1979). Infant visual perception. In J. Osofsky (Ed.), *Handbook of infant development*. New York: Wiley.

Cohen, S., & Parmelee, A. (1983). Prediction of five-year Stanford-Binet scores in preterm infants. *Child Development, 54*, 1242–1253.

Coie, J. D., & Pennington, B. F. (1976). Children's perceptions of deviance and disorder. *Child Development, 47*, 407–413.

Colby, A., & Kohlberg, L. (1975). The relation between logical and moral development. Unpublished manuscript, Harvard Graduate School of Education, Cambridge, MA.

Colby, A., Kohlberg, L., Gibbs, J., & Lieberman, M. (1983). A longitudinal study of moral judgment. *Monographs of the Society for Research in Child Development, 48*(1–2) Serial #200.

Coleman, J. S. (1961). *The adolescent society*. New York: Free Press.

Coleman, J. S., Campbell, E. Q., Hobson, C. J., McPartland, J. M., Mood, A. M., Weinfeld, P. V., & York, R. L. (1966). *Equality of educational opportunity* (2 vols.). Washington, DC: U.S. Government Printing Office.

Collins, W. A. (Ed.) (1984a). *Development during middle childhood: The years from six to twelve*. Washington, DC: National Academy Press.

Collins, W. A. (1984b). Inferences about the actions of others: Developmental and individual differences in the use of social knowledge. In J. Masters & K. Yarkin (Eds.), *Boundary areas in psychology: Social and developmental psychology*. New York: Academic Press.

Collins, W. A. (1990). Parent-child relationships in the transition to adolescence: Continuity and change in interaction, affect, and cognition. In R. Montemayor, G. Adams, & T. Gullotta (Eds.), *From childhood to adolescence: A transitional period?* (pp. 85–106), Beverly Hills, CA: Sage.

Collins, W. A., & Gunnar, M. R. (1990). Social and personality development. *Annual Review of Psychology, 41*, 387–416.

Collins, W. A., & Korac, N. (1982). Recent progress in the study of the effects of television viewing on social development. *International Journal of Behavioural Development, 5*, 171–193.

Collins, W. A., & Russell, G. (1991). Mother-child and father-child relationships in middle childhood and adolescence. *Developmental Review*.

Collins, W. A., Wellman, H., Keniston, A. H., & Westby, S. D. (1978). Age related aspects of comprehension and inference from a televised dramatic narrative. *Child Development, 49*, 389–399.

Conel, J. (1939). *The postnatal development of the human cerebral cortex, Vol. 1, The cortex of the newborn*. Cambridge, MA: Harvard University Press.

Conel, J. (1941). *The postnatal development of the one-month infant*. Cambridge MA: Harvard University Press.

Connell, J. (1976). *Individual differences in attachment: An investigation into stability, implications, and relationships to structure of early language development*. Unpublished doctoral dissertation, Syracuse University, Syracuse, NY.

Cooney, E. (1977). Social-cognitive development: Applications to intervention and evaluation in the elementary grades. *Counseling Psychologist, 6*, 6–9.

Cooper, C., Grotevant, H., & Condon, S. (1984). Individuality and connectedness in the family as a context for adolescent identity formation and role-taking skill. In H. Grotevant & C. Cooper (Eds.), *Adolescent development in the family: New directions for child development* (pp. 43–60). San Francisco, CA: Jossey-Bass.

643

Cooper, H. M. (1979). Pygmalion grows up: A model for teacher expectation, communication and performance influence. *Review of Educational Research, 49,* 389–410.

Corah, N., Anthony, E., Painter, P., Stern, J., & Thurston, P. (1965). Effects of perinatal anoxia after seven years. *Psychological Monographs, 79*(Whole No. 596).

Cornell, E., & McDonnell, P. (1986). Infants' acuity at twenty feet. *Investigative Ophthalmology & Visual Science, 27,* 1417–1420.

Corter, C., Trehub, S., Boukydis, C., Ford, L., Celhoffer, L., & Minde, K. (1978). Nurses' judgments of the attractiveness of premature infants. *Infant Behavior and Development, 1,* 373–380.

Costanzo, P. R. (1970). Conformity development as a function of self-blame. *Journal of Personality and Social Psychology, 14,* 366–374.

Costanzo, P. R., Coie, J. D., Grumet, J. F., & Farnill, D. (1973). A reexamination of the effects of intent and consequence on children's moral judgments. *Child Development, 44,* 154–161.

Cote, J., & Levine, C. (1988). A critical examination of the Ego Identity Status paradigm. *Developmental Review, 8,* 147–184.

Covell, K., & Abramovitch, R. (1987). Understanding emotion in the family: Children's and parents' attributions of happiness, sadness, and anger. *Child Development, 58,* 985–991.

Cowan, P., Langer, J., Heavenrich, J., & Nathanson, M. (1969). Social learning and Piaget's cognitive theory of moral development. *Journal of Personality and Social Psychology, 11,* 261–274.

Cowart, B. (1981). Development of taste perception in humans: Sensitivity and preference throughout the life span. *Psychological Bulletin, 90,* 43–73.

Cowen, E., Pederson, A., Babigan, H., Izzo, L., & Prost, M. (1973). Long-term follow-up of early detected vulnerable children. *Journal of Consulting and Clinical Psychology, 41,* 438–446.

Crites, J. (1962). Parental identification in relation to vocational interest development. *Journal of Educational Psychology, 53,* 262–270.

Crnic, K., Ragozin, A., Greenberg, M., Robinson, N., & Basham, R. (1983). Social interaction and developmental competence of preterm and full-term infants during the first year of life. *Child Development, 54,* 1199–1210.

Crockenberg, S. (1981). Infant irritability, mother responsiveness, and social support influences on the security of infant attachment. *Child Development, 52,* 857–865.

Crockenberg, S., & McCluskey, K. (1986). Change in maternal behavior during the baby's first year of life. *Child Development, 57,* 746–753.

Crook, C. (1978). Taste perception in the newborn infant. *Infant Behavior and Development, 1,* 52–69.

Csikszentmihalyi, M., & Larson, R. (1984). Being adolescent: *Conflict and growth in the teenage years.* New York: Basic Books.

Cvetkovich, G., & Grote, B. (1981). Psychosocial maturity and teenage contraceptive use: An investigation of decision-making and communication skills. *Population and Environment, 4,* 211–226.

Cvetkovich, G., & Grote, B. (1983). Adolescent development and teenage fertility. In D. Byrne & W. A. Fisher (Eds.), *Adolescents, sex, and contraception* (pp. 109–123). Hillsdale, NJ: Erlbaum.

Dale, P. S. (1976). *Language development* (2nd ed.). New York: Holt, Rinehart & Winston.

Damon, W. (1977). *The social world of the child.* San Francisco, CA: Jossey-Bass.

Damon, W. (1983). *Special and personality development.* New York: Norton.

Damon, W., & Hart, D. (1982). The development of self-understanding from infancy to adolescence. *Child Development, 53,* 841–864.

Damon, W., & Hart, D. (1988). *Self-understanding: In childhood and adolescence.* New York: Cambridge University Press.

Daniels, D., Dunn, J., Furstenberg, F. F., Jr., & Plomin, R. (1985). Environmental differences within the family and adjustment differences within pairs of adolescent siblings. *Child Development, 56,* 764–774.

Darvill, D., & Cheyne, J. A. (1981, April). *Sequential analysis of response to aggression: Age and sex effects.* Paper presented at the meeting of the Society for Research in Child Development, Boston, MA.

Darwin, C. (1975). *The expression of the emotions in man and animals.* Chicago: University of Chicago Press (original work published 1872).

Darwin, C. (1977). Biographical sketch of infants. *Mind, 2,* 285–294.

Davids, A., & Hainsworth, P. (1967). Maternal attitudes about family life and childrearing as avowed by mothers and perceived by their under-achieving and high-achieving sons. *Journal of Consulting Psychology, 31,* 29–37.

Dawe, H. C. (1934). The influence of size of kindergarten group upon performance. *Child Development, 5,* 295–303.

Dawkins, R. (1976). *The selfish gene.* New York: Oxford University Press.

Deaux, K., & Emswiller, T. (1974). Explanations of successful performance on sex-linked tasks: What is skill for the male is luck for the female. *Journal of Personality and Social Psychology, 29,* 80–85.

Debus, R. (1970). Effects of brief observation of model behavior on conceptual tempo of impulsive children. *Developmental Psychology, 2,* 22–32.

DeCasper, A., & Fifer, W. (1980). Of human bonding: Newborns prefer their mother's voices. *Science, 208,* 1174–1176.

Dekaban, A., O'Rourke, J., & Corman, T. (1958). Abnormalities in offspring related to maternal rubella during pregnancy. *Neurology, 8,* 387–392.

DeLaguna, G. (1927). *Speech: Its function and development.* Bloomington: Indiana University Press.

de Lissovoy, V. (1973). Child care by adolescent parents. *Children Today, 14,* 22.

DeLoache, J. (1986). Memory in very young children: Exploitation of cues to the location of a hidden object. *Cognitive Development, 1,* 123–138.

DeLoache, J. (1987). Rapid change in the symbolic functioning of very young children. *Science, 238,* 1556–1557.

DeLoache, J., & Brown, A. (1987). The early emergence of planning skills in children. In J. Bruner & H. Harte (Eds.), *Making sense: The child's construction of the world.* London: Methuen.

DeLoache, J., Cassidy, D., & Brown, A. (1985). Precursors of mnemonic strategies in very young children's memory for the location of hidden objects. *Child Development, 56,* 125–137.

DeLoache, J., Sugarman, S., & Brown, A. (1985). The development of error correction strategies in young children's manipulative play. *Child Development, 56,* 928–939.

Deutsch, F. (1974). Female preschoolers' perceptions of affective responses and interpersonal behavior in videotaped episodes. *Developmental Psychology, 10,* 733–740.

Deutsch, M., & Gerard, H. (1955). A study of normative and informational social influences upon individual judgment. *Journal of Abnormal and Social Psychology, 51,* 629–636.

Deutsch, W., & Pechmann, T. (1982). Social interaction and the development of definite descriptions. *Cognition, 11,* 159–184.

de Villiers, P. A., & de Villiers, J. G. (1979). Form and function in the development of sentence negation. *Papers and Reports in Child Language, 17,* 57–64. Stanford, CA.

DeVolder, M., & Lens, W. (1982). Academic achievement and future time perspective as a cognitive-motivational concept. *Journal of Personality and Social Psychology, 43,* 566–571.

Diamond, A. (1985). Development of the ability to use recall to guide action as indicated by infants' performance on AB. *Child Development, 56,* 868–883.

Dickstein, S., & Parke, R. (1988). Social referencing in infancy: A glance at fathers and marriage. *Child Development, 59,* 506–511.

Dion, K. K. (1973). Young children's stereotyping of facial attractiveness. *Developmental Psychology, 9,* 183–198.

Dion, K. K., & Berscheid, E. (1974). Physical attractiveness and peer perception among children. *Sociometry, 37,* 1–12.

DiPietro, J. A. (1981). Rough and tumble play: A function of gender. *Developmental Psychology, 17,* 50–58.

Dlugokinski, E. L., & Firestone, I. J. (1974). Other centeredness and susceptibility to charitable appeals: Effects of perceived discipline. *Developmental Psychology, 10,* 21–28.

Dockrell, J., & Campbell, R. (1986). Lexical acquisition strategies in the preschool child. In S. Kuczaj & M. Barrett (Eds.), *The development of word meaning.* New York: Springer-Verlag.

Dodge, K. A. (1980). Social cognition and children's aggressive behavior. *Child Development, 51,* 162–170.

Dodge, K. A. (1983). Behavioral antecedents of peer social status. *Child Development, 54,* 1386–1399.

Dodge, K. A. (1985). Attributional bias in aggressive children. *Advances in Cognitive Behavioral Research and Therapy, 4,* 73–110.

Dodge, K. A., & Frame, C. L. (1982). Social cognitive biases and deficits in aggressive boys. *Child Development, 53,* 620–635.

Dodge, K. A., & Newman, J. P. (1981). Biased decision-making processes in aggressive boys. *Journal of Abnormal Psychology, 90,* 375–379.

Dodge, K. A., & Somberg, D. (1987). Hostile attributional biases among aggressive boys are exacerbated under conditions of threats to the self. *Child Development, 58,* 213–224.

Dodge, K. A., & Tomlin, A. (1984). *The role of cue-utilization in attributional biases among aggressive children.* Presented at the second Invitational Conference on Social Cognition, Nags Head, NC.

Dodwell, P., Muir, D., & DiFranco, D. (1976). Responses of infants to visually presented objects. *Science, 194,* 209–211.

645

Doland, D. J., & Adelberg, K. (1967). The learning of sharing behavior. *Child Development, 38*, 696–700.

Dollard, J., & Miller, N. (1950). *Personality and psychotherapy*. New York: McGraw-Hill.

Dollard, J., Doob, L. W., Miller, N. E., Mowrer, O. H., & Sears, R. R. (1939). *Frustration and aggression*. New Haven, CT: Yale University Press.

Dornbusch, S. M., Carlsmith, J. M., Gross, R., Martin, J., Jennings, D., Rosenberg, A., & Duke, P. (1981). Sexual development, age, and dating: A comparison of biological and social influences upon one set of behaviors. *Child Development, 52*, 179–185.

Dornbusch, S. M., Ritter, P. L., Leiderman, P. H., Roberts, D. F., & Fraleigh, M. J. (1987). The relation of parenting style to adolescent school performance. *Child Development, 58*, 1244–1257.

Douvan, E., & Adelson, J. (1966). *The adolescent experience*. New York: Wiley.

Drillien, C. (1964). *The growth and development of the prematurely born infant*. Edinburgh: Livingstone.

Dubanoski, R., & Parton, D. (1971). Effect of the presence of a human model on imitative behavior in children. *Developmental Psychology, 4*, 463–468.

Dubois, P. H. (1970). *A history of psychological testing*. Boston, MA: Allyn & Bacon.

Dubow, E., Huesmann, L. R., & Eron, L. (1987). Childhood correlates of adult ego development. *Child Development, 58*, 859–869.

Duncan, O. D., Schuman, H., & Duncan, B. (1973). *Social change in a metropolitan community*. New York: Russell Sage.

Duncan, P., Ritter, P., Dornbusch, S., Gross, R., & Carlsmith, J. M. (1985). The effects of pubertal timing on body image, school behavior, and deviance. *Journal of Youth and Adolescence, 14*, 227–235.

Dunn, J. (1983). Sibling relationships in early childhood. *Child Development, 54*, 787–811.

Dunn, J. (1988). *The beginnings of social understanding*. Cambridge, MA: Harvard University Press.

Dunn, J., & Kendrick, C. (1979). The arrival of a sibling: Changes in patterns of interaction between mother and firstborn child. *Journal of Child Psychology and Psychiatry, 21*, 119–132.

Dunn, L. M. (1959). *Peabody Picture Vocabulary Test manual*. Minneapolis, MN: American Guidance Service.

Dunn, L. M. (1965). *Expanded manual for the Peabody Picture Vocabulary Test*. Minneapolis, MN: American Guidance Service.

Durfee, J. T., & Lee, L. C. (1973, August). *Infant-infant interaction in daycare setting*. Paper presented at the meeting of the American Psychological Association, Montreal, Canada.

Dusek, J., & Flaherty, J. (1981). The development of the self-concept during the adolescent years. *Monographs of the Society for Research in Child Development, 46*, (4) Serial #191.

Dweck, C. S. (1975). The role of expectations and attributions in the alleviation of learned helplessness. *Journal of Personality and Social Psychology, 31*, 674–685.

Dweck, C. S. (1986). Motivational processes affecting learning. *American Psychologist, 41*, 1040–1048.

Dweck, C. S., & Bush, E. S. (1976). Sex differences in learned helplessness: I. Differential debilitation with peer and adult evaluators. *Developmental Psychology, 12*, 147–156.

Dweck, C. S., Davidson, W., Nelson, S., & Enna, B. (1978). Sex differences in learned helplessness: II. The contingencies of evaluative feedback in the classroom, and III. An experimental analysis. *Developmental Psychology, 14*, 268–276.

Dweck, C. S., & Gilliard, D. (1975). Expectancy statements as determinants of reactions to failure: Sex differences in persistence and expectancy change. *Journal of Personality and Social Psychology, 32*, 1077–1084.

Dye, N., & Very, P. (1968). Developmental changes in adolescent mental structure. *Genetic Psychology Monographs, 78*, 55–88.

East, P. (1986). *Peers as providers of social support in early adolescence*. Paper presented at the biennial meeting of the Society for Research on Adolescence, Madison, WI.

Easterbrook, J. (1959). The effect of emotion on cue utilization and the organization of behavior. *Psychological Review, 66*, 183–201.

Easterbrooks, M. A., & Lamb, M. E. (1979). The relationship between quality of infant-mother attachment and infant peer competence in initial encounters with peers. *Child Development, 50*, 380–387.

Eaton, W. O., & Keats, J. G. (1982). Peer presence, stress, and sex differences in the motor activity levels of preschoolers. *Developmental Psychology, 18*, 534–540.

Eaton, W. O., & von Bargen, D. (1981). Asynchronous development of gender understanding in preschool children. *Child Development, 52*, 1020–1027.

Eckerman, C. O., & Whatley, J. L. (1977). Toys and social interaction between infant peers, *Child Development, 48*, 1645–1656.

Eckerman, C. O., Whatley, J. L., & Kutz, S. L. (1975). The growth of social play with peers during the second year of life. *Developmental Psychology*, 11, 42–49.

Edelman, G. (Ed.). (1984). *The cell in contact*. New York: Wiley.

Edwards, L., Steinman, M., Arnold, K., & Hakanson, E. (1980). Adolescent pregnancy prevention services in high school clinics. *Family Planning Perspectives*, 12, 6–14.

Egeland, B. (1983). Discussion of Kopp et al.'s paper, Patterns of self-control in young handicapped children. In M. Perlmutter (Ed.), *Development and policy concerning children with special needs: Minnesota Symposia on Child Psychology* (Vol. 16, pp. 129–136). Hillsdale, NJ: Erlbaum.

Egeland, B., Breitenbucher, M., Rosenberg, D. (1980). Prospective study of the significance of life stress in the etiology of child abuse. *Journal of Consulting and Clinical Psychology*, 48, 195–205.

Egeland, B., Jacobvitz, D., & Sroufe, L. A. (1988). Breaking the cycle of abuse: Relationship predictors. *Child Development*, 59, 1080–1088.

Egeland, B., & Sroufe, L. A. (1981). Attachment and early maltreatment. *Child Development*, 52, 44–52.

Eimas, P. (1985). The perception of speech in early infancy. *Scientific American*, 252, 46–61.

Eimas, P. D., Siqueland, E. R., Jusczyk, P. W., & Vigorito, J. (1971). Speech perception in infants. *Science*, 171, 303–306.

Eisenberg, N., Fabes, R., Bustamante, D., Mathy, R., Miller, P., & Lindholm, E. (1988). Differentiation of vicariously induced emotional reactions in children. *Developmental Psychology*, 24, 237–246.

Eisenberg, N., & Miller, P. A. (1987). The relation of empathy to prosocial and related behaviors. *Psychological Bulletin*, 102, 91–119.

Eisenberg, N., Pasternack, J., Cameron, E., & Tryon, K. (1984). The relation of quantity and mode of prosocial behavior to moral cognitions and social style. *Child Development*, 55, 1479–1485.

Eisenberg, N., Shell, R., Pasternack, J., Lennon, R., Beller, R., & Mathy, R. M. (1987). Prosocial development in middle childhood: A longitudinal study. Developmental Psychology, 23, 712–718.

Ekman, P. (1980). Biological and cultural contributions to body and facial movement in the expression of emotions. In A. Rorty (Ed.), *Explaining emotions*. Berkeley: University of California Press.

Ekman, P., Friesen, W., O'Sullivan, M., Chan, A., Diacoyanni-Tarlatzis, I., Heider, K., Krause, R., LeCompte, W., Pitcairn, T., Ricci-Bitti, P., Scherer, K., Tomita, M., & Tzavaras, A. (1987). Universals and cultural differences in the judgments of facial expressions of emotion. *Journal of Personality and Social Psychology*, 53, 712–717.

Elardo, P. (1974). *Project AWARE: A school program to facilitate the social development of children*. Paper presented at the fourth annual H. Blumberg Symposium, Chapel Hill, NC.

Elder, G. H., Jr. (1963). Parental power legitimation and its effect on the adolescent. *Sociometry*, 26, 50–65.

Elder, G. H., Jr. (1974). *Children of the great depression*. Chicago, IL: University of Chicago Press.

Elder, G. H., Jr., Caspi, A., & Burton, L. (1988). Life transition in developmental perspective: Sociological and historical insights on adolescence. In M. Gunnar & W. A. Collins (Eds.), *Development in the Transition to Adolescence: The Minnesota Symposia on Child Psychology* (Vol. 21). Hillsdale, NJ: Erlbaum.

Elder, G. H., Jr., Downey, G., & Cross, C. (1986). Family ties and life chances: Hard times and hard choices in women's lives since the Great Depression. In N. Datan (Ed.), *Life-span developmental psychology: Socialization and intergenerational relations* (pp. 151–183). Hillsdale, NJ: Erlbaum.

Elkind, D. (1967). Egocentrism in adolescence. *Child Development*, 38, 1025–1034.

Elkind, D. (1968). Cognitive development in adolescence. In J. F. Adams (Ed.), *Understanding adolescence*. Boston, MA: Allyn & Bacon.

Elkind, D., & Bowen, R. (1979). Imaginary audience behavior in children and adolescents. *Developmental Psychology*, 15, 38–44.

Ellis, G. T., & Sekyra, F. (1972). The effect of aggressive cartoons on the behavior of first grade children. *Journal of Psychology*, 81, 37–43.

Emanuel, I. (1977). Need for future epidemiologic research: Studies for prevention and intervention. In D. Reed & F. Stanley (Eds.), *The epidemiology of prematurity*. Munich: Urban & Schwarzenberg.

Emde, R., Harmon, R., Metcalf, D., Koenig, K., & Wagonfeld, S. (1971). Stress and neonatal sleep. *Psychosomatic Medicine*, 33, 491–497.

Emde, R., & Koenig, K. (1969). Neonatal smiling and rapid eye movement states. *American Academy of Child Psychiatry*, 8, 57–67.

Engen, T., Lipsitt, L., & Kaye, H. (1963). Olfactory response and adaptation n the human neonate.

Journal of Comparative and Physiological Psychology, 56, 73–77.

Epstein, J. L. (1980). *After the bus arrives: Resegregation in desegregated schools.* Paper presented at the meetings of the American Educational Research Association, Boston, MA.

Epstein, J. L. (1983). Longitudinal effects of family-school-person interactions on student outcomes. In A. Kerckhoff (Ed.), *Research in sociology of education and socialization* (Vol. 4, pp. 90–130). Greenwich, CT: JAI Press.

Erdelyi, M. (1974). A new look at the New Look: Perceptual defense and vigilance. *Psychological Review, 81,* 1–25.

Erickson, M., Farber, E., & Egeland, B. (1982, August). *Antecedents and concomitants of compliance in high-risk preschool children.* Paper presented at the annual meeting of the American Psychological Association, Washington, DC.

Erickson, M., Sroufe, L. A., & Egeland, B. (1985). The relationship between quality of attachment and behavior problems in preschool in a high-risk sample. *Monographs of the Society for Research in Child Development, 50* (Nos. 1–2).

Erikson, E. (1950). *Childhood and society.* New York: Norton.

Erikson, E. (1963). *Childhood and society* (2nd ed.). New York: Norton.

Erikson, E. (1968). *Identity: Youth and crisis.* New York: Norton.

Eron, L. D. (1963). Relationship with TV viewing habits and aggressive behavior in children. *Journal of Abnormal and Social Psychology, 67,* 193–196.

Eron, L. D., Huesmann, L. R., Lefkowitz, M. M., & Walder, L. O. (1972). Does television violence cause aggression? *American Psychologist, 27,* 253–263.

Escalona, S. (1968). *The roots of individuality: Normal patterns of individuality.* Hawthorne, NY: Aldine.

Etaugh, C. (1974). Effects of maternal employment on children: A review of recent research. *Merrill-Palmer Quarterly of Behavior and Development, 20,* 71–98.

Etaugh, C., Collins, G., & Gerson, A. (1975). Reinforcement of sex-typed behaviors of two-year-old children in a nursery school setting. *Developmental Psychology, 11,* 255.

Fabes, R., Eisenberg, N., McCormick, S., & Wilson, M. (1988). Preschoolers' attributions of the situational determinants of others' naturally occurring emotions. *Developmental Psychology, 24,* 376–385.

Fabricius, W., Sophian, C., & Wellman, H. (1987). Young children's sensitivity to logical necessity in their inferential search behavior. *Child Development, 58,* 409–423.

Fagan, J. (1973). Infant's delayed recognition memory and forgetting. *Journal of Experimental Child Psychology, 16,* 424–450.

Fagan, J. (1984). The relationship of novelty preferences during infancy to later intelligence and recognition memory. *Intelligence, 8,* 339–346.

Fagan, J., & McGrath, S. (1981). Infant recognition memory and later intelligence. *Intelligence, 5,* 121–130.

Fagot, B. I. (1973). Influence of teacher behavior in the preschool. *Developmental Psychology, 9,* 198–206.

Fagot, B. I. (1977a). Consequences of moderate cross-gender behavior in preschool children. *Child Development, 48,* 902–907.

Fagot, B. I. (1977b). Teachers' reinforcement of sex-preferred behaviors in Dutch preschools. *Psychological Reports, 41,* 1249–1250.

Fagot, B. I. (1978a). Reinforcing contingencies for sex-role behaviors: Effect of experience with children. *Child Development, 49,* 30–36.

Fagot, B. I. (1978b). The influence of sex of child parental reactions to toddler children. *Child Development, 49,* 459–465.

Fagot, B. I. (1978c). *Sex determined consequences of different play styles in early childhood.* Paper presented at the American Psychological Association, Toronto, Canada.

Fagot, B. I. (1985). Changes in thinking about early sex role development. *Developmental Review.*

Fagot, B. I., Leinbach, M. D., & Hagan, R. (1986). Gender labeling and the adoption of sex-typed behaviors. *Developmental Psychology, 22,* 440–443.

Fagot, B. I., & Patterson, G. R. (1969). An *in vivo* analysis of reinforcing contingencies for sex-role behaviors in the preschool child. *Developmental Psychology, 1,* 563–568.

Fantz, R. (1961). The origin of form perception. *Scientific American, 204*(5), 66–72.

Fantz, R. (1963). Pattern vision in newborn infants. *Science, 140,* 296–297.

Fantz, R. (1965). Visual perception from birth as shown by pattern selectivity. *Annals of the New York Academy of Sciences, 118,* 793–814.

Farber, S. L. (1981). *Identical twins reared apart: A reanalysis.* New York: Basic Books.

Farran, D., & Ramey, C. (1977). Infant day care and attachment behaviors toward mothers and teachers. *Child Development, 48,* 1112–1116.

Farwell, C. (1975). The language spoken to children. *Human Development*, *18*, 288–309.

Faust, M. S. (1960). Developmental maturity as a determinant in prestige of adolescent girls. *Child Development*, *31*, 173–184.

Feffer, M. H. (1959). The cognitive implications of role-taking behavior. *Journal of Personality and Social Psychology*, *27*, 152–168.

Feingold, A. (1988). Cognitive gender differences are disappearing. *American Psychologist*, *43*, 95–103.

Feiring, C., Lewis, M., & Jaskir, J. (1983). Birth of a sibling: Effect on mother-first born child interaction. *Developmental Behavioral Pediatrics*, *4*, 190–195.

Feldman, N. S., Klosson, E. C., Parsons, J. E., Rholes, W. S., & Ruble, D. N. (1976). Order of information presentation and children's moral judgments. *Child Development*, *47*, 556–559.

Felleman, E., Barden, C., Carlson, C., Rosenberg, L., & Masters, J. (1983). Children's and adults' recognition of spontaneous and posed emotional expressions in young children. *Developmental Psychology*, *19*, 405–413.

Feltham, R., Doyle, A., Schwartzman, A., Serbin, L., & Ledingham, J. (1985). Friendship in normal and socially deviant children. *Journal of Early Adolescence*, *5*, 371–382.

Fenema, E., & Sherman, J. (1977). Sex-related differences in mathematics achievement, spatial visualization, and affective factors. *American Education Research Journal*, *14*, 51–71.

Ferguson, C. A. (1989). Individual differences in language learning. In M. Rice & R. Schiefelbusch (Eds.), *The teachability of language*. Baltimore, MD: Brookes.

Feshbach, N. D. (1978). Studies of empathic behavior in children. In B. A. Maher (Ed.), *Progress in experimental personality research* (Vol. 8). New York: Academic Press.

Feshbach, N. D. (1979). Empathy training: A field study in affective education. In S. Feshbach & A. Fraczek (Eds.), *Aggression and behavior change: Biological and social processes*. New York: Praeger.

Feshbach, N. D., & Feshbach, S. (1982). Empathy training and the regulation of aggression: Potentialities and limitations. *Academic Psychology Bulletin*, *4*, 399–413.

Feshbach, S. (1956). The catharsis hypothesis and some consequences of interaction with aggressive and neutral play objects. *Journal of Personality*, *24*, 449–462.

Feshbach, S. (1970). Aggression. In P. H. Mussen (Ed.), *Carmichael's manual of child psychology* (3rd ed., Vol. 2). New York: Wiley.

Field, J. (1977). Coordination of vision and prehension in young infants. *Child Development*, *48*, 97–103.

Field, T. (1982). Individual differences in the expressivity of neonates and young infants. In R. Feldman (Ed.), *Development of nonverbal behavior in children*. New York: Springer-Verlag.

Field, T. (1983). Early interactions and interaction coaching of high-risk infants and parents. In M. Perlmutter (Ed.), *Development and policy concerning children with special needs: The Minnesota Symposia on Child Psychology* (Vol. 16). Hillsdale, NJ: Erlbaum.

Field, T., Woodson, R., Cohen, D., Greenberg, R., Garcia, R., & Collins, K. (1983). Discrimination and imitation of facial expressions by term and pre-term neonates. *Infant Behavior and Development*, *6*, 485–489.

Field, T., Woodson, R., Greenberg, R., & Cohen, D. (1982). Discrimination and imitation of facial expressions by neonates. *Science*, *218*, 179–181.

Finkelstein, N. W., Dent, C., Gallagher, K., & Ramey, C. T. (1978). Social behavior of infants and toddlers in a daycare environment. *Developmental Psychology*, *14*, 257–262.

Fischer, K. W., Carnochan, P., & Shaver, P. R. (in press). *Cognition and Emotion*.

Flapan, D. (1968). *Children's understanding of social interaction*. New York: Teacher's College Press.

Flavell, J. H. (1963). *The developmental psychology of Jean Piaget*. New York: Van Nostrand.

Flavell, J. H. (1966). *The development of role-taking and communication skills in children*. New York: Wiley.

Flavell, J. H. (1970). Developmental studies of mediated memory. In H. Reese & L. Lipsitt (Eds.), *Advances in child development and behavior* (Vol. 5). New York: Academic Press.

Flavell, J. H. (1974). The development of inferences about others. In T. Mischel (Ed.), *Understanding other persons*. Oxford: Blackwell, Basil, Mott.

Flavell, J. H. (1982). Structures, stages, and sequences in cognitive development. In W. A. Collins (Ed.), *The Concept of Development: Minnesota Symposia on Child Psychology* (Vol. 15, pp. 1–28). Hillsdale, NJ: Erlbaum.

Flavell, J. H. (1985). *Cognitive development* (2nd ed.). Englewood Cliffs, NJ.: Prentice-Hall.

Flavell, J. H., Beach, D., & Chinsky, J. (1966). Spontaneous verbal rehearsal in a memory task as a function of age. *Child Development*, *37*, 283–299.

Flavell, J. H., Botkin, P., Fry, C., Wright, J., & Jarvis,

P. (1968). *The development of role-taking and communication skills in children.* New York: Wiley.

Flavell, J. H., Flavell, E., & Green, F. (1987). Young children's knowledge about the apparent-real and pretend-real distributions. *Developmental Psychology, 23,* 816–822.

Flavell, J. H., Friedrichs, A., & Hoyt, J. (1970). Developmental changes in memorization processes. *Cognitive Psychology, 1,* 324–340.

Flavell, J. H., Green, F., & Flavell, E. (1986). Development of knowledge about the appearance-reality distinction. *Monographs of the Society for Research in Child Development, 51*(1, Serial No. 212).

Flavell, J. H., Zhang, X.-D., Zou, H., Dong, Q., & Qi, S. (1983). A comparison between the development of the appearance-reality distinction in the People's Republic of China and the United States. *Cognitive Psychology, 15,* 459–466.

Flerx, V. C., Fidler, D., & Rogers, R. W. (1976). Sex role stereotypes: Developmental aspects and early intervention. *Child Development, 47,* 998–1007.

Foley, M., Johnson, M., & Raye, C. (1983). Age-related changes in confusion between memories for thoughts and memories for speech. *Child Development, 54,* 51–60.

Fontaine, R. (1983). Imitative skill between birth and six months. *Infant Behavior and Development, 7,* 323–333.

Foot, H. C., Chapman, A. J., & Smith, J. R. (1977). Friendship and social responsiveness in boys and girls. *Journal of Personality and Social Psychology, 35,* 401–411.

Ford, C., & Beach, F. (1951). *Patterns of sexual behavior* (pp. 167–198). New York: Harper & Row.

Ford, M. E. (1982). Social cognition and social competence in adolescence. *Developmental Psychology, 18,* 323–340.

Ford, M. E., Miura, I., & Masters, J. C. (1984). Effects of social stimulus value on academic achievement and social competence: A reconsideration of children's first-name characteristics. *Journal of Educational Psychology, 76,* 1149–1158.

Forehand, G., Ragosta, J., & Rock, D. (1976). *Condition and processes of effective school desegregation.* Final Report, Washington, D.C.: U.S. Office of Education.

Forehand, R., Faust, J., & Baum, C. (1985). Accuracy of weight perception among young adolescent girls: An examination of personal and interpersonal correlates. *Journal of Early Adolescence, 5,* 239–245.

Forsterling, F. (1985). Attributional retraining: A review. *Psychological Bulletin, 98,* 495–512.

Fox, L. H. (1976). Sex differences in mathematical precocity: Bridging the gap. In D. P. Keating (Ed.), *Intellectual talent: Research and development.* Baltimore, MD: Johns Hopkins University Press.

Fox, N., & Davidson, R. (1988). Patterns of brain electrical activity during facial signs of emotion in 10-month-old infants. *Developmental Psychology, 24,* 230–236.

Fox, R., Aslin, R., Shea, S., & Duais, S. (1979). Stereopsis in human infants. *Science, 207,* 323–324.

Frantz, R. L., Ordy, J. M., & Udelf, M. S. (1962). Maturation of pattern vision in infants during the first six months. *Journal of Comparative Physiological Psychology, 55,* 907–917.

Frederiksen, N. (1986). Toward a broader conception of human intelligence. *American Psychologist, 41,* 445–452.

Freedman, J. L. (1965). Long-term behavioral effects of cognitive dissonance. *Journal of Experimental Social Psychology, 1,* 145–155.

Freedman, J. L. (1983). Effect of television violence on aggressiveness. *Psychological Bulletin, 96,* 227–246.

Fremgen, A., & Fay, D. (1980). Overextensions in production and comprehension: A methodological clarification. *Journal of Child Language, 7,* 205–211.

Freud, A. (1969). Adolescence as a developmental disturbance. In G. Caplan & S. Lebovici (Eds.), *Adolescence: Psychological perspectives.* New York: Basic Books.

Freud, S. (1938). *The basic writings of Sigmund Freud* (A. A. Brill, Trans.). New York: Random House.

Frey, K. S., & Ruble, D. N. (1987). What children say about classroom performance: Sex and grade differences in perceived competence. *Child Development, 58,* 227–246.

Friedenberg, E. (1965). *Dignity of youth and other atavisms.* Boston, MA: Beacon Press.

Friedman, M., Meltzer, R., & Miller, C. (Eds.). (1979). *New perspectives on school integration.* Philadelphia, PA: Fortress.

Friedrich, L. K., & Stein, A. H. (1973). Aggressive and prosocial TV programs and the natural behavior of preschool children. *Monographs of the Society for Research in Child Development, 38*(4, Serial No. 151).

Frodi, A. M., & Lamb, M. E. (1980). Child abusers' responses to infant smiles and cries. *Child Development, 51,* 238–241.

Frydman, O., & Bryant, P. (1988). Sharing and number equivalence by young children. *Cognitive Development, 3,* 323–340.

Frye, D., Braisby, N., Lowe, J., Maroudas, C., & Nicholls, J. (1989). Young children's understanding of counting and cardinality. *Child Development, 60,* 1158–1171.

Fulker, D., Eysenck, S. B. G., & Zuckerman, M. (1980). A genetic and environmental analysis of sensation seeking. *Journal of Research in Personality, 14,* 261–281.

Furman, W., & Bierman, K. (1984). Children's conceptions of friendship: A multimethod study of developmental changes. *Developmental Psychology, 20,* 925–931.

Furman, W., & Buhrmester, D. (1985). Children's perceptions of the qualities of sibling relationships. *Child Development, 56,* 148–161.

Furman, W., & Masters, J. C. (1980). Peer interactions, sociometric status, and resistance to deviation in young children. *Developmental Psychology, 16,* 229–236.

Furman, W., Rahe, D. F., & Hartup, W. W. (1979). Rehabilitation of socially withdrawn preschool children through mixed-age and same-age socialization. *Child Development, 50,* 915–922.

Furstenberg, F. F., Jr. (1976). *Unplanned parenthood: The social consequences of teenage childbearing.* New York: Free Press.

Furstenberg, F. F., Jr., et al. (1985). Sex education in school and family: Effects on adolescent sexual behavior. *American Journal of Public Health, 75,* 908–920.

Furstenberg, F. F., Jr., Lincoln, R., & Menken, J. (Eds.) (1981). *Teenage sexuality, pregnancy, and childbearing.* Philadelphia: University of Pennsylvania Press.

Furstenberg, F. F., Jr., Moore, K. A., & Peterson, J. L. (1986). Sex education and sexual experience among adolescents. *American Journal of Public Health, 75,* 1221–1222.

Gagnon, J. (1974). Scripts and the coordination of sexual conduct. In J. Cole & R. Dienstbier (Eds.), *Nebraska Symposium on Motivation* (Vol. 21). Lincoln: University of Nebraska Press.

Gaite, A. J. H. (1977). Teachers' perceptions of ideal male and female students: male chauvinism in the schools. In J. Pottker & A. Fishel (Eds.), *Sex bias in the schools: The research evidence.* Cranbury, NJ: Associated University Presses.

Galton, F. (1889). *Natural inheritance.* New York: Macmillan.

Ganchrow, J., Steiner, J., and Daher, M. (1983). Neonatal facial expressions in response to different qualities and intensities of gustatory stimuli. *Infant Behavior and Development, 6,* 189–200.

Gans, H. (1962). *The urban villagers.* Glencoe, IL: Free Press.

Garcia, J. (1981). The logic and limits of aptitude testing. *American Psychologist, 36,* 1172–1180.

Garn, S., Shaw, H., & McCabe, K. (1977). Effects of socioeconomic status and race on weight-defined and gestational prematurity in the United States. In D. Reed & F. Stanley (Eds.), *The epidemiology of prematurity.* Baltimore, MD: Urban and Schwarzenberg.

Garner, R., & Haynes, J. (1982). *Acquisition of text lookback expertise.* Unpublished paper, University of Maryland, Baltimore.

Garris, L., Steckler, A., & McIntire, J. (1976). The relationship between oral contraceptives and adolescent sexual behavior. *Journal of Sex Research, 12,* 135–146.

Garvey, C. (1975). Requests and responses in children's speech. *Journal of Child Language, 2,* 41-63.

Garvey, C., & BenDebba, M. (1974). Effects of age, sex, and partner on children's dyadic speech. *Child Development, 45,* 1159–1161.

Garvey, C., & Hogan, R. (1973). Social speech and social interaction: Egocentrism revisited. *Child Development, 44,* 562–568.

Gelfand, D. M., Hartmann, D. P., Cromer, C. C., Smith, C. L., & Page, B. C. (1975). The effects of instructional prompts and praise on children's donation rates. *Child Development, 46,* 980–983.

Gelman, R. (1972). The nature and development of early number concepts. In H. W. Reese (Ed.), *Advances in child development and behavior* (Vol. 7). New York: Academic Press.

Gelman, R. (1982). Basic numerical abilities. In R. Sternberg (Ed.), *Advances in the psychology of human intelligence* (Vol. 2). Hillsdale, NJ: Erlbaum.

Gelman, R., & Gallistel, R. (1978). *The child's understanding of number.* Cambridge, MA: Harvard University Press.

Gelman, R., & Meck, E. (1983). Preschoolers' counting: Principles before skill. *Cognition, 13,* 343–359.

Gelman, R., & Shatz, M. (1977). Appropriate speech adjustments: The operation of conversational constraints on talk to two-year-olds. In M. Lewis & L. Rosenblum (Eds.), *Friendship and peer relations.* New York: Wiley.

Gentner, D. (1982). Why nouns are learned before verbs: Linguistic relativity versus natural language partitioning. In S. Kuczaj (Ed.), *Language development: Vol 2. Language, thought, and culture.* Hillsdale, NJ: Erlbaum.

Gerber, P. J. (1977). Awareness of handicapping con-

651

ditions and sociometric status in an integrated pre-school setting. *Mental Retardation*, 15, 24–25.

Gewirtz, J., & Baer, D. (1958). Deprivation and satiation of social reinforcers as drive conditions. *Journal of Abnormal and Social Psychology*, 56, 49–56.

Gibbs, J., Arnold, K., & Burkhart, J. (1984) Sex differences in the expression of moral judgment. *Child Development*, 55, 1040–1043.

Gibson, E., & Spelke, E. (1983). The development of perception. In P. H. Mussen, J. H. Flavell, & E. M. Markman (Eds.), *Handbook of child psychology: Vol. 3. Cognitive development* (4th ed.). New York: Wiley.

Gibson, E., & Walker, A. (1982, March). *Intermodal perception of substance*. Paper presented at the meeting of the International Conference on Infant Studies, Austin, TX.

Gibson, E., & Walker, A. (1984). Development of knowledge of visual-tactual affordances of substance. *Child Development*, 55, 453–460.

Gibson, E. J., & Walk, R. D. (1960). The "visual cliff." *Scientific American*, 202, 64–71.

Gil, D. (1970). *Violence against children: Physical child abuse in the United States*. Cambridge, MA: Harvard University Press.

Gilligan, C. F. (1963). *Responses to temptation: An analysis of motives*. Unpublished doctoral dissertation, Harvard University, Cambridge, MA.

Gilligan, C. F. (1977). In a different voice: Women's conceptions of self and morality. *Harvard Educational Review*, 47, 481–517.

Gilligan, C. F. (1979). Woman's place in man's life cycle. *Harvard Educational Review*, 49, 431–446.

Gilligan, C. F. (1982). *In a different voice: Psychological theory and women's development*. Cambridge, MA: Harvard University Press.

Gilligan, C. F., & Attanucci, J. (1988). Two moral orientations: Gender differences and similarities. *Merrill-Palmer Quarterly*, 34, 223–237.

Ginsburg, H. J., & Miller, S. M. (1982). Sex differences in children's risk-taking behavior. *Child Development*, 53, 426–428.

Gjerde, P. E., Block, J., & Block, J. H. (1985). Longitudinal consistency of matching Familiar Figures Test performance from early childhood to preadolescence. *Developmental Psychology*, 21, 262–271.

Glass, G. V., Cohen, L. S., Smith, M. L., & Filby, N. N. (1982). *School class size: Research and policy*. Beverly Hills, CA: Sage.

Gleason, J., & Weintraub, S. (1978). Input language and the acquisition of communicative competence. In K. E. Nelson (Ed.) *Children's language* (Vol. 1). New York: Gardner Press.

Gluck, J. P., & Sackett, G. P. (1976). Extinction deficits in socially isolated Rhesus monkeys (Macaca Mulatta). *Developmental Psychology*, 12, 173–174.

Glueck, S., & Glueck, E. (1950). *Unraveling juvenile delinquency*. Cambridge: Harvard University Press.

Gnepp, J. (1983). Children's social sensitivity: Inferring emotions from conflicting cues. *Developmental Psychology*, 19, 805–814.

Gnepp, J., & Chilamkurti, C. (1988). Children's use of personality attributions to predict other people's emotional and behavioral reactions. *Child Development*, 59, 743–754.

Gnepp, J., & Gould, M. (1985). The development of personalized inferences: Understanding other people's emotional reactions in light of their prior experiences. *Child Development*, 56, 1455–1464.

Gnepp, J., McKee, E., & Domanic, J. (1987). Children's use of situational information to infer emotion: Understanding of emotionally equivocal situations. *Developmental Psychology*, 23, 114–123.

Goelman, H. (1986). The language environments of family day care. In S. Kilmer (Ed.), *Advances in early education and day care* (Vol. 4). Greenwich, CT: JAI Press.

Gold, D., & Andres, D. (1978a). Relations between maternal employment and development of nursery school children. *Canadian Journal of Behavioural Science*, 10, 116–129.

Gold, D., & Andres, D. (1978b). Comparisons of adolescent children with employed and nonemployed mothers. *Merrill-Palmer Quarterly*, 24, 243–254.

Goldberg, S. (1983). Parent-infant bonding: Another look. *Child Development*, 54, 1355–1382.

Golden, M., & Birns, B. (1975). Social class and infant intelligence. In M. Lewis (Ed.), *Origins of intelligence: Infancy and early childhood* (pp. 299–351). New York: Plenum.

Goldfarb, W. (1945). Effects of psychological deprivation in infancy and subsequent stimulation. *American Journal of Psychiatry*, 102, 18–33.

Goldfarb, W. (1955). Emotional and intellectual consequences of psychological deprivation in infancy: A revaluation. In P. Hock & J. Zubin (Eds.), *Psychopathology of childhood*. New York: Grune & Stratton.

Goldman-Rakic, P. (1987). Development of cortical circuitry and cognitive function. *Child Development*, 58, 601–622.

Goldsmith, H. H., Buss, A., Plomin, R., Rothbart, M., Thomas, A., Chess, S., Hinde, R., & McCall, R. (1987). Roundtable: What is temperament? Four approaches. *Child Development*, *58*, 505–529.

Goldsmith, H. H., & Campos, J. (1982, August). *Infant temperament: Genetics and generalizability*. Paper presented at the meeting of the American Psychological Association, Washington, DC.

Gollin, E. S. (1958). Organizational characteristics of social judgment: A developmental investigation. *Journal of Personality*, *26*, 139–154.

Good, T. L. (1980). *Teacher expectations, teacher behavior, student perceptions, and student behavior: A decade of research*. Paper presented at the meeting of the American Educational Research Association, Boston, MA.

Goodenough, F. L. (1931a). The expression of the emotions in infancy. *Child Development*, *2*, 96–101.

Goodenough, F. L. (1931b). *Anger in young children*. Minneapolis: University of Minnesota Press.

Goodenough, F. L. (1934). *Developmental psychology*. New York: D. Appleton-Century.

Goodlad, J. I. (1984). *A place called school: Prospects for the future*. New York: McGraw-Hill.

Goodman, P. (1956). *Growing up absurd*. New York: Random House.

Goodnow, J. J., & Collins, W. A. (1990). *Development according to parents: The nature, sources, and consequences of parents' ideas*. London: Erlbaum.

Goodsit, J., Morse, P., Ver Hoeve, J., & Cowan, N. (1984). Infant speech recognition in multisyllabic contexts. *Child Development*, *55*, 903–910.

Goossens, L. (1984). Imaginary audience behavior as a function of age, sex, and formal operational thinking. *International Journal of Behavioral Development*, *7*, 77–93.

Gopnik, A., & Meltzoff, A. (1987). The development of categorization in the second year and its relation to other cognitive and linguistic developments. *Child Development*, *58*, 1523–1531.

Goren, C., Sarty, J., & Wu, P. (1975). Visual following and pattern discrimination of face-like stimuli by newborn infants. *Pediatrics*, *56*, 544–549.

Gottlieb, G., & Krasnegor, N. (1985). *Measurement of audition and vision in the first year of postnatal life: A methodological overview*. Norwood, NJ: Ablex Press.

Gottlieb, J. (1975). Public, peer and professional attitudes toward mentally retarded persons. In M. J. Begab & S. A. Richardson (Eds.), *The mentally re-tarded and society: A social science perspective*. Baltimore, MD: University Park Press.

Gottman, J. M. (1983). How children become friends. *Monographs of the Society for Research in Child Development*, *48*(Serial No. 201).

Gottman, J. M., & Parkhurst, J. (1980). A developmental theory of friendship and acquaintanceship processes. In W. A. Collins (Ed.), *Minnesota Symposia on Child Psychology* (Vol. 13, pp. 197–224). Hillsdale, NJ: Erlbaum.

Graham, P., & Rutter, M. (1985). Adolescent disorders. In M. Rutter & L. Hersov (Eds.), *Child and adolescent psychiatry: Modern approaches* (2nd ed., pp. 351–367). Oxford: Blackwell.

Granrud, C., & Yonas, A. (1984). Infants' perception of pictorially specified interposition. *Journal of Experimental Child Psychology*, *37*, 500–511.

Gray, W., & Hudson, L. (1984). Formal operations and the imaginary audience. *Developmental Psychology*, *20*, 619–627.

Green, R. (1974). *Sexual identity conflict in children and adults*. New York: Basic Books.

Green, R. (1987). *The ''sissy-boy'' syndrome and the development of homosexuality*. New Haven, CT: Yale University Press.

Green, R., & Money, J. (Eds.), *Transsexualism and sex reassignment*. Baltimore: Johns Hopkins University Press.

Greenberg, M., & Crnic, K. (1988). Longitudinal predictors of developmental status and social interaction in premature and full-term infants at age two. *Child Development*, *59*, 554–570.

Greenberger, E., & Steinberg, L. (1982, July). *Statement on proposed changes in child labor regulations*. Testimony presented before the House Subcommittee on Labor Standards, Washington, DC.

Greenfield, P., & Smith, J. (1976). *The structure of communication in early language development*. New York: Academic Press.

Greenough, W., Black, J., & Wallace, C. (1987). Experience and brain development. *Child Development*, *58*, 539–559.

Greif, E., & Ulman, K. (1982). The psychological impact of menarche on early adolescent females: A review of the literature. *Child Development*, *53*, 1413–1430.

Grim, P., Kohlberg, L., & White, S. (1968). Some relationships between conscience and attentional processes. *Journal of Personality and Social Psychology*, *8*, 239–253.

Grossmann, K., & Grossmann, K. (1982). *Maternal sensitivity to infants' signals during the first year as related to the year old's behavior in Ainsworth's strange situation in a sample of Northern German families*. Paper presented at the meeting of the International Conference on Infant Studies, Austin, TX.

Grotevant, H., & Cooper, C. (1985). Patterns of interaction in family relationships and the development of identity exploration in adolescence. *Child Development*, *56*, 415–428.

Grotevant, H., Scarr, S., & Weinberg, R. (1977). Patterns of interest similarity in adoptive and biological families. *Journal of Personality and Social Psychology*, *35*, 667–676.

Gruendel, J. M. (1977). Referential extension in early child language. *Child Development*, *42*, 1567–1576.

Grueneich, R. (1982). Issues in the developmental study of how children use intention and consequences information to make moral evaluations. *Child Development*, *53*, 29–43.

Guilford, J. P. (1967). *The nature of human intelligence*. New York: McGraw-Hill.

Guilford, J. P. (1988). Some changes in the structure-of-the-intellect model. *Educational and Psychological Measurement*, *48*, 1–4.

Gunnar, M. R. (1980). Control, warning signals and distress in infancy. *Developmental Psychology*, *16*, 281–289.

Gunnar, M. R., & Donahue, M. (1980). Sex differences in social responsiveness between six months and twelve months. *Child Development*, *51*, 262–265.

Gunnar, M. R., Malone, S., Vance, G., & Fisch, R. (1985). Coping with aversive stimulation in the neonatal period: Quiet sleep and plasma cortisol levels during recovery from circumcision. *Child Development*, *56*, 824–834.

Gunnar, M. R., Mangelsdorf, S., Larson, M., & Hertsgaard, L. (1989). Attachment, temperament, and adrenocortical activity in infancy: A study of psychoendocrine regulation. *Developmental Psychology*, *25*, 355–363.

Guralnick, M. J. (1981). The social behavior of preschool children of different developmental levels: Effects of group composition. *Journal of Experimental Child Psychology*, *31*, 115–130.

Guttmacher, A. (1973). *Pregnancy, birth, and family planning: A guide for expectant parents in the 1970's*. New York: Viking Press.

Haaf, R., Smith, P., & Smitley, S. (1983). Infant response to facelike patterns under fixed-trial and infant-control procedures. *Child Development*, *54*, 172–177.

Haan, N. (1985). Processes of moral development: Cognitive or social disequilibrium? *Developmental Psychology*, *21*, 996–1006.

Haith, M. (1980). *Rules that babies look by*. Hillsdale, NJ: Erlbaum.

Hale, R. (1978). The WISC-R as a predictor of WRAT performance. *Psychology in the Schools*, *15*, 172–175.

Hallinan, M. T., & Texeira, R. A. (1987). Opportunities and constraints: Black white differences in the formation of interracial friendships. *Child Development*, *58*, 1358–1371.

Halpern, D. (1986). *Sex differences in cognitive abilities*. Hillsdale, NJ: Erlbaum.

Hanson, J. W., Streissguth, A. P., & Smith, D. W. (1981). The effects of moderate alcohol consumption during pregnancy on fetal growth and morphogenesis. *Journal of Pediatrics*, *92*, 457–460.

Hargreaves, D. H. (1967). *Social relations in a secondary school*. London: Routledge and Kegan Paul.

Harlow, H. F., & Harlow, M. K. (1977). The young monkeys. In P. Cramer (Ed.), *Readings in developmental psychology today* (2nd ed.). Del Mar, CA: CRM Books.

Harlow, H. F., Harlow, M. K., Dodsworth, R. O., & Arling, G. L. (1960). Maternal behavior in rhesus monkeys deprived of mothering and peer association as infants. *Proceedings of the American Philosophical Society*, *110*, 88–98.

Harlow, H. F., & Zimmermann, R. (1959). Affectional responses in the infant monkey. *Science*, *130*, 421–432.

Harris, L. (1986). *American teens speak: Sex myths, TV, and birth control*. New York: Louis Harris & Associates, Project No. 864012.

Harris, L. A. (1967). A study of altruism. *Elementary School Journal*, *68*, 135–141.

Harris, M. B. (1970). Reciprocity and generosity: Some determinants of sharing in children. *Child Development*, *41*, 313–328.

Harris, N., Jackson, N., & Rydingsword, C. E. (Eds.). (1975). *The integration of American schools: Problems, experiences, solutions*. Boston, MA: Allyn & Bacon.

Harris, P., Donnelly, K., Guz, G., & Pitt-Watson, R. (1986). Children's understanding of the distinction between real and apparent emotion. *Child Development*, *57*, 895–909.

Harry, J. (1982). *Gay children grown up: Gender culture and gender deviance*. New York: Praeger.

Hart, D. (1988). The development of personal identity in adolescence: A philosophical dilemma approach. *Merrill-Palmer Quarterly, 34,* 105–114.

Harter, S. (1982). Children's understanding of multiple emotions: A cognitive developmental approach. In W. F. Overton (Ed.), *The relationship between social and cognitive development* (pp. 147–194). Hillsdale, NJ: Erlbaum.

Harter, S. (1983). Developmental perspectives on the self-system. In P. H. Mussen & E. M. Hetherington (Eds.), *Handbook of child psychology: Vol. 4. Socialization, personality, and social development* (4th ed., pp. 285–386). New York: Wiley.

Harter, S., & Connell, J. P. (1982). A comparison of alternative models of the relationships between academic achievement and children's perceptions of competence, control, and motivational orientation. In J. Nicholls (Ed.), *The development of achievement-related cognitions and behaviors.* Greenwich, CT: JAI Press.

Hartshorne, H., & May, M. S. (1928). *Studies in the nature of character: Vol. 1. Studies in deceit.* New York: Macmillan.

Hartshorne, H., & May, M. S. (1930). *Studies in the nature of character: Vol. 3. Studies in the organization of character.* New York: Macmillan.

Hartshorne, H., May, M. A., & Maller, J. B. (1929). *Studies in the nature of character: Vol. 2. Studies in service and self-control.* New York: Macmillan.

Hartup, W. W. (1964). Friendship status and the effectiveness of peers as reinforcing agents. *Journal of Experimental Child Psychology, 1,* 154–162.

Hartup, W. W. (1979). Two worlds of childhood. *American Psychologist, 34,* 944–950.

Hartup, W. W. (1983). Peer relations. In P. H. Mussen & E. M. Hetherington (Eds.), *Handbook of child psychology: Vol 4. Socialization, personality, and social development* (4th ed., pp. 103–196). New York: Wiley.

Hartup, W. W. (1984). The peer context in middle childhood. In W. A. Collins (Ed.), *Development during middle childhood: The years from six to twelve* (pp. 240–282). Washington, DC: National Academy Press.

Hartup, W. W. (1988). Developmental universals childhood socialization. *Singapore Journal of Education, 9,* 9–18.

Hartup, W. W. (1989). Social relationships and their developmental significance. *American Psychologist, 44,* 120–126.

Hartup, W. W., & Coates, B. (1967). Imitation of a peer as a function of reinforcement from the peer group and rewardingness of the model. *Child Development, 38,* 1003–1016.

Hartup, W. W., Glazer, J. A., & Charlesworth, R. (1967). Peer reinforcement and sociometric status. *Child Development, 38,* 1017–1024.

Harvey, O. J., & Consalvi, C. (1960). Status and conformity to pressures in informal groups. *Journal of Abnormal and Social Psychology, 60,* 182–187.

Harvey, O. J., & Rutherford, J. (1960). Status in the informal group: Influence and influencibility at differing age levels. *Child Development, 31,* 377–385.

Hastings Center Project. (1987). Imperiled newborns. *Hastings Center Report, 17,* 5–32.

Hauser, S., Powers, S., Noam, G., Jacobson, A., Weiss, B., & Follansbee, D. (1984). Familial contexts of adolescent ego development. *Child Development, 55,* 195–213.

Hawkins, R. P., & Pingree, S. (1982). Television's influence on constructions of social reality. In D. Pearl, L. Bouthilet, & J. Lazar (Eds.), *Television and human behavior: Ten years of scientific progress and implications for the '80's.* Washington, DC: U.S. Government Printing Office.

Hayes, C. (Ed.). (1987). *Risking the future: Adolescent sexuality, pregnancy, and childbearing.* Washington, DC: National Academy Press.

Hayes, L., & Watson, J. (1981). Neonatal imitation: Fact or artifact. *Developmental Psychology, 17,* 655–660.

Haynes, H., White, B., & Held, R. (1965). Visual accommodation in human infants. *Science, 148,* 528–530.

Hecox, K., & Deegan, D. (1985). Methodological issues in the study of auditory development. In G. Gottlieb & N. Krasnegor (Eds.), *Measurement of audition and vision in the first year of life: A methodological overview.* Norwood, NJ: Ablex Publishing.

Heibeck, T., & Markman, E. (1987). Word learning in children: An examination of fast mapping. *Child Development, 58,* 1021–1034.

Herold, E., Goodwin, M., & Lero, D. (1979). Self-esteem, locus of control, and adolescent contraception. *Journal of Psychology, 101,* 83–88.

Herold, E., & Samson, L. (1980). Differences between women who begin pill use before and after first intercourse: Ontario, Canada. *Family Planning Perspectives, 12,* 304–305.

Hershenson, M., Munsinger, H., & Kessen, W. (1965). Preferences for shapes of intermediate variability in the newborn human. *Science, 147,* 630–631.

Hersov, L., & Berg, I. (Eds.). (1980). *Out of school: Modern perspectives in truancy and school refusal.* Chichester, England: Wiley.

Hess, R., & Goldblatt, I. (1957). The status of adolescents in American Society: A problem in social identity. *Child Development, 28,* 459–468.

Hetherington, E. M., Camara, K. A., & Featherman, D. L. (1982). *Cognitive performance, school behavior and achievement of children from one-parent households.* Washington, DC: National Institute of Education.

Hetherington, E. M., Cox, M., & Cox, R. (1979). Play and social interaction in children following divorce. *Journal of Social Issues, 35,* 26–49.

Hetherington, E. M., Cox, M., & Cox, R. (1982). Effects of divorce on parents and children. In M. Lamb (Ed.), *Nontraditional families.* Hillsdale, NJ: Erlbaum.

Hetherington, E. M., Stanley-Hagan, M. S., & Anderson, E. R. (1989). Marital transitions: A child's perspective. *American Psychologist, 44*(2), 303–312.

Hicks, D. J. (1965). Imitation and retention of film-mediated aggressive peer and adult models. *Journal of Personality and Social Psychology, 2,* 97–100.

Hicks, J., & Hayes, M. (1938). Study of the characteristics of 250 junior high school children. *Child Development, 9,* 219–242.

Hill, J. (April, 1986). *Research on adolescents and their families: Past and prospect.* Invited address to the National Conference on Health Futures for Adolescents, Daytona Beach.

Hill, J. (1980a). The family. In NSSE yearbook, *Toward adolescence: The middle school years.* Chicago, IL: University of Chicago Press.

Hill, J. (1980b). *Understanding early adolescence: A framework.* Chapel Hill, NC: Center for Early Adolescence.

Hill, J. (1987). Research on adolescents and their families: Past and prospect. In *New directions for child development, 37,* 13–31.

Hill, J. (1988). Adapting to menarche: Familial control and conflict. In M. Gunnar & W. A. Collins (Eds.), *Development during the transition to adolescence: The Minnesota Symposia on Child Psychology* (Vol. 21). Hillsdale, NJ: Erlbaum.

Hill, J., Holmbeck,G., Marlow, L., Green, T., & Lynch, M. (1985). Menarcheal status and parent-child relations in families of seventh-grade girls. *Journal of Youth and Adolescence, 14,* 301–316.

Hill, J. P., & Holmbeck, G. N. (1986). Attachment and autonomy during adolescence. *Annals of Child Development, 3,* 145–189.

Himmelweit, H., Oppenheim, A. N., & Vince, P. (1958). Television and the child: *An empirical study of the effects of television on the young.* London: Oxford University Press.

Hindley, C. B., & Owen, C. F. (1978). The extent of individual changes in IQ for ages between 6 months and 17 years in a British longitudinal sample. *Journal of Child Psychology and Psychiatry, 19,* 329–350.

Hirsh-Pasek, K., Treiman, R., & Schneiderman, M. (1984). Brown and Hanlon revisited: Mother's sensitivity to ungrammatical forms. *Journal of Child Language, 11,* 81–88.

Hobbs, N. (1975). *The futures of children.* San Francisco, CA: Jossey-Bass.

Hock, H., Romanski, L., Galie, A., & Williams, C. (1978). Real world schemata and scene recognition in adults and children. *Memory and Cognition, 6,* 423–431.

Hofferth, S. L., & Hayes, C. D. (Eds.). (1987). *Risking the future: Adolescent sexuality, pregnancy, and childbearing: Vol. 2. Working papers and statistical reports.* Washington, DC: National Academy Press.

Hoff-Ginsberg, E. (1983). Sound-based errors in early word use. *Journal of Child Language, 10,* 459–464.

Hoffman, L. W. (1984). Work, family, and the socialization of the child. In R. Parke (Ed.), *Review of child development research: Vol. 7. The family* (pp. 223–282). Chicago, IL: University of Chicago Press.

Hoffman, M. L. (1970). Moral development. In P. H. Mussen (Ed.), *Carmichael's Manual of Child Psychology* (3rd ed., Vol. 2). New York: Wiley.

Hoffman, M. L. (1975). Developmental synthesis of affect and cognition and its implications for altruistic motivation. *Developmental Psychology, 11,* 605–622.

Hokanson, J. E., Wilers, K. R., & Koropsak, E. (1968). Modification of autonomic responses during aggressive interchange. *Journal of Personality, 36,* 386–404.

Holstein, C. B. (1976). Irreversible, stepwise sequence in the development or moral judgment: A longitudinal study of males and females. *Child Development, 47,* 51–61.

Honzik, M. P. (1983). Measuring mental abilities in infancy: The value and limitations. In M. Lewis (Ed.), *Origins of intelligence: Infancy and early childhood.* New York: Plenum.

Honzik, M. P., MacFarlane, J. W., & Allen, L. (1948). The stability of mental test performance between two and eighteen years. *Journal of Experimental Education, 17,* 309–324.

Horn, J. L., & Cattell, R. B. (1967). Age differences in fluid and crystallized intelligence. *Acta Psychologica, 26,* 107–129.

Horn, J. L., & Cattell, R. B. (1982). Whimsy and misunderstandings of gf-gc theory: A comment on Guilford. *Psychological Bulletin, 91,* 623–633.

Horn, J. L., & Donaldson, G. (1976). On the myth of intellectual decline in adulthood. *American Psychologist, 31,* 701–719.

Horn, J. L., & Knapp, J. (1974). Thirty wrongs do not make a right: A reply to Guilford. *Psychological Bulletin, 81,* 502–504.

Hornick, J., Doran, L., & Crawford, S. (1979). Premarital contraceptive usage among male and female adolescents. *Family Coordinator, 28,* 181–190.

Hornik, R. (1981). Out-of-school television and schooling: Hypothesis and methods. *Review of Educational Research, 51,* 199–214.

Hornik, R., & Gunnar, M. (1988). A descriptive analysis of infant social referencing. *Child Development, 59,* 626–634.

Horowitz, F. (1987). *Exploring developmental theories: Toward a structural/behavioral model of development.* Hillsdale, NJ: Erlbaum.

Horowitz, F. (Ed.). (1974). Visual attention, auditory stimulation, and language discrimination in young infants. *Monographs of the Society for Research in Child Development, 39*(Serial No. 158).

Horowitz, F., & O'Brien, M. (1986). Gifted and talented children: State of knowledge and directions for research. *American Psychologist, 41,* 1147–1152.

Hoving, K. L., Hamm, N., & Galvin, P. (1969). Social influence as a function of stimulus ambiguity at three age levels. *Developmental Psychology, 1,* 631–636.

Howes, C. (1988). Relations between early child care and schooling. *Developmental Psychology, 24,* 53–57.

Huesmann, L. R., Eron, L. D., Lefkowitz, M. M., & Walder, L. O. (1984). Stability of aggression over time and generations. *Developmental Psychology, 20* (6), 1120–1134.

Hughes, L. W., Gordon, W. M., & Hillman, L. W. (1980). *Desegregating America's schools.* New York: Longman.

Humphreys, L. G. (1971). Theory of intelligence. In R. Cancro (Ed.), *Intelligence: Genetic and environmental influences* (pp. 31–42). New York: Grune & Stratton.

Hunter, F. (1984). Socializing procedures in parent-child and friendship relations during adolescence. *Developmental Psychology, 20,* 1092–1099.

Hunter, F. (1985a). Adolescents' perception of discussions with parents and friends. *Developmental Psychology, 21,* 433–440.

Hunter, F. (1985b). Individual adolescents' perceptions of interactions with friends and parents. *Journal of Early Adolescence, 5,* 295–305.

Huston, A. C. (1983). Sex typing. In P. H. Mussen & E. M. Hetherington (Eds.), *Handbook of child psychology: Vol. 4. Socialization, personality, and social development.* New York: Wiley.

Huston, A. C., Carpenter, C. J., Atwater, J. B., & Johnson, L. M. (1986). Gender, adult structuring of activities, and social behavior in middle childhood. *Child Development, 57,* 1200–1209.

Huston, A. C., Watkins, B. A., & Kunkel, D. (1989). Public policy and children's television. *American Psychologist, 44,* 424–433.

Hutt, S. J., Hutt, C., Leonard, H. G., Benuth, H. V., & Montjewerff, W. J. (1968). Auditory response in the newborn. *Nature (London), 218,* 888–890.

Huttenlocher, J. (1974). The origins of language comprehension. In R. L. Solso (Ed.), *Theories in cognitive psychology.* New York: Wiley.

Huttenlocher, J., & Lui, F. (1979). The semantic organization of some simple nouns and verbs. *Journal of Verbal Learning and Verbal Behavior, 18,* 141–162.

Huttenlocher, P. (1979). Synaptic density in human frontal cortex-developmental changes and effects of aging. *Brain Research, 163,* 195, 205.

Iannotti, R. (1985). Naturalistic and structured assessments of prosocial behavior in preschool children: The influence of empathy and perspective taking. *Developmental Psychology, 21,* 46–55.

Imperato-McGinley, J. (1981). The impact of androgens on the evolution of male gender identity. In S. Kogan & E. Hafez (Eds.), *Clinics in andrology, Vol. 7. Pediatric andrology.* Boston, MA: Nijhoff.

Ingram, D. (1986). Phonological development: Production. In P. Fletcher & M. Garman (Eds.), *Language acquisition* (2nd ed.). Cambridge: Cambridge University Press.

Inhelder, B., & Piaget, J. (1958). *The growth of logical thinking from childhood to adolescence.* New York: Basic Books.

Inoff-Germain, G., Arnold, G., Nottelmann, E., Susman, E., Cutler, G., Jr., & Chrousos, G. (1988). Relations between hormone levels and observational measures of aggressive behavior of young adolescents in family interactions. *Developmental Psychology, 24,* 129–139.

Isen, A. (1984). Toward understanding the role of affect in cognition. In R. Wyer & T. Strull (Eds.), *Handbook of social cognition* (Vol. 3, pp. 179–236). Hillsdale, NJ: Erlbaum.

Isen, A., & Shalker, T. (1982). The influence of mood state on evaluation of positive, neutral, and negative stimuli: When you "accentuate the positive," do you "eliminate the negative"? *Social Psychology Quarterly*, *45*, 58–63.

Ishiyama, F., & Chabassol, D. (1985). Adolescents' fear of social consequences of academic success as a function of age and sex. *Journal of Youth and Adolescence*, *14*, 37–46.

Iwawaki, S., Sonoo, K., Williams, J. E., & Best, D. L. (1978). Color bias among young Japanese children. *Journal of Cross-cultural Psychology*, *9*, 61–73.

Izard, C. E., Hembree, E. A., & Huebner, R. R. (1987). Infant's emotional expressions to acute pain: Developmental change and stability of individual differences. *Developmental Psychology*, *23*, 105–113.

Izard, C. E., & Malatesta, C. Z. (1987). Perspectives on emotional development. I. Differential emotions theory of early emotional development. In J. D. Osofsky (Ed.), *Handbook of infant development* (2nd ed.). New York: Wiley.

Jacklin, C. M., & Maccoby, E. E. (1978). Social behavior at thirty-three months in same-sex and mixed-sex dyads. *Child Development*, *49*, 557–569.

Jacobson, J., & Wille, D. (1986). The influence of attachment pattern on developmental changes in peer interaction from the toddler to the preschool period. *Child Development*, *57*, 338–347.

Jacobson, S. W. (1979). Matching behavior in the young infant. *Child Development*, *50*, 425–430.

Jakobson, R. (1968). Child language, aphasia, and phonological universals. The Hague, Netherlands: Mouton.

James, W. (1884). What is emotion? *Mind*, *4*, 188–204.

James, W. (1890). *Principles of psychology*. New York: Henry Holt.

James, W. (1961). *Psychology: The briefer course*. New York: Harper. (Original work published 1892.)

Janos, P., Sanfilippo, S., & Robinson, N. (1986). "Underachievement" among markedly accelerated college students. *Journal of Youth and Adolescence*, *15*, 303–313.

Jelinek, M. M., & Brittan, E. M. (1975). Multiracial education: I. Inter-ethnic friendship patterns. *Educational Research*, *18*, 44–53.

Jencks, C. (1985). How poor are the poor? *The New York Review*, May, 41–43.

Jencks, C. S., Smith, M., Acland, H., Bane, M. J., Cohen, D., Gintis, H., Heyns, B., & Michelson, S. (1972). *Inequality: A reassessment of the effects of family and schooling in America*. New York: Basic Books.

Jensen, A. R. (1969). How much can we boost IQ and scholastic achievement? *Harvard Educational Review*, *39*, 1–123.

Jensen, A. R. (1980). *Bias in mental testing*. New York: Free Press.

Jensen, A. R. (1985). The nature of black-white difference on various psychometric tests: Spearman's hypothesis. *Behavioral and Brain Sciences*, *8*, 193–263.

Jensen, A. R. (1989). Raising IQ without raising g? A review of the Milwaukee Project: Preventing mental retardation in children at risk. *Developmental Review*, *9*, 234–258.

Jersild, A. T. (1954). Emotional development. In L. Carmichael (Ed.), *Manual of child psychology* (2nd ed.). New York: Wiley.

Jersild, A. T., & Markey, F. C. (1935). Conflicts between preschool children. *Child Development Monographs* (No. 21). New York: Columbia University, Teachers College.

Jespersen, O. (1922a). *Language: Its nature, development, and origin*. London: Allen & Unwin.

Jespersen, O. (1922b). Language: Its nature, development, and English as a second language. *Cognitive Psychology*, *21*, 60–99.

Johnson, D. W., Maruyama, G., Johnson, R., Nelson, D., & Skon, L. (1981). Effects of cooperative, competitive, and individualistic goal structures on achievement: A meta-analysis. *Psychological Bulletin*, *89*, 47–62.

Johnson, J., & Newport, E. (1989). Critical period effects in second language learning: The influence of maturational state on the acquisition of English as a second language. *Cognitive Psychology*, *21*, 60–99.

Johnston, L., O'Malley, P., & Bachman, J. (1985). *Use of licit and illicit drugs by America's high school students, 1975–1984*. Washington, DC: U.S. Government Printing Office.

Jones, E., Forest, J. D., Goldman, N., Henshaw, S., Lincoln, R., Rosoff, J., Westoff, C., & Wulf, D. (1985). Teenage pregnancy in developed countries: Determinants and policy implications. *Family Planning Perspectives*, *17*(2), 53–63.

Jones, M. C. (1957). The later careers of boys who were early or late maturing. *Child Development*, *28*, 113–128.

Jones, M. C., & Bayley, N. (1950). Physical maturing among boys as related to behavior. *Journal of Educational Psychology*, *41*, 129–148.

Josselson, R. (1980). Ego development in adolescence. In J. Adelson (Ed.), *Handbook of adolescent psychology* (pp. 188–210). New York: Wiley.

Jurkovic, G. (1980). The juvenile delinquent as a moral philosopher: A structural-developmental perspective. *Psychological Bulletin*, *88*, 709–727.

658

Jusczyk, P., Pisoni, D., Fernald, A., Reed, M., & Myers, M. (1983, April). *Durational context effects in the processing of non-speech sounds by infants.* Paper presented at the meeting of the Society for Research in Child Development, Detroit, MI.

Kagan, J. (1971). *Change and continuity in infancy.* New York: Wiley.

Kagan, J. (1976). Resistance and continuity in psychological development. In A. M. Clarkeand & A. D. B. Clarke (Eds.), *Early experience: Myth and evidence.* New York: Free Press.

Kagan, J. (1978). On emotion and its development: A working paper. In M. Lewis & L. Rosenblum (Eds.), *The development of affect.* New York: Plenum.

Kagan, J. (1983). Stress and coping in early development. In N. Garmezy & M. Rutter (Eds.), *Stress, coping, and development in children.* New York: McGraw-Hill.

Kagan, J. (1984). *The nature of the child.* New York: Basic Books.

Kagan, J., Kearsley, R., & Zelazo, P. (1978). *Infancy: Its place in human development.* Cambridge, MA: Harvard University Press.

Kagan, J., & Klein, R. (1973). Cross-cultural perspectives on early development. American Psychologist, 28, 947–961.

Kagan, J., & Moss, H. (1962). *Birth to maturity.* New York: Wiley.

Kagan, J., Rosman, B. L., Day, D., Albert, J., & Philips, W. (1964). Information processing in the child: Significance of analytic and reflective attitudes. *Psychological Monographs,* 78(No. 278).

Kalyan-Masih, V. (1985). Cognitive performance and cognitive style. *International Journal of Behavioral Development,* 8, 39–54.

Kamin, L. J. (1974). *The science and politics of IQ.* Potomac, MD: Erlbaum.

Kamin, L. J. (1981). Commentary. In S. Scarr (Ed.), *Race, social class, and individual differences in IQ.* Hillsdale, NJ: Erlbaum.

Kandel, D. (1973). Adolescent marijuana use: Role of parents and peers. *Science,* 181, 1067–1070.

Kandel, D., & Lesser, G. (1972). *Youth in two worlds.* San Francisco, CA: Jossey-Bass.

Kanfer, F. H., & Duerfeldt, P. H. (1968). Comparison of self-reward and self-criticism as a function of types of prior external reinforcement. *Journal of Personality and Social Psychology,* 8, 261–268.

Kaplan, E. L. (1969). *The role of intonation in the acquisition of language.* Unpublished doctoral dissertation, Cornell University, Ithaca, NY.

Kaplan, E. L., & Kaplan, G. A. (1971). The prelinguistic child. In J. Eliot (Ed.), *Human development and cognitive processes.* New York: Holt, Rinehart, & Winston.

Kaplan, R. (1985). The controversy related to the use of psychological tests. In B. Wolman (Ed.), *Handbook of intelligence.* New York: Wiley.

Karniol, R., & Ross, H. (1976). The development of causal attributions in social perception. *Journal of Personality and Social Psychology,* 34, 455–464.

Karp, L. (1976). *Genetic engineering: Threat or promise.* Chicago: Nelson-Hall.

Katchadourian, H. (1975). *The biology of adolescence.* San Francisco, CA: Freeman.

Kaufman, A., Kamphaus, R., & Kaufman, N. (1985). New directions in intelligence testing: The Kaufman Assessment Battery for Children (K-ABC). In B. Wolman (Ed.), *Handbook of intelligence.* New York: Wiley.

Kaufman, J., & Zigler, E. (1987). Do abused children become abusive parents? *American Journal of Orthopsychiatry,* 57, 186–197.

Kaye, K. (1982). *The mental and social life of babies: How parents create persons.* Chicago, IL: University of Chicago Press.

Kaye, K., & Charney, R. (1980). How mothers maintain "dialogue" with two-year-olds. In D. Olson (Ed.), *The social foundations of language and thought.* New York: Norton.

Keasey, C. B. (1971). Social participation as a factor in the moral development preadolescents. *Developmental Psychology,* 5, 216–220.

Keasey, C. B. (1977). Young children's attribution of intentionality to themselves and others. *Child Development,* 48, 261–264.

Keating, D. P. (1980). Thinking processes in adolescence. In J. Adelson (Ed.), *Handbook of adolescent psychology* (pp. 211–246). New York: Wiley.

Keating, D. P. (Ed.). (1976). *Intellectual talent: Research and development.* Baltimore, MD: Johns Hopkins University Press.

Keeney, T., Cannizzo, S., & Flavell, J. (1967). Spontaneous and induced verbal rehearsal in a recall task. *Child Development,* 38, 953–966.

Kempe, C. H., Silverman, F. N., Steele, B. B., Droegemueller, W., & Silver, H. K. (1962). The battered-child syndrome. *JAMA, Journal of the American Medical Association,* 181, 17–24.

Kessen, W. (1965). *The child.* New York: Wiley.

Kirby, D. (1984). *Sexuality and education: An evaluation of programs and their effects.* Santa Cruz, CA: Network Publications.

Kisilevsky, B., & Muir, D. (1984). Neonatal habituation

and dishabituation to tactile stimulation during sleep. *Developmental Psychology, 20*, 367–373.

Klaus, M., & Kennell, J. (1976). *Maternal-infant bonding.* St. Louis, MO: Mosby.

Kligman, D., Smyrl, R., & Emde, R. (1975). A "nonintrusive" longitudinal study of infant sleep. *Psychosomatic Medicine, 37*, 448–453.

Klinnert, M., Campos, J., Sorce, J., Emde, R., & Svejda, M. (1983). Emotions as behavior regulators: Social referencing in infancy. In R. Plutchik & H. Kellerman (Eds.), *Emotions in early development: Vol. 2. The emotions.* New York: Academic Press.

Klinnert, M., Emde, R., Butterfield, P., & Campos, J. (1986). Social referencing: The infant's use of emotional signals from a friendly adult with mother present. *Developmental Psychology, 22*, 427–432.

Knobloch, H., & Pasamanick, B. (Eds.). (1974). *Gesell and Amatruda's developmental diagnosis.* Hagerstown, MD: Harper & Row.

Koch, H. L. (1955). Some personality correlates of sex, sibling position, and sex of siblings among 5- and 6-year-old children. *Genetic Psychology Monographs, 52*, 3–50.

Koch, H. L. (1956). Some emotional attitudes of the young child in relation to characteristics of his sibling. *Child Development, 27*, 393–426.

Koepke, J., Hamm, M., Legerstee, M., & Russell, M. (1983). Neonatal imitation: Two failures to replicate. *Infant Behavior and Development, 6*, 97–102.

Kogan, N. (1983). Stylistic variation in childhood and adolescence: Creativity, metaphor, and cognitive style. In P. H. Mussen, J. H. Flavell, & E. M. Markman (Eds.), *Cognitive development: Vol. 3. Handbook of child psychology* (4th ed.), New York: Wiley.

Kohlberg, L. (1964). The development of moral character and ideology. In M. Hoffman & L. Hoffman (Eds.), *Review of child development research* (Vol. 1, pp. 383–431). New York: Russell Sage.

Kohlberg, L. (1966). A cognitive-developmental analysis of children's sex-role concepts and attitudes. In E. E. Maccoby (Ed.), *The development of sex differences* (pp. 82–173). Stanford, CA: Stanford University Press.

Kohlberg, L. (1969). Stage and sequence: The cognitive-developmental approach to socialization. In D. A. Goslin (Ed.), *Handbook of socialization theory and research.* Chicago, IL: Rand McNally.

Kohlberg, L. (1976). Moral stages and moralization: The cognitive developmental approach. In T. Lickona (Ed.), *Moral development and behavior: Theory, re-search, and social issues* (pp. 31–53). New York: Holt, Rinehart, & Winston.

Kohlberg, L. (1981). *Essays on moral development* (Vol. 1). New York: Harper & Row.

Kohlberg, L., & Gilligan, C. (1971). The adolescent as a philosopher: The discovery of the self in a post-conventional world. In J. Kagan & R. Coles (Eds.), *Twelve to sixteen: Early adolescence* (pp. 1051–1086). New York: Norton.

Kohlberg, L., & Kramer, R. (1969). Continuities and discontinuities in childhood and adult moral development. *Human Development, 12*, 93–120.

Kohn, M. L. (1976). Social class and parental values: Another confirmation of the relationship. *American Sociological Review, 41*, 533–545.

Kopp, C. (1974). Fine motor abilities of infants. *Developmental Medicine and Child Neurology, 16*, 629–636.

Kopp, C. (1983). Risk factors in development. In P. H. Mussen, M. Haith, & J. J. Campos (Eds.), *Handbook of child psychology: Vol. 2. Infancy and Developmental Psychobiology* (4th ed., pp. 1081–1188). New York: Wiley.

Kopp, C., & Parmelee, A. (1979). Prenatal and perinatal influences on infant behavior. In J. Osofsky (Ed.), *Handbook of infant development.* New York: Wiley.

Korner, A. F. (1972). State as variable, as obstacle and as mediator of stimulation in infant research. *Merrill-Palmer Quarterly, 18*, 77–94.

Korner, A. F., Hutchinson, C., Koperski, J., Kraemer, H., & Schneider, P. (1981). Stability of individual differences of neonatal motor and crying patterns. *Child Development, 52*, 83–90.

Kornfield, J. R. (1971). Theoretical issues in child phonology. In the Proceedings of the Seventh Annual Meeting of the Chicago Linguistic Society (pp. 454–468). Chicago, IL: University of Chicago.

Krebs, D. L. (1969). *Some relations between moral judgment, attention, and resistance to temptation.* Unpublished doctoral dissertation, University of Chicago, Chicago, IL.

Kremenitzer, J., Vaughn, H., Kurtzberg, D., & Dowling, K. (1979). Smooth-pursuit eye movements in the newborn infant. *Child Development, 50*, 441–448.

Kreutzer, M., Leonard, C., & Flavell, J. (1975). An interview study of children's knowledge about memory. *Monographs of the Society for Research in Child Development, 40*(1, Serial No. 159).

Krosnick, J., & Judd, C. (1982). Transitions in social

influence at adolescence: Who induces cigarette smoking? *Developmental Psychology, 18,* 359–368.

Kuczaj, S. (1975). On the acquisition of a semantic system. *Journal of Verbal Learning and Verbal Behavior, 14,* 340–358.

Kuczaj, S. (1977). The acquisition of regular and irregular past tense forms. *Journal of Verbal Learning and Verbal Behavior, 16,* 589–600.

Kuczaj, S. (1978). Why do children fail to overgeneralize the progressive inflection? *Journal of Child Language, 5,* 167–171.

Kuczaj, S. (1979). Evidence for a language learning strategy: On the relative ease of acquisition of prefixes and suffixes. *Child Development, 50,* 1-13.

Kuczaj, S. (1982a). Children's overextensions in comprehension and production: Support for a prototype theory of object word meaning acquisition. *First Language, 3,* 93–105.

Kuczaj, S. (1982b). The acquisition of word meaning in the context of the development of the semantic system. In C. Brainerd & M. Pressley (Eds.), *Progress in cognitive development research: Vol. 2. Verbal processes in children.* New York: Springer-Verlag.

Kuczaj, S. (1982c). Language play and language acquisition. In H. Reese (Ed.), *Advances in child development and child behavior* (Vol. 17). New York: Academic Press.

Kuczaj, S. (1983). "I mell a kunk!"—Evidence that children have more complex representations of word pronunciations which they simplify. *Journal of Psycholinguistic Research, 12,* 69–73.

Kuczaj, S. (1986). Thoughts on the intentional basis of early object word extension: Evidence from comprehension and production. In S. Kuczaj & M. Barrett (Eds.), *The development of word meaning.* New York: Springer-Verlag.

Kuczaj, S., & Borys, R. (1989). The overgeneralization of morphological forms as a function of experience. *Language Sciences, 10,* 111–122.

Kuhl, P., & Miller, J. (1975). Speech perception by the chinchilla: Voiced-voiceless distinction in alveolar plosive consonants. *Science, 190,* 69–72.

Kuhl, P., & Padden, D. (in press). Enhanced discriminability at the phonetic boundary for the place feature in Macaques. *Journal of the Acoustical Society of America.*

Kunkel, D. (1988). Children and host-selling television commercials. *Communication Research, 15,* 71–92.

Kuo, Z. Y. (1930). The enesis of the cat's response to the rat. *Journal of Comparative and Physiological Psychology, 11,* 1–35.

Kurdek, L. A., & Rodgon, M. M. (1975). Perceptual, cognitive, and affective perspective taking in kindergarten through sixth-grade children. *Developmental Psychology, 11,* 643–650.

Kurtines, W., & Grief, E. B. (1974). The development of moral thought: Review and evaluation of Kohlberg's approach. *Psychological Bulletin, 81,* 453–470.

Labouvie-Vief, G. (1977). Adult cognitive development: In search of alternative interpretations. *Merrill-Palmer Quarterly, 23,* 227–263.

Ladd, G., & Emerson, E. (1984). Shared knowledge in children's friendships. *Developmental Psychology, 20,* 932–940.

Lamb, M. E. (1977). Father-infant and mother-infant interaction in the first year of life. *Child Development, 48,* 167–181.

Lamb, M. E. (1978a). Qualitative aspects of mother- and father-infant attachments. *Infant Behavior and Development. 1,* 265–275.

Lamb, M. E. (1978b). Social interaction in infancy and development of personality. In M. Lamb (Ed.), *Social and personality development.* New York: Holt, Rinehart & Winston.

Lamb, M. E. (1981). The development of father-infant relationships. In M. E. Lamb (Ed.), *The role of the father in child development.* New York: Wiley.

Lamb, M. E. (1986). The changing role of fathers. In M. Lamb (Ed.), *The fathers' role: Applied perspectives* (pp. 3–28). New York: Wiley.

Lamb, M. E., & Campos, J. (1982). *Development in infancy.* New York: Random House.

Lamb, M. E., Thompson, R., Gardner, W., Charnov, E., & Estes, D. (1985). *Patterns of attachment reassessed.* Hillsdale, NJ: Erlbaum.

Lancaster, J. B., Altmann, J., Rossi, A. S., & Sherrod, L. R. (1987). *Parenting across the life span: Biosocial dimensions.* New York: de Gruyter.

Landsbaum, J. B., & Willis, R. H. (1971). Conformity in early and late adolescence. *Developmental Psychology, 4,* 334–337.

Langlois, J. H., & Downs, A. C. (1979). Peer relations as a function of physical attractiveness: The eye of the beholder or behavioral reality? *Child Development, 50,* 409–418.

Langlois, J. H., & Downs, A. C. (1980). Mothers, fathers, and peers as socialization agents of sex-typed play behaviors in young children. *Child Development, 51,* 1237–1247.

Langlois, J. H., & Stephan, C. (1977). The effects of physical attractiveness and ethnicity on children's behavioral attributions and peer preferences. *Child Development, 48,* 1694–1698.

Lantos, J. (1987). Baby Doe five years later: Implications for child health. *The New England Journal of Medicine, 317,* 444–447.

Lapsley, D., Milstead, M., Quintana, S., Flannery, D., & Buss, R. (1986). Adolescent egocentrism and formal operations: Tests of a theoretical assumption. *Developmental Psychology, 22,* 800–807.

Larry P. v. Riles. (1979). 495 F. Supp. 926.

Larson, L. (1972). The relative influence of parent-adolescent affect in predicting the salience hierarchy among youth. *Pacific Sociological Review, 15,* 83–102.

LaVigne, M. (1982). Rubella's disabled children: Research and rehabilitation. *Columbia, 7,* 10–17.

Layzer, D. (1972). Science or superstition: A physical scientist looks at the IQ controversy. *Cognition, 1,* 265–300.

Lazar, I., & Darlington, R. B. (1978). *Lasting effects after preschool. A report of the Consortium for Longitudinal Studies.* Ithaca: Cornell University, New York State College of Human Ecology, Cornell University.

Leahy, R. (1976a). Development of preferences and processes of visual scanning in the human infant during the first 3 months of life. *Developmental Psychology, 12,* 250–254.

Leahy, R. (1976b). Developmental trends in qualified inferences and descriptions of self and others. *Developmental Psychology, 12,* 546–547.

Leahy, R., & Huard, C. (1976). Role-taking and self-image disparity in children. *Developmental Psychology, 12,* 504–508.

Leboyer, F. (1975). *Birth without violence.* New York: Knopf.

Lee, L. C. (1973). *Social encounters of infants: The beginnings of popularity.* Paper presented at the meeting of the International Society for Behavioral Development, Ann Arbor, MI.

Lehrer, L. (1967). *Sex differences in moral behavior and attitudes.* Unpublished doctoral dissertation, University of Chicago, Chicago, IL.

Leifer, A. D., Leiderman, P. H., Barnett, C., & Williams, J. (1972). Effects of mother-infant separation on maternal attachment behavior. *Child Development, 43,* 1203–1218.

Lempers, J., Flavell, J. H., & Flavell, E. (1977). The development in very young children of tacit knowledge concerning visual perception. *Genetic Psychology Monographs, 95,* 3–53.

Lenneberg, E. (1967). *Biological foundations of language.* New York: Wiley.

Lenneberg, E., Rebelsky, F., & Nichols, I. (1965). The vocalizations of infants born to deaf and hearing parents. *Human Development, 8,* 23–37.

Lenz, W. (1962). Thalidomide and congenital abnormalities. *Lancet, 2,* 38–49.

Leon, M. (1984). Rules mothers and sons use to integrate intent and damage information in their moral judgments. *Child Development, 55,* 2106–2113.

Leopold, W. F. (1949). *Speech development of a bilingual child: A linguist's record* (Vol. 3). Evanston, IL: Northwestern University Press.

Lepper, M. R. (1981). Intrinsic and extrinsic motivation in children: Detrimental effects of superfluous social controls. In W. A. Collins (Ed.), *Aspects of the development of competence: Minnesota Symposia on Child Psychology* (pp. 155–214). Hillsdale, NJ: Erlbaum.

Lepper, M. R., Greene, D., & Nisbett, R. E. (1973). Undermining children's intrinsic interest with extrinsic rewards. *Journal of Personality and Social Psychology, 28,* 129–137.

Lerner, J., & Lerner, R. M. (1982). Temperament and adaptation across life. Theoretical and empirical issues. In P. Baltes & O. Brim, Jr. (Eds.), *Life-span development and behavior* (Vol. 5). New York: Academic Press.

Lerner, R. M. (1969). The development of stereotyped expectancies of body build–behavior relationships. *Child Development, 40,* 137–141.

Lerner, R. M. (1984) *On the nature of human plasticity.* New York: Cambridge University Press.

Lerner, R. M., Karson, M., Meisels, M., & Knapp, J. (1975). Actual and perceived attitudes of late adolescents and their parents: The phenomenon of the generation gaps. *Journal of Genetic Psychology, 126,* 195–207.

Lesser, G., & Kandel, D. (1969). Parent-adolescent relationships and adolescent independence in the United States and Denmark. *Journal of Marriage and the Family, 31,* 348–358.

Lester, B. (1983). A biosocial model of infant crying. In L. Lipsitt (Ed.), *Advances in infant behavior and development.* New York: Ablex.

Lester, B., Hoffman, J., & Brazelton, T. B. (1985). The rhythmic structure of mother-infant interaction in term and preterm infants. *Child Development, 56,* 15–27.

Leung, E., & Rheingold, H. (1981). Development of pointing as a social gesture. *Developmental Psychology, 17,* 215–220.

LeVine, R., & LeVine, B. (1967). *Nyansongo: A Gusii community in Kenya*. New York: Wiley.

Levy, D. (1943). *Maternal overprotection*. New York: Columbia University Press.

Levy, R. (1973). *Tahitians*. Chicago, IL: University of Chicago Press.

Levy, R. (1983). The attack on Mead. *Science, 220,* 829–832.

Lewin, K. (1939). The field theory approach to adolescence. *American Journal of Sociology, 44,* 868–897.

Lewin-Epstein, N. (1981). *Youth employment during high school*. Washington, DC: National Center for Educational Statistics.

Lewis, C. (1981). How adolescents approach decisions: Changes over grades seven to twelve and policy implications. *Child Development, 52,* 538–544.

Lewis, M., Feiring, C., McGuffog, C., & Jaskir, J. (1984). Predicting psychopathology in six-year-olds from early social relations. *Child Development, 55,* 123–136.

Lewis, M., & Rosenblum, L. A. (1975). *Friendship and peer relations*. New York: Wiley.

Lewis, M., & Sullivan, M. (1985). Infant intelligence and its assessment. In B. Wolman (Ed.), *Handbook of human intelligence*. New York: Wiley.

Lewotin, R. C. (1976). Race and intelligence. In N. J. Block & G. Dworkin (Eds.), *The IQ controversy*. New York: Pantheon.

Leyens, J. L., Camino, L., Parke, R. D., & Berkowitz, L. (1975). Effects of movie violence on aggression in a field setting as a function of group dominance and cohesion. *Journal of Personality and Social Psychology, 32,* 346–360.

Lieberman, A. F. (1977). Preschoolers' competence with a peer: Relations with attachment and peer experience. *Child Development, 48,* 1277–1287.

Lieberman, P. (1984). *The biology and evolution of language*. Cambridge, MA: Harvard University Press.

Liebert, R. M., & Baron, R. A. (1972a). Some immediate effects of televised violence on children's behavior. *Developmental Psychology, 6,* 469–475.

Liebert, R. M., & Baron, R. A. (1972b). Short-term effects of televised aggression on children's aggressive behavior. In J. P. Murray, E. A. Rubenstein, & G. A. Comstock (Eds.), *Television and social behavior: 2. Television and social learning*. Washington, DC: U.S. Government Printing Office.

Lightfoot, D. (1989). The child's trigger experience: Degree-0 learnability. *Behavioral and Brain Sciences, 12,* 189–210.

Linn, M. C. (1978). Influence of cognitive style and training on tasks requiring the separation of variables schema. *Child Development, 49,* 874–877.

Linney, J. A., & Seidman, E. (1989). The future of schooling. *American Psychologist, 44,* 336–340.

Lipsitt, L. (1978). Assessment of sensory and behavioral functions in infancy. In H. Pick, Jr., H. Leibowitz, J. E. Singer, A. Steinschneider, & H. Stevenson (Eds.), *Psychology: From research to practice* (pp. 9–28). New York: Plenum.

Lipsitt, L., Engen, T., & Kaye, H. (1963). Developmental changes in the olfactory threshold of the neonate. *Child Development, 34,* 371–376.

Livesley, W., & Bromley, D. (1973). *Person perception in childhood and adolescence*. New York: Wiley.

Livson, N., & Peskin, H. (1980). Perspectives on adolescence from longitudinal research. In J. Adelson (Ed.), *Handbook of adolescent psychology* (pp. 47–98). New York: Wiley.

Locke, J. L. (1979). The child's processing of phonology. In W. A. Collins (Ed.), *Children's language and communication: Minnesota Symposia on Child Psychology* (Vol. 12). Hillsdale, NJ: Erlbaum.

Lockwood, A. (1978). The effects of values clarification and moral development curricula on school age subjects: A critical review of recent research. *Review of Educational Research, 48,* 325–364.

Loevinger, J. (1976). *Ego development*. San Francisco, CA: Jossey-Bass.

Londerville, S., & Main, M. (1981). Security of attachment, compliance and maternal training methods in the second year of life. *Developmental Psychology, 17,* 289–299.

Lorenz, K. (1957). Companionship in bird life. In C. Schiller (Ed.), *Instinctive behavior*. New York: International Universities Press.

Lorenz, K. (1966). *On aggression*. New York: Harcourt, Brace, & World.

Lorenz, K. (1973). The comparative study of behavior. In K. Lorenz & P. Leyhausen (Eds.), *Motivation of human and animal behavior: An ethological view*. New York: Van Nostrand.

Lougee, M. D., Grueneich, R., & Hartup, W. W. (1977). Social interaction in same- and mixed-age dyads of preschool children. *Child Development, 48,* 1353–1361.

Lundy, J. (1972). Some personality correlates of contraceptive use among unmarried female college students. *Journal of Psychology, 80,* 9–14.

Luria, A. R. (1961). *The role of speech in the regulation of normal and abnormal behavior*. New York: Liveright.

Lutkenhaus, P., Grossmann, K. E., & Grossmann, K. (1985). Infant-mother attachment at twelve months

663

and style of interaction with a stranger at the age of three years. *Child Development, 56,* 1538–1542.

Lutz, C. (1982). The domain of emotion words on Ifaluk. *American Ethologist, 9,* 113–128.

Lyons-Ruth, K., Connell, D., Zoll, D., & Stahl, J. (1987). Infants at social risk: Relations among infant maltreatment, maternal behavior, and infant attachment behavior. *Developmental Psychology, 23,* 223–232.

Maccoby, E. E. (1980). *Social development.* San Diego, CA: Harcourt, Brace, Jovanovich.

Maccoby, E. E. (1984). Middle childhood in the context of the family. In W. A. Collins (Ed.), *Development during middle childhood: The years from six to twelve.* Washington, D.C: National Academy Press.

Maccoby, E. E., & Feldman, S. (1972). Mother-attachment and stranger reactions in the third year of life. *Monographs of the Society for Research in Child Development, 37,* (1)Serial No. 146.

Maccoby, E. E., & Jacklin, C. M. (1974). *The psychology of sex differences.* Stanford, CA: Stanford University Press.

Maccoby, E. E., & Jacklin, C. M. (1980). Sex differences in aggression: A rejoinder and reprise. *Child Development, 51,* 964–980.

Maccoby, E. E., & Martin, J. (1983). Socialization in the context of the family. In P. H. Mussen, E. M. Hetherington (Eds.), *Handbook of child psychology: Vol. 4. Socialization, personality, and social development* (4th ed.) New York: Wiley.

Maccoby, E. E., & Wilson, W. C. (1957). Identification and observational learning from films. *Journal of Abnormal Social Psychology, 55,* 76–87.

MacFarlane, A. (1975). Olfaction in the development of social preferences in the human neonate. *Ciba Foundation Symposium, 33,* 103–113.

Macken, M., & Ferguson, C. A. (1983). Cognitive aspects of phonological development: Model, evidence, and issues. In K. Nelson (Ed.), *Children's language.* Hillsdale, NJ: Erlbaum.

Mackenzie, B. (1984). Explaining race differences in IQ: The logic, the methodology, and the evidence. *American Psychologist, 39,* 1214–1233.

MacWhinney, B. (1987). The competition model. In B. MacWhinney (Ed.), *Mechanisms of language acquisition.* Hillsdale, NJ: Erlbaum.

Madsen, M. C. (1967). Cooperative and competitive motivation of children in three Mexican sub-cultures. *Psychological Reports, 20,* 1307–1320.

Mahler, M., Pine, F., & Bergman, A. (1975). *The psychological birth of the human infant.* New York: Basic Books.

Main, M. (1973). *Exploration, play and level of cognitive functioning as related to child-mother attachment.* Unpublished doctoral dissertation, Johns Hopkins University, Baltimore, MD.

Main, M., & Weston, D. (1981). The quality of the toddler's relationship to mother and father: Related to conflict behavior and readiness to establish new relationships. *Child Development, 52,* 932–940.

Mandler, J., & Robinson, C. (1978). Developmental changes in picture recognition. *Journal of Experimental Child Psychology, 26,* 122–136.

Mann, I. (1964). *The development of the human eye.* London: British Medical Association.

Maratsos, M. P. (1981). Problems in categorical evolution: Can formal categories arise from semantic ones? In W. Deutsch (Ed.), *The child's construction of language.* London: Academic Press.

Maratsos, M. P. (1983). Some current issues in the study of the acquisition of grammar. In J. Flavell & E. Markman (Eds.), *Handbook of child psychology: Vol. 3. Cognitive development.* New York: Wiley.

Maratsos, M. P. (1989). Innateness and plasticity in language acquisition. In M. Rice & R. Schiefelbusch (Eds.), *The teachability of language.* Baltimore, MD: Brooks.

Maratsos, M., & Chalkley, M. (1980). The internal language of children's syntax. The ontogenesis and representation of syntactic categories. In K. Nelson (Ed.), *Children's language* (Vol. 2). New York: Gardner Press.

Marcia, J. (1966). Development and validation of ego identity status. *Journal of Personality and Social Psychology, 3,* 551–558.

Marcia, J. (1980). Identity in adolescence. In J. Adelson (Ed.), *Handbook of adolescent psychology.* New York: Wiley.

Markman, E. (1973). *Factors affecting the young child's ability to monitor his memory.* Doctoral dissertation, University of Pennsylvania, Philadelphia.

Markman, E., Cox, B., & Machida, S. (1981). The standard object-sorting task as a measure of conceptual organization. *Developmental Psychology, 17,* 115–117.

Markus, H., & Nurius, P. (1984). Self-understanding and self-regulation in middle childhood. In W. A. Collins (Ed.), *Development during middle childhood: The years from six to twelve* (pp. 147–183). Washington, DC: National Academy Press.

Marshall, H. R., & McCandless, B. R. (1957). A study

in prediction of social behavior of preschool children. *Child Development, 28,* 149–159.

Marshall, R., Porter, F., Rogers, A., Moore, J., Anderson, B., & Boxerman, S. (1982) Circumcision: II. Effects on mother-infant interaction. *Early Human Development, 7,* 367–374.

Marshall, W. A., & Tanner, J. M. (1970). Variations in the pattern of pubertal changes in boys. *Archives of the Diseases of Childhood, 45,* 13–23.

Marshall, W. A., & Tanner, J. M. (1974). Puberty. In J. A. Douvis & J. Dobbing (Eds.), *Scientific foundations of pediatrics.* London: Heinemann.

Martin, J. A. (1980). A longitudinal study of the consequences of early mother-infant interaction: A microanalytic approach. *Monographs of the Society for Research in Child Development, 46*(3, Serial No. 190).

Martin, R. (1975). Effects of familiar and complex stimuli on infant attention. *Developmental Psychology, 11,* 178–185.

Masters, J. C, Barden, R. C., & Ford, M. (1979). Affective states, expressive behavior, and learning in children. *Journal of Personality and Social Psychology, 37,* 380–390.

Masters, J. C., & Wilkinson, A. (1976). Concensual and discriminative stereotype of sex-type judgments by parents and children. *Child Development, 47,* 208–217.

Masur, E., McIntyre, C., & Flavell, J. (1973). Developmental changes in apportionment of study time among items in a multitrial free recall task. *Journal of Experimental Child Psychology, 15,* 237–246.

Matas, L., Arend, R., & Sroufe, L. A. (1978). Continuity of adaptation in the second year: The relationship between quality of attachment and later competence. *Child Development, 49,* 547–556.

Matheny, A. P. (1989). Children's behavioral inhibition over age and across situations: Genetic similarity for a trait during change. *Journal of Personality, 57,* 215–236.

Maurer, D., & Adams, R. (1987). Emergence of the ability to discriminate a blue from gray at one month of age. *Journal of Experimental Child Psychology, 44,* 147–156.

McCabe, A., Siegel, L., Spence, I., & Wilkinson, A. (1982). Class-inclusion reasoning: Patterns of performance from three to eight years. *Child Development, 53,* 780–785.

McCall, R. B. (1977). Children's IQ as predictors of adult educational and occupational status. *Science, 197,* 482–483.

McCall, R. B. (1983). A conceptual approach to early mental development. In M. Lewis (Ed.), *Origins of intelligence: Infancy and early childhood.* New York: Plenum.

McCall, R. B., Applebaum, M. I., & Hogarty, P. S. (1973). Developmental changes in mental performance. *Monographs of the Society for Research in Child Development, 38*(Serial No. 150).

McCandless, B. R., & Hoyt, J. M. (1961). Sex, ethnicity and play preferences of preschool children. *Journal of Abnormal and Social Psychology, 62,* 683–685.

McCandless, B. R., & Marshall, H. R. (1957). Sex differences in social acceptance and participation of preschool children. *Child Development, 28,* 421–425.

McCarthy, D. (1954). Language development in children. In L. Carmichael (Ed.), Manual of child psychology (2nd ed.). New York: Wiley.

McCord, W., McCord, J., & Howard, A. (1961). Familial correlates of aggression in non-delinquent male children. *Journal of Abnormal and Social Psychology, 62,* 79–93.

McCormick, R. (1974). To save or let die: The dilemma of modern medicine. *JAMA, Journal of the American Medical Association, 229*(2), 172–176.

McCoy, C., & Masters, J. (1985). The development of children's strategies for the social control of emotion. *Child Development, 56,* 1214–1222.

McDavid, J. W., & Harari, H. (1966). Stereotyping of names and popularity in grade-school children. *Child Development, 37,* 453–459.

McDonald, L., & Pien, D. (1982). Mother conversational behavior as a function of interactional intent. *Journal of Child Language, 9,* 337–358.

McFall, R. M. (1982). A review of reformulation of the concept of social skills. *Behavioral Assessment, 4,* 1–33.

McFall, R. M., & Dodge, K. A. (1982). Self-management and interpersonal skills learning. In P. Karoly & F. H. Kanfer (Eds.), *Self-management and behavior change.* New York: Pergamon.

McGhee, P. E. (1971a). Cognitive development and children's comprehension of humor. *Child Development, 42,* 123–138.

McGhee, P. E. (1971b). The role of operational thinking in children's comprehension and appreciation of humor. *Child Development, 42,* 733–744.

McGrew, W. (1972). *An ethological study of children's behavior.* New York: Academic Press.

McKenry, P., Walters, L., & Johnson, D. (1979). Adolescent pregnancy: A review of the literature. *Family Coordinator, 28,* 23–34.

McKenzie, B., & Over, R. (1983). Young infants fail to imitate facial and manual gestures. *Infant Behavior and Development, 6,* 85–95.

McKenzie, B., Tootell, H., & Day, R. (1980). Development of visual size constancy during the first year of human infancy. *Developmental Psychology, 16,* 163–174.

McMichael, P. (1980). Reading difficulties, behavior, and social status. *Journal of Educational Psychology, 72,* 76–86.

McNamara, J. (1982). *Names for things: A study of human learning.* Cambridge, MA: MIT Press.

McNeill, D. (1970). The development of language. In P. Mussen (Ed.), *Carmichael's manual of child psychology* (3rd ed., Vol. 1). New York: Wiley.

McPartland, J. M. (1968). *The segregated student in desegregated schools: Sources of influence on Negro secondary students* (Report 21). Baltimore, MD: Johns Hopkins University, Center for the Study of Social Organization of Schools .

McTear, M. (1980). Getting it done: The development of children's abilities to negotiate request sentences in peer interaction. *Belfast Working Papers in Language and Linguistics, 4,* 1–29.

Mead, G. H. (1935). *Sex and temperament in three primitive societies.* New York: Morrow.

Mead, M. (1961). *Coming of age in Samoa.* New York: Morrow.

Mehler, J., Lambertz, G., Jusczyk, P., & Amiel-Tison, C. (1986). Discrimination de la langue maternelle par le nouveau-ne. *Comptes Rendus des Seances de l'Academie de Sciences, Serie 3, 303,* 637–640.

Melody, W. (1973). *Children's television: The economics of exploitation.* New Haven, CT: Yale University Press.

Meltzoff, A. (1985). Immediate and deferred imitation in fourteen- and twenty-four-month-old infants. *Child Development, 56,* 62–72.

Meltzoff, A. (1988). Infant imitation and memory: Nine-month olds in immediate and deferred tests. *Child Development, 56,* 62–72.

Meltzoff, A., & Borton, R. (1979). Intermodal matching by human neonates. *Nature (London), 282,* 403–404.

Meltzoff, A., & Moore, M. K. (1977). Imitation of facial and manual gestures by human neonates. *Science, 198,* 75–78.

Meltzoff, A., & Moore, M. (1983). Newborn infants imitate adult facial gestures. *Child Development, 54,* 702–709.

Meltzoff, A., & Moore, M. (1985). Cognitive foundations and social functions of imitation and intermodal representation in infancy. In J. Mehler & R. Fox (Eds.), *Neonate cognition: Beyond the blooming buzzing confusion.* Hillsdale, NJ: Erlbaum.

Mendelson, M., & Haith, M. (1976). The relation between audition and vision in the human newborn. *Monographs of the Society for Research in Child Development, 41*(Serial No. 167).

Menyuk, P. (1971). *The acquisition and development of language.* Englewood Cliffs, NJ: Prentice-Hall.

Merriman, W. & Bowman, L. (1989). The mutual exclusivity bias in children's word learning. *Monographs of the Society for Research in Child Development, 54*(Serial No. 220).

Mervis, C. B., & Canada, K. (1983). On the existence of competence errors in early comprehension: A reply to Fremgen and Fay and Chapman and Thompson. *Journal of Child Language, 10,* 431–440.

Messer, S. B. (1976). Reflection-impulsivity: A review. *Psychological Bulletin, 83,* 1026–1053.

Messer, S. B., & Brodzinsky, D. M. (1981). Three-year stability of reflection-impulsivity in young adolescents. *Developmental Psychology, 17,* 848–850.

Metcoff, J. (1974). Biochemical markers of intrauterine malnutrition. In M. Winick (Ed.), *Nutrition and fetal development.* New York: Wiley.

Meyer, W. J., & Thompson, G. G. (1956). Sex differences in the distribution of teacher approval and disapproval among sixth-grade children. *Journal of Educational Psychology, 47,* 385–396.

Midlarsky, E., & Bryan, J. H. (1967). Training charity in children. *Journal of Personality and Social Psychology, 5,* 408–415.

Miller, J., Cisin, I., Gardner-Keaton, H., Harrell, A., Wirtz, P., Abelson, H., & Fishbourne, P. (1983). *National survey on drug abuse: Main findings, 1982.* Rockville, MD: National Institute on Drug Abuse.

Miller, P., & Simon, W. (1980). The development of sexuality in adolescence. In J. Adelson (Ed.), *Handbook of adolescent psychology* (pp. 383–407). New York: Wiley.

Miller, P., & Sperry, L. (1987). The socialization of anger and aggression. *Merrill-Palmer Quarterly, 33,* 1–31.

Miller, P. H., Kessel, F. S., & Flavell, J. H. (1970). Thinking about people thinking about people thinking about . . . : A study of social cognitive development. *Child Development, 41,* 613–623.

Milowe, J. D., & Lourie, R. S. (1964). The child's role in the battered child syndrome. *Journal of Pediatrics, 65,* 1079–1081.

666

Minton, C., Kagan, J., & Levine, J. A. (1971). Maternal control and obedience in the two-year-old child. *Child Development, 42,* 1873–1894.

Minton, H. L., & Schneider, F. W. (1980). *Differential psychology.* Pacific Grove, CA: Brooks/Cole.

Minuchin, P., & Shapiro, E. (1983). The school as a context for social development. In P. H. Mussen & M. Hetherington (Eds.), *Handbook of child psychology: Vol. 4. Socialization, personality, and social development* (4th ed.). New York: Wiley.

Mischel, H., & Mischel, W. (1983). The development of children's knowledge of self-control strategies. *Child Development, 54,* 603–619.

Mischel, W. (1958). Preference for delayed reinforcement: An experimental study of a cultural observation. *Journal of Abnormal and Social Psychology, 56,* 57–61.

Mischel, W. (1984). Convergences and challenges in the search for consistency. *American Psychologist, 39,* 351–364.

Mischel, W., & Baker, N. (1973). *Cognitive appraisals and transformations in delay behavior.* Unpublished manuscript, Stanford University, Stanford, CA.

Mischel, W., Coates, B., & Raskoff, A. (1968). Effects of success and failure on self-gratification. *Journal of Personality and Social Psychology, 10,* 381–390.

Mischel, W., & Ebbesen, E. (1970). Attention in delay of gratification. *Journal of Personality and Social Psychology, 16,* 329–337.

Mischel, W., Ebbesen, E., & Zeiss, A. (1972). Cognitive and attentional mechanisms in delay of gratification. *Journal of Personality and Social Psychology, 21,* 204–218.

Mischel, W., & Gilligan, C. (1964). Delay of gratification, motivation for the prohibited gratification, and responses to temptation. *Journal of Abnormal and Social Psychology, 69,* 411–417.

Miyake, K. (1983). *Relation of temperamental disposition to attachment classification.* Paper presented at the meeting of the Society for Research in Child Development, Detroit, MI.

Money, J. (1965a). Influence of hormones on sexual behavior. *Annual Review of Medicine, 16,* 67–82.

Money, J. (1965b). Psychosexual differentiation. In J. Money (Ed.), *Sex research, new developments* (pp. 3–23). New York: Holt, Rinehart & Winston.

Money, J., & Clopper, R., Jr. (1974). Psychosocial and psychosexual aspects of errors of pubertal onset and development. *Human Biology, 46,* 173–181.

Money, J., & Ehrhardt, A. A. (1972). *Man and woman. Boy and girl.* Baltimore, MD: Johns Hopkins University Press.

Money, J., Hampson, J. G., & Hampson, J. L. (1957). Imprinting and the establishment of gender role. *AMA Archives of Neurology and Psychiatry, 77,* 333–336.

Montemayor, R. (1982). The relationship between parent-adolescent conflict and the amount of time adolescents spend alone with parents and peers. *Child Development, 53,* 1512–1519.

Montemayor, R. (1983). Parent-adolescent conflict: All of the families some of the time, or some of the families all of the time? *Journal of Early Adolescence, 3,* 1–20.

Montemayor, R., & Brownlee, J. (1987). Fathers, mothers, and adolescents: Gender-based differences in parental roles during adolescence. *Journal of Youth and Adolescence, 16,* 281–291.

Montemayor, R., & Van Komen, R. (1980). Age segregation of adolescents in and out of school. *Journal of Youth and Adolescence, 9,* 371–381.

Montemayor, R., & Van Komen, R. (1985). The development of sex differences in friendship patterns and peer group structure during adolescence. *Journal of Early Adolescence, 5,* 285–294.

Montour, K. (1977). William James Sidis, the broken twig. *American Psychologist, 32,* 265–279.

Moore, K. L. (1982). *The developing human: Clinically oriented embryology* (3rd ed.). Philadelphia, PA: Saunders.

Moore, K. L., & Burt, M. (1982). *Private crisis, public cost: Policy perspectives on teenage childbearing.* Washington, DC: Urban Institute Press.

Morrison, D. (1985). Adolescent contraceptive behavior: A review. *Psychological Bulletin, 98,* 538–599.

Morrongiello, B., & Clifton, R. (1984). Effects of sound frequency on behavioral and cardiac orienting in newborn and five-month-old infants. *Journal of Experimental Child Psychology, 38,* 429–446.

Motti, E. (1986). *Relationship of preschool teachers with children of varying developmental histories.* Unpublished doctoral dissertation, University of Minnesota, Minneapolis.

Mueller, E., & Lucas, T. A. (1975). A developmental analysis of peer interaction among toddlers. In M. Lewis & L. A. Rosenblum (Eds.), *Friendship and peer relations.* New York: Wiley.

Mueller, E., & Rich, A. (1976). Clustering and socially-directed behaviors in a play-group of 1-year-old boys. *Journal of Child Psychology and Psychiatry, 17,* 315–322.

Muir, D., & Field, J. (1978). Newborn infants orient to sound. *Child Development, 50,* 431–436.

Muller, E., Hollien, H., & Murry, T. (1974). Perceptual responses to infant crying: Identification of cry types. *Journal of Child Language, 1,* 89–95.

Murray, J. P., & Kippax, S. (1978). Children's social behavior in three towns with differing television experience. *Journal of Communication, 28*(1), 19–29.

Mussen, P. H., & Jones, M. C. (1957). Self-conceptions, motivations, and interpersonal attitudes of late and early maturing boys. *Child Development, 28,* 243–256.

Mussen, P. H., & Jones, M. C. (1958a). The behavior inferred motivations of late and early maturing boys. *Child Development, 29,* 61–67.

Mussen, P. H., & Jones, M. C. (1958b). Self-conceptions, motivations, and interpersonal attitudes of early and late-maturing girls. *Child Development, 29,* 491–501.

Muste, M. J., & Sharpe, D. F. (1947). Some influential factors in the determinants of aggressive behavior in preschool children. *Child Development, 18,* 11–28.

Myers, B. (1982). Early intervention using Brazelton training with middle-class mothers and fathers of newborns. *Child Development, 53,* 462–471.

Nadelman, L. (1974). Sex identity in American children: Memory, knowledge, and preference tests. *Developmental Psychology, 10,* 413–417.

Nakazima, S. (1962). A comparative study of the speech developments of Japanese and American English in children. *Studies in Phonology, 2,* 27–39.

Nannis, E., & Cowan, P. (1987). Emotional understanding: A matter of age, dimension and point of view. *Journal of Applied Developmental Psychology, 8,* 289–304.

Nasby, W., & Yando, R. (1982). Clinical and developmental implications of memory and affect in children. *New Directions for Child Development, 7,* 21–44.

Nathans, J. (1989). The genes for color vision. *Scientific American, 260,* 42–49.

Nawas, M. M. (1971). Change in efficiency of ego functioning and complexity from adolescence to young adulthood. *Developmental Psychology, 4,* 412–415.

Nelsen, E. A., Grinder, R. E., & Mutterer, M. L. (1969). Sources of variance in behavioral measures of honesty in temptation situations: Methodological analyses. *Developmental Psychology, 1,* 265–279.

Nelson, C. (1987). The recognition of facial expressions in the first two years of life: Mechanisms of development. *Child Development, 58,* 889–909.

Nelson, K. (1973). Structure and strategy in learning to talk. *Monographs of the Society for Research in Child Development, 38*(Serial No. 149).

Nelson, K. (1974). Concept, word, and sentence: Interrelations in acquisition and development. *Psychological Review, 81,* 267–285.

Nelson, K. (1979). Exploration in the development of a functional system. In W. Collins (Ed.), *Children's language and communication: The Minnesota Symposia on Child Psychology* (Vol. 12). Hillsdale, NJ: Erlbaum.

Nelson, K., Rescorla, L., Gruendel, J. M., & Benedict, H. (1978). Early lexicons: What do they mean? *Child Development, 49,* 960–968.

Nelson, K. E., & Bonvillian, J. (1973). Concepts and words in the 18-month-old. Acquiring concept names under controlled conditions. *Cognition, 2,* 435–450.

Nelson, K. E., Carskaddon, G., & Bonvillian, J. (1973). Syntax acquisition: Impact of experimental variation in adult interaction. *Child Development, 44,* 497–504.

Nelson, K. E., Denninger, M., Kaplan, B., & Bonvillian, J. (1979, March). *Varied angles on how children progress in syntax.* Paper presented at the biennial meeting of the Society for Research in Child Development, San Francisco, CA.

Newberg, N. (1980). *Affective education addresses the basics.* Paper presented at the meetings of the American Educational Research Association, Boston, MA.

Newcomb, A. F., Brady, J. E., & Hartup, W. W. (1979). Friendship incentive condition as determinants of children's task-oriented social behavior. *Child Development, 50,* 878–881.

Newcomb, M., Huba, G., & Bentler, P. (1983). Mothers' influence on the drug use of their children: Confirmatory tests of direct modeling and mediational theories. *Developmental Psychology, 19,* 714–726.

Newcomb, M., Huba, G., & Bentler, P. (1986). Determinants of sexual and dating behaviors among adolescents. *Journal of Personality and Social Psychology, 50,* 428–438.

Newcombe, N., & Dubas, J. (1987). Individual differences in cognitive ability: Are they related to timing of puberty? In R. Lerner & T. Foch (Eds.), *Biological-psychosocial interactions in early adolescence* (pp. 249–302). Hillsdale, NJ: Erlbaum.

Newport, E. L., Gleitman, L. R., & Gleitman, H. (1975, September). *A study of mother's speech and child lan-*

guage acquisition. Paper presented at the 7th Child Language Research Forum, Stanford University, Stanford, CA.

Newson, J., & Newson, E. (1976). *Seven years old in the home environment*. London: Allen & Unwin.

Nilsson, L., Furuhjelm, M., Ingelman-Sundbert, A., & Wirsen, C. (1977). *A child is born*. New York: Delacorte Press.

Novak, M. A., & Harlow, H. F. (1975). Social recovery of monkeys isolated for the first year of life: I. Rehabilitation and therapy. *Developmental Psychology, 11,* 453–465.

Nowakowski, R. (1987). Basic concepts of CNS development. *Child Development, 58,* 568–595.

Nucci, L., & Nucci, M. (1982). Children's responses to moral and social conventional transgressions in free-play settings. *Child Development, 53,* 1337–1342.

Nummedal, S. G., & Bass, S. C. (1976). Effects of the salience of intention and consequence on children's moral judgments. *Developmental Psychology, 12,* 475–476.

Nunnally, J. C. (1967). *Psychometric theory*. New York: McGraw-Hill.

Oakland, T., & Parmelee, R. (1985). Mental measurement of minority-group children. In B. Wolman (Ed.), *Handbook of intelligence*. New York: Wiley.

O'Brien, M., & Huston, A. C. (1985). Development of sex-typed play behavior in toddlers. *Developmental Psychology, 21,* 866–871.

Ochs, E. (1982). Talking to children in Western Samoa. *Language in Society, 11,* 77–104.

Ochs, E., & Schieffelin, B. (1984). Language acquisition and socialization. Three developmental stories and their implications. In R. Shweder & R. LeVine (Eds.), *Culture theory*. Cambridge: Cambridge University Press.

O'Connor, R. (1969). Modification of social withdrawal through symbolic modeling. *Journal of Applied Behavior Analysis, 2,* 15–22.

Offer, D., & Offer, J. (1975). *From teenage to young manhood: A psychological study*. New York: Basic Books.

Oller, D., & Eilers, R. (1988). The role of audition in infant babbling. *Child Development, 59,* 441–449.

Olson, D., McCubbin, H., Barnes, H., Larsen, A., Muxen, M., & Wilson, M. (1983). *Families: What makes them work*. Beverly Hills, CA: Sage.

Olson, G., & Sherman, T. (1983). Attention, learning, and memory in infants. In P. H. Mussen, M. Haith, & J. J. Campos (Eds.), *Handbook of child psychology:*

Vol. 2. Infancy and developmental psychobiology (4th ed., pp. 1001–1080). New York: Wiley.

Olweus, D. (1980). Familial and temperamental determinants of aggression behavior in adolescents—A causal analysis. *Developmental Psychology, 16,* 644–660.

Oskamp, S., & Mindick, B. (1983). Personality and attitudinal barriers to contraception. In D. Byrne & W. A. Fisher (Eds.), *Adolescents sex, and contraception* (pp. 65–107). Hillsdale, NJ: Erlbaum.

Ounsted, C., Oppenheimer, R., & Lindsay, J. (1974). Aspects of bonding failure: The psychopathology and psychotherapeutic treatment of families of battered children. *Developmental Medicine and Child Neurology, 16,* 447–452.

Owen, M., & Chase-Lansdale, L. (1982). *The relationship between mother-infant and father-infant attachments*. Paper presented at the Southwestern Society for Research in Human Development, Galveston, TX.

Palkovitz, R. (1985). Fathers' birth attendance, early contact, and extended contact with their newborns: A critical review. *Child Development, 56,* 392–406.

Papini, D., & Datan, N. (1983, April). *Transition into adolescence: An interactionist perspective*. Paper presented at the biennial meeting of the Society for Research in Child Development, Detroit, MI.

Parke, R. D. (1967). Nurturance, nurturance-withdrawal and resistance to deviation. *Child Development, 38,* 1101–1110.

Parke, R. D. (1969). Effectiveness of punishment as an interaction of intensity, timing, agent nurturance and cognitive structuring. *Child Development, 40,* 213–236.

Parke, R. D. (1973). Explorations in punishment, discipline, and self-control. In P. J. Elich (Ed.), *Social learning*. Bellingham: Western Washington State Press.

Parke, R. D. (1981). *Fathers*. Cambridge, MA: Harvard University Press.

Parke, R. D. (1988). Families in life-span perspective: A multilevel developmental approach. In E. M. Hetherington, R. M. Lerner, & M. Perlmutter (Eds.), *Child development in life-span perspective* (pp. 159–190). Hillsdale, NJ: Erlbaum.

Parke, R. D. & Murray, S. (1971). *Re-instatement: A technique for increasing stability of inhibition in children*. Unpublished manuscript, University of Wisconsin, Department of Psychology, Madison.

Parke, R. D., & Slaby, R. (1983). The development of aggression. In P. H. Mussen & E. M. Hetherington

(Eds.), *Handbook of child psychology: Vol. 4. Socialization, personality, and social development* (4th ed.). New York: Wiley.

Parke, R. D., & Walters, R. H. (1967). Some factors determining the efficacy of punishment for inducing response inhibition. *Monographs of the Society for Research in Child Development, 32*(Serial No. 109).

Parker, J. G., & Asher, S. R. (1987). Peer relations and later personal adjustment: Are low-accepted children at risk? *Psychological Bulletin, 102*, 357–389.

Parsons, J. E., Adler, T. F., & Kaczala, C. M. (1982). Socialization of achievement attitudes and beliefs: Parental influences. *Child Development, 53*, 310–321.

Parten, M. B. (1932). Social participation among preschool children. *Journal of Abnormal and Social Psychology, 27*, 243–269.

Parten, M. B., & Newhall, S. W. (1943). Social behavior of preschool children. In R. G. Baker, J. S. Kounin, & H. F. Wright (Eds.), *Child behavior and development.* New York: McGraw-Hill.

Pastor, D. (1981). The quality of mother-infant attachment and its relationship to toddlers' initial sociability with peers. *Developmental Psychology, 27*, 326–335.

Patterson, G. R. (1982). *Coercive family process.* Eugene, OR: Castalia Publications.

Patterson, G. R., & Bank, C. L. (1989). Some amplifying mechanisms for pathologic processes in families. In M. Gunnar & E. Thelen (Eds.), *Systems and development: Minnesota Symposia on Child Psychology,* (Vol. 22, pp. 167–209). Hillsdale, NJ: Erlbaum.

Patterson, G. R., Littman, R. A., & Brocker, W. (1967). Assertive behavior in children: A step toward a theory of aggression. *Monographs of the Society for Research in Child Development, 32*(Serial No. 113).

Patterson, G. R., & Reid, J. (1984). Social interactional processes within the family: The study of the moment-by-moment family transactions in which human social development is imbedded. *Journal of Applied Developmental Psychology, 5*, 237–262.

Pavlov, I. (1927). *Conditional reflexes.* Oxford: Oxford University Press.

Pawlby, S. J. (1977). Imitative interaction. In H. R. Schaffer (Ed.), *Studies in mother-infant interaction.* London: Academic Press.

Pearl, D., Bouthilet, L., & Lazar, J. (Eds.). (1982). *Television and behavior: Ten years of scientific progress and implications for the 80s* (Vol. 1). Washington, DC: National Institute of Mental Health.

Peevers, B. H., & Secord, P. F. (1973). Developmental changes in attribution of descriptive concepts to persons. *Journal of Personality and Social Psychology, 27,* 120–128.

Peiper, A. (1924). Untersuchungen über den glalvanischenltautreflex. *Annales Paediatrici, 107,* 139–150.

Peiper, A. (1927). Über das unterscheid ungsvermögen des kleinkindes. *Annales Paediatrici, 117,* 350–363.

Pellegrini, D. (1985). Social cognition and competence in middle childhood. *Child Development, 56,* 253–264.

Perlmutter, M. (1984). Continuities and discontinuities in early human memory paradigms, processes, and performances. In R. Kail & N. Spear (Eds.), *Comparative perspectives or the development of memory.* Hillsdale, NJ: Erlbaum.

Peskin, H. (1967). Pubertal onset and ego functioning. *Journal of Abnormal Psychology, 72,* 1–15.

Petersen, A., & Taylor, B. (1980). The biological approach to adolescence. In J. Adelson (Ed.), *Handbook of adolescent psychology* (pp. 117–158). New York: Wiley.

Peterson, L., Hartmann, D. P., & Gelfand, D. M. (1977). Developmental changes in the effects of dependency and reciprocity cues on children's moral judgments and donation rates. *Child Development, 48,* 1331–1339.

Pettit, G. S., Brown, M. M., & Dodge, K. A. (1988). Early family experiences: Social problem patterns and children's social competence. *Child Development, 59,* 107–120.

Phillips, S., King, S., & Dubois, L. (1978). Spontaneous activities of female versus male newborns. *Child Development, 49,* 590–597.

Piaget, J. (1932). *The moral judgment of the child.* New York: Harcourt.

Piaget, J. (1951). *Play, dreams and imitation in childhood.* New York: Norton.

Piaget, J. (1952a). *The child's conception of number.* New York: Humanities Press.

Piaget, J. (1952b). *The origins of intelligence in children.* New York: International Universities Press.

Piaget, J. (1955). *The language and thought of the child.* Cleveland, OH: Meridian Books.

Piaget, J. (1962). *Play, dreams, and imitation in childhood.* New York: Norton.

Piaget, J. (1965). *The moral judgment of the child.* New York: Free Press.

Piaget, J., & Inhelder, B. (1956). *The child's conception of space.* London: Routledge & Kegan Paul.

Piaget, J., & Inhelder, B. (1969). *The psychology of the child.* New York: Basic Books.

Piaget, J., & Inhelder, B. (1973). *Memory and intelligence.* New York: Basic Books.

Pick, H. L., Jr. (1976). Comments on the transactional constructionist approach to environmental knowing. In G. Moore & R. Golledge (Eds.), *Environmental knowing*. Stroudsberg, PA: Dowden, Hutchinson, and Ross.

Pilling, D., & Pringle, M. K. (1978). *Controversial issues in child development*. New York: Schocken Books.

Pingree, S. (1978). The effect of nonsexist television commercials and perceptions of reality on children's attitudes about women. *Psychology of Women Quarterly, 2*, 262–277.

Pinker, S. (1984). *Language learnability and language development*. Cambridge, MA: Harvard University Press.

Platt, J., Spivack, G., Altman, N., Altman, D., & Peizer, S. (1974). Adolescent problem-solving thinking. *Journal of Consulting and Clinical Psychology, 42*, 787–793.

Plomin, R. (1989). Environment and genes: Determinants of behavior. *American Psychologist, 44*, 105–111.

Plomin, R., & DeFries, J. C. (1980). Genetics and intelligence: Recent data. *Intelligence, 4*, 15–24.

Plomin, R., & Dunn, J. (Eds.). (1986). *The study of temperament: Changes, continuities, and challenges*. Hillsdale, NJ: Erlbaum.

Plomin, R., & Foch, T. (1981). Sex differences and individual differences. *Child Development, 52*, 383–385.

Plomin, R., & Rowe, D. C. (1981). The importance of nonshared (E) environmental influences in behavioral development. *Developmental Psychology, 17*, 517–531.

Plutchik, R. (1980). A general psychoevolutionary theory of emotion. In R. Plutchik & H. Kellerman (Eds.), *Emotion: Theory, research, and experience* (Vol. 1, pp. 3–33). New York: Academic Press.

Pollitt, E., Garza, C., & Leibel, R. (1984). Nutrition and public policy. In H. Stevenson & A. Siegel (Eds.), *Child development research and social policy* (pp. 421–470). Chicago, IL: University of Chicago Press.

Potts, C. R. (1983). *Role of positive and negative effect in children's comprehension of televised social behavior*. Unpublished doctoral dissertion, University of Kansas, Lawrence.

Pratt, K., Nelson, A., & Sun, K. (1930). The behavior of the newborn infant. *Ohio State University Studies, Contributions in Psychology*, No. 10.

Prechtl, H. F. R. (1977). *The neurological examination of the full-term newborn infant* (2nd ed., No. 63). London: Heinemann.

Prechtl, H. F. R., & Beintema, D. (1965). The neurological examination of the full-term newborn infant. London: William Heinemann Books.

President's Commission for the Study of Ethical Issues in Biomedical and Behavioral Research. (1983). *Deciding to forego life-sustaining treatment*. Washington, DC: U.S. Government Printing Office.

Preyer, W. (1988). *The mind of the child*, Part I. *The senses and will*. New York: Appleton.

Proskauer, S., & Rolland, R. (1973). Youth who use drugs. *Journal of the American Academy of Child Psychiatry, 12*, 32–47.

Provence, S., & Lipton, R. (1976). *Infants in institutions*. New York: International Universities Press.

Psathas, G. (1958). Ethnicity, social class, and adolescent independence from parental control. *American Sociological Review, 22*, 415–523.

Pulkkinen, L. (1982). Self-control and continuity from childhood to adolescence. In P. B. Baltes & O. G. Brin (Eds.), *Life-span development and behavior* (Vol. 4). New York: Academic Press.

Pulos, E., Teller, D., & Buck, S. (1980). Infant color vision: A search for short wavelength-sensitive mechanisms by means of chromatic adaptation. *Vision Research, 20*, 485–493.

Radke-Yarrow, M., Cummings, M., Kuczynski, L., & Chapman, M. (1985). Patterns of attachment in two and three year olds in normal families and families with parental depression. *Child Development, 56*, 884–893.

Radke-Yarrow, M., Zahn-Waxler, C., & Chapman, M. (1983). Children's prosocial dispositions and behavior. In P. H. Mussen & E. M. Hetherington (Eds.), *Handbook of child psychology: Vol. 4. Socialization, personality, and social development* (4th ed.). New York: Wiley.

Rakic, P. (1985). Contact regulation of neuronal migration. In G. M. Edelman (Ed.), *The cell in contact*. New York: Wiley.

Ramsey, P. (1978). *Ethics at the edges of life*. New Haven, CT: Yale University Press.

Rapaport, D. (1961). *Emotions and memory*. New York: Science Editions.

Rapaport, D. (1967). On the psychoanalytic theory of thinking. In M. M. Gill (Ed.), *The collected papers of David Rapaport*. New York: Basic Books.

Rauh, V., Achenbach, T., Nurcombe, B., Howell, C., & Teti, D. (1988). Minimizing adverse effects of low birthweight: Four-year results of an early intervention program. *Child Development, 59*, 544–553.

Raymond, C. L., & Benbow, C. P. (1986). Gender differences in mathematics: A function of parental support and student sex typing? *Developmental Psychology, 22,* 809–819.

Reisman, J. (1985). Friendship and its implications for mental health or social competence. *Journal of Early Adolescence, 5,* 383–391.

Rescorla, L. (1980). Category development in early language. *Journal of Child Language, 8,* 225–238.

Rest, J. R. (1974). The cognitive developmental approach to morality: The state of the art. *Counseling and Values, 18,* 64–77.

Rest, J. R. (1983). Morality. In P. H. Mussen, J. H. Flavell, & E. M. Markman (Eds.), *Handbook of child psychology: Vol. 3. Cognitive development* (4th ed., pp. 556–629). New York: Wiley.

Rest, J. R., Davison, M., & Robbins, S. (1978). Age trends in judging moral issues: A review of cross-sectional, longitudinal, and sequential studies of the Defining Issues Test. *Child Development, 49,* 263–279.

Rest, J. R., & Thoma, S. (1985). Relation of moral judgment development to formal education. *Developmental Psychology, 21,* 709–714.

Revelle, G., Karabenick, J., & Wellman, H. (1981). *Comprehension monitoring in preschool children.* Paper presented at the meeting of the Society for Research in Child Development, Boston, MA.

Rheingold, H. L. (1985). Development as the acquisition of familiarity. *Annual Review of Psychology, 36,* 1–17.

Rheingold, H. L., & Cook, K. V. (1975). The contents of boys' and girls' rooms as an index of parents' behavior. *Child Development, 46,* 459–463.

Rheingold, H. L., & Eckerman, C. (1973). Fear of the stranger: A critical examination. In H. Reese (Ed.), *Advances in child development and behavior* (Vol. 8). New York: Academic Press.

Rheingold, H. L., Gewirtz, J. L., & Ross, H. W. (1959). Social conditioning of vocalizations in the infant. *Journal of Comparative and Physiological Psychology, 52,* 68–73.

Rheingold, H. L., Hay, D. F., & West, M. J. (1976). Sharing in the second year of life. *Child Development, 47,* 1148–1158.

Rhoden, N. (1985). Treatment dilemmas for imperiled newborns: Why quality of life counts. *Southern California Law Review, 58,* 1283–1347.

Rholes, W., & Ruble, D. (1984). Children's understanding of dispositional characteristics of others. *Child Development, 55,* 550–560.

Rice, M. L., Huston, A. C., & Wright, J. C. (1982). The forms of television: Effects on children's attention, comprehension, and social behavior. In D. Pearl, L. Bouthilet, & J. Lazar (Eds.), *Television and behavior: Ten years of scientific progress and implications for the eighties* (Vol. 2). Washington, DC: U.S. Government Printing Office.

Richards, J., & Rader, N. (1981). Crawling-onset age predicts visual cliff avoidance in infants. *Journal of Experimental Psychology: Human Perception and Performance, 7,* 383–387.

Richardson, R., Galambos, N., Schulenberg, J., & Petersen, A. (1984). Young adolescents' perceptions of the family environment. *Journal of Early Adolescence, 4,* 131–153.

Richardson, S. A., Goodman, U., Hastorf, A. H., & Dornbush, S. A. (1961). A cultural uniformity in reaction to physical disabilities. *American Sociological Review, 26,* 241–247.

Ricks, D. (1972). *The beginnings of vocal communication in infants and autistic children.* Unpublished doctorate of medicine thesis, University of London.

Rierdan, J., & Koff, E. (1985). Timing of menarche and initial menstrual experience. *Journal of Youth and Adolescence, 14,* 237–244.

Rioux, J. W. (1968). The disadvantaged child in school. In J. Helmuth (Ed.), *The disadvantaged child.* New York: Brunner/Mazel.

Rist, R. C. (1970). Student social class and teacher expectations: The self-fulfilling prophecy in ghetto education. *Harvard Educational Review, 40,* 411–451.

Rist, R. C. (1978). *Invisible children: School integration in American society.* Cambridge, MA: Harvard University Press.

Rist, R. C. (Ed.). (1979). *Desegregated school: Appraisals of an American experiment.* New York: Academic Press.

Roberts, C. W., Green, R., Williams, K., & Goodman, M. (1987). Boyhood gender identity development: A statistical contrast of two family groups. *Developmental Psychology, 23,* 544–557.

Roberts, D. F., & Maccoby, N. (1984). Effects of mass media. In G. Lindzey & E. Aronson (Eds.), *Handbook of social psychology.* Menlo Park, CA: Addison-Wesley.

Roberts, E., Kline, D., & Gagnon, J. (1978). *Family life and sexual learning: A study of the role of parents in the sexual learning of children.* Cambridge, MA: Population Education.

Roberts, G., Block, J. H., & Block, J. (April, 1981). *Continuity and change in parents' child-rearing practices.* Paper presented at the Society for Research in Child Development, Boston.

Robinson, B., Rowland, R., & Coleman, M. (1986). *Latchkey kids: Unlocking doors for the children and their families*. Lexington, MA: Lexington Books.

Robinson, E. J. (1981). The child's understanding of inadequate messages and communication failure: A problem of ignorance or egocentrism? In W. P. Dickson (Ed.), *Children's oral communication skills*. New York: Academic Press.

Roff, M., & Sells, S. (1970). Some life-history factors in relation to various types of adult maladjustment. In M. Roff & D. Ricks (Eds.), *Life history research in psychopathology* (Vol. 1). Minneapolis: University of Minnesota Press.

Roff, M., Sells, S. B., & Golden, M. M. (1972). *Social adjustment and personality development*. Minneapolis: University of Minnesota Press.

Roffwarg, H., Muzio, J., & Dement, W. (1966). Onto-genetic development of the human sleep-dream cycle. *Science, 152*, 604–619.

Rogoff, B., Sellers, M., Pirrotta, S., Fox, N., & White, S. (1975). Age of assignment of roles and responsibilities in children: A cross-cultural survey. *Human Development, 18*, 353–369.

Rosch, E., Mervis, C. B., Gray, W., Johnson, D., & Boyes-Braem, P. (1976). Basic objects in natural categories. *Cognitive Psychology, 8*, 382–439.

Rose, S. A., Feldman, J., McCarton, C., & Wolfson, J. (1988). Information processing in seven-month-old infants as a function of risk status. *Child Development, 59*, 589–603.

Rose, S. A., & Wallace, I. F. (1985). Visual recognition memory: A predictor of later cognitive functioning in preterms. *Child Development, 56*, 843–856.

Rosenbach, D., Crockett, W., & Wapner, S. (1973). Developmental level, emotional involvement, and the resolution of inconsistency in impression formation. *Developmental Psychology, 8*, 120–130.

Rosenbaum, J. E. (1978). The structure of opportunity in school. *Social Forces, 57*, 236–256.

Rosenbaum, J. E. & Presser, S. (1978). Voluntary racial integration in a magnet school. *School Review, 86*, 156–186.

Rosenberg, M. (1979). *Conceiving the self*. New York: Basic Books.

Rosenhan, D. L., & White, G. M. (1967). Observation and rehearsal as determinants of prosocial behavior. *Journal of Personality and Social Psychology, 5*, 424–431.

Rosenthal, R., & Jacobsen, L. (1968). *Pygmalion in the classroom*. New York: Holt, Rinehart & Winston.

Ross, A. O. (1967). Learning difficulties of children: Dysfunctions, disorders, disabilities. *Journal of School Psychology, 5*, 82–92.

Ross, H. S., & Goldman, B. M. (1976). Establishing new social relations in infancy. In L. Krames & P. Pliner (Eds.), *Advances in communication and affect* (Vol. 4). New York: Plenum.

Ross, R. P., Campbell, T. A., Huston-Stein, A., & Wright, J. C. (1981). Nutritional misinformation of children: A developmental and experimental analysis of the effects of televised food commercials. *Journal of Applied Developmental Psychology, 1*, 329–345.

Ross, R. P., Campbell, T. A., Wright, J. C., Huston, A. C., Rice, M. L., & Turk, P. (1984). When celebrities talk, children listen: An experimental analysis of children's responses to TV ads with celebrity endorsement. *Journal of Applied Developmental Psychology, 5*, 185–202.

Rothbart, M., & Derryberry, D. (1981). Development of individual differences in temperament. In M. Lamb & A. Brown (Eds.), *Advances in developmental psychology* (Vol. 1). Hillsdale, NJ: Erlbaum.

Rothbart, M. K. (1971). Birth order and mother-child interaction in an achievement situation. *Journal of Personality and Social Psychology, 17*, 113–120.

Rothbart, M. K., & Maccoby, E. E. (1966). Parents' differential reactions to sons and daughters. *Journal of Personality and Social Psychology, 4*, 237–243.

Rothbart, M. K., & Rothbart, M. (1976). Birth order, sex of child, and maternal helpgiving. *Sex Roles, 2*, 39–46.

Rowe, D., & Plomin, R. (1981). The importance of nonshared (E) environmental influences in behavioral development. *Developmental Psychology, 17*, 517–531.

Rubin, K. H. (1972). Relationship between egocentric communication and popularity among peers. *Developmental Psychology, 7*, 364.

Rubin, K. H., Fein, G. G., & Vandenberg, B. (1983). Play. In P. H. Mussen & E. M. Hetherington (Eds.), *Handbook of child psychology: Vol. 4. Socialization, personality, and social development* (4th ed., pp. 693–774). New York: Wiley.

Rubin, K. H., & Krasnor, L. (1985). Social-cognitive and social behavioral perspectives on problem solving. In M. Perlmutter (Ed.), *Social cognition and social behavior: The Minnesota Symposia on Child Psychology* (Vol. 18). Hillsdale, NJ: Erlbaum.

Rubin, R. A., Maruyama, G., & Kingsbury, G. G. (1979, September). Self-esteem and educational achievement: A causal-model analysis. Paper presented at the annual convention of the American Psychological Association, New York.

Ruble, D., Balaban, T., & Cooper, J. (1981). Gender constancy and the effects of sex-typed televised toy commercials. *Child Development*, 52, 667–673.

Ruble, D., & Brooks-Gunn, J. (1982). The experience of menarche. *Child Development*, 53, 1557–1566.

Ruble, D., & Rholes, W. (1982). The development of children's perceptions and attributions about their social world. In J. Harvey, W. Ickes, & W. Kidd (Eds.), *New directions in attribution research* (Vol. 3). Hillsdale, NJ: Erlbaum.

Ruff, H., & Halton, A. (1977). Is there directed reaching in the human neonate. *Developmental Psychology*, 17, 460–473.

Rush, D., Stein, Z., Christakis, G., & Susser, M. (1974). The prenatal project: The first 20 months of operation. In M. Winick (Ed.), *Nutrition and fetal development*. New York: Wiley.

Russell, G., & Russell, A. (1987). Mother-child and father-child relationships in middle childhood. *Child Development*, 58, 1573–1585.

Russell, G. F. M. (1985). Anorexia and bulimia nervosa. In M. Rutter & L. Hersov (Eds.), *Child and adolescent psychiatry: Modern approaches* (2nd ed., pp. 625–637). Oxford: Blackwell.

Russell, J., & Ridgeway, D. (1983). Dimensions underlying children's emotion concepts. *Developmental Psychology*, 19, 795–804.

Rutter, M. (1979). Maternal deprivation, 1972–1978: New findings, new concepts, new approaches. *Child Development*, 50, 283–305.

Rutter, M. (1986). The developmental psychopathology of depression: Issues and perspectives. In M. Rutter, C. E. Izard, & P. B. Read (Eds.), *Depression in young people: Developmental and clinical perspectives* (pp. 3–30). New York: Guilford Press.

Rutter, M., & Garmezy, N. (1983). Developmental psychopathology. In P. H. Mussen & E. M. Hetherington (Eds.), *Handbook of child psychology: Vol. 4. Socialization, personality, and social development* (4th ed.). New York: Wiley.

Rutter, M., Graham, P., Chadwick, O., & Yule, W. (1976). Adolescent turmoil: Fact or fiction? *Journal of Child Psychology and Psychiatry*, 17, 35–56.

Rutter, M., Maughan, B., Mortimore, P., & Ouston, J. (1979). *Fifteen thousand hours: Secondary schools and their effects on children*. Cambridge, MA: Harvard University Press.

Saarni, C. (1979). Children's understanding of display rules for expressive behavior. *Developmental Psychology*, 15, 424–429.

Saarni, C. (1984). An observational study of children's attempts to monitor their expressive behavior. *Child Development*, 55, 1504–1513.

Saarni, C. (1987). Cultural rules of emotional experience: A commentary on Miller and Sperry's study. *Merrill-Palmer Quarterly*, 33, 535–540.

Saarni, C., & Harris, P. (Eds.). (1989). *Children's understanding of emotion*. New York: Cambridge University Press.

Sachs, J., & Devin, J. (1976). Young children's use of age-appropriate speech styles in social interaction and role-playing. *Journal of Child Language*, 3, 81–98.

Sagar, H. A., Schofield, J. W., & Snyder, H. N. (1983). Race and gender barriers: Preadolescent peer behavior in academic classrooms. *Child Development*, 54, 1032–1040.

Saghir, M. T., & Robins, E. (1973). *Male and female homosexuality: A comprehensive investigation*. Baltimore: Williams and Wilkins.

Sagi, A., Lamb, M., Lewkowicz, K., Shoham, R., Dvir, R., & Estes, D. (1985). Security of infant-mother, -father, and -metapelet attachments among kibbutz-reared Israeli children. *Monographs of the Society for Research in Child Development*, 50, 257–275 (1–2) Serial #209.

Salapatek, P. (1975). Pattern perception in early infancy. In L. Cohen & P. Salapatek (Eds.), *Infant perception: From sensation to cognition: Vol. 1. Basic visual processes*. New York: Academic Press.

Salapatek, P., & Kessen, W. (1966). Visual scannings of triangles by the human newborn. *Journal of Experimental Child Psychology*, 3, 155–157.

Salkind, N., & Nelson, C. (1980). A note on the development of reflection-impulsivity. *Developmental Psychology*, 16, 237–238.

Saltzstein, H., Diamond, R., & Belenky, M. (1972). Moral judgment level and conformity behavior. *Developmental Psychology*, 7, 327–335.

Sameroff, A. (1981). Longitudinal studies of preterm infants: A review of chapters 17–20. In S. L. Friedman & M. Sigman (Eds.), *Preterm birth and psychological development*. New York: Academic Press.

Sameroff, A., & Abbe, L. (1978). The consequences of prematurity: Understanding and therapy. In H. Pick, Jr., H. Leibowitz, J. E. Singer, A. Steinschneider, & H. Stevenson (Eds.), *Psychology: From research to practice* (pp. 197–226). New York: Plenum.

Sameroff, A., & Cavanaugh, P. (1979). Learning in

674

infancy: A developmental perspective. In J. D. Osofsky (Ed.), *Handbook of infant development*. New York: Wiley.

Sameroff, A., & Chandler, M. (1975). Reproductive risk and the continuum of caretaking casualty. In F. Horowitz (Ed.), *Review of child development research* (Vol. 4, pp. 187–244). Chicago, IL: University of Chicago Press.

Sarnat, H. (1978). Olfactory reflexes in the newborn infant. *Journal of Pediatrics*, 92, 624–626.

Sattler, J. (1988). *Assessment of children's intelligence and special abilities* (3rd ed.). San Diego, CA: Jerome M. Sattler.

Savin-Williams, R. C. (1979). Dominance hierarchies in groups of early adolescents. *Child Development*, 50, 923–935.

Savin-Williams, R. C. (1987). *Adolescence: An ethological perspective*. New York: Springer-Verlag.

Sawin, D. (1979). Assessing empathy in children: A search for an elusive construct. Symposium presented at the meeting of the Society for Research in Child Development, San Francisco, CA.

Scarlett, H., Press, A., & Crockett, W. (1971). Children's descriptions of peers: A Wenerian developmental analysis. *Child Development*, 42, 434–454.

Scarr, S. (1969). Social introversion-extroversion as a heritable response. *Child Development*, 40, 823–832.

Scarr, S., & Kidd, K. K. (1983). Developmental behavior genetics. In P. H. Mussen, M. Haith, & J. J. Campos (Eds.), *Handbook of child psychology: Vol. 2. Infancy and developmental psychobiology* (4th ed.). New York: Wiley.

Scarr, S., & McCartney, K. (1983). How people make their own environments: A theory of genotype-environment effects. *Child Development*, 54, 424–435.

Scarr, S., & Salapatek, P. (1970). Patterns of fear development during infancy. *Merrill-Palmer Quarterly*, 16, 53–90.

Scarr, S., & Weinberg, R. A. (1976). IQ test performance of black children adopted by white families. *American Psychologist*, 32, 726–739.

Scarr, S., & Weinberg, R. A. (1977). Intellectual similarities within families of both adopted and biological children. *Intelligence*, 1, 170–191.

Scarr, S., & Weinberg, R. A. (1983). The Minnesota adoption studies: Genetic differences and malleability. *Child Development*, 54, 260–267.

Schachter, R., Panel, E., Glassman, G., & Zweibelson, I. (1971). Acne vulgaris and psychologic impact on high school students. *New York State Journal of Medicine*, 71, 2886–2890.

Schachter, S., & Singer, J. (1962). Cognitive, social, and physiological determinants of emotional state. *Psychological Review*, 69, 379–399.

Schaefer, E. S. (1959). A circumplex model for maternal behavior. *Journal of Abnormal and Social Psychology*, 59, 226–235.

Schaffer, H. R., & Emerson, P. E. (1964). The development of social attachments in infancy. *Monographs of the Society for Research in Child Development*, 29 (3) Serial #94.

Schaffer, H. R. (1971). *The growth of sociability*. London: Penguin.

Schaffer, H. R., Greenwood, A., & Parry, M. (1972). The onset of wariness. *Child Development*, 43, 165–176.

Schaie, K. W. (1979). The primary mental abilities in adulthood: An exploration in the development of psychometric intelligence. In P. B. Baltes & O. G. Brim, Jr. (Eds.), *Life-span development and behavior* (Vol. 2). New York: Academic Press.

Schaie, K. W., & Hertzog, C. (1983). Fourteen-year cohort sequential analyses of adult intellectual development. *Developmental Psychology*, 19, 531–543.

Schaie, K. W., & Hertzog, L. (1986). Toward a comprehensive model of adult intellectual development: Contributions of the Seattle longitudinal study. In R. J. Sternberg (Ed.), *Advances in the psychology of human intelligence* (Vol. 3). Hillsdale, NJ: Erlbaum.

Schank, R. C., & Abelson, R. P. (1977). *Scripts, plans, goals, and understanding*. Hillsdale, NJ: Erlbaum.

Schatten, G., & Schatten, H. (1983). The energetic egg. *Sciences*, 23, 28–37.

Schleifer, M., Weiss, G., Cohen, N., Elman, M., Cvejic, H., & Kruger, E. (1975). Hyperactivity in preschoolers and the effect of mythylphenidate. *American Journal of Orthopsychiatry*, 45, 38–50.

Schofield, J. W. (1978). School desegregation and intergroup relations. In D. Bar-Tal & L. Saxe (Eds.), *Social psychology of education: Theory and research*. Washington, DC: Hemisphere.

Schofield, J. W., & Sagar, H. A. (1977). Peer interaction patterns in an integrated middle school. *Sociometry*, 40, 130–138.

Schwartz, R. G., & Terrell, B. Y. (1983). The role of input frequency in lexical acquisition. *Journal of Child Language*, 10, 57–64.

Scott, L. H. (1981). Measuring intelligence with the

Goodenough-Harris Drawing Test. *Psychological Bulletin*, *89*, 483–505.

Sears, R. R., Maccoby, E. E., & Levin, H. (1957). *Patterns of child rearing*. Evanston, IL: Row, Peterson.

Sears, R. R., Rau, L., & Alpert, R. (1965). *Identification and child rearing*. Stanford, CA: Stanford University Press.

Secord, P., & Peevers, B. (1974). The development and attribution of person concepts. In T. Mischel (Ed.), *Understanding other persons*. Oxford: Blackwell, Basil, Mott.

Seligman, M. (1975). *Helplessness*. San Francisco, CA: Freeman.

Seligman, M., & Peterson, C. (1984). A learned helplessness perspective on childhood depression: Theory and research. In M. Rutter, C. Izard, & P. Read (Eds.), *Depression in childhood: Developmental perspectives*. New York: Guilford Press.

Selman, R. (1976). Toward a structural analysis of developing interpersonal relations concepts: Research with normal and disturbed preadolescent boys. In A. D. Pick (Ed.), *Minnesota Symposia on Child Psychology* (Vol. 10, pp. 156–200). Minneapolis: University of Minnesota Press.

Selman, R. (1980). *The growth of interpersonal understanding: Developmental and clinical applications*. New York: Academic Press.

Selman, R., Beardslee, W., Schultz, L., Krupa, M., & Podorefsky, D. (1986). Assessing adolescent interpersonal negotiation strategies: Toward the integration of structural and functional models. *Developmental Psychology*, *22*, 450–459.

Selman, R. L., & Byrne, D. F. (1974). A structural-developmental analysis of levels of role taking in middle childhood. *Child Development*, *45*, 803–806.

Serbin, L. A., O'Leary, K. D., Kent, R. N., & Tonick, I. J. (1973). A comparison of teacher response to the preacademic and problem behavior of boys and girls. *Child Development*, *44*, 796–804.

Seyfarth, R., Cheney, D., & Marler, P. (1980). Vervet monkey alarm calls: Semantic communication in a free-ranging primate. *Animal Behaviour*, *28*, 1070–1094.

Shantz, C. U. (1975). The development of social cognition. In E. M. Hetherington (Ed.), *Review of child development research*, Vol. 5 (pp. 257–324). Chicago, IL: University of Chicago Press.

Shantz, C. U. (1983). Social cognition. In P. H. Mussen, J. H. Flavell, & E. M. Markman (Eds.), *Handbook of child psychology: Vol. 3. Cognitive development* (4th ed.). New York: Wiley.

Sharabany, R., Gershoni, R., & Hofman, J. (1981). Girlfriend, boyfriend: Age and sex differences in intimate friendship. *Developmental Psychology*, *17*, 800–808.

Shatz, M. (1983). Communication. In P. H. Mussen, J. H. Flavell, & E. M. Markman (Eds.), *Handbook of child psychology: Vol. 3. Cognitive development* (4th ed.). New York: Wiley.

Shatz, M., & Gelman, R. (1973). The development of communication skills: Modifications in the speech of young children as a function of listener. *Monographs of the Society for Research in Child Development*, *38*(5, Serial No. 152).

Shaver, P., Schwartz, J., Kirson, D., & O'Connor, C. (1987). Emotion knowledge: Further exploration of a prototype approach. *Journal of Personality and Social Psychology*, *52*, 1061–1086.

Shelton, J., & Hill, J. P. (1969). Effects on cheating of achievement anxiety and knowledge of peer performance. *Developmental Psychology*, *1*, 449–455.

Shepard, R. (1967). Recognition memory for words, sentences, and pictures. *Journal of Verbal Learning and Verbal Behavior*, *6*, 156–163.

Sherif, M., Harvey, O. J., White, B. J., Wood, W. R., & Sherif, C. W. (1961). *Intergroup conflict and cooperation: The Robbers Cave experiment*. Norman: University of Oklahoma Press.

Sherif, M., & Sherif, C. W. (1953). *Groups in harmony and tension*. New York: Harper.

Sherif, M., & Sherif, C. W. (1966). *Groups in harmony and tension*. New York: Octagon Press. (Originally published in 1953.)

Sherif, M., & Sherif, C. (1969). Adolescent attitudes and behavior in their reference groups within differing sociocultural settings. In J. P. Hill (Ed.), *Minnesota Symposia on Child Psychology* (Vol. 3). Minneapolis: University of Minnesota Press.

Sherman, M., Sherman, I., & Flory, C. (1936). Infant behavior. *Comparative Psychology Monographs*, *12* (4) Serial #59.

Sherrod, L. (1979). Social cognition in infants: Attention to the human face. *Infant Behavior and Development*, *2*, 279–294.

Shiffenbauer, A. (1974). Effect of observer's emotional state on judgments of the emotional state of others. *Journal of Personality and Social Psychology*, *30*, 31–35.

Shigetomi, C. C., Hartmann, D. P., & Gelfand, D. M. (1981). Sex differences in children's altruistic behavior and reputations for helpfulness. *Developmental Psychology*, *17*, 434–437.

Shiller, V., Izard, C. E., & Hembree, E. A. (1986).

Patterns of emotion expression during separation in the Strange-Situation procedure. *Developmental Psychology, 22,* 378–382.

Shinn, M. (1907). *Notes on the development of a child.* Berkeley, CA: University of California Publications in Education.

Shipley, E., Kuhn, I., & Madden, E. (1983). Mother's use of superordinate category terms: *Journal of Child Language, 10,* 571–588.

Shonkoff, J. P. (1984). The biological substrate and physical health in middle childhood. In W. A. Collins (Ed.), *Development during middle childhood: The years from six to twelve.* Washington, DC: National Academy Press.

Shultz, T. (1972). The role of incongruity and resolution in children's appreciation of cartoon humor. *Journal of Experimental Child Psychology, 13,* 456–477.

Shure, M. B., Spivack, G., & Jaeger, M. (1971). Problem-solving thinking and adjustment among disadvantaged preschool children. *Child Development, 42,* 1791–1803.

Siegel, L. S. (1981). Infant tests as predictors of cognitive development at two years. *Child Development, 52,* 545–557.

Siegler, R. (1986a). *Children's thinking.* Englewood Cliffs, NJ: Prentice-Hall.

Siegler, R. (1986b). Unities across domains in children's strategy choices. In M. Perlmutter (Ed.), *Minnesota Symposium on Child Development* (Vol. 19). Hillsdale, NJ: Erlbaum.

Siegler, R. (1989a). Mechanisms of cognitive development. *Annual Review of Psychology, 40,* 353–379.

Siegler, R. (1989b). How domain-general and domain-specific knowledge interact to produce strategy choices. *Merrill-Palmer Quarterly, 35,* 1–26.

Siegler, R., & Richards, D. (1980, August). *College students' prototypes of children's intelligence.* Paper presented at the meeting of the American Psychological Association, New York.

Siegler, R., & Richards, D. (1982). The development of intelligence. In R. Sternberg (Ed.), *Handbook of intelligence.* Cambridge: Cambridge University Press.

Siegler, R., & Robinson, M. (1982). The development of numerical understandings. In H. Reese & L. Lipsitt (Eds.), *Advances in child development and behavior:* (Vol. 16). New York: Academic Press.

Silverberg, S. B. (1989). *A longitudinal look at parent-adolescent relations and parents' evaluations of life and self.* Paper presented at the tenth biennial meeting of the International Society for the Study of Behavioural Development, Jyvaskyla, Finland.

Silverberg, S. B., & Steinberg, L. (1987). Adolescent autonomy, parent adolescent conflict, and parental well-being. *Journal of Youth and Adolescence, 16,* 293–312.

Simmons, R. G., & Blyth, D. A. (1987). *Moving into adolescence: The impact of pubertal change and school context.* New York: Aldine de Gruyter.

Simmons, R. G., Blyth, D. A., & McKinney, K. L. (1983). The social and psychological effects of puberty on white females. In J. Brooks-Gunn & A. Petersen (Eds.), *Girls at puberty: Biological and psychosocial perspectives* (pp. 229–272). New York: Plenum.

Simmons, R. G., Blyth, D. A., Van Cleave, E., & Bush, D. (1979). Entry into early adolescence: The impact of school structure, puberty, and early dating on self-esteem. *American Sociological Review, 44,* 948–967.

Simmons, R. G., Burgeson, R., Carlton-Ford, S., & Blyth, D. A. (1987). The impact of cumulative change in early adolescence. *Child Development, 58*(5), 1220–1234.

Simmons, R., Rosenberg, F., & Rosenberg, M. (1973). Disturbance in the self-image at adolescence. *American Sociological Review, 38,* 553–568.

Simon, W., & Gagnon, J. H. (1969). On psychosexual development. In D. A. Goslin (Ed.), *Handbook of socialization theory and research* (pp. 733–752). Chicago, IL: Rand McNally.

Sinclair, J., Saigal, S., & Yeung, C. (1974). Early postnatal consequences of fetal malnutrition. In M. Winick (Ed.), *Nutrition and fetal development.* New York: Wiley.

Singer, J. L. (1973). *The child's world of make-believe: Experimental studies of imaginative play.* New York: Academic Press.

Singleton, L. C., & Asher, S. R. (1979). Racial integration and children's peer preferences: An investigation of developmental and cohort differences. *Child Development, 50,* 936–941.

Sinnott, J., Pisoni, D., & Aslin, R. (1983). A comparison of pure tone auditory thresholds in human infants and adults. *Infant Behavior and Development, 6,* 3–17.

Siqueland, E., & Lipsitt, L. (1966). Conditioned head-turning in human newborns. *Journal of Experimental Child Psychology, 3,* 356–376.

Sizer, T. (1984). *Horace's compromise: The dilemma of the American high school.* Boston, MA: Houghton-Mifflin.

Skeels, H. (1966). Adult status of children with contrasting early life experiences. *Monographs of the Society for Research in Child Development, 31* (3) Serial #105.

Skinner, B. F. (1938). *The behavior of organisms*. New York: Appleton-Century-Crofts.

Skinner, B. F. (1953). *Science and human behavior*. New York: Macmillan.

Skinner, B. F. (1957). *Verbal behavior*. New York: Appleton-Century-Crofts.

Slaby, R. G., & Frey, K. S. (1975). Development of gender constancy and selective attention to same-sex models. *Child Development*, 46, 849–856.

Slaby, R. G., & Guerra, N. (1988). Cognitive mediators of aggression in adolescent offenders: 1. Assessment. *Developmental Psychology*, 24, 580–588.

Slater, A., & Morison, V. (1985). Shape constancy and slant perception at birth. *Perception*, 14, 337–344.

Slavin, R. E. (1983). *Cooperative learning*. New York: Longman.

Slavin, R. E. (1987). Developmental and motivational perspectives on cooperative learning: A reconciliation. *Child Development*, 58, 1161–1167.

Slavin, R. E., & Madden, N. A. (1979). School practices that improve race relations. *American Educational Research Journal*, 16, 169–180.

Slobin, D. I. (1973). Cognitive prerequisites for the acquisition of grammar. In C. A. Ferguson & D. I. Slobin (Eds.), *Studies of child language development*. New York: Holt, Rinehart & Winston.

Slobin, D. I. (1975). On the nature of talk to children. In E. Lenneberg & E. Lenneberg (Eds.), *Foundations of language development* (Vol. 1). New York: Academic Press.

Slobin, D. I. (1979). *Psycholinguistics*. Dallas, TX: Scott, Foresman.

Slobin, D. I. (1986). Cross-linguistic evidence for the language-making capacity. In D. Slobin (Ed.), *The cross-linguistic study of language acquisition: Vol. 2. Theoretical issues*. Hillsdale, NJ: Erlbaum.

Smetana, J. G. (1985). Children's impressions of moral and conventional transgressors. *Developmental Psychology*, 21, 715–724.

Smetana, J. G. (1986). Preschool children's conceptions of sex-role transgressions. *Child Development*, 57, 862–871.

Smetana, J. G. (1988). Adolescents' and parents' conceptions of parental authority. *Child Development*, 59, 321–335.

Smith, H. (1973). Some developmental interpersonal dynamics through childhood. *American Sociological Review*, 38, 343–352.

Smith, J. D., & Nelson, D. G. (1988). Is the more impulsive child a more holistic processor? A reconsideration. *Child Development*, 59, 717–719.

Smith, J. R., Foot, H. C., & Chapman, A. J. (1977). Non-verbal communication among friends and strangers sharing humor. In A. J. Chapman & H. C. Foot (Eds.), *It's a funny thing, humor*. Oxford: Pergamon.

Smith, M. (1975). Children's use of the multiple sufficient cause schema in social perception. *Journal of Personality and Social Psychology*, 32, 737–747.

Snarey, J. (1985). Cross-cultural universality of social-moral development: A critical review of Kohlbergian research. *Psychological Bulletin*, 97, 202–232.

Snow, C. E. (1977). The development of conversation between mothers and babies. *Journal of Child Language*, 4, 1–22.

Snow, C. E. (1983). *Research findings on quality of day care, 1976–1983*. Paper presented at the annual conference of the National Association for the Education of Young Children, Washington, DC.

Snow, C. E., & Hoefnagel-Hohle, M. (1978). The critical period for language acquisition: Evidence from second language learning. *Child Development*, 49, 1114–1128.

Snow, C. E., & Tomasello, M. (1989). Data on language input: Incomprehensible omission indeed! *Behavioral and Brain Sciences*, 12, 357–358.

Snow, R., & Yalow, E. (1982). Education and intelligence. In R. Sternberg (Ed.), *Handbook of human intelligence*. Cambridge: Cambridge University Press.

Snyderman, M., & Rothman, S. (1987). Survey of expert opinion on intelligence and aptitude testing. *American Psychologist*, 42, 137–144.

Sodian, B., & Wimmer, H. (1987). Children's understanding of inference as a source of knowledge. *Child Development*, 58, 424–433.

Sones, G., & Feshbach, N. (1971). Sex differences in adolescent reactions toward newcomers. *Developmental Psychology*, 4, 381–386.

Sonnenschein, S. (1986). Development of referential communication skills: How familiarity with a listener affects a speaker's production of redundant messages. *Developmental Psychology*, 22, 549–552.

Sontag, L., Baker, C., & Nelson, V. (1958). Mental growth and personality development: A longitudinal study. *Monographs of the Society for Research in Child Development*, 23(Whole No. 2).

Sontag, L., & Wallace, R. (1935). The movement response of the human fetus to sound stimuli. *Child Development*, 6, 253–258.

Sorce, J., Emde, R., Campos, J., & Klinnert, M. (1981). *Maternal emotional signaling: Its effect on the visual cliff behavior of one-year-olds*. Paper presented at the meeting of the Society for Research in Child Development, Boston, MA.

Sorenson, R. (1973). *Adolescent sexuality in contemporary America*. New York: World.

Spearman, C. (1927). *The abilities of man*. New York: Macmillan.

Spelke, E. (1976). Infant's intermodal perception of events. *Cognitive Psychology*, 8, 533–560.

Spelke, E. (1979). Perceiving bimodally specified events in infancy. *Developmental Psychology*, 15, 626–636.

Spitz, R. (1946). Anaclitic depression. *Psychoanalytic Study of the Child*, 2, 313–342.

Spitz, R. (1965). *The first year of life*. New York: International Universities Press.

Spitz, R., Emde, R., & Metcalf, D. (1970). Further prototypes of ego formation: A working paper from a research project on early development. *Psychoanalytic Study of the Child*, 25, 417–441.

Spivack, G., & Shure, M. (1974). *Social adjustment of young children: A cognitive approach to solving real-life problems*. San Francisco, CA: Jossey- Bass.

Sroufe, L. A. (1979). Socioemotional development. In J. Osofsky (Ed.), *Handbook of infancy*. New York: Wiley.

Sroufe, L. A. (1983). Infant-caregiver attachment and patterns of adaptation in preschool: The roots of maladaptation and competence. In M. Perlmutter (Ed.), *Development and policy concerning children with special needs: The Minnesota Symposia on Child Psychology* (Vol. 16, pp. 41–84). Hillsdale, NJ: Erlbaum.

Sroufe, L. A. (1985). Attachment classification from the perspective of infant caregiver relationships and infant temperament. *Child Development*, 56, 1–14.

Sroufe, L. A. (1987). The role of infant-caregiver attachment in development. In J. Belsky & T. Nezworski (Eds.), *Clinical implications of attachment*. Hillsdale, NJ: Erlbaum.

Sroufe, L. A., Fox, N., & Pancake, V. (1983). Attachment and dependency in developmental perspective. *Child Development*, 54, 1615–1627.

Sroufe, L. A., & Waters, E. (1976). The ontogenesis of smiling and laughter: A perspective on the organization of development in infancy. *Psychological Review*, 83, 173–189.

Sroufe, L. A., & Waters, E. (1977). Attachment as an organizational construct. *Child Development*, 48, 1184–1199.

Sroufe, L. A., Waters, E., & Matas, L. (1974). Contextual determinants of infant affective response. In M.

Lewis & L. Rosenblum (Eds.), *The origins of fear*. New York: Wiley.

St. John, N. H. (1975). *School desegregation*. New York: Wiley.

Staffieri, J. R. (1967). A study of social stereotype of body image in children. *Journal of Personality and Social Psychology*, 7, 101–104.

Stanley, J. C., Keating, D. P., & Fox, L. H. (Eds.). (1974). *Mathematical talent: Discovery, description, and development*. Baltimore, MD: Johns Hopkins University Press.

Starkey, P., Spelke, E., & Gelman, R. (1980, April). *Number competence in infants: Sensitivity to numerical invariance and numeric change*. Paper presented at the meeting of the International Conference on Infant Studies, New Haven, CT.

Starkey, P., Spelke, E., & Gelman, R. (1981). *Detection of intermodal numerical correspondences by human infants*. Unpublished manuscript, University of Pennsylvania, Philadelphia.

Staub, E. (1970a). A child in distress: The effect of focusing responsibility on children on their attempts to help. *Developmental Psychology*, 2, 152–153.

Staub, E. (1970b). A child in distress: The influence of age and number of witnesses on children's attempts to help. *Journal of Personality and Social Psychology*, 14, 130–140.

Staub, E. (1971). A child in distress: The influence of nurturance and modeling on children's attempts to help. *Developmental Psychology*, 5, 124–132.

Staub, E. (1972). Effects of persuasion and modeling on delay of gratification. *Developmental Psychology*, 6, 166–177.

Stayton, D., Hogan, R., & Ainsworth, M. D. S. (1971). Infant obedience and maternal behavior: The origins of socialization reconsidered. *Child Development*, 42, 1057–1069.

Steele, B. F. (1975). *Working with abusive parents from a psychiatric point of view*. (U.S. Department of Health, Education and Welfare Publication No. [OHD] 75-70). Washington, DC: U.S. Government Printing Office.

Stein, J., Newcomb, M., & Bentler, P. (1987). An 8-year study of multiple influences on drug use and drug use consequences. *Journal of Personality and Social Psychology*, 53, 1094–1105.

Steinberg, L. (1981). Transformations in family relations at puberty. *Developmental Psychology*, 17, 833–840.

Steinberg, L., & Silverberg, (1986). The vicissitudes of autonomy. *Child Development*, 57, 841–850.

679

Steinberg, M. D., & Dodge, K. A. (1983). Attributional bias in aggressive adolescent boys and girls. *Journal of Social and Clinical Psychology*, *1*, 312–321.

Steiner, J. (1979). Human facial expression in response to taste and smell stimulation. In H. Reese & L. Lipsitt (Eds.), *Advances in child development and behavior* (Vol. 13). New York: Academic Press.

Steinlauf, B. (1979). Problem-solving skills, locus of control, and the contraceptive effectiveness of young women. *Child Development*, *50*, 268–271.

Steinschneider, A. (1975). Implications of the sudden infant death syndrome for the study of sleep in infancy. In A. Pick (Ed.), *The Minnesota Symposia on Child Psychology* (Vol. 9). Minneapolis: University of Minnesota Press.

Steinschneider, A., Lipton, E., & Richmond, J. (1966). Auditory sensitivity in the infant: Effect of intensity on cardiac and motor responsivity. *Child Development*, *37*, 233–252.

Stenberg, C., & Campos, J. (1983). The development of the expression of anger in human infants. In M. Lewis & C. Saarni (Eds.), *The socialization of affect*. New York: Plenum.

Stephan, W. G., & Feagin, J. R. (1980). *School desegregation: Past, present and future*. New York: Plenum.

Steri, A., & Pecheux, M. (1986). Tactual habituation and discrimination of form in infancy: A comparison with vision. *Child Development*, *57*, 100–104.

Sternberg, R. J. (Ed.). (1982). *Handbook of human intelligence*. New York: Cambridge University Press.

Sternberg, R. J. (1985). *Beyond IQ: A triarchic theory of human intelligence*. New York: Cambridge University Press.

Sternberg, R. J. (1988). *The nature of creativity*. New York: Cambridge University Press.

Sternberg, R. J., Conway, B. E., Ketron, J. L., & Bernstein, M. (1981). People's conceptions of intelligence. *Journal of Personality and Social Psychology, 41,* 37–55.

Sternberg, R. J., & Powell, J. (1983). The development of intelligence. In P. Mussen (Ed.), J. Flavell & E. Markman (Vol. Eds.), *Handbook of child psychology*, Vol. 3: *Cognitive development* (pp. 341–419). New York: Wiley.

Stevenson, D. L., & Baker, D. P. (1987). The family-school relation and the child's school performance. *Child Development*, *58*, 1348–1357.

Stevenson, H. (1965). Social reinforcement of children's behavior. In L. Lipsitt & C. Spiker (Eds.), *Advances in child development and behavior* (Vol. 2, pp. 97–126). New York: Academic Press.

Stevenson, R. (1977). *The fetus and newly born infant: Influence of the prenatal environment* (2nd ed.). St. Louis, MO: Mosby.

Stoddart, T., & Turiel, E. (1985). Children's conceptions of cross-gender activities. *Child Development*, *56*, 861–865.

Stoel-Gammon, C., & Otomo, K. (1986). Babbling development of hearing-impaired and normally hearing subjects. *Journal of Speech and Hearing Disorders*, *51*, 33–41.

Stoller, R. J. (1968). *Sex and gender: On the development of masculinity and femininity*. New York: Science House.

Strayer, J., Bigelow, A., & Ames, E. W. (1973). "I," "you," and point of view. Unpublished manuscript, Simon Fraser University, Burnaby, British Columbia.

Struhsaker, T. (1967). *The red colobus monkey*. Chicago, IL: University of Chicago Press.

Stucki, M., Kaufmann-Hayoz, R., & Kaufmann, F. (1987). Infants' recognition of a face revealed through motion: Contribution of internal facial movement and head movement. *Journal of Experimental Child Psychology*, *44*, 80–91.

Styczynski, L. E., & Langlois, J. H. (1980). *Judging the book by its cover: Children's attractiveness and achievement*. Unpublished manuscript, University of Texas at Austin.

Sugarman, S. (1987). Young children's spontaneous inspection of negative instances in a search task. *Journal of Experimental Child Psychology*, *44*, 170–191.

Sullivan, H. S. (1953). *The interpersonal theory of psychiatry*. New York: Norton.

Suomi, S. J. (1977). Development of attachment and other social behaviors in rhesus monkeys. In T. Alloway, P. Pliner, & I. Kramer (Eds.), *Attachment behavior*. New York: Plenum.

Suomi, S. J., & Harlow, H. F. (1972). Social rehabilitation of isolate-reared monkeys. *Developmental Psychology*, *6*, 487–496.

Surber, C. (1977). Developmental processes in social inference: Averaging of intentions and consequences in moral judgment. *Developmental Psychology*, *13*, 654–665.

Susman, E. J., Inoff-Germain, G., Nottelmann, E. D., Loriaux, D. L., Cutler, G. B., Jr., & Chrousos, G. P. (1987). Hormones, emotional dispositions, and aggressive attributes in young adolescents. *Child Development*, *58*(4), 1114–1134.

Svejda, M., & Campos, J. (1982, March). *The mother's voice as a regulator of the infant's behavior*. Paper presented at the meeting of the International Conference on Infant Studies, Austin, TX.

Takahashi, K. (1986). Examining the Strange Situation procedure with Japanese mothers and 12-month-old infants. *Developmental Psychology, 22*, 265–270.

Tanner, J. (1978). *Fetus into man: Physical growth from conception to maturity.* Cambridge, MA: Harvard University Press.

Tanner, J. M., Whitehouse, R., & Takaishi, M. (1966). Standards from birth to maturity for height, weight-height velocity and weight velocity; British children, 1965. *Archives of the Diseases of Childhood, 41*, 455–471.

Taylor, D., & Harris, P. (1983). Knowledge of the link between emotion and memory among normal and maladjusted boys. *Developmental Psychology, 19*, 832–838.

Taylor, M. (1988). Conceptual perspective taking: Children's ability to distinguish what they know from what they see. *Child Development, 59*, 703–718.

Templin, M. C. (1957). *Certain language skills in children: Their development and interrelationships.* Minneapolis: University of Minnesota Press.

Terman, L. M. (1916). *The measurement of intelligence.* Boston, MA: Houghton Mifflin.

Terman, L. M., & Oden, M. H. (1959). *Genetic studies of genius*, Vol. 4: *The gifted group at midlife.* Stanford, CA: Stanford University Press.

Termine, N., & Izard, C. (1988). Infants' responses to their mothers' expressions of joy and sadness. *Developmental Psychology, 24*, 223–229.

Terr, L. C. (1970). A family study of child abuse. *American Journal of Psychiatry, 223*, 102–109.

Thomas, A., & Chess, S. (1977). *Temperament and development.* New York: Brunner/Mazel.

Thompson, J. R., & Chapman, R. S. (1977). Who is "daddy?" The status of two-year-old's overextended words in use and comprehension. *Journal of Child Language, 4*, 359–375.

Thompson, R., Lamb, M., & Estes, D. (1982). Stability of infant-mother attachment and its relationship to changing life circumstances in an unselected middle class sample. *Child Development, 53*, 144–148.

Thompson, S. K. (1975). Gender labels and early sex role development. *Child Development, 46*, 339–347.

Thorndike, R., Hagen, E., & Sattler, J. (1986). *The Stanford-Binet Intelligence Scale: Guide for administering and scoring* (4th ed.). Chicago, IL: Riverside.

Thurstone, L. L. (1938). Primary mental abilities. *Psychometric Monographs*, No. 1, Chicago: University of Chicago Press.

Tiktin, S., & Hartup, W. W. (1965). Sociometric status and the reinforcing effectiveness of children's peers. *Journal of Experimental Child Psychology, 2*, 306–315.

Tinbergen, N. (1951). *The study of instinct.* New York: Oxford University Press.

Tisak, M., & Turiel, E. (1988). Variation in seriousness of transgressions and children's moral and conventional concepts. *Developmental Psychology, 24*, 352–357.

Tobin-Richards, M., Boxer, A., & Petersen, A. (1983). Early adolescents' perceptions of their physical development. In J. Brooks-Gunn & A. Petersen (Eds.), *Girls at puberty: Biological and psychological perspectives* (pp. 127–154). New York: Plenum.

Toder, N. L., & Marcia, J. E. (1973). Ego identity status and response to conformity pressure in college women. *Journal of Personality and Social Psychology, 26*, 287–294.

Tomlinson-Keasey, C., & Keasey, C. B. (1974). The mediating role of cognitive development in moral judgment. *Child Development, 45*, 291–298.

Torrance, E. (1966). *Torrance tests of creative thinking.* Princeton, NJ: Personnel Press.

Torrance, E. (1976). Creativity research in education: Still alive. In I. A. Taylor & J. Getzels (Eds.), *Perspectives in creativity.* Chicago, IL: Aldine.

Toth, S. A. (1981). *Blooming: A small town girlhood.* Boston, MA: Little, Brown.

Tramontana, M., Hooper, S., & Selzer, S. (1988). Research on the preschool prediction of later academic achievement: A review. *Developmental Review, 8*, 89–146.

Trickett, P., & Kuczynski, L. (1986). Children's misbehaviors and parental discipline strategies in abusive and nonabusive families. *Developmental Psychology, 22*, 115–123.

Trincker, D., & Trincker, I. (1955). Die ontogenetische entwicklung des helligkeits und farbensehens beim menschen. I. Die entwicklung des helligeitssehens. *Albrecht von Graefes Archiv fue Klinische und Experimentele Ophthalmologie, 156*, 519–534.

Tuchmann-Duplessis, H. (1969). Foetal reactions to drugs taken by the mother. In G. Wolstenholme & M. O'Connor (Eds.), *Foetal autonomy.* London: Churchill.

Turiel, E. (1978). The development of concepts of social structure: Social convention. In J. Glick & A. Clarke-Stewart (Eds.), *The development of social understanding.* New York: Gardner Press.

Turiel, E. (1983). *The development of social knowledge: Morality and convention.* Cambridge: Cambridge University Press.

Tyler, L. (1963). *Tests and measurements.* Englewood Cliffs, NJ: Prentice-Hall.

Udry, J. R., Newcomer, S., & Cameron, F. (1983). Adolescent sexual behavior and popularity. *Adolescence, 18*, 515–522.

Udry, J. R., & Talbert, L. M. (1988). Sex hormone effects on personality at puberty. *Journal of Personality and Social Psychology, 54*, 291–295.

Ugurel-Semin, R. (1952). Moral behavior and moral judgment of children. *Journal of Abnormal and Social Psychology, 47*, 463–474.

Underwood, B., & Moore, B. (1982). Perspective-taking and altruism. *Psychological Bulletin, 91*, 143–173.

U.S. Department of Education (1988). *Digest of Education Statistics*. Washington, DC.

Valentine, C. W. (1930). The psychology of imitation with special reference to early childhood. *British Journal of Psychology, 21*, 105–132.

Vandell, D. L., Minnett, A. M., & Santrock, J. W. (1987). Age-differences in sibling relationships during middle childhood. *Journal of Applied Developmental Psychology, 8*, 247–257.

Vandell, D. L., & Mueller, E. C. (1980). Peer play and friendships during the first two years. In H. C. Foot, A. J. Chapman, & J. R. Smith (Eds.), *Friendship and social relations in children*. New York: Wiley.

Vandell, D. L., Wilson, K. S., & Buchanan, N. R. (1980). Peer interaction in the first year of life: An examination of its structure, content, and sensitivity to toys. *Child Development, 51*, 481–488.

Vaughn, B. E., Egeland, B., Sroufe, L. A., & Waters, E. (1979). Individual differences in infant-mother attachment at 12 and 18 months: Stability and change in families under stress. *Child Development, 50*, 971–975.

Vaughn, B. E., Kopp, C. B., Krakow, J. B., Johnson, K., & Schwartz, S. S. (1986). Process analyses of the behavior of very young children in delay tasks. *Developmental Psychology, 22*, 752–759.

Vihman, M. (1981). Phonology and the development of the lexicon: Evidence from children's errors. *Journal of Child Language, 8*, 239–264.

Vihman, M., Macken, M., Miller, R., Simmons, H., & Miller, J. (1985). From babbling to speech: A re-assessment of the continuity issue. *Language, 61*, 397–445.

Vinter, A. (1986). The role of movement in eliciting early imitations. *Child Development, 57*, 66–71.

Volpe, E. (1984). *Patient in the womb*. Macon, GA: Mercer University Press.

Volpe, J. (1977). *Observing the infant in the early hours after asphyxia. Intrauterine asphyxia*. Chicago, IL: Year Book Medical Publishers.

Vorhees, C., & Mollonow, E. (1987). Behavior teratogenesis: Long-term influences on behavior. In J. Osofsky (Ed.), *Handbook of infant development* (2nd ed.). New York: Wiley.

Wachs, T. (1976). Utilization of a Piagetian approach in the investigation of early experience. *Merrill-Palmer Quarterly, 22*, 11–30.

Wachs, T., & Gruen, G. (1982). *Early experience and human development*. New York: Plenum.

Wahler, R. G. (1967). Infant social attachments: A reinforcement theory interpretation and investigation. *Child Development, 38*, 1079–1088.

Waite, L. (1979, March). *Early imitation with several models: An example of socio-cognitive and socio-affective development*. Paper presented at the biennial meeting of the Society for Research in Child Development, San Francisco, CA.

Walker, A. (1982). Intermodal perception of expressive behaviors by human infants. *Journal of Experimental Child Psychology, 33*, 514–535.

Walker, L. J. (1980). Cognitive and perspective-taking prerequisites for moral development. *Child Development, 51*, 131–139.

Walker, L. J. (1983). Sources of cognitive conflict for stage transition in moral development. *Developmental Psychology, 19*, 103–110.

Walker, L. J. (1984). Sex differences in the development of moral reasoning: A critical review. *Child Development, 55*, 677–691.

Walker, L. J. (1986). Sex differences in the development of moral reasoning: A rejoinder to Baumrind. *Child Development, 57*, 522–526.

Walker, L. J., de Vries, B., & Bichard, S. (1984). The hierarchical nature of stages of moral development. *Developmental Psychology, 20*, 960–966.

Wallach, M. A. (1970). Creativity. In P. Mussen (Ed.), *Carmichael's manual of child psychology* (3rd ed., Vol. 1) New York: Wiley.

Wallach, M. A., & Kogan, N. (1965). *Modes of thinking in young children*. New York: Holt, Rinehart & Winston.

Wallerstein, J. S., Corbin, S. B., & Lewis, J. M. (1988). Children of divorce: A ten-year study. In E. M. Hetherington & J. Araseth (Eds.), *Impact of divorce, single-parenting and stepparenting on children* (pp. 198–214). Hillsdale, NJ: Erlbaum.

Wallerstein, J. S., & Kelly, J. B. (1980). *Surviving the break-up: How children and parents cope with divorce*. New York: Basic Books.

Wallis, C. (1985, December). Children having children. *Time, 9*, 78–90.

Walters, J., Pearce, D., & Dahms, L. (1957). Affectional and aggressive behavior of preschool children. *Child Development, 28,* 15–26.

Walters, R. H., & Brown, M. (1963). Studies of reinforcement of aggression: Transfer of responses to an interpersonal situation. *Child Development, 34,* 562–571.

Walters, R. H., Parke, R. D., & Cane, V. A. (1965). Timing of punishment and the observation of consequences to others as determinants of response inhibition. *Journal of Experimental Child Psychology, 2,* 10–30.

Wartella, E., & Hunter, L. (1983). Children and the formats of television advertising. In M. Meyer (Ed.), *Children and the formal features of television* (pp. 144–165). Munich: K. G. Saur.

Waterman, A. (1985). Identity in adolescence: Processes and contents. *New Directions of Child Development* (pp. 12–13, 18). San Francisco: Jossey-Bass.

Waterman, A. S. (1988). Identity status theory and Erikson's theory: Communalities and differences. *Developmental Review, 8,* 185–208.

Waterman, A. S., & Waterman, C. K. (1970). A longitudinal study of changes in ego identity status during the freshman year in college. *Developmental Psychology, 5,* 167–173.

Waterman, A. S., Geary, P. S., & Waterman, C. K. (1974). Longitudinal study of changes in ego identity status from the freshman to senior year at college. *Developmental Psychology, 10,* 387–392.

Waters, E. (1978). The reliability and stability of individual differences in infant-mother attachment. *Child Development, 48,* 489–494.

Waters, E., Hay, D., & Richters, J. (1986). Infant-parent attachment and the origins of prosocial and antisocial behavior. In D. Olweus, J. Block, & M. Radke-Yarrow (Eds.), *Development of antisocial and prosocial behavior: Research, theories, and issues* (pp. 97–125). Orlando, FL: Academic Press.

Waters, E., & Sroufe, L. A. (1983). Social competence as a developmental construct. *Developmental Review, 3,* 79–97.

Waters, E., Vaughn, B., & Egeland, B. (1980). Individual differences in infant mother attachment relationships at age one: Antecedents in neonatal behavior in an urban, economically disadvantaged sample. *Child Development, 51,* 208–216.

Waters, E., Wippman, J., & Sroufe, L. A. (1979). Attachment, positive affect, and competence in the peer group: Two studies in construct validation. *Child Development, 50,* 821–829.

Watson, J. B, & Rayner, R. (1920). Conditioned emotional reactions. *Journal of Experimental Psychology, 3,* 1–14.

Watson, J. (1979). Perception of contingency as a determinant of social responsiveness. In E. B. Thomas (Ed.), *Origins of the infant's social responsiveness.* Hillsdale, NJ: Erlbaum.

Watson, J., & Ramey, C. (1972). Reactions to responsive contingent stimulation in early infancy. *Merrill-Palmer Quarterly, 18,* 219–227.

Weber, D., Redfield, R., & Lemon, S. (1986). Acquired immunodeficiency syndrome: Epidemiology and significance for the obstetrician and gynecologist. *American Journal of Obstetrics and Gynecology, 155,* 235–239.

Weber, R., Levitt, M., & Clark, M. C. (1986). Individual variation in attachment security and Strange Situation behavior: The role of maternal and infant temperament. *Child Development, 57,* 56–65.

Wechsler, D. (1949). *Manual for the Wechsler Intelligence Scale for Children.* New York: Psychological Corporation.

Wechsler, D. (1967). *Manual for the Wechsler Preschool and Primary Scale of Intelligence.* New York: Psychological Corporation.

Wechsler, D. (1974). *Manual for the Wechsler Intelligence Scale for Children—Revised.* New York: Psychological Corporation.

Weikert, D. P. (1983). A longitudinal view of a preschool research effort. In M. Perlmutter (Ed.), *Development and policy concerning children with special needs: Minnesota Symposia on Child Psychology* (Vol. 16, pp. 175–196). Hillsdale, NJ: Erlbaum.

Weinberg, R. (1989). Intelligence and IQ: Landmark issues and great debates. *American Psychologist, 44,* 98–104.

Weiner, I. (1980). Psychopathology in adolescence. In J. Adelson (Ed.), *Handbook of adolescent psychology.* New York: Wiley.

Weinraub, M., & Brown, L. (1983). Crushing realities: Development of children's sex role knowledge. In V. Franks & E. Rothblum (Eds.), *The stereotyping of women: Its effects on mental health.* New York: Springer.

Weir, R. (1966). Some questions on the child's learning of phonology. In F. Smith & G. Miller (Eds.), *The genesis of language.* Cambridge, MA: MIT Press.

Weisberg, P. (1963). Social and nonsocial conditioning of infant vocalizations. *Child Development, 34,* 377–388.

Weitzman, L. J., Eifler, D., Hokada, E., & Ross, C.

(1972). Sex role socialization in picture books for preschool children. *American Journal of Sociology, 77,* 1125–1150.

Wellman, H., Cross, D., & Bartsch, K. (1986). Infant search and object permanence: A meta-analysis of the A-not-B error. *Monographs of the Society for Research in Child Development, 51* (3, Serial No. 214).

Wellman, H., Fabricius, W., & Chuan-Wen, W. (1987). Considering every available instance: The early development of a fundamental problem solving skill. *International Journal of Behavioral Development, 10,* 485–500.

Wells, G. (1985). *Language development in preschool children.* Cambridge: Cambridge University Press.

Werker, J. (1989). Becoming a native listener. *American Scientist, 77,* 54–59.

Werner, E., Bierman, J., & French, F. (1971). *The children of Kauai.* Honolulu: University of Hawaii.

Werner, E., & Smith, R. (1977). *Kauai's children come of age.* Honolulu: University of Hawaii.

Werner, E., & Smith, R. (1982). *Vulnerable but invincible: A study of resilient children.* New York: McGraw-Hill.

Werner, H. (1948). *Comparative psychology of mental development.* New York: International Universities Press.

Werner, N. E., & Evans, I. M. (1968). Perception of prejudice in Mexican-American preschool children. *Perceptual and Motor Skills, 27,* 1039–1046.

Wertheimer, M. (1961). Psychomotor coordination of auditory and visual space at birth. *Science, 134,* 1692.

Whalen, C., Henker, B., Dotemoto, S., & Hinshaw, S. (1983). Child and adolescent perceptions of normal and atypical peers. *Child Development, 54,* 1588–1598.

Whitam, F. L. (1986). *Male homosexuality in four societies: Brazil, Guatemala, the Phillipines, and the United States.* New York: Praeger.

White, K., Speisman, J., & Costos, D. (1984). Young adults and their parents: Individuation to mutuality. In H. Grotevant & C. Cooper (Eds). *Adolescent development in the family. New directions for child development.* San Francisco, CA: Jossey-Bass.

Whitehorn, L. A., & Campbell, S. (1982). The competency of children and adolescents to make informed treatment decisions. *Child Development, 53,* 1589–1598. (Excerpt © The Society for Research in Child Development, Inc.)

Wiesenfeld, A., Malatesta, C., & DeLoach, L. (1981). Differential parental response to familiar and unfamiliar infant distress signals. *Infant Behavior and Development, 4,* 281–295.

Wikoff, R. (1979). The WISC-R as a predictor of achievement. *Psychology in the Schools, 16,* 364–366.

Williams, J. E., & Moreland, J. K. (1976). *Race, color, and the young child.* Chapel Hill: University of North Carolina Press.

Williams, R. L. (1974, May). Scientific racism and IQ: The silent mugging of the black community. *Psychology Today, 101,* 32–41.

Williams, T. H. (Ed.). (1986). *The impact of television: A natural experiment in three communities.* Orlando, FL: Academic Press.

Wilson, E. O. (1975). *Sociobiology: The new synthesis.* Cambridge, MA: Harvard University Press.

Wilson, W. J. (1987). *The truly disadvantaged.* Chicago, IL: University of Chicago Press.

Winchester, A. (1972). *Genetics: A survey of the principles of heredity* (4th ed.). New York: Houghton Mifflin.

Winick, M. (Ed.). (1974). *Nutrition and fetal development.* New York: Wiley.

Wintz, P. W., Rohrbeck, C. A., Charner, I., & Fraser, B. S. (1988). Employment of adolescents while in high school: Employment intensity, interference with schoolwork, and normative approval. *Journal of Adolescent Research, 3,* 97–105.

Wishart, J., Bower, T., & Dunkeld, J. (1978). Reaching in the dark. *Perception, 7,* 507–512.

Witkin, H. A., Dyk, R. B., Faterson, H. F., Goodenough, D. R., & Karp, S. A. (1962). *Psychological differentiation.* New York: Wiley.

Witkin, H. A., Goodenough, D. R., & Karp, S. A. (1967). Stability of cognitive style from childhood to young adulthood. *Journal of Personality and Social Psychology, 7,* 291–300.

Witryol, S. L., & Thompson, G. G. (1953). A critical review of the stability of social acceptability sources obtained with the partial-rank-order and the paired-comparison scales. *Genetic Psychology Monographs, 48,* 221–260.

Wolff, P. (1966). The causes, controls, and organization of behavior in the neonate. *Psychological Issues, 5*(1, Whole No. 17).

Wolff, P. (1969a). Crying and vocalization in early infancy. In B. Foss (Ed.), *Determinants of infant behavior* (Vol. 4). New York: Wiley.

Wolff, P. (1969b). The natural history of crying and other vocalizations in early infancy. In B. Foss (Ed.), *Determinants of infant behavior* (Vol. 4). New York: Wiley.

Wolosin, R. J., Sherman, S. J., & Mynatt, C. R. (1975).

When self-interest and altruism conflict. *Journal of Personality and Social Psychology, 32*, 752–760.

Yando, S., Seitz, V., & Zigler, E. (1978). *The development of imitation*. New York: Erlbaum.

Yarrow, L., Rubinstein, J., & Pedersen, F. (1975). *Infant and environment*. New York: Halsted.

Yarrow, M. R., Scott, P. M., & Waxler, C. Z. (1973). Learning concern for others. *Developmental Psychology, 8*, 240–260.

Yonas, A. (1981). Infants' responses to optical information for collision. In R. Aslin & Petersen (Eds.), *Development of perception: Psychobiological perspectives* (Vol. 2). New York: Academic Press.

Yonas, A., Cleaves, W., & Pettersen, L. (1978). Development of sensitivity to pictorial depth. *Science, 200*, 77–79.

Yonas, A., Granrud, C., Atterberry, M., & Hanson, B. (1986). Infant's distance perception from linear perspective and texture gradients. *Infant Behavior and Development, 9*, 247–256.

Yonas, A., Pettersen, L., & Lockman, J. (1979). Young infants' sensitivity to optical information for collision. *Canadian Journal of Psychology, 33*, 268–276.

Yonas, A., Pettersen, L., Lockman, J., & Eisenberg, N. (1980). *The perception of impending collision in 3-month-old infants*. Paper presented at the International Conference on Infant Studies, New Haven, CT.

Yoshida, H., & Kuriyama, K. (1986). The numbers 1 to 5 in the development of children's number concepts. *Journal of Experimental Child Psychology, 41*, 251–266.

Young, W. C., Goy, R. W., & Phoenix, C. H. (1964). Hormones and sexual behavior. *Science, 143*, 212–218.

Youniss, J. (1980). *Parents and peers in social development*. Chicago: University of Chicago Press.

Youniss, J., & Smollar, J. (1985). *Adolescent relations with mothers, fathers, and friends*. Chicago, IL: University of Chicago Press.

Yussen, S., & Levy, V. (1975). Developmental changes in predicting one's own span of memory. *Journal of Experimental Child Psychology, 19*, 502–508.

Zabin, L. S., Hirsch, M. B., Smith, E. A., Strett, R., &

Hardy, J. B. (1986). Evaluations of a pregnancy prevention program for urban teenagers. *Family Planning Perspectives, 18*, 119–126.

Zahn-Waxler, C., Friedman, S., & Cummings, E. M. (1983). Children's emotions and behaviors in response to infants' cries. *Child Development, 54*, 1522–1528.

Zajonc, R. B., & Markus, G. B. (1975). Birth order and intellectual development. *Psychological Review, 82*, 74–88.

Zaporozhets, A. (1965). The development of perception in the preschool child. *Monographs of the Society for Research in Child Development, 30*(Serial No. 100).

Zarbatany, L., Hartmann, D. P., Gelfand, D. M., & Vinciguerra, P. (1986). Gender differences in altruistic reputation: Are they artifactual? *Developmental Psychology, 21*, 97–101.

Zelazo, P., Zelazo, N., & Kolb, S. (1972). "Walking" in the newborn. *Science, 176*, 314–315.

Zelnik, M., & Kantner, J. (1979). Reasons for non-use of contraception by sexually active women aged 15–19. *Family Planning Perspectives, 11*, 289–296.

Zelnik, M., & Kim, Y. J. (1982). Sex education and its association with teenage sexual activity, pregnancy and contraceptive use. *Family Planning Perspectives, 14*(3), 117–126.

Zelnik, M., & Shah, F. K. (1983). First intercourse among young Americans. *Family Planning Perspectives, 15*(2), 64–70.

Zelniker, T., & Jeffrey, W. E. (1976). Reflective and impulsive children: Strategies of information processing underlying differences in problem solving. *Monographs of the Society for Research in Child Development, 41*(Serial No. 168).

Zeskind, P. S. (1983). Cross-cultural differences in maternal perceptions of cries of low- and high-risk infants. *Child Development, 54*, 1119–1128.

Zigler, E., & Seitz, V. (1982). Social policy and intelligence. In R. Sternberg (Ed.), *Handbook of human intelligence*. Cambridge: Cambridge University Press.

Zill, N. (1985). *Happy, healthy, and insecure: A portrait of middle childhood in the United States*. New York: Cambridge University Press.

Photo Credits

Title Page Robert Henri, "Laughing Child," oil, 24 × 20, 1907 Whitney Museum, Gift of Gertrude Vanderbilt Whitney, Acq #31.240.

Part One Opener (page 2), Mary Cassatt, "Mother With Child," pastel. Louvre, Paris. Giraudon/Art Resource, Acq #LAC96774.

Chapter 1 Page 5, © Mary Kate Denny/Photo Edit; page 9, © Gale Zucker/Stock Boston; page 10, The Granger Collection; page 15, © Paul Sequeria/Rapho/Photo Researchers, Inc.; page 17, © Bob Daemmrich/Stock Boston; page 22, © Cary Wolinsky/Stock Boston.

Chapter 2 Page 29, © Burton McNeely; page 34, Dr. Merlin G. Butler, Vanderbilt University; page 34, Dr. Merlin G. Butler, Vanderbilt University; page 38, © Alan Carey/The Image Works; page 58, © David Witbeck/The Picture Cube; page 62, © Erika Stone; page 62, © Eric Liebowitz.

Chapter 3 Page 69, © Elizabeth Crews; page 73, Joel Gordon Photography; page 87, © Frederick Bodin/Stock Boston; page 89, © Erika Stone; page 90, Museum of the City of New York.

Chapter 4 Page 101, © Michael Hayman/Stock Boston; page 103, Joel Gordon Photography; page 105, Joel Gordon Photography; page 116, © Rick Smolan/Stock Boston; page 119, © Jeffrey Myers/Stock Boston; page 122, Harlow Primate Lab, University of Wisconsin, Madison, Wisconsin; page 125, © Elizabeth Crews.

Part Two Opener (page 130), Duverger Theophile-Emmanuel, "Alone." Guildhall Art Gallery, London. The Bridgeman Art Library/Art Resource.

Chapter 5 Page 133, © James R. Rolland/Stock Boston; page 136, The Prelearning Institute; page 141, Dr. Patricia Kuhl; page 141, Dr. Patricia Kuhl; page 157, William Vandivert/Scientific American.

Chapter 6 Page 167, © Elizabeth Crews/The Image Works; page 174, © Elizabeth Crews; page 178, © Elizabeth Crews; page 181, © Kaufman Moon/Stock Boston; page 186, © Gabor Demjen/Stock Boston; page 201, © Elizabeth Crews.

Chapter 7 Page 205, © Elizabeth Crews; page 209, Brown Brothers, Sterling, PA; page 220, © Charles Gatewood/Stock Boston.

Chapter 8 Page 241, Joel Gordon Photography; page 248, Courtesy of Dr. Tiffany Field; page 251, © Zimbel/Monkmeyer Press Photo; page 251, © Zimbel/Monkmeyer Press Photo; page 255, Bill Wiegand/University of Illinois; page 258, © Elizabeth Crews; page 263, Professor Benjamin Harris; page 275, © Elizabeth Crews.

Part Three Opener (page 280), Maris Bashirtseff, "The Meeting." Musée d'Orsay, Paris. Giraudin/Art Resource.

Chapter 9 Page 283, Joel Gordon Photography; page 300, © Michael Hayman/Stock Boston; page 303, © Alan Carey/The Image Works.

Chapter 10 Page 313, Joel Gordon Photography; page 321, © Stuart Cohen/Comstock; page 333, © Carolyn Hine/The Picture Cube; page 348, © Erika Stone; page 351, © Judy Gelles/Stock Boston.

Chapter 11 Page 355, © Elizabeth Crews/Stock Boston; page 359, © David A. Krathwohl/Stock Boston; page 361, © Jean-Claude Lejeune/Stock Boston; page 361, © Nita Winter/The Image Works; page 361, Rapho/Photo Researchers; page 366, © Beryl Goldberg; page 369, © Elizabeth Crews/Stock Boston; page 383, Joel Gordon Photography.

Part Four Opener (page 390), © James Van der Zee

Chapter 12 Page 393, Joel Gordon Photography; page 399, © Nancy J. Pierce/Photo Researchers, Inc.; page 407, © Blair Seitz/Photo Researchers, Inc.; page 410, New York Newsday; page 414, © Susan Lapides/Design Conceptions; page 427, © Michael McGovern/The Picture Cube.

Chapter 13 Page 433, Joel Gordon Photography; page 436, © Elizabeth Crews; page 439, © Alan Carey/The Image Works; page 457, © Stan Goldblatt/Photo Researchers, Inc.

687

Chapter 14 Page 471, © Lynn Johnson/Stock Boston; page 480 © Alan Carey/The Image Works; page 480, © Elizabeth Crews/The Image Works; page 488, © Elizabeth Crews; page 491, Joel Gordon Photography; page 493, © Hazel Hankin/Stock Boston; page 497, © Hayman/Photo Researchers, Inc.

Chapter 15 Page 501, Joel Gordon Photography; page 509, © Elizabeth Crews; page 512, Joel Gordon Photography; page 519, © Elizabeth Crews/Stock Boston; page 526, © Susan Lapides/Design Conceptions.

Part Five Opener (page 534), Mary Cassatt, "Girl Arranging Her Hair," 1886. Chester Dale Collection. National Gallery of Art, Washington, D.C.

Chapter 16 Page 537, © Susan Lapides/Design Conceptions; page 543, © Peter Southwick/Stock Boston; page 553, © Robert Kalman/The Image Works; page 558, © Susan Rosenberg/Photo Researchers, Inc.; page 559, © Barbara Rios/Photo Researchers, Inc.; page 560 © Gale Zucker/Stock Boston; page 567, © Billy E. Barnes/Stock Boston; page 575, Courtesy of Bob McConnin.

Chapter 17 Page 581, Joel Gordon Photography; page 587 © Peter Menzel/Stock Boston; page 599 © Spencer Grant/Stock Boston; page 601 © Kindra Clineff/The Picture Cube; page 609 © Alan Carey/The Image Works.

Color Insert 1 © Lennart Nilsson/Bonnier Fakta.

Color Insert 2 Courtesy of Christine Cardone; © Linda Benedict Jones/The Picture Cube; © Elizabeth Crews; © Elizabeth Crews/The Image Works; © J. da Cunha/Petit Format; © Julie O'Neil/The Picture Cube; © Erika Stone; © Willie Hill, Jr./The Image Works; © Elsa Peterson.

Color Insert 3 © Susie Fitzburgh; © Blair Seitz/Photo Researchers, Inc.; © Jeff Jacobson/Archive Pictures, Inc.; © Nancy Sheehan; © Lawrence Migdale/Photo Researchers, Inc.; © Erika Stone; Comstock; © Bob Daemmrich/The Image Bank; Comstock; © Elsa Peterson; © Jim Anderson/Woodfin Camp & Associates; © Michael Heron/Woodfin Camp & Associates.

Color Insert 4 © Dick Van Halsema/KPC Photography; © Richard Hutchings/Info Edit; © Mark Antm/The Image Works; © Erika Stone; © Bob Daemmrich/The Image Works; © David R. Fraizer/Photo Researchers, Inc.; © Abe Renzy/The Image Works; University of California Lawrence Berkeley Laboratory/Photographic Services; © Elsa Peterson.

Name Index

Subject Index